# Comparative Defamation and Privacy Law

Defamation and privacy are now two central issues in media law. While defamation law has long posed concerns for media publications, the emergence of privacy as a legal challenge has been relatively recent in many common law jurisdictions outside the US. A number of jurisdictions have seen recent defamation and privacy law reforms, which have often drawn on, or reacted against, developments elsewhere. This timely book examines topical issues in defamation and privacy law focussed on media, journalism and contemporary communication. Aimed at a wide legal audience, it brings together leading and emerging analysts of media law to address current and proposed reforms and the impact of changes in communication environments and to re-examine basic principles such as harm and free speech. This book will be of interest to all those working on commonwealth or US law, as well as comparative scholars from wider jurisdictions.

ANDREW T. KENYON is Professor of Law and a Director of the Centre for Media and Communications Law at the University of Melbourne, Australia.

*Cambridge Intellectual Property and Information Law*

As its economic potential has rapidly expanded, intellectual property has become a subject of front-rank legal importance. *Cambridge Intellectual Property and Information Law* is a series of monograph studies of major current issues in intellectual property. Each volume contains a mix of international, European, comparative and national law, making this a highly significant series for practitioners, judges and academic researchers in many countries.



A list of books in the series can be found at the end of this volume.

# Comparative Defamation and Privacy Law

*Edited by*

**Andrew T. Kenyon**

*Centre for Media and Communications Law, Melbourne Law School, University of Melbourne, Australia*

CAMBRIDGE
UNIVERSITY PRESS

**CAMBRIDGE**
**UNIVERSITY PRESS**

University Printing House, Cambridge CB2 8BS, United Kingdom

Cambridge University Press is part of the University of Cambridge.

It furthers the University's mission by disseminating knowledge in the pursuit of education, learning and research at the highest international levels of excellence.

www.cambridge.org
Information on this title: www.cambridge.org/9781107123649



First published 2016

*A catalogue record for this publication is available from the British Library*

*Library of Congress Cataloguing in Publication Data*
Kenyon, Andrew T., editor.
Comparative defamation and privacy law / edited by Andrew T. Kenyon.
Cambridge, United Kingdom ; New York : Cambridge University Press, 2016. | Series: Cambridge intellectual property and information law ; 32 | Includes papers presented at a workshop held at the Centre for Media and Communications Law at the University of Melbourne. – ECIP preface and acknowledgements.
LCCN 2015048603 | ISBN 9781107123649 (hardback)
LCSH: Freedom of expression – Congresses. | Privacy – Congresses. | Libel and slander – Congresses.
LCC K3253. A6 C658 2016 | DDC 346. 03/4–dc23
LC record available at http://lccn.loc.gov/2015048603

ISBN 978-1-107-12364-9 Hardback

# Contents

*List of contributors* *page* vii
*Acknowledgements* ix

1 Defamation and privacy in an era of 'more speech'
ANDREW T. KENYON 1

2 'Anyone . . . in any medium'? The scope of Canada's responsible communication defence
HILARY YOUNG 17

3 *Ceci n'est pas une pipe*: the autopoietic inanity of the single meaning rule
ANDREW SCOTT 40

4 *New York Times* v. *Sullivan* at fifty years: defamation in separate orbits
DAVID PARTLETT 58

5 Defamation and democracy
RUSSELL L. WEAVER 82

6 'A reasonable expectation of privacy': a coherent or redundant concept?
ERIC BARENDT 96

7 Media intrusion into grief: lessons from the Pike River mining disaster
N.A. MOREHAM AND YVETTE TINSLEY 115

8 Press freedom, the public interest and privacy
GAVIN PHILLIPSON 136

9 The Atlantic divide on privacy and free speech
KIRSTY HUGHES AND NEIL M. RICHARDS 164

10 The 'right to be forgotten' by search engines under data privacy law: a legal and policy analysis of the *Costeja* decision
DAVID LINDSAY 199

11 Privacy for the weak, transparency for the powerful
MELISSA DE ZWART 224

12 The trouble with dignity
AMY GAJDA 246

13 The uncertain landscape of Article 8 of the ECHR: the protection of reputation as a fundamental human right?
TANYA APLIN AND JASON BOSLAND 265

14 Vindicating reputation and privacy
DAVID ROLPH 291

15 Divining the dignity torts: a possible future for defamation and privacy
URSULA CHEER 309

16 Reverberations of *Sullivan*? Considering defamation and privacy law reform
ANDREW T. KENYON AND MEGAN RICHARDSON 331

*Bibliography* 354
*Index* 373

# Contributors

TANYA APLIN, Professor, The Dickson Poon School of Law, King's College London, United Kingdom

ERIC BARENDT, Emeritus Professor, Faculty of Laws, University College London, United Kingdom

JASON BOSLAND, Senior Lecturer, Melbourne Law School, University of Melbourne, Australia

URSULA CHEER, Professor of Law, University of Canterbury School of Law, New Zealand

AMY GAJDA, Professor of Law, Tulane University Law School, New Orleans, Louisiana, United States

KIRSTY HUGHES, University Lecturer in Public Law, University of Cambridge, United Kingdom

ANDREW T. KENYON, Professor, Melbourne Law School and Joint-Director, Centre for Media and Communications Law, University of Melbourne, Australia

DAVID LINDSAY, Associate Professor, Faculty of Law, Monash University, Australia

N.A. MOREHAM, Reader in Law, Victoria University of Wellington, New Zealand

DAVID PARTLETT, Asa Griggs Candler Professor of Law, Emory University School of Law, United States

GAVIN PHILLIPSON, Professor of Law, Durham Law School, University of Durham, United Kingdom

NEIL M. RICHARDS, Professor of Law, Washington University School of Law, United States

MEGAN RICHARDSON, Professor, Melbourne Law School and Joint-Director, Centre for Media and Communications Law, University of Melbourne, Australia

DAVID ROLPH, Associate Professor, Faculty of Law, University of Sydney, Australia

ANDREW SCOTT, Associate Professor, Department of Law, London School of Economics and Political Science, United Kingdom

YVETTE TINSLEY, Reader in Law, Victoria University of Wellington, New Zealand

RUSSELL L. WEAVER, Professor of Law and Distinguished University Scholar, University of Louisville Louis D Brandeis School of Law, United States

HILARY YOUNG, Assistant Professor, Faculty of Law, University of New Brunswick, Canada

MELISSA DE ZWART, Professor, Adelaide Law School, University of Adelaide, Australia

# Acknowledgements

It has been a privilege to work with academic colleagues from five common law countries in developing this collection. Contributions address issues in defamation and privacy law, examining UK, US, Canadian, New Zealand and Australian developments. The project was made possible through support from the Australian Research Council and its Discovery programme (Kenyon DP0985337). A two-day workshop was held at the Centre for Media and Communications Law at the University of Melbourne, Australia, where almost all contributors participated, along with further colleagues whose valuable contributions greatly helped the final development of the chapters, participated. Many thanks to everyone who took part, as well as to those whose work is seen in the pages that follow; thanks also to Roy Baker, Eric Descheemaeker, Steve Friedland, Lyrissa Lidsky, Barbara McDonald and Andrew Roberts. Wide-ranging debate and discussion at the workshop led to revised chapters and substantially improved the final collection.

Thanks to all at Cambridge University Press for their support of the publication; to James Nunez and Hamish Carr, who assisted me with some of the editorial tasks; and to the Melbourne Law School for its continuing support of the Centre for Media and Communications Law. But above all, thanks to the contributors for their thought, care and engagement in addressing a range of evolving and challenging issues in media law.

As readers will see, a wide range of views are presented in the chapters that follow, and it should be clear that I could not agree with all of them. Given my interest in diverse public speech, however, it should not be surprising that I think it is valuable for these varied analyses to be presented. I hope readers also find much of value in the work.

# 1 Defamation and privacy in an era of 'more speech'

*Andrew T. Kenyon*

Defamation and privacy are now two central issues in media law. While defamation law has long posed concerns for media publications, the emergence of privacy as a legal challenge has been relatively recent in many common law jurisdictions. The detailed consideration of both defamation and privacy by the Australian Law Reform Commission in its 1979 report *Unfair Publication: Defamation and Privacy* stands as an exception more than a rule in Commonwealth jurisdictions.[1]

In Australia, privacy had long received some protection under defamation law through the requirement in five states and territories to prove the 'public benefit' or 'public interest' in publishing the matter in question, as well as its truth to establish the justification defence. Merely proving truth was not enough in Queensland, New South Wales, Tasmania and the Australian Capital Territory until the commencement of substantially uniform defamation laws across Australia in 2006.[2] Before then, true private facts that were also defamatory might receive protection where law recognised no public interest or public benefit in publication. In practice, the extra requirement was examined rarely in litigation, although some observers suggested it changed particular media decisions about what to publish. In any event, that particular legal position makes the detailed consideration of *both* defamation and privacy in 1970s Australia law reform less remarkable. The Australian Law Reform Commission aside, however, there was generally tangential engagement

This research has benefited from Australian Research Council funding (Kenyon, DP0985337).

[1] Australian Law Reform Commission, *Unfair Publication: Defamation and Privacy*, Report 11 (Canberra: Australian Government Publishing Service, 1979).

[2] On the early history, see, e.g., Paul Mitchell, 'The Foundations of Australian Defamation Law' (2006) 28 *Sydney Law Review* 477; for overviews of Australia's uniform defamation laws when introduced, see, e.g., David Rolph, 'A Critique of the National, Uniform Defamation Laws' (2008) 16 *Torts Law Journal* 207; and more recently, Matt Collins, 'Five Years on: A Report Card on Australia's National Scheme Defamation Laws' (2011) 16 *Media & Arts Law Review* 317.

by Australian law with privacy and media publications. US law saw more direct consideration of both defamation and privacy during the 1960s with Supreme Court decisions about the First Amendment's effect on defamation law, followed by its effect on aspects of privacy law.[3] The law in England and Wales, and many jurisdictions in that tradition, did not have such developed legal treatment of privacy. It received haphazard and tangential protection through other legal actions. Privacy was not a day-to-day legal concern for the media, unlike matters such as contempt of court, reporting restrictions and defamation.

## 1.1 Rights, courts and legislative proposals

Historically, detailed analyses of journalism law did not often refer explicitly to privacy, as Australian and New Zealand examples illustrate. One could begin with the multiple editions of Geoffrey Sawer's pioneering monograph on law and journalism in Australia. The book's three editions, published between 1949 and 1984, do not directly address privacy, secrecy or even confidential information as legal concerns. Matters such as contempt of court, copyright and defamation are examined,[4] but privacy was largely a foreign concept. Some references exist in work from the 1980s, but the analysis then tended to focus on confidential information and protecting creative ideas rather than privacy as such.[5]

More recently, however, privacy has not been so foreign to antipodean media law. Texts have gradually given detailed consideration to actions that can protect privacy interests against media publication.[6] The change

[3] See, in particular, *New York Times* v. *Sullivan*, 376 US 254 (1964); *Time* v. *Hill*, 385 US 374 (1967). It is reasonably common for US privacy and defamation claims to be brought against the same publication, even though they both often face formidable hurdles: e.g., David A Anderson, 'An American Perspective' in Simon Deakin, Angus Johnston and Basil Markesinis (eds), *Markesinis and Deakin's Tort Law*, 5th edn (Oxford: Clarendon Press, 2003) 721, 735.

[4] See Geoffrey Sawer, *A Guide to Australian Law for Journalists, Authors, Printers and Publishers* (Melbourne: Melbourne University Press, 1949); 2nd edn (Melbourne: Melbourne University Press, 1968); 3rd edn (Melbourne: Melbourne University Press, 1984).

[5] For example, Colin Golvan and Michael McDonald, *Writers and the Law* (Sydney: Law Book Co, 1986); Sally Walker, *The Law of Journalism in Australia* (Sydney: Law Book Co, 1989). Similarly, concern with confidential information and its use against material leaked to the media was addressed in professional media law seminars: see, e.g., Anthony F Smith, 'Actions for Breach of Confidence' in Carol Bartlett (ed), *Current Legal Developments: Media Law Seminars* (Clayton: Monash Law Press, 1985) 223.

[6] See, e.g., Mark Pearson, *The Journalist's Guide to Media Law* (St Leonards: Allen & Unwin, 1997) and subsequent editions (jointly written by Mark Pearson and Mark Polden from 4th edn 2011) which initially dealt with matters more in terms of journalistic ethics. See also, e.g., Paul Chadwick and Jennifer Mullaly, *Privacy and the Media* (Sydney: Communications Law Centre, 1997).

is illustrated by the leading New Zealand work by John Burrows, more recent editions of which have been co-authored with Ursula Cheer. The first edition from 1974 – with detailed chapters on defamation, copyright and contempt of court among other matters – contained no explicit discussion of privacy, although it did outline breach of confidence and made brief reference to the lack of clear legal avenues to protect privacy.[7] In 1990, the third edition took a similar approach. It provided a chapter-long analysis of breach of confidence, but it dealt directly with privacy and media publications in only two pages in another chapter.[8] By the end of that decade, the fourth 1999 edition contained a full chapter addressing privacy in addition to an updated chapter on breach of confidence.[9] That approach has continued in subsequent editions.[10]

Unlike privacy, defamation has long been a central legal topic for journalism and other public speech. This was true in the nineteenth century and has remained so.[11] In many jurisdictions, the greatest changes to defamation law appear to have followed increased legal recognition of public speech's value. That can be seen in notable historical changes – such as the introduction of defamation codes in four Australian defamation jurisdictions from the late 1800s and case law under them which gradually established strong protection for public speech.[12] Equally, it is evident in more recent developments, such as the broader qualified privilege defences that have emerged in many common law jurisdictions during the last two decades.[13] In many places, more critical speech can now be published than a century ago without liability for defamation.[14] Free speech has moved

[7] John F Burrows, *News Media Law in New Zealand* (Wellington: Sweet & Maxwell, 1974) 337; there are also brief references to, e.g., obtaining information.

[8] John F Burrows, *News Media Law in New Zealand*, 3rd edn (Auckland: Oxford University Press, 1990) 187–9.

[9] John Burrows and Ursula Cheer, *Media Law in New Zealand*, 4th edn (Auckland: Oxford University Press, 1999) 171–98.

[10] John Burrows and Ursula Cheer, *Media Law in New Zealand*, 5th edn (Auckland: Oxford University Press, 2005); 6th edn (Wellington: LexisNexis NZ, 2010).

[11] See, e.g., *Wason* v. *Walter* (1868) LR 4 QB 73 and discussion in Andrew T Kenyon and Sophie Walker, 'The Cost of Losing the Code: Historical Protection of Public Debate in Australian Defamation Law' (2014) 38 *Melbourne University Law Review* 554, 559–67.

[12] See Kenyon and Walker, above n 11.

[13] Select examples include in Australia: *Theophanous* v. *Herald & Weekly Times* (1994) 182 CLR 104 and *Lange* v. *Australian Broadcasting Corporation* (1997) 189 CLR 520; Canada: *Grant* v. *Torstar Corporation* [2009] 3 SCR 640; Malaysia: *Anwar Bin Ibrahim* v. *Mahathir Bin Mohamad* [2001] 2 MLJ 65 and *Irene Fernandez* v. *Utusan Melayu* [2008] 2 CLJ 814; New Zealand: *Lange* v. *Atkinson* [2000] 3 NZLR 385; South Africa: *National Media* v. *Bogoshi* [1999] 1 Butterworths Constitutional Law Report 1; and the UK: *Reynolds* v. *Times Newspapers* [2001] 2 AC 127; *Flood* v. *Times Newspapers* [2012] 2 WLR 760 (now see Defamation Act 2013 (UK) s 4).

[14] I am thinking here of many common law systems, but there have been some reforms that have limited defences, notably the abolition in Australia's uniform defamation laws of a

from being a residual value – that is, a space left untouched by all the laws that restrict speech – to a value protected, to a degree at least, as a basic element of the constitutional order. In the UK, for example, that constitutional value is clearly established and one could chart much of its evolution through the successive editions of Eric Barendt's major work on free speech.[15] In the US, the First Amendment became a foundational element of the constitutional order through twentieth-century case law and dramatically reshaped defamation law.

In contrast, privacy has not received the same degree of legal attention overall. Even so, the relevance of privacy for media publications has been recognised for a very long time. I am not thinking just of Warren and Brandeis' late nineteenth-century scholarship about an action against media invasions of privacy, later adopted by US courts.[16] That is certainly significant, especially for US law and commentary. But England offers another example of long-term concern about media publication of private information and about media intrusion during newsgathering. For decades, there have been Bills debated in parliament and official enquiries into privacy. The Younger Committee, for example, 'received more complaints about the activities of the press than on any other aspect' of privacy.[17] Even so, enquiries repeatedly recommended against a general tort action for privacy,[18] preferring instead to call for improved media self-regulation.[19] After English courts established a privacy action against media publication during the last decade, great attention continued to be

public interest-style defence that existed under Australian defamation codes (see Kenyon and Walker, above n 11), and in some Commonwealth jurisdictions, free speech retains a lesser value than in places like England; see, e.g., Clive Walker and Russell L Weaver, 'Libelocracy' (2014) 41 *Journal of Malaysian and Comparative Law* 69; David Tan, 'The Reynolds Privilege in a Neo-Confucianist Communitarian Democracy: Reinvigorating Freedom of Political Communication In Singapore' [2011] *Singapore Journal of Legal Studies* 456; Andrew T Kenyon, 'Investigating Chilling Effects: News Media and Public Speech in Malaysia, Singapore, and Australia' (2010) 4 *International Journal of Communication* 440.

15 Eric Barendt, *Freedom of Speech* (Oxford: Clarendon Press, 1996) and 2nd edn (Oxford: Oxford University Press, 2005).

16 Samuel D Warren and Louis D Brandeis, 'The Right to Privacy' (1890) 4 *Harvard Law Review* 193. See also William L Prosser, 'Privacy' (1960) 48 *California Law Review* 383.

17 UK, Committee on Privacy, *Report of the Committee on Privacy*, Cmnd 5012 (1972) [116] ('Younger Committee').

18 *Ibid.*; UK, Committee on Privacy and Related Matters, *Report of the Committee on Privacy and Related Matters*, Cmnd 2135 (1990) ('Calcutt Committee').

19 *Ibid.* See also the earlier UK, Royal Commission on the Press, *Royal Commission on the Press, 1947–1949: Report*, Cmnd 7700 (1949). From the same period, interesting comparisons could be drawn with the US experience from the Hutchins Commission on Freedom of the Press; see, e.g., Victor Pickard, *America's Battle for Media Democracy: The Triumph of Corporate Libertarianism and the Future of Media Reform* (New York: Cambridge University Press, 2015).

given to improving press regulation.[20] During the same period from the 1960s, there were at least five Bills as well as draft Bills produced by civil society organisations.[21] The Bill that perhaps has the highest profile was introduced by Lord Mancroft in 1961. It proposed an action against publication by press, broadcasting or film that related to personal affairs or conduct and that would cause distress or embarrassment. The Bill received strong support in the House of Lords but not from the Lord Chancellor. Even so, the general aim retained currency, with Zelman Cowen later writing:

> While I am fully aware of the difficulty of formulating an effective and workable legal remedy to protect privacy, I should on balance like to see the enactment of legislation following broadly the lines of Lord Mancroft's proposals. I do not believe that it will encourage a flood of frivolous litigation, and it will not and should not bring solace to all wounded susceptibilities. But I believe it may do a useful job.[22]

Some calls for privacy protection were motivated by human rights concerns, with references made to the Universal Declaration of Human Rights and the International Covenant on Civil and Political Rights.[23] While the Younger Committee noted the human rights issues, the role of human rights is most clear in the minority report of Donald Ross QC. Unlike the majority, he concluded that a privacy action was needed. He started 'from the point of view of principle', noting these international instruments as well as the European Convention on Human Rights, and said that UK law 'should now be brought into line with these important declarations' through a statutory privacy action.[24] Those human rights pressures gradually increased and reshaped the law, an influence which also became apparent in defamation.

The situation was broadly as Raymond Wacks had predicted. In 1980, he suggested that 'the most powerful catalyst for change [in the UK] may either be the European Convention for the Protection of Human Rights and Fundamental Freedoms . . . or the adoption by Parliament of a Bill of

[20] See Right Honourable Lord Justice Brian Leveson, *An Inquiry into the Culture, Practices and Ethics of the Press*, HC 780 (2012).

[21] Younger Committee, above n 17, discusses Bills introduced by Lord Mancroft (1961), Alexander Lyon (1967), Brian Walden (1969), as well as draft Bills from Justice and the National Council for Civil Liberties. All these Bills are reproduced in Younger Committee, Appendix F. Calcutt Committee, above n 18, also discusses Bills from William Cash (1987) and John Browne (1989).

[22] Zelman Cowen, *The Private Man: The Boyer Lectures 1969* (Sydney: Australian Broadcasting Commission, 1969) 27.

[23] See, e.g., *ibid.*, 11; Younger Committee, above n 17, 5.

[24] DM Ross, 'Minority Report' in Younger Committee, above n 17, 213.

Rights which incorporates a "right to privacy"'.[25] Wacks then called for a carefully drafted statutory action protecting personal information against publicity.[26] By 1995, his prediction had developed slightly: while he continued to press for a statutory action against disclosure of private information, Wacks concluded that if politicians would not act, 'the courts must'.[27] And courts could do this by drawing on sources including developments in breach of confidence and decisions from Strasbourg under the Convention.[28] As Ross had called for at the start of the 1970s, courts eventually did just this.

Thus, one pressure for change in privacy law has been the gradual recognition of privacy as a human right, protected in international, regional and national instruments. The approach, on occasion, linked privacy and reputation conceptually, in a manner that calls to mind more recent statements of the European Court of Human Rights (analysed later in this collection). For example, the 1967 Nordic Conference on the Right to Privacy defined privacy in terms of a right to be let alone and made reference to 'private, family and home life', as well as being protected against 'disclosure of irrelevant embarrassing facts' about private life and attacks on 'honour and reputation'.[29] While incorporating reputation so explicitly has not been common when describing privacy in common law jurisdictions, a basis in human rights has been a more frequent reference. Of course, as part of that human rights' awareness, there has also been recognition of free speech. As a result, English developments in privacy law may well have been more tempered than was the case for its defamation law in earlier periods – when those who could afford to sue were offered extremely strong protection for reputation.

## 1.2 Technologies, data, communication

Another point of pressure, relevant to both defamation and privacy law, has been technology. Invasive technologies have long been an issue for privacy – the concern of Warren and Brandeis with media intrusion was linked to reporting technologies.[30] But technology has

[25] Raymond Wacks, *The Protection of Privacy* (London: Sweet & Maxwell, 1980) 9–10.
[26] *Ibid.*, 179.
[27] Raymond Wacks, *Privacy and Press Freedom* (London: Blackstone Press, 1995) 173.
[28] *Ibid.*; see also Raymond Wacks, *Privacy and Media Freedom* (Oxford: Oxford University Press, 2013), which contains a draft Protection of Privacy Bill, added to those produced earlier by law reform bodies, civil society organisations or debated in parliament; see above n 21.
[29] International Commission of Jurists, *Conclusions of the Nordic Conference, May 1967, on the Right to Privacy* (Geneva: ICJ, 1967) 2.
[30] Warren and Brandeis, above n 16.

probably gained particular significance for privacy since the 1960s, when privacy was seen to face threats of a new 'nature and scale' due 'chiefly' to technological change.[31] Technological concerns exist in many publications from the period and, perhaps most influentially, in Alan Westin's US analysis of surveillance.[32] Since then, issues related to computers, databanks and surveillance have gained ever-greater traction. Even by 1980, the literature on information collection and storage was described as 'astonishingly prodigious'.[33] If that was the descriptor thirty-five years ago, it is difficult to settle on an appropriate one now, after WikiLeaks, Edward Snowden and more. Defamation law has also seen change linked with digital communication networks, transnational litigation being an important example. It has, at times, led to important reforms via case law or legislation – consider, for example, decisions such as *Jameel* v. *Wall Street Journal Europe*[34] and the various statutory responses to 'libel tourism'.[35] Somewhat similar issues involving transitional publication can also be seen in recent privacy litigation.[36]

Changes in the environment for public speech, allied to networked communications, provide further impetus for doctrinal reform. When commenting on defamation in 2014, I noted that opportunities clearly exist for 'more speech':

> Public speech is changing. Institutional media remains significant, but in a very different context than even 10 years ago, let alone what is often called the era of broadcast news. With internet-based communications, many more people can reach a public directly with less editorial influence on their speech . . . [T]here are clear opportunities for 'more speech' and, it seems plausible to think,

[31] International Commission of Jurists, 'The Legal Protection of Privacy: A Comparative Survey of Ten Countries' (1972) 24 *International Social Science Journal* 413, 418 (survey of nearly 200 pages commissioned by UNESCO).

[32] Alan F Westin, *Privacy and Freedom* (New York: Atheneum, 1967). See also, e.g., Cowen, above n 22; ICJ, above n 31; Younger Committee, above n 17, which includes chapters on surveillance devices and computers; and WL Morison, *Report on the Law of Privacy* (Sydney: Government Printer NSW, 1973).

[33] Wacks, above n 25, 18. [34] [2007] 1 AC 359.

[35] See, e.g., SPEECH (Securing the Protection of our Enduring and Established Constitutional Heritage) Act 2010 (US) § 4102(a); Defamation Act 2013 (UK) s 9. The issue is older than this recent debate: see, e.g., Kyu Ho Youm, 'The Interaction between American and Foreign Libel Law: US Courts Refuse to Enforce English Libel Judgements' (2000) 49 *International and Comparative Law Quarterly* 131. Evolving approaches to jurisdiction and choice of law can be traced through, e.g., Mathew Collins, *The Law of Defamation and the Internet* (Oxford: Oxford University Press, 2001); 2nd edn (Oxford: Oxford University Press, 2005); 3rd edn (Oxford: Oxford University Press, 2010) and now *Collins on Defamation* (Oxford: Oxford University Press, 2014).

[36] See, e.g., *Weller* v. *Associated Newspapers* [2014] EWHC 1163 (QB).

opportunities for speech of more varied styles from a wider variety of speakers to circulate in more public forms than was commonplace in twentieth-century mass media.[37]

These opportunities for 'more speech' change the context for both defamation and privacy law. They prompt renewed consideration of the forms and availability of legal actions and, perhaps particularly, remind one of long-standing calls to address deficiencies in existing remedies.[38] The changes do not remove the significance of political economy nor the host of other factors that influence the creation, dissemination and reception of public speech. Far from it, rather the entities warranting attention in scholarly analysis and the questions raised are evolving as the environment for speech changes.

## 1.3 Comparative analysis

One final prompt for change may be greater comparative legal analysis. This has been seen both in legal scholarship and many judgements. And it is consistent with the move to comparative analysis in media studies.[39] The legal development would appear to have been influenced by changes in communications technologies, particularly the development of digital networked communication – another aspect of the 'more speech' that now exists.[40] An illustration of the trend in judgements is provided by defamation law decisions developing qualified privilege defences for matters of public interest (or political communication in the Australian instance). In the decisions, reference was frequently made to a host of Commonwealth decisions and, even if not always directly, to the iconic

[37] Andrew T Kenyon, 'Protecting Speech in Defamation Law: Beyond *Reynolds*-Style Defences' (2014) 6 *Journal of Media Law* 21, 21 (note omitted).

[38] See, e.g., John G Fleming, 'Retraction and Reply: Alternative Remedies for Defamation' (1978) 12 *University of British Columbia Law Review* 15; David A Barrett, 'Declaratory Judgements for Libel: A Better Alternative' (1986) 74 *California Law Review* 847; Marc A Franklin, 'A Declaratory Judgement Alternative to Current Libel Law' (1986) 74 *California Law Review* 809; Rodney A Smolla and Michael J Gaertner, 'The Annenberg Libel Reform Proposal: The Case for Enactment' (1989) 31 *William & Mary Law Review* 25; John Soloski and Randall P Bezanson (eds), *Reforming Libel Law* (New York: Guilford Press, 1992); New South Wales Law Reform Commission, *Defamation*, Report 75 (Sydney: NSW Law Reform Commission, 1995); Alastair Mullis and Andrew Scott, 'Tilting at Windmills: The Defamation Act 2013' (2014) 77 *Modern Law Review* 87, 107–8.

[39] Among a very large literature, see e.g., Daniel C Hallin and Paolo Mancini, *Comparing Media Systems: Three Models of Media and Politics* (Cambridge: Cambridge University Press, 2004); Toril Aalberg and James Curran (eds), *How Media Inform Democracy: A Comparative Approach* (New York: Routledge, 2012).

[40] The leading legal website Austlii (the Australasian Legal Information Institute) and its host of international parallels appear to have an important part in that history.

US decision in *Sullivan*.[41] One could see similar tendencies in privacy developments, as well as in calls for comparative privacy scholarship.[42]

These interests – in defamation, privacy and speech – and the changing context in which law addresses them, have prompted this book. Contributors draw from one or more of the developments to address legal issues in defamation, privacy or their relationship, focussing on media in a range of common law jurisdictions. Many of the jurisdictions have seen defamation law reforms and privacy law developments in recent years, or extensive consideration of them. The changes have often drawn on, or reacted against, approaches or ideas in other jurisdictions. In addition, the emergence of divergent views about the legal protection of reputation and privacy – prompted in part by case law under Article 8 of the European Convention on Human Rights – raises challenging conceptual questions about the interests involved. The developments in each area of law and the ways in which they display similarities and differences have led to a comparative collection encompassing both areas of law.

## 1.4 Defamation: comparative reform, constitutions and common law

The law of defamation traditionally offered limited protection to matters of public interest published widely. Defences would protect some speech – it might be proven to be true, it might be an honest comment based on facts that are proven true, it might be a fair report of a statement made in parliament, and so forth. The law took a categorical approach, with free speech interests considered, so far as they were, in the formulation of defences. Arguably, the law in England and some other jurisdictions is moving towards a more flexible approach where the overall interests in speech and reputation will be given more attention in any particular case. To date, one way in which that flexibility has been pursued is through reformed privilege defences that have emerged in many common law countries since the mid-1990s.[43] This style of change in defamation

[41] For example, in *Reynolds* v. *Times Newspapers* [2001] 2 AC 127, direct reference was made to the earlier House of Lords decision in *Derbyshire County Council* v. *Times Newspapers* [1993] AC 534 (which prevented elected government bodies from suing in defamation). In *Derbyshire*, English law explicitly endorsed the chilling effect rationale of *Sullivan*.

[42] See, e.g., Ronald J Krotoszynski Jr, 'Responding to a World Without Privacy: On the Potential Merits of a Comparative Law Perspective' in Austin Sarat (ed), *A World Without Privacy: What Law Can and Should Do?* (New York: Cambridge University Press, 2015) 234.

[43] See above n 13.

law, as well as the US *Sullivan* model that preceded it, is addressed in various chapters.

Hilary Young examines Canadian developments in defamation law through *Grant* v. *Torstar*[44] and subsequent case law on the responsible communication defence. Her analysis suggests that courts may interpret the defence too conservatively, perhaps especially when dealing with non-journalistic publications. The Canadian situation offers some echoes of English experience, with less flexibility in assessing the 'responsibility' of communication than appears warranted by the defence's rationale. This leads Young to suggest the defence should become focussed on a 'reasonableness' standard, as in negligence law, developing ideas seen in some commentary after *Reynolds*.[45]

Andrew Scott addresses an omission from the reforms in the Defamation Act 2013 (UK), which focussed on areas of substantive law, rather than dispute management, resolution and remedies. He examines how ending the single meaning rule in defamation, along with introducing discursive remedies, could lead to a much better 'triangulation' of social and individual interests in reputation and free speech. Finding ways to deal more effectively with a publication's meaning in defamation law certainly has great potential for ameliorating some of the law's worst problems.[46] Scott suggests how reconsidering the single meaning rule along with remedial reform offers a relatively simple way of providing most litigants with 'mutually acceptable' and quicker results in defamation disputes. Under the current approach, defamation litigation becomes 'strategy and semantics' more than 'the attempt to address any core dispute'. Notably, changing the single meaning rule could be pursued by courts, not merely by legislation. While the argument of principle is independent of the recent statutory reforms, it may be that reform to the single meaning rule becomes more palatable for courts after jury trials have become the exception in English defamation law.[47]

The analyses of Young and Scott both have wider resonance: their concerns and suggested approaches could have application in a host of Commonwealth jurisdictions at the least. But the US, in many ways, remains a place apart for matters of media law. Commentators, however, differ as to the degree to which that separation does, or should, exist. In

[44] [2009] 3 SCR 640.

[45] See, e.g., Eric Descheemaeker, 'Protecting Reputation: Defamation and Negligence' (2009) 29 *Oxford Journal of Legal Studies* 603.

[46] Much of my own earlier research has addressed other ways in which the treatment of a publication's meaning creates unwarranted complexities in defamation law; see, e.g., Andrew T Kenyon, *Defamation: Comparative Law and Practice* (Abingdon: UCL Press, 2006).

[47] Defamation Act 2013 (UK) s 11.

this collection, David Partlett starts from the observation that the Supreme Court's approach to the First Amendment has had little direct 'legal resonance elsewhere in the western world' and emphasises the particular civil rights context underlying *New York Times* v. *Sullivan*.[48] That context may be more persuasive in understanding the decision than simply ideas about free speech. For Partlett, the constitutionalisation of defamation law through *Sullivan* is problematic, removing defamation from its 'common law culture'. He criticises the US approach for its reliance on a 'marketplace' model of truth and questions how the doctrine accords with contemporary modes of producing, circulating and accessing public information. Journalistic standards of news production are not so easy to apply to digital communication technologies and networked public speech. For Partlett, all those factors suggest that *Sullivan*'s international influence will lessen – as US law remains 'frozen in constitutional stasis' – even though the US decision has to date 'framed' free speech debates in many places.

The idea that greater space should be left for speech on democratic grounds is what has had most purchase internationally from *Sullivan*, and that is the point of departure for Russell Weaver. He considers the varied doctrinal methods taken in defamation reform in the US, the UK and Australia and summarises earlier research into the law's practical effects on publication. He concludes that while some may find that the US approach offers too little protection to reputation, it is not clear that the defamation law reforms elsewhere have found an appropriate balance. In short, for Weaver, the other reforms have not done enough to promote speech and, through that, democratic values.

One of the things done by the US valuation of speech has been to sideline privacy protection. In contrast, privacy has emerged as an important area of law for media publications in many common law jurisdictions.[49] Some of those changes frame the next group of chapters.

## 1.5 Privacy: expectations, impacts and rationales

Eric Barendt addresses a question that is not often considered in relation to English privacy law. Is it useful to have, as the law currently does, a threshold test of whether claimants had 'a reasonable expectation of privacy'? There is not, for example, a question of whether 'reasonable

[48] 376 US 254 (1964).

[49] In several notable Commonwealth jurisdictions, the developments have emerged recently and are ongoing. But there are exceptions, as some older statutory provisions protecting privacy attest; see, e.g., the Canadian provincial examples discussed in Younger Committee, above n 17 and Calcutt Committee, above n 18.

expectation of reputation' exists when the cause of action is defamation. Barendt explores why it could be thought necessary in privacy law in an interesting analysis which, as the chapter suggests, generated much discussion among other contributors to this book. Barendt argues that the reasonable expectation test is misconceived and should be abandoned. Among other weaknesses, it enables or even 'tempts' courts, when deciding if Article 8 of the European Convention on Human Rights has been *engaged*, to consider arguments that are relevant to the later task of *balancing* any privacy interest against free speech, protected by Article 10. This could lead to 'an unconscious double-counting' of factors supporting free speech against the interests of claimants, as well as reduce the law's predictability. Barendt suggests that, if an objective limit to the scope of privacy is needed, only serious or non-trivial infringements of privacy should ground an action.

Nicole Moreham and Yvette Tinsley explore another topic that is not often seen in the privacy law literature. Their study of media coverage of a New Zealand coal mining disaster is a revealing examination of 'grief journalism' and some of its effects. As part of larger research, Moreham and Tinsley focus here on how families and close friends of the miners experienced the media's physical presence in the days after an explosion trapped workers underground. There was a second explosion five days after the first, which none of those underground could have survived. Participants in the study had many negative feelings about the conduct of photographers and reporters. These findings support an understanding of privacy in terms of dignity, security and autonomy. Moreham and Tinsley draw out three main effects of the media's physical intrusiveness: it undermined dignity through communicating a 'lack of respect' for 'people who were suffering deeply'; it undermined security by causing many family and close friends to feel physically unsafe; and it undermined individual autonomy in terms of freedom of action, expression and connecting with others.

Something that might be drawn from such research is an understanding of media free speech as being distinct from individual free speech. That is Gavin Phillipson's starting point. When the value of media speech is understood in terms of audience interests, some types of regulation that might otherwise be thought to restrict speech can be recognised as publicly beneficial. Phillipson addresses how that understanding of press freedom would affect judicial approaches to the concept of 'public interest' in privacy claims, evaluating decisions from English courts and the European Court of Human Rights. Among other things, the analysis is used to critique the idea of public figures having reduced expectations of privacy. He argues that the treatment of public figures would be better approached more precisely, avoiding 'lumping together into one category pop stars and prime ministers'. He goes further to critique recent English decisions that suggest there is a 'freedom to criticise',[50] which could protect disclosure of conduct where it could reasonably be argued that the conduct 'ought to be' contrary to contemporary social standards.[51] It is suggested that this undermines the very values sought to be protected by privacy and amounts to an invitation for judges to apply their own moral judgements to privacy claims.

Kirsty Hughes and Neil Richards consider how the balance struck between privacy and free speech in UK and US law can be so different, despite general similarities in the legal systems and their common origins. Their analysis focusses on two points: the domestic 'cultural power' of the First Amendment is quite different from that of free speech for English judges, especially in cases involving media defendants, and the conceptualisation of privacy actions differ in the two countries. This second point is less commonly explored but appears equally valuable in understanding the overall differences in law. The action is understood as a private law tort in the US, while it is seen as an action based on a significant human right in England. That difference changes the free speech interests that are sufficient to outweigh a privacy claim. Hughes and Richards explore these differences in several typical scenarios involving disclosure under US and European principles. The analysis reveals more nuances than might initially be apparent. And it highlights the importance of carefully examining the different approaches – including their effects on parties in national or transnational privacy disputes – in any future attempt to bridge this Atlantic divide.

## 1.6 Privacy: data, surveillance and journalistic practice

David Lindsay examines another transnational issue, although here focussed legally on Europe, in analysing the 'right to be forgotten' following the European Court of Justice's *Costeja* decision.[52] Lindsay examines legal and policy questions about applying the 1995 European Data Protection Directive to search engines. After explaining the relevant background, he explores gaps and ambiguities in the decision, especially in relation to the scope of rights held by data subjects. His analysis

[50] See, e.g., *Hutcheson* v. *News Group Newspapers* [2011] EWCA Civ 808, [35] (Gross LJ, Lord Neuberger MR and Etherton LJ agreed).

[51] See, e.g., *Goodwin* v. *News Group Newspapers* [2011] EWHC 1437 (QB), [133] (Tugendhat J).

[52] Case 131/12, *Google Spain SL* v. *Agencia Española de Protección de Datos (AEPD) and Mario Costeja González* [2014] 3 CMLR 50 (ECJ (Grand Chamber)).

focusses on three points: the Directive's territorial scope; whether search engines that engage in automated processing can be data controllers under the Directive; and the extent to which search engines would need to remove relevant links from search results if the Directive does apply to their activities. Lindsay explains some of the central challenges for search engines in implementing the decision and highlights the importance that different interpretations of the social value of internet intermediaries have for digital communications and law.

Particular implications of digital communications are also addressed by Melissa de Zwart. She explores what role concepts of privacy could have in a digital surveillance society. Starting from publications by and about Julian Assange and warnings made in 2012 of mass online surveillance, De Zwart reviews more recent US events as well as changes to Australian security legislation that affect whistle-blowing and media reporting and plans for statutory data retention. For de Zwart, a central message coming from the activities of Edward Snowden and WikiLeaks is the need to distinguish institutional and individual privacy. In short, 'personal privacy is paramount' and should be protected against indiscriminate surveillance. One option that appears plausible to achieve protection is encryption, a form of privacy by choice. De Zwart concludes that encryption 'may need to become the new standard, replacing common law or statutory concepts of privacy which have proven too vague and too unenforceable' in relation to individual privacy interests.

Amy Gajda tackles a different aspect of contemporary privacy, focussing on media disclosures of private information. She examines the extremely wide protection given to such disclosures under US law, but suggests that the legal position could change in response to some contemporary media practices. Those practices ignore the journalistic ethics that have long played an important role in US publications. Gajda argues for greater legal respect for privacy, but not by focussing solely on the human dignity values often linked to privacy. Dignity for her is a powerful, but dangerous, concept in relation to media freedom. She suggests that US courts need to find ways to consider both dignity and speech values. That might amount to taking something from Europe and adapting it to US soil.

## 1.7 Connections and contrasts: defamation and privacy

Another development in defamation and privacy law is the way in which they are coming to be seen as intertwined, in some circumstances at least. The issue has perhaps been flagged most clearly in Europe during recent years, with the European Court of Human Rights finding – in different and not entirely consistent ways – that reputation can fall within the 'private life' protected by Art 8 of the Convention. Tanya Aplin and Jason Bosland tackle this development, beginning with a review of theoretical rationales for protecting reputation, particularly those related to dignity and sociality. They suggest there is some resonance between those ideas and the concept of private life. They then examine the European decisions to show how the court's analyses do not entirely accord with these apparent rationales for protection. This leads to a suggested approach for understanding how reputational harm can affect private life that draws carefully from existing case law. In their analysis, Aplin and Bosland seek to advance what is likely to remain an important debate, with potentially significant legal results.

David Rolph engages with another aspect of reputation and privacy by focussing on the concept of vindication, in a comparative analysis of English, Australian and New Zealand developments. He examines an often-stated difference between defamation and privacy; namely that vindication by damages is possible for harm to reputation but not for privacy. For Rolph, the distinction is flawed and he suggests that coherent legal development may require change in the approach to injunctions in defamation, as well as the approach to damages in privacy.

Ursula Cheer offers another view of a possible legal future for defamation and privacy, suggesting the two actions could merge. Primarily using examples from New Zealand and the UK, she investigates how the law currently treats 'complex damaging speech' – speech that appears to affect both reputational and privacy interests – and examines the expansion of the privacy tort since its comparatively recent development. Cheer suggests that the actions share conceptual bases, as both seek protection for dignity and autonomy. This leads to two possible models for merging the actions, one statutory, adapted from NZ's Harmful Digital Communications Act 2015, the other constitutional in the form of amending the New Zealand Bill of Rights Act 1990. As Cheer notes, each model offers interesting ideas for comparative consideration and, in that, the chapter illustrates one of the primary aims underlying this collection.

Andrew Kenyon and Megan Richardson return to US law and its influence in the UK and Australia, examining the very different reverberations of *New York Times* v. *Sullivan*[53] in terms of defamation law and privacy. As with Partlett, they note the social and political setting that underpinned the Supreme Court decision. One of the elements they draw out is the way in which, of two important rationales expressed by Brennan J in *Sullivan*, only one has been recognised and accepted by

[53] 376 US 254 (1964).

Commonwealth courts when they have developed defamation law. That is, the recognition of traditional defamation law's chilling effect has been accepted, but the profound US commitment to 'uninhibited, robust and wide-open'[54] public debate has not been addressed in Commonwealth defamation law. Thus reforms have taken a very different shape than under US law. In contrast, the US Supreme Court's application of *Sullivan* to privacy law has not registered to any great degree in Commonwealth law and reform. English judgements have drawn on constitutional-style rights to private life *and* free speech in developing privacy, while Australian courts have taken a more incremental approach, without an explicit rights framework, to long-standing causes of action relevant to privacy. While in relation to privacy law the US is clearly distinct from jurisdictions like Australia and the UK, for defamation law the US is distinct *but only in part* because the idea of the chilling effect that was recognised in *Sullivan* has been enormously influential.

The collection, examining a wide range of issues in defamation and privacy law and their reform, seeks to make clear the importance of both areas of law, their relationships and their evolution. It suggests the value in engaging with developments and challenges within and across multiple jurisdictions in relation to such areas of media law. One of the pressures for reform has been increased recognition of the claims of human rights, which has certainly supported reform to defamation and the development of privacy law in a jurisdiction such as England, as well as revealing challenges in understanding the relations between reputation and privacy. But there have also been important pressures for reform arising from digital and networked communications technologies and their uses; whether in terms of data collection and surveillance or the greater possibilities for public speech, the context in which the law operates has changed. In addition, a third prompt to the legal developments is mirrored in the collection; namely, the comparative legal analysis that has become an important element of media law in many places. While I would not seek to suggest that law now deals adequately with interests in reputation, free speech and privacy, it is clear that the debate about the appropriate elements in these areas of law has changed. In defamation law, for example, the debate has shifted substantially through the gradual recognition of free speech as a valuable interest deserving greater protection in law. The tensions, links and developments in law that are examined in this collection suggest ways in which the debate – and perhaps defamation and privacy law – will change again.

[54] *Ibid.*, 270.

# 2 'Anyone ... in any medium'? The scope of Canada's responsible communication defence

*Hilary Young*

In *Grant* v. *Torstar*,[1] Canada finally got its own *Reynolds* v. *Times Newspapers* defence to defamation: 'responsible communication on matters of public interest'. With the benefit of other common law countries' experience, Canada's Supreme Court created a complete defence where communications on matters of public interest are published responsibly. It justified this change in the law on the basis that the existing balance between freedom of expression and reputation insufficiently protected factual communications on matters of public interest.

*Grant* was heralded as a 'historic' victory for freedom of expression.[2] Its impact, however, will depend on how courts understand and apply it. I examine the first five years of case law on the '*Grant* defence' to see whether its stated aims are being achieved. Although it is still in its infancy, there are signs that courts are applying the *Grant* defence conservatively – especially when it comes to non-journalistic publications. Since it was intended to apply broadly, there is a risk that the promise of *Grant* will not be met.

I propose that the best way to understand the *Grant* defence is as a broad defence available in regard to any factual communication in the public interest, and not limited to journalism or to widely published statements. That said, the less like traditional journalism a communication is, the harder it may be sensibly to apply a defence that defines

I wish to thank Bohdana Tkachuk for her research assistance and the UNB Faculty of Law for funding this work. I also wish to thank Andrew Kenyon and the participants of the 'Defamation and Privacy: Comparative Law, Media and Public Speech' workshop for their valuable comments.

[1] *Grant* v. *Torstar*, 2009 SCC 61 (CanLII), [2009] 3 SCR 640 ('*Grant*'). *Grant* had a companion case, *Quan* v. *Cusson*, 2009 SCC 62 (CanLII); [2009] 3 SCR 712, in which the new defence was applied. See, generally, *Reynolds* v. *Times Newspapers* [1999] 4 All ER 609 ('*Reynolds*').

[2] See, e.g., Richard Dearden and Wendy Wagner, 'Canadian Libel Law Enters the 21st Century: The Public Interest Responsible Communication Defence' (2009–2010) 41 *Ottawa Law Review* 351 at 373.

responsible communication largely in terms of journalistic standards. If the *Grant* defence is to develop as a defence of *communication* on matters of public interest, the factors that determine whether communication is responsible will have to be applied flexibly. Given courts' tendency to apply the factors rigidly, I conclude that the language of 'responsible communication' and its journalism-based indicia should be replaced by negligence's 'reasonableness' standard.

## 2.1 Canada gets a responsible communication defence

*Grant* v. *Torstar* was a defamation action against media defendants. A Toronto businessman was seeking government approval to develop a private golf course. There was some resistance in the community, and the *Toronto Star* newspaper published an article quoting a resident of the area who said people there thought Grant would get his approval (it was a 'done deal') because of his government connections. Grant alleged that was defamatory of him.[3]

Before the Supreme Court of Canada, the principal issue was whether Canada should adopt a new defence to defamation of responsible journalism, and if so, what its parameters should be. It was the first time the Supreme Court had addressed this question[4] since the United Kingdom adopted its defence of responsible journalism in *Reynolds* v. *Times Newspapers*,[5] and since Australia, New Zealand and South Africa had adopted their own public interest communication defences.[6] Critics had long argued that Canadian defamation law strikes a balance that is too protective of reputation at the expense of free speech, and particularly so where matters of public interest are at stake.[7]

*Grant* adopted a new defence to defamation, similar to that set out in *Reynolds*. Responsible Communication on Matters of Public Interest is

[3] *Grant* [4].

[4] In *WIC Radio* v. *Simpson*, 2008 SCC 40 (CanLII); [2008] 2 SCR 420, the Supreme Court dedicated eight paragraphs to the issue of responsible communication defences but declined to decide whether Canada should adopt one because *WIC Radio* was a fair comment case.

[5] *Reynolds* modified in *Jameel* v. *Wall Street Journal Europe* [2006] UKHL 44; [2007] 1 AC 359, reversing [2005] EWCA Civ 74, [2005] 4 All ER 356 ('*Jameel*'). It should be noted, however, that as of 2013, the United Kingdom has enacted the Defamation Act 2013 [Defamation Act]. Section 4 abolishes the *Reynolds* defence in favour of a public interest defence that requires reasonable belief that publication was in the public interest.

[6] For Australia, see *Lange* v. *Australian Broadcasting Corporation* (1997) 145 ALR 96 (HC) ('*Lange*'). For New Zealand, see *Lange* v. *Atkinson* [2000] 3 NZLR 385 (CA) and its predecessors. For South Africa, see *Du Plessis* v. *De Klerk*, 1996 (3) SA 850 (CC); *National Media* v. *Bogoshi*, 1998 (4) SA 1196 (SCA).

[7] See, e.g., Denis Boivin, 'Accommodating Freedom of Expression and Reputation in the Common Law of Defamation' (1997) 22 *Queen's Law Journal* 229.

essentially a fault-based defence that applies (a) where the matter is of public interest and (b) where the defendant has acted responsibly in publishing.

### 2.1.1 *Public interest*

The Supreme Court made it clear that the defence applies only to communication on matters of public interest,[8] but that 'public interest' is to be understood broadly:

> the subject matter 'must be shown to be one inviting public attention, or about which the public has some substantial concern because it affects the welfare of citizens, or one to which considerable public notoriety or controversy has attached' ... mere curiosity or prurient interest is not enough. Some segment of the public must have a genuine stake in knowing about the matter published.[9]

The court was explicit that: 'Public interest is not confined to publications on government and political matters, as it is in Australia and New Zealand'.[10] As Eric Descheemaeker notes, '"public interest" is an old category within the law of defamation' which *Reynolds* did not alter.[11] Neither, would it seem, did *Grant*.

Communications on matters of public interest are singled out because they are more worthy of protection. *Grant* discussed the three reasons why freedom of expression is constitutionally protected: democratic discourse, truth-finding and self-fulfilment.[12] Of these, the first two are clearly implicated even by false and defamatory speech on matters of public interest.[13] According to the Supreme Court, existing defamation law had a chilling effect on speech on matters of public interest. It therefore did not strike the correct balance between reputation and freedom of expression: 'When proper weight is given to the constitutional value of free expression on matters of public interest, the balance tips in favour of broadening the defences available to those who communicate facts it is in the public's interest to know'.[14]

### 2.1.2 *Responsible communication*

The second element of the defence is that communication be responsible. This is assessed with regard to indicia drawn largely from the United

[8] *Grant* [98], [99]. [9] *Ibid.*, [105]. [10] *Ibid.*, [106].

[11] Eric Descheemaeker, '"A Man Must Take Care Not to Defame His Neighbour": The Origins and Significance of the *Reynolds* Defence' (University of Edinburgh School of Law, Research Paper No 2013/07, 13 February 2013) 2.

[12] *Grant* [47]. [13] *Ibid.*, [51], [52]. [14] *Ibid.*, [65].

Kingdom's *Reynolds* defence. *Grant* states that publication is responsible where:

The publisher was diligent in trying to verify the allegation, having regard to:

(a) the seriousness of the allegation;
(b) the public importance of the matter;
(c) the urgency of the matter;
(d) the status and reliability of the source;
(e) whether the plaintiff's side of the story was sought and accurately reported;
(f) whether the inclusion of the defamatory statement was justifiable;
(g) whether the defamatory statement's public interest lay in the fact that it was made rather than its truth ('reportage'); and
(h) any other relevant circumstances.[15]

These factors differ from the indicia of responsible journalism in *Reynolds* only in relatively trivial respects. For example, *Grant* explicitly includes consideration of reportage (g) while *Reynolds* does not,[16] and *Grant* lists 'other' as a criterion, while *Reynolds* achieves the same effect by stating that the list is not exhaustive. Both mention the seriousness of the allegation, public importance, urgency, the source of the publication and whether the plaintiff's side was sought and reported. Both are grounded in standards of professional journalism.[17]

Despite this list, the court makes clear that the indicia of responsible communication are not a checklist, but simply 'relevant factors that may aid in determining whether a defamatory communication on a matter of public interest was responsibly made'.[18] They are 'non-exhaustive but illustrative guides. Ultimately, all matters relevant to whether the defendant communicated responsibly can be considered'.[19] This warning was perhaps considered necessary given British courts' tendency to apply the *Reynolds* factors like a checklist.[20]

### 2.1.3 Scope

Although the *Reynolds* defence is frequently invoked by media defendants and closely associated with the media, both the United Kingdom's

[15] *Ibid.*, [126]. [16] Although see *Jameel* [62].
[17] 'The common law does not seek to set a higher standard than that of responsible journalism, a standard the media themselves espouse.' *Reynolds* [1999] 4 All ER 609, 623. In particular, the indicia related to reliability of sources, reporting the plaintiff's views and reportage reflect a journalistic emphasis in the test. Further, the 'urgency' criterion takes into account the fact that news is a 'perishable commodity' (*Grant* [113]).
[18] *Grant* [110]. [19] *Ibid.*, [122].
[20] *Ibid.*, [71]; Andrew T Kenyon, *Defamation: Comparative Law and Practice* (Abingdon: UCL Press, 2006) at 205; Marin Scordato, 'The International Legal Environment for Serious Political Reporting Has Fundamentally Changed: Understanding the Revolutionary New Era of English Defamation Law' (2007) 40 *Connecticut Law Review* 165, 175.

defence[21] and the new Canadian defence can apply to any communication on a matter of public interest – not only those published by journalists and not only those published to the world at large. The Chief Justice stated:

> I agree with Lord Hoffmann [in *Jameel*] that the new defence is 'available to anyone who publishes material of public interest in any medium'.[22]

In this section, I demonstrate that the *Grant* defence is meant to be limited neither to journalists nor to those who publish to the world at large.

*2.1.3.1 Not strictly a journalism defence* Given the constant references to journalism in *Reynolds* and *Grant*, one would be forgiven for thinking that the responsible communication defence only applies to media communications. In *Grant*, the Chief Justice refers to responsible journalism as the 'essence of the defence'.[23] She named the defence 'responsible communication' to note that non-journalists are included, but relied primarily on the distinction between old and new media (bloggers, for example).[24] This suggests a defence that applies to communication *complementary* or analogous to the traditional media, as opposed to all communication – my letter to a friend, for example, or a citizen speaking at a town council meeting. The Supreme Court continues by referring to 'disseminators of news and information',[25] again suggesting a focus on journalism.

Another reason to think that *Grant* creates a media defence is that, as noted earlier, the standards to be applied are drawn largely from professional standards of journalism.[26]

Further, *Grant* makes frequent reference to the importance of free speech for the press in its freedom of expression rationale for the defence (the 'argument from principle'). For example, the court takes note of the constitutional protection granted specifically to the freedom of expression of 'the press and other media of communication'.[27] It notes that: 'it is vital that the media act responsibly in reporting facts on matters of public concern, holding themselves to the highest journalistic standards'.[28] 'Media', in the sense of journalists, are referred to throughout *Grant*[29]

[21] *Jameel* [54]; Alastair Mullis and Richard Parkes (eds), *Gatley on Libel and Slander*, 12th edn (London: Sweet & Maxwell, 2013) [15.20].

[22] *Grant* [96]. [23] *Ibid.* [24] *Ibid.* [25] *Ibid.* [26] *Reynolds*, 623.

[27] *Grant* [43] citing s 2b of the *Canadian Charter of Rights and Freedoms*. The court repeats the importance of free speech for the press at [52].

[28] *Ibid.*, [53]. [29] *Ibid.*, [53], [57], [62].

and few if any non-journalistic examples are given other than bloggers – an example to which we will return.

There is no doubt that the Supreme Court seems frequently to have journalism in mind in creating the *Grant* defence, just as the House of Lords had journalism in mind in creating the *Reynolds* defence. However, *Grant* makes it reasonably clear that the defence can apply to any defamatory statement of fact on a matter of public interest, not only to those communicated by journalists.

First, *Grant* explicitly rejects the *Reynolds* 'responsible journalism' approach in favour of a test of 'responsible communication'.[30] The court indicates that the defence applies more broadly than to journalists. The plain meaning of the court's words, taken from *Jameel* ('anyone . . . in any medium'), suggests that the defence applies quite broadly.

Second, there is no apparent reason to limit the defence to statements made by journalists. Although freedom of the press is important, as the Supreme Court noted, the primary impetus for the change was the importance of communication on matters of public interest. An argument could perhaps be made that journalism deserves special protection, but *Grant* does not rely on any such argument. Instead, it suggests that the press is important because it communicates on matters of public interest. It is the fact of being on a matter of public interest, combined with defamation law's chilling effect on communicating such content, that justifies a fault-based defence.

I therefore conclude that the *Grant* defence applies beyond the context of journalism.

*2.1.3.2 Not limited to publications to the world at large* One might alternately conclude that the *Grant* defence only applies to communications to the world at large. The defence (like the *Reynolds* defence) was justified in part because qualified privilege is unavailable to those who publish to the world at large. In justifying the new defence in principle, the Supreme Court stated: 'the law of defamation currently accords no protection for statements on matters of public interest published to the world at large if they cannot, for whatever reason, be proven to be true'.[31]

Qualified privilege protects communications based on the occasion of publication. Occasions are privileged where 'the person who makes a communication has an interest or a duty, legal, social, or moral, to make it to the person to whom it is made, and the person to whom it is so made has a corresponding interest or duty to receive it'.[32] Courts have

[30] *Ibid.*, [96]. [31] *Ibid.*, [65].
[32] *Hill* v. *Church of Scientology of Toronto*, 1995 CanLII 59 (SCC), [1995] 2 SCR 1130 [143].

generally held that those who publish indiscriminately, or to the 'world at large', exceed the scope of the privilege by communicating to those to whom a duty is not owed and who have no interest in receiving the communication.[33]

While it is true that one reason for creating the *Grant* defence was the lack of defences for those who publish to the world at large, especially the media, the Supreme Court refused to treat the *Grant* defence as a new type of qualified privilege.[34] This is because its purpose is not to protect certain occasions of communication but rather to promote freedom of expression on matters of public interest. Qualified privilege's duty/interest approach makes sense if one is trying to identify protected occasions, but makes little sense as an approach to determining when freedom of expression on matters of public interest should be protected.[35] The Supreme Court held that, given the importance of speech on matters of public interest, the law of defamation did not sufficiently reflect the value of freedom of expression protected in the Canadian Constitution. As a result, *Grant* created a new defence rather than a subset of qualified privilege.

If the duty/interest approach is rejected, so too should the distinction between publishing narrowly (to someone owed a duty and with an interest) and publishing to the world at large. The size of the audience may be relevant to whether communication is responsible, but the defence should not a priori be limited to those who publish widely. Although the Supreme Court expressed an intent to include those who publish to the world at large, by mentioning bloggers and new communications media, this in no way suggests it intended to exclude those who do not publish widely.

To summarise, the *Grant* defence protects responsible communication on matters of public interest regardless of whether it is journalism and regardless of the size of the audience. The defence simply requires that publications relate to matters of public interest, defined broadly, and that communication itself be responsible.

### *2.1.4 Jury question*

Whether the *Grant* defence is made out is to be determined by a jury.[36] This differs from the approach in the United Kingdom and Australia, where the question is one for the judge.[37] One criticism of *Reynolds* is that

[33] *Jones* v. *Bennett*, [1969] SCR 277, 2 DLR (3d) 291, 284–5. [34] *Grant* [88]–[95].
[35] *Ibid.*, [94]. [36] *Ibid.*, [130]–[135].
[37] For the UK, see Mullis and Parkes, above n 21, at [15.22]. For Australia, see *Herald & Weekly Times* v. *Popovic* (2003) VSCA 161 [111].

it creates a complex and unworkable situation in which the question of what is responsible is left to the judge, based on numerous factual findings by the jury. The jury task has been described as setting 'an examination paper',[38] as 'clumsy and unsatisfactory'[39] and as 'subvert[ing juries'] traditional role of delivering general verdicts'.[40] *Grant* referred to these criticisms in deciding that the defence would be left to the jury.

## 2.2 The *Grant* defence in practice

In the first five years of its existence, there were thirty-four reported cases in which the *Grant* defence was pleaded or argued.[41] About half (sixteen) have not yet been decided or settled, as best I can determine from the case law and media coverage. This is hardly surprising given the time it takes for civil actions to work their way through the courts and given that defamation actions are often heard by juries rather than judges, such that the only reported decision in a case may be a decision on a motion. Eighteen have been decided.

Although the sample size is too small and incomplete[42] to permit strong empirical conclusions, the cases nevertheless provide clues as to how courts are interpreting *Grant*.

### *2.2.1 Pleading the* Grant *defence*

Consider first the types of defendants who are pleading the *Grant* defence. Traditional journalists are certainly availing themselves of the defence. Fourteen of the thirty-four cases involved a traditional media defendant (newspapers and television or radio broadcast media) or a press release. In fact, newspapers or newspaper reporters were defendants in eleven of these cases.[43]

That means, however, that most cases involved defendants who are not traditional media defendants.[44] Four of these were bloggers. This is

38 *Loutchansky* v. *Times Newspapers (No 4)* [2001] EMLR 898, 912 (Gray J).

39 Andrew T Kenyon, '*Lange* and *Reynolds* Qualified Privilege: Australian and English Defamation Law and Practice' (2004) 28 *Melbourne University Law Review* 406 at 426, citing a British barrister.

40 *Ibid.* Although note that under s 11 of the United Kingdom's Defamation Act, the default is judge-alone trials, and so the problems with juries should be greatly reduced.

41 As of 13 June 2014. I have counted closely related cases reported separately as one case. Cases with multiple reported decisions (e.g., appeals) are counted as one.

42 Defamation actions tried by jury are underrepresented in the reported cases.

43 That said, some of these newspapers are student-run or small community papers, such that it cannot be assumed that the defendants are professional media corporations.

44 I am aware of no statistics regarding the proportion of defamation cases against media versus non-media in Canada. In the United Kingdom and Australia, media are defendants in between 60 and 75 per cent of defamation actions (Kenyon, above n 20, 257). If

unsurprising given the Supreme Court's explicit mention of bloggers in *Grant*. The remaining sixteen cases involve a range of defendants including a public official,[45] a pornography business,[46] the Ontario SPCA,[47] and a candidate for City Council.[48]

Given the nature of the defendants pleading the *Grant* defence, lawyers seem to have gotten the message that it applies broadly (or at least that it *may*). Although many of the cases still involve traditional media defendants, most do not. Some defendants have communicated to a small number of people, and others to a large number. Lawyers would presumably not plead the *Grant* defence in relation to oral communications,[49] letters[50] and ads in the local paper,[51] if they thought it only applied to journalists or to those who publish to the world at large. Section 2.2.2 suggests, however, that judges have perhaps not understood *Grant* in the same way as lawyers.

### 2.2.2 *Applying the* Grant *defence*

Of the eighteen decided cases in which the *Grant* defence has been argued, only three have been successful on that basis.[52] That said, in six additional cases, the defendant won on other grounds, such as that the publication was not *prima facie* defamatory or was protected by qualified privilege. Further, in three of those six cases, it was not the case that the *Grant* defence failed – the court simply refused to consider it given that the defendant won on other grounds. Still, given the breadth of the defence and the optimism that it would be a game changer,[53] it is worth noting that the *Grant* defence was only made out in three of eighteen cases.[54]

the proportion is similar for Canada, the fact most *Grant* defences are being argued by non-media defendants is perhaps significant.

45 *Hunter* v. *Chandler*, 2010 BCSC 729 (CanLII) ('*Hunter*').

46 *Asselin* v. *McDougall*, 2013 ONSC 1716 (CanLII) ('*Asselin*').

47 *Robinson* v. *Ontario Society for the Prevention of Cruelty to Animals*, 2012 ONSC 3647 (CanLII) ('*Robinson*').

48 *Foulidis* v. *Baker*, 2012 ONSC 7295 (CanLII) ('*Baker*').

49 *Roshard* v. *St Dennis*, 2013 BCSC 1388 (CanLII) ('*Roshard*'); *Hunter*.

50 *Rubin* v. *Ross*, 2010 SKQB 249 (CanLII) ('*Rubin*'); *Baker*.

51 *Daboll* v. *DeMarco*, 2011 ONSC 1 (CanLII) ('*Daboll*').

52 *Hadjor* v. *Sault Ste Marie Chamber of Commerce* 2011 ONCA 811 (CanLii); see also David Hedwig, *Jury dismisses libel suit against City Police, SooToday.com* (13 September 2010) sootoday.com, www.sootoday.com/content/news/full_story.asp?StoryNumber=48377; *Shavluk* v. *Green Party of Canada*, 2011 BCCA 286 (CanLII) ('*Shavluk appeal*'); and *Vellacott* v. *Saskatoon Starphoenix Group Inc*, 2012 SKQB 359 (CanLII) ('*Vellacott*').

53 See, e.g., Robert Danay, 'The Medium is Not the Message: Reconciling Reputation and Free Expression in Cases of Internet Defamation' (2010) 56 *McGill Law Journal* 1 at 35–7.

54 One would want to know more about success rates for defamation defences generally in order to conclude that the *Grant* defence is relatively unsuccessful. Unfortunately,

Consider some of the reasons why the defence failed. Predictably, some defendants were held not to have published reasonably with reference to the indicia of responsible communication set out in *Grant*. Specifically, the *Grant* defence failed because of: the seriousness of the allegations (five cases);[55] the status and reliability of the source (three cases);[56] a lack of urgency in the matter (four cases);[57] and insufficient public importance (distinct from public interest – two cases).[58] It failed because including defamatory material was not justifiable (three cases);[59] and because the plaintiff's side of the story was not accurately sought or reported (six cases).[60] As has been noted in other jurisdictions, obtaining/reporting the plaintiff's side of the story seems to be especially important for a defendant to succeed with the *Grant* defence.[61]

In one case, the *Grant* defence failed in part because of insufficient public interest in the matter.[62] This would seem to support the conclusion that the threshold for public interest is relatively low. That is, the *Grant* defence is rarely rejected on the grounds that the communication was not on a matter of public interest.

Another reason the defence is failing is that the defendant is not a journalist or new media communicator. The three cases in which the defence succeeded all involved journalism.[63] The *Grant* defence was rejected in three cases in whole or in part because they were not 'media' cases.

*Foulidis* v. *Baker* was a defamation action brought by a businessman against a candidate for Toronto City Council. Mr. Baker had delivered a letter to the mayor and councillors alleging that Mr Foulidis influenced City Council to obtain favours regarding his business. The judge held that the defendant could not avail himself of the *Grant* defence because the

Canadian courts do not collect data regarding success rates for particular causes of action and since many defamation cases are unreported, it is virtually impossible to calculate a precise success rate.

55 *Hanson* v. *Harder*, 2010 BCCA 482 (CanLII) ('*Hanson*'); *Hunter; James* v. *Black Press Group*, 2012 BCSC 1969 (CanLII) ('*James*'); *Vigna* v. *Levant*, 2010 ONSC 6308 (CanLII) ('*Vigna*'); *Roshard.*

56 *Hanson; James; Vigna.* 57 *Hunter; James; Vigna; Roshard.* 58 *Vigna; Roshard.*

59 *James; Reaburn* v. *Langen* [2009] BCCA 465 (CanLii)*; Vigna.*

60 *Daboll; Hanson; Hunter; James; Reaburn; Vigna.*

61 The Supreme Court stated that whether the plaintiff's side of the story is reported is 'perhaps the core *Reynolds* factor': *Grant* at [116] citing Patrick Milmo and W.V.H. Rogers, *Gatley on Libel and Slander*, 11th edn (London: Sweet & Maxwell, 2008) at 535. See also Kenyon, above n 39, at 412, 424.

62 *Daboll.* Note, however, that the court held there was no public interest in 'targeting Mr. Daboll in this fashion' (at [43]). In my view, that is a misapplication of the test. At issue were statements that a lawyer had criminal convictions. This is surely a matter of public interest. Whether the allegations were true or were reasonably conveyed is a separate matter.

63 Above n 52.

case did not involve 'traditional media or new media dissemination of information':

[69]... McLachlin CJ considered at paragraph 96 to whom the defence should be available. The court observed that 'the traditional media are rapidly being complemented by new ways of communicating on matters of public interest, many of them online, which do not involve journalists. These new disseminators of news and information should, absent good reason for exclusion, be subject to the same laws as established media outlets.' ...

[70] In my view, there are several related reasons why this defence is not available to the defendant. This case does not involve either traditional media or new media dissemination of information. It involves communication which is almost antiquated in nature: a letter, delivered by hand. The letter was not published generally, as is the case with media publication, but to a select and focused few. Further, in a case of widespread media publication, the defence of qualified privilege is often unavailable. That was a reason given in *Grant* v. *Torstar* (*supra*) for the development of this new defence. ... In my view, it adds unnecessary complexity to this area of the law to hold that this important new defence is available to a non-media defendant to whom the defence of qualified privilege has been found to apply.[64]

MacDonald J interprets *Grant* as creating a defence applicable only to media or to those who communicate to the world at large. He seems especially persuaded that, because the qualified privilege origins of responsible communication defences, the *Grant* defence applies only in circumstances where the defendant has published broadly.

Similarly, in *Rubin* v. *Ross*, the defendants were a union, the head of that union's grievance committee and a grievance officer. They were alleged to have defamed a veterinarian by posting details of a grievance on workplace bulletin boards, in a union newsletter and on the union's website. The *Grant* defence was rejected. The complete discussion of the defence was very short, comprising only the following:

In my view, the case of *Grant* v. *Torstar Corp.* is not applicable to this situation. This is not a case of a broad-based media seeking the protection of the defence granted under that decision.[65]

Finally, *Roshard* v. *Saint Denis* involved municipal politicians. In a media interview, the defendant, a candidate for town council, accused the plaintiff mayoral candidate of being in a conflict of interest with regard to a grape-growing initiative.

Schultes J rejected the *Grant* defence on its merits, but noted that:

It would really make a mockery of this defence, which was carefully crafted by the Supreme Court of Canada primarily to protect journalists who have done their

[64] *Baker* [70]. [65] *Rubin* [91].

best to get the story right on matters of great public importance, if it became a shield for petty and malicious sniping of this kind.[66]

Schultes J seems to share the views of Keene and MacDonald JJ that the *Grant* defence's scope is limited to journalism and new media.[67]

This view is also reflected in the fact that some courts are calling the *Grant* defence 'responsible journalism',[68] despite *Grant*'s explicit rejection of that name in favour of 'responsible communication'.[69]

These three decisions are from different provinces (Ontario, British Columbia and Saskatchewan), and it is therefore not simply a matter of the same judge or court taking a narrow view of the *Grant* defence.

This narrow approach is not uniform, however. Although there are no cases to date in which the defence has *successfully* been applied in non-media cases,[70] some courts have applied the *Grant* defence on its merits to non-media cases (including cases where the publication is not made to the world at large), or explicitly state that the defence is not limited to media.[71]

In *Hunter* v. *Chandler* a public official, speaking to a politically active constituent, impugned another public official's ethics and alleged a conflict of interest.[72] Although the communication was held not to be responsible, there was no suggestion in this case that it could not apply because the case did not involve 'media' or widespread publication.

In *Daboll* v. *DeMarco*, the defendant was a former client of the plaintiff lawyer. DeMarco took out ads in a local shopping newspaper alleging that the lawyer had committed criminal acts.[73] Although newspaper publication is involved, this can hardly be said to be a case involving journalism. Nor are new media involved. And yet there was no suggestion that the *Grant* defence could not apply to such publications. Rather, as in *Hunter*, the defence failed on its merits.

There is therefore inconsistency in how courts have interpreted the scope of the *Grant* defence. Some suggest that the defence applies only to old and new media cases. Others explicitly state that the defence is not

[66] *Roshard* [72].

[67] This is perhaps especially surprising given that in *Roshard*, the defamatory statements were made in the context of an interview with a partisan public interest newsletter, where the statements were ultimately published. Depending on whether Schultes J considers the interviewer to have been a journalist, he may be implying that the source of a journalistic publication is not entitled to the protection of the *Grant* defence.

[68] *Kent* v. *Postmedia Network*, 2011 ABQB 479 (CanLII); *Nazerali* v. *Mitchell*, 2013 BCSC 698 (CanLII).

[69] *Grant* [97].

[70] In *Shavluk*, the defendant was a political party, but the statement in question was made in a press release.

[71] *Casses* v. *Backer*, 2012 BCSC 17 (CanLII) at [52]. [72] *Hunter*. [73] *Daboll*.

limited to journalism and apply it in contexts far removed from traditional journalism, including contexts in which publication is not widespread. Although it is too early to say which view will ultimately prevail in the case law, it is worth addressing this issue now, since limiting the *Grant* defence to journalists or widely published statements threatens to undo much of what I argue the Supreme Court intended to do in *Grant*.

It is also worth noting that Canadian courts have tended to stick closely to the enumerated indicia in *Grant*, even in non-journalism cases. Of course, there is nothing wrong with a court addressing each of the *Grant* factors. However, this may result in a responsible communication analysis that overemphasises certain factors and ignores relevant ones – especially where the defendant is not a professional journalist.

In *Vigna, James, Tilley*[74] and *Vellacott*, the court addressed each *Grant* factor in turn. (In the first three, the courts did so without considering 'any other relevant circumstances'. In *Vellacott*, 'tone' was considered under the last factor.) In the trial decision in *Shavluk*,[75] all criteria were addressed except reportage and 'other'. In *Vigna* and *Vellacott*, the courts implied that each criterion was an element of the defence by referring to the *Grant* criteria as 'required elements'.[76] After listing and applying each of the eight criteria, Danyliuk J in *Vellacott* stated that: 'The defendants have met all the criteria required to establish the defence of responsible journalism'.[77] Other than 'tone', very few 'other' criteria were considered.[78] The Saskatchewan Court of Appeal referred to the *Grant* factors as an 'eight-part test'.[79] While one should be cautious not to read too much into the 'elements' wording, or into reliance on the *Grant* criteria, these cases suggest that Canadian courts may be no better at applying *Grant* flexibly than British courts were at applying *Reynolds* flexibly.

## 2.3 Ensuring a broad scope for the *Grant* defence

Assuming that the *Grant* defence is best understood as applicable to any factual communication on a matter of public interest, and that it should be applied flexibly with regard to the overarching question of whether

[74] In *Tilley*, the trial court applied the *Reynolds* factors rather than the *Grant* factors, but the Court of Appeal in *Hanson* applied the *Grant* approach.
[75] *Shavluk* v. *Green Party of Canada*, 2010 BCSC 804 (CanLII) ('*Shavluk trial*').
[76] *Vellacott* [80]; *Vigna* [43]. [77] *Vellacott* [83].
[78] Although decided before *Grant*, *Hanson* v. *Tilley* 2009 BCSC 360 (CanLII) ('*Tilley*') considered whether student newspaper 'journalists' should be held to the same standard as professional journalists. The court concluded that they should. See [65].
[79] *Caswell* v. *Buckle*, 2010 SKCA 116 (CanLII).

publication was responsible, this section examines how best to ensure that the *Grant* defence is applied broadly and flexibly.

### 2.3.1 *Eliminate the reference to journalistic standards*

First, determining whether a communication is responsible with reference to criteria drawn largely from professional journalism is problematic. It makes less and less sense the less like traditional journalism a publication is.

Consider the effect of applying the *Grant* criteria to non-journalistic communications such as tweets, blogs and oral communications. There are hundreds of millions of Twitter users and 500 million tweets are sent every day.[80] In his article, 'A Defence of Responsible Tweeting', Paul Bernal notes that criteria of responsible journalism such as including the plaintiff's side of the story and verifying sources may not be relevant to the responsible use of Twitter:

> Many of the features of Twitter run counter to traditional ideas of professional, 'responsible' journalism. The 140-character limit makes it very hard to give both sides of the story. The immediacy of Twitter – both in terms of spontaneity of use and in terms of contributing to current, real-time events – mean that what in traditional terms would be considered 'responsible' levels of fact-checking or gathering of alternative sources is all but impossible. The fact that it can be and is used by non-journalists (indeed, that it can be used by anyone) means that knowledge of the law and of professional ethics cannot reasonably be expected – but it is the way that it can be used by non-journalists that gives it its strength and makes it ideal for allowing those non-journalists an opportunity to exercise their freedom of expression.[81]

Bernal does not suggest that tweeting is never irresponsible. Rather, he argues that responsible tweeting is different from responsible journalism. For example, responsible tweeters are broadly aware of who their followers are and consider how they might react to a tweet.[82]

Bloggers may similarly be disadvantaged by the indicia of responsible journalism set out in *Grant*. Although the Supreme Court made it clear that the *Grant* defence can be applied to bloggers, the indicia do not necessarily reflect the way in which bloggers (responsibly) communicate.

For example, the *Grant* defence failed in *Vigna* v. *Levant*. Despite a public interest in whether the plaintiff lawyer lied to the Human Rights Commission and otherwise acted unethically, the court decided the matter was not one of high importance and there was no urgency in publishing. Further, it concluded that Levant did not try to contact the plaintiff

[80] https://about.twitter.com/company (accessed 25 March 2014). [81] *Ibid.*, 17.
[82] *Ibid.*

for his side of the story and he insufficiently investigated the truth of the impugned statements.

Although *Vigna* was likely correctly decided given the seriousness of the allegations and Levant's wide audience and credibility, we should not always expect bloggers to maintain journalistic standards in order that their communication is found to be responsible. The degree to which bloggers should be expected to verify the truth of their statements or request and publish the plaintiff's side of the story presumably varies considerably depending on the kind of blog. As Bernal suggests in relation to tweeting, what is responsible will depend on factors such as the defendant's following and the effect the blog is likely to have on its audience.

Consider a final example involving slander. Recall that in *Hunter* v. *Chandler*, a public official made an oral statement about another public official impugning his professional ethics and alleging a conflict of interest.[83] These statements were made by telephone to a politically active constituent. As with tweeting and blogging, what amounts to a responsible oral statement to a constituent is different from what would be responsible in publishing the same allegation in a newspaper.

For example, it is odd to think about seeking the plaintiff's side and 'publishing' it when the communication in question is an oral statement. Journalists must maintain a degree of objectivity and neutrality when reporting,[84] but the same is not true of non-journalists: even when making statements of fact we expect individuals to communicate their own priorities and values. Similarly, disclosing a factual basis for a statement makes reporting fairer, but failing to do so does not make it unreasonable for individuals to speak their mind. Finally, the 'urgency' criterion makes less sense when applied to oral statements – it will sometimes be unreasonable to speak your mind before you have gathered sufficient facts, but the context of deadlines, 'scoops' and the competitive nature of the news business is not relevant.

Yet in *Hunter*, the court considered most of the *Grant* indicia in turn. It held that there was no urgency to publication (the defendant should have waited for a legal opinion, which was being prepared), that the matter was a serious one, that the defendant did not disclose the facts on which the statements were based,[85] and so on.

[83] *Hunter*.

[84] For example, the Canadian Association of Journalists publishes a set of ethics guidelines for journalists. They include: 'We do not allow our own biases to impede fair and accurate reporting'; 'We are accountable to the public for the fairness and reliability of our reporting'; and 'We serve the public interest, and put the needs of our audience – readers, listeners or viewers – at the forefront of our newsgathering decisions'. (Canadian Association of Journalists Ethics Guidelines, online: www.caj.ca/?p=1776.)

[85] *Hunter* [145].

I do not suggest that the case was wrongly decided, but simply that rigid application of the *Grant* criteria is not the best way to assess whether communication is responsible where oral statements are involved. And although the *Grant* defence's test of responsible communication is meant to be applied flexibly, with regard to the overarching question of whether the publisher was sufficiently diligent in trying to verify the allegation, the United Kingdom's experience with its *Reynolds* defence suggests that the criteria tend to be applied as a checklist.[86] The limited experience in Canada to date may reflect the same tendency. The risk in applying the *Grant* criteria rigidly is to set a high bar for the defence that may undermine the goals *Grant* sought to achieve.

### 2.3.2 *A new test of reasonableness*

The rest of this section addresses how the test of responsible communication should change to reflect communications as varied as a personal letter, an article in a newspaper, a blog entry and an oral communication.

Before examining the proposed test of responsible communication, however, it is important to review what 'responsible communication' means. According to *Grant*, it means that the defendant acted with reasonable diligence in verifying the truth of the communication to justify publishing it.[87] Eric Descheemaeker has stated that *Reynolds* privilege 'boils down to what is essentially an idea of reasonable belief in truth'[88] and there is no doubt that much of the focus is on steps taken to assess whether a statement is true. However, this does not mean that the only relevant considerations are those that relate to steps to establish truth. As examined in more detail later, the question should be whether publishing was reasonable given the risk that the statement is false, the extent of injury that would result if it were, and any benefits of publishing despite the risk.

To get at this question, I recommend that Canadian law abandon the *Reynolds*-based indicia of responsible journalism. Instead of asking: 'Was publication of the defamatory communication responsible?'[89] with regard to the listed indicia, the second element of the defence should be framed in terms of 'reasonableness'. Given my understanding of *Grant*, this would not amount to a significant shift. 'Responsible' would not seem to be meaningfully different from 'reasonable'[90] and the second element

[86] *Grant*; Kenyon, above n 20; Scordato, above n 20. [87] See *Grant* [111], [112], [126].

[88] Descheemaeker, above n 11, at 2. [89] *Grant* [110].

[90] Others have referred to *Reynolds* responsible communication defences as importing a negligence standard into defamation. See Eric Descheemaeker, 'Protecting Reputation: Defamation and Negligence' (2009) 29 *Oxford Journal of Legal Studies* 603 at 639: 'Responsible journalism' may or may not, in this instance, be synonymous with the

of the *Grant* defence has always targeted the question of whether facts were responsibly communicated – not whether communication met the indicia set out in *Grant*. However, since the 'responsible communication' approach is linked to the indicia in *Grant* and *Reynolds*, and since the indicia risk leading courts to rigidly apply criteria of varying relevance to the facts, or leading courts to weigh certain indicia too heavily, it is appropriate to provide different guidance.

Reasonableness should be assessed with regard to the likelihood and severity of foreseeable harm to reputation (understood as harm to reputation caused by *false* statements rather than true statements), the costs of avoiding that harm, and any social benefits to publishing potentially false statements. This is, of course, the approach to assessing whether there has been a breach of the standard of care in negligence. (I will return to the question of custom in establishing reasonable conduct.)

An initial objection might be that a negligence standard amounts to an impermissible incursion of the law of negligence into the law of defamation. Much has been written about the intersection between defamation and negligence law.[91] Some jurisdictions maintain a strict distinction between the causes of action.[92] In Canada, the law of negligence can apply to defamatory statements so long as there is an injury the law of negligence recognises (reputational injury alone is insufficient) and the other elements of negligence are met.[93] However, one must distinguish between the availability of the negligence action in relation to reputational injuries and the introduction of aspects of negligence into defamation law itself. Eric Descheemaeker demonstrates that features of negligence law, especially in relation to fault, have long been creeping into defamation law,[94] although the responsible communications defences in *Lange, Reynolds* and *Grant* are the clearest example. Given that the *Grant* defence is already based on a fault standard of responsibility, not meaningfully different from reasonableness, I see no inconsistency with the spirit of

taking of reasonable care; but it is clear from *Loutchansky* that it cannot be very different' at 639. See also Descheemaeker, above n 11, at 15.

91 See, e.g., Descheemaeker, above n 90.

92 This tendency is more apparent in some jurisdictions than in others. Mullis and Parkes, above n 21, at [23.4] notes that Australia and New Zealand guard the distinction more jealously than the United Kingdom and Canada.

93 *Young v Bella*, [2006] 1 SCR 108; 2006 SCC 3 (CanLII).

94 Descheemaeker, above n 90. Note also that since *Gertz* v. *Robert Welch, Inc*, 418 US 323, at 347 (1974), American defamation law has applied the negligence standard to most cases involving private plaintiffs. See Douglas R Gould, 'Is Editing What Judges Are For? Judicial Review of Journalists' Editorial Decisions in Defamation Cases in the United Kingdom and European Court of Human Rights' (2008) 46 *Columbia Journal of Transnational Law* 732 at 756–7.

*Grant* in overtly applying a negligence standard to the 'responsible communication' element of the *Grant* defence.

Consider how a negligence standard would apply to defamatory statements of fact. The 'likelihood of harm' relates primarily to the likelihood that the statement is, in fact, false.[95] Factors relevant to assessing the likelihood of harm therefore include steps taken to establish the truth of the defamatory allegation. This is already reflected in some of the *Grant* criteria (e.g., status and reliability of the source; whether the plaintiff's side was sought). Instead of focussing narrowly on these criteria, however, a trier of fact should consider all evidence available to the defendant at the time of publication for believing the allegation to be true or false.

The 'severity of harm' relates to the degree of damage to the plaintiff's reputation as a result of publication. The *Grant* criterion of 'seriousness of the allegation' gets at that question, but commentators have noted that this criterion has been interpreted in a way that disadvantages the defendant. If the matter is serious, more diligence is required in verifying it, but if it is not serious, that weighs against having communicated it at all.[96] In other words, the fact that an allegation is serious is not only a reason to take extra care in publishing, but also a reason to publish even if you cannot prove truth with certainty. (This is different from public interest in that matters of public interest range in seriousness.) *Grant* notes the former implication, but not the latter. Not surprisingly, all of the Canadian cases that mention the relevance of the seriousness of the allegation mention it in the former context – seriousness weighs against publication, not in favour of it. A proper balancing approach might ensure that both consequences of a matter's seriousness are considered.

Other factors relevant to the severity of harm are the nature and scope of the audience and the credibility of the defendant.[97] These may not have been included in *Reynolds* or *Grant* because in traditional media cases the wide scope of publication and credibility of the publisher is generally assumed. However, if the *Grant* defence is to apply beyond traditional

[95] Whether the statement is likely to be believed could also be considered relevant to the likelihood of harm, but as I have argued elsewhere, statements that are not credible should not be considered *prima facie* defamatory. Hilary Young, 'But Names Won't *Necessarily* Hurt Me: Considering the Effect of Disparaging Statements on Reputation' (2011) 37 *Queen's Law Journal* 1 at 21–7.

[96] Ian Cram, 'Political Expression, Qualified Privilege and Investigative Journalism – An Analysis of Developments in English Defamation Law Post *Reynolds* v. *Times Newspapers*' (2005) 11 *Canterbury Law Review* 143 at 157; Roy Baker, 'Extending Common Law Qualified Privilege to the Media: A Comparison of the English and Australian Approaches' (2002) 7 *Media & Arts Law Review* 87 at 99.

[97] This is similar to Paul Bernal's assertion that responsible tweeting takes into account the size of the audience and a tweet's likely effect on it. Paul Bernal, 'A Defence of Responsible Tweeting' (2014) 19 *Communications Law* 12 at 17.

media, we cannot assume widespread publication or a credible defendant.

Further, the language used in the publication is relevant to the severity of harm. A fair and balanced statement may cause less harm to a person's reputation than a one-sided communication or one that draws tenuous inferences from facts. *Grant* suggests the importance of the 'fairness' of the publication in referring to the factor of whether the plaintiff's side of the story was sought and reported.[98] However, fairness also relates to the tone of the communication (tone being one of the *Reynolds* factors). By focussing on the broader questions of the likelihood and severity of the harm, the trier of fact can assess responsible communication without over-relying on factors such as whether the plaintiff's side of the story was reported.

The 'cost of risk avoidance' relates to the costs to the defendant of not publishing or of delaying publication. These include tangible costs such as lost sales and the cost of actually verifying (e.g., reporters' time). The *Grant* (and *Reynolds*) factor of 'the urgency of the matter' invokes the possibility of costs to the defendant in making further efforts to verify. However, the cost of risk avoidance may also include less tangible costs such as interference with autonomy or losing a political advantage.

Finally, a standard of care analysis sometimes concludes with an enquiry into whether there are any social benefits in engaging in risky behaviour. In the context of communications on matters of public interest, there will often be a social benefit to taking the risk that the publication is untrue. Benefits to the public interest include promoting democratic discourse and truth-finding.[99] The *Grant* factors of 'seriousness of the allegation' and the 'public importance of the matter' reflect such benefits to the public, but as indicated earlier, this aspect of 'seriousness' tends not to be considered.

Another possible social benefit is the benefit of reportage: communicating that an allegation was made because of the public importance of that statement rather than because one believes it to be true. There is a risk that simply repeating the allegation, even without the defendant adopting it, could injure the plaintiff's reputation. However, where it is in the public interest to know the allegation was made, there is some social benefit to taking that risk.

Of the factors listed in *Grant*, all but one would effectively be subsumed within the reasonableness approach proposed: 'whether the inclusion of the defamatory statement was justifiable'. This question asks the trier of fact to engage in a balancing exercise not unlike the broader question of

[98] *Grant* [116]. [99] *Ibid.*, [51]–[52].

whether publishing was reasonable. If it was not justifiable to include the defamatory statement, how could publishing be reasonable/responsible? Similarly, if it was justifiable to include the defamatory statement, does that not mean that the risk to the plaintiff's reputation was outweighed by the benefits of publishing? While the questions of justifiability and responsible communication are technically different, I believe the former factor is already accounted for by the very nature of the reasonableness enquiry, which involves balancing the risks and benefits of publishing defamatory statements of fact.

As is the case with the standard of care in negligence, malice would not be a separate enquiry, but publishing facts known to be false (or with reckless disregard as to truth) would almost inevitably be unreasonable.

As for the role of custom, I propose the same approach as in negligence. The reasonableness of a professional's conduct may be assessed with regard to the customary standards of that profession, so long as they are not fraught with obvious risk.[100] *Reynolds* and *Grant* in some ways suggest that journalists (and perhaps others) should be held to the standard of reasonable journalism – no more and no less.[101] And yet commentators have noted that British courts have generally not shown deference to professional standards.[102]

Douglas R Gould nicely canvasses the pros and cons of applying a custom standard. On the one hand, custom is consensus-based and representative, demonstrates feasible practice, is not assessed with hindsight, and may be easier to prove than individuals' own criteria of reasonableness. On the other hand, custom might not reflect all the relevant costs and benefits of an act, the need for expert evidence may burden smaller parties, and there may be disputes about the appropriate level of generality.[103]

I agree with Gould that the advantages of a custom standard outweigh the disadvantages, given that custom need not be determinative of reasonableness. As Gould notes, if custom does not reflect all the relevant

[100] *Ter Neuzen* v. *Korn* [1995] 3 SCR 674.

[101] Above n 17. Further, Scordato, above n 20, at 179 states: 'Consistent with a classic negligence analysis, Lord Hoffmann notes that the court in conducting this enquiry can benefit from a comparison of the defendant's actions with industry standards of good journalistic practice'.

[102] See, e.g., Paul Mitchell, 'The Nature of Responsible Journalism' (2011) 3 *Journal of Media Law* 19 at 26: 'In short, the decision in *Flood* v. *Times Newspapers Ltd* looks more like the Court of Appeal setting the standard, not deferring to journalists' own views'; Kenyon, above n 39, at 426: 'Judges and journalists appear to hold markedly different views about standards: "the highest level of journalistic endeavour" achieved in the media is seen as being "miles short of where the court sets the lowest standard for journalistic endeavour"'.

[103] Gould, above n 94, at 762.

costs and benefits, and is therefore unreasonable in the circumstances, it can be found to be unreasonable.[104]

Custom could therefore be relied on in assessing reasonableness, not only in the context of journalism, but of other professionals' communications, such as those of lawyers or politicians, if there are relevant professional standards of conduct.

I do not suggest that a 'reasonableness' approach will cure all the problems I have identified with how the *Grant* defence is or may be applied. Ultimately, although I do think it offers a better way to identify whether communication was responsible, a 'reasonableness' test is still extremely subjective and provides less concrete guidance than the *Grant* factors. Triers of fact uncomfortable with the possibility that a communication may be false may apply a reasonableness test conservatively.

That has certainly been the case in Australia, where a reasonableness standard has long been applied to some states' statutory qualified privilege defence and common law *Lange* privilege.[105] Defendants rarely succeed in establishing the high threshold for reasonableness that judges impose. According to Andrew Kenyon: '[t]he history of statutory privilege under s. 22 of the Defamation Act 1974 (NSW) suggests that reasonableness [under *Lange* privilege] will be hard to meet.[106] He continues: '[t]he [s. 22] defence appears to be commonly pleaded, but has succeeded in only a handful of cases since 1974'.[107] With regard to *Lange* privilege specifically, Kenyon cites defamation lawyers who consider the defence ineffective – not despite but because of its reasonableness requirement: 'reasonableness is the "killer"'.[108]

Other potential problems with a reasonableness standard include uncertainty. Whereas there is a large body of negligence case law to guide us regarding reasonable conduct in specific contexts such as driving, practicing medicine and manufacturing products, there would be little such guidance regarding journalistic communication or other kinds of communication until a sufficient body of case law emerges. Journalistic codes of conduct would likely provide guidance, but journalistic practices vary.[109] That said, they probably vary less in Canada than they do in the United Kingdom, with its robust tabloid news industry.

104 *Ibid.*, 763.

105 For the history of 'reasonableness' in Australian defamation defences, see Descheemaeker, above n 11, at 8–15.

106 Kenyon, above n 39, at 417. 107 *Ibid.*, 418. 108 *Ibid.*, 429.

109 The European Court of Human Rights has stated that: 'the methods of objective and balanced reporting may vary considerably, depending among other things, on the form of media in question': Marie McGonagle, *A Textbook on Media Law*, 2nd edn (Dublin: Thomson Round Hall, 2003) at 126.

At least with *Reynolds* privilege, the checklist approach allowed journalists to change their conduct in order to '*Reynolds*-proof' their stories.[110] Under the reasonableness test I have proposed, meeting criteria such as reporting the plaintiff's side of the story might be less important than it is under *Reynolds* and *Grant*. It might be harder to '*Reynolds*-proof' a story and consequently, the chilling effect associated with uncertainty and high litigation costs might increase.

Nevertheless, taking a negligence approach has sufficient advantages to justify it over an indicia-based approach. It has the potential to avoid overreliance on indicia that may or may not be relevant in a particular case, to make triers of fact consider other factors that *are* relevant, to avoid applying journalistic standards when journalism is not at issue and to apply *actual* journalistic standards (custom) when they are at issue. The reasonableness standard reflects the apparent intent of *Grant*. Further, whether conduct is reasonable is a well-known test with a long record of being put to triers of fact. Unlike the standard of 'responsible journalism', it is flexible and has been applied to all manner of conduct.

## 2.4 Conclusion

When *Reynolds* was first decided, it was heralded as an important development in the law of defamation, and the same is true of Canada's *Grant* defence. Since 2008, Canada's Supreme Court has been altering defamation law to make it more protective of freedom of expression and *Grant* is perhaps the most significant example of this trend. But whether the defence lives up to its promise will depend on how the courts interpret it.

Although there is relatively little case law to date on which to judge the application of the *Grant* defence, there is reason for concern. Courts understand the scope of the defence differently: some view it as broadly applicable, others consider it to apply only to publications akin to journalism or to those who publish broadly. Further, in applying the defence, courts tend to stick rigidly to the enumerated indicia of responsible communication, which focus on journalistic standards and ignore other considerations. For example, although 'other' is an enumerated criterion, other factors are rarely considered.

The Supreme Court should clarify the scope of the defence and modify the approach to assessing responsible communication. I have argued that a broad interpretation best reflects the language and aims of *Grant*. If the

110 Russell L Weaver, Andrew T Kenyon, David F Partlett and Clive P Walker, *The Right to Speak Ill: Defamation, Reputation and Free Speech* (Durham, NC: Carolina Academic Press, 2006) at 222.

defence is understood as applicable to any communication, however, it becomes hard to justify a list of indicia of responsible communication drawn from professional journalism. Although these are meant only to guide triers of fact, in the United Kingdom they have become a checklist of hurdles for defendants to meet and the same may be happening in Canada. It is time to explicitly acknowledge that the defence is a fault-based one, and the fault standard is that of reasonableness, just as in negligence. Applying the test of reasonableness both reflects the spirit of *Grant* and provides a number of advantages over an indicia-based approach, although it cannot prevent courts from applying the defence conservatively, should they be so inclined.

# 3 '*Ceci n'est pas une pipe*': the autopoietic inanity of the single meaning rule

*Andrew Scott*

The Defamation Act 2013 was the culmination of a phenomenally successful political campaign. The changes in the law of defamation that it has introduced are notable, although it is not yet clear precisely how significant they will prove. It is sufficiently clear, however, that the reforms are unlikely to address the core problem with libel law: the juridification and over-complication of public sphere disputes, and the attendant cost of embroilment in legal proceedings.[1] Too much effort was focussed on revising elements of the substantive law; not enough on how to design a regime for the resolution of arguments that might best triangulate the individual and social interests in reputation and free speech.

A more sensible and effective, although perhaps counter-intuitive, target for reform may have been the long-standing 'single meaning rule'. Allied with the introduction of a range of discursive remedies – corrections, retractions and rights of reply – the jettisoning of that rule might have gone far towards ending the 'casino' element in libel proceedings. The fundamental contention of this chapter is that the single meaning rule is a device that pushes the law into a form of autopoietic over-simplification, into damaging mischaracterisations, of real-world disputes. Simplification in this sense does not equate to good public policy. Due to the single meaning rule, the process of transposing a dispute from the public sphere to the legal forum provides opportunities for parties and their lawyers to indulge in obscurantist, cost-generating game-playing. The rule may also encourage some publishers unconscionably to game-play in the way they craft their stories. This is all

The author wishes to thank the participants in workshops in Melbourne and in Edinburgh, and especially Andrew Kenyon, for helpful comments on earlier versions of this chapter.

[1] See, generally, Alastair Mullis and Andrew Scott, 'Tilting at Windmills: the Defamation Act 2013' (2014) 77 *Modern Law Review* 87; Gavin Phillipson, 'The "Global Pariah", the Defamation Bill and the Human Rights Act' (2012) 63 *Northern Ireland Legal Quarterly* 149.

perplexing to non-lawyers,[2] not so much on account of their ignorance in the face of the technical sophistication of a complex body of law, but rather because it seems so fundamentally unnecessary.[3] Justice is not served. The imbalance between wealthy and relatively impecunious litigants is exacerbated.[4]

This chapter proceeds in four parts. First, it briefly sets out the issues that might confront a court when determining meaning and explains the single meaning rule. Second, it considers the justifications that have been offered for the rule over time, as articulated most recently in a judgement delivered by Lord Neuberger in the Hong Kong Final Court of Appeal.[5] That judgement offered an implied rejoinder to criticism of the rule previously aired in the English Court of Appeal.[6] Third, the chapter considers what might be the practical ramifications of any withdrawal of the single meaning rule. It is suggested that such a move, coupled with the introduction of appropriate discursive remedies, would offer the best means possible of providing the parties to most potential libel disputes with mutually acceptable outcomes quickly, while focussing intractable disputes immediately on the core points of contention. Finally, and by way of conclusion, the chapter addresses the question of whether the opportunity for reform of the type contemplated in this chapter has not been missed in England and Wales.[7] It suggests that while statutory amendment would be preferable, there is

[2] Anecdotally, it is also very curious from the perspective of lawyers from other jurisdictions – notably the US – in the extent to which the determination of meaning becomes such a focus of defamation litigation in the UK and comparable jurisdictions. If this premise holds good (that is, if the anecdote is accurate), it begs the question as to why so little time is spent on this issue in American litigation. One explanation may be that because in the US the burden of proof lies on the claimant and the standard of proof required is higher, there is an incentive for claimants to present only obviously sustainable meanings to the court.

[3] Speaking during Parliamentary debate, the eminent scientist Lord May expressed the prescient concern that 'what is being described ... [is] not easily going to be translated into anything that is not almost as expensive as what is currently being used as a weapon ... [when most disputes] could have been settled by a judge in half an hour'; Hansard, HL, vol. 741, col. 429, 17 December 2012. He was referring specifically to the rule in clause 1 of the Bill (the 'serious harm' threshold), but might easily have been speaking more generally.

[4] Despite the emphasis placed on the harm posed to free speech by defamation law, the key imbalance in this area is not that in favour of reputation over free speech or vice versa. Rather, it is that between litigants who can afford to defend their publications or to vindicate their reputations, and those who cannot.

[5] *Oriental Daily Publisher* v. *Ming Pao Holdings* [2012] HKCFA 59 ('*Oriental Daily*'). Lord Neuberger's comments on the single meaning rule comprised an excursus. The case focussed rather on the relevance of the credibility of the original publisher to the determination of meaning and the quantum of damages in 'repetition rule' libel cases.

[6] *Ajinomoto Sweeteners* v. *ASDA Stores* [2010] EWCA Civ 609 ('*Ajinomoto*').

[7] Manifestly, the logic of the argument applies to all common law jurisdictions in which the single meaning rule is deployed.

reason to expect that the courts might act on this point come the appropriate case.

### 3.1 The single meaning rule: explanation and critique

Disputes about meaning are often central to libel actions; they are 'very often if not always the most important issue'.[8] If a court is able to determine meaning early in proceedings, very often the dispute will be settled.[9] Outside of legal innuendo cases, there is no attempt to divine the actual inferences drawn by recipients of the publication at issue. Determination of meaning is not an empirical question.[10] Neither is the publisher's intended meaning directly relevant. The test is that of how the words would have been understood by the ordinary, reasonable recipient of the publication in question.[11] In accordance with the single meaning rule, the court is required to pretend that only one interpretation of each imputation involved will have been inferred by all such ordinary, reasonable people. Thereafter, this choice will form the basis of the disposal of (that element of) the case.

Plainly, this involves a legal abstraction from reality.[12] This abstraction is often explicitly recognised by the courts. In *Slim* v. *Daily Telegraph*, Lord Justice Diplock acknowledged that:

> everyone outside a court of law recognises that words are imprecise instruments for communicating the thoughts of one man to another. The same words may be understood by one man in a different meaning from that in which they are understood by another and both meanings may be different from that which the author of the words intended to convey . . . [and] where . . . words are published to the millions of readers of a popular newspaper, the chances are that if the words are reasonably capable of being understood as bearing more than one meaning, some readers will have understood them as bearing one of those meanings and some will have understood them as bearing others of those meanings.[13]

[8] Joint Committee on the Draft Defamation Bill, *Oral and associated written evidence* (2011 HL Paper 203 / HC 930-II) Q 622 (Tugendhat J).

[9] For a recent example, see *RBoS Shareholders Action Group* v. *News Group Newspapers* [2014] EWHC 130 (QB). For discussion, see 'Sun settles claim by RBoS Shareholders Action Group', *Inforrm*, 19 February 2014: http://inforrm.wordpress.com/2014/02/19/news-sun-settles-claim-by-rbos-shareholders-action-group/.

[10] *Hough* v. *London Express Newspapers* [1940] 2 KB 507 (Goddard LJ).

[11] An 'impeccable synthesis of the authorities' on this theme offered by Eady J was reiterated by the Court of Appeal in *Gillick* v. *Brooke Advisory Centre* [2001] EWCA Civ 1263 (Lord Phillips MR).

[12] The extent of that abstraction has recently been made plain by Alan Durant; see *Meaning in the Media: Discourse, Controversy and Debate* (Cambridge: Cambridge University Press, 2010).

[13] *Slim* v. *Daily Telegraph* [1968] 2 QB 157, 171–3 ('*Slim*').

One might add that many readers will recognise the ambiguity of language where it exists, and reach no firm conclusion as to what message the author was intending to convey. A similar point was made by Lord Nicholls in *Bonnick* v. *Morris*:

> language is inherently imprecise. Words and phrases and sentences take their colour from their context. The context often permits a range of meanings, varying from the obvious to the implausible. Different readers may well form different views on the meaning to be given to the language under consideration.[14]

In short, language is complicated and human communication rarely achieved perfectly.

Having assumed the task of determining the meaning of imputations, the courts have been compelled to develop wide-ranging tools with which to divine singular meanings. In the simplest – and relatively unusual – cases, publications may comprise forms of words that are susceptible to only one possible interpretation, or may involve both a literal and an innuendo meaning that can be inferred from the words themselves (false or popular innuendo). Also relatively straightforward are the cases in which a publication or broadcast includes a number of separate and distinct allegedly defamatory imputations. In principle, these imputations will be independently actionable, and must be separately defended if the claimant chooses to sue.[15] In these first two scenarios, the defence of truth is straightforward in concept: each imputation is either substantially true or not, and the dispute will be determined by reference to the evidence that each party adduces.

Beyond this, however, there is a range of more complicated scenarios in which the determination of meaning is more difficult. In these areas, the insistence that the law proceed to identify a single meaning of the words becomes more problematic. One such scenario is that where what appear to be a number of separate and distinct imputations might arguably be understood as instances of the same general, singular imputation.[16] That is, the seemingly separate allegations can be said to possess a 'common sting'.[17]

[14] *Bonnick* v. *Morris* [2002] UKPC 31, [20] ('*Bonnick*').

[15] A claimant accused of being a thief and an adulterer, for instance, might choose to sue on the accusation of adultery only, in which case the defendant cannot then seek to justify the charge of theft. 'It is no defence to a charge that "You called me A" to say, "Yes, but I also called you B on the same occasion and that was true"'; *Cruise* v. *Express Newspapers* [1999] QB 931, 954 (Brooke LJ); *Warren* v. *Random House Ltd* [2008] EWCA Civ 834.

[16] This is distinct from the circumstances in which a party is permitted to rely on evidence of other examples of poor conduct, which have not been alluded to in what was published, in order to prove a general imputation of which the specific published allegation is said to be illustrative – see, for example, *Williams* v. *Reason* [1988] 1 WLR 96.

[17] This is the basis of the *Polly Peck* justification defence. A useful illustration is that where failure to prove one specific allegation of adultery on which the claimant sued may not

Others arise where the same form of words is semantically capable of bearing a number of slightly differing, and progressively more serious, interpretations. The words may elicit a number of 'shades of meaning'.[18] Naturally, in such cases the defendant will seek to persuade the court to select a less serious meaning as that which would be inferred by the reasonable reader. This is known as the '*Lucas-Box*' meaning.[19] Relatedly, an allegation can be published with varying force in that it is made with a greater or lesser degree of certitude: the '*Chase* levels' of meaning.[20] Finally, a seemingly anodyne form of words may bear an innuendo meaning for a section of the wider audience the members of which possess some special, extraneous knowledge that informs only their interpretation of the phrase in question (legal innuendo).[21]

The need to select one from among an array of possible meanings has resulted in complex rules and practice on the pleading of meanings. At present in English law, the claimant must specify in the statement of case the defamatory meaning that he or she believes the contested words hold.[22] Claimants tend to plead only a narrow range of meanings. On occasion, he or she may 'hedge bets' by offering different arguments in the alternative. As the litigation develops, the court is not bound to the claimant's pleaded meaning,[23] save that it will not find that the words

undermine a defence of truth if other instances of adultery that have been alleged can be proved and the common sting of the allegations is read as one of adulterous promiscuity; see *Khashoggi* v. *IPC Magazines* [1986] 1 WLR 1412. Sometimes, of course, it may be of the utmost importance to the claimant that one particular allegation of adultery is disproven.

18 For example, the statement 'X is helping police with their inquiries into a murder' could be taken to mean any or all of the following: that X murdered someone else, that he or she was complicit in the murder, that he or she knew about the murder, that the police believe that he or she might know something about the murder or about its surrounding circumstances, or that he or she was a forensic psychologist involved in suspect profiling.

19 *Lucas-Box* v. *News Group Newspapers* [1986] 1 WLR 147.

20 *Chase* v. *News Group Newspapers* [2002] EWCA Civ 1772 ('*Chase*'). These strengths of allegation are (i) that the claimant is guilty of X; (ii) that there are grounds to suspect that the claimant is guilty of X, and (iii) that there are grounds for investigating whether the claimant is guilty of X.

21 This last scenario has become a special case: it is the only situation in which the defamatory meaning of a libel is in any sense tested empirically through adduced evidence.

22 Civil Procedure Rules 1998 (UK) (SI 1998 No. 3132 as amended), Pt 53, PD, at 2.3(1). It is suggested in the Pre-Action Protocol for Defamation that claimants should also include the meaning(s) attributed to the words complained of in the 'letter before action' – at [3.3].

23 *Lucas-Box* v. *News Group Newspapers* [1986] 1 WLR 147, at 153 (per Ackner LJ). See, generally, Andrew T Kenyon, *Defamation: Comparative Law and Practice* (Abingdon: UCL Press 2006) at 54–60 (which includes a comparison with the position in Australia). A caveat exists in relation to pleaded legal innuendo meanings; *Ibid.*, 54, footnote 292.

bear a meaning more serious than that contended for.[24] The claimant is free, therefore, to offer additional argument related to meanings other than those first presented in response to defences that speak to lesser meanings. Indeed, not to do so may be self-defeating as the judge or jury may ultimately tend towards the defendant's view when deciding on the single meaning to be attributed. The defendant must set out any lesser meaning he or she wishes to plead in the statement of case, and must do so with sufficient particularity to allow the claimant to know the case he or she faces.[25]

In cases where the meaning of the impugned publication is ambiguous or multifarious, the abstraction from reality involved in applying the single meaning rule will always result in a measure of injustice. The potentially pathological consequences of the rule were highlighted by the Court of Appeal in *Ajinomoto Sweeteners*:

> if the single meaning rule does achieve a fair balance in defamation law between the parties' competing interests, that would appear to be the result of luck rather than judgment ... the application of the rule can also be said to carry with it the potential for swinging the balance unfairly against one party or the other, resulting in no compensation in cases when fairness might suggest that some should be due, or in over-compensation in others.[26]

A similar point has been made in other jurisdictions: 'to insist upon an innocent interpretation where any reasonable person could, and many reasonable people would, understand a sinister meaning is to refuse reparation for a wrong that has in fact been committed'.[27] Clearly, the converse also applies.

The consideration of the single meaning rule offered by the unanimous Court of Appeal in *Ajinomoto Sweeteners* v. *ASDA Stores* was excoriating.[28] That case concerned the application of the rule in the context of claims for malicious falsehood. In the course of his judgement, however, Rimer LJ reflected that 'if the single meaning rule did not exist, I doubt if any modern court would invent it, either for defamation or any other tort'.[29] Sedley LJ described it as 'anomalous, frequently otiose and, where not otiose, unjust'.[30] In his half-hearted, but seminal, affirmation of the rule in *Slim* v. *Daily Telegraph*, Diplock LJ described the law of libel as 'artificial and archaic' in this respect.[31] Commentators have described it

24 *Cook* v. *Telegraph Media Group* [2011] EWHC 1134 (QB), at [11].
25 For a forceful demonstration of this requirement, see *Lord Ashcroft* v. *Foley* [2011] EWHC 292 (QB).
26 *Ajinomoto* [2010] EWCA Civ 609, at [43] (Rimer LJ).
27 *Entienne* v. *Festival City Broadcasters* [2001] SASC 60.
28 *Ajinomoto* [2010] EWCA Civ 609. 29 *Ibid.*, at [43]. 30 *Ibid.*, at [31].
31 *Slim* v. *Daily Telegraph* [1968] 2 QB 157, at 171.

as a legal fiction 'the existence of which owes much to accidents of history rather than legal principle or policy'.[32]

### 3.2 Justifications for the single meaning rule

Yet, the single meaning rule is incontrovertibly a facet of English libel law. In *Lait* v. *Evening Standard*,[33] the Court of Appeal traced the origins of the rule back as far as *Merivale* v. *Carson*, a case decided in the late nineteenth century.[34] The House of Lords affirmed it in *Charleston* v. *News Group Newspapers* ('*Charleston*') as 'too well established to require citation of authority',[35] while its use was described as 'unexceptional' by Lord Nicholls in *Bonnick* v. *Morris*.[36] The question must be asked, therefore, as to why the law has embraced a rule that generates a focus on counter-factual artifice instead of plain fact. Seldom have justifications been articulated by the courts. In light of that fact, Lord Neuberger's recent judgement is a welcome contribution.

When Lord Neuberger sat recently as a member of the Hong Kong Final Court of Appeal in *Oriental Daily Publisher* v. *Ming Pao Holdings*, the sole purpose behind his contribution in a concurring judgement was to affirm the single meaning rule as an 'essential' feature of defamation law that 'makes obvious good sense'.[37] From his Lordship's speech, but also other sources, it is possible to divine a range of putative justifications that have been advanced by the courts and others over time.

A first justification is that ascribing singular meanings to words is part and parcel of legal practice. In *Slim* v. *Daily Telegraph*, Diplock LJ explained that:

> the argument between lawyers as to the meaning of words starts with the unexpressed major premise that any particular combination of words has one meaning which is not necessarily the same as that intended by him who published them or understood by any of those who read them but is capable of ascertainment as being the 'right' meaning by the adjudicator to whom the law confides the responsibility of determining it.[38]

This was echoed by Lord Neuberger in *Oriental Daily* v. *Ming Pao*. He explained that the determination of the meaning of words 'is a question which arises in many areas of law, most notably perhaps in cases involving the interpretation of statutes, contracts and notices'.[39]

[32] Cameron Doley and Alastair Mullis (eds), *Carter-Ruck on Libel and Privacy*, 6th edn (London: LexisNexis, 2010) at xx.
[33] [2011] EWCA Civ 859. [34] (1887) 20 QBD 275.
[35] [1995] 2 AC 65, at 71 (Lord Bridge). [36] *Bonnick* [2002] UKPC 31 at [21].
[37] *Oriental Daily* [2012] HKCFA 59, at [141]. [38] *Slim* [1968] 2 QB 157, at 172.
[39] *Oriental Daily* [2012] HKCFA 59, at [140].

For the most part, this explanation is manifestly misdirected. The lawyers' interpretative task to which Diplock LJ referred is most often that of assisting the court in determining the meaning of words as terms of law. In contrast, the determination of the meaning of words in a publication is a matter of fact, not law. Lord Neuberger is of course correct to highlight the fact that allowing legal terms to have multiple meanings would 'self-evidently lead to chaos and uncertainty in many cases'.[40] There is simply no correspondence, however, between the discussion of statutory or contractual interpretation and the single meaning rule in libel law.

To be fair, Lord Neuberger's version of the point was not limited to legal interpretation. His reference to 'notices', and his invocation of *Mannai Investment* v. *Eagle Star Life Assurance* extended his argument to cover instances outside of libel where the need to interpret ambiguous words might arise as a question of fact.[41] In the case cited, the House of Lords was required to decide whether a tenant had properly given notice as required under a break clause in his lease in order to bring a tenancy to a close. On their face, the words in the notice were not in fact ambiguous: read strictly, it was clear that the tenant had not done what was required of him. The issue was rather whether the words should be understood by reference to their context, which was that the tenant had obviously intended to act as required under the contract but had erred. Their Lordships split on that issue.

It is of course interesting that the imperfection of communication can bear on legal issues in different contexts, but the strength of this analogy as a justification for the single meaning rule in libel law is nugatory. The reason why the words in *Mannai Investment* had to be interpreted one way or the other as a matter of fact was to allow the court to decide whether the contract persisted or not (and impliedly to determine whether there had been a subsequent breach of contract). This requires a binary determination. There is no equivalent necessity in the libel context that might explain why one meaning only must be attributed to impugned words. To argue otherwise is tautologous. If this were the only justification offered for the state of the law, the single meaning rule would be a rule of law only because it has been a rule of law.

Incidentally, a closer analogy to the context in which the single meaning rule is used in defamation law is the determination of whether there might be confusion between commercial signs or symbols among consumers in European and domestic trade mark law. In that context, the High Court recently roundly rejected the suggestion that European precedent

[40] *Ibid.*, at [141]. [41] [1997] AC 749.

compelled the recognition of a single meaning rule.[42] In debunking the proposition, Arnold J noted that he was 'not aware of any textbook or academic commentary which supports the existence of a single meaning rule in trade mark law ... nor am I aware of any authority from the superior courts of the other Member States to support the existence of such a rule'.[43] Moreover, he added that 'the single meaning rule which exists in English defamation law is widely regarded as anomalous'.[44] As already noted, the Court of Appeal has also rejected the notion of a single meaning rule in the closely analogous context of malicious falsehood.[45]

It may be that pragmatic justifications for the single meaning rule are more persuasive. Indeed, in *Lait* v. *Evening Standard*, Laws LJ introduced the rule precisely as 'a fiction adopted by the law for practical reasons'.[46] Even so, such reasons have generally been more assumed than expressed. It is possible to draw out three main, somewhat interrelated, practical justifications for the single meaning rule, however, from the jurisprudence and wider literature.

The first of these is based upon the fact that libel involves jury trials. In *Slim* v. *Daily Telegraph*, Diplock LJ noted that:

> the recognition that there may be more than one meaning which reasonable men might understand words to bear does not absolve the jury from the duty of deciding upon one of those meanings as being the only 'natural and ordinary meaning' of the words. Juries, in theory, must be unanimous upon every issue on which they have to adjudicate; and since the damages that they award must depend upon the defamatory meaning that they attribute to the words, they must all agree upon a single meaning as being the 'right' meaning.[47]

There is an obvious rejoinder to this justification: juries have become more or less obsolete in the libel context in England and Wales. Even if this contention might once have justified the single meaning rule, it cannot do so for the future.

There is also room to be sceptical about Diplock's LJ premise on its own terms. It is a contestable assertion, and one again tainted by tautology. It seems an unnatural exercise to require a group of twelve individuals to fix on one interpretation when, if anything, they would be better-placed than a single adjudicator to appreciate the multiplicity of meanings. Such limited evidence as is available on juries' undertaking of the task suggests that they are often unwilling or unable to agree on singular meanings, or that they engage in compromise between meanings.[48] Certainly, the abstraction of

[42] *Interflora* v. *Marks & Spencer* [2013] EWHC 1291 (Ch), [213][224].
[43] *Ibid.*, at [221]. [44] *Ibid.*, at [224]. [45] *Ajinomoto* [2010] EWCA Civ 609.
[46] [2011] EWCA Civ 859. [47] *Slim* [1968] 2 QB 157, at 174.
[48] See, e.g., Kenyon, above n 23, 120–3; Richard Shillito and Eric Barendt, 'Libel Law' (1999) 4 *Yearbook of Copyright and Media Law* 370.

the single meaning rule must make the task of the jury no less difficult, but much less natural, than asking the group to proceed on the basis that multiple reasonable meanings were possible. Under that second approach, the jury would be required to determine the relative likelihood that given meanings would be inferred by the reasonable readers, and to determine the appropriate level of damages by aggregating separate 'probability ×-seriousness' calculations in accordance with their nuanced findings.

In *Oriental Daily*, Lord Neuberger offered two further pragmatic arguments in favour of the single meaning rule. Both suggested that removing the rule would result in an obviously undesirable increase in legal costs in libel litigation. His Lordship's first point was an elaboration of Diplock's LJ premise. Lord Neuberger asserted that abolition of the rule would 'lead to the dispiriting, expensive, and time-consuming prospect of many witnesses being called by each party, to explain how they understood the statement in question'.[49] A similar assertion was made in *Charleston*.[50] This assumption that evidentiary practice would necessarily have to change if the single meaning rule was excised from the law, however, is ungrounded. It is not obvious why the presumption that harm flows from defamatory meanings should be affected, or that a court would be unable to attribute quantums of harm to different meanings recognised.

If the question was whether any given interpretation could reasonably be inferred from the impugned words, with all such reasonable interpretations remaining on the table, then the exercise reverts to one of easy impression. There would be no need for any evidence on how a publication was in fact interpreted. To reiterate Diplock's LJ statement of the rather obvious, 'the chances are that if the words are reasonably capable of being understood as bearing more than one meaning, some readers will have understood them as bearing one of those meanings and some will have understood them as bearing others of those meanings'.[51] A presumption that all reasonable meanings will have been inferred by at least some recipients of a publication is in fact much more legitimate than a presumption that all reasonable recipients will have inferred a single meaning. It is not beyond the wit of a court to ascribe relative likelihoods that a given interpretation will have been drawn to different possible interpretations of a given publication.

Lord Neuberger's second pragmatic argument in favour of the extant rule was that jettisoning it would 'lead to greater uncertainty in outcome ... [as] instead of a statement with two possible meanings giving rise to a problem requiring a binary resolution, it would give rise to a problem

49 *Oriental Daily* [2012] HKCFA 59, at [142].
50 [1995] 2 AC 65, at 71 (Lord Bridge).
51 *Slim* [1968] 2 QB 157, at 173.

which had a multiplicity of potential answers, along what might be seen as a continuous spectrum'.[52] Lord Neuberger appears to presume that without the single meaning rule the determination of disputes would become by degrees more complex than at present. As discussed later, this need not be the case.

Lord Neuberger's argument also seems almost wilfully to underplay the reality of how pleading and argument over meaning in libel cases currently proceeds. At present, both sides proffer meanings to the court that best serve their own interests in the libel game. The very fact that the court must settle on a single meaning has the result that obfuscation and complication become a worthwhile exercise. It is no stretch of the imagination to suppose that the insight once afforded by an interviewee to Andrew Kenyon is generalisable to all libel practitioners:

> when I get a claim, I would have a look at that article and do two things. One is I would form my own view [about its meaning], as any person in the world would ... and the second thing I'd do is [ask] what meaning can I extract out of it which is most helpful to my clients. The two things are often quite different.[53]

As things stand, all reasonable meanings already remain on the table until the single meaning is determined by the court.[54] The context created by the single meaning rule encourages the parties to enter into a legal game, rather than to address concerns raised and to mollify them quickly and effectively – if appropriate – through real-world action. Parties are incentivised poorly by the existing law. The process discourages defendants in particular from responding appropriately to claimants' complaints. It encourages claimants to plead over-broadly on meanings. Much argument between parties is focussed on meaning in the hope that the court will select one that is favourable to this side or that. The tenor of the libel game becomes one of strategy and semantics, rather than the attempt to address any core dispute. Costs are significantly increased.

52 *Oriental Daily* [2012] HKCFA 59, at [142].

53 Kenyon, above n 23, 119–20. Furthermore, on the strength of interviewees' comments Kenyon notes that the meanings pleaded by defendant's are often verbose and general, not because the lawyers wish to establish those meanings per se, but rather because the general meaning provides a wider gateway to evidence (at 120).

54 In recent times, the tendency of English courts to consider libel disputes without a jury has expedited the determination of meaning, often placing the exercise in the preliminary stage of litigation. This tendency will likely accelerate under the 2013 Act. Relative to the previous position, where meaning was determined by the jury only at the endpoint of a trial, this is a very significant advance. Even after the shift, however, much time and effort – and correspondingly cost – prior to and in the early stages of litigation must still be dedicated towards the meaning issue. Even this minimised commitment places libel out of the realms of the possible for many claimants, and threatens defendants with a financial chill that is impossible to withstand.

## 3.3 Libel law in the absence of the single meaning rule

Absent the single meaning rule, the determination of meaning issue and the complicated associated rules on pleading would effectively disappear. In principle, a judge could still be asked to decide whether a given form of words was capable of bearing a meaning attributed to it by the claimant. Indeed, in the absence of a jury, the test could be applied more stringently by the judge unrestrained by constitutional niceties.[55] It might be, for instance, whether a pleaded meaning was 'tenable', in the sense that it could have been taken – perhaps among others – by a 'significant' proportion of readers.[56] Importantly, however, there would seldom be any need for a judge to engage in such an exercise. The parties themselves could easily distinguish meanings that are tenable from those that are not.

This is not to say that there would never be cases in which multiple meanings would remain in play. As discussed, human communication is rarely perfect. Retaining a range of meanings in libel actions could become unfair, particularly in circumstances where a publisher simply did not intend the more damaging interpretations.[57] It might be expected that two related practices would develop wherein, first, publishers would seek to eradicate ambiguity of language to the furthest extent possible. This could be stultifying, both in terms of how stories would be authored and in terms of the contribution of journalism to the democratic public sphere. Second, it might be expected that publishers would seek to placate claimants as swiftly as possible with corrections and retractions where unintended meanings could be inferred. In itself, this would be very desirable, but as things stand it would clearly give claimants an undeserved 'whip-hand'.

[55] When the task of determining meaning was left as a question of fact for the jury, judges naturally tended towards over-inclusion of meanings at the capability stage. The question of capability was understood as 'an exercise in generosity, not in parsimony ... [as] the long stop is the jury' – see *Berezovsky* v. *Forbes* [2001] EWCA Civ 1251, at [16] (Sedley LJ). There is a desire not to usurp the fact-finding function. For the same reason, appeal courts were reticent to reverse inclusive findings – see, for example, *Cruise* v. *Express Newspapers* [1999] QB 931, at 936 (Brooke LJ); *Jameel* v. *Wall Street Journal Europe (No 1)* [2003] EWCA Civ 1694, at [14] (Simon Brown LJ) – and 'a little less reluctant to interfere' where trial judges had excluded meanings from consideration by a jury – see, for example, *Geenty* v. *Channel Four Television Corporation* [1998] EMLR 524, at 532 (Hirst LJ). With the effective obsolescence of the jury, the basis for this judicial tendency towards generosity of interpretation dissolves.

[56] That significant proportion would also normally have to comprise an arithmetically sizeable number of individuals to satisfy the serious harm threshold.

[57] Anecdotally, this was the experience in New South Wales prior to the uniform defamation acts of 2005. As the cause of action rested upon possible imputations, publishers were sometimes left to defend meanings that they had never contemplated when publishing the impugned words.

This need not be an argument for retaining the counterfactual single meaning rule, however. Indeed, as noted by the judges of the Court of Appeal in *Ajinomoto*, the adoption of such an approach afresh would seem almost perverse. Avoiding the dystopian vision does require some further intervention. The law can be used to facilitate good outcomes. One option would be to couple the removal of the single meaning rule with the introduction of appropriate 'discursive remedies' that might provide an attractive 'way out' for defendants. That is, the law might recognise, applaud and promote the tendency of publishers to provide a discursive solution to disputes generated by publication. The jettisoning of the single meaning rule and the introduction of discursive remedies together could take all but the intractable disputes out of the legal forum. Those cases that rested on some fundamental dispute of fact would still go to court. All others might be resolved through enhanced public sphere engagement, not bowdlerising legal chill.

Discursive remedies – corrections, retractions, rights of reply and apologies – have long been identified as being of potential utility in the defamation context.[58] The potential of such options has grown enormously in the context of online and social media.[59] In some respects, they are already commonplace in the United Kingdom. Their use is haphazard however, and their availability as a matter of law is limited.[60] In contrast, in many European jurisdictions discursive remedies are the primary mechanism utilised.[61] It is often said that the primary aim of

[58] See, John G Fleming, 'Retraction and Reply: Alternative Remedies for Defamation' (1978) *University of British Columbia Law Review* 12, 15–31; Randall P Bezanson, Gilbert Cranberg and John Soloski, *Libel Law and the Press: Myth and Reality* (New York: Free Press, 1987).

[59] See, generally, David S Ardia, 'Reputation in a Networked World: Revisiting the Social Foundations of Defamation Law' (2010) 45 *Harvard Civil Rights-Civil Liberties Law Review* 261.

[60] Declarations of falsity have been said to be unavailable at common law (see *Loutchansky* v. *Times Newspapers (Permission to Amend Particulars of Claim)* [2002] EMLR 44), although a publication of summary of judgement remedy was imposed recently by the Court of Appeal in *Samsung Electronics (UK)* v. *Apple* [2012] EWCA Civ 1339 in resolution of an intellectual property dispute. There is some provision for a declaration of falsity and publication of a suitable correction and apology under ss. 8–9 of the Defamation Act 1996 (UK) on the summary disposal of a claim, for the stipulation of a suitable correction and a sufficient apology as part of the 'offer of amends' procedure set out in ss. 2–4 of the 1996 Act, and most recently in the power of the court under s. 12 of the Defamation Act 2013 (UK) to order publication of a summary of its judgement. Libel claims that are settled will often include an agreement that an appropriate correction and/or apology will be published, and sometimes that an apologetic statement in open court will be made.

[61] Hugh Tomlinson, 'Libel, damages and declarations of falsity', *Inforrm*, 2 November 2010 http://inforrm.wordpress.com/2010/11/02/libel-damages-and-declarations-of-falsity/. See, generally, Gert Brüggemeier, Aurelia Ciacchi and Patrick O'Callaghan (eds), *Personality Rights in European Tort Law* (Cambridge: Cambridge University Press, 2010); Helmut

claimants is to obtain a swift correction of misleading publications concerning themselves.[62] It is also a tenet of good journalism that errors should be corrected. Clause 1 of the Press Complaints Commission Editors' Code of Practice states that 'a significant inaccuracy, misleading statement or distortion once recognised must be corrected, promptly and with due prominence, and – where appropriate – an apology published'.[63] Broadcasters can be compelled by Ofcom to carry summaries of fairness and standards complaints and the regulator's adjudications.[64]

Clearly, a key question becomes what forms of discursive remedy might serve this purpose.[65] Rights of reply, retractions and corrections, and apologies are each different in character. A right of reply allows a claimant the opportunity to 'set the record straight', but it clearly does not also amount to any admission on the part of a publisher that what has been said was inaccurate. Apologies, if sincere, may do much to salve the hurt felt by a claimant, but as a mandated remedial device they invite cynicism both in their use and their appreciation.[66] From a wider perspective, the existence or otherwise of contrition on the part of a publisher seems somewhat beside the point. In contrast, a voluntary retraction or

Koziol and Alexander Warzilek (eds), *The Protection of Personality Rights against Invasions by Mass Media* (New York: Springer Wein, 2005).

62 This idea was oft-cited by claimants' lawyers during the debates on libel reform that culminated in the Defamation Act 2013 (UK). It was also a core finding of the Iowa Libel Research project that claimants were motivated by this desire, and not by the prospect of a financial windfall, see Randall P Bezanson, 'Libel Law and the Realities of Litigation: Setting the Record Straight' (1985) 71 *Iowa Law Review* 215; Randall P Bezanson, 'The Libel Suit in Retrospect: What Plaintiffs Want and What Plaintiffs Get' (1986) 74 *California Law Review* 789. This general preference among libel claimants for a discursive remedy is also recognised in the English Pre-Action Protocol for Defamation (at [1.4]).

63 Press Complaints Commission, Editors' Code of Practice, www.pcc.org.uk/cop/practice.html. Cl. 1 (iv) provides that 'a publication must report fairly and accurately the outcome of an action for defamation to which it has been a party'. Similarly, clause 3 of the NUJ *Code of Conduct* provides that '[a journalist] does her/his utmost to correct harmful inaccuracies'. Interestingly, as regards the 'Comment is free' section of its website, the *Guardian* newspaper provides an automatic right of reply to any person mentioned in a published article (see www.guardian.co.uk/commentisfree/series/response). The failure to ensure the correction of misinformation can also be seen as a shortcoming of the American approach to the defamation of public figures. Traditionally, this concern has been addressed by a relatively high and generalised commitment to journalistic ethics that insists upon fact-checking and the correction of error. It may be, however, that the inadequacies of this 'cultural' form of regulation are exposed when confronted with more 'populist' forms of media content such as that reflected in publications such as the *National Enquirer*, television channels such as Fox News, or the proliferation of online gossip websites.

64 Broadcasting Act 1996 (UK) ss. 119, 120.

65 Strictly, the nomenclature of 'remedy' in this context is inappropriate, given that the action taken by the publisher would pre-empt any determination of a dispute by a court.

66 Joint Committee on the Draft Defamation Bill, above n 8, at Q 604 (per Desmond Browne QC and Hugh Tomlinson QC).

correction provided 'promptly' and 'prominently', with its explicit recognition of error, would often – perhaps generally – be sufficient to provide a good measure of vindication. The most effective way of vindicating a person's reputation must be to ensure that the truth is fully and quickly aired, and misrepresentations corrected. Certainly, a substantive intervention in the public sphere that pre-empted litigation would deliver more effective vindication than a compelled payment of damages following a protracted and contested legal dispute.[67]

In the absence of any compulsion to correct or retract, or of any advantage to publishers from having done so, it might reasonably be questioned why – barring ethical rectitude – they might take the trouble. To incentivise the use of such tools, the law might stipulate that the prompt and prominent correction or retraction of an error following receipt of a complaint would preclude any further action in respect of the meaning in question. Claimants could be obliged to communicate the imputations complained of and the meaning ascribed to the words in question to the publisher in advance of bringing any suit. Alongside assessing the capability of any meanings over which remedial action was not taken by the publisher, provision could be made for a court to assess whether the meaning complained of had been properly corrected before any action could proceed. While such a scheme might easily be gamed by publishers, both the value of their own reputations for accuracy and credibility and the potential availability of a claim for malicious falsehood might be expected to militate against abuses. Moreover, any inadequacy in the discursive remedy afforded would permit the claimant to proceed to court. Whether any similar prompt to allowing rights of reply – for example, an associated cap on damages – should be introduced is more a moot point.[68]

To appreciate the potential utility of this approach in the absence of a single meaning rule, one can consider the outcomes in cases involving ambiguous or multifarious potential meanings. For example, in a case involving *Chase* levels of meaning (the descending scale from the firm allegation, through an allegation of reasonable suspicion, to the suggestion that there is reason to investigate further), the claimant might suggest that all three meanings can be taken from a

[67] The recent illustration of the libelling of the late Lord McAlpine as a paedophile provides a useful illustration. Within days of the publications occurring, retractions and apologies published by broadcasters and social media commentators could have left few people unclear that the allegations had been mistaken.

[68] On the development of a Convention jurisprudence on the right of reply, see Ronan Ó Fathaigh, 'The Recognition of a Right of Reply under the European Convention' (2012) 4 *Journal of Media Law* 322. See also, András Koltay, *Freedom of Speech: The Unreachable Mirage* (Budapest: CompLex, 2013), ch.2.

publication.[69] On receipt of a complaint, the defendant might respond that the form of words used could not tenably be interpreted as the most serious meaning (A). He or she might agree, on reflection, that the words could be understood as amounting to an allegation of reasonable suspicion (B), but assert that no such meaning was in fact intended. Instead, he or she might posit that all that was intended was the identification of a need to investigate some matter further (C). In those circumstances, he or she might publish a note to the effect that there had been no intention to suggest (A) or (B) thereby providing vindication on those meanings insofar as this was necessary.[70] He or she might also say that it is not considered tenable that (A) could be inferred, and – importantly – that (C) absolutely was intended. Should the claimant then wish to proceed to litigate on meaning (C), this would remain possible. Indeed, this would comprise a honing of the dispute onto the territory of the allegation made and intended.[71] This would be achieved prior to going to court, and without any expensive technical lawyering on the pleading of meanings.

Other types of cases involving complexity of meaning would also be easily refined so as either to dissolve or to focus quickly on core disputes of fact. For instance, in the – surely infrequent – cases in which it was important for a claimant to differentiate between individual allegations that carried a common sting – 'I may be an adulterer, but I was not unfaithful with *that* man' – this could be easily accommodated with a retraction of the contested particular allegation if it could not be stood up. Similarly, the parsing of 'shades of meaning' and the correction of any unintended misrepresentation would see *Lucas-Box* pleadings – where the defendant contends that the claimant's meaning is not conveyed at all, and proposes instead to justify an alternative meaning – become an artefact of legal history.

## 3.4 Codicil: prospects for reform of the single meaning rule

Statutory reform of libel laws, we are told, is a once-in-a-generation phenomenon, and so – in terms of the prospects for further reform in England and Wales – there must be a question whether this chapter

[69] Similar exercises might be conducted in respect of the scenario in which 'shades of meaning' can be inferred from a publication.

[70] The publisher might also simply ignore the complaint in respect of meaning (A), thereby inviting the claimant to sue. The expectation would be that a judge would in any event strike out the meaning early on capability grounds.

[71] Notably, in those circumstances, the claimant would have to be able to explain why he or she considered that any significant harm had been caused by meaning (C) when that impliedly attributed by him or her to meanings (A) and (B) had been taken off the table. This would itself introduce an incentive for claimants to 'go in low', or perhaps 'realistically', in the original letter of complaint.

reflects any more than a lament for lost opportunities. Presented with an appropriate case, however, judges may be expected to confirm or withdraw the single meaning rule as a facet of English libel law. As discussed, the appropriateness of the rule has recently been identified by the Court of Appeal as a theme worthy of reconsideration. Given that the rule is venerable, and that it has been affirmed by the House of Lords and the Privy Council in the past, any such judicial reconsideration must be taken by the Supreme Court if anywhere.

A specific opportunity for such reconsideration has been generated, albeit indirectly, by the 2013 Act.[72] The approach taken in the statutory restatement of the main defences in sections 2, 3 and 4 was abolition of the precursor common law defences. Hence, whenever a case involving a 'rule' of law relevant to one of these defences arises, the court will have to consider whether that rule has survived abolition.[73] A rule might survive either because it was not in fact part of the defence at issue, or because the court determines positively that it should continue to be followed. It seems likely that the single meaning rule would fall into the former category, but it is arguable that determination of meaning is so tied up with the pleading and proof of the defence of truth that the court may legitimately determine whether it should continue to form part of the law. Conservatism may, but will not necessarily, hold sway. Either way, come the apposite case, the approach adopted in the statute could provide the opportunity for the single meaning rule to be reassessed.

A further feature of the new legislation may also lend weight to the need to reassess the rule. When the determination of meaning is undertaken by a jury, the meaning actually selected remains unstated. The outcome of the exercise is obscured in the black box of jury deliberations, with no reasons for the outcome subsequently being given. When standard practice sees judges acting alone and providing reasoned explanations as to how meaning has been determined, this may throw a searching light upon the artificiality of the process.[74] Also relevant to any reconsideration of the

[72] This prospect has been noted in both Richard Parkes and Alastair Mullis (eds), *Gatley on Libel and Slander*, 12th edn (London: Sweet & Maxwell, 2013) at [11.2], and James Price and Felicity McMahon (eds), *Blackstone's Guide to the Defamation Act 2013* (Oxford: Oxford University Press, 2013), ch.3.

[73] Examples might include the 'repetition rule', or the 'conduct rule' that is relevant to the proof of *Chase* level two meanings.

[74] There is a growing number of such reasoned decisions on meaning: see, for example, *Rothschild* v. *Associated Newspapers* [2012] EWHC 177 (QB), at [29]–[31]; *Bento* v. *Chief Constable of Bedfordshire* [2012] EWHC 1525 (QB), at [10]; *El Naschie* v. *Macmillan Publishers (t/a Nature Publishing Group)* [2012] EWHC 1809 (QB), at [20]–[30]; *Mengi* v. *Hermitage* [2012] EWHC 3445 (QB), at [49]–[50]. In *Rothschild*, the Court of Appeal was then in a position to assess the appropriateness of the judge's determinations, see [2013] EWCA Civ 197, at [9]–[11].

single meaning rule will be the question of whether the rule permits adequate account to be taken, in any given case, of plausible arguments based on Article 10 or Article 8 ECHR. Conceivably more important may be the overriding objective of the Civil Procedure Rules: 'enabling the court to deal with cases justly and at proportionate cost'.[75] Whether that imperative can be brought to bear at all on what is a substantive aspect of the law of libel is a moot point. If it can be demonstrated that the procedural ramifications of the extant rule run diametrically opposite to this golden rule, then it would be remarkable if a court were to turn its face against the advantages of a more 'realistic' law.

By way of tangent, as regards the Northern Irish jurisdiction there is perhaps a stronger prospect that statutory reform may occur in the near future. The question as to whether the single meaning rule should continue in place has been raised in the context of the study being undertaken by the NI Law Commission as to the future of libel law in that jurisdiction. One option there is clearly retention of the status quo. Some measure of reform is also foreseeable, and in that case one might expect the adoption of (all or parts of) the Defamation Act 2013, with or without the inclusion of other reform options. Far from becoming the new haven for libel tourists, that jurisdiction has the opportunity to introduce progressive defamation laws that might serve as an exemplar for its larger neighbour and other common law jurisdictions.

[75] Civil Procedure Rules 1998 (UK), r. 1.1.

# 4 *New York Times* v. *Sullivan* at fifty years: defamation in separate orbits

*David Partlett*

In one respect it is passing strange that *New York Times* v. *Sullivan*[1] should have any comparative component. The case grew from the unique soil of the United States Constitution and the American Civil Rights movement. Nothing better shows the specialised meld of social conditions, politics, text and convention, than the rise of the First Amendment. Of the Bill of Rights provisions, it was to become, in the second half of the twentieth century, the one that rules them all.[2] Most Bill of Rights freedoms and protections have had their seasons. The First Amendment's season has had different colours and emphases; in present days it presents a vivid social and political salience, the vanguard of the Roberts Court's power as the third branch. The Supreme Court, after initial insouciance towards free speech protection, took a stance checking governmental zeal in quelling the tide of the union movement and of reactions to perceived external communist and anarchistic threats in the early twentieth century. Dramatically important in American jurisprudence, this Holmes- and Brandeis-led promotion of the First Amendment as dominant had little legal resonance elsewhere in the Western world.[3]

1 376 US 254 (1964).

2 Ellen D Katz, 'Hobby Lobby and the Pathology of Citizens United' (2014) 9 *Duke Journal of Constitutional Law and Public Policy* 23.

3 See Thomas Healy, *The Great Dissent: How Oliver Wendell Holmes Changed his Mind – and Changed the History of Free Speech in America* (New York: Henry Holt and Company, 2013) (describing how Holmes and Brandeis shifted the prism of analysis). Healy at 370, discussing the influence of Holmes's dissent in *Abrams v United States*, 250 US 616, 624 (1919), rightly says that it influences deeply: '[Holmes's] metaphor of the marketplace of ideas and his concept of "clear and present danger" have worked their way into our collective consciousness, becoming part of our language, our view of the world, and our identity as a nation'. See also G Edward White, 'Justice Holmes and the Modernization of Free Speech Jurisprudence: The Human Dimension' (1992) 80 *California Law Review* 391 (discussing the Holmes / Brandeis / Hand relationship); Lyrissa Barnett Lidsky, 'Nobody's Fool: The Rational Audience as First Amendment Ideal' [2010] *University of Illinois Law Review* 799, 813 (reasoning that 'radical speakers', like the defendants in *Abrams*, do not create a clear and present danger by urging their audience to take action: 'Justice Holmes' opinion rests on faith in rational deliberation as an antidote to violence').

Fifty years ago in another particularly American dilemma, the Civil Rights movement, the Court would respond by again invoking the First Amendment. In Montgomery, Alabama, Dr Martin Luther King and other civil rights leaders took a stand against the deprivation of civil rights faced by African American citizens. Sullivan was a commissioner of the city who had supervisory duties over, inter alia, the police. In an effort to support the embattled Civil Rights movement, an advertisement was published in the *New York Times* on 29 March 1960. Certain facts reported in the ad were false. Sullivan brought an action in defamation against some of the signers of the advertisement – African American clergymen – and the *New York Times*. The jury awarded damages of \$500,000 against the *New York Times*, an award that was upheld on appeal to the Alabama Supreme Court. The US Supreme Court took the appeal and handed down its unanimous decision overruling the Alabama Supreme Court with remarkable speed. It adopted the reasoning and many of the words in the petitioner's brief, written by Professor Wechsler of Columbia Law School, in finding that the First Amendment imposed a constitutionally mandated requirement to prove, by clear and convincing evidence, that the piece was published with actual malice.

The case was noteworthy in its bold holding that put aside the Supreme Court's past support of the common law of defamation, and even more for its attack on the structure and tenets of the American republic. It ignored the federal structure that at its core resided in state laws, sovereignty in relations among citizens governed by the common law. It put aside too an institution at the heart of republican ideals – the jury. Drawing on its earlier boldness and broad-brush assertions about free speech, the court upheld a fundamentally important, but often flouted, ideal: equality.

The fault lines were not apparent to the casual observer back in those heady days of the 1960s. Most foreign observers nodded in approval when the Supreme Court sallied forth under the banner of the First Amendment into Alabama state law. It seemed plain that Alabama's defamation law chilled free speech in the critical arena of civil rights. That is, one should be able to criticise government officials thwarting the exercise of civil rights without fear of libel damage awards. At least that is so where assertions of fact, directed to public officials, are not actuated by malice. I need not repeat the sonorous rhetoric that carried the justices to their displacement of the common law of defamation as it had been applied until that time. It was a powerful statement of the right to free speech in the cauldron of a troubled period.

Fifty years allows a perspective that rightly situates *Sullivan* as a singular civil rights case. I venture, however, that as a case that constitutionalised defamation law, its legacy is weaker. That is the purpose of this essay. The Supreme Court, distracted by the exigencies of an American dilemma,[4] weakened the common law and shunted aside three tenets of the Constitution.

First, the Alabama law was dismissed with little regard for the prime place of defamation in the fabric of the common law. Its doctrine, evolved over centuries, had balanced free speech and the individual's interest in reputation. It certainly was not blind to the need for free speech, rather, it had championed it through its defences. Here, however, the court crafted a new path despite no experience in providing the normative guidance of the common law. In addition, the structural assumptions of federalism were put asunder.[5] To federalise an important tract of the common law was an enormous step.

Second, a republican institution was deemed too dangerous. The republic depends on a citizenry that is autonomous and capable of self-rule. The jury, with its republican roots, the lens of community norms, was found to be an unruly element in the protection of rights.[6]

The third is that the newly minted law turned on an assumption untested and easily contested: free speech, unshackled from other norms like privacy and community precepts, would further democratic values, drive us to truth, or make us better citizens. It would too perhaps make us more realised human beings. This raises two questions: (1) Why should free speech be the trump card among other modes of nurturing these values? (2) If free speech is prime, was the court serious in claiming any empirical backing for its 'chilling of speech' claim, for its faith in the marketplace of ideas, and for the curative waters of more speech in furthering the search for truth? The empirical uncertainty of the claim puts at issue whether the court was actually not making this claim but

[4] See Gunnar Myrdal, *An American Dilemma: The Negro Problem And Modern Democracy* (New York: Harper & Row, 1962). This book was enormously influential in framing American society at the time.

[5] There is irony here, for the Australian Constitution was influenced by the United States, especially in terms of a federal structure. See Helen Irving, 'The Over-Rated Mr Clark: Putting Andrew Inglis Clark's Contribution to the Constitution into Perspective' in '*The Truest Patriotism': Andrew Inglis Clark and the Building of an Australian Nation* (Papers on Parliament No. 61, May 2014) www.aph.gov.au/About_Parliament/Senate/Research_and_Education/~/link.aspx?_id=466D7B081D21483D9368859B07DA824D&_z=z (noting the influence of Inglis Clark of Tasmania in persuading the convention to follow the American model of federalism and of judicial review).

[6] This same distrust of the jury arose in the mind of Holmes J when he ignored the jury's finding of intent in *Abrams* and failed to distinguish *Debs* v. *United States*, 249 US 211 (1919). Healy puts it down to the winning arguments of Hand and Freund on the dangers of the Sedition Act: Healy, above n 3, at 298. The institution of the jury had been contested since the founding of the nation. See Donald M Middlebrooks, 'Reviving Thomas Jefferson's Jury: *Sparf and Hansen* v. *United States*, Reconsidered' (2004) 46 *American Journal of Legal History* 353.

rather expressing the aspirations of law. That it was expressing, as Holmes J had done in his *Abrams* dissent, the values of the republic. It is law explicated by its highest court in the highest dudgeon. The law is not endeavouring to guide behaviour but to express its deepest values.[7]

I will examine these points in the rest of this essay. At the outset however, it is worth noting the international salience of the great case. If one takes these elements, a reasonable assumption may have been that the doctrine in *Sullivan* was unfit for export. It articulated American values in a peculiar American setting. Its use of the marketplace metaphor, its lack of attention to other 'free countries', and a parochial line of scholarship underpinning the case and doctrines, like Meiklejohn's New England town meeting,[8] underline its Americanness.

However, *Sullivan* initially prevailed against these headwinds to establish an international beachhead for the free speech ideal. One reason is the resonance of the call for free speech in a time when the cry for human rights was at its height. Another is an internationalisation of the conversation that took place as scholars looked for a basis to extend rights. More foreign lawyers came to American law schools for postgraduate training and took back the framing conversation. In the 1970s, many Western countries looked to written constitutions and basic law to instantiate human rights.[9] Third, the power of a first mover should not be underemphasised. If written constitutions were the mode of protection, the long experience of the United States was a ready model. A fourth is a place of leadership, as the United States took human rights stances. The reaction against human rights abuses in the Second World War led to international and domestic normative changes that still ring loud. President Carter, it may be recalled, put this at the heart of American foreign policy.[10] When the European

[7] See Robert L Tsai, *Eloquence and Reason: Creating a First Amendment Culture* (New Haven: Yale University Press, 2008) (explaining how the guarantees of the First Amendment are expressive of culture and social norms forging a nationwide commitment).

[8] See, e.g., Alexander Meiklejohn, *Political Freedom: The Constitutional Powers of the People* (New York: Oxford University Press, 1960) 23 ('The meeting has assembled, not primarily to talk, but primarily by means of talking to get business done. And the talking must be regulated and abridged as doing of the business under actual conditions may require').

[9] See Mary Dudziak, 'The Global Impact of *Brown* v. *Board of Education*', SCOTUSBlog, (18 February 2010) www.scotusblog.com/2010/02/the-global-impact-of-brown-v-board-of-education/ (Mary Dudziak, arguing that the American move to protect racial minorities was in part motivated by the vulnerability of the United States in its treatment of racial minorities.); Mary Dudziak, '*Brown* as a Cold War Case' (2004) 91 *Journal of American History* 32.

[10] Jimmy Carter, 'Universal Declaration of Human Rights Remarks at a White House Meeting Commemorating the 30th Anniversary of the Declaration's Signing, Address before the East Room in the White House' (6 December 1978), transcribed by Gerhard Peters & John T Woolley, *The American Presidency Project* www.presidency.ucsb.edu/ws/?pid=30264 ('Human rights is the soul of our foreign policy. And I say this with assurance, because human rights is the soul of our sense of nationhood').

Community was being formed, it was ripe for inculcation of rights rhetoric, and free speech under Article 10 of the European Convention on Human Rights took pride of place. We also in that age embraced the notion that courts ought to take the lead in fashioning rights where other institutions of government proved to be feckless. *Brown* v. *Board of Education*[11] was a beacon for those avid for change in human rights.

*Sullivan* frames any conversation about free speech. In *The Right to Speak Ill*,[12] a book I co-authored, *Sullivan* was the point of reference as we examined the growing free speech norm in Western nations.[13] There it can be seen that the case has been influential in all Western nations, from Canada, Australia and New Zealand to England and Europe. It has not provided precise doctrine, but rather it has inspired the powerful notion that free speech is critical for democracy. Thus, it follows that when considering the role of defamation liability in a modern democracy, room should be ceded for political and public speech. What is resisted elsewhere in the Anglo-American tradition is the cleavage between defamation law and its roots in the common law. And even more in those systems, where government is not a *bête noir*, policy makers and courts have been unimpressed with the vast implications of a burgeoning First Amendment doctrine, as it invades seemingly endless interstices of public and private ordering. For example, its reach into regulation of election financing and corporate speech[14] seems remarkable to foreign observers. To the extent that the case launched that movement against broad swathes of public ordering, it is a peculiarly American creature.[15]

Part 1 of this chapter will examine two themes: first, the gains made in the remainder of the Western world towards securing the place of free speech in the law of defamation. This has been especially marked over the last two decades, and has been accomplished within the common law in those nations in the Anglo-American tradition. Second, I will elaborate on the American developments that root the law within the First Amendment discourse. The *Sullivan* revolution deprived affected persons of effective tort recourse. It led to haphazard doctrine that raises serious questions of its coherence. It is grounded on a First Amendment

[11] 347 US 483 (1954).

[12] Russell L Weaver, Andrew T Kenyon, David F Partlett and Clive P Walker, *The Right to Speak Ill: Defamation, Reputation and Free Speech* (Durham, NC: Carolina Academic Press, 2006).

[13] See also Eric Barendt, *Freedom of Speech*, 2nd edn (Oxford: Oxford University Press, 2005).

[14] See *Citizens United* v. *Federal Election Commission*, 558 US 310 (2010).

[15] Ronald Reagan, US President, Remarks Accepting the Presidential Nomination at the Republican National Convention in Dallas, TX (23 August 1984) ('We proclaimed a dream of an America that would be a "shining city on a hill"').

epistemology that is problematic. Lastly, it in effect bypasses the function of courts in speaking to truth.

In Part 2, I submit that the law has ignored the institutions that produce information. Both *Sullivan* and the emerging law elsewhere focus on information production by way of the traditional press, cabined in discrete jurisdictions. The definition of the press as a guardian requires a constant updating. By dint of the Internet, we see that *Sullivan* has been tested and found wanting in the time of worldwide publication. Legal norms have limited power.[16] Moreover, far more muscular in protecting free speech in the United States is section 230 of the Communications Decency Act of 1996,[17] which gives immunity to internet service providers from lawsuits. Google, Yahoo and the like are immune. As Marvin Ammori reports, internet service providers dub the Act their *New York Times* v. *Sullivan*.[18] The market for information is difficult to tame; liability rules play less a part than we lawyers suppose.[19] The argument for common law liability is that balanced rules nurtured by courts will foster confidence and undergird other important democratic norms beyond free speech.

Part 3 proposes that the journey of *Sullivan* has impoverished American common law. A court with no experience in the subtleties of the law has given little weight to tort doctrine designed to promote the same self-interests of citizens. *Sullivan*, decided under the pressure of civil rights abuses in Alabama, alluded to the common law in a cursory and dismissive way. The stamp of the great case is seen most recently in *Snyder* v. *Phelps*,[20] the Westboro Baptist Church case. The law of intentional infliction of emotional distress was dismissed without attention to the limits and evolution of that tort, which was designed to protect human dignity. That function of the tort is not acknowledged in the blinding light of the First Amendment. In this part, I probe the reasons for the Supreme Court's neglect of private law.

From this I will conclude that the international influence of *Sullivan* will weaken, while at the same time the place of free speech in the development of the law in the Anglo-American sphere will prosper within the common law that takes rights seriously. American defamation law will

[16] See David F Partlett, 'The Libel Tourist and the Ugly American: Free Speech in an Era of Modern Global Communications' (2009) 47 *University of Louisville Law Review* 629.

[17] Communications Decency Act of 1996, Pub. L. No. 104–104, Title V, 110 Stat. 133 (1996), codified at 18 USC §§1462 and 1465 (2012).

[18] Marvin Ammori, 'The "New" New York Times: Free Speech Lawyering in the Age of Google and Twitter' (2014) 127 *Harvard Law Review* 2259.

[19] See Partlett, above n 16 (observing the internationalisation of information flow and the limits of liability).

[20] 562 U.S. ___ Docket No. 09-751, 131 S. Ct. 1207 (2011).

be isolated from reforms relating to remedies and procedure. The orbits of our law will separate to the detriment of constructive conversations between our courts and a mutual understanding of a critical tract of the law in a globalising world.

## 4.1 *New York Times* v. *Sullivan:* the accidental tourist

I show first the awareness of courts, not in the thrall of the First Amendment, to adhere to the importance of free speech. The focus has been on the rights of citizens to access vital information and to cast light into the recesses of the body politic. In the second place I note how the great case left the American jurisprudence to grow without its common law culture. Its epistemological roots are uncertain and its ideological suppositions are at odds with the moderate libertarian roots of the common law. *Sullivan* usurps common law rights and may diminish the role of courts in convincingly speaking to truth.

### *4.1.1 New gains for free speech*

The Australian High Court attempted to find a right to free speech under the Australian Constitution. This implied right was founded upon the core understanding that the Constitution was based on representative government, and thus a right of free speech in political matters was necessary to effectuate that understanding. The implication of this constitutional protection was roundly criticised, and the development more represents an acknowledgment that free speech is critical to democratic government than launching a new wave of jurisprudence.[21] It was found to limit governmental action, but not create private rights.[22] The case that first fixed the High Court's mind on the *Sullivan* principle is *Lange.*[23] That case recognised that existing doctrine of qualified privilege did not give sufficient scope to political free speech. The qualified privilege defence had been confined to communications in which the publisher and recipient had a mutual interest to publish and receive. The *locus classicus* is the letter of reference. The courts had always set their face against a publication to the world at large in drawing protection from the defence. In *Lange*, the court held

[21] See Leslie Zines, 'A Judicially Created Bill of Rights' (1994) 16 *Sydney Law Review* 166; Leslie Zines, *The High Court and the Constitution*, 5th edn (Annandale, NSW: Federation Press, 2008).

[22] See David Rolph, 'A Critique of the National, Uniform Defamation Laws' (2008) 16 *Torts Law Journal* 207.

[23] *Lange* v. *Australian Broadcasting Corporation* [1997] HCA 25; (1997) 189 CLR 520.

that a qualified privilege could exist where the publication to the world at large was reasonable. This was drawn from legislation in New South Wales and looked to the process through which the story was produced. The principle has now been adopted in a broader form in national legislation on defamation.[24] *Lange* has not encouraged the press, and while still early, the new reforms do little to free the hand of the press to engage in broader criticism.[25] Of course, it is very hard to predict its future impact.

It is telling that the Australian High Court does not view *Sullivan* as transplantable to Australian soil. In the well-known *Gutnick*[26] case, the court was invited to adopt *Sullivan* and the American single publication rule when Gutnick, who lived in Victoria, brought an action against Dow Jones, who published Barron's online. The story found its way to Victoria by way of the online publication. The court found that each time an internet user accessed the piece in Victoria, it had been, in effect, published in Victoria. There was no forum non conveniens issue since Gutnick, although a world traveller and businessman, was certainly domiciled in that state. He had interests there to which his reputation appertained. The High Court stressed that the balance, given these interests by Australian law, was not reflected in *Sullivan*.

Australian law is now subject to uniform defamation law that came into force in early 2006. The approach of the law – to grant a qualified privilege in order to protect public speech – derives from early law and represents no radical departure.[27] It does not appear to have provided great solace to the media avid for freedom from liability rules.[28] Attention is paid to strengthening the defence of truth through more liberal pleading rules and providing a wider array of remedies, such as amends and speedy trial. The legislation has unleashed a wave of close examination of the law that will shine light on the furtherance of critical interests at play.[29]

[24] See David Rolph, above n 22; Kenyon, below n 27 re uniform legislation.

[25] David Rolph, 'Splendid Isolation? Australia as a Destination for Libel Tourism' (2012) 18 *Australian International Law Journal* 79, at 84 (describing the protection of speech under *Lange* as 'largely unsuccessful').

[26] *Dow Jones* v. *Gutnick* [2002] HCA 56; (2002) 210 CLR 575. For an excellent examination and update, see David Rolph, 'Publication, Innocent Dissemination and the Internet after *Dow Jones & Co* v. *Gutnick*' (2010) 33 *University of NSW Law Journal* 562.

[27] See Andrew T Kenyon, 'Six Years of Australian Uniform Defamation Law: Damages, Opinion and Defence Meanings' (2012) 35 *University of NSW Law Journal* 31.

[28] See Kim Gould, 'Statutory Qualified Privilege Succeeds, But Too Early for the Media to Go "Dancing in the Streets"' (2011) 16 *Media & Arts Law Review* 241.

[29] *Ibid.* See also Rolph, above n 22, who opines that Australian law in terms of its jurisdictional rules and substantives rules provides more capacious protection for reputation is more attractive for plaintiffs than is the present law in England.

*4.1.1.1* Reynolds *and* Jameel The English law has been influenced by section 10 of the European Charter on Human Rights.[30] The protection given to free speech must be part of member states' laws. The English law had been found wanting earlier.[31] In *Reynolds*,[32] the English law was motivated by these obligations and partly by the approach taken in *Lange*. In particular, scope for free speech on public matters was given greater license through the defence that provided a multifactorial test that seeks to measure the reasonableness of the publication in the circumstances. It is a test that is more capacious than that found in *Lange*. In the later case of *Jameel*,[33] the House of Lords voiced its frustration that these factors were too narrowly construed, given the intent of *Reynolds* to free speech. Long tradition is not easily put aside. In accord with the argument I set forth here, that tradition might make sense.

It may be noted that the test draws on the practices of the established and responsible press. The professional journalistic standard is used to determine the balance of liability for a defamatory story. It was aligned to the large national press, yet failed to recognise the limitations of smaller media organisations. This is a considerable misstep because the capacity to verify information depends on the size and investigative capabilities of the outlet, yet much of our public information now comes from these smaller operators.

*4.1.1.2 The Defamation Act 2013* After some intense broadsides from across the Atlantic about the English courts being used to gag speech, a Parliamentary Report recommended changes. An important provision reflecting the need for more scope for speech is section 4(1) of the Act.[34]

It is a defence to an action for defamation for the defendant to show that—

(a) the statement complained of was, or formed part of, a statement on a matter of public interest; and
(b) the defendant reasonably believed that publishing the statement complained of was in the public interest.

Although this test is a descendant of *Reynolds*, it is expressed more flexibly, commanding that a 'court have regard to all the circumstances of the case'.[35] Although a checklist is discouraged, the standards appeal to

[30] See Jacob Rowbottom, 'In the Shadow of the Big Media: Freedom of Expression, Participation and the Production of Knowledge Online' (2014) *Public Law* 491.
[31] See *London Artists* v. *Littler* [1969] 2 QB 375; *Campbell* v. *Spottiswoode* [1863] 122 ER 288.
[32] *Reynolds* v. *Time Newspapers* [2001] 2 AC 127.
[33] *Jameel* v. *Wall Street Journal Europe* [2007] 1 AC 359.
[34] Defamation Act 2013 (UK) cl 26. [35] *Ibid.*, s 4(2).

courts avid for certainty.[36] Indeed, if the spirit of the legislation is taken account of, courts should give a greater scope to editorial discretion and recognise the exigencies of different circumstances. It is the stepping away from big media that has been the focus of efforts to liberalise speech that I want to now address. We find, then, that much is anticipated as the courts take on the task of defining the open-textured commands of section 4. In addition, to deter forum shopping the rules on jurisdiction have been tightened.

The lesson is that although the steps are halting and, as we will see, grounded in outmoded models of the production of public information, the efforts have been strenuous. It is true that, as the House of Lords in *Jameel* opined, the courts have been conservative and likewise, the press tends to proceed in a risk-averse fashion. Reform is always constrained by the habits and procedures well entrenched in the bar and the established press.[37]

### 4.1.2 *Concerns on home turf*

*4.1.2.1 Isolation costs* Like Adam and Eve, the common law was banished in *Sullivan*.[38] In core public speech, the liability rule was expelled and in most circumstances the traduced public official or figure is left to lump misstatements of fact. The rules of liability offered by the Court have proven to be, as Russell Weaver has shown,[39] a boon for the press. It is rarely sued, and suits are even more rarely successful. The unmooring in the United States of defamation from its common law roots has been baleful. The law of defamation is subject to an impossible standard with respect to public officials and public figures. At the same time, it has robbed a changing and developing law of the ability to sample reforms and reflect new precepts in a society undergoing dynamic changes. For example, the courts have been precluded from experimenting with an array of remedies that would more delicately balance free speech and reputational interests. Untested is the old assumption that bad,

36 See Rowbottom, above n 30, at 11–12 (setting forth statements in the parliamentary debate hoping for more flexibility).

37 Defamation practice is arcane and specialised. It is also lucrative and incentives are strongly conservative. See Kenyon, above n 27 (commenting on reform in the Australian setting).

38 It was to return in a modest way for the publication of information of no public concern, such as in *Dun & Bradstreet* v. *Greenmoss Builders*, 472 US 749 (1985), for information listing bankruptcies paid for by consumers. It is plain that accuracy of this information is essential in commercial intercourse and the common law strict liability rule is a guarantor of accuracy. The payment for the information will reflect the cost of liability in the supplier.

39 See Weaver et al., above n 12.

untruthful information directed at public officials dissuades the best persons from entering public service.[40] If falsehoods about those avid for public careers go uncorrected, it is reasonable to assume that rehabilitation will be a fatuous exercise as the spotless, supported by election funds, spread falsehoods, half-truths and acontextual true assertions.[41] In *Sullivan*, none of this rated detailed analysis. The Supreme Court was faced with a civil rights dilemma that called out for a solution. No argument of weighing interests and subtle constitutional interests could stand against the trumping power of the First Amendment because any harm to persons, processes and tradition was a small price to pay for the robust discussion of public affairs.

While these are impediments in the ability of the law to perform its job, the constitutionalisation of the tort, as Fred Schauer[42] and others have pointed out, had a dramatic effect on putative public officials and public figures. Those persons were deprived, without compensation, of rights they enjoyed at common law in the name of a public good.

*4.1.2.2 Lumpy doctrine and epistemological problems* It is trite but true to say that to refashion the law of defamation as it relates to public speech is a large job. It is made difficult by the court having to pay fealty to the soaring rhetoric of the originating case. Moreover, the law was separated from its common law roots. Accordingly, the progeny have been scattered and the law uncertain. One need only observe the law that has grown around the defence of opinion.[43] Once we were told that an opinion stated no fact and was not actionable.[44] Now we are told that the words in *Gertz* were dicta and should not be credited with the law that followed.[45] Once we were told that *Rosenbloom*,[46] which held that actual malice

[40] The mention of this rationale is usually met with ridicule as having been disproved. Yet there is much economic analysis on the market for lemons that favours the conclusion that the bad drives out the good. If consumers are not seized with information allowing them to differentiate the good from the bad they will not buy as confidently in the market; the good will have less incentive to invest in developing reputations when distinctions cannot be made. Baron Bramwell had this insight in the famous case of *Derry* v. *Peek* [1889] 14 AC 337, where he opined that a liability rule should not be so strict as to sweep up the good and honest with the bad and fraudulent.

[41] The phenomenon can be seen in Supreme Court nominees where the incentives for the president are not excellence but a candidate without a past that can be attacked. Nominees are coached to provide the most anodyne of answers.

[42] Frederick Schauer, 'Harm(s) and the First Amendment' [2011] *Supreme Court Review* 81; Daniel Farber, 'Afterword: Property and Free Speech' (1999) 93 *Northwestern University Law Review* 1239.

[43] See, e.g., *Milkovich* v. *Lorain Journal Co*, 497 US 1 (1990).

[44] See *Gertz* v. *Robert Welch*, 418 US 323, 347–9 (1974).

[45] *Milkovich* v. *Lorain Journal Co*, 497 US 1 (1990).

[46] *Rosenbloom* v. *Metromedia*, 403 US 29 (1971).

applied to any matter of public or general interest, was too restrictive of state's rights, yet in *Phelps*, we see *Rosenbloom* appear from the grave. Adding to this miasma is the uncertainty of the distinction between public figures and private persons, the fundamental legal principle involved here.

A marketplace of ideas is critical to the emergence of truth in a democracy – and more broadly to the advancement of knowledge. This premise found such powerful champions as Holmes[47] and Brandeis.[48] The marketplace of ideas, sitting at the centre of *Sullivan* is much repeated and often misused. This is a most important matter.[49] Does competition of the most robust and vehement type, although it makes us uncomfortable, serve a higher purpose of exposing truth through the fire of contending views? If this is true and if democracy is made the stronger for it, the fulsome interpretation of the First Amendment ought to be upheld. For our purposes, the press ought to be unfettered and, perhaps, an even greater scope ought to be afforded public speech. Here lie the epistemological problems.

Two points are salient. Why is it that free speech has attained a trumping power when the interests it is protecting, say liberty or democracy, are not seen as standing on their own feet? There are other rights that may play as important a role in sustaining the ultimate value.[50] It may be tactically justifiable to employ a powerful version of free speech but that does not make it philosophically sound.[51] The recitation of an express right must signal that the right, as part of a wider right, was absent or threatened especially. That makes the right historically contingent and its form will vary in time and place. Thus, to punish speech denying the holocaust is understandable in Europe but not in the United States. To criticise European laws prohibiting such denial under First Amendment grounds fails to attend to the historic grounding of the prohibition.

What is more, the rhetoric of the marketplace implants unfortunate elements of laissez-faire ideology that allow antiregulatory assumptions to be translated as accepted versions of constitutional free speech rights. In accepting the metaphor, under the view that the right is to protect an audience or listener's rights, the US Supreme Court assumes the

47 See *Abrams* v. *United States*, 250 US 616, 624 (1919) (Holmes J dissenting).

48 See *Whitney* v. *California*, 274 US 357, 372 (1927) (Brandeis J concurring).

49 It has not fared well in contemporary commentary. See, e.g., Alvin I Goldman and James C Cox, 'Speech, Truth, and the Free Market for Ideas' (1996) 2 *Legal Theory* 1.

50 See Frederick Schauer, 'Free Speech on Tuesdays' (University of Virginia Public Law and Legal Theory Research Paper Series, Paper No. 2014–10) http://ssrn.com/abstract=2387009; Opinion, Bruce Ackerman, 'Dignity Is a Constitutional Principle', *NY Times*, 30 March 2014 at SR5, http://nyti.ms/1hKKIVx (championing human dignity as a base constitutional value).

51 See Schauer, above n 50, at 22.

truth-producing powers of the 'free market'. Thus, the court relies on the free market to strike down not only campaign financing restrictions in *Citizens United*[52] and *McCutcheon*[53] but also the dissemination of false information on military decorations in *Alvarez*.[54] Such a market also is available to those traduced by defamatory imputations, even private persons, it is supposed, under *Phelps*.[55] Like the abandoned *Lochner*[56] decision that threw its lot in with laissez-faire freedom of contract under substantive due process, the First Amendment rhetoric marginalises the role of government and the common law.

In the second place, the rhetoric of truth production through the operation of the free market flies in the face of research showing that the public, receiving information, is not composed of rational actors. The listener rights theory is premised on the assumption that individuals faced with a range of competing information on topics may rationally sift through that information and come to conclusions that, when grossed across a population, will express truth. Research reported by Glaeser and Sunstein shows that persons faced with truth that does not fit their preconceived ideas and persuasions will reject the truth.[57] For example, people given a mock news article, where President Bush defends the Iraq War by citing the risks of weapons being passed to terrorists, were given the Duelfer Report,[58] which documented the lack of weapons of mass destruction in Iraq. Those people were then asked on a five-point scale their agreement with the statement that Iraq had 'an active weapons of mass destruction program'.[59] Noting the subjects' political ideology, one finds a remarkable result. Liberals shifted modestly to disagree while for

[52] *Citizens United* v. *Federal Election Commission*, 558 US 310 (2010).

[53] *McCutcheon* v. *Federal Election Commission*, 572 US ___ Docket No. 12–536, 134 S. Ct. 1434 (2014) ('*McCutcheon*').

[54] *US* v. *Alvarez*, 567 US ___Docket No. 11-210, 132 S. Ct. 2537 (2012). See also Thomas W Joo, 'The Worst Test of Truth: The "Marketplace of Ideas" as a Faulty Metaphor' (2014) 89 *Tulane Law Review* 383. First Amendment jurisprudence may justify the protection either in the rights of the speaker (an exercise in autonomy) or in the rights of the audience or listener (the sustenance of democratic values or republican ideals). Republican theory may base certain rights in protecting ideals of citizens' participation. See Andrew J Roberts, 'A Republican Account of the Value of Privacy' (University of Melbourne, Melbourne Legal Studies Research Paper No. 673, 2013) http://ssrn.com/abstract=2369680.

[55] *Snyder* v. *Phelps*, 562 US ___ Docket No. 09-751, 131 S. Ct. 1207 (2011).

[56] *Lochner* v. *NY*, 198 US 45 (1905).

[57] See Edward Glaeser and Cass R Sunstein, 'Does More Speech Correct Falsehoods?' (2014) 43 *Journal of Legal Studies* 65.

[58] Charles Duelfer, *Comprehensive Report of the Special Advisor to the DCI on Iraq's WMD* (Washington, DC: Central Intelligence Agency, 2004) www.cia.gov/library/reports/general-reports-1/iraq_wmd_2004/index.html.

[59] See Glaeser and Sunstein, above n 57, '2.1: Backfiring Corrections' at 68.

conservatives, there was a significant shift to agreeing with the statement. In other words, the correction backfired.

The authors cite similar studies. In recent research about immunisation, parents given scientific facts about the dangers of immunisation still persist in believing falsehoods about connections to autism.[60] Cognitive explanations may encourage people to cling to false information. To change one's views leads to uncertainty in how one views the world, which comes at a cost in accessing memories. Glaeser and Sunstein base an explanation on what they label 'asymmetric Bayesianism'.[61] A speaker conveys the information and the identity of that speaker is critical. The speaker may be interested in persuading to a viewpoint or independent. Given that listeners have preconceptions, information is filtered as to conform to a pre-existing, settled view of the world. The authors state that 'corrections may backfire if people have strong antecedent convictions and understand purported corrections of those convictions as evidence that those convictions must be right'.[62] Alternatively, the authors also model the 'memory boomerang', which, in the face of an asserted fact, acts to surface a host of lost memories that were the basis of forming a contrary view. Those past memories, now recalled, will move a person to reject the new information. The argument holds that the only speaker who is likely to shift these antecedent convictions is the 'surprising validator', the speaker who is representative of the ingrained view but takes the other unexpected view. The surprising validator has special credibility in counteracting asymmetric Bayesianism. Rather than a competition convincing listeners of truth, the authors find that the most convincing vehicle is the opinion of a person with a similar and shared worldview who vouches for the truth. Dan Kahan has shown through exhaustive empirical research that perceptions of risks arising in socially contested areas like gun control, disposal of nuclear wastes and climate change, are mediated by values rather than scientific fact.[63]

Similarly, the new behaviouralism in social sciences has alerted us to the limits of the rational actor model of human actions. Humans are decision-makers that are energy conserving. They depend on shortcuts to make decisions that are usually good enough but which break down in contexts where tough rational thought is called for.[64] The ordinary person relies on

[60] Brendan Nyhan, Jason Reifler, Sean Richey and Gary L Freed, 'Effective Messages in Vaccine Promotion: A Randomized Trial' (2014) 133 *Pediatrics* e835 DOI: 10.1542/peds.2013-2365.

[61] See Glaeser and Sunstein, above n 57, '3: Asymmetric Bayesianism' at 72ff.

[62] *Ibid.*, at 90.

[63] Dan M Kahan, Hank Jenkins-Smith and Donald Braman, 'Cultural Cognition of Scientific Consensus' (2011) 14 *Journal of Risk Research* 147.

[64] See Daniel Kahneman, *Thinking Fast and Slow* (New York: Farrar, Straus and Giroux, 2011).

certain decision-making heuristics to get by. This is a problem, as Paul Horwitz points out: 'Much of our current free speech jurisprudence is based on the assumption that the government should not regulate speech because, in an unregulated marketplace, people will be perfectly capable of responding rationally to speech'.[65] Distinguished commentators like Lyrissa Lidsky concede the flaws but urge that it is a noble model, serving the purpose of guarding against the dangers of an overweening government.[66] Another argument in rescue of the possible emergence of truth is that humans evolved to make and evaluate arguments. One would assume they show biases in order to make persuasive arguments. This would be the reason for resistance to truthful statements.[67] If one believes in the veracity of an idea or fact, one is more convincing and persuasive. Yet, these arguments cannot be pursued here. What is plain is that the First Amendment will be under attack as rotten in its foundations. Like Lidsky's contention, the repair work will take the form of treating the marketplace as a theoretical construct – a metaphor – for a principle that eschews government regulation as dangerous to democracy, to the rights of the public audience and to the speakers in the public forum. One cannot ground this in behaviour but rather in faith. That sceptic Holmes never thought truth would emerge. Everything in his world was up for grabs.

These qualifications on the marketplace support a judicial role in correcting error. If a validator has a role in correcting falsehoods, it would seem that defamation is a powerful tool. The truth of the facts is subjected to independent review through court proceedings. May this – non-market – process be an effective vehicle to convey the truth? If listeners often agree with courts when they support a worldview, say, in support of the Second Amendment, will those listeners be more amenable when the court speaks to truth that does not conform to the preconceived beliefs? Since defamation litigation is centred on the truth of allegations, would the courts as an institution play a powerful part in correcting mistaken information? The court room as a neutral and trusted forum for dispute resolution and diversion of warring camps has great advantage.

[65] Paul Horwitz, 'Free Speech as Risk Analysis: Heuristics, Biases, and Institutions in the First Amendment' (2003) 76 *Temple Law Review* 1. See also Paul Horwitz, 'The First Amendment's Epistemological Problem' (2012) 87 *Washington Law Review* 445. For a comprehensive listing of the role of the marketplace device/metaphor see Derek E Bambauer, 'Shopping Badly: Cognitive Biases, Communications, and the Fallacy of the Marketplace of Ideas' (2006) 77 *University of Colorado Law Review* 649.

[66] Lidsky, above n 3.

[67] See Drew Westen, *The Political Brain: The Role of Emotion in Deciding the Fate of the Nation* (New York: Public Affairs, 2007) (neuroscience establishing that political choices are driven by emotional portions of the brain, thus people may vote against their objective self-interests).

One matter follows from this discussion: we cannot think that the cacophony of voices in the public marketplace will tack public debate towards truth. Further, the very metaphor may be biased against reasonable regulation and the use of liability rules to balance rights in speech. Moreover, as I propose to canvass in the next part, the assumptions about the production of public information are frozen in the times of major news outlets and are not reflective of modern technology and methods by which citizens garner information about the world around them.

## 4.2 Public information then and now

In this part, I want to make two points. First, *Sullivan* adopts an old model of the way public speech is generated. In 1964, the market for news was print-based and dominated by newspapers in the major metropolitan areas. Nowadays the situation of once great newspapers is parlous.[68] Second, the distribution of information on the Internet changes the usual way that news relating to public officials and figures emerges in the public domain.[69]

The classic model for journalism acting as the fourth estate was the investigative journalist, who bravely garnered information, tracked down its reliability and published it fearlessly. The *Washington Post*'s stories about Watergate are usually cited as the exemplar.[70] Certainly the Pentagon Papers case[71] emboldened the press to intrude on government secrecy even where national security was claimed. This precedent has given the *New York Times* in particular space and freedom to publish when the press elsewhere has been crimped by government prerogatives.[72] The test for false information that should not be protected has been acceptable

[68] See 'Who Killed the Newspaper?', *The Economist* (online) (24 August 2006), www.economist.com/node/7830218.

[69] See Rowbottom, above n 30 (pointing to the uneasy place of low level speech in the protections provided for speech).

[70] The reporting made the careers of Bob Woodward and Carl Bernstein. 'Deep Throat', whose identity was recently revealed, fed the story to them and it did not require the kind of in depth research that is often claimed as the marker of this journalism. See, generally, David von Drehle, 'FBI's No 2 Was 'Deep Throat': Mark Felt Ends 30-Year Mystery of The Post's Watergate Source', *Washington Post* (online) (1 June 2005) www.washingtonpost.com/politics/fbis-no-2-was-deep-throat-mark-felt-ends-30-year-mystery-of-the-posts-watergate-source/2012/06/04/gJQAwseRIV_story.html.

[71] *NY Times* v. *US*, 403 US 713 (1971).

[72] Note *The Guardian*'s compunctions and reliance on the *New York Times*' greater legal freedoms in the Snowden disclosures. See Lisa O'Carroll, 'Guardian partners with New York Times over Snowden GCHQ files', *Guardian* (online) (24 August 2013), http://gu.com/p/3t98j; Editorial, 'British Press Freedom under Threat', *NY Times*, 14 November 2013, at A28, www.nytimes.com/2013/11/15/opinion/british-press-freedom-under-threat.html?smid=pl-share.

standards of journalistic and press behaviour. In *Sullivan*, the absolutist free speech camp, headed by Black and Douglas JJ, was thwarted by Harlan J, who agreed to join his brethren only on the condition that Brennan J couch his opinion, and therefore the court's opinion, in terms of the actual malice standard. That test turns on the issue of whether the publisher knew the falsity of the information or turned a blind eye to its truth. Immediately the test requires that a light be shone on the journalistic process preceding publication.[73]

Whether it is progeny of *Sullivan* or other courts in the Anglo-American tradition, the desire to draw in journalistic standards has been fraught. In a context of traditional publications, the standards are clearer. For example, to vet stories and seek comment from those traduced is articulated in the *Reynolds* test and found to be critical in the application of *Lange*. In post-*Sullivan* law the enquiry focusses on proof of 'actual malice'. This approach places a heavy burden on the plaintiff to show recklessness by producing 'obvious reasons to doubt the veracity of the informant or the accuracy of his reports'.[74] The difficulty in applying the standard can be seen in *Masson*,[75] which also highlights the nature of the publication and the standard of journalism to be expected. That will be a constant issue with online publications and the expectations that are made on accuracy. Even the use of the term 'journalist' now creates problems.[76] Costless entry to the blogosphere has set up different expectations. Additionally, the privacy concerns are grave given that electronic media remains retrievable well past its date of publishing.[77] So the question is posed: how do we establish any kind of reliability in public discourse? Is that a forlorn hope that used to be relevant when we could talk about responsible journalism? Or perhaps it is that the press carries the imprimatur of reliability even more strongly, given that there is so much dross around.

The First Amendment adherent would say that all the information should be published and the competition of the marketplace of ideas will root out the truth. As noted earlier, this rhetorical flourish has been the mainstay of the march of First Amendment jurisprudence. Although the

[73] See Anthony Lewis, '*New York Times* v. *Sullivan* Reconsidered: Time to Return to "The Central Meaning of the First Amendment"' (1983) 83 *Columbia Law Review* 603 (arguing that *Sullivan* has been insufficiently protective of free speech).

[74] *St Amant* v. *Thompson*, 390 US 727, 732 (1968).

[75] *Masson* v. *New Yorker Magazine*, 501 US 496 (1991).

[76] See Kelvin Hiu Fai Kwok, 'Liability of Online Service Providers for Defamatory Content: The Case of Online Discussion Forums' (2014) 130 *Law Quarterly Review* 206; Anne SY Cheung, 'Liability of Internet Host Providers in Defamation Actions: From Gatekeepers to Identifiers' (University of Hong Kong Faculty of Law Research Paper No. 2014/013, 2014) http://ssrn.com/abstract=2428566.

[77] Daniel J Solove, *The Future of Reputation: Gossip, Rumor, and Privacy on the Internet* (New Haven: Yale University Press, 2007).

metaphor of the triumph of truth in a struggle goes back to the venerable John Milton, the backing for the proposition that truth will win out has never been made. Of course the common law liability chilled speech but that is just part of the analysis. A liability rule in respect of defective products also chills the production of goods. Yet the story of product liability law has been to sharpen the impact of the rule to the benefit of consumers and the public. Now the major move of the law under *Sullivan* was to reject the old adage that the First Amendment was not intended to protect the distribution of false information.[78] Can this be asserted in an era when information is frictionless? Where the citizen depended on newspapers and a restricted electronic media, it may rightly be said that a liability rule may be targeted effectively to restrain publication. And perhaps the chill would be real. The world of blogs, of instantaneous communications, is distinguishable from this model. Google, Yahoo and others have powers that can range beyond the nation state. These private entities are the norm entrepreneurs and much of the action involves nation states attempting to influence their activities. Here I contend that *Sullivan* joins *Reynolds* in presenting a quaint version of the world frozen in time. To be sure, the traditional press still has power, but it is in competition with new and rapidly evolving ways in which the public receives its information.[79]

## 4.3 The First Amendment *deus ex machina*[80]

### 4.3.1 *The fate of common law rights*

American law is now separated from defamation law as it is developing elsewhere in the common law world. Experimentation with remedies and the level of damages is foreclosed by constitutional doctrine. Over the years American scholars have made suggestions that have been planted in foreign law but not in the native soil.[81] The law of defamation has been a

78 Mary-Rose Papandrea, 'Citizen Journalism and the Reporter's Privilege' (2007) 91 *Minnesota Law Review* 515.

79 See David Partlett and Barbara McDonald, 'International Publications and Protection of Reputation: A Margin of Appreciation but not Subservience' (2011) 62 *Alabama Law Review* 477, 483 n 25; Partlett, above n 16. Ironically, it is the traditional press that ought to invite a quality-ensuring defamation liability rule as an efficient means of differentiating its product from that of blogs and other electronic evanescent information; see above n 76.

80 When a character or entity enters a story and suddenly solves a previously difficult or perplexing problem usually in an unconvincing way. The timely appearance of a god mechanically lowered onto the stage to bring a closure dates in Greek and Roman theatre from the fifth century BC.

81 See David Anderson, 'Is Libel Law Worth Reforming' (1991) 140 *University of Pennsylvania Law Review* 487, 550–4; *Proposal for Reform of Libel Law: The Report of the*

fertile field for reform in the common law world, with courts and parliaments playing active parts in modifying the law both in its substance and remedies. Australia has adopted national legislation, while England has been ready to change the law according to the exigencies of social change and attitude. At the same time, privacy law has been developed to protect the interests of individuals in societies that possess great power to impugn the scope of its citizen's privacy.[82] The to and fro has bypassed the United States, frozen in constitutional stasis.[83]

The surprising element is that the court, caught in a maelstrom of contradictory doctrine and shifting premises, dismisses the common law as chaotic and unruly. As a *deus ex machina*, constitutional law settles the debate. The law of defamation was found to be constitutionally infirm, and this swept aside the developing law of privacy at a time when it was enjoying growth in other common law nations.[84] Well-recognised torts such as trespass to land were given limited scope in the face of the First Amendment.[85] Even negligent statements leading to physical harm were examined under the rubric of the First Amendment.[86] Important for the protection of dignitary interests, the law of intentional infliction of emotional distress has been developed separately but with close governing principles.[87] This is especially the case in respect of situations where

*Libel Reform Project of the Annenberg Washington Program* (Washington, DC: Annenberg Washington Program [in] Communications Policy Studies, Northwestern University, 1988).

82 See Australian Law Reform Commission, *Serious Invasions of Privacy in the Digital Era*, Discussion Paper No. 80 (2014); NSW Law Reform Commission, *Invasion of Privacy*, Consultation Paper No 1 (2007).

83 This is not to say that creative judges have not attempted to work around constitutional strictures by restructuring the litigation process to reflect the values inherent in the tort of defamation. See *Sharon* v. *Time*, 575 F Supp 1162 (SDNY 1983); *Westmoreland* v. *CBS*, 596 F Supp 1170 (SDNY 1984).

84 David Partlett, 'Fifty Years Decline in Privacy: The Forgotten Right to be Forgotten and Forgiven', Uppsala University Sweden, September 2014.

85 See, e.g., *Food Lion* v. *Capital Cities/ABC*, 194 F.3d 505 (4th Cir. 1999) (limiting the scope of damages).

86 See *Winter* v. *GP Putnam's Sons*, 938 F.2d 1033 (9th Cir. 1991) (finding liability for misleading and negligent statements about harvestable mushrooms).

87 In the United States the leading case is *State Rubbish Collectors Association* v. *Siliznoff*, 240 P.2d 282 (Ca. 1952); in England and the Commonwealth it is *Wilkinson v Downton* [1897] 2 QB 57 and the law stemming from it. Noting the development of the cause of action, see *Giller* v. *Procopets* (2008) 24 VR 1. Cf David F Partlett, 'Tort Liability and the American Way: Reflections on Liability for Emotional Distress' (1997) 45 *American Journal of Comparative Law* 171 (reviewing Nicholas J Mullany and Peter R Handford, *Tort Liability For Psychiatric Damage: The Law of 'Nervous Shock'*, and discussing categories of cases in which American courts have found liability for emotional distress), with Peter Handford, 'Intentional Negligence: A Contradiction in Terms?' (2010) 32 *Sydney Law Review* 29, 55 (discussing the increasing importance of negligence as a remedy for intentional conduct in Australia generally, as well as the mental harm context specifically).

people are most vulnerable.[88] In two landmark cases, plaintiffs raised the tort in order to found liability for words and actions that were pleaded to have caused emotional distress. The first was *Hustler Magazine* v. *Falwell*,[89] wherein the Reverend Jerry Falwell complained of a parody replete with sexual innuendos published in Larry Flint's Hustler Magazine. The Supreme Court found that pleading the tort rather than defamation could not circumvent the restraints of *Sullivan*. Considering that Falwell was by any measure a public figure, the decision is easily justifiable. The tort of intentional infliction of emotional distress could not be allowed to do an end run around the constitutional prescriptions. The speech fell within the heart of political speech. Parody was well recognised as a legitimate form of political commentary. The common law would have dealt with this case under the principle that the publication would have been read by the ordinary reader as not asserting any fact.[90] Further, the Commonwealth law on intentional infliction of emotional distress, the case of *Wilkinson* v. *Downton*,[91] would not have provided relief for Falwell.[92]

In *Phelps*, a case corrosive of privacy rights and human dignity, the court precluded the application of the tort of intentional infliction of emotional distress in a corner of personal life where the tort had been long and carefully applied, that is, mourning the death of loved ones. Nothing touches the raw human nerve more. The facts give a window into a remarkable sector of American civic life. The Westboro Baptist Church

[88] See Jane Stapleton for an exposition of the role of vulnerability in founding tort liability. Jane Stapleton, 'Duty of Care and Economic Loss: A Wider Agenda' (1999) 107 *Law Quarterly Review* 249, 266; Jane Stapleton, 'In Restraint of Tort' in Peter Birks (ed), *The Frontiers of Liability*, vol 2. (Oxford: Oxford University Press, 1994) 83, 92–3; Jane Stapleton, 'Duty of Care: Peripheral Parties and Alternative Opportunities for Deterrence' (1995) 111 *Law Quarterly Review* 301, at 303, 305, 331, 342, 345; Jane Stapleton, 'Duty of Care Factors: A Selection from the Judicial Menus' in Peter Cane and Jane Stapleton (eds), *The Law of Obligations: Essays in Honour of John Fleming* (Oxford: Clarendon Press, 1998) 59, 79–80, 83–7; Jane Stapleton, 'Comparative Economic Loss: Lessons from Case-Law Focused "Middle Theory"' (2002) 50 *UCLA Law Review* 531; Jane Stapleton, 'The Golden Thread at the Heart of Tort Law: Protection of the Vulnerable' (2003) 24 *Australian Bar Review* 135. See also *Woolcock Street Investments* v. *CDG* (2004) 216 CLR 515; *Harriton* v. *Stevens* (2006) 226 CLR 52 n. 156; *D'Orta-Ekenaike* v. *Victoria Legal Aid* (2005) 223 CLR 1 n. 313; *Cole* v. *South Tweed Heads Rugby League Football Club* (2004) 217 CLR 469 n. 54 (Austl.).

[89] 485 US 46 (1988).

[90] See, e.g., *Pring* v. *Penthouse International*, 695 F.2d 438 (10th Cir. 1982), cert. denied; 462 US 1132 (1983).

[91] [1897] 2 Q.B. 57.

[92] The tort requires intent that the statement be believed. This was never on a proper construction of the ad parody, a statement, in its literal form, that Flint intended the reader to believe. For discussion of this tort, see *Tame* v. *New South Wales* (2002) 211 CLR 317.

is a small splinter church based in Topeka, Kansas. A guiding tenet of its belief was the destructive effect of tolerance of gays on American society. Members of the Church attended funerals of fallen soldiers nationwide to promote their belief that God was wreaking revenge on America for its liberal ways. To protest at the funerals of deceased veterans was seen as a way of highlighting this message. The plaintiffs were the mother and father of a soldier who had been killed in Iraq and whose memory was being honoured. They sought damages from the church pursuant to the tort.

Roberts CJ devoted less than a paragraph of his majority opinion to the tort, opining that the element of '"[o]utrageousness" . . . is a highly malleable standard with "an inherent subjectiveness about it which would allow a jury to impose liability on the basis of the jurors' tastes or views, or perhaps on the basis of their dislike of a particular expression"'.[93] The case extends beyond the boundaries of *Falwell* because here, in *Phelps*, the plaintiff was a private figure. Yet the Chief Justice tells us that the speech was of 'public concern' and thus attracts the full protection of the First Amendment. Hurt real and palpable must be endured to serve the greater good. Roberts CJ admits that ' public concern' is itself vague.[94] In fact, as was brought to the attention of the court, the tort had been developed carefully for over a hundred years and applied particularly where humans are at their most vulnerable: grieving the loss of a loved one. Zipursky had written a careful and persuasive article supporting the application of the tort[95] but we see none of this given any weight by the Chief Justice. The court then decrees that when persons acting for their political ends wish to exploit private activities of private persons, those private persons must concede privacy in the name of the First Amendment. The Chief Justice was forthright in saying these actions are distasteful but must be given protection because they air matters of public concern.[96] The test of public concern reintroduces a wider notion once scotched in the landmark case of *Gertz*.[97] Thus, the prodigy of *Sullivan* welcomes a new and unruly cousin. The Chief Justice admits that the law will take time to absorb and refine this new test.

93 *Snyder* v. *Phelps*, 562 U.S. ___ Docket No. 09-751, 131 S. Ct. 1207, 1219 (2011) (quoting *Hustler Magazine* v. *Falwell*, 485 US 46, 55 (1988)).

94 See *ibid.*, at 1216 ('"the boundaries of the public concern test are not well defined"' (quoting *San Diego* v. *Roe*, 543 US 77, 83 (2004)).

95 See Benjamin C Zipursky, '*Snyder* v. *Phelps*, Outrageousness, and the Open Texture of Tort Law' (2011) 60 *DePaul Law Review* 473.

96 See *Snyder* v. *Phelps*, 131 S. Ct. 1207 (2011) at 1220 (noting that Westboro's funeral picketing is 'hurtful', may contribute little to public discourse, and in this case, 'inflict[ed] great pain', but that hurtful speech on public issues is protected to prevent 'stifl[ing] public debate').

97 *Gertz* v. *Robert Welch*, 418 US 323 (1974).

### 4.3.2 *The limits of constitutional courts: blindness to the common law*

The trumping power of the First Amendment also expunges other interests that are vital for citizens in a modern democracy. The most notable fatality is the law of privacy that found its start in American law.[98] Before *Sullivan*, privacy law was robust and protected persons from public disclosure of intimate private facts.[99] That law has been reduced to uncertain rump. This has occurred at a time when other Western democracies are looking carefully at increasing the range of liability for privacy invasions.

The major problem is to conflate the presumptions against government regulation with the common law. Unfortunately, legal realism and, in particular, the law and economics movement have contributed to this categorical mistake by conceptualising the law of torts as a form of regulation.[100] This is a wooden view of the function and foundations of the common law that are normatively generated within constraints of history and tradition in order to allow citizens to interact and to uphold fundamental values of society. It is a form of normative guidance. The categorical mistake was an original sin of *Sullivan*. The Supreme Court readily accepts that the common law of defamation is governmental action indistinguishable from governmental fiat.[101] The failure of the court to respect the salience of the common law crimps the nurture it owes to liberty interests that are equally as fundamental as the First Amendment.

In the recent decision on campaign financing, *McCutcheon*, Roberts CJ opens by asserting that public taste is not a value that would allow the government to regulate. The role of money in politics may seem 'repugnant',[102] but that should not allow a crimping of the free speech rights of contributors. The court, he says, has allowed flag burning, Nazi parades and funeral protests, all of which are in bad taste.[103] The Chief Justice makes no distinction in this list between governmental measures and rights asserted through the common law. The last, as we have seen, involved citizens' torts rights. The government did not step in and

[98] See Samuel D Warren and Louis D Brandeis, 'The Right to Privacy' (1890) 4 *Harvard Law Review* 193. The law was organised into its tort frame by Dean Prosser; see William L Prosser, 'Privacy' (1960) 48 *California Law Review* 383. The interest in providing room for an individual to make a new beginning in life has changed radically. The old law that would support that interest, shown in *Melvin* v. *Reid*, 297 P. 91 (Cal Dist. Ct. App. 1931), is superseded by modern First Amendment jurisprudence. For a discussion of the decline in the right to be forgotten and forgiven, see Partlett, above n 84.

[99] See above n 84.

[100] See *Riegel* v. *Medtronic*, 552 US 312 (2008) (pre-emption case in which state tort law is conceived as a form of regulation). But cf *Wyeth* v. *Levine*, 555 US 555 (2009) (majority opinion of Stevens J gives state tort law a greater salience, requiring clear and manifest congressional intent before pre-emption could be implied).

[101] *New York Times* v. *Sullivan*, 376 US 254, 291–3 (1964).

[102] See *McCutcheon*, 134 S. Ct. 1434, 1441 (2014).

[103] *Ibid*.

prohibit demonstrations; the tort, long and carefully defined, attempted to protect individual interests, not any governmental sense of outrage. Later in the plurality opinion, the Chief Justice cites *Cohen* v. *California*[104] for the foundational notion that '[t]he First Amendment is designed and intended to remove governmental restraints from the arena of public discussion, putting the decision as to what views shall be voiced largely in the hands of each of us ... in the belief that no other approach would comport with the premise of individual dignity and choice upon which our political system rests'.[105]

This is remarkable in its amnesia on the foundation of our law in the common law. The very value that is touted, 'individual dignity', which is preserved by the common law, is crowded out by a freedom to express views without government restraint. It is possible to sympathise that government regulation often overreaches, but courts should not sweep up common law protections with the same table-clearing swipe. Individual dignity is at the centre of privacy protection: are tort actions to fall because some matter of public concern is invoked? Are constraints on the identification of victims of sexual abuse to be abolished because each of us can decide? To talk about 'governmental restraints' as enfolding both regulations and the common law is rude and intrusive of individual rights.[106]

## 4.4 Conclusion

*Sullivan* is unlikely to continue to be transnationally influential. Foreign courts will see it as strident and not sufficiently attentive to competing values. The Supreme Court, isolated from common law developments,

[104] 403 US 15 (1971).

[105] *McCutcheon*, 134 S. Ct. 1434, 1448 (2014) (quoting *Cohen* v. *California*, 403 US 15, 24 (1971)).

[106] It is clear that legislative judgements about citizens' rights, as in protection of privacy, are subject to the pre-emptive powers of the First Amendment. See, e.g., *Sorrell* v. *IMS Health, Inc*, 564 US ___ Docket No. 10-779, 131 S.Ct. 2653 (2011). This case involved a practice now at issue in Australia, where data miners compile and sell bulk information about the prescription habits of doctors. Vermont attempted to regulate this practice, arguing that it was detrimental to doctors' faithfulness to patients and privacy. This is not a tort case but has implications for the assertion of privacy rights in tort. The wane of privacy interests in the United States is ironical when elsewhere even as the value of free speech is increasingly fortified, the courts and legislatures have moved to provide citizens direct protection for privacy. The High Court of Australia for example supports a recognition of the interest given the right conditions: *Australian Broadcasting Corporation* v. *Lenah Game Meats* (2001) 208 CLR 199, and *Giller* v. *Procopets* (2008) 24 VR 1. For discussion of law and future directions, see Barbara McDonald, 'Tort's Role in Protecting Privacy: Current and Future Directions' in Simone Degeling, James Edelman and James Goudkamp (eds), *Torts in Commercial Law* (Pyrmont, NSW: Thomson Reuters, 2011) 63.

will develop a jurisprudence that ignores the tenets of the republic. It will be unable to engage in experimentation with remedies and provide little space for legislative reform.

Foreign law will draw from an increasingly rich and diverse discourse in defamation and the scope of public speech. It will, through legislation and court opinions, develop a jurisprudence of privacy when the Supreme Court under the engine of the First Amendment has scotched most of that court-created law. It is more likely that courts in developing the law under the aegis of the common law will have a richer source of material from which to draw and that judges will understand one another. American legal discourse will be viewed as idiosyncratic and inaccessible. The marketplace of ideas metaphor, weakened by its unreality, will have little suasion in the rest of the Anglo-American legal world. To paint responsible government as a *bête noir*, and to give short shrift to accepted and well-developed tort rights designed to uphold individual dignity, is far removed from the prevailing public attitudes and evolving legal standards in the remainder of the Western world.

Fifty years have seen a change, from civil rights in the 1960s in the shadow of the Second World War, to speech and privacy in the anxious age of international terrorism and a distrust of civil and human rights. Moreover, modern communications have weakened domestic legal norms as they have ceded ground to the realities of the Internet. The static world of journalism of 1964 is remote from the dynamics of information generation, collection and dissemination today.[107] Pragmatically, in a world of accelerating information flows, the role of traditional media optimally should be as an assured and reliable source of information. The enfeebling of defamation liability rules under the First Amendment, however, perversely inclines in the opposite direction, to reduce reliability and accuracy. Energetic and influential in early life, the case – a great case in its time – has fallen into old age and decrepitude on the international stage.

[107] See Jack M Balkin, 'The Future of Free Expression in a Digital Age' (2009) 36 *Pepperdine Law Review* 427 (noting the shifting paradigms for the protection of free speech).

# 5 Defamation and democracy

*Russell L. Weaver*

Over the last half a century, judicial decisions have revolutionised defamation law in the United States,[1] Australia,[2] New Zealand,[3] Canada[4] and England,[5] but often through divergent approaches. The United States Supreme Court opted to provide greater protection to the media by focussing on categories of defamation plaintiffs (e.g., distinguishing between public officials, public figures and private individuals), and varying the burden of proof depending on the category (and, to some extent, varying the burden of proof based on the relationship of the issues to the public interest).[6] By contrast, most Commonwealth countries opted to extend qualified common law privilege protections, in an effort to provide greater protection for public speech, but defining the extension in different ways.[7] Recently, Britain replaced its judicial decisions with a statutory amendment.[8]

This evolution of defamation standards was long overdue, and has brought the affected nations more into conformity with modern notions of government. At one point in history, some monarchies of Europe were regarded as ruling by 'divine right'[9] in the sense that the monarchs had

[1] See *New York Times* v. *Sullivan*, 376 US 254 (1964).
[2] See *Lange* v. *Australian Broadcasting Corporation* (1997) 189 CLR 520, 521.
[3] See *Lange* v. *Atkinson* [1997] 2 NZLR 22, 27.
[4] See *Cusson* v. *Quan*, [2009] 3 SCR 712; *Grant* v. *Torstar*, [2009] 3 SCR 640; *WIC Radio* v. *Simpson*, [2008] 2 SCR 420.
[5] See *Jameel* v. *Wall Street Journal Europe* [2006] UKHL 44; *Reynolds* v. *Times Newspapers* [2001] 2 AC 127.
[6] See *Dun & Bradstreet* v. *Greenmoss Builders*, 472 US 749 (1985) (liability standards for purely private individuals in matters of purely private interest); *Gertz* v. *Robert Welch*, 418 US 323 (1974) (liability standards for other private individuals); *Associated Press* v. *Walker*, 388 US 130 (1967) (liability standards for public figures); *New York Times* v. *Sullivan*, 376 US 254 (1964) (liability standards for public officials).
[7] See Russell L Weaver, Andrew T Kenyon, David F Partlett and Clive P Walker, *The Right to Speak Ill: Defamation, Free Speech and Reputation* (Durham, NC: Carolina Academic Press, 2006) 35–6.
[8] See Defamation Act 2013 (UK) cl 26.
[9] See *Seminole Tribe of Florida* v. *Florida*, 517 US 44, 96 (1996) (noting that 'centuries ago' there was a 'belief that the monarch served by divine right').

been placed on their thrones by God,[10] and were carrying out God's will through their actions.[11] Most modern nations reject the concept of divine right in favour of democratic principles. The US Declaration of Independence, a document premised on the ideas of English and French philosophers, illustrates the modern approach. That document implicitly rejects the concept of divine right, and articulates a democratic view of government:[12] 'Governments are instituted among Men, deriving their just powers from the consent of the governed'.[13]

As governments evolved from monarchy to democracy (and those monarchies that survived were usually forced to exercise limited powers consistent with democratic ideals), societal attitudes towards freedom of expression evolved as well. Following Gutenberg's invention of the printing press in the fifteenth century, many European governments tried to limit the ability of private individuals to use the press to communicate their ideas. In addition to placing limits on the total number of presses that could exist,[14] governments also imposed licensing restrictions on the content of publications.[15] Further, some governments criminalised speech. For example, in 1606, England's Star Chamber created the crime of seditious libel in *de Libellis Famosis*.[16] That decision made it a crime to criticise the King and other governmental officials (and, at one point, the clergy as well).[17] The crime was enforced by 'threats of punishment, litigation costs, and stigma',[18] and was justified by the notion that criticism of the government 'inculcated a disrespect for public authority'.[19] 'Since maintaining a proper regard for government was the goal of this new offense, it followed that truth was just as reprehensible as falsehood' and therefore was not a defence.[20] Indeed, truthful criticisms were punished more severely than false criticisms because it was assumed that true criticisms were potentially more

10 *Ibid.* 11 *Ibid.*

12 See *Employees of the Department of Public Health & Welfare* v. *Department of Public Health & Welfare*, 411 US 279, 323 (1973).

13 *Ibid.*

14 See Russell L Weaver, Catherine Hancock, Donald E Lively and John C Knechtle, *The First Amendment: Cases, Problems and Materials*, 3rd edn (New Providence, NJ: LexisNexis, 2011) 5.

15 See *Thomas* v. *Chicago Park District*, 534 US 316, 320 (2002).

16 77 Eng Rep 250 (Star Chamber 1606).

17 See William T Mayton, 'Toward a Theory of First Amendment Process: Injunctions of Speech, Subsequent Punishment, and the Costs of the Prior Restraint Doctrine' (1982) 67 *Cornell Law Review* 245, 248. Indeed, in *de Libellis Famosis*, the defendants had ridiculed high clergy.

18 *Ibid.*

19 *Ibid.*, at 103; see also Matt J O'Laughlin, 'Exigent Circumstances: Circumscribing the Exclusionary Rule in Response to 9/11' (2002) 70 *UMKC Law Review* 707.

20 *Ibid.*

damaging to the government.[21] While the concept of divine right was in vogue, and the monarch was presumed to be carrying out God's will, such restrictions might have made sense. After all, why should ordinary people be allowed to criticise a divinely inspired monarch who was carrying out God's will? However, as democratic principles took root, suppression of speech became anathema to a free society, and restrictions like seditious libel and licensing became anomalies.[22]

Defamation litigation poses a very real threat to the functioning of modern democracies.[23] When media outlets are sued for defamation, they must expend resources to defend themselves, and they risk being subjected to substantial monetary judgements, thereby potentially chilling reporting on matters of public concern. Of course, defamation litigation inevitably involves a balance between the societal interest in freedom of expression, and the societal and individual interest in providing compensation to those who have been injured by defamatory statements, and nations have historically chosen to cut the balance between those two interests in different ways.

This chapter examines the defamation standards recently adopted in the US, UK and Australia, and offers some reflection on the efficacy of those standards in terms of promoting free speech and democratic values.

## 5.1 The common law of defamation

The common law of defamation was decidedly pro-plaintiff, and erred decisively in favour of reputation over freedom of expression. Without attempting to summarise fully the common law, something that would be difficult or impossible in the context of a short chapter, the English common law of defamation was decidedly pro-plaintiff,[24] and saddled plaintiffs with only limited burden of proof obligations.[25] Although English law provided various privileges to defendants,[26] including the

[21] See Stanton D Krauss, 'An Inquiry into the Right of Criminal Juries to Determine the Law in America' (1998) 89 *Journal of Criminal Law & Criminology* 111, 183 n 290.

[22] See *New York Times* v. *Sullivan*, 376 US 254 (1964); *see also* C Edwin Baker, 'Scope of the First Amendment Freedom of Speech' (1978) 25 *UCLA Law Review* 964; Robert H Bork, 'Neutral Principles and Some First Amendment Problems' (1971) 47 *Indiana Law Journal* 1; Thomas I Emerson, 'Toward a General Theory of the First Amendment' (1963) 72 *Yale Law Journal* 877; Alexander Meiklejohn, 'The First Amendment is an Absolute' [1961] *Supreme Court Review* 245; Russell L Weaver, *Understanding the First Amendment*, 5th edn (New Providence, NJ: LexisNexis, 2014) 10–3.

[23] See *New York Times* v. *Sullivan*, 376 US 254 (1964).

[24] See Weaver et al., above n 7, at 17.

[25] *Ibid.*, at 21–5 (e.g., plaintiff must show that the material was 'published', that the material identified him or her, and that the publication carried a defamatory meaning).

[26] *Ibid.*, at 31–4.

defence of 'fair comment',[27] the burden of proving 'truth' rested squarely on the defendant.[28] The net effect, as one British commentator noted, was that English law was 'too jealous of defending the reputations of politicians and insufficiently alert to the legitimate interests of the electorate in consuming political information about those who govern us'.[29]

## 5.2 The US's departure from the common law

For much of US history, defamation law tracked the English common law. Under the system of dual governmental authority that exists under the US Constitution,[30] the individual states possessed the authority to define the tort of defamation (meaning, of course, that defamation standards could vary from state to state),[31] and most states tended to track the English common law.[32] In theory, since defamation rules affect speech, the authority of the states to regulate defamation liability might have been circumscribed by the First Amendment to the Constitution, which contains the guarantee of free speech. However, for most of US history, the Supreme Court precedents had held that the First Amendment did not apply to the states.[33]

In 1940, when the United States Supreme Court decided *Cantwell* v. *Connecticut*,[34] it extended First Amendment protections to the states. However, nothing much changed in regard to defamation. In *Chaplinsky* v. *New Hampshire*,[35] in dicta, the Supreme Court flatly rejected the notion that defamatory speech was entitled to any constitutional protection under the First Amendment. *Chaplinsky* stated that there are 'certain well-defined and narrowly limited classes of speech, the prevention and punishment of which have never been thought to raise any constitutional problem. These include the lewd and obscene, the profane, the libellous, and the insulting or "fighting" words-those which by their very utterance inflict injury or tend to incite an immediate breach of the peace'.[36] Likewise, in *Smith* v. *People of the State of California*,[37] the Supreme Court held that the First Amendment does not 'prohibit the States from abridging free speech by the enactment of defamation or libel laws'.[38]

[27] *Ibid.*, at 28–30. [28] *Ibid.*, at 25–8.
[29] Ian Loveland, *Political Libels: A Comparative Study* (Oxford: Hart Publishing, 2000) p. ix.
[30] See Russell L Weaver, Catherine Hancock, Donald E Lively, Steven I Friedland and Wendy B Scott, *Inside Constitutional Law: What Matters and Why* (Austin, TX: Wolters Kluwer Law & Business, 2009) 48–9.
[31] See Weaver et al, above note 7, at 35–9. [32] *Ibid.*, at 39–43.
[33] See *Chaplinsky* v. *New Hampshire*, 315 US 568 (1942). [34] 310 US 296, 303 (1940).
[35] 315 US 568 (1942). [36] *Ibid.*, at 571–2. [37] 361 US 147, 157 n 2 (1959).
[38] *Ibid.*

US law began to radically diverge from the common law with two landmark constitutional decisions handed down in 1964 by the United States Supreme Court. In *Garrison* v. *Louisiana*,[39] the Supreme Court flatly rejected the idea that individuals (or the media, for that matter) could be criminally prosecuted for libellous statements. *Garrison* effectively abolished the crime of seditious libel in the United States. At the same time, the court decided *New York Times* v. *Sullivan*, and imposed significant constitutional restrictions on the ability of the states to impose liability for defamation. In particular, the Supreme Court held that public officials could not recover for defamation unless they could prove that the defendant had acted with 'actual malice',[40] and the court shifted the burden of proof from the defendant to the plaintiff.[41] The actual malice standard required plaintiffs to prove either that the defendant knew that the defamatory statement was false, or had acted with reckless disregard for whether it was true or false.[42] In addition, in suits by public officials, the Supreme Court rejected the common law presumption of damages, and forced defamation plaintiffs to prove actual damages.[43]

In rendering the *New York Times* decision, the United States Supreme Court was fully conscious of the relationship of speech to the political process. The case arose during the tumult of the 1960s civil rights movement, and involved a paid advertisement by civil rights leaders who made allegations regarding how the police had responded to civil rights demonstrations on a college campus. Mindful of this context, and the potential impact on speech, the Supreme Court chose to move the balance between speech and reputation in favour of free expression.[44] The court emphasized that the United States, as a nation, had made 'a profound national commitment to the principle that debate on public issues should be uninhibited, robust, and wide-open', and the court recognised that speech on public issues 'may well include vehement, caustic, and sometimes unpleasantly sharp attacks on government and public officials'.[45] Indeed, the Supreme Court noted that the advertisement in question had been commissioned as part of an 'expression of grievance and protest on one of the major public issues of our time'.[46] Recognising that a certain amount of erroneous statement is inevitable in public debate, the court held that constitutional liability standards must be limited in order to provide 'breathing space' for freedom of expression.[47] In articulating the 'actual malice' standard, the court flatly stated that it intended to make it much more difficult for public officials to recover for injury to reputation.

[39] 379 US 64 (1964). [40] *New York Times* v. *Sullivan* 376 US 254, 277 (1964).
[41] *Ibid.* [42] *Ibid.*, at 279–80. [43] *Ibid.* [44] *Ibid.*, at 270–1. [45] *Ibid.*, at 271.
[46] *Ibid.* [47] *Ibid.*, at 271–2.

The Supreme Court took particular note of the fact that seditious libel prosecutions had repressed speech, and emphasised that libel judgements could have a similarly repressive effect on freedom of expression.[48] Indeed, in the court's view, the mere fact that an official's reputation had suffered injury 'affords no more warrant for repressing speech'.[49]

In subsequent cases, the Supreme Court expanded on the *New York Times* decision by requiring 'public figures' to satisfy the actual malice standard in defamation cases.[50] However, the court refused to extend the actual malice standard to suits brought by private individuals.[51] The court did draw distinctions between categories of private individuals based on whether they were 'purely private individuals'[52] or private individuals involved in matters of public interest.[53] The states were given latitude to apply less difficult burden-of-proof standards to private individuals,[54] especially individuals involved in matters of purely private interest.[55]

## 5.3 The extensions of qualified common law privilege in Australia and England

As noted, the Australian High Court and the British House of Lords chose not to follow the lead of the US Supreme Court, and instead chose to provide greater protection through an extension of common law qualified privilege. However, the Australian and British courts chose somewhat different approaches to that extension. In its recent statutory enactment, the UK abolished the *Reynolds* defence, but adopted an approach that was premised on that decision's underlying ideas.

### *5.3.1* Lange *and Australia's expansion of qualified common law privilege*

The legal landscape in Australia is quite different from the landscape in the United States. The Australian Constitution does not contain a bill of rights, and has no explicit provision protecting freedom of expression, and provides no explicit basis for providing protections to defamation

[48] *Ibid.*, at 273. [49] *Ibid.*, at 272.
[50] See *Curtis Publishing* v. *Butts*, 388 US 130, 154–5 (1967); *Associated Press* v. *Walker*, 388 US 130, 154–5 (1967).
[51] See *Gertz* v. *Robert Welch*, 418 US 323 (1974).
[52] See *Dun & Bradstreet* v. *Greenmoss Builders*, 472 US 749 (1985).
[53] See *Gertz* v. *Robert Welch*, 418 US 323 (1974).
[54] See *Dun & Bradstreet* v. *Greenmoss Builders*, 472 US 749 (1985); *Gertz* v. *Robert Welch*, 418 US 323 (1974).
[55] See *Dun & Bradstreet* v. *Greenmoss Builders*, 472 US 749 (1985).

defendants. Indeed, the omission of a bill of rights was not an oversight, but instead reflected the constitutional framers' conscious rejection of the need for such protections in deference to legislative supremacy.[56] Moreover, not only were explicit rights omitted from the Australian Constitution, Australian courts had historically been hostile to the idea of 'implied rights'.[57]

Australian jurisprudence began to shift in the 1990s. In two decisions, *Australian Capital Television* v. *Commonwealth*[58] and *Nationwide News* v. *Wills*,[59] the High Court recognised an implied guarantee of free speech. In doing so, the High Court 'distilled from the provisions and structure of the Constitution, particularly from the concept of representative government which is enshrined in the Constitution, an implication of freedom of communication'.[60] This freedom of communication did not create an unrestricted right to free expression, but did provide citizens and the media the freedom to communicate 'in relation to public affairs and political discussion'.[61]

The High Court then decided *Theophanous* v. *Herald & Weekly Times*,[62] and *Stephens* v. *Western Australian Newspapers*,[63] in which it defined the guarantee of freedom of expression to include protections against defamation liability. In *Theophanous*, the High Court purported to adopt a modified version of the *New York Times* v. *Sullivan* 'actual malice' standard, which included a slightly different burden of proof, and a shift of the burden to the defendant.[64] However, the High Court limited the scope of its decision to discussions of government or political matters, or discussions regarding the suitability and performance of governmental officials or, presumably, those seeking office.[65]

[56] See *Australian Capital Television* v. *Commonwealth* (1992) 177 CLR 106, 136 ('[The] prevailing sentiment of the framers [was] that there was no need to incorporate a comprehensive Bill of Rights in order to protect the rights and freedoms of citizens'.).

[57] See *ibid.* ('It is difficult, if not impossible, to establish a foundation for the implication of general guarantees of fundamental rights and freedoms. To make such an implication would run counter to the prevailing sentiment of the framers that there was no need to incorporate a comprehensive Bill of Rights in order to protect the rights and freedoms of citizens'.).

[58] (1992) 177 CLR 106. [59] (1992) 177 CLR 1. [60] *Ibid.* [61] *Ibid.*

[62] (1994) 182 CLR 104 ('*Theophanous*'). [63] (1994) 182 CLR 211.

[64] See *Theophanous*, (1994) 182 CLR 104, 137. The court allowed recovery only if the defendant failed to establish: (1) that it was unaware of the falsity of the material published; (2) that it had not published the material recklessly without concern for whether the material was true or false; and (3) the publication was reasonable under the circumstances. See *ibid.*

[65] See *ibid.*, at 124. The decision applied to discussions of government and political matters, to discussions of members of parliament relating to the performance of their duties in parliament or on parliamentary committees, and to the suitability of persons for office as members of the parliament. See *ibid.*

Because of these prior decisions, *Lange* was not quite as far a stretch as it might otherwise have been (although *Lange* is generally regarded as having replaced *Theophanous*). In *Lange*, the Australian High Court simply extended common law qualified privilege to matters relating to political and governmental matters.[66] In particular, *Lange* provided a defence against defamation liability when the plaintiff had reasonable grounds to believe that the defamatory allegations were true, did not believe that they were false, and made proper enquiry to verify the allegations.[67]

### 5.3.2 *Reynolds* and England's expansion of qualified privilege

Following *Lange*, England's House of Lords handed down its decision in *Reynolds* v. *Times Newspapers*[68] (which has since been overruled by statute). Like *Lange*, that decision extended the scope of common law qualified privilege in order to provide greater protection for free expression. Under *Reynolds*, defendant's publication must relate to a matter of public interest.[69] Even if it does, the communication was not automatically protected by qualified privilege. On the contrary, in deciding whether to extend protection, the House of Lords suggested that various factors should be considered, including the following:

> Depending on the circumstances, the matters to be taken into account include the following. The comments are illustrative only. (1) The seriousness of the allegation. The more serious the charge, the more the public is misinformed and the individual harmed, if the allegation is not true. (2) The nature of the information, and the extent to which the subject matter is a matter of public concern. (3) The source of the information. Some informants have no direct knowledge of the events. Some have their own axes to grind, or are being paid for their stories. (4) The steps taken to verify the information. (5) The status of the information. The allegation may have already been the subject of an investigation which commands respect. (6) The urgency of the matter. News is often a perishable commodity. (7) Whether comment was sought from the plaintiff. He may have information others do not possess or have not disclosed. An approach to the plaintiff will not always be necessary. (8) Whether the article contained the gist of the plaintiff's side of the story. (9) The tone of the article. A newspaper can raise queries or call for an investigation. It need not adopt allegations as statements of fact. (10) The circumstances of the publication, including the timing.
>
> This list is not exhaustive. The weight to be given to these and any other relevant factors will vary from case to case. Any disputes of primary fact will be a matter for the jury, if there is one. The decision on whether, having regard to the admitted or proved facts, the publication was subject to qualified privilege is a matter for the judge. This is the established practice and seems sound. A

[66] *Lange* v. *Australian Broadcasting Corporation* 189 CLR 520, 562–4.
[67] See Weaver et al., above n 7, at 82–7. [68] [2001] 2 AC 127. [69] *Ibid.*

balancing operation is better carried out by a judge in a reasoned judgement than by a jury. Over time, a valuable corpus of case law will be built up.[70]

Although the new Defamation Act purports to abolish the *Reynolds* defence,[71] the Act relies on the *Reynolds* approach and its later interpretation in *Flood* v. *Times Newspapers*[72] in creating a defence for publication on matters of 'public interest'. Section 4(1) provides a defence where the defendant shows:

(a) the statement complained of was, or formed part of, a statement on a matter of public interest; and
(b) the defendant reasonably believed that publishing the statement complained of was in the public interest.

As with *Reynolds*, 'the court must have regard to all the circumstances of the case' in determining if the defence has been established.[73] However, unlike *Reynolds*, the Act does not explicitly list a number of factors to be considered in determining whether the test is met, although in determining point (b), the court must make allowance for editorial judgement 'as it considers appropriate'.[74] A list in the style of *Reynolds* had been proposed in the Bill,[75] but it was removed because of concerns that it would see the defence applied more restrictively than intended. The degree to which the defence has been strengthened through these changes remains to be determined by case law. The origin of the provision in *Reynolds* may see substantially the same approach continue.

## 5.4 Impact of the defamation reforms

How have these judicial decisions affected defamation litigation? More importantly, how have those decisions affected public debate and the functioning of the democratic process?

[70] *Ibid.*, at 205. [71] See Defamation Act 2013 (UK), cl 26, s 4(6).
[72] *Flood* v. *Times Newspapers* [2012] 2 AC 273. [73] Defamation Act 2013, s 4(2).
[74] *Ibid.*, s 4(4). There is also express provision of a 'reportage' defence in s 4(3).
[75] The Bill had provided, in cl 4(2), that the factors would include: '(a) the nature of the publication and its context; (b) the seriousness of the imputation conveyed by the statement; (c) the relevance of the imputation conveyed by the statement to the matter of public interest concerned; (d) the importance of the matter of public interest concerned; (e) the information the defendant had before publishing the statement and what the defendant knew about the reliability of that information; (f) whether the defendant sought the claimant's views on the statement before publishing it and whether an account of any views the claimant expressed was published with the statement; (g) whether the defendant took any other steps to verify the truth of the imputation conveyed by the statement; (h) the timing of the statement's publication; (i) the tone of the statement'.

### 5.4.1 *British reporting prior to the recent decisions*

Prior to the judicial decisions, there was little doubt but that defamation litigation had a significant impact on the willingness of the media to report on matters of public interest.[76] The British media, in particular, was chilled by the threat of defamation litigation. For those who have observed the British media in action, this assertion might seem remarkable. Indeed, some might view the British media as particularly aggressive and particularly willing to publish defamatory allegations despite the potential for an adverse defamation judgement. Our interviews did not bear out this view of the British media, and indeed suggested that the British media was nowhere near as aggressive or bold as one might have assumed. On the contrary, the British media significantly limited its publication practices in order to avoid the threat of defamation liability.[77]

Many factors reveal how pre-*Reynolds* defamation law affected the British media's publication practices. One significant indicator was the threat of suits, and actual suits, brought against British media outlets.[78] Even quality newspapers, which were less inclined to sensationalise, regularly received threatening letters from solicitors regarding their coverage. These letters could average two or more per week.[79] If the paper or broadcaster felt that a statement was inaccurate, it would usually offer to retract the statement[80] and might even offer a small damage payment.[81] Some papers made such retractions in response to about one-third of the letters they received.[82] Of course, some matters could not be settled, and 5 per cent to 10 per cent of all letters ultimately resulted in litigation.[83]

Because of the threat of litigation, the British media tended routinely to involve lawyers in the publication and editorial process, and engaged in a more thorough and careful pre-publication editorial process.[84] Most newspapers employed teams of lawyers, so-called 'night barristers', who were charged with reviewing each day's paper or program for material

[76] See Weaver et al, above n 7, at 131–50. [77] *Ibid.* [78] *Ibid.*, at 139–41.

[79] *Ibid.*, at 139, n 28 (*The Times* was receiving letters from solicitors at the rate of two to three a fortnight, and a writ was being issued against it about once a month. *News International* was receiving three to four letters from solicitors per week, or 150–200 letters per year. *The Guardian* was receiving somewhere between 100 and 120 letters from solicitors per year. Thames Television was receiving about 100 letters from solicitors per year).

[80] *Ibid.*, at 139. [81] *Ibid.*

[82] *Ibid.*, at 139–40 (Of the 100–120 letters that *The Guardian* received from solicitors per year, it paid a small settlement sum in about forty cases. However, Thames Television finds that they have an adequate defence, and are able to convince opposing solicitors of this fact, in nearly 99 per cent of all cases).

[83] *Ibid.*, at 140 (Of the 150–200 letters that News International received per year, about 10 per cent evolved into writs. For every 100 or so demand letters received by Thames Television, about five writs were issued).

[84] *Ibid.*, at 141–2.

that might be defamatory. When one of the night barristers identified potentially defamatory material, he or she would then trigger an intensive review process that was focussed on whether there was 'legally admissible evidence' to support any defamatory allegations.[85] Moreover, the British media made efforts to assess the risks of an adverse judgement. As a result, participating lawyers would focus on the quality of the evidence available to support the allegations (e.g., would the witness be willing to go into the box and testify? Is the witness someone who would be believable? Is the witness someone who is likely to go 'wobbly').[86] Fearing potential liability, especially the possibility of being forced to pay costs, British media organisations were reluctant to publish allegations that they believed to be true, but for which sufficient 'legally admissible evidence' was lacking.[87] As a result, they might withhold publication or water down the nature of the allegations.

Because of the potential for suits, and the possibility of being forced to pay costs, British media outlets were reluctant to publish allegations against particularly litigious individuals.[88] Regarding someone like the late Robert Maxwell, who was regarded as being willing to sue if the media got so much as a word wrong, the media was particularly cautious.[89] As a result, the British media failed to report on concerns regarding the stability of Maxwell's empire, thereby causing great loss to pensioners and others when that empire suddenly collapsed.[90] By contrast, if someone was particularly disinclined to sue (for example, the Queen or Rupert Murdoch), the media tended to be a bit more relaxed in their reporting about that individual.[91]

The other interesting aspect of English defamation law at this time was the fact that there was a very active group of lawyers who specialised in plaintiff's defamation litigation. In other words, defamation litigation was sufficiently lucrative to lure lawyers into that field of practice.[92]

### 5.4.2 *The US media post-*NY Times

In the post-*NY Times* era, the US media functioned quite differently from the British media pre-*Reynolds* (and, presumably, quite differently from the US media pre-*NY Times*).[93] Although the British media seemed quite 'chilled' by the possibility of defamation liability, US media outlets were not chilled at all.[94] The reason that US newspapers and broadcasters were less concerned about defamation litigation was because they were being threatened with suit, and actually sued, far less frequently than

[85] *Ibid.*, at 141. [86] *Ibid.*, at 142–3. [87] *Ibid.* [88] *Ibid.*, at 144–6.
[89] *Ibid.*, at 145–6. [90] *Ibid.* [91] *Ibid.*, at 146. [92] *Ibid.*, at 250–2.
[93] *Ibid.*, at 183–200. [94] *Ibid.*, at 131–200.

their British counterparts.[95] As a result, US media outlets involved lawyers in the publication process far less frequently than did British media outlets. US newspapers had no equivalent to the 'night barrister' system in the UK.[96] Most US papers and broadcasters did not routinely involve lawyers in the publication process, but instead allowed editors and producers to decide for themselves whether material was potentially defamatory, and whether to consult or involve counsel.[97] In the few instances when US media outlets did involve lawyers in the publication process, they used a process that was similar to that used by their English counterparts.[98] Although the possibility of defamation suits had some impact on reporting in the United States, most interviewees indicated that the impact was minimal, and some indicated that it had no impact at all.[99]

Consistent with the much lower level of defamation litigation in the United States, the US media did not seem concerned about particularly litigious individuals.[100] This lack of concern was interesting because they often reported on some of the same individuals that the British media regarded as litigious, but without the same concern or skittishness regarding the potential for defamation liability.[101] Unlike Australia, defamation suits by politicians were virtually non-existent.[102]

Perhaps the most striking difference between the United States and Britain is the absence of a plaintiff's defamation bar in the United States.[103] This absence is striking given that Americans have a reputation for being more litigious than the Australians or the English, particularly in regard to tort litigation.[104] Given that the United States allows contingency fee arrangements between lawyers and their clients, and does not require the losing party to pay costs, one might have expected a significant number of tort lawyers to have been willing to bring tort defamation litigation.[105] The reality is that the *New York Times* decision made defamation litigation an unwise bet for a good tort lawyer.[106] The chances of recovery are low, damages awards are generally limited to actual (rather than presumed) damages, and most defamation judgements are overturned on appeal.[107] As a result, lawyers had little incentive to take defamation cases on a contingency fee basis.

[95] *Ibid.*, at 185–7.

[96] *Ibid.*, at 190–1 (there are some exceptions. CBS routinely asks legal counsel to review investigative programs. In addition, those who publish internationally may be more inclined to use pre-publication lawyer reviews as a matter of routine, but they do so because of the risk under foreign laws).

[97] *Ibid.* [98] *Ibid.*, at 191–2. [99] *Ibid.*, at 185–7. [100] *Ibid.*, at 193–4. [101] *Ibid.*

[102] *Ibid.* [103] *Ibid.*, at 250–2. [104] *Ibid.* [105] *Ibid.* [106] *Ibid.* [107] *Ibid.*

### 5.4.3 *The Australian media post-*Lange

How did *Lange* affect the Australian media and its willingness to report on matters of public interest? Interestingly, the evidence suggested that *Lange* did not significantly alter how the Australian media reported on matters of public interest, and the Australian media continued reporting in much the same way that the British media reported prior to *Reynolds*.[108]

Post-*Lange*, virtually all Australian media companies continued to apply a 'legally admissible evidence' standard in deciding what to publish,[109] and were 'fairly reluctant to publish allegations that they believed to be true, but for which they lacked legally admissible evidence'.[110] The source of the problem was *Lange*'s focus on 'reasonableness'. Most media outlets felt that it was quite risky to assume that, if they reported incorrectly in making a defamatory allegation, the finder of fact would conclude that they had acted 'reasonably' – no matter how careful they had been.[111] As a result, post-*Lange* interviews suggested that the Australian media continued to function in much the same way that it had functioned pre-*Lange*.[112]

### 5.4.4 *British post-*Reynolds *interviews*

Even though *Reynolds* marked a sea change in English defamation law, the evidence suggests that it did not have a huge impact on British media practices.[113] Although one British newspaper decided to chart a new journalistic course following that decision,[114] the overwhelming majority of British newspapers and media outlets continued to function as before.[115] In other words, they continued to apply the 'legally admissible evidence' standard in deciding whether to publish or to withhold information.[116]

*Reynolds*'s shortcomings are attributable to the fact that the decision articulated multiple criteria to be considered, and therefore created uncertainty for media outlets regarding when and how expanded common law qualified privilege would be applied.[117] How could an editor, in deciding whether to publish allegations, accurately assess all of those factors and make an informed assessment regarding the potential for liability?[118] The overwhelming majority of interviewees suggested that they tended to be cautious post-*Reynolds*, and made publication decisions in much the same way that they had made them pre-*Reynolds*.[119] In other words, they continued to apply the legally admissible evidence standard,

108 *Ibid.*, at 201–14. 109 *Ibid.*, at 211–2. 110 *Ibid.* 111 *Ibid.*, at 211.
112 *Ibid.*, at 201–14. 113 *Ibid.*, at 215–42. 114 *Ibid.*, at 222–3.
115 *Ibid.*, at 215–42. 116 *Ibid.*, at 223–6. 117 *Ibid.* 118 *Ibid.* 119 *Ibid.*

and to be cautious regarding the potential for liability. The net effect is that (with one exception) the British media did not feel free to report on matters that they believed to be in the public interest without fear of defamation liability.

Although the new Defamation Act replaces *Reynolds*, the essence of the test generally follows the *Reynolds* approach, with a focus on responsible journalism. There is no reason to believe that the Act will have much impact either.

## 5.5 Conclusion

Over the last half a century, courts around the world have tweaked (or, sometimes, radically altered) their defamation laws to make them more consistent with the underlying values of democracy. The direction of these efforts have varied considerably from country to country. Whereas the United States Supreme Court sought to constitutionalise defamation law, and thereby provide substantial protection against the potential chilling effect of defamation litigation based on the status of the plaintiff, Australia and the United Kingdom opted instead to expand common law qualified privilege. The results have also varied. The *New York Times* decision provided very substantial protection to the media, and has largely freed it from the threat and vagaries of defamation litigation. With one limited exception, the *Lange, Reynolds* and *Jameel* decisions have not had a similar impact.

Of course, defamation rules inevitably involve a trade-off between society's desire to protect individual reputation, and its corresponding desire to protect freedom of expression.[120] While the big advantage of the *New York Times* decision is that it provides very real and substantial protection for free expression, it provides very little protection for reputation.[121] Defamation plaintiffs, especially public officials and public figures, rarely prevail in defamation litigation.[122] Even when they obtain judgements at the trial court level, those judgements are almost routinely overturned on appeal.[123] As a result, one might have hoped that the Australian and English extensions of qualified common law privilege might have provided a pathway for a better balance between speech and reputation. Thus far, neither extension seems to have struck the proper balance.[124]

[120] *Ibid.*, at 3. [121] *Ibid.*, at 243–66. [122] *Ibid.*, at 252–5. [123] *Ibid.*
[124] *Ibid.*, at 201–92.

# 6 'A reasonable expectation of privacy': a coherent or redundant concept?

*Eric Barendt*

## 6.1 Introduction

It is now familiar English law that the first question for a court to resolve in a misuse of private information case is whether the claimant had a reasonable expectation of privacy. A court must find there was such a reasonable expectation to conclude that the claimant's right to respect for his or her private life under Article 8 of the European Convention on Human Rights (ECHR) is engaged before it proceeds to balance that right against the media's (or other defendant's) right to freedom of expression. As Lord Nicholls said in the leading case, *Campbell* v. *MGN*, '[e]ssentially the touchstone of private life is whether in respect of the disclosed facts the person in question had a reasonable expectation of privacy'.[1] In other words, the 'reasonable expectation' test determines the scope of the privacy right. The test has subsequently been developed and applied by the courts in a number of cases, notably by the Court of Appeal in *Murray* v. *Express Newspapers*,[2] so that it may seem much too late to question its role in English privacy law.

Nevertheless, in this chapter I argue that the test is misconceived, and that it should now be abandoned. It makes no sense to attempt to apply it where the claimant is a child, as in the *Murray* case itself; more importantly, it does not, as its defenders argue, lead to certainty in the law, and it may lead a court to consider factors, which should only be taken into account at the second stage of a privacy case – when the claimant's privacy rights are balanced against the media's interest in freedom of expression. The test may, therefore, require a claimant in some circumstances to establish that he or she has a privacy claim, when the burden should be on the defendant to show that the claim is a spurious one, or that the

1 [2004] 2 AC 457 [21] ('*Campbell*').

2 [2009] Ch 481 ('*Murray*'). It has also been adopted in other jurisdictions, and recently the Australian Law Reform Commission (ALRC) has recommended that it should be a requirement of the new privacy tort it is proposing for Australia: ALRC, *Serious Invasions of Privacy in the Digital Era*, Discussion Paper No 80, (2014), [1.89]–[1.99].

privacy claim is outweighed by the defendant's interest in freedom of expression.

Although my argument is heterodox, I am not sure I can claim much originality for it. Raymond Wacks has made some of the points I will be making in this chapter in his recent book, *Privacy and Media Freedom*,[3] published last year. But at places his argument is a little unclear, so I am unsure whether he has totally abandoned all attachment to the test.[4] Like the defenders of the 'reasonable expectation' test, he argues that some objective test is required, in order to limit the kinds of information which claimants can reasonably wish to withhold from the public;[5] it may be hard to distinguish such a test from the reasonable expectation test developed in English law. I am not convinced that any objective test is necessary for this purpose, but will leave that point to later when I consider the implications of abandoning the 'reasonable expectation' test (see Section 6.6).

Section 6.2 of this chapter outlines the origins of the 'reasonable expectation' test in English law, exploring how it has developed from tests formulated in other Commonwealth jurisdictions, notably by the New Zealand Court of Appeal in its famous ruling in *Hosking* v. *Runting*.[6] This section also examines the adoption and development of the test in the English cases. Section 6.3 briefly examines the use of 'reasonable' and 'legitimate expectation' formulations by the European Court of Human Rights, when it has decided whether the right to private life guaranteed by ECHR Art. 8 is engaged or not. The core of the chapter is contained in Sections 6.4 and 6.5, which respectively discuss the justifications for the test (Section 6.4) and its drawbacks or weaknesses (Section 6.5). In my view the weaknesses of the test clearly outweigh the arguments which have been made in its favour. But whether or not that conclusion is accepted, there must be doubts whether it is the most appropriate device for limiting the circumstances in which privacy claims can properly be brought. The final section of the chapter considers the implications for privacy law of abandoning the 'reasonable expectation' test. It will be

[3] Raymond Wacks, *Privacy and Media Freedom* (Oxford: Oxford University Press, 2013).

[4] *Ibid.* For example, he writes (at 122): 'rather than seeking to discover what the victim's reasonable expectations were . . . the court would ask whether the complaint refers to facts, communications, or opinions about the claimant which it would be reasonable to expect him or her to regard as intimate or sensitive and therefore to want to withhold, or at least to restrict their collection, use, or circulation.' This passage suggests a reformulation of the 'reasonable expectations' test, rather than its abandonment.

[5] *Ibid.*, 125. Wacks argues that an objective test is necessary to preclude a claim for privacy in respect of disclosure of the registration documents or other information concerning a claimant's car.

[6] [2005] 1 NZLR 1.

argued that the test does not provide the best means for determining the scope of a right to keep personal information private. Moreover, if it is considered necessary to impose an objective limit on the circumstances in which privacy claims can be brought, it should be formulated in terms of 'a serious' or 'non-trivial' infringement of privacy, rather than in terms of whether the claimant had a reasonable expectation that his or her privacy would be respected.

## 6.2 The 'reasonable expectation' test in case law

### 6.2.1 *Origins in Commonwealth and other precedents*

I should begin with the Australian case, *Australian Broadcasting Corporation* v. *Lenah Game Meats*,[7] even though the High Court did not formulate a reasonable expectation test. The High Court rejected the claimant company's application for an injunction to stop the broadcast of a film showing the stunning and killing of possums at its processing facilities. In a much quoted passage, Gleeson CJ said that while certain types of information, such as those relating to health, personal relationships and finances, were 'easy to identify as private', other activities could be so regarded if 'a reasonable person, applying contemporary standards of morals and behaviour, would understand [them] to be meant to be unobserved'. The disclosure of information 'highly offensive to a reasonable person of ordinary sensibilities' provided a useful practical test of what is private.[8] As Lord Hope pointed out in *Campbell*,[9] the 'highly offensive' test is of assistance only when there is room for doubt whether the information is private; it is not needed when the information is clearly private. Moreover, as will be seen when *Campbell* is discussed, the test is unsatisfactory because it seems to allow the consideration of factors relevant only at the second stage of a privacy case, when privacy rights are balanced against freedom of expression.

Of greater importance in exploring the origins of the 'reasonable expectation' test is the decision, a few months before *Campbell*, of the New Zealand Court of Appeal in *Hosking* v. *Runting*.[10] On facts strikingly similar to those in *Murray*, it declined to grant an injunction to stop the publication of photographs taken of the twin children of two celebrity parents, while they were all out on the street. The judgements of both Gault J (with whom Blanchard J concurred) and of Tipping J held that a claimant must be able to show a reasonable expectation of privacy in

[7] (2001) 208 CLR 199. [8] *Ibid.* [42]. [9] [2004] 2 AC 457 [94].
[10] [2005] 1 NZLR 1 ('*Hosking*').

respect of the information or material as an initial requirement of a privacy claim; in this case neither parents nor children had a reasonable expectation, as the photographs did not disclose any sensitive information about them. Moreover, the photos had been taken when the claimants were out in public. The greater the celebrity of a claimant, the less reasonable was his or her expectation of privacy; the families of famous parents also had a reduced expectation of privacy.[11] The judgement of Tipping J is particularly instructive, for he explored the underlying rationale for the 'reasonable expectation' test. It introduced an objective element to control the subjective expectations of claimants. Nor was it too amorphous or ill-defined. Nothing more precise could be formulated at this stage in the development of privacy law.[12] It should be emphasised that this was the first occasion in which the New Zealand courts had recognised an independent tort of privacy, so it was perhaps understandable that they were nervous that many claims would be made for trivial infringements of the new right.

The NZ Court of Appeal and the High Court of Australia both referred to US law in formulating the 'reasonable expectation' and the 'highly offensive' tests. The latter has been significant in the development – some would say the decline[13] – of the privacy tort in American law, where it has had to struggle against the strong protection afforded in the USA to freedom of speech. A reasonable expectations test in contrast has been used in constitutional law to demarcate the scope of Fourth Amendment protection 'against unreasonable searches and seizures'. In *Katz* v. *US*[14] the Supreme Court held that a claimant was entitled to be protected under the Amendment against the interception of telephone communications from a public telephone booth, on the ground that he had a reasonable expectation that their contents would be kept private. It was not enough that subjectively he had an expectation of privacy; the expectation must be recognised in society as reasonable.[15] Here the test was used to determine the scope of protection against an *intrusion*, rather than a *disclosure* or *publication* infringing privacy. It may be that, as Wacks argues,

[11] *Ibid.* [122]–[123] (Gault J). [12] *Ibid.* [249]–[250].

[13] See David A Anderson, 'The Failure of American Privacy Law' in Basil S Markesinis (ed), *Protecting Privacy* (Oxford: Oxford University Press, 1999) p. 141; Paul Gewirtz, 'Privacy and Speech' (2001) *Supreme Court Review* 139.

[14] 389 US 347 (1967).

[15] *Ibid.* 361 per Harlan J, concurring. The 'reasonable expectations' test formulated by Harlan J has been adopted in subsequent Supreme Court decisions on the constitutionality of intrusions under the Fourth Amendment: see, for example, *US* v. *Miller* 425 US 435 (1976) and *Smith* v. *Maryland* 442 US 735 (1979). For criticism of the application of the test in these decisions, see Daniel J Solove, 'Conceptualizing Privacy' (2002) 90 *California Law Review* 1087, 1152.

there is a stronger case for a reasonable expectation test in the intrusion context than in publication cases, because it is harder to see what other test could be employed in the former set of circumstances to decide when an intrusion was illegitimate.[16] As will be seen in Section 6.6 of this chapter, it is relatively easy to formulate less problematic requirements than the 'reasonable expectation' test in disclosure of private facts cases.

### *6.2.2 The test in the English courts*

It is unnecessary for the purpose of my principal argument to analyse exhaustively the English case law on the 'reasonable expectation' test. Reference will be made only to a few leading decisions where the rationale or content of the test was explored. In the landmark *Campbell* case, Lords Nicholls and Hope, and Baroness Hale, all preferred the test to the 'highly offensive to a reasonable person' formulation of Gleeson CJ in the High Court of Australia. For Lord Nicholls the 'highly offensive' formula was stricter than a reasonable expectation of privacy and it brought into consideration factors which should be taken into account only at the second stage when privacy was balanced against freedom of expression.[17] Baroness Hale considered an objective reasonable expectation test 'simpler and clearer' than the test formulated by Gleeson CJ.[18] Lord Hope's approach was slightly different. Gleeson CJ's test was useful in borderline cases where it was unclear whether the information or activity was private, but was not needed when the information was obviously private, as it was in the *Campbell* case itself. And if the information is clearly private, then it followed that there was a reasonable expectation of privacy.[19] On this approach, whether there is a reasonable expectation of privacy is perhaps a conclusion, rather than a test for determining whether the disclosed information or conduct was private or confidential.

In some early decisions after *Campbell*, it is unclear whether the courts required satisfaction of the test in order to classify the information as private and so covered by ECHR Art. 8. In *Douglas* v. *Hello!*[20] the Court of Appeal paid little attention to it. When considering whether the publication of the wedding photographs in the defendant's magazine infringed the claimants' privacy (or confidentiality), Lord Phillips MR said simply that private information must include 'information that is personal to the person who possesses it and that he does not intend shall be imparted to the general public'. The nature of the information and the form in which it is kept may usually be adequate to show that it meets these criteria.[21] Nor did the 'reasonable expectation' test play much part

[16] See Wacks, above n 3, 115–9. [17] *Campbell* [2004] 2 AC 457 [121]. [18] *Ibid.* [135]. [19] *Ibid.* [94]–[96]. [20] [2006] QB 125. [21] *Ibid.* [84].

in the reasoning of the Court of Appeal in *McKennitt* v. *Ash*,[22] when it upheld Eady J's decision that Ms Ash's book infringed the claimant's privacy and the relationship of confidence between the parties. The book disclosed information concerning the claimant's personal and sexual relationships, her feelings about her fiancé's death, and her health; these were all regarded without difficulty as private matters and so were covered by ECHR Art. 8. It was only in relation to the disclosure of details concerning a property dispute between the claimant, Ms Ash and other parties that the courts referred to the claimant's entitlement to expect that these matters would remain private even after the end of the confidential relationship between the singer and her agent.[23]

The most important decision establishing the need for satisfaction of the test is *Murray* v. *Express Newspapers*.[24] The Court of Appeal allowed the appeal of the parents of David Murray – the author, JK Rowling, and her partner – against a decision striking out his claim for misuse of private information when photographs of him in a buggy with his parents on the streets of Edinburgh were published in the *Sunday Express* and in other newspapers. Sir Anthony Clarke MR, giving the Court of Appeal's judgement, held that after *Campbell* the first question for a court was whether there is a reasonable expectation of privacy, an objective question.[25] The question is a broad one, which should be answered taking 'account of all the circumstances of the case', including the claimant's attributes, the nature of the activity in which he or she was engaged, the place where it was happening, the nature and purpose of the intrusion, and whether there was an absence of consent and that was known. The effect on the claimant and the circumstances in which the publisher obtained the information are also relevant.[26]

The Court of Appeal agreed with the judge's remark that a reasonable expectation of privacy could be attributed to a child claimant, as in this case, but it was relevant to take into account his parents' conduct and the extent to which they had courted publicity.[27] In fact JK Rowling and her partner had deliberately avoided exposing their son to publicity. However, in a later case,[28] a child claimant's case was significantly weakened by the fact that her mother had given an interview to a magazine in which she allowed speculation about the child's paternity, which the child was trying to keep private: 'the result has been to compromise the claimant's reasonable expectation of privacy on the issue of her paternity'.[29]

[22] [2008] QB 73. [23] *Ibid.* [76] (Buxton LJ). [24] *Murray* [2009] Ch 481.
[25] *Ibid.* [35]. [26] *Ibid.* [36]. [27] *Ibid.* [37]–[38].
[28] *AAA v Associated Newspapers* [2013] EMLR 2 (Nicola Davies J) ('*AAA*'). The decision has been upheld by the Court of Appeal which approved the judge's reasoning on the claimant's expectation of privacy: [2013] EWCA Civ 554.
[29] *AAA* [2013] EMLR 2, [116].

The general practice of the courts now is to consider misuse of private information claims in two stages: the first question is whether the claimant had a reasonable expectation of privacy, and the second, which need be answered only if the answer to the first is in the affirmative, is how the privacy claim should be balanced against the right to freedom of expression. That was the approach taken, for example, in *Mosley* v. *News Group Newspapers*,[30] *Ferdinand* v. *MGN*,[31] *Hutcheson (previously 'KGM')* v. *News Group Newspapers*,[32] *Spelman* v. *Express Newspapers*,[33] and *McLaren* v. *News Group Newspapers*;[34] this is far from an exhaustive list. The question has been raised whether the 'reasonable expectation' test is satisfied automatically once the court has determined that ECHR Art. 8 is engaged because the right to respect for private and family life is in issue. Or are they two separate questions? In *Hutcheson*, the Court of Appeal upheld the approach of Eady J; he had been right to treat them as distinct questions. Even if ECHR Art. 8 is in play or engaged, the critical question is whether the claimant has a reasonable expectation of privacy with regard to the information or other material for which privacy (or confidentiality) is claimed.[35]

One other case should be mentioned at this point. The issue in *Wood* v. *Commissioner of Police of the Metropolis*[36] was whether the police had infringed the rights of the claimant, a media coordinator for Campaign against the Arms Trade, to privacy when it took (and retained) photographs of him on the street after he had left a meeting of an arms company. Allowing the claimant's appeal against the rejection of his application for judicial review, the Court of Appeal ruled that his rights under ECHR Art. 8 had been infringed, and further that the police had not justified the infringement under ECHR Art. 8(2). The judgement of Laws LJ (who dissented on the justification for the infringement) is particularly interesting. He began by examining whether the appellant's right under ECHR Art. 8 had been infringed. Decisions of the European Court of Human Rights showed that this right has a broad scope, encompassing the personal autonomy of an individual to 'master' (or have control over) facts about his or her personal identity and to engage in close personal relationship with others.[37] But this broad right is limited in three ways: first, any interference with it must be sufficiently serious to merit protection under the ECHR, second, the claimant should have on the facts a reasonable expectation of privacy, and third, the right is limited by the restrictions which may be imposed under ECHR Art. 8(2) on the

[30] [2008] EMLR 20. [31] [2011] EWHC 2454 (QB) ('*Spelman*').
[32] [2012] EMLR 2 ('*Hutcheson*'). [33] [2012] EWHC 355 (QB).
[34] [2012] EMLR 33. [35] *Hutcheson*, [2012] EMLR 2, 38–9.
[36] [2010] EMLR 1 ('*Wood*'). [37] *Ibid.* [16]–[21].

exercise of the right, for example, in order to safeguard national security or public order or to protect the rights of others (in particular freedom of expression).[38] This is perhaps the clearest explanation given by an English court for the 'reasonable expectations' test. It 'may operate as a factor limiting the scope of the Art. 8 right'.[39] The *Wood* case concerned an intrusion on the claimant's privacy through the taking, rather than the publication, of his photograph. In that context, there may be an argument for a reasonable expectations test;[40] Laws LJ's reasoning is less persuasive, as will be argued in Section 6.5, in the context of misuse of personal information cases.

## 6.3 'Reasonable expectation' in the jurisprudence of the European Court of Human Rights

In a handful of cases the European Court of Human Rights has considered whether the applicant had a reasonable expectation of privacy when determining whether his or her rights under ECHR Art. 8 were engaged. These have generally involved intrusion or interception of communications, rather than the publication of private facts or photographs. In *Halford* v. *UK*,[41] for example, the court said that the applicant, an Assistant Chief Constable, would 'have had a reasonable expectation of privacy for ... calls' made on an internal telephone system at Police Headquarters, because she had sole use of an office where she had two telephones, one of which was specifically allocated for her private use, and she had been assured that she could use her office phones for the purpose of her case alleging employment discrimination against her on the basis of sex.[42] So she could invoke ECHR Art. 8 when the police authorities tapped her phone.[43] The reasonable expectations of the applicant were also decisive in *Perry* in holding that ECHR Art. 8 was engaged when a camera installed in a police custody suite took photographs of him; they were subsequently used in an identity parade. The applicant could not have expected that the police would use the photographs for this purpose, which went beyond the usual or expected use of the camera.[44]

Similar reasoning was used in the well-known *Peck* case.[45] The applicant accepted that his midnight walk through the Brentwood shopping

[38] *Ibid.* [22]. [39] *Ibid.* [25]. [40] See Wacks, above n 3, 115–9.
[41] (1997) 24 EHRR 523. [42] *Ibid.* [45].
[43] The same approach was taken in *Copland* v. *UK* (2007) 45 EHRR 37, when it was held that telephone calls and emails sent from a place of work are prima facie covered by ECHR, Art. 8; an applicant in these circumstances has a reasonable expectation of privacy unless warned that his or her communications may be monitored.
[44] *Perry* v. *UK* (2004) 39 EHRR 3. [45] *Peck* v. *UK* [2003] EMLR 15.

mall in a state of great distress and his suicide attempt might have been witnessed by passers-by and would be picked up by CCTV cameras without engaging ECHR Art. 8. But the distribution to the media of the footage of him after his suicide attempt without disguising his image, and its subsequent reproduction by the press and on television broadcasts was unforeseen. It was this unexpected use of his image which engaged ECHR Art. 8. In *Von Hannover* the court referred to the 'legitimate expectations' of everyone, including those known to the general public, to the protection of their private life,[46] but the concept was not used in this case to distinguish those cases covered by the right to respect for private and family life from those which fall outside it.

It is important, however, to note that in a number of important ECHR Art. 8 cases the court seems to have been completely unconcerned whether the interference infringed the reasonable or legitimate expectations of the applicant. In its view any medical information relating to a patient falls within the scope of Article 8; this is particularly true with regard to confidential information about an individual's HIV infection.[47] When in *Fressoz and Roire* v. *France*[48] the court held that information in the tax assessment of the chairman of Peugeot was not confidential, so the press was free to reproduce copies of the assessments, it did not trouble to ask whether the head of the car company did or did not have a reasonable expectation of privacy in this context. The information was simply not private. In these cases the court appears to have been able easily to determine whether information was covered by ECHR Art. 8 without resort to the concept of 'a reasonable expectation of privacy'. The cases where the idea has been invoked for the most part concern intrusion, rather than the disclosure of private information; only in *Peck* did the unexpected use of the images of the applicant play a role in determining the scope of the right to respect for private life.

## 6.4 The argument for the 'reasonable expectation' test

The argument for a test of 'a reasonable expectation of privacy' to determine the scope of the privacy right has been well made by Nicole Moreham in a law review article.[49] She explores the theoretical foundations of privacy. In her view privacy is best regarded as a state of 'freedom

[46] *Von Hannover* v. *Germany* [2004] EMLR 21 [51], [69].
[47] *Z* v. *Finland* (1997) 25 EHRR 371; *I* v. *Finland* (2009) 48 EHRR 31.
[48] (2001) 31 EHRR 2.
[49] NA Moreham, 'Privacy in the Common Law: A Doctrinal and Theoretical Analysis' (2005) 121 *Law Quarterly Review* 628.

from unwanted access'.[50] The key elements are the *desire* of claimants to be free from unwanted physical and informational *access* (my emphasis); informational access 'encompasses the collection, storage and dissemination of *information* about X' (emphasis in the original).[51] At the theoretical level any information which someone wants to keep to him- or herself can be regarded as private. It is impossible to determine categories of inherently private or personal information. In the first place, that is because the desires or preferences of people for the privacy of different types of information vary; some people, for example, regard any disclosure of their income as a misuse of private information, while others freely discuss it with their colleagues and friends. Second, any attempt to determine categories of information is bound to fail because it cannot draw a line between trivial and serious information; if we regard, as the European Court of Human Rights certainly seems to, any disclosure of medical information as infringing privacy, then we are compelled to the conclusion that disclosure of a report that X suffers from a cold or a headache is a breach of privacy.[52]

On this argument the reasonable expectation test can be justified as providing the best way of determining the scope of the right to privacy in personal information cases, because the principal alternative – an attempt to list categories of personal or private information – is doomed to failure. Kirsty Hughes also justifies the reasonable expectation of privacy test, partly on the ground that it reflects 'an objectively recognised social norm that privacy should be respected'.[53] On this view, which seems quite consistent with Moreham's argument, we can conclude that a claimant has a reasonable expectation of privacy when contemporary society considers the information to be of the type or kind which he or she is entitled to keep private. The test is an objective one. It contrasts with a subjective one, which might focus on the claimant's desire to control the spread of what he or she regards as private information as determinative of the scope of the privacy right.

This last point leads to a second justification for a reasonable expectation test, though it is really one side of the coin, the other of which is the determination of the scope of privacy: as Moreham argues, there is a need for an *objective check* on the scope of any privacy right recognised in law. Otherwise, even allowing for public interest and other defences, an

[50] *Ibid.* 636. [51] *Ibid.* 640. [52] *Ibid.* 641–2.

[53] Kirsty Hughes, 'A Behavioural Understanding of Privacy and its Implications for Privacy Law' (2012) 75 *Modern Law Review* 806, 824. Hughes, however, argues that on the behavioural approach which she advocates, a claimant would also have a reasonable expectation of privacy when the claimant has taken steps to erect physical or behavioural barriers to protect personal privacy.

enormous range of disclosures would be covered.[54] She then considers the three possible objective checks which the courts in England have considered, notably in the landmark decision in *Campbell:*[55] the 'reasonable expectation' test, the 'highly offensive' test, and the 'obviously private' test. The 'highly offensive' test is rejected, to some extent for the reasons given by Lord Nicholls in *Campbell* itself;[56] moreover, 'offensive' is an inappropriate term for describing the harm suffered by an invasion of privacy.[57] I have no problem with her dismissal of the 'highly offensive' test. (I am not persuaded, however, by Nicole Moreham's treatment of the 'obviously private' test which she regards as depending on the judge's own value judgements of what is private. I will discuss this disagreement in Section 6.6.) The 'reasonable expectation' test strikes the right balance between the consideration due to the subjective expectations of the claimant and the provision of an objective check on their reasonableness.[58] It ensures that claimants will not be able to claim an infringement of privacy whenever any information about them which they would prefer to keep undisclosed is revealed by the media. Moreham's conclusion reflects the justifications for the test sometimes given by the judiciary, notably by Tipping J in the New Zealand *Hosking* case[59] and by Laws LJ in *Wood.*[60] Its role in ensuring that non-serious privacy claims are not actionable has also been emphasised by the Australian Law Reform Commission when recommending the reasonable expectation test as a required element for a new privacy tort.[61]

Nicole Moreham herself points to a difficulty in her argument when she considers how the 'reasonable expectation' test should be developed.[62] A focus on the claimants' reasonable expectations carries the risk that some consideration will be given to whether privacy is likely to be respected on the facts, and this may mean that attention is paid to the usual conduct of the media in the circumstances. She discusses the Californian case, *Shulman* v. *Group W Productions,*[63] where it was held that the claimants, who had been filmed being attended on the highway after a very serious accident, could have no reasonable expectation of privacy because it is usual practice for journalists to turn up and film serious traffic accidents. It was not unexpected for them to behave in that way.[64] The reasonable expectation test also leaves the door open to an argument that the

[54] Moreham, above n 49, 643–4. [55] *Campbell* [2004] 2 AC 457. [56] *Ibid.* [121].

[57] Moreham, above n 49, 646–8.

[58] *Ibid.* Also see Hughes, above n 53, 824–32, where she argues that the test should have both normative and subjective components.

[59] *Hosking,* [2005] 1 NZLR 1 [249]–[250]. [60] *Wood* [2010] EMLR 1 [22], [25].

[61] Australian Law Reform Commission, *Serious Invasions of Privacy in the Digital Era,* Discussion Paper No 80, (2014) [1.99].

[62] Moreham, above n 49, 647. [63] 74 Cal Rpter 2nd 843 (Cal 1998). [64] *Ibid.* 864.

claimant is a public figure who has courted attention and has used the media to disseminate his or her views on earlier occasions, so the claimant cannot therefore reasonably expect that they will treat his or her correspondence or diaries as private. This argument was made unsuccessfully in *Prince of Wales* v. *Associated Newspapers*; the courts rightly treated it as more relevant to balancing the claimant's privacy and confidentiality rights against the newspaper's right to freedom of expression.[65] Nicole Moreham suggests that it would be better to reformulate the test in terms of the claimant's *desires*, rather than his or her *expectations*. In her view the meaning of *reasonable* should also be clarified; it should be considered from the claimant's perspective, and '*all* the claimant's circumstances should be taken into account' (emphasis in the original), including his or her attitude to media publicity.[66] These points may be acceptable, but they would surely reduce the effectiveness of the 'reasonable expectations' test as providing an objective check on inappropriate privacy claims. They may also suggest, as will now be argued, that it is fundamentally flawed and should be replaced by another approach which does more justice to the privacy right.

## 6.5 The incoherence of the 'reasonable expectation of privacy' test

The test requires courts to determine whether the claimant had an expectation of privacy with regard to the information (or photographs) and whether that expectation was reasonable. The question is one of fact.[67] Whether a claimant actually had an expectation is essentially a subjective matter, while the reasonableness of that expectation imposes an objective check on whether the claimant's subjective wishes or desires are to be satisfied. This approach is surely highly artificial. In many cases a claimant will have had no actual expectations at the time his or her privacy was infringed, whether that occurred by intrusion or by publication, although subsequently he or she might say something like: 'Yes, of course, I would have expected that to be treated as private'. The artificiality of the approach is most obvious in cases where the claim is brought on behalf of a child as in *Murray*, in the New Zealand *Hosking* case, and most recently in *AAA* v. *Associated Newspapers*. It makes no sense to ask whether a child, a year or so old, had an actual expectation of privacy, or whether his or her expectation was reasonable. But as Patten J said in *Murray* in a passage

[65] [2007] 2 All ER 139, [44]–[45]. [66] Moreham, above n 49, 647–8.
[67] *Murray* [2009] Ch 481 [41].

approved by the Court of Appeal,[68] the court can attribute to the child reasonable expectations about his or her private life based on matters such as how that life has been conducted by the child's parents or others responsible for the child's upbringing. He added that it may be immaterial whether the child was even aware that his or her photograph was being taken, while the reasonable expectations of the parents in the privacy of their child must be taken into account.

The apparent relevance of the parents' expectations leads to the bizarre conclusion that a child may have no, or only a reduced, reasonable expectation of privacy, when his or her parents – or the parent claiming privacy on the child's behalf – have courted publicity. That was in effect the conclusion reached by Nicola Davies J in the *AAA* case, when she held that the reasonable expectation of the claimant, a very young child, in keeping her paternity private was entitled to less weight, because her mother had discussed the matter with friends, and acquaintances at a country house party, and had allowed speculation about the claimant's father in a magazine interview.[69] For that reason, the publication of the story about the child's paternity – her father is a famous political figure, notorious for extramarital liaisons – was justified as in the public interest.[70] The result in that case may have been right; it has been upheld by the Court of Appeal. But the conclusion that a child's privacy rights may be reduced by the conduct of his or her parents is surely very unattractive; it was rightly criticised by a Joint Committee of the House of Lords and House of Commons.[71] One drawback of the 'reasonable expectation' test is that it enables, even though it does not compel, this reasoning; the conduct of the parents is considered relevant to determining the privacy expectations of the child, itself a thoroughly artificial concept.

Another, and a major, drawback of the test is that it too easily enables – one might say, tempts – courts to consider arguments at the first stage – whether the claimant has a right under ECHR Art. 8 – which should properly be taken into account only at the second stage of a privacy action, when the right is balanced against the right to freedom of expression. So it may be held that the claimant, as a public figure, does not have a reasonable expectation of privacy, or has only a reduced expectation.[72] Previous

[68] [2007] EMLR 22–3, approved in *Murray* [2009] Ch 481 at [38].

[69] *AAA* [2013] EMLR 2 [98]–[101], [116].

[70] In the Court of Appeal [2013] EWCA Civ 554, the politician was identified as Boris Johnson, the Mayor of London and a prominent Conservative.

[71] Joint Committee on Privacy and Injunctions, *Privacy and Injunctions*, House of Lords Paper No 273, House of Commons Paper No 1443, Session 2010–2012 (2012) [81].

[72] See *Spelman* [2011] EWHC 2454 (QB), where Tugendhat J held that a sportsman has no, or only a low, expectation of privacy with regard to a health matter which affects his ability to participate in national and international sport.

conduct in courting publicity on the matter he or she now wants to keep private may be taken into account, as it was in the *AAA* case. In *Ferdinand* v. *MGN*, Nicol J suggested that in extreme cases the extensive discussion by a claimant of aspects of his or her private life might mean that the claimant had no reasonable expectation of privacy with regard to them.[73] Sir Anthony Clarke MR in *Murray* left the door open for courts to take account of these factors at the first stage of a privacy action, when he issued a non-exhaustive list of a number of circumstances they should consider in determining whether there was a reasonable expectation of privacy.[74] As a result, a claimant may have to show, for example, that he or she has an expectation of privacy, despite the claimant's status as a public figure or celebrity or despite the fact that he or she has given frequent interviews to the press about the matter, when it should be for the media defendant to show that, as a result of one of these factors, freedom of expression trumps the privacy right. Consequently, there may be an unconscious double-counting of these factors; they may be used both to weaken the claimant's case and also to strengthen the media argument for publication. Further, as Nicole Moreham admitted, a claimant may be held to have no reasonable expectation because he or she should have appreciated that the media would take photographs or publish a privacy infringing story of interest to the public.[75] It is sobering to remember that Lord Nicholls preferred the reasonable expectation test to the 'highly offensive' formulation of Gleeson CJ in the High Court of Australia, because the latter could 'too easily bring into account, when deciding whether the disclosed information was private, considerations which go more properly to issues of proportionality ... This could be a recipe for confusion'.[76] But the reasonable expectation test has also produced confusion of this kind.

A hypothetical case can be used to illustrate this argument. In the course of discussion of the paper on which this chapter is based during the Melbourne workshop, I was asked by Barbara McDonald whether a member of a government suffering from the early stages of dementia would have a reasonable expectation of privacy, if he or she wanted to prevent the media revealing this to the public. The implication was, I think, that the test would be an appropriate one in these circumstances. Of course, the expectation of privacy could be said to be reduced, perhaps even non-existent. But that would not be because the person's privacy interest was any less than it would be if he or she were an ordinary person;

[73] *Ibid.* [58]. [74] *Murray* [2009] Ch 481 [36].
[75] *Shulman* v. *Group W Productions* 74 Cal Rpter 2nd 843 (Cal 1998), 864.
[76] *Campbell* [2004] 2 AC 457 [22].

the expectation of privacy could be said to be weaker only because the public has a real freedom of expression interest in knowing the health of members of the government. Now that interest should be considered when freedom of expression is balanced against the privacy right. If it is also taken into account at the first stage of a privacy case, the media (or other defendant) is given two opportunities to make the freedom of expression argument. That is surely wrong.

The final count in the indictment of the reasonable expectation of privacy test is that, if it were taken seriously, it would lead to uncertainty in the law.[77] It is inherently uncertain because the boundaries of what amounts to a *reasonable* expectation of privacy shift over time. One generation may find acceptable disclosures which earlier generations would almost certainly have found a clear infringement of privacy; this is perhaps most clear now with regard to the publication of information about income or personal wealth, but it is surely also the case for many people so far as a revelation that they are gay or bisexual is concerned. A similar change has occurred with regard to disclosures concerning a politician's health. The English press did not reveal that Churchill suffered a severe stroke in June 1953 and was for several weeks incapable of discharging his duties as prime minister;[78] it is inconceivable that it would not now fully report a comparable matter affecting the conduct of government. Of course, any attempt to delineate the boundaries of private life is susceptible to social and cultural change, but the 'reasonable expectation' test in principle makes the judiciary responsible for deciding when such a change has occurred. There is another, better solution (see Section 6.6). Application of the test is also more difficult, and the result less predictable, insofar as judges feel compelled to consider the wide range of circumstances listed in *Murray*.[79] It may be said that the test works well enough in practice; there are relatively few reported cases in which the court has found it hard to apply. I suspect that this is because it has become a formula – almost an incantation – which is unimportant in litigation when the matter is obviously private, because, for example, it concerns the claimant's health or details of his or her sexual life. In that case, it has no advantage over the 'obviously private' test for determining the scope of private life, which has itself been considered inappropriate because it leaves too much to judicial discretion.[80]

[77] This point is also made by Wacks, above n 3, 250.
[78] Roy Jenkins, *Churchill* (London: Macmillan, 2001) 861–8.
[79] See *Murray* [2009] Ch 481 [36]. In this context it may be noted that Kirsty Hughes, who supports the reasonable expectation test is critical of the range of factors listed in *Murray:* Hughes, above n 53, 828.
[80] Moreham, above n 49, 646.

## 6.6 Implications of abandoning the 'reasonable expectation' test

Would anything be lost if English law were to abandon the 'reasonable expectation' test, and courts simply asked whether the claimant's rights under ECHR Art. 8 were engaged? Would there be a flood of privacy cases because the law had lost an objective check on the making of trivial, or silly, claims? I doubt it, though these questions are not without point, particularly if the recommendations in the Leveson Report are implemented, so it becomes relatively easy without the risk of incurring much cost to require the press to submit to arbitration of privacy claims.[81] In this context, it is worth pointing out that the Data Protection Act (DPA) 1998 – a privacy law in all but name – does not impose any threshold requirement for the type of 'personal data' which are subject to the requirement of fair and lawful processing and the other data protection principles. It is enough that the data relate to an individual who can be identified from those data. (On the other hand, the 'sensitive personal data', which are subject to stricter processing principles, are defined in the statute;[82] some of the sensitive data concern matters which are typically treated as private, for example, information about physical or mental health, sexual life, and religious or comparable beliefs.) Data protection law, however, may not provide a good guide for the framing of privacy law, primarily because of the generous defence under the DPA available to the media in respect of the processing of data for 'journalistic purposes',[83] and the difficulties in obtaining an award of compensation under the legislation.[84]

The need for an objective check is felt because the content and scope of the right to privacy is contested, even within the context of media law where what is at issue are the particular rights of individuals to be free from unwanted intrusion and the publication of personal information. But stated in such terms these rights may also be considered too broad, and their recognition, without qualification, may be thought to endanger freedom of speech and of the press. Hence the need for an objective check, expressed in terms of a reasonable expectation of privacy. But defamation law has existed without any comparable check on the reputation right, such as a reasonable expectation of protection for reputation; moreover, we have been satisfied with courts determining the content of

[81] Right Honourable Lord Justice Brian Leveson, *An Inquiry into the Culture, Practices and Ethics of the Press*, HC 780 (2012), Part K, chapter 7 [4.46].
[82] Data Protection Act 1998, s. 2. [83] *Ibid.* s. 32.
[84] *Ibid.* s. 13, on which see Mark Warby, Nicole Moreham and Iain Christie (eds), *Tugendhat and Christie: The Law of Privacy and the Media*, 2nd edn (Oxford: Oxford University Press, 2011), [6.85]–[6.88].

the right, although its precise scope remains contested.[85] The same can be said of the right to freedom of expression: the law does not require that speakers must have a reasonable expectation of freedom to exercise it, in order to control its use. Checks on the right to reputation have been imposed by the defences to a defamation action, defences which now instantiate the right to freedom of expression, while checks on that right are provided by the laws of libel and privacy and by the other interests which may justify restrictions on its exercise. No further objective checks are necessary.

Even if an objective check on the making of inappropriate privacy claims is necessary, it should be asked whether a reasonable expectations test is the best means of achieving that end. And it should be asked whether the test provides the best delimitation of the scope of the privacy right. As we have seen,[86] it has been preferred to an 'obviously private' test, on the ground that this test leaves too much discretion to the judge in determining what information is covered by the right to privacy. That argument is unconvincing. For a start, the European Court of Human Rights does not appear to have had any difficulty in holding that health data are covered by ECHR Art. 8, or, it seems, that accessible financial information falls outside it.[87] Moreover, the argument completely collapses if the categories of private information were to be listed in legislation. While there is something in the argument that the judiciary are not well placed to determine what is generally, and should be, regarded as private, it can hardly be objected that the legislature is incompetent to do this. Parliament is well placed to determine what matters should be treated as 'private' for the purposes of a disclosure of private facts tort; moreover, as cultural attitudes change, any legislative list can be revised from time to time, while flexibility can be provided by drafting the list of private matters non-exhaustively, so there is room for an argument that material not on the list should be protected as private.

Perhaps there would be a place for a reasonable expectation of privacy test to determine privacy claims where the matter was not covered by a non-exhaustive list set out in legislation? In these circumstances there would be room for argument whether the information was private. But it is doubtful whether the test is particularly helpful, let alone necessary, for resolving these cases. Consider as an example of such a case the *Author of a Blog* case, where the claimant blogger argued that he had a reasonable expectation of privacy in preserving his anonymity, so he could stop *The*

[85] See the various formulations of the meaning of 'defamatory' considered in *Berkoff* v. *Burchill* [1996] 4 All ER 1008 (CA).

[86] See Moreham, above n 49, 646.

[87] See the cases discussed in Section 6.3.

*Times* from revealing his identity.[88] Eady J rejected this argument, pointing out that the information was quite different from that for which privacy rights had been upheld in earlier cases: information of a personal nature concerning sexual relationships, health, financial affairs and the claimant's family or other relationships. In contrast the claimant here was trying to keep private the identity of a person communicating to the public through his blog.[89] The judge concluded that 'blogging is essentially a public rather than a private activity'.[90] Although the reasonable expectation test was mentioned at places in the judgement,[91] it is hard to believe that it played much part in Eady J's reasoning, or that it was necessary to invoke it to dispose of the case. The identity of a blogger engaging in public communication was rightly, in my view, not treated as analogous to the personal information for which privacy can be claimed.[92]

It can also be objected that the reasonable expectation test is needed as a check to preclude the bringing of trivial claims, for example, in respect of a disclosure that a celebrity missed an opening night because she had a heavy cold or a headache. But this can be done without invoking the test. All that is needed is a requirement of 'non-triviality' or 'seriousness', so redress could not be obtained for a banal story, say, that the claimant was having dinner out with a married man or woman – quite apart from any freedom of expression or public interest argument that might be made in these circumstances. This requirement has been applied in breach of confidence cases, even those concerning the disclosure of personal information, without difficulty.[93] In *McKennitt* v. *Ash*, for example, Eady J at first instance rejected the breach of confidence claim in respect of some passages in the defendant's book, because the disclosures in them were trivial or anodyne, and unlikely to cause the claimant any distress.[94] In assessing the triviality of a disclosure, whether it has caused or is likely to cause serious distress is a relevant factor, but it would be wrong to treat it as decisive, as it is now in determining whether a statement is defamatory for the purpose of a libel action.[95] For cases can be envisaged in which a claimant should be able to stop, or even secure nominal damages, for the

[88] *Author of a Blog* v. *Times Newspapers* [2009] EMLR 22. [89] *Ibid.* [9]. [90] *Ibid.* [11].

[91] *Ibid.* [2], [7], [10].

[92] For a different view, see Kirsty Hughes, 'No Reasonable Expectation of Anonymity?' (2010) 2 *Journal of Media Law* 169. She argues that a claimant should be able to claim privacy in respect of some activities conducted in public, and that the court should have placed greater weight on the steps the claimant had taken to protect his or her anonymity. There is much in both these points, but it is unclear whether it would be necessary to invoke the reasonable expectation of privacy to support this case for the claimant.

[93] Warby, Moreham and Christie, above n 84, [4.81]–[4.83].

[94] [2006] EMLR 10 [131]–[158]. His approach was approved by the Court of Appeal, *McKennitt* v. *Ash* [2008] QB 73 at [12].

[95] Defamation Act 2013, s. 1.

publication of a story about his or her health or his personal relationships, even though their revelation would be unlikely to cause the claimant serious distress.

So nothing would be lost if the 'reasonable expectation of privacy' test were abandoned, particularly if a privacy law provided a broad list of categories of private information and formulated a requirement of 'non-triviality'. The continued existence of the test is tolerable, only because it is almost always a ritual incantation; courts decide that information about, say, the claimant's health, or family or sexual relationship, is covered by ECHR Art. 8, because it is clearly or obviously private, without seriously considering whether it is information in respect of which he or she had a reasonable expectation of privacy. Even more difficult cases like *Author of a Blog* can be, and are, resolved without unpacking the elements of a reasonable expectation test. But it will not do to argue that the vast majority of cases would be decided in exactly the same way if the test were abandoned, so it might as well be kept.[96] Much would be gained if it went. In the first place, the test is incoherent, and there is surely much to be said for coherence and integrity in the formulation of legal principles. More importantly, if it were applied seriously, the test carries the real risk that a claimant will be required to prove that his or her privacy expectations were reasonable, for instance, in the context of great media interest in any story about someone of the claimant's status, when it should be for the media to make the freedom of expression argument in these circumstances. It then becomes much harder than it should be for a claimant to assert his or her privacy rights.

The origins and survival of the reasonable expectation of privacy requirement are almost certainly attributable to nervousness about privacy rights, both generally and in the media context: uncertainty about their basis and scope, and their relationship to the right to freedom of expression. That has been quite understandable. After all, an independent privacy right against media disclosures has only been established in English law in the last ten years, while the general right has still not been recognised.[97](Neither right has yet been recognised in Australia.) But now that, as the Leveson Report has shown, the value of privacy rights, and the importance of protecting them against media intrusion, have been widely accepted – at least outside the tabloid press – the time has surely come to discard a test which significantly weakens the coherence and effectiveness of privacy law.

[96] This, I think, is the argument made by Gavin Phillipson in the course of discussion of the original paper at the Melbourne workshop.

[97] See the decision of the House of Lords in *Wainwright* v. *Home Office* [2004] 2 AC 406.

# 7 Media intrusion into grief: lessons from the Pike River mining disaster

*N.A. Moreham and Yvette Tinsley*

## 7.1 Introduction

At 3:45 pm on 19 November 2010, an explosion occurred underground in the Pike River coal mine on the West Coast of New Zealand. Thirty-one men were working in the mine at the time. Two escaped within forty-five minutes. The remaining twenty-nine, aged between seventeen and sixty-two, were trapped underground. Their bodies remain in the mine.

In the aftermath of the explosion, members of the national and international media flocked in large numbers to the small town of Greymouth. Much of their attention was directed towards the anxiety of friends and relatives who were waiting for news. As a result, friends and family members were subjected to persistent door knocking, telephone calls, photography, and occasional 'dirty tricks' in their homes; photographed and approached for comment as they moved from vehicles to information sessions; and followed as they moved around the town. This kind of 'grief journalism' is typical in the aftermath of a disaster: journalists need stories and those relating to grief and anxiety are thought to grab the public's attention. But what is the impact of this kind of reporting on its subjects?

This chapter provides some answers to this question by setting out the preliminary results of a study into the effect of intense media interest on the family and friends of the men lost at Pike River. The study raises a plethora of legal and ethical questions about the behaviour of journalists and reporters in the aftermath of tragedy. This chapter focusses on just one of them: the participants' concerns about the media's *physical* presence in the aftermath of the explosions. The discussion will explain the nature of those concerns and show how the participants' responses to them reinforce theorists' views about the importance of privacy in

Readers in Law, Victoria University of Wellington. The authors would like to thank participants in the Pike River study for sharing their experiences. They also thank Andrew Kenyon and the participants at the Centre for Media and Communications Law's Defamation and Privacy Workshop, University of Melbourne, April 2014 (at which an earlier version of this chapter was presented) for their helpful feedback.

maintaining a sense of dignity, security, and autonomy. The chapter furthers the study's ultimate aim of using the experience of the Pike River families to gain a deeper understanding of the effect of the media on those experiencing trauma and loss and to ask what, if anything, should be done to change media behaviour.

## 7.2 The Pike River disaster

Pike River Coal's response to the first explosion in the mine was initially faltering. Although the explosion took place at 3:45 pm, the Mines Rescue Service was not called until 4:26 pm. Emergency services were called at 4:35 pm, with the first police officer arriving on the scene some forty minutes later. As there was little reliable evidence of conditions inside the mine, and therefore nothing to determine that it was safe, no rescue was attempted.

There was no individual communication from the company to the family members of the trapped men.[1] They received news of the explosion in an *ad hoc* way, mostly though friends or family.[2] The company issued statements at 7:14 pm and 9:12 pm but there was confusion about the number of men missing; reports from Pike River Coal ranged from twenty-seven to thirty-three men.[3] That night, a welfare centre was established at the Red Cross Hall in Greymouth so that families could gather and receive support while awaiting news.

At 7:30 am on the day after the explosion, the first of a number of information meetings for close friends and family was held at the welfare centre. It was immediately followed, at 8 am, by a press conference at Greymouth Police Station. By this stage, most families knew if their relative was missing – on account of his failure to return from work – but there was still no formal advice from the company about who was underground.[4] At the family meeting, the CEO of Pike River Coal, Peter Whittall, provided information about portable self-rescuers and air being

[1] Pike River Coal decided not to contact next of kin until accurate information was available. Unfortunately, that took approximately sixteen hours while media reports began just over an hour after the first explosion: New Zealand, Royal Commission on the Pike River Coal Mine Tragedy, *Commission's Report: Volume 2*, chapter 17 'The families of the men', 236.

[2] For example, female participant 01 heard about the explosion from friends and family members and female participant 10 heard from a journalist friend. See also Rebecca Macfie, *Tragedy at the Pike River Mine: How and Why 29 Men Died* (Wellington: Awa Press, 2013), 198.

[3] See Royal Commission, above n 1, 236. On the evening of the first explosion, the police reported that thirty-six tags remained on the board (the company had reported that thirty-two tags remained): see www.police.govt.nz/news/release/26081.

[4] Some families never received a call from the Pike River Mine company: Macfie, above n 2, 199.

pumped into the mine, and stated that he had no information about fatalities. Similar meetings were held twice a day in the five days which followed the first explosion. The tone of the early meetings was optimistic and, especially for those families who did not come from a mining background, they were seen by some to have generated false hopes.[5]

At 3 pm on 24 November 2010, next of kin were told in a text message that there would be a significant update at the afternoon family meeting and that all families were encouraged to attend. Peter Whittall began the briefing with the positive news that earlier that day gas levels had improved and Mines Rescue Service had been preparing to enter the mine. The families' optimism soon turned to devastation, however, when they were told that at 2:37 pm there had been a second explosion at the mine which none of the men could have survived.

The Pike River disaster generated a level of national and international media interest which, although more common internationally, had not previously been seen in New Zealand.[6] That, combined with days of uncertainty about the fate of the men, meant that friends and family members were subjected to ongoing and intense media interest.[7] Some were persistently approached in their homes for news. Many were photographed and approached in public places, particularly following the family information meetings and on other occasions when the families came together, including the one instance (on the morning of 21 November) when they were taken up to the mine site in buses. Dozens of film clips and photographs showing family members in an emotional state appeared in the media during that period and in the weeks and months that followed.

## 7.3 The Pike River study

The aim of the Pike River study is to find out what it is like to be caught up in a media frenzy while also dealing with acute anxiety and/or loss. More

[5] Royal Commission, above n 1, 238; Macfie above n 2, 198–9.

[6] The Pike River explosion occurred just one month after the rescue of thirty-three men who had been trapped for sixty-nine days in a gold and copper mine in Chile. This might well have heightened international interest in the story: for a report of the Chile miners' rescue see www.reuters.com/article/2010/10/13/us-chile-miners-idUSN0925972620101013.

[7] It has been observed that what determines the extent of media coverage of a disaster is not the level of destruction or loss of life, but geopolitics and the extent of local connection: Mervi Pantti, Karin Wahl-Jorgensen and Simon Cottle, *Disasters and the Media* (New York: Peter Lang Publishing, 2012), 41. As well as men from New Zealand, the Pike River disaster involved men from Australia and the United Kingdom which created a local connection to the disaster in those countries.

specifically, the study investigates how media interest affected the participants' external behaviour in the days following the explosions, what impact it had on their ability to cope with the situation, whether their responses to the role of the media changed over time, and whether there were any respects in which they thought members of the media should have conducted themselves differently. Limited research has previously been conducted into the impact of intense media interest on grieving or traumatised individuals.[8] As far as the authors are aware, the Pike River project is the first study to examine victims' experience of grief journalism from a legal perspective,[9] although the study also draws on research from other disciplines including media studies, trauma studies, social science and, to a limited extent, psychology.[10] The project's ultimate objective is to assess whether there is a need for change – legal, regulatory or ethical – in respect of the media's treatment of people affected by grief and anxiety.

8 Other studies include Denis Muller and Michael Gawenda, *Black Saturday: In the Media Spotlight* (Melbourne: Cussonia Press, 2011), 219; Kim Walsh-Childers, Norman Lewis and Jeff Neely 'Listeners, not Leeches: What Virginia Tech Survivors Needed from Journalists' (2011) 26 *Journal of Mass Media Ethics* 191; Deni Elliott, 'Family Ties: A Case Study of Coverage of Families and Friends during the Hijacking of TWA Flight 847' (1988) 5 *Political Communication and Persuasion* 67; Liselotte Englund, Rebecca Forsberg and Britt-Inger Saveman, 'Survivors' Experience of Media Coverage after Traumatic Injury Events' (2013) 22 *International Emergency Nursing* 25; and R McAlister and C Meehan, 'An Exploration of Media Reporting of Victims of Murder and Manslaughter in Northern Ireland' (Research Report for Support After Murder Manslaughter Northern Ireland, University of Ulster, 2011).

9 The Leveson Inquiry also touched on this issue: see Right Honourable Lord Justice Brian Leveson, *An Inquiry into the Culture, Practices and Ethics of the Press*, HC 780 (2012), vol. II, pt. F, Chapter 6. Ursula Cheer and Sarah Rosanowski's useful work on the Christchurch earthquake examines media coverage from the journalists' perspective: Ursula Cheer and Sarah Rosanowski, 'The Impact of Law on Media Reporting of Earthquakes in Christchurch 2010–2011' (2013) 18 *Media & Arts Law Review* 220.

10 Media studies scholars have considered the ethical questions raised by reporting on the aftermath of disasters (see, e.g., Denis Muller, 'Ethics and Trauma: Lessons from Media Coverage of Black Saturday' (2010) 18 *Australian Journal of Rural Health* 5; T Joseph Scanlon, Rudy Luukko and Gerald Morton, 'Media Coverage of Crises: Better than Reported, Worse than Necessary' (1978) 55 *Journalism Quarterly* 68; Wendy Bilboe, 'The Thredbo Landslide: Was it only Media Ethics that came Tumbling Down?' (1998) 20 *Australian Journalism Review* 88); social scientists consider the role of the media as disseminator of information and public watchdog (see, e.g., Peter Vasterman, C Joris Yzermans and Anja JE Dirkzwager, 'The Role of the Media and Media Hypes in the Aftermath of Disasters' (2005) 27 *Epidemiologic Reviews* 107; Christopher F Payne, 'Handling the Press' (1994) 3 *Disaster Prevention and Management* 24); and trauma experts examine the relationship between media reporting and trauma symptoms (see, e.g., Betty Pfefferbaum, Robin H Gurwitch, Nicholas B McDonald, Michael JT Leftwich, Guy M Sconzo, Anne K Messenbaugh and Rosemary A Schultz, 'Posttraumatic Stress among Young Children after the Death of a Friend or Acquaintance in a Terrorist Bombing' (2000) 51 *Psychiatric Services* 386; J David Kinzie, James Boehnlein, Crystal Riley and Lisa Sparr, 'A Cross-cultural Study of Reactivation of Posttraumatic Stress Disorder Symptoms: American and Cambodian Psychophysiological Response to Viewing Traumatic Video Scenes' (1998) 186 *Journal of Nervous and Mental Disease* 670).

### 7.3.1 *Methodology*

Each of the seventeen participants in the Pike River study had a close relationship to one of the men who died. They include wives, mothers, fathers, brothers, sisters, sisters-in-law, brothers-in-law and close friends.[11] All of the participants were present in Greymouth at some stage between the first and second explosions, although some lived in other parts of New Zealand or overseas. The researchers also interviewed a social worker who was closely involved with many family members in the period immediately following the disaster.

Participants were given a choice of methods for their participation: face-to-face interview; telephone or Skype interview; or e-mail questionnaire. Fifteen participants took part in in-depth, open-ended interviews. Twelve of these were conducted face-to-face and three were conducted by telephone. The two remaining participants completed written e-mail questionnaires which asked open-ended questions similar to those used in the interviews.

Interviews lasted between forty-five and ninety minutes. Eleven of them, plus the interview with the social worker, took place during a one-week period in June 2012. These were all conducted face-to-face. Of the remaining four interviews, three were conducted by telephone (one in March 2013 and two in May 2013) and one face-to-face in April 2013. The participants who completed written questionnaires did so in March and July 2013.

In both the interviews and questionnaires, participants were invited to explain what contact they had with members of the media in the aftermath of the explosions, how they felt about that contact (both initially and after the passage of time), what effect that contact had had on their behaviour, what response they had to images of or reports about themselves or their loved ones in the media (both initially and after the passage of time), what distinguished any positive media experiences from any negative ones, and what, if anything, they would have changed about their media experience. Since the interviews and questionnaires were open-ended, participants themselves identified which issues were most important to them and sometimes touched on matters which were not expressly raised by the researchers.

### 7.3.2 *Strengths of this study*

The experience of the Pike River families is a particularly clear example of grief journalism in action. This is because all the participants were

[11] Although one participant was a close friend of one of the explosion victims, participants will sometimes be referred to as 'family' in this chapter for the sake of brevity.

experiencing a similar kind of emotional stress at the time of the media's interest.[12] All had lost a close friend or family member in the disaster and were therefore dealing with similar types of emotion – extreme anxiety, distress and grief. Since media attention often focussed on the families as a group, many of the participants had at least some common media experiences. Also, the Pike River disaster was not a situation, like the Christchurch earthquake or London bombings, where images of grieving or traumatised individuals were caught as part of general reporting of the event. As there were no images of or information about the disaster scene itself, the emotions of the Pike River families *were* the story; or at least the main story the media was telling.[13] Public interest considerations relating to disaster *scene* coverage therefore do not intrude on the analysis.[14]

### 7.3.3 Limitations of the study

Like all empirical work, however, this study has some potential limitations. First, because invitations to participate in the study were sent via a central family liaison contact, participants were self-selected.[15] Those who elected to take part might, therefore, be those with the strongest views about their media experience; perhaps those with strongly negative views. In reality, though, media experience was rarely recounted in black-and-white terms: most participants reported both negative and positive media interactions. It also became clear during interviews that other community members had had negative media experiences; participants in this study were not the only ones.[16] Second, some might argue there is a risk of stress transference in a situation like Pike River – that negative emotional reactions to the media will

[12] In contrast, participants in Muller and Gawenda's research on media coverage of the Black Saturday bushfires had lost property while others had lost friends or family members (see Muller and Gawenda, above n 8, 219). Similarly, some of the participants in a study into the aftermath of the Virginia Tech shootings were survivors and some were family members of the victims: Walsh-Childers et al, above n 8, 191.

[13] The entrance to the Pike River mine is remote and inaccessible and no reporters had access to it in the days following the explosion. Further, the two men who survived the blast were not available for comment and there was a general shortage of information.

[14] Some media interviewees in Cheer and Rosanowski's study felt that obtaining potentially distressing images and information was 'justified on the basis of the overall scale of the disaster, and that they were recording history': Cheer and Rosanowski, above n 9, 16.

[15] This approach was adopted so that interviews could be conducted in an ethical and sensitive manner and so that that no-one felt pressured to take part in the study. For an alternative approach using randomly selected participants, see Muller and Gawenda, above n 8, 216.

[16] Participants provided the names of other people they knew to have had concerns, assuming that they were taking part in the study. It was to be expected, however, that there would be people who were tired of approaches from the media who did not wish to speak to researchers either.

have been caused by the immensely stressful situation the families were facing rather than by anything that the media was doing. To ameliorate this risk, participants were specifically asked to identify the impact of the media's conduct in the aftermath of the explosions. Psychological research has also confirmed that media behaviour can exacerbate already traumatic situations.[17] Third, since the interviews related to a time of extreme stress which had occurred some months earlier, there is a risk that memories could have been distorted or that feelings could have changed or taken on a different complexion. Participants were therefore asked about more recent media contact so potential distortion effects could be identified and a fuller picture obtained. Fourth, it should be reiterated that analysis of the interviews is still in progress. Although the authors conducted all of the interviews themselves and have re-read all transcripts, full analysis has not yet been completed. As a result, the quotes in this chapter are drawn from just five of the seventeen interviews.

The 'media' is often referred to in this chapter as a collective group. It is acknowledged that there is a degree of artificiality in describing the many individual reporters, journalists, editors and photographers covering the Pike River story in this way. It is also acknowledged that only some of those covering the Pike River story engaged in the practices described in this chapter. The study is, however, concerned with how the acts of reporters, journalists, editors and photographers were experienced by those in whom they were interested. Since those individuals experienced the media as a group, they will sometimes be so characterised here. Further, although many of the experiences described in this chapter are negative, it is recognised that media has an important public interest role to play in the aftermath of disasters[18] and that media interaction can be a

[17] Henna Haravuori, Laura Suomalainen, Noora Berg, Olli Kiviruusu and Mauri Marttunen, 'Effects of Media Exposure on Adolescents Traumatized in a School Shooting' (2011) 24 *Journal of Traumatic Stress* 70, 75 which suggests that merely being approached by journalists, and especially being interviewed, had a significant effect on posttraumatic distress in traumatised adolescents. See also, Judith A Libow 'Traumatized Children and the News Media' (1992) 62 *American Journal of Orthopsychiatry* 379; Englund et al, above n 8, 27; J Sykes and K Green, 'The Dangers of Dealing with Journalists' (Paper presented at the Australian and New Zealand Communications Association conference, Brisbane, July 2003) 7; Alexander McFarlane, 'Victims of Trauma and the News Media' (letter to editor) (1986) 145 *Medical Journal of Australia* 664; Kari Koljonen, Pentti Raittila and Jari Väliverronen, 'Crisis Journalism at a Crossroads? Finnish Journalists' Reflections on their Profession after Two School Shooting Cases' (2011) 5 *Journalism Practice* 719, 724 (where the authors note that crisis psychologists have recommended that journalists avoid interviewing victims or, at least, refrain from asking emotionally loaded questions).

[18] Many participants acknowledged, for example that the media was a vital source of information for them in the hours following the explosion (see also, Ann Shearer, *Survivors and the Media* (London: Broadcasting Standards Council, 1991), 13 and

positive experience, especially if family members and survivors maintain their sense of control over the interview process.[19]

Finally, as the number of participants is small, this research does not produce quantitative data or generate any statistically significant results. The material is, however, rich in depth and detail and offers real insight into the subjective experiences and responses of the participants. With care, the responses can be used to draw conclusions about the likely impact of media attention on people who experience stress, trauma and grief in future accidents, disasters and other tragedies.

## 7.4 What the study tells us: preliminary observations about the media's physical presence

### *7.4.1 The media's physical presence – how was it experienced?*

Nearly every participant in the Pike River study spoke of the oppressive presence of photographers, reporters and journalists both in public and in or around their homes.[20] They explained, and contemporaneous footage shows, that on any occasion when the families came together as a group – for example, for information meetings in Greymouth or for the bus trip up to the mine – reporters, journalists and photographers would gather in

Marla Perez-Lugo 'Media Uses in Disaster Situations: A New Focus on the Impact Phase' (2004) 74 *Sociological Inquiry* 210, 217) and that it played an important role in raising mine safety awareness and communicating to the public the families' desire for body recovery (see, on related issues, Di Powell 'Media Intrusion into Grief' (1990) 57 *Media Information Australia* 24, 28–9; Pantti et al, above n 7, 156–7; Richard D Waters 'Tracing the Impact of Media Relations and Television Coverage on US Charitable Relief Fundraising: An Application of Agenda-Setting Theory across Three Natural Disasters' (2013) 25 *Journal of Public Relations Research* 329; Ano Lobb, Nancy Mock and Paul L Hutchinson, 'Traditional and Social Media Coverage and Charitable Giving following the 2010 Earthquake in Haiti' (2012) 27 *Prehospital and Disaster Medicine* 319; Zarqa S Ali, 'Media Myths and Realities in Natural Disasters' (2013) 2 *European Journal of Business and Social Sciences* 125, 127; Mihye Seo, Shaojing Sun, Andy J Merolla and Shuangyue Zhang, 'Willingness to Help Following the Sichuan Earthquake: Modelling the Effects of Media Involvement, Stress, Trust, and Relational Resources' (2012) 39 *Communication Research* 3, 4).

19 See Sykes and Green, above n 17; Joseph Scanlon and Conrad McCallum, 'Media Coverage of Mass Death: Not Always Unwelcome' (1999) 14(3) *Australian Journal of Emergency Management* 55, 57.

20 The 'pack' phenomenon occurs because different domestic and international media organisations send their own reporters, photographers, and camera operators to enable them to capture the story for themselves: Kim Walsh-Childers, Norman Lewis and Jeff Neely, 'Twice Victimized: Lessons from the Media Mob at Virginia Tech' (Research Paper, University of Florida, August 2008), 4–5; Philip Castle, 'Journalism and Trauma: Proposals for Change' (1999) 7 *Asia Pacific Media Educator* 143, 147. Walsh-Childers et al, above n 8, 198–9, characterised the influx of journalists in the aftermath of the Virginia Tech shootings as an 'invasion'.

large numbers. Family members would then be approached for interviews as they walked to and from their vehicles. Some participants also believed that members of the media knew their car number plates and were following people to and from the meetings.[21] In addition, photographers would crowd around family members in public places to take photographs, or use zoom lenses to capture images from a distance.[22]

All participants in the study found these activities to be stressful and unwelcome. A typical description was provided by male participant 02:

> Yeah there was cameras, cameras going off everywhere I'd say hundreds of cameras. Some of them had two or three they were just like this click click click at all different angles at you. We had to hold my [relative] back from sconing one. He was just ready to go over and kick over their gears. They were just right in their face he could feel the zoom just zoom right into him.

Another participant said:

> Actually we couldn't even get off of our bus, I don't know what the other buses were like but when we first arrived the media were right up against the door of the bus and the police had to come and move people away and then they only removed them enough for just basically a person to make a tunnel between the bus and the Pike River building in town ... That was really wrong because the pressure of the people and the main road was all media, and because all you could see was microphones and cameras and everything else, and we only had this short little distance to get into the building, that I stood at the top of the step and I was fearful to actually go through there, it was like going through a tunnel of I dunno, claustrophobic ... It was the worst experience. (Female 06)

Some of the participants in the study also received multiple telephone calls and visits from reporters and photographers in their homes. In the most extreme case, these visits began as early as 6 am and continued until very late at night for several days.[23] An example is the experience of male participant 02's family:

> Yeah so that started and then there was knocks on the door and bangs on the windows from morning to night, late at night 11 and 12 at night we were getting bangs on the doors and windows ... It was miles too too much...One day we counted 19 [reporters and photographers] here at once.

[21] Female participants 06 and 09 both expressed this view.

[22] For discussion of the intrusive impact of recording equipment, see Roger Simpson and William Coté, *Covering Violence: A Guide to Ethical Reporting about Victims and Trauma*, 2nd edn (New York: Columbia University Press, 2006), 144–6.

[23] Door knocking, frequent phone calls and 'setting up camp' outside a person's home are all behaviours noted in other studies: see, e.g., Walsh-Childers et al, above n 8, 198; Elliott, above n 8, 68. The Pike River study supports the view, expressed by Walsh-Childers et al, above n 8, 201, that, '[e]ven journalists who adhere to ethical codes that urge professionals to treat victims with respect ... can unwittingly create harm through their sheer numbers'.

Persistent telephone calls from reporters were also common. For example:

> Oh gosh yes, we had, and my kids said, 'We've had so many people' and I said, 'Well how many people?' and they said, 'Well probably about 6 or 7 people knocking on the door' and then yeah the phone calls were just non-stop . . . they just they were exhausted by the phone calls because it they never stopped. And okay a lot of them were friends and community members wanting to check that everything was okay with us and, um, but there was also a lot of media and radio stations ringing up and they just had enough. (Female 01)

Many participants used the word 'privacy' to explain what they were seeking – and being denied – in the days following the explosion. And although it is not suggested that all the media's activities in the aftermath of Pike River would be actionable breaches of privacy, many of them conform to theoretical descriptions of privacy interference. Those definitions connecting privacy to a desire for accessibility are particularly apposite. For example, it seems clear that on occasions the media undermined what James Rachels identifies as the cornerstone of privacy: 'our ability to control who has access to us and to information about us'.[24] Likewise, to use Moreham's own definition of the privacy interest, individual members of the media obtained both unwanted sensory access and informational access to the participants.[25]

The study also supports the view of theorists who argue that *physical* privacy – freedom from unwanted watching, listening, recording – should be recognised as a vital part of the privacy interest.[26] Concern that private

[24] James Rachels, 'Why Privacy is Important' (1975) 4 *Philosophy & Public Affairs* 323, 326.

[25] NA Moreham, 'Privacy in the Common Law: A Doctrinal and Theoretical Analysis' (2005) 121 *Law Quarterly Review* 628. See also Ruth E Gavison 'Privacy and the Limits of the Law' (1980) 89 *Yale Law Journal* 421, 423; Tom Gerety 'Redefining Privacy' (1977) 12 *Harvard Civil Rights-Civil Liberties Law Review* 233, 265; Judith Wagner DeCew, 'The Scope of Privacy in Law and Ethics' (1986) 5 *Law and Philosophy* 145, 155–9; Kirsty Hughes, 'A Behavioural Understanding of Privacy and its Implications for Privacy Law' (2012) 75 *Modern Law Review* 806, 808–11; Chris DL Hunt, 'Conceptualizing Privacy and Elucidating its Importance: Foundational Considerations for the Development of Canada's Fledgling Privacy Tort' (2011) 37 *Queen's Law Journal* 167, 196–201.

[26] As well as 'informational privacy' which relates to unwanted access to private information about a person: see Moreham, above n 25 and NA Moreham 'Beyond Information: Physical Privacy in English Law' (2014) 73 *Cambridge Law Journal* 350. See also Gavison, above n 25, 428–40; Daniel J Solove, 'A Taxonomy of Privacy' (2006) 154 *University of Pennsylvania Law Review* 477, 489 ff; Gerety, above n 25, 261 ff; Stanley I Benn, 'Privacy, Freedom and Respect for Persons', in J Roland Pennock and John W Chapman (eds), *Privacy*, NOMOS vol XIII (New York: Atherton Press, 1971) 1, 3–4; Rachels, above n 24, 326; DeCew, above n 25, 153–8; Ernest van den Haag, 'On Privacy' in J Pennock and J Chapman (eds) *Privacy*, NOMOS vol XIII (New York: Atherton Press, 1971) 149, 149–53; Rachel Mulheron, 'A Potential Framework for Privacy? A Reply to *Hello!*' (2006) 69 *Modern Law Review* 679, 696–701; Hunt, above n 25, 201;

images of or information about them might be published was clearly part of participants' objection to the media's constant presence but it was consistently expressed as a secondary concern.[27] The principal objection was to the media's physical presence and their persistent attempts to get something from the grieving friends and families that they did not want to give. To use Warren and Brandeis's words, participants wanted to be 'let alone'.[28] These sentiments accord with the view of academics such as Ernest van den Haag that a key part of the privacy interest is the right to exclude others from watching, utilising or invading one's private realm[29] and, as Judith Wagner De Cew says, that people's privacy is diminished when someone gains physical proximity to them by *inter alia* observing their body, behaviour or interactions.[30] Indeed, the strength of the participants' objections to the physical presence of the media suggests that Tom Gerety is right to say that physical intrusion 'brings us to the core of our expectations and intuitions about privacy and hence of our rights to it'.[31]

### *7.4.2 The effect of the media's physical encroachment*

The physical intrusiveness of the media in the early aftermath of the explosions had a significant impact upon the participants' experience of, and ability to cope with, an already stressful situation.[32] This section will

Raymond Wacks, *Privacy and Media Freedom* (Oxford: Oxford University Press, 2013), ch. 6; Hughes, above n 25, 810–1. See also Richard B Parker, 'A Definition of Privacy' (1974) 27 *Rutgers Law Review* 275, 275–88.

27 There has been little research done on the impact of images of emotional pain on those who appear in them, but see Joan Deppa, with Maria Russell, Dona Hayes, and Elizabeth Lynne Flocke, *The Media and Disasters: Pan Am 103* (New York: New York University Press, 1994), 33. It has also been argued that media consumers often view such images as an unwarranted breach of privacy: Jennifer E Brown, 'News Photographs and the Pornography of Grief' (1987) 2 *Journal of Mass Media Ethics* 75, 78. In contrast, Muller and Gawenda, above n 8, 173–4, said that survivors of the Black Saturday bushfires were unconcerned if they cried spontaneously during media encounters unless they felt that the interviewer was trying to make them break down.

28 Samuel D Warren and Louis D Brandeis, 'The Right to Privacy' (1890) 4 *Harvard Law Review* 193.

29 van den Haag, above n 26, 149.

30 DeCew, above n 25, 156.

31 Gerety, above n 25, 265.

32 This is consistent with previous studies showing that an 'over-abundance' of journalists at an incident causes considerable additional stress for victims. See, e.g., Walsh-Childers et al, above n 20, 9 (reporting that students felt 'stalked' by the media in the aftermath of the Virginia Tech mass shooting); Walsh-Childers et al, above n 8, 201; Agustín Palacios, José Cueli, José Camacho, Ramón Clériga, Pablo Cuevas, Jaime Ayala, and Linda Cossoff, 'The Traumatic Effect of Mass Communication in the Mexico City Earthquake: Crisis Intervention and Preventive Measures' (1986) 13 *International Review of Psycho-Analysis* 279, 282 (in relation to the effect on victims and the wider community from a saturation of television and radio reporting). It should be stressed that this study has not investigated signs or assessed participants for clinical trauma symptoms.

explore these impacts, suggesting that that media attention adversely affected family members in three main ways: first, it communicated a lack of respect for family members as people who were suffering deeply; second, it caused fear and anxiety; and third, it undermined individuals' freedom of action, self-expression and ability to connect with others. The relationship between these reasons, as described by participants, and the reasons for protecting privacy advanced by privacy theorists, will also be explored.

*7.4.2.1 Seeing the story, not the person – undermining dignity* Interviewees' responses to the media's behaviour in the aftermath of the Pike River explosions reinforced the relationship between privacy and dignity recognised by theorists and judges alike. According to Immanuel Kant, the principle that one should respect the intrinsic value of all persons and seek, insofar as possible, to further their ends as well as one's own is 'the supreme limiting condition of every man's freedom of action'.[33] It demands that you should, '[a]ct in such a way that you treat humanity, whether in your own person or in the person of another, always at the same time as an end and never simply as a means'.[34] It is this entitlement to respect, to be treated as an 'end' and not simply as a 'means', that many theorists argue underpins the privacy interest. For example, Stanley Benn argues that that the 'general principle of privacy' is grounded upon a more general 'principle … of respect for persons'.[35] To treat a person merely as something to be looked at, listened to, found out about, or reported against his or her wishes is to ignore his or her right to respect as a person. It is to

> treat people as objects or specimens – like 'dirt' – and not as subjects with sensibilities, ends, and aspirations of their own, morally responsible for their own decisions, and capable, as mere specimens are not, of reciprocal relations with the observer …[36]

Others agree. In their celebrated article on the American law, Warren and Brandeis describe the interests protected by privacy as 'spiritual' and as closely connected to an individual's 'inviolate personality'.[37] And in

[33] Immanuel Kant, *Grounding for the Metaphysics of Morals; with On a Supposed Right to Lie Because of Philanthropic Concerns*, translated by J Ellington, 3rd edn (Indianapolis: Hackett Publishing, 1993), 430–1.

[34] *Ibid.*, 429. [35] Benn, above n 26, 8–9. [36] *Ibid.*, 6–7.

[37] Warren and Brandeis, above n 28, 205 and 197 respectively. See also Jeffrey H Reiman, 'Privacy, Intimacy and Personhood' (1976) 6 *Philosophy & Public Affairs* 26, 39; David Feldman, 'Secrecy, Dignity or Autonomy? Views of Privacy as a Civil Liberty' (1994) 47 *Current Legal Problems* 41, 54–8 (especially 55); Harry Kalven Jr, 'Privacy in Tort Law – were Warren and Brandeis wrong?' (1966) 31 *Law and Contemporary Problems* 326; Edward Schils, 'Privacy: Its Constitution and Vicissitudes' (1966) 31 *Law and Contemporary Problems* 281, 306. In the doctrinal context, see Peter Cane, *The Anatomy*

the New Zealand Supreme Court case of *Brooker* v. *Police*, Thomas J held that privacy is 'closely allied to the fundamental value underlying and supporting all other rights: the dignity and worth of the human person'.[38]

It is suggested that the objection to being treated as simply something to be looked at, found out about, photographed and reported on was at the heart of many participants' dislike of the media's conduct following the Pike River disaster. Indeed, the language of participants often echoed that of Kant and Benn: as male participant 02 said: '[w]e just seemed violated by them all the time'.[39] Participants also repeatedly expressed objections to a perceived lack of respect, humanity and empathy from some members of the media; they felt that they were 'just a story'.[40] As one female participant said:

> You're being robbed of your privacy really in that you're being watched the whole time. And you know we're all, as you can imagine, just so upset and even when you're sort of wiping your tear away they would be clicking in their cameras. Like they didn't even care, they just wanted a story.
>
> ... And yeah I can remember hearing them yeah not taking no for an answer and kept on talking and talking you know even though they'd been asked to leave the property. Oh but you know can you say a few comments on this? No consideration for how the family was feeling.

This theme of a lack of empathy or acknowledgement of the immensely difficult situation they were in was expressed strongly by almost all participants in the Pike River study:

*of Tort Law* (Oxford: Hart Publishing, 1997), 71–4 and Edward J Bloustein, 'Privacy as an Aspect of Human Dignity: An Answer to Dean Prosser' (1964) 39 *NYU Law Review* 962, 1002–3.

[38] *Brooker* v. *Police* [2007] 3 NZLR 91, [252]. See also *Hosking* v. *Runting* [2004] NZCA 34; [2005] 1 NZLR 1, [239] (Tipping J) ('*Hosking*') and *Campbell* v. *Mirror Group Newspapers* [2004] UKHL 22, [2004] 2 AC 457, [12] (Lord Nicholls) and [51] (Lord Hoffmann) ('*Campbell*').

[39] This language has also been used by participants in previous studies and Inquiries: see, e. g., Leveson, above n 9, vol. II, pt. F, 505 (para. [3.2]), 540 (paras. [1.7] and [1.10]), 548 (para. [3.4]), 553 (para. [3.27]) and 602 (para. [2.44])) where Leveson LJ spoke of the 'commodification' of individuals by the media; Walsh-Childers et al, above n 8, 202 (where the authors speak of the '"trauma ... experienced when journalists treated them [survivors and grieving family] as means to an end"'); and Englund et al, above n 8, 27 (who say that some participants felt 'violated' by the media's behaviour).

[40] Male participant 02. The same sentiment was also expressed by female participants 01, 06, 07 and 09. The importance of being treated as people, rather than merely the subjects of an interview, has been repeatedly expressed by participants in previous studies: see, e.g., Muller and Gawenda, above n 8, 163 et seq; W Bilboe, above n 10, 94–7; Walsh-Childers et al, above n 8, 195–8; J Deppa et al, above n 27, 29. Further, participants in the Pike River project and earlier studies make it clear that journalists are more likely to get interviews when they approach people respectfully and convey genuine concern: see Muller and Gawenda, above n 8, 163–8.

As for trying to get to the cars [following news of the second explosion], I mean we were approached by media people ... And I think I got quite short with one of them and I said for God's sake just leave us alone ... it's like can't you see that I'm holding someone who is physically collapsed and can't you see that? ... It was all too fast; it was too oh they were awful. The media were awful. And we were in just such a horrendous state, all of us ... (Female 07)

Another participant said:

I remember a woman collapsing at the meeting when she was told of the second explosion and she was carried out ... it was her husband that was in the mine. She was carried out to a waiting ambulance and the cameras got that and it's just it was just so intrusive. (Female 01)

There was a clear sense from many participants that members of the media wanted something from them; that journalists and photographers were there to further their own ends and uninterested in the needs or pain of the people they were covering. Female participant 01 objected to both the process of obtaining the information and the resulting story generated:

I know it's their job and without a good story they don't get paid but ... it's horrible, it's like they're hounds to a wolf, they'll be straight for it: click, click, click. No permission to use my photo or anything else like that ....

... they want the glory of it, they just. One thing I've learnt you give a newspaper a story and they take what they want, take it out of context and print anything that sells a good paper or good magazine article ... They take it out of context. You might say something, add something later on, but that something later on would fit nicely with what I said first and they sort of the connect the two and they've got a story ...[41]

*7.4.2.2 Feelings of insecurity and lack of safety* A second theme to emerge strongly from preliminary analysis of the interviews is the connection between persistent media interest – following, photography, telephone calls and interview requests – and physical fear and insecurity. The word 'safety' was used time and again as participants, particularly women, described their responses to the media presence. For example, describing what she called a 'physical attack' on a young woman present, female participant 07 said:

[41] Previous studies appear to support this participant's impression that material that is the most painful to grieving relatives is often the most attractive to journalists and their editors. Research from the 1980s shows that more than half of 'Pictures of the Year' recognised by the National Press Photographers Association and the University of Missouri School of Journalism from 1944 to 1982 depicted violence and tragedy: Brown, above n 27, 76 (citing H Goodwin, *Groping for Ethics in Journalism* (Ames: Iowa State University, 1983)).

One of the journalists who was trying to get this microphone into their face stood on the back of [X's] shoe. She almost fell over but her shoe got broken in the process and . . . I just felt physically frightened for all the family members who were there . . . The physical presence . . . meant that everybody was more congested and so it was harder to feel physically safe . . . these journalists were getting physically too close it was totally inappropriate and if she if [X] hadn't had her arm linked with one or at least one of the other [people] on one side and maybe the other side as well . . . she actually would have fallen over . . . That's how full on, physical it was . . . And I felt quite angry about that because were dealing with enough, we don't need you guys coming in and doing this.

Another explained why she stayed in groups during that period:

[I]f you were walking out by yourself, well this is what I thought if I were walking by myself, you wouldn't feel safe to walk to the car by yourself 'cause you, you know . . .

they'd sort of pounce on you and start asking you questions. You know? That's what you felt like . . . And makes you quite anxious too. A lot of people that have anxiety through this media. Sort of pouncing on you all the time. You sort of become a bit paranoid . . . When we needed to go to town and that we had to go pick up some food, stuff, you were sort of looking around sort of paranoid, you didn't know who to trust. Because they were following, they were following people. (Female 09)

In an example reminiscent of Stanley Benn – who says that if an unknown stranger sat watching your house all day, you might become concerned that he or she was 'casing the joint'[42] – one participant explained the feeling of being watched in her home:

We also had a situation of where our house . . . had a vacant block of land at the back of it and it was noted that there was a vehicle at the back of that block of land with a camera pointed on the back door of the house . . . Now I don't know the reason for that but to me that's really invasion of privacy . . . It's so scary because you don't know what that's being used for. (Female 06)

But perhaps the most acute effects of this physical encroachment were felt by a pre-teenage boy. His mother explained the impact on him of the media surrounding the bus after they had been up to the entrance of the mine on the morning of Sunday 21 November:

He just fell to bits and was crying and all that sort of side of it but he was scared to get off the bus as well because I don't know why because he just felt he didn't know what was going on, ah well he knew but, how do I explain it . . . We had just been up to the mine, and so all the other emotions and everything else were running through our adrenaline and everything . . . it was just a matter of wanting to get into that building so that we could get a cup of tea or relax or do whatever we were

[42] Benn, above n 26, 6.

going to do next, that it was like we couldn't move, we couldn't do anything, it was a fear, ah we just didn't know what was going to happen next ... I had never had that feeling before it's just that, just scary to go forward. (Female 06)

The conduct of photographers had long-term effects on that boy:

Well after the business with the bus my [son] just had a total freak out of cameras. It didn't matter, even friends would take photos and that went on for a year and a half afterwards. Every time he saw a camera he would hide, he would cover his face, he didn't want it to be used. We had a situation ... the media were at the airport ... trying to get information on [a public interest event], they were doing their normal reports ... a particular TV camera was there with one of the ladies who had approached us a couple of times during the Pike River situation. So my son knew her face and he bolted and hid ... We could not find him. I had to get the people to do with Air New Zealand to give me a hand to try and find him. And he had hidden himself ... And I said to him why have you done that, and he said camera was going to be on TV – I don't want to be on TV, I don't want to, I don't want to. Something simple as that getting him into a frenzy and that was months after like it happened in November and this was towards the middle of January, end of January ... He just totally hid himself ... For at least twelve months we had problems with even just trying to get friends to take photos. (Female 06)

Given that one psychological study has shown 'that being approached by journalists and especially being interviewed had a significant effect on posttraumatic distress in traumatised adolescents', this boy's reaction is perhaps unsurprising.[43] The responses of the adult female participants are also consistent with Sheila Brown's observations, in her study of the reactions of women to the use of CCTV surveillance in public space, that exaggerated visibility can create insecurity[44] and with statements by female celebrities about the fear induced by 'stalking' photographers.[45] The connection between observation and physical fear is also implicitly recognised in criminal measures combating harassment and voyeurism both in New Zealand and the United Kingdom.[46] Academic discussion of

[43] Haravuori et al., above n 17, 75. See also Libow, above n 17; Englund et al, above n 8, 27; Sykes and Green, above n 17, 7; McFarlane, above n 17; Koljonen et al, above n 17, 724.

[44] Sheila Brown, 'What's the Problem, Girls? CCTV and the Gendering of Public Safety' in Clive Norris, Jade Moran and Gary Armstrong (eds), *Surveillance, Closed Circuit Television and Social Control* (Aldershot: Ashgate, 1998) 207, 218. She therefore criticised the widespread use of CCTV in public places on the basis that in one sense it perpetuated the problem of the 'male gaze' which many of the women had complained was a factor making them feel uncomfortable in the town centre.

[45] See, e.g., actress Sienna Miller's evidence to the Leveson Inquiry (Inquiry transcript, Day 7 (AM) 24 November 2011, 24) and singer Lorde's comments at www.nzherald.co.nz/entertainment/news/article.cfm?c_id=1501119&objectid=11249341.

[46] See, in New Zealand, the Harassment Act 1997 (NZ) and the Crimes (Intimate Covert Filming) Amendment Act 2006 (NZ) and in England, section 67 of the Sexual Offences Act 2003 (UK) (the voyeurism provision), and Protection from Harassment Act 1998 (UK).

this important connection is, however, surprisingly limited. The strength with which safety concerns were communicated in this study indicates that further investigation is needed.

### 7.4.3 *Undermining autonomy – restricting freedom of action, expression and intimacy*

Finally, the study supports the view – also expressed by theorists and judges – that privacy facilitates freedom of action, expression and intimacy. The relationship between privacy and autonomy is well articulated in the case law. For example, in New Zealand's leading privacy case *Hosking* v. *Runting*, Tipping J held that '[i]t is the essence of the dignity and personal autonomy and wellbeing of all human beings that some aspects of their lives should be able to remain private if they so wish'.[47] Similar observations were made in *Campbell* v. *MGN*, the leading English privacy decision. Lord Hoffmann there said that the breach of confidence/privacy action is about 'the protection of human autonomy and dignity – the right to control the dissemination of information about one's private life and the right to the esteem and respect of other people'.[48]

Commonwealth courts have yet to articulate what is meant by 'autonomy' in this context but it is clearly something narrower than the decisional, liberty-based conception of autonomy applied in many European Court of Human Rights and United States privacy cases.[49] Instead, where privacy relates to an individual's right to preserve inaccessibility, it supports autonomy in a more limited sense; it creates a right to determine whether and in what circumstances others have access to one's personal affairs. Cobb J describes 'liberty' in this sense in the American misappropriation case of *Pavesich* v. *New England Life Insurance*:

> Liberty includes the right to live as one will, so long as that will does not interfere with the rights of another or of the public. One may desire to live a life of seclusion; another may desire to live a life of publicity; still another may wish to live a life of privacy as to certain matters, and of publicity as to others. One may wish to live a life of toil, where his work is of a nature that keeps him constantly before the public gaze, while another may wish to live a life of research and contemplation, only moving before the public at such times and under such circumstances as may be necessary to his actual existence. Each is entitled to a liberty of choice as to his manner of life, and neither an individual nor the public has a right to arbitrarily take away from this liberty.[50]

[47] *Hosking* [2005] 1 NZLR 1, [239].
[48] *Campbell* [2004] 2 AC 457, [12] (Lord Nicholls) and [51] (Lord Hoffmann).
[49] See, e.g., *Roe* v. *Wade*, 410 US 113 (1974) and *Pretty* v. *United Kingdom* [2002] 35 EHRR 1.
[50] *Pavesich* v. *New England Life Insurance*, 50 SE 68, 70 (SC Ga 1905).

If the word 'autonomy' is substituted for 'liberty' (and it is suggested that they are interchangeable in this context), this passage nicely expresses the relationship between autonomy and privacy in the English and New Zealand context. It also provides a framework for understanding many of the difficulties that intense media attention caused for the participants in the Pike River study.

*7.4.3.1 Avoiding the media – cut yourself off or submit to unwanted media attention* Participants felt that they had two choices in the immediate aftermath of the Pike River explosions: to submit to unwanted photography and media approaches or hide themselves away from others. This had a significant impact on their freedom of action, especially since many responded to the dilemma by staying at home as much as possible. For example:

> You know speaking out loud if you were speaking to [my husband] about something, about Pike River things, and you were out in public like the supermarket you sort of become more aware of that you sort of didn't talk about it until you were behind closed doors sort of like that you know? Yeah it was terrible. There's only so many places you felt safe really . . . [It was] sort of like [being] a hostage in your own environment . . . It was a bit on your privacy. Nothing was a secret anymore . . . (Female 09)

Many also avoided telecommunications. Male participant 02 became so frustrated with persistent media calls that he threw his mobile telephone in the Otira River. Another said:

> And I know that when I come back to [place of residence] you know I just sort the children out, we were getting phone calls here asking if, if this was the [X] household we were told basically that to hang up on them sort of phone calls, and not get into conversation but I know, our number wasn't even listed at the time so we were you know . . . [wondering] how the numbers were leaking . . . I just said that at the moment, I'd answer the phone sort of thing and don't handle the phone calls. (Female 09)

At Pike River, the fact that many participants felt that they could only go out in public or answer their telephones if they were prepared to deal with the media had the effect of cutting them off from their community and support networks. This is a significant loss given that communities have been shown to be an important source of both emotional and practical support in times of crisis.[51] One mother explained that her

[51] Nikki A Hawkins, Daniel N McIntosh, Roxane Cohen Silver and E Alison Holman, 'Early Responses to School Violence: A Qualitative Analysis of Students' and Parents' Immediate Reactions to the Shootings at Columbine High School' (2007) 4 *Journal of Emotional Abuse* 197, 212–3.

teenaged children did not want to answer the phone even though she was trying to ring them with support and information:

> Because I was [somewhere else] and I was saying to them, I will ring you with information as it comes to hand so . . . I don't have caller display or anything . . . [But when I came back] they said, 'Mum we're just not answering any more phone calls. We're just not', because they just felt like every time they put the phone down the phone'd ring again and they were just over it, so over it. (Female 01)

Media attention also prevented many participants from obtaining one-on-one contact with others. One participant explained that just walking down the road to visit a friend involved dealing with unwanted media attention:

> We wandered down to [X's] which is [Y's] friend, we went down there to see whether she was okay. This was about three days later and we were followed by a camera walking out of our place to their place. If we can't do that there's something wrong you know? (Male 02)

Another explained how it prevented her from reaching out to other family members after the meeting informing them of the second explosion:

> I really hated it because it was a really private moment for the families. We just wanted to be with one another and support one another but we couldn't do that outside because when you stopped and talked to another family member and you had your arms around them the cameras were on you and they were just there. (Female 01)

These comments highlight the importance of the observation, made by many privacy scholars, that although it is sometimes regarded as an individualistic right, privacy plays an important role in the formation of maintenance of relationships and social networks. As Stanley Benn says: 'one cannot carry on personal conversations under the same condition as an open seminar'.[52] It follows that friendship and wider social interactions are dependent on people's ability to include some and exclude others from their inner circle.[53] The study shows how strong that need can be in the aftermath of a fatal disaster and how intense media interest can prevent it from being met.

[52] Benn, above n 26, 18. See also Charles Fried, 'Privacy' (1968) 77 *Yale Law Journal* 475; Rachels, above n 24, 330; Feldman, above n 37, 5; Graeme Laurie, *Genetic Privacy: A Challenge to Medico-Legal Norms* (Cambridge: Cambridge University Press, 2002), 7; Thomas Nagel, 'Concealment and Exposure' (1998) 27 *Philosophy & Public Affairs* 3; Paul Freund, 'Privacy: One Concept or Many?' in J Roland Pennock and John W Chapman (eds), *Privacy*, NOMOS vol XIII (New York: Atherton Press, 1971) 195–6; Hughes, above n 25, 821–3; Hunt, above n 25, 213–7.

[53] Feldman, above n 37.

*7.4.3.2 Hiding one's emotions* Many respondents also felt that because of the media attention, they needed to put a brave face on when they were out in public. As male participant 02 explained: 'sometimes you just felt like dissolving into tears but you couldn't 'because they are on you'. Concern about being filmed in private moments of grief or anguish was particularly distressing.[54] For some, this was due in part to a belief that the media preyed on those who displayed emotion:

> You've got to go out you've got to portray yourself as coping and everything else that won't sell a story, 'Oh she's just getting on with her life' and so that's a lot of the reason why I go out there .... You show them any emotion and then the camera's there and guarantee you'll they'll get a shot ... If you're crying, you're grieving, it's a good story, there's a good photo in that. If you're portrayed as just the average everyday person that won't sell. (Female 01)

Another participant said:

> I kept my emotions at bay, because I know once you start, the media put in something, but to be honest they do play on the emotional side of situations they look for the downhearted, the sorrowing and all that side of it because it sells the story. And I knew if I gave in to that side of it, it would be worse ... I put a barrier up. (Female 06)

These experiences are consistent with the connection that sociologists and theorists have identified between privacy and emotional release. As Nagel says, the requirements of self-presentation inherent in the gaze are incompatible with the natural expression of strong or intimate feeling.[55] People who wish to comply with societal expectations around emotional display or to avoid revealing their emotions to strangers are therefore likely to censor their emotions in the face of unwanted observation.[56] This is exactly what many family members did after the explosions.

Theorists and psychologists are therefore right to stress the important role that privacy plays in facilitating emotional release. As Westin acknowledges, this emotional release is particularly important in times of loss, grief and sorrow, such as that experienced by the participants in this study.[57] And Thomas Nagel rightly says that, by allowing people to retreat to an environment where they can 'be themselves', privacy ensures

[54] Media filming of such private moments caused the greatest discomfort after Black Saturday: Muller and Gawenda, above n 8, 178–9. See also the discussion above, page 133.

[55] Nagel, above n 52, 19–20.

[56] See Sidney M Jourard, 'Some Psychological Aspects of Privacy' (1966) 31 *Law and Contemporary Problems* 307, 309.

[57] Alan F Westin acknowledges the importance of privacy in providing emotional release in times of loss, shock or sorrow: *Privacy and Freedom* (New York: Atheneum, 1967), 36. Non-consensual filming of moments of grief interferes with that process: see Brown, above n 27, 78

that the 'full private reality' of emotions such as such as grief, anger, self-doubt and pain are protected from the knowledge and, more importantly, the direct perception of others. This in turn facilitates their expression.[58]

The Pike River study shows that sometimes people need opportunities for private emotional release outside the confines of their home. This is particularly the case where, as at Pike River, they have no choice but to receive news of their loved ones' fate in a public setting. Many family members were understandably reluctant to show the full extent of their emotions with the world's media looking on. However, the study demonstrates that the cost of emotional suppression following trauma and loss can be high. As female participant 06 explained:

> I put a barrier up . . . it got me through it but it meant when it came to the grieving process it took a heck of a lot longer, yeah, and everything I bottled up was finally able to start coming out.

## 7.5 Conclusion

The impact of media coverage of the Pike River mine explosion on the families and friends of those who died reveals a great deal about the effects of intense media interest on its subjects. This chapter offers a preliminary snapshot of one aspect of the Pike River study: the effect of the media's physical presence in the days following the explosion. The large numbers of reporters and photographers outside homes and family meetings, the persistent following and requests for comment, constant telephone calls and door-knocking intruded on family members who wished to be left alone to deal with the tragedy in private. On a practical level, this interfered with family members' ability to communicate with one another, to access practical and emotional support, and to engage with their communities. On an emotional level, it undermined their sense of dignity, safety, security, and autonomy at a time of great vulnerability.

The effect of the media's conduct at Pike River suggests that society still has many questions to ask about media treatment of individuals who are coming to terms with immense personal loss. This discussion of physical privacy – the first of many publications to be generated by the Pike River study – is designed to increase awareness of the effects of grief journalism, contribute to an assessment of the adequacy of current legal and regulatory responses to it, and, ultimately, to support arguments for change.

[58] See Nagel, above n 52, 18–20 and Westin, above n 57, 36.

# 8 Press freedom, the public interest and privacy

*Gavin Phillipson*

## 8.1 Introduction

It is generally accepted that the critical issue in most press-privacy cases is the balance struck between privacy and press freedom, and in particular, the view taken by the courts of the value to attach to press freedom in general and how strongly a particular publication engages the public interest. In explaining how conflicts between Articles 8 and 10[1] of the European Convention of Human Rights – respectively protecting privacy and freedom of expression – should be resolved, the European Court of Human Rights in Strasbourg has made the following key pronouncement:

> the decisive factor in balancing the protection of private life against freedom of expression should lie in the contribution that the published photos and articles make to a debate of general interest.[2]

English courts have generally followed this line. The chapter by Hughes and Richards in this volume[3] explains the methodology the English courts

I am particularly grateful to Andrew Kenyon for his patience and very helpful advice as an editor and organiser of the conference at Melbourne University at which an earlier version of this chapter was delivered.

1 Convention for the Protection of Human Rights and Fundamental Freedoms, opened for signature 4 November 1950, 213 UNTS 221 (entered into force 3 September 1953) ('European Convention of Human Rights'). Article 8 provides: '(1) Everyone has the right to respect for his private and family life, his home and his correspondence'. The second paragraph provides for restrictions only as they are provided for by law, in pursuit of a legitimate aim, such as the prevention of disorder or crime, or 'protection of the rights and freedoms of others' and are necessary in a democratic society to protect these other rights and interests and proportionate. Article 10 provides in para 1 that 'Everyone has the right to freedom of expression'; the second paragraph provides a similar set of exceptions to para 2 of Art. 8. Under the UK's Human Rights Act 1998, effect is given in domestic law to the Convention. Legislation must be interpreted compatibly with it if possible (s 3) while courts as public authorities under section 6(3)(a) must act compatibly with the Convention rights, something which requires regard to be had at the least, to the Convention rights when developing the common law, in this case, the extended action in breach of confidence.

2 The leading decision in *Von Hannover* v *Germany* (2005) 40 EHRR 1, [76].

3 Kirsty Hughes and Neil M Richards, 'The Atlantic Divide on Privacy and Free Speech'.

and Strasbourg use in weighing up the two rights against each other and some of the criteria employed in doing so. The purpose of this chapter is not to make a general exposition of the case law in this area; instead it seeks to isolate a number of trends in the jurisprudence that it argues are reconfiguring the balance the law strikes between the two rights. Indeed this essay makes what I hope is an unduly pessimistic argument: that privacy is starting to lose its fight with the press; not of course to the extent that it has decisively lost its ill-matched contest with the First Amendment in the US – English courts, unlike American ones, are still prepared to assess the 'value' of speech and some cases are still won by claimants[4] – but losing it nevertheless. Cases like *Naomi Campbell*,[5] *McKennitt* v. *Ash*,[6] *Mosley* v. *News Group Newspapers*[7] and – at Strasbourg – *Von Hannover* v. *Germany*[8] showed the courts taking a fairly robust line in protecting privacy from press public interest claims. However, I will argue that more recent cases – both domestic and at Strasbourg – disclose a number of emerging tendencies that are tilting the balance quite strongly in favour of press freedom, even in instances where I would contend that no real public interest is present. Strikingly, the way in which this has happened has strong parallels with the way that US judges in the 1940s and 1950s, under the growing influence of the First Amendment, began to expand the level of protection given to the press in privacy cases, as noted by Richards and Hughes's chapter in this volume.[9] They quote one study which found an

> expansion of the definition of 'the news' to encompass a wide variety of information, including private facts, and a reassessment of the significance of the news media to modern social life. We see the emergence of the concept of 'the public's right to know' about the world through the news media, and the ideas that the purpose of the news is not only to inform citizens about the complex workings of modern society but to generate public discourse.[10]

As will appear below, the English courts and Strasbourg are engineering a similar change, through expansion of the notion of 'public interest', and coming up with new or expanded reasons to find no reasonable

[4] Two recent examples, albeit in cases in which there was no attempt to advance a public interest justification for the particular publication were *Rocknroll* v. *News Group Newspapers* [2013] EWHC 24 (Ch) and *Weller* v. *Associated Newspapers* [2014] EWHC 1163. It is also noticeable that cases in which the judges advert clearly to possible harm to the children of the claimant have also been won: eg *K* v. *News Group Newspapers* [2011] EWCA Civ 439, esp [17].

[5] [2004] 2 WLR 1232.

[6] *McKennitt* v. *Ash* [2006] EWCA Civ 1714; [2008] QB 73, [8].

[7] [2008] EWHC 1777 (QB); [2008] EMLR 20.

[8] Above n 2.

[9] Above n 3, 166–9.

[10] Samantha Barbas, 'The Death of the Public Disclosure Tort: A Historical Perspective' (2010) 22 *Yale Journal of Law and the Humanities* 171, 173.

expectation of privacy in the first place. This chapter will identify six trends in the case law, each of which favours the press and weakens protection for privacy.

Before doing so, however, it is necessary to set out some brief observations about the main free speech rationales and how far they are engaged by stories that consist of disclosures of private facts. It is also necessary to say something about the distinction between the individual right to free speech on the one hand, and press freedom on the other.

## 8.2 Free speech, press freedom and the free speech rationales

Although newspapers often present the notion of press freedom and free speech interchangeably,[11] simply conflating the two like this is simplistic.[12] In order to see why this is so, we have to first ask why we value free speech in the first place. The answer lies in the insight legal philosophers have provided[13]: free speech can perform or vitally aid certain classical and valuable functions – the discovery of truth,[14] democratic deliberation,[15] the development of individuals, and the holding of government to account. It then becomes apparent that some of the most important of these free speech rationales – those that rest on arguments concerning the autonomy[16] and self-actualisation[17] of the speaker – are not generally applicable to speech produced by media corporations. While these rationales *are* generally engaged by individual speech, they cannot normally be considered as underpinning exercises of press freedom by large

[11] See, e.g., the headline of the *Sunday Times*' recent Leader on press regulation: 'Free Speech, Warts and All', 6 October 2013.

[12] I have set out this argument in full in 'Leveson, The Public Interest and Press Freedom' (2013) 5 *Journal of Media Law* 220.

[13] See generally Kent Greenwalt, 'Free Speech Justifications' (1989) 89 *Columbia Law Review* 119; Frederick Schauer, *Free Speech: A Philosophical Enquiry* (Cambridge: Cambridge University Press, 1982).

[14] Classically put forward in Mill's *On Liberty* in M Cowling (ed), *Selected Writings of John Stuart Mill* (Cambridge: Cambridge University Press, 1968) 121; for discussion see Greenwalt, above n 13, 130–41.

[15] Perhaps the most influential theory: see Alexander Meiklejohn, 'The First Amendment is an Absolute' [1961] *Supreme Court Review* 245; *Political Freedom: The Constitutional Powers of the People* (New York: Oxford University Press, 1960) esp 115–24. Eric Barendt, *Freedom of Speech*, 2nd edn (Oxford: Oxford University Press, 2005), 68.

[16] See, e.g., Ronald Dworkin's basic postulate of the state's duty to treat its citizens with equal concern and respect, *Taking Rights Seriously* (Harvard University Press, 1978), and Thomas Scanlon's influential approach set out in 'A Theory of Freedom of Expression' (1972) 1 *Philosophy & Public Affairs* 204, 216.

[17] Thomas I Emerson, 'Towards a General Theory of the First Amendment' (1963) 72 *Yale Law Journal* 877, 879–80; Martin H Redish, *Freedom of Expression: A Critical Analysis* (Charlottesville: Michie Co, 1984) 20–30; Greenwalt, above n 13, 143–5.

newspapers.[18] It is worth noting that section 12 of the Human Rights Act 1998 (UK) appears to be in harmony with this view: section 12(4) requires the court to consider 'the extent to which it is, or would be, in the public interest for the material to be published' but only where the matter published is 'journalistic, literary or artistic material'. This suggests parliamentary acceptance of the notion that, in assessing the legal weight to be given to journalistic speech in particular, its contribution to the public interest is key.

This is in line with the judicial view – and that adopted in the Leveson[19] report – that our reasons for valuing speech in the mass media are different from those applying to individual free speech, being less concerned with the rights of the 'speaker' and more to do with the benefits obtained by the audience. In *McCartan Turkington Breen* v. *Times Newspapers*[20] Lord Bingham said:

> The majority [of citizens] can participate only indirectly, by exercising their rights as citizens to vote, express their opinions, make representations to the authorities, form pressure groups and so on. But [they] cannot participate in the public life of their society in these ways if they are not alerted to and informed about matters which call or may call for consideration and action. It is very largely through the media, including of course the press, that they will be so alerted and informed. The proper functioning of a modern participatory democracy requires that the media be free, active, professional and inquiring. For this reason the courts, here and elsewhere, have recognised the cardinal importance of press freedom ...

Lord Justice Laws has recently made this distinction even clearer. In the *Miranda* case – which concerned the seizure from journalist Glenn Greenwald's partner of material obtained by Edward Snowden – he spoke of

> ... an important difference between the general justification of free expression and the particular justification of its sub-class, journalistic expression. The former is a right which belongs to every individual for his own sake. But the latter is given to serve the public at large ... The journalist enjoys no heightened protection for his own sake, but only for the sake of his readers or his audience.[21]

Similarly, Ward LJ recently stressed the particular importance of press freedom, arguing that

[18] The same does not of course apply to much online speech by individual bloggers and on social media. My concern in this paper is with the mass media.

[19] Right Honourable Lord Justice Brian Leveson, *An Inquiry into the Culture, Practices and Ethics of the Press*, HC 780 (2012), discussed in Phillipson, n 12 above. For a contrary view, critical of Leveson's stance on this point, see P. Wragg, 'The Legitimacy of Press Regulation' [2015] PL 290.

[20] [2001] 2 AC 277, 290.

[21] *R (Miranda)* v. *Secretary of State for the Home Department and another (Liberty and others intervening)* [2014] 1 WLR 3140, [46]

everyone has the right to freedom of expression but the ones with the greatest need for this constitutionally vital freedom are the organs of the media. In the interests of our democratic society we – and that includes the judges – must ensure that the press are freely able to inquire, investigate and report matters of interest. The press is the public watchdog.[22]

The above dicta exhibit a striking level of agreement on the notion that press freedom has particular value *because* it serves the public interest. This signals judicial concurrence with the view expressed above, that mass media can only rely upon those justifications for free speech that are *consequentialist and societal*, such as the discovery of truth or promotion of self-governance. It also suggests that journalism that does *not* serve the public interest will attract relatively little weight.[23]

In contrast, the favoured press line is that *any* restriction on even tawdry stories – such as one featuring photos of a prince's bare bottom – puts these precious values at stake.[24] This, however, depends upon the fallacy that all speech in the press performs or contributes to the furtherance of all these values; but it is very difficult to argue that much of the kind of (often salacious) gossip-journalism that runs into conflict with individual privacy does much to advance noble goals like democratic self-government. The standard judicial approach recognises this. As Baroness Hale put it in a leading case, for the public to 'have a right to be told'

there must be a real public interest in communicating and receiving the information. This is, as we all know, very different from saying that it is information which interests the public – the most vapid tittle-tattle about the activities of footballers' wives and girlfriends interests large sections of the public but no-one could claim any real public interest in our being told all about it.[25]

There is a contrary argument – that such material provides a kind of generalised benefit to the individual in helping to personalise information about a range of topics.[26] This argument was originally made in the First Amendment context by Dianne Zimmerman and Eugene Volokh;[27] in

[22] *K* v. *News Group Newspapers* [2011] EWCA Civ 439, [13].

[23] Unless, that is, it was thought that all journalism should be afforded a high value because the judges cannot be trusted to distinguish 'high' from 'low value' journalism: see text to n 30.

[24] See discussion in Phillipson, above n 12, 222–3.

[25] *Jameel* v. *Wall Street Journal* [2006] UKHL 44, [148].

[26] In essence the argument is that the media *can* use stories concerning celebrities to highlight issues such as eating disorders, abortion, attitudes to sexuality, education and the like, thus 'inform[ing] the social, political, moral and philosophical positions of individual citizens': Dianne Zimmerman, 'Requiem for a Heavyweight: A Farewell to Warren and Brandeis's Privacy Tort' (1983) 68 *Cornell Law Review* 291, 346.

[27] Eugene Volokh, 'Freedom of Speech and Information Privacy: The Troubling Implications of a Right to Stop People from Speaking about You' (2000) 52 *Stanford Law Review* 1049, 1089–90.

the English law context it has been advanced by Paul Wragg.[28] I have previously expressed some scepticism about it:[29] as a rationale it seems to be extremely weak: any given piece of information is likely to have only the most marginal impact on the individual's development and moreover something very similar would likely have been obtainable without intruding on anyone's privacy, given the vast amount of personal information that is made available quite consensually, through social media, chat shows, consensual celebrity coverage, reality TV and the like. Hence it is very hard to see how lack of access to any particular item of gossip is a tangible loss to a citizen, at least one that is sufficiently strong to justify plain violations of the individual's right to control their own personal information and the clear harms to self-development that may come from actual or threatened exposure of morally controversial choices concerning their private lives. There is perhaps implicit recognition of the weakness of the argument in the fact that US lawyers and judges tend to fall back on more general First Amendment arguments concerning distrust of the judicial role in drawing lines between valuable and non-valuable speech – what Hughes and Richards refer to as 'an ethic of judicial self-doubt'.[30]

However, my purpose here is primarily to consider the *judicial* approach to these matters in Strasbourg and in the English courts. This relies, as Baroness Hale's dicta makes clear, on the notion that courts *can* sift stories that make a real contribution to the public interest from those that do not. (Without such an ability there would indeed be no 'balancing act' since speech would tend to win nearly every case, as in the US.) But the judicial approach also seems to show some receptiveness to the 'generalised benefit' argument just considered;[31] certainly it discloses a substantial broadening of the general approach to assessing 'public interest', though I contend later that much of the 'reasoning' underpinning this development remains obscure, and is perhaps little more than a set of largely unarticulated judicial intuitions. These points will become clearer

[28] Paul Wragg, 'The Benefits of Privacy-Invading Expression' (2013) 64 *Northern Ireland Legal Quarterly* 187, 194. 'Privacy-invading expression may be said to encourage self-reflection, personal growth and maturity in its audience, particularly where it is disapproving of celebrity excess. It may also help develop positive personality traits and generally enhance a deeper understanding of what it is to be a member of society and to be human'. Wragg goes on that it may also develop one's moral sense, make one feel better about oneself or simply provide something to talk about with others, thus helping to develop relationships.

[29] See Helen Fenwick and Gavin Phillipson, *Media Freedom under the Human Rights Act* (Oxford: Oxford University Press, 2006), 683–8 and 792–4.

[30] See in this volume, 172.

[31] As Wragg himself argues: above n 28.

as we consider the six factors that together are changing how the courts configure the priority between privacy and press freedom.

## 8.3 The economic survival argument[32]

The first factor is the increasing use of an argument that posits an instrumental value simply in the press being free to print stories that sell; if accepted, it weighs in on the press side of the balance, even where it is hard or impossible to find any specific public interest justification for the particular story in question. I have termed this the 'economic survival' argument because it contends, in a nutshell, that a factor in favour of tabloid celebrity coverage that invades people's privacy is that the survival of newspapers depends on it. It is frequently advanced by the press[33] and has received some judicial support. Thus Lord Woolf, in the Gary Flitcroft case, *A* v. *B*, said:

> The courts must not ignore the fact that if newspapers do not publish information which the public are interested in, there will be fewer newspapers published, which will not be in the public interest.[34]

Similar comments were made by two of their Lordships in the *Campbell* case. Lady Hale said:

> One reason why press freedom is so important is that we need newspapers to sell in order to ensure that we still have newspapers at all. It may be said the newspapers should be allowed considerable latitude in their intrusions into private grief so that they can maintain circulation and the rest of us can then continue to enjoy the variety of newspapers . . . which are available in this country.[35]

Lord Hoffmann reminded us that, 'We value the freedom of the press but the press is a commercial enterprise and can flourish only by selling newspapers'.[36]

Much more recently, Gross LJ in the Court of Appeal, giving the leading judgement in the *Hutcheson* case, said:

> for sections of the media, developments in privacy law impinging on their ability to publish such matters may not only give rise to issues of principle as to freedom of

[32] I draw in this section on Phillipson, above n 12, 232–4.

[33] See, e.g., the speech by Paul Dacre at the Society of Editors Conference, 9 November 2008: 'if mass-circulation newspapers, which, of course, also devote considerable space to reporting and analysis of public affairs, don't have the freedom to write about scandal, I doubt whether they will retain their mass circulations, with the obvious worrying implications for the democratic process': http://image.guardian.co.uk/sys-files/Media/documents/2008/11/07/DacreSpeech.pdf.

[34] [2002] 3 WLR 542, 552. [35] *Campbell* v. *MGN* [2004] 2 WLR 1232, [162].

[36] *Ibid.*, [77].

expression in the individual case but also to real commercial concerns – which, at least to the extent of the general public interest in having a thriving and vigorous newspaper industry, representing all legitimate opinions, may also be argued to give rise to a relevant factor for the court to take into account.[37]

These dicta were cited in a subsequent decision of the High Court, concerning a story about an illegitimate child of the London Mayor, Boris Johnson. Noting Gross LJ's view, Davies J said firmly that 'the commercial imperative to sell newspapers is a relevant factor to be taken into account when conducting the art 8/10 balancing exercise'.[38] Similarly, in *K* v. *News Group Newspapers* Ward LJ also said:

> we have to enable sales if we want to keep our newspapers. Unduly to fetter their freedom to report as editors judge to be responsible is to undermine the pre-eminence of the deserved place of the press as a powerful pillar of democracy.[39]

The same argument was accepted in the *Paul Weller* case,[40] in which the judge explicitly endorsed the earlier dicta. Notably in that case, the press's counsel attempted explicitly to liberalise the standards applied by UK courts to privacy-invading stories through the argument that publications like the Daily Mail online (the most visited newspaper website in the world) have to compete in 'a highly competitive global market' with bigger news portals, all of which are based in the US, and therefore benefit from the more 'unfettered' free speech guarantee provided by the First Amendment; hence the *Mail*'s ability to compete would be weakened if it could not publish the kind of celebrity stories that were immune from liability in the US.[41] The judge said simply, 'I accept [this] evidence about some of the difficulties faced by UK newspapers and websites in attempting to compete in a global market';[42] however, his conclusion was that '[t]he balance of the general interest of having a vigorous and flourishing newspaper industry does not outweigh the interests of the children in this case'.

It is fair to say that the economic survival argument does not (yet) appear to have won a case on its own;[43] rather its function has probably

[37] *Hutcheson* v. *News Group* [2011] EWCA Civ 808, [34] ('*Hutcheson*').
[38] *AAA* v. *Associated Newspapers* [2013] EWCA Civ 554, [102].
[39] *K* v. *News Group Newspapers* [2011] EWCA Civ 439, [13].
[40] *Weller* v. *Associated Newspapers* [2014] EWHC 1163. The case concerned photos taken non-consensually of the Wellers' children in a public place.
[41] *Ibid.*, [146]. See also [145], [147]. On appeal to the Court of Appeal Counsel likewise argued 'there is a public interest in freedom of expression itself and in having a vibrant press, which in turn requires the press to be able to compete in the online global news market' [2015] EWCA Civ 1176, [54]. The appeal was dismissed.
[42] *Ibid.*, [149].
[43] *Weller* was a case in which it might have, since the newspaper did not attempt to argue any particular public interest in the story itself (which concerned anodyne pictures of the couples' children).

been to bolster what have been sometimes flimsy-looking – but successful – public interest or other press arguments in favour of publication, or to maximise the discretion given to editors in deciding how to present intrusive stories, including the level of detail articles go into.[44]

To be clear, one way in which this argument may be used is unobjectionable and simply reminds us that, in the real world, not all journalism can be high minded and serious. Newspapers have to be sold, and celebrity gossip and the like helps to sell them. As Lord Leveson put it:

> purely entertaining stories [as well as giving pleasure to readers] have a corollary function in attracting readers to the newsstand and in maintaining circulation; and the advantageous by-product of both these functions is that readers will participate more in the democratic process by being drawn to the news and comment pages of the paper which are often skilfully interwoven with the lighter sections.[45]

This argument only becomes objectionable when it is used – as some of the dicta earlier suggest it may be – to justify particular stories that intrude into people's private lives and which appear otherwise to lack, or have only very weak, specific public interest value. The proposition then logically must be that even where particular stories are otherwise not justifiable or have only a very weak specific justification, they should nevertheless be permitted *because* of their economic value to newspapers – or at least that their economic value is a relevant factor for the court to consider, as Gross LJ and Davies J put it. Bluntly, the contention is that the press must be allowed to invade privacy and publish worthless gossip in order to make money to subsidise more valuable journalism. There are two key objections to it.

First of all, it should be recognised that it makes a factual claim about the world; as such it should be accompanied by proper evidence, which, however, never seems to be adduced. While it is doubtless true that publishing celebrity gossip per se is very lucrative, I have never seen evidence adduced to support the specific proposition that newspapers can *only* survive financially if they publish private information *without the consent of the person concerned* (a huge amount of celebrity gossip is very profitably published in the media on a consensual basis, as is generally the case, for example, in *Hello!* magazine).

[44] The argument has also been endorsed by a parliamentary body: the Joint Committee on Privacy and Injunctions noted that: 'As gossip in newspapers can help sales and thus enable journalism to continue to perform its essential role in a democracy, it might follow that the commercial viability of the press should be a factor when balancing the public interest in a story against an individual's right to privacy', *Report from the Joint Committee on Privacy and Injunctions* (2010–12 HL Paper 273, HC 1443), [82]

[45] Leveson, above n 19, 454.

The second and more important point is as follows: even if the proposition is empirically correct (which may be doubted), it still does not justify tipping the balance in favour of press freedom in privacy cases where there is no, or only a weak, public interest justification. The reason is this: the contention that the press should be allowed to invade people's privacy in order to make enough money to ensure their continued existence means that the burden of ensuring that the general social good of having newspapers falls on that very small minority of individuals whose privacy they invade: they are to be denied the remedy they would otherwise be entitled to, in order to ensure the survival of the press. Thus this small group alone pays the cost of ensuring the continuation of our free press. But if the existence of newspapers is a social good from which everyone benefits, then everyone should contribute to it, not just the victims of gossip journalism. The easiest way for everyone to contribute to it would be via the tax system or some other form of public subsidy.[46] There is no reason why one small group in society should pay, by having their rights diminished and their private lives treated as commodities, in order to subsidise the media for the benefit of everyone else.[47]

## 8.4 Acceptance/expansion of the 'Public Figure' doctrine

The second trend is that the Strasbourg Court in both *Von Hannover (no 2)*[48] and *Axel Springer*[49] has started to fully embrace the notion that 'public figures' have a reduced expectation of privacy, and, importantly, expanded the notion of 'public figure' to encompass those who are simply well known to the public. These two decisions are of particular importance, not only because they were both delivered by the Grand Chamber, but because in them the Court sought to lay down comprehensive guidance on balancing Articles 8 and 10 in similar cases, and have indicated in subsequent cases that, provided domestic courts make use of that guidance, they will be granted a substantial margin of appreciation in

[46] Building on the zero VAT-rating for newspapers in the UK.

[47] Andrew Kenyon has pointed out to me that Frederick Schauer has made a similar argument: see Andrew T Kenyon, 'Protecting Speech in Defamation Law: Beyond *Reynolds*-Style Defences' (2014) 6 *Journal of Media Law* 21, 44 discussing Frederick Schauer, 'Uncoupling Free Speech' (1992) 92 *Columbia Law Review* 1321.

[48] *Von Hannover* v. *Germany (no 2)* (European Court of Human Rights, Grand Chamber, Application Nos 40660/08 and 60641/08, 7 February 2012) ('*Von Hannover (no 2)*'). The later decision in *Von Hannover* v. *Germany (no 3)* (European Court of Human Rights, Application No 8772/10 19 September 2013) ('*Von Hannover (no 3)*') largely confirmed the trends apparent in the Grand Chamber decision, though in some respects taking them further.

[49] *Axel Springer* v. *Germany* (European Court of Human Rights, Grand Chamber, Application No 39954/08, 7 February 2012) ('*Axel Springer*').

reaching their conclusions.[50] Thus in *Von Hannover (no 2)*, which concerned Princess Caroline of Monaco, the Grand Chamber said that, 'the applicants and her partner, who are undeniably very well known, [cannot be viewed as] ordinary private individuals. They must, on the contrary, be regarded as public figures' and hence afforded a somewhat reduced expectation of privacy.[51] It is notable that the reason the Court gave for this finding was not that Caroline is a member of a royal family, or that she perform official functions (she does not) but simply because of her celebrity status. Similarly, in *Axel Springer*, the claimant 'X' was well known to the public because he played one of the main characters in a popular TV series.[52] The Grand Chamber judgement remarked:

> that role was, moreover, that of a police superintendent, whose mission was law enforcement and crime prevention. That fact was such as to increase the public's interest in being informed of X's arrest for a criminal offence. Having regard to those factors and to the terms employed by the domestic courts in assessing the degree to which X was known to the public, *the Court considers that he was sufficiently well known to qualify as a public figure.* That consideration thus reinforces the public's interest in being informed of X's arrest and of the criminal proceedings against him.[53]

This adoption by the Strasbourg Court of the notion that 'public figures' – broadly defined – have a sharply reduced expectation of privacy, is problematic. The essence of the objection is that the concept of 'public figures' is analytically imprecise and therefore not conducive of clear judicial reasoning. It acts as a relatively crude and generalised proxy for three more precise arguments that by their nature should be fact-sensitive: first, that aspects of the lives of some well-known people may become so widely publicised that they can no longer meaningfully be

[50] As noted by Hughes and Richards in this volume: see 179–80 and 186.

[51] *Von Hannover (no 2)* (European Court of Human Rights, Grand Chamber, Application Nos 40660/08 and 60641/08, 7 February 2012), [91], [120]; the finding was confirmed in *Von Hannover (no 3)*

[52] The facts of *Axel Springer* that gave rise to the application to Strasbourg are of a kind that common law observers will find rather startling. A well-known actor was arrested and convicted for possession of cocaine; first the arrest and then the conviction were reported in a newspaper and German courts injuncted both articles, finding the report to be on a matter insufficiently serious to warrant the intrusion into private life. The Strasbourg Court, perhaps not surprisingly, found a violation of Article 10. As the Court pointed out, 'the articles did not ... reveal details of X's private life but mainly concerned the circumstances of and events following his arrest': [108]. Thus it is not the outcome of the case that I contest but some of the reasoning deployed in support of the outcome. The simple way to decide the case would have been to find that Article 8 was not engaged by the reporting at all, since the working of the criminal justice system is presumptively a public matter.

[53] *Axel Springer* (European Court of Human Rights, Grand Chamber, Application No 39954/08, 7 February 2012), [99] (emphasis added).

considered private; second, that they may reasonably be considered to have consented to publicity about their private life; third that there is a degree of legitimate public interest in aspects of their private lives, as in the case of politicians. The problem is that the 'public figure' concept doesn't deal with any of these three separate arguments well. Far more analytical clarity can be obtained by asking each of these questions separately and precisely and in a highly fact-sensitive way. This gives rise to a more sophisticated methodology that avoids lumping together into one category pop stars and prime ministers, footballers and chairmen of global financial institutions.

We can tease out these problems in more detail by examining how Dean Prosser – whose well-known work 'brought the privacy torts into the mainstream of American tort law'[54] – analysed the issue of public figures. His analysis was given great weight in the ground-breaking decision in *Hoskings* v. *Runting*,[55] which introduced a common law tort of privacy into New Zealand law, largely adopted from the US 'private facts' tort. Gault P and Blanchard J introduced their consideration of the issue of 'public figures' by citing the US perspective:

> Prosser identified three reasons why, in the United States context, public figures are held to have lost, at least to some extent, their right of privacy:
>
> (1) by seeking publicity they have consented to it;
> (2) their personalities and affairs are already public facts not private ones; and
> (3) there is a legitimate public interest in the publication of details about public figures.[56]

All three of these reasons are, it is suggested, problematic. Proposition (1) makes two mistakes: first, it *assumes* that all public figures seek publicity voluntarily – which is by no means the case – and second, it draws no distinction between seeking publicity for one's *private* life, and seeking publicity in relation to one's vocation, surely an elementary distinction. As we will see, Strasbourg has not gone quite as far as this, but the English courts have come close to it in at least one decision.[57] Proposition (2) is ambiguous, but either meaning is deeply problematic. If we are concerned with the question whether personal information is *worthy* of protection, then it seeks to answer a normative question with a factual answer and therefore amounts to a category mistake. If it is instead indicating simply that information about certain public figures is so well known that it cannot any longer be considered 'private', then it is no more than an unhelpful generalisation. All that can be said is that in certain

[54] Hughes and Richards in this volume, 169. [55] [2005] 1 NZLR 1. [56] *Ibid.*,[120].
[57] *Spelman* v. *Express Newspapers* [2012] EWHC 355 ('*Spelman*').

cases particular facts about a person's private life may be so widely known that they can no longer be considered 'private'. But this clearly will not always be the case and cannot be decided in advance of examining the particular situation before the court. Nevertheless, a softened version of proposition 2 – that being well known to the public per se *diminishes* your reasonable expectation of privacy – captures exactly what Strasbourg and the English courts now assume to be the case.

Proposition (3) is not a reason for reducing the scope of the protection given to public figures, but rather a description of a countervailing consideration to be weighed in the balance against their right to protection for privacy. Even put in those terms it is flawed, because it again amounts to a perverse generalisation: whether there is a legitimate public interest in the life of the public figure will depend upon the nature of the information in question, the role of the public figure and whether the information contributes significantly to an important public debate. Had the New Zealand court recognised that the effect of Prosser's work was, as Hughes and Richards put it, to 'marginalise' the privacy torts,[58] perhaps they would have placed less weight on it.

Unfortunately, English courts in recent decisions appear also to be both using and expanding the concept of 'a public figure' – broadening it out from covering 'those who exercise public or official functions', as Tugendhat J thought it had been defined in the leading case of *Campbell*,[59] to people who are simply well known to the public.[60] Thus in the *Trimingham* case,[61] the judge denied that the claimant – a press officer for a senior government minister who became the minister's lover – was a purely private person, because her job consisted (in effect) of placing a certain image of her employer before the public and asking the public to trust him – and, implicitly, herself. This, without more, was deemed to reduce her expectation of privacy. As one commentator has argued, while one can perhaps tease out a more specific argument for a public interest in the fact of the affair between the claimant and the minister, merely noting that her job was in communications amounted to a crude proxy for the more nuanced argument about the public interest

[58] At 169.

[59] See Tugendhat J in *Spelman* v. *Express Newspapers* [2012] EWHC 355 (QB), [44], citing Baroness Hale in *Campbell* v. *MGN* [2004] AC 457, [158], [159].

[60] See further Eric Barendt, 'English Privacy Law in the Light of the Leveson Report' in Normann Witzleb, David Lindsay, Moira Paterson and Sharon Rodrick (eds), *Emerging Challenges in Privacy Law: Comparative Perspectives* (Cambridge: Cambridge University Press, 2014).

[61] *Trimingham* v. *Associated Newspapers* [2012] EWHC 1296 (QB), [249]–[250]. See further on this case Sophie Matthiesson and Eric Barendt, '*Carina Trimingham* v. *Associated Newspapers:* A Right to Ridicule?' (2012) 4 *Journal of Media Law* 309.

in the story that should have been made.[62] Similarly, Barendt has noted the dubious finding in the *Spelman*[63] case – which concerned a seventeen-year-old national junior rugby player[64] – that the claimant was 'to be regarded as exercising a public function' and as inevitably accepting, by 'participating in high level sport', the 'condition' that he 'give up control over many aspects of private life'.[65] Thus again status was deemed, through the fallacious notion of an implied agreement (and by a minor, to boot!), to strip away a great deal of protection for private life. In another case, concerning Steve McClaren, the judge found that, 'as a former England football manager and a current club manager, the claimant was undoubtedly a public figure' in the UK;[66] this was so, even though the football club McClaren managed was a Dutch, not an English one.

Thus the notion of 'public figure' has, in the space of a few years, extended beyond politicians and other figures exercising real public power, to encompass those who are simply famous, for whatever reason – the worst example of this tendency being the *Von Hannover* and *Axel Springer* cases, in which 'public figure' meant simply a person in whose doings the public are interested. Used in this way, the 'public figure' doctrine can mean that the right to privacy is surrendered or sharply reduced by reference simply to public whim; thus the supposedly sacrosanct distinction between the public interest and what interests the public comes close to being (indirectly) collapsed.

In short then, the public figure concept is objectionable because it seeks to answer a general question when it is meaningful only to answer more specific ones about reasonable expectations of privacy in the particular circumstances and whether there is a sufficient public interest in the disclosure so as to justify the prima facie interference in privacy. The public figure doctrine doesn't in itself help answer these questions: even very senior politicians may reasonably be taken to have reasonable expectations of privacy in relation to *some* areas of their life (e.g., how often they have sex with their spouses)[67] and there may well be many mundane areas of their private lives over which the public cannot be said to have a

[62] *Ibid.*, 312–14. [63] *Spelman* [2012] EWHC 355 (QB). Barendt, above n 60.

[64] Specifically, a 17 year old who had played rugby for the England Under 16 side and a nationally known Rugby Club.

[65] *Spelman*, [70] and [72].

[66] *McClaren* v. *News Group Newspapers* [2012] EWHC 2466 (QB); [2012] EMLR 33, [38] ('*McClaren*').

[67] Possibly something like this explains the doubtful decision in *Ruusunen* v. *Finland* (European Court of Human Rights, Chamber, Application No 73579/10, 14 January 2014), discussed by Hughes and Richards in this volume, 185–7. An application based on the same facts by the publisher of the disputed book alleging a breach of Art. 10 also failed: *Ojala and Etukeno Oy* v. *Finland*, Application No 69939/10, 14 January 2014.

legitimate interest (e.g., the colour of their underwear). Hence not only is the public figure doctrine an unhelpful proxy for more distinct and precise questions, concerning public interest and reasonable expectation of privacy, it unhelpfully generalises an enquiry that must by its nature be fact-specific to yield meaningful conclusions.

## 8.5 Strasbourg acceptance of implied 'waiver' of privacy rights

The third problematic tendency in recent case law lies in the fact that Strasbourg has for the first time unequivocally accepted the so-called 'waiver argument' (often known in US privacy law as 'implied consent'):[68] that since in the past the applicant has sought publicity for herself (when put more specifically, for her private life), she should not be allowed to complain about the current intrusive publication. I have argued previously[69] that the notion that a voluntary disclosure of private information prevents an individual from being able to complain about an *involuntary* disclosure is wholly incompatible with the core privacy value of the individual's right to *control* over the release of personal information. All of us exercise this right to selective disclosure in our social lives: we may tell one friend an intimate secret and not another; at times be open, at others more reticent. But someone who is shown a personal letter on one occasion does not assume that they have thereby acquired the right to read, uninvited, all other such letters. In other words, to suggest that public figures should be treated as estopped from complaining about unwanted publicity because they had previously sought it would deny them the very *control* over personal information that is inherent in the notion of personal autonomy; previous disclosures amount not to an *abandonment* of the right to privacy, but an exercise of it.[70]

Up until very recently, privacy claimants in England could argue that the 'waiver' notion was not endorsed by Strasbourg and provided no clear

[68] See, e.g., John P Ellwood, 'Outing, Privacy and the First Amendment' (1992) 102 *Yale Law Journal* 747.

[69] Gavin Phillipson and Helen Fenwick, 'Breach of Confidence as a Privacy Remedy in the Human Rights Act Era' (2000) 63 *Modern Law Review* 660, 680.

[70] There may be extreme situations in which the applicant has, so voluntarily, thoroughly and repeatedly placed details about the same subject matter which it is now proposed to publish, that it may be inferred that the information in question is not any longer, to that person, truly private or personal. Where the information has, as it were been sold 'for gain', this inference would be stronger: there is a clear difference between confiding a private fact to certain people in order to enhance one's relationship with them, and simply selling it. Thus in cases where a celebrity has quite genuinely commodified an aspect of their personal life, it may be concluded that it has lost its private character. However, it is suggested that such an approach would be apposite only in fairly extreme cases.

basis for limiting Article 8 rights (it is generally hard to make the argument that someone has voluntarily waived their rights under the Convention). The position has, however, changed as a result of the *Von Hannover (no 2)* and *Axel Springer* decisions. In the first, the Court made clear that one relevant factor in assessing the weight of any privacy claim was the claimant's 'prior conduct'; seemingly this referred to their previous attitude to publicity. The Court added that the mere fact of having cooperated with the press could not deprive a person of *all* protection,[71] but this will be of little comfort to privacy advocates, since all this does is rule out the extreme (and implausible) 'blanket' version of waiver, in which any prior disclosures to the press negate all protection for private life. The Court put the position more clearly in *Axel Springer*, in which it said that the applicant's 'legitimate expectation' of protection for his private life was reduced by virtue of the fact that he had himself informed the media of details of his private life in several interviews and had, therefore, 'actively sought the limelight'.[72] No reasoning was given for this, nor was its apparent incompatibility with notions of informational autonomy acknowledged, still less explained away.

The acceptance of the waiver doctrine by Strasbourg is a highly significant tilt towards the press, because, where a newspaper can make the waiver argument out, the claimant is found to have no reasonable expectation of privacy in the first place and therefore the press has no need to provide any public interest justification for the story. Like the 'economic survival' argument and the 'public figure doctrine' it thus opens the door to privacy-invading stories that lack any public interest dimension at all. It is only if these arguments fail that the press must advance any specific public interest arguments based on the particular information disclosed. We now turn to consider the three different ways in which courts have made it considerably easier for the press to do so.

## 8.6 Broadening and blurring of the notion of the 'public interest'

The first of these changes is that, as a result of the same two key Grand Chamber decisions considered earlier, the Strasbourg court has rendered its stance on what constitutes the public interest simultaneously much broader and much vaguer. To appreciate this change we must recall some of the key findings of the first *Von Hannover* decision. In that case the

[71] *Von Hannover (no 2)* (European Court of Human Rights, Grand Chamber, Application Nos 40660/08 and 60641/08, 7 February 2012) [111] (emphasis added).

[72] *Axel Springer* (European Court of Human Rights, Grand Chamber, Application No 39954/08, 7 February 2012) [101].

Court reasoned in three stages: *first*, generally speaking, the press does *not* fulfil its vital function in a democracy when reporting on someone's private life – even when that person is well known to the public, like Princess Caroline of Monaco; therefore, *second*, such speech is for that reason generally to be given a low weight; therefore, *third*, it will normally be outweighed by the claims of privacy. This decision thus gave presumptive priority to privacy in cases in which the media publishes private facts about a person: it did so, by narrowing the effective scope of the free speech right, thereby allowing the privacy right to generally win in such cases. The rationale was that the press's role is to act as a watchdog in a democracy; therefore reporting on the private life of a person who exercises no official duties was not usually something that attracted any real protection under the Article 10 free speech guarantee.[73] This was a rather austere, high-minded view of the role of the press in a democracy – a narrow view, some would say.

What Strasbourg did in *Von Hannover (no 2)* was to expand the effective scope of Article 10 by finding that it does, after all, cover photographic gossip-journalism, *provided* that the text accompanying the photo makes some link with a topic that can conceivably be considered to be of general interest. The picture in dispute at Strasbourg showed Princess Caroline with her husband in the street in the fashionable skiing resort, St Moritz. The text accompanying the photo (which was not in itself something considered to have any public interest value) noted the serious illness of her father, the Prince of Monaco, and informed readers that his children were worried about him, and were taking it in turn to look after him, while also seeking to maintain their social life, including holidays. The text thus made a connection (albeit a tenuous one) between the photograph of Caroline on her skiing vacation and the health of the reigning Prince of Monaco. The German Courts had found that the latter topic was clearly a matter of legitimate public concern and that the article contributed to a debate on it by discussing 'how the Prince's family reconciled the obligations of family solidarity with the legitimate needs of their private life, among which was the desire to go on holiday'.[74] This was their key reason for finding in favour of the press and against the Princess in relation to this

[73] The Court considers that a fundamental distinction needs to be made between reporting facts . . . capable of contributing to a debate in a democratic society, relating to politicians in the exercise of their functions, for example, and reporting details of the private life of an individual who, moreover, as in this case, does not exercise official functions. While in the former case the press exercises its vital role of 'watchdog' in a democracy by contributing to 'impart[ing] information and ideas on matters of public interest . . . it *does not do so* in the latter case: *Von Hannover* v. *Germany* (2005) 40 EHRR 1, [63] (emphasis added).

[74] *Von Hannover (no 2)* (European Court of Human Rights, Grand Chamber, Application Nos 40660/08 and 60641/08, 7 February 2012), [49].

publication. Strasbourg agreed, finding that the photo-article did indeed engage with a debate of general interest about the Prince's health and contributed to it, 'at least to some degree'.[75]

Not only does this open the door to editors to link otherwise valueless photographs to some public debate via a few lines of text, it also reduces the right to private life to the weakest of interests. If a so-called 'human right' to privacy can be overridden by the public interest in seeing a picture of Princess Caroline on holiday, so that Germans can ponder on how often relatives of another country's ailing Monarch are visiting him and how often they are going on holiday, then it is hardly a right at all. Strasbourg would have done better simply to find that the photo (which it found was anodyne, inoffensive and taken without pursuit or harassment) did not engage Article 8 at all, rather than to create a vague, woolly mess by continuing to insist that anodyne photos taken in public *do* engage Article 8, but can then be overridden by whatever connection to some possible public interest debate an ingenious editor can think up.[76] The case is probably explicable, given its particular facts, by the Court's (implicit) view that the privacy claim was only a weak one, therefore fairly easily overridden by even a weak public interest claim. But that nuance may be lost in translation, particularly where it is cited in domestic courts by newspaper lawyers, arguing that publication of a disputed picture of a bikini-clad female celebrity considered over- or under-weight by the critical reporter, is in the public interest because the text briefly discussed the dangers of anorexia – or obesity. In this respect, Paul Wragg's seeming approval of the reasoning here – 'the subject matter in *Von Hannover (no 2)* speaks to the audience's emotional development by observing how others handle grief'[77] – seems equally unpersuasive. As a rationale, it would of course cover *any* press intrusion into grief; and ironically the more intrusive it was – the more starkly portraying the suffering of the bereaved – the more insight it would presumably give. Moreover, given the rich resources of film, literature, theatre and music dealing with the subject of grief, it is unclear why citizens need to see pictures of Princess Caroline's skiing trip in order to assist their emotional development.

[75] *Ibid.*, [118].

[76] In the subsequent case of *Lillo Steinberg* v. *Norway* (European Court of Human Rights, Chamber, Application No. 13258/09, 16 January 2014), as Hughes and Richards discuss, the Court seemed to relieve the press of even that burden, inventing through sheer assertion an 'element of general interest' in an article about a wedding, where no connection to any broader debate was suggested: see 189 in this volume. Moreover, no link at all was apparent between the article and photograph in the later *Von Hannover (no 3)* with the Court seeming to suggest that only where the purported link between the two was wholly artificial and arbitrary would it be minded to object (at [50]).

[77] Wragg, above n 28, 207.

Thus what Strasbourg has done, by accepting such a broad and undefined notion of the public interest, is rob that notion of any coherent boundaries it might once have had. The fuzziness at work here is particularly evident where the Grand Chamber discusses its general guidance on this point, reminding us that Strasbourg has recognised a public interest not only in relation to 'political issues or crimes' but 'also sporting issues or performing artists' and, we might add, how often the members of another royal family go on holiday when their father is sick and the tendency of celebrities nowadays to rent out their properties as holiday homes.[78] The fuzziness in judicial reasoning is particularly apparent in the way the Court here lumps together categories of *speech* – those concerned with 'political issues', 'crimes', and 'sporting issues' with a category of *people* – 'performing artists'; the latter phrase also giving the somewhat bizarre impression that speech about performing artists must somehow always be in the public interest. In the same paragraph, however, the Court goes on to remind us that 'the rumoured marital difficulties of a president of the Republic or the financial difficulties of a famous singer were not deemed to be matters of general interest'; since 'famous singers' are obviously performance artists, this seems simply to contradict the earlier dicta, while leaving the distinctly odd impression that stories about some performing artists are more likely to be in the public interest than those about presidents.[79]

## 8.7 The 'role model' argument

One sub-set of the 'public interest' argument justifying privacy-invading stories is the so-called 'role model' argument, beloved of tabloid editors. It is popular because it provides a justification for stories about 'public figures' who have no formal power at all (i.e., celebrities or ordinary people suddenly thrust into the limelight by tragedy), on the basis that they may be considered to be influential figures in society (although no

[78] *Von Hannover (no 2)* (European Court of Human Rights, Grand Chamber, Application Nos 40660/08 and 60641/08, 7 February 2012) [109]. The disputed article in *Von Hannover (no 3)* discussed the latter topic re the Von Hannover family villa in Kenya.

[79] Hughes and Richard's analysis also hints at a similar incoherence in some of the later case law applying this guidance: see this volume, 184–90. The recent Grand Chamber decision in *Couderc and Hachette Filipacchi Associés* v. *France*, Application No 40454/07), by contrast concerned a matter of more substantial interest: the relationship of the Prince of Monaco with his lover and the fact that he had had a son by her. This was relevant both to the possibility of dynastic succession if the son was legitimated by marriage and because the information could spark public debate on the fact that the rules of succession in Monaco prevented children born out of wedlock from succeeding to the throne [108-111]. Hughes and Richards discuss the case briefly at 187.

concrete evidence is ever offered for such influence). As with the 'waiver' argument, this was a principle that has for some time had purchase in English courts, but which had not hitherto been specifically endorsed by Strasbourg and which had seemed to be in retreat even in English law. Its most well known exposition in an English decision had been made by Lord Woolf in the Court of Appeal decision in *A* v. *B*, concerning the revelation of a football player's infidelity:

> [A] public figure may hold a position where higher standards of conduct can be rightly expected by the public. [He] may be a role model whose conduct could well be emulated by others. He may set the fashion.[80]

Applying this to the facts before him, Lord Woolf found that:

> . . . it is not self-evident that how a well-known premiership football player chooses to spend his time off the football field does not have a modicum of public interest. Footballers are role models for young people and undesirable behaviour on their part can set an unfortunate example.[81]

Essentially, as the above quotation reveals, the argument tells us that where a celebrity claimant is influential on the behaviour and attitudes of his or her fans, it is in the public interest to report his or her antisocial or immoral conduct to their easily led followers. It is not clear why: one might think that fans deemed to be under the influence of a role model might be likely to imitate their antisocial behaviour, although how this could possibly count as being 'in the public interest' is anyone's guess.

However, it was precisely such an argument that the Grand Chamber endorsed in *Axel Springer*. The Court there gave weight to the fact that the claimant played the protagonist in a highly popular detective television series and, therefore, had a substantial fan base, which, it was said, could have been influenced into imitating his drug-taking had the offence been committed in public view.[82] If one accepts the factual premises underlying the Grand Chamber's argument (that the fans of the actor would be likely to imitate his drug-taking if they knew about it), one would presumably conclude the likely outcome of the story to be that some of his many fans would, as a result of learning that their idol is fond of cocaine, be more likely to try it themselves. While a hedonist libertarian or a drug dealer would perhaps agree that an increase in the number of people using cocaine is a good thing, it is strange to see an

[80] [2002] 3 WLR 542, [11] (xiii). [81] *Ibid.*, [45].

[82] *Ibid.*, [98]: the Court referred with approval to the view of the German Court of Appeal that 'his admirers could have been encouraged to imitate him by taking drugs, if the offence had not been committed out of public view'.

international court reason in a way that appears to leads to such a conclusion.

Given the criticism of Lord Woolf's dicta, and its marginalisation by subsequent courts,[83] it might have been expected that the role model argument would have disappeared from domestic judgements. But *au contraire*: in recent times, it has played a significant role in a trio of cases involving football players (*Terry*,[84] *Ferdinand*[85]) and managers (*McClaren*).[86] For example, in the latter, it was said that:

> the claimant belongs to the category of those from whom the public could reasonably expect a higher standard of conduct . . . He is clearly still a prominent public figure who has held positions of responsibility in the national game.[87]

Much the same was said about Ferdinand, then captain of the England national team. Leaving aside the implausibility of the courts' view that members of the public expect famous footballers to behave better than they do themselves, the more serious objection is that in neither case did the court go on to explain *why it mattered* if the public had an incorrect impression about the private lives of such people, nor, conversely, why the public benefitted from knowing that someone who was likely to influence their own behaviour (so the court thought) had been unfaithful in the past. As with the actor in *Springer*, might we not think the likely outcome of the revelation would be that the fans of these role models would now become more likely themselves to be unfaithful?

Paul Wragg gives a perhaps more plausible account: that readers of such stories: 'might modify their behaviour in respect of the well-known figure publicly, for example, by not purchasing associated products or not providing support in some other way (booing at a football match, say), or, privately, in their discussions with friends about that figure'.[88] However, it is still not clear why this is a desirable result – why it matters whether some fans boo, as opposed to applauding a football player – or indeed modify what they say about the footballer in private conversation. If I were to learn, through a betrayal of confidence, or coming across a private letter, that a colleague's marriage was in trouble, or that another was having money problems, I might treat them somewhat differently – I would perhaps talk about them differently with my friends (even if I didn't pass on the particular information) – yet if this is a reason for invading

83 See, e.g., dicta of Court of Appeal in *Campbell* v. *MGN* [2003] 2 WLR 80, [40].
84 *Terry (previously LNS)* v. *Persons Unknown* [2010] EMLR 16 ('*Terry*').
85 *Ferdinand* v. *MGN* [2011] EWHC 2454 (QB) ('*Ferdinand*').
86 *McClaren* [2012] EWHC 2466; [2012] EMLR 33. 87 *Ibid.*, [34].
88 Wragg, above n 28, 196.

privacy it applies to virtually any kind of disclosure, except the ultra-anodyne (which few would object to anyway).

Thus the notion that it is important for the public not to be misled about the personal lives of 'role models' and to learn of their improper conduct continues simply to be asserted by judges, without explication. Perhaps this normative gap is attributable to a (perhaps unconscious) belief that it is just bad for people to believe things that aren't true, a notion in turn perhaps linked to John Stuart Mill's famous argument for free speech as a means to gaining the truth.[89] Philosophical investigations of Mill's argument have, however, cast strong doubt on the (manifestly weak) argument that simply knowing more truthful facts, regardless of their importance, is an obvious good.[90] Moreover, unless we tell people, immediately we meet them, everything about our private lives, they are bound to have *some* mistaken impressions about us. But presumably their interest in not holding erroneous beliefs about our marriages, or sex lives, or health, does not override our right to control which aspects of our private lives to share with them. If that is right, why is it any different when the press corrects such mistaken beliefs about more well-known people? There may be answers to these questions, but the courts have certainly not provided them.

## 8.8 'The right to criticise?'[91]

Probably the most worrying development in English privacy law is the birth of a seemingly novel way of satisfying the 'public interest' requirement, which may be termed the 'right to criticise' – a notion previously espoused by newspaper editors, but not previously expressly endorsed by the courts. We will look first at how the editors put it. Paul Dacre is not only the editor of the best-selling middle market British tabloid newspaper, *The Daily Mail*; he was also Chair of the Editors' Code Committee of the Press Complaints Commission and now performs that role for its successor, the Independent Press Standards Organisation (IPSO), which has the role of setting standards for most of the English print media on the obtaining and publishing of private information by newspapers and adjudicating upon complaints.[92] In a public lecture given in 2008 he strongly attacked the courts – and a particular judge, Justice Eady – for developing

[89] See above n 14.

[90] See, e.g., Frederick Schauer, 'Reflections on the Value of Truth' (1991) 41 *Case Western Reserve Law Review* 699, 708–9.

[91] See generally, Paul Wragg, 'A Freedom to Criticise? Evaluating the Public Interest in Celebrity Gossip after *Mosley* and *Terry*' (2010) 2 *Journal of Media Law* 295.

[92] See n 110.

a right to privacy.[93] Among other points, the lecture expressed Dacre's view that it is for the press – not the courts – to decide when a person's private life should be laid bare to the public, on the basis that some might take the view that what he or she had done, while perfectly legal, was contrary to their own standards of morality. Thus he argued:

> From time immemorial public shaming has been a vital element in defending the parameters of what are considered acceptable standards of social behaviour, helping ensure that citizens ... adhere to them for the good of the greater community. For hundreds of years, the press has played a vital role in that process. It has the freedom to identify those who have offended public standards of decency ... and hold the transgressors up to public condemnation.[94]

Since it is clear that in modern pluralistic societies there is huge variation in terms of moral standards on intimate matters of judgement such as sexual conduct, what the editor is asserting in effect is a right for newspaper editors to decide for themselves what conduct is immoral and should therefore be revealed to the public. This puts privacy at the mercy of the moral judgements of the editors of tabloid newspapers – a precarious place for it indeed and plainly not a place that affords it the status of a fundamental right.

Now compare Justice Tugendhat in the *John Terry* case, which concerned the revelation that a married footballer had had an affair:

> Freedom to live as one chooses is one of the most valuable freedoms. But so is the freedom to criticise ... the conduct of other members of society as being socially harmful, or wrong ... It is as a result of public discussion and debate that public opinion develops.[95]

The judge expanded somewhat upon this rationale, in a judgement concerning an affair between Fred Goodwin, the notorious Chairman of the bank RBS, and a woman who also worked for the bank:

> in my judgement it is in the public interest that there should be public discussion of the circumstances in which it is proper for a chief executive (or other person holding public office or exercising official functions) should be able to carry on a sexual relationship with an employee in the same organisation. It is in the public interest that newspapers should be able to report upon cases which raise a question as to what should or should not be a standard in public life. The law, and standards in public life, must develop to meet changing needs. *The public interest cannot be confined to exposing matters which are improper only by existing standards and laws, and not by standards as they ought to be, or which people can reasonably contend that they ought to be.*[96]

[93] Dacre, above n 33. [94] *Ibid.* [95] *Terry* [2010] EMLR 16, [100].
[96] *Goodwin* v. *News Group Newspapers* [2011] EWHC 1437 (QB); [2011] EMLR 27, [133] (emphasis added).

The *Terry* passage has had a strong influence on subsequent judgements: it was endorsed as 'powerful' by the Court of Appeal in a judgement in which Gross LJ, giving the leading judgement, said: 'The judge must . . . balance the claim to privacy with the equally fundamental art. 10 right to freedom of expression, in the public interest *and including the freedom to criticise*'.[97] In turn, Nicol J in the *Ferdinand* case noted the Court of Appeal's approval of the *Terry* dictum and said that he respectfully agreed with it too.[98] Why then may it be considered problematic?

First of all, it puts the issue in a misleading way: what was at issue in all these cases was not the freedom to *criticise* as such, but rather the claimed right to reveal certain private facts. To conflate the two is to treat as identical the revelation or allegation of facts with the expression of opinion about them. But the law of defamation, for example, treats these two very differently, with the defence of 'honest opinion' as it is now called,[99] affording a very broad measure of protection for evaluative statements – protection not afforded to bare factual allegations. Tugendhat J's dicta give the impression that privacy law runs the danger of censoring people who wish to express their opinions. But it does no such thing: it merely in some circumstances provides protection from the revelation of private facts.

The second and more fundamental problem with 'the right to criticise' is that it *prima facie* provides a general licence to reveal virtually any private behaviour in order to be able to criticise it, provided only that the behaviour either might generally be considered improper or even, following the more expansive *Goodwin* dicta, that some people *reasonably consider* that it *ought* to be regarded as improper. This is a staggeringly broad proposition. It would seem to follow, for example that, since most traditional religious believers of the Abrahamic faiths still consider homosexual sex immoral, this would give them the right to criticise any sexually active gay or lesbian and therefore a right to the press to disclose the homosexuality of anyone the public is interested in, given that criticism from some quarters might then be expected to follow. Presumably the same would follow about any woman in the public eye who has had an abortion. Further examples could be multiplied. While such a rationale

[97] *Hutcheson* [2011] EWCA Civ 808, [35] (emphasis added).

[98] *Ferdinand* [2011] EWHC 2454, [64]. It does not always appear, however: it was not mentioned in *K* v. *News Group Newspapers* [2011] EWCA Civ 439, despite that case involving adultery.

[99] Following the Defamation Act 2013 (UK). See section 3 of the Act, which provides that no liability arises from the expression of opinion, even if defamatory, provided that (a) the statement complained of indicated, whether in general or specific terms, the [factual] basis of the opinion and (b) the opinion is one that an honest man could have held on the basis of a fact that existed at the time of the statement.

might be seen as applicable to revelations about elected officials – on the basis that it is not for the courts to determine what factors voters should and should not consider when engaging in self-government[100] – it seems extraordinary to apply it to any (public?) figure.

But there is a deeper problem here: this 'freedom to criticise' is flatly incompatible not only with a right to privacy but with the very reasons we seek to protect privacy in the first place. The right to criticise seems to be envisaged by Tugendhat J as extending to even the inner core of private conduct, namely sexual relations; as such, it seems simply incompatible with a right to privacy. The very reason that people *need* a right to privacy in the first place is to guarantee a sphere of private, autonomous action, in which they may develop their own personality and choices, in a self-directed way, free from the censorious gaze of the crowd. Particularly where the formation of such relations, and certain modes of development, may be controversial in the 'judgement of the mob',[101] privacy allows for the exercise of individual liberty, for what DeCew has termed 'experiments in living'.[102] While control over private property allows for the physical space in which such 'experiments' can occur, if there was no ability to withhold information about them from the disapproving majority, not only would such exercises of individual choice be penalised by the reaction of others, many would be likely to be deterred by the anticipation of it (e.g., a person who wishes to explore their sexual identity might be deterred from visiting a gay bar for fear of being 'outed'). As Ruth Gavison has put it, without privacy, '[w]e also shall have [fewer] chances to experiment ... through trial and error, and fewer opportunities to experiment with behaving differently'.[103] The 'right to criticise' doctrine thus turns the ethical case for a right to privacy on its head by using the very reason that we need privacy as the reason for denying it. It also threatens to allow us privacy only for activities or decisions that are so innocuous that no one would think of criticising us for them – taking our children shopping for example.[104]

[100] For example, as Schauer has put it, 'in a democracy there appears to be a right to base one's voting decisions on criteria that other people take to be wrong': Frederick Schauer, 'Can Public Figures Have Private Lives?' in Ellen Frankel Paul, Fred D Miller, Jr and Jeffrey Paul (eds), *The Right to Privacy* (Cambridge: Cambridge University Press, 2000) 297–306; see also Volokh, above n 27, 1089–90.

[101] Nicholas W Barber, 'A Right to Privacy' [2003] *Public Law* 602, 605.

[102] Judith Wagner DeCew, 'The Scope of Privacy in Law and Ethics' (1986) 5 *Law and Philosophy* 145, 166–70.

[103] Ruth Gavison, 'Too Early for a Requiem: Warren and Brandeis were Right on Privacy vs Free Speech' (1992) 43 *South Carolina Law Review* 437, 461.

[104] A case that was won recently, by Paul Weller: *Weller* v. *Associated Newspapers* [2014] EWHC 1163.

Therefore, third, the notion of a 'right to criticise' is problematic because it will nearly always be present, and is not fact-specific: whereas the conventional public interest test requires a court to identify a specific gain to public debate in learning that particular information, the 'right to criticise' simply asserts that in every case there is a right to criticise the behaviour, provided only, presumably, that some members of the public might (reasonably) consider it to be immoral. It would be amusing to watch the judges embark on the task of trying to decide which moral views are reasonable and which are not: those of the Catholic Church on the use of artificial contraceptives?; those of right-wing Evangelicals on pre-marital sex? It is hard to escape the conclusion that these judges have simply lapsed into moralism – that their personal disapproval of the conduct in question has coloured their judgement, as it has in many judgements given by other judges in the past. Justice Eady was quite right, in the *Mosley* and other cases, to lay down a principle of moral neutrality for judges in deciding such cases, since otherwise the outcome may depend on the particular moral view of the judge,[105] an outcome that would be both unjust, and contrary to the rule of law. His lesson appears to be being rapidly forgotten.

## 8.9 Conclusion

The cases discussed in this chapter show not only that the press is starting to win the privacy battle but also the poor quality of the judicial reasoning that is allowing them to do so. Courts are increasingly relying on vague portmanteau notions like 'public figure' as proxy for more precise arguments; they have seemingly not noticed how accepting the notion that becoming well known to the public means giving up a large portion of your privacy threatens to collapse the distinction they claim to hold dear – between the public interest and what interests the public. They have started again using 'waiver' arguments, without any enquiry as to whether this notion is compliant with the core value they have identified as underlying claims to privacy. And, in a spectacularly fuzzy piece of thinking, they have embraced the notion that we have 'a right to criticise' people in

[105] 'It is not for the state or for the media to expose sexual conduct which does not involve any significant breach of the criminal law. That is so whether the motive for such intrusion is merely prurience or a moral crusade. It is not for journalists to undermine human rights, or for judges to refuse to enforce them, merely on grounds of taste or moral approval. Everyone is naturally entitled to espouse moral or religious beliefs to the effect that certain types of sexual behaviour are wrong or demeaning to those participating. That does not mean that they are entitled to hound those who practise them or to detract from their right to live life as they choose' (*Mosley* [2008] EWHC 1777 (QB); [2008] EMLR 20, [127]).

the public eye – an idea straight from the Paul Dacre handbook – as a justification for ferreting out and revealing to the public details of the private behaviour that someone may subsequently wish to criticise. And they have done so again without acknowledging any limits to a principle that is straightforwardly incompatible with any right to privacy. They have done all this while continuing to recite the mantra that the twin rights to privacy and speech are presumptively equal, and must be 'balanced' against each other – while allowing speech with any conceivable public interest to trump privacy claims without the slightest attempt to explain why one, in the circumstances, outweighs the other.

Meanwhile perhaps partly because of this, partly for other reasons, the practical effectiveness of our privacy law seems to be diminishing. It is widely acknowledged that interim injunctions are the only really effective means of protecting privacy, since they prevent the private information entering the public domain; damages awards are generally quite small[106] and accompanied by a frenzy of destructive publicity about the revelations, which then proliferate across the world via the Internet, as Max Mosley has found to his cost. The Inforrm blog noted in December last year the awarding of what was the first privacy injunction for nearly two years.[107] We can only guess at the reasons for this. It may perhaps be that the press are, at least for a while, behaving slightly less intrusively.[108] But claimants may also be more reluctant to seek injunctions these days; the recent trend of the case law is not encouraging, but another reason may be the growing perception that, in the age of the Internet, social media and instant cross-jurisdictional posting, it is nowadays hard if not impossible to keep an injunction secure, as Ryan Giggs found to his cost: he was identified in Parliament as the footballer who had had an affair, in breach of an anonymised injunction, after 75,000 Twitter users had named him.[109] I hope I am wrong, but all the above seems to suggest that real hope for improved privacy protection in practice may now lie not with the courts, but

[106] Even when substantial – the highest award was given to Max Mosley (*ibid.*) – they will generally be insufficient to cover even the inevitable portion of unrecovered costs: Mosley won £60,000 damages but, on his own account, the litigation left him substantially about of pocket.

[107] 'News: Privacy injunction granted against 'Sun on Sunday', first against the media for nearly two years' *Inforrm* (7 December 2014): https://inforrm.wordpress.com/2014/12/07/news-privacy-injunction-granted-against-sun-on-sunday-first-against-the-media-for-nearly-two-years. The previous injunction was awarded in Jan 2013 in the case of *Rocknroll* v. *News Group Newspapers* [2013] EWHC 24 (Ch).

[108] Certain practitioners suggested this to me at a conference organised by Newcastle Law School entitled 'The Campbell Legacy: A Decade of "Misuse of Private Information"' (April 2015).

[109] See 'Ryan Giggs named by MP as injunction footballer', *BBC News* (23 May 2011) www.bbc.com/news/uk-13503847.

with robust, independent press regulation in accordance with the criteria laid down by Leveson.[110] The only real hope for that appears to lie with the nascent press regulator, IMPRESS.[111] If privacy remedies are not working and the law is undermining protection for privacy, perhaps the only real hope is a change in ethical standards in the press that would mean that such gross violations would not occur in the first place.

[110] Most major newspapers have now signed up to regulator IPSO, www.ipso.co.uk/IPSO/index.html, which is dominated by the big newspaper companies, is not Leveson-compliant and has no intention of seeking 'recognition' as a Leveson-compliant regulator by the Press Recognition Panel: http://pressrecognitionpanel.org.uk/word.

[111] The Impress Project, http://www.impress.press/. It will also of course require the government to bring into force ss 40, 41, 42 of the Courts and Crimes Act 2013 (UK), to activate the statutory costs incentives for newspapers to sign up to a recognised regulator.

# 9 The Atlantic divide on privacy and free speech

*Kirsty Hughes and Neil M. Richards*

## 9.1 Introduction

When does a right to privacy become a right of censorship? Conversely, when does freedom of speech become a *carte blanche* to violate the dignity and autonomy of others? Discussions of privacy throughout the world frequently boil down to these questions. Indeed these issues have bedevilled privacy from its earliest recognition in the law. As long ago as 1890, Warren and Brandeis's seminal article framed 'The Right to Privacy' as the right to protect an 'inviolate personality' from the prying and disclosure of the new Yellow Press.[1] Leading legal authorities in both England and the United States continue to reflect this tension. Despite the parallel relationships between privacy and speech, and despite their shared legal heritage, the two legal systems have struck the balance in radically different ways. In the United States, decisions balancing privacy and the First Amendment have invariably favoured the free speech interest, at least where a press defendant published lawfully obtained 'newsworthy' content. Thus, the publication of names of rape victims or the transcripts of illegally intercepted phone conversations have been protected against privacy claims as 'matters of public concern'.[2] By contrast, numerous

[1] Samuel D Warren and Louis D Brandeis, 'The Right to Privacy' (1890) 4 *Harvard Law Review* 193; see also Neil M Richards, 'The Puzzle of Brandeis, Privacy and Speech' (2010) 63 *Vanderbilt Law Review* 1295; Neil M Richards, *Intellectual Privacy: Rethinking Civil Liberties in the Digital Age* (Oxford: Oxford University Press, 2015) Chapters 1–3.

[2] See, e.g., *Bartnicki* v. *Vopper*, 532 US 514, 526–8 (2001) (holding that a radio station cannot be prohibited from publishing newsworthy information of public concern, even where such information had been illegally obtained by a third party); *Florida Star* v. *BJF*, 491 US 524, 526 (1989) (holding that a state statute prohibiting the publication of the name of a rape victim was unconstitutional as applied to a newspaper that had obtained the name from a 'publicly released police report'); *Smith* v. *Daily Mail Publishing*, 443 US 97 (1979) (holding the First Amendment prohibits a state from punishing a newspaper for publishing the name of a juvenile murder suspect because the press lawfully obtained the information); *Oklahoma Publishing* v. *Oklahoma County District Court*, 430 US 308 (1977) (holding the First Amendment prevents a state court from prohibiting the media from publishing the name of a juvenile in a proceeding that a reporter attended); *Cox Broadcasting* v. *Cohn*, 420 US 469 (1975) (holding the name of a rape victim obtained

English cases under the Human Rights Act have protected privacy interests against press disclosure even when the facts alleged constituted front-page news.[3]

Our purpose in this chapter is to make some sense of this divergence. How could two similar legal systems apply rules sharing a common origin and reach such different results? Our methodology is explanatory and comparative. We conclude that the divergence is a function of at least two factors. First, the cultural power of the First Amendment in the United States as it has emerged from defamation law has meant that American judges have been particularly reluctant to trust themselves in ruling in ways which might infringe on freedom of speech. This reluctance is especially pronounced when the press is before the court as a defendant. By contrast, English judges are required by legislation to engage actively in balancing the two rights under the Human Rights Act 1998 and the European Convention on Human Rights. Ironically enough, the English approach is much truer to the method Warren and Brandeis suggested 125 years ago as the best way to manage this tension.

Second, we find that the two jurisdictions diverge on what privacy means, and in how the privacy interest is framed. In the United States, the right to privacy is often conceptualised as a tort right protecting little more than hurt feelings. By contrast, while English law protects privacy as a tort (through the law of misuse of private information), the structure and content of that tort is grounded upon the fundamental human right protected by Article 8 of the European Convention of Human Rights. The nature of this framing affects the ways courts approach speech-privacy cases. In the United States, the constitutional primacy and cultural power of the First Amendment makes it supreme over most private-law interests. Under such a framing, only weakened free speech interests (like private, non-mainstream press expression) or compelling privacy injuries (like the disclosure of sex videos) are regularly capable of withstanding the power of the First Amendment. By contrast, when privacy is framed in England as a human right protecting the universal dignity of all human beings, it is much better able to withstand a free speech challenge, as the cases reflect.

by the press from public records cannot be prevented from being published by statute or made the basis for liability under the nondisclosure tort).

[3] See for example the protection offered to supermodel Naomi Campbell, prohibiting photographs of her outside a Narcotics Anonymous clinic and details of her drug rehabilitation treatment, in *Campbell* v. *Mirror Group Newspapers* [2004] UKHL 22 ('*Campbell*'); Max Mosley, President of the Fédération Internationale de l'Automobile, protecting details of his sado-masochistic sex life, in *Mosley* v. *News Group Newspapers* [2008] EWHC 1777; and footballer Ryan Giggs, protecting details of his extra-marital affair, in *CTB* v. *News Group Newspapers* [2011] EWHC 1326.

Some qualifications are in order at this point. First, while there are important differences, we should be careful not to overlook the many similarities, even on the substantive question of the balance between privacy and free speech. Both are common-law jurisdictions, both have largely judge-made traditions of privacy and free speech law, and both consider privacy and free speech to be important values, and the line between them to be a difficult one.

In this chapter, we do not ultimately recommend which way the law should evolve in each jurisdiction, nor which of the two approaches is superior. In full disclosure, we disagree on some of these normative questions, which may be a reflection of our professional acculturation in American (Richards) and English (Hughes) law. But we maintain that there is value to be had in exploring the points of disagreement as well as those of similarity. If any trans-Atlantic or global conversation on privacy is to be fruitful, it will depend on first carefully identifying the variables and points of contention. It is in this spirit that we present this piece of scholarship.

We develop our argument in three parts. First, we show how the American position is a function of political commitments made initially in the context of defamation cases involving issues of racial equality in the 1960s. Second, we show how the position in English law is a product of involvement with European Human Rights Law. Third, we examine these differences through a series of case studies mapping out how each jurisdiction deals with the publication of stories involving (i) government officials; (ii) celebrities; (iii) private individuals; and (iv) video footage and photographs. We conclude by considering the ramifications of those differences. We argue that bridging the divide is essential as international conversations about privacy in a wide variety of contexts take on an increasingly critical political and economic importance; however, if any progress is to be made, such movements must be premised on a clear understanding of why and how these different approaches emerged.

## 9.2 The American approach

### *9.2.1 The development of American privacy and free speech law*

The American approach to the right to privacy is conventionally traced back to the *Harvard Law Review* publication of 'The Right to Privacy' by Louis Brandeis and Samuel Warren in December of 1890.[4] Although there were many English and American antecedents to the tort the two

[4] Warren and Brandeis, above n 1.

men proposed, it was the publication of 'The Right to Privacy' and the star power of Brandeis that led to the recognition of the tort in its modern form.[5] But although the article inspired many different conceptions of privacy, its core argument was squarely one that targeted the press. The proposed tort captured *press defendants* publishing *true facts* that caused *emotional harm.*[6] Recognising that this tort would run into claims of infringing a free press, the authors suggested that courts could separate matters of public concern from those of private matters that were not fit to print through well-established principles of common-law balancing. Judges, in their view, could be trusted with the job of keeping the press focussed on its role of informing the public and not straying into lucrative but inappropriate matters of salacious gossip.[7]

Although the United States is famed for the protectiveness of its First Amendment free speech guarantee, strong protection for free speech is newer than the right to privacy. When Warren and Brandeis penned their article in 1890, American notions of free speech were far less developed than they are today. The United States was bound by the First Amendment, but there was essentially no First Amendment jurisprudence at the Supreme Court level until after the First World War.[8] Even then, American free speech law remained much less protective of expression for most of the twentieth century, as the right to privacy and freedom of speech and press developed together over the decades. It became clear only after the landmark decision of *New York Times* v. *Sullivan* in 1964 that speech and privacy would assume their now familiar position when they conflict over matters of public interest, with free speech dominant and the right to privacy subordinate.[9]

First Amendment law did not develop until its evolution was spurred by the persecution and prosecution of leftist dissidents during the First World War. Before the war (and for some time afterwards) American free speech law could be summed up by three basic principles. First, relying on Blackstone,[10] the First Amendment was little more than a protection against prior restraints, and did not prevent the government from punishing 'bad' speech once it was uttered. Second, the standard for

[5] Neil M Richards and Daniel J Solove, 'Privacy's Other Path: Recovering the Law of Confidentiality' (2006) 96 *Georgetown Law Journal* 123. For the original suggestion of the 'star power' thesis, see Harry Kalven Jr, 'Privacy in Tort Law – Were Warren and Brandeis Wrong?' (1966) 31 *Law & Contemporary Problems* 326, 327.

[6] Richards, *Intellectual Privacy*, above n 1, 18. [7] Warren and Brandeis, above n 1.

[8] David M Rabban, *Free Speech in its Forgotten Years, 1870–1920* (Cambridge: Cambridge University Press, 1997).

[9] Richards, *Intellectual Privacy*, above n 1, 46–7.

[10] William Blackstone, *Commentaries on the Laws of England* (1765–69) 151–2 (Chicago: University of Chicago Press, facsimile edition, 2002).

government punishment of 'bad' speech was highly deferential to the state. And third, though implicit in the cases, the First Amendment only restrained the government in acting as censor, and did not restrain private parties from using civil law to seek liability based upon speech.[11]

These principles were illustrated well by *Patterson* v. *Colorado* (1907), involving a newspaper editor who had committed the grave error of 'reflecting upon the motives and conduct of the Supreme Court of Colorado in cases still pending' and been cited for contempt of court.[12] In upholding the conviction, Justice Oliver Wendell Holmes also said two very interesting things that revealed the state of First Amendment law at the time. First, he stated, referring to the protections of the First Amendment that 'the main purpose of such constitutional provisions is "to prevent all such previous restraints upon publications as had been practiced by other governments" and they do not prevent the subsequent punishment of such as may be deemed contrary to the public welfare'.[13] This, of course, is the standard principle from Blackstone about the prohibition on prior restraints but not subsequent punishments. Second, Holmes concluded that courts had an interest in prohibiting interference with the 'course of justice'.[14] He explained that 'if a court regards, as it may, a publication concerning a matter of law pending before it, as tending towards such an inference, it may punish it'.[15] This is a statement of the general view of the judiciary on the freedom of speech in the nineteenth century through the First World War, which scholars have termed the 'bad tendency test'.[16] Under this principle, government had the power to punish speech that had any tendency, however remote, to bring about violations of law that it had the power to prevent. This principle is also flatly inconsistent with the subsequent course of American free expression law.

Holmes, of course, famously changed his mind about free speech.[17] In this conversion, he was joined by Louis Brandeis. In a series of dissents after the First World War, the two men outlined a more protective theory of First Amendment law that required a 'clear and present danger' before the state could regulate expression.[18] Most notable were Holmes's dissent in *Abrams* v. *United States* (1919),[19] which justified special protection for free speech in terms of the search for truth and Brandeis' concurrence

[11] Rabban, above n 10. [12] 205 US 454 (1907) ('*Abrams*').

[13] *Ibid.*, 462 (internal citations omitted). [14] *Ibid.* [15] *Ibid.* [16] *Ibid.*

[17] Rabban, above n 10. See also Gerald Gunther, 'Learned Hand and the Origins of Modern First Amendment Doctrine: Some Fragments of History' (1975) 27 *Stanford Law Review* 719, 720.

[18] G Edward White, 'The First Amendment Comes of Age: The Emergence of Free Speech in Twentieth-Century America' (1996) 95 *Michigan Law Review* 299, 313.

[19] 250 US 616 (1919).

in *Whitney* v. *California* (1927), which justified it in terms of its relationship to democratic self-government.[20]

The Holmes–Brandeis theory of special protection for free expression was outlined in dissents and separate opinions, and took several decades to be adopted by a majority of the court. Yet throughout the middle years of the twentieth century, both privacy and free speech were evolving simultaneously in the lower courts. An important recent study of these cases by Samantha Barbas has demonstrated that lower court cases from the end of the First World War through the beginnings of the Cold War were grappling with privacy and free speech, often at the same time, as they sought to reconcile the two rights in a modern society that was beginning to tie free expression and the notion of 'the public interest' to basic commitments of democratic self-governance.[21] As Barbas puts it well, judges in these cases were recognising an

> expansion of the definition of 'the news' to encompass a wide variety of information, including private facts, and a reassessment of the significance of the news media to modern social life. We see the emergence of the concept of 'the public's right to know' about the world through the news media, and the ideas that the purpose of the news is not only to inform citizens about the complex workings of modern society but to generate public discourse. For the news media to achieve this function, there must be robust legal and constitutional protection for a free press, and news content must be as extensive as the public's interests and concerns.[22]

Privacy scholars were also affected by the cultural ascendancy of free speech. In his seminal 1960 article 'Privacy', William Prosser, the dean of American tort law, announced his four privacy torts of intrusion, disclosure, appropriation and false light.[23] Each of these torts was defined in terms of emotional harm that was 'highly offensive to a reasonable person'. At the same time, Prosser strongly hinted that disclosure and false light were probably unconstitutional due to the First Amendment. Prosser finally brought the privacy torts into the mainstream of American tort law, but did so while suggesting their basic inconsistency with the rising tide of protection for free expression, especially truthful expression by the establishment press.[24] He tamed and marginalised them at the same time.

[20] 274 US 357 (1927).
[21] Samantha Barbas, 'The Death of the Public Disclosure Tort: A Historical Perspective' (2010) 22 *Yale Journal of Law and the Humanities* 171, 173.
[22] *Ibid.* [23] William L Prosser, 'Privacy' (1960) 48 *California Law Review* 383.
[24] Neil M Richards and Daniel J Solove, 'Prosser's Privacy Law: A Mixed Legacy' (2010) 98 *California Law Review* 1887.

Prosser's suggestions of privacy's unconstitutionality were prophetic. Just four years later, the Supreme Court decided the seminal case of *New York Times* v. *Sullivan* (1964), which laid down the foundations for First Amendment law in general, and the conflict between privacy and the media in particular.[25] *Sullivan* transformed the landscape upon which the torts like privacy interacted with the First Amendment, and adopted an interpretation of both free speech and the role of judges in free speech cases that has much to do with the transatlantic divide on privacy and the press.

*Sullivan* involved a libel suit brought by LB Sullivan, the Alabama state police commissioner, against the *Times* for running an inaccurate political advertisement by civil rights leaders. The ad sought financial support from *Times* readers for the legal defence of Martin Luther King, Jr, against persecution by the Alabama authorities, and it described the tactics of racial persecution that the Alabama authorities had levied against King and his supporters. While the charges made in the advertisement against the State of Alabama were substantially true, they contained several factual inaccuracies. Sullivan brought suit for defamation in his capacity as a private citizen and won a large award of damages in the Alabama state courts. The US Supreme Court understood the case to be one of a state official using the civil tort system as a tool of political censorship and reversed the decision.

Two aspects of the holding in *Sullivan* are significant for present purposes. First, is the frequently overlooked holding that the First Amendment applies to tort lawsuits between private parties that impose liability on the basis of spoken or printed words. Commissioner Sullivan had argued, consistent with over a century of American case law, that civil suits between private parties could not possibly implicate the First Amendment's restriction on government power. The court rejected this argument, noting that

> Although this is a civil lawsuit between private parties, the Alabama courts have applied a state rule of law which petitioners claim to impose invalid restrictions on their constitutional freedoms of speech and press. It matters not that that law has been applied in a civil action and that it is common law only, though supplemented by statute. The test is not the form in which state power has been exercised but, whatever the form, whether such power has in fact been exercised.

Thus, because Alabama's liability rule in defamation cases was being used to chill political dissent and organisation, it was 'state action' within the meaning of the First Amendment and needed to be assessed for its compatibility with that constitutional guarantee.

[25] 376 US 254, 270 (1964) ('*Sullivan*').

That assessment formed the second dimension of *Sullivan's* holding; its famous rule that a government official suing in defamation must prove that the defendant acted with 'actual malice'. 'Actual malice' does not mean animus or hatred towards the defendant but rather spoke to the defendant's state of mind about the truth of the allegedly defamatory speech. The rule requires the plaintiff to prove that the defendant printed defamatory falsehoods knowing that they were false or at least printed them with a reckless disregard for the truth. But the importance of actual malice is not its doctrinal formulation; however, protective of false political speech, but rather the background assumptions about free speech on which the holding rested. These were fundamental assumptions about the importance of public debate in a democracy and the requirement that such debate be 'uninhibited, robust, and wide-open'. This proposition that public speech must receive substantial protection and deference lest it chill public debate has become the core of American First Amendment law. Writing shortly after the *Sullivan* opinion, Harry Kalven termed it 'the central meaning of the First Amendment',[26] while more recently Lee Bollinger has called it the 'The First Pillar' of American free speech law; its 'extraordinary protection from censorship'.[27] Under this theory, developed from the theories of Holmes, Brandeis, and others, and developed in the common law cases from the 1920s to the 1960s, the fragility of public debate in a democracy means that judges must be especially hesitant in censoring or imposing liability for speech involving public matters, lest they chill it and deprive listeners and readers of its insight.

*Sullivan* was a defamation case rather than a privacy case, but its two central principles applied directly to the privacy torts, especially the tort of the disclosure of private facts. This was a logical extension of the holding in *Sullivan* made even easier because Warren and Brandeis themselves had closely modelled their proposed tort on defamation.[28] Yet privacy had one additional problem that defamation did not – while defamation law punished falsehoods, the privacy torts impose liability for publicly circulated truth. Thus, in *Time* v. *Hill* (1967), the court largely gutted the 'false light' tort, an offshoot of tort privacy remedying publications that place a defendant in a 'false light' in an offensive way.[29] The court reasoned that because false light suits raise many of the same threats to public debate that defamation does, false light plaintiffs in cases on

26 Harry Kalven, Jr, 'The New York Times Case: A Note on "The Central Meaning of the First Amendment"' [1964] *Supreme Court Review* 191, 208.

27 Lee C Bollinger, *Uninhibited, Robust, and Wide-Open: A Free Press for a New Century* (New York: Oxford University Press, 2010).

28 Richards and Solove, above n 5.

29 American Law Institute, Restatement (Second) of Torts (1977) § 652E.

matters of public concern must also prove actual malice.[30] Similar constitutional limitations (though not always actual malice) have been placed on disclosures of true but newsworthy facts that are offensive to a reasonable person, as well as on infliction of emotional distress cases in which newsworthy speech is the alleged legal wrong.[31]

### 9.2.2 *American free speech methodology*

With this background in mind, it is possible to understand not only *how* American cases approach the balance between public disclosures of private facts, but also *why*. Such cases ask courts to decide whether the imposition of tort liability based upon words is constitutional. The basic approach is to measure the tort interest in preventing emotional harm against the paramount constitutional interest from *Sullivan* of ensuring that public debate remains 'uninhibited, robust, and wide-open'.[32] Courts thus do not really balance the two interests, at least not in the sense of anything resembling proportionality analysis in European cases. The American approach is much more of a measuring of the theory of liability in the case against a fixed constitutional yardstick, with any verdicts that do not measure up thrown out as unconstitutional. In practice, this is likely to be most verdicts.

Further driving the analysis in favour of the First Amendment interest is an ethic of judicial self-doubt in free speech cases. Because of the cultural and legal power of the First Amendment guarantee, American judges are by and large reluctant to create new categories of exemption from the First Amendment,[33] or to skirt too close to press regulation in close cases. American judges err on the side of free speech because they doubt their ability to police the line between acceptable and unacceptable speech without infringing *Sullivan*'s foundational commitment to unregulated and unrestricted public discussion. At least where there is a colourable claim that the disclosure at issue involves a matter of public concern, courts (even the Supreme Court) are reluctant to find liability except in the most outrageous of cases. This epistemic doubt has a long pedigree. In the most important section of his seminal dissent in *Abrams*, Justice Holmes explained that

> Persecution for the expression of opinions seems to me perfectly logical. If you have no doubt of your premises or your power, and want a certain result with all your heart, you naturally express your wishes in law, and sweep away all

[30] 385 US 374, 390–1 (1967).

[31] For example, *Cox Broadcasting* v. *Cohn*, 420 US 469, 495–6 (1975) (disclosure); *Hustler Magazine* v. *Falwell*, 485 US 46, 56 (1988).

[32] *Sullivan*, 376 US 254, 270 (1964).

[33] *United States* v. *Stevens*, 559 US 460 (2010).

opposition. To allow opposition by speech seems to indicate that you think the speech impotent, as when a man says that he has squared the circle, or that you do not care wholeheartedly for the result, or that you doubt either your power or your premises. But when men have realized that time has upset many fighting faiths, they may come to believe even more than they believe the very foundations of their own conduct that the ultimate good desired is better reached by free trade in ideas[34]

Justice Holmes' historical warning is still a central pillar of modern First Amendment law. In its most recent free speech and privacy case, the funeral protest case of *Snyder* v. *Phelps* (2011),[35] the court accepted the argument dubious to many that a military funeral protest involving signage including 'God Hates You' and 'You're Going to Hell' was a matter of public concern because it was surrounded by other signs such as 'God Hates the USA'. The court's abiding concern in that case was that tort liability (including privacy liability) not be used to chill public debate, even public debate that most people would find distasteful or offensive. In so doing, the court (which seemed to believe that the speaker's arguments were nonsense) steadfastly refused to act on that belief in case the speaker was right. As we will see in section 9.4, in practice this means that the First Amendment is highly likely to prevail unless we have private figures, private speech, sex tapes, or a theory of liability sounding not in tort privacy but in confidentiality.

## 9.3 The English approach

### *9.3.1 The development of privacy law and the relationship with human rights*

Although Americans might think of English law as pro-privacy, the right to privacy in the United Kingdom is a relatively recent development. Traditionally English law had no right to privacy. Indeed as recently as the 1990s, the courts had very little to offer privacy claimants. This is illustrated by the case of *Kaye* v. *Robertson.*[36] Gordon Kaye was a well-known actor from the BBC television sitcom *'Allo 'Allo!* He suffered a serious head injury after a piece of wood fell through his car windscreen during a storm. Kaye was in hospital following extensive brain surgery when journalists gained access to his room, interviewed him and took photographs. Shortly afterwards Kaye had no recollection of the 'interview'. A notorious tabloid newspaper called *The Sunday Sport* sought to

[34] *Abrams* 205 US 454, 630 (Holmes, J, dissenting) (1907).
[35] 562 US ___ (2011) (No. 09-751) ('*Snyder*'). [36] [1991] FSR 62 (CA)

publish the interview and photographs and an injunction was sought on Kaye's behalf. The case went to the Court of Appeal but although the Judges plainly wished to halt publication, they were powerless to do so. Under the law at the time there was no right to privacy, no general tort of privacy, and unlike American law, not even a tort of intrusion into solitude. All the court could offer was an injunction through the law of malicious falsehood prohibiting the newspaper from publishing material that implied that Kaye had voluntarily permitted the photographs to be taken and/or participated in the interview. The injunction could not preclude the publication of the story, or the photographs, nor could the court award damages for what was regarded by the judges as a 'monstrous invasion of privacy' – namely the initial intrusion into the hospital room.[37] At that time English law simply did not protect these interests.

The judges in *Kaye* were so concerned about the gap in legal protection that they requested legislative intervention to protect privacy.[38] However, no legislation was forthcoming. On a number of occasions committees considered the possibility of introducing various statutory privacy laws, but none of these proposals resulted in legislation.[39] At the same time the courts refused to develop a general tort of privacy.[40] Thus there was no right to privacy and no general tort of privacy.

[37] *Ibid.*, 70 (Bingham LJ).

[38] *Ibid.*, 66 (Glidewell LJ), 70 (Bingham LJ) and 71 (Leggatt LJ).

[39] For example, in 1972 the Younger Committee decided against the introduction of a tort of disclosure of unlawfully acquired information (Kenneth Gilmour Younger, Report of the Committee on Privacy, Cmnd. 5012 (1972)). The first Calcutt Committee also decided against recommending a new tort (David Calcutt, Report of the Committee on Privacy and Related Matters, Cmnd. 1102 (1990)), while the second Calcutt Committee decided that the government needed to consider the issue further (David Calcutt, Review of Press Self-Regulation, Cmnd. 2135 (1993)). In the same year the National Heritage Select Committee recommended the introduction of a tort (Privacy and Media Intrusion, Fourth Report (1993 HC 291), while the Lord Chancellor's Green Paper recommended a wider tort encompassing 'infringement of privacy causing substantial distress' (Infringement of Privacy: consultation paper (1993)). In 2003 a select committee again recommended that the government reconsider its position (House of Commons Culture, Media and Sport Select Committee, Privacy and Media Intrusion, Fifth Report (2003 HC 458)).

[40] The House of Lords was asked to develop a general tort of privacy in *Wainwright* v. *Home Office* [2003] UKHL 53; [2004] 2 AC 406, but they declined to do so. See Angus Johnston, 'Putting the Cart Before the Horse? Privacy and the Wainwrights' (2004) 63 *Cambridge Law Journal* 15. It should be noted that Tugendhat J recently suggested in *Goodwin* v. *MGN* [2011] EWHC 1437 (QB), [85]–[87] and [113]–[130], that intrusion is part of English law. This discussion appears to be limited to cases which involve the publication of private information. In other words, the courts may issue an injunction to prevent disclosure of information where although the information itself is not strictly private, the disclosure of information is an intrusion into private life. This is desirable, but it is not a full-blown privacy tort. Moreover, this is only a first instance decision and is currently on appeal. It should be noted that the United States has a tort of seclusion and a number of Canadian states have statutory torts of invasion of privacy.

The vehicles for development of the law in this area were the law of breach of confidence and the introduction of the Human Rights Act 1998 (HRA). While the courts were developing breach of confidence, the law was ambiguous and the courts had not yet provided protection for the sort of personal information that the courts now routinely protect under the law of misuse of private information. Commentators at the time noted that pre-HRA there were very few cases concerning personal as opposed to commercial information.[41]

This background is important for a number of reasons. First, it highlights the fact that up until the 1990s English law provided less protection for privacy than American law. It provided less protection not because the balance between free speech and privacy was struck differently but rather because there was no cause of action even remotely resembling a right to privacy. Second, that position changed largely because of the introduction of the Human Rights Act 1998.

Unlike the right to privacy, freedom of expression has long been recognised in English law. As noted earlier, freedom of the press had been a concern of Blackstone, as it had been for John Milton and John Stuart Mill.[42] By the twentieth century, as in the United States, freedom of expression was regarded as a common law constitutional right[43] and the courts advocated the role of free speech in a democracy. This was evident in *R* v. *Secretary of State for the Home Department ex parte Simms*, in which Lord Steyn could assert that

> *freedom of speech is the lifeblood of democracy. The free flow of information and ideas informs political debate. It is a safety valve: people are more ready to accept decisions that go against them if they can in principle seek to influence them. It acts as a brake on the abuse of power by public officials. It facilitates the exposure of errors in the governance and administration of justice of the country.*[44]

Following the Human Rights Act 1998 freedom of expression is protected by Article 10 ECHR, although some scholars have suggested that the

[41] Gavin Phillipson and Helen Fenwick, 'Breach of Confidence as a Privacy Remedy in the Human Rights Act Era' (2000) 63 *Modern Law Review* 660. Fenwick and Phillipson were only able to identify one case at the interlocutory stage, *Francome* – in which an obligation of confidentiality was imposed without an express or implied promise of confidentiality and without a pre-existing relationship between the claimant and the defendant. Apart from *Francome* all of the surreptitious takings of information were commercial cases. They offered two reasons for why the HRA was needed: (i) provide an organising principle around which uncertainties in the cause of action may be addressed; and (ii) normative impetus for the consolidation of the pre-HRA developments – while confidence had the potential to be applied in privacy cases the developments were tentative and insecure.

[42] See John Milton, *Areopagitica* (1644); John Stuart Mill, *On Liberty* (1869).

[43] See, e.g., Browne-Wilkinson LJ dissent in *Wheeler* v. *Leicester City Council* [1985] AC 1054, 1065.

[44] [2000] 2 AC 115, 126.

impact on cases is often a cosmetic one.[45] Yet one should be cautious about the extent to which freedom of expression was embedded in and protected by the common law as Lord Bingham stated in a later case following the enactment of the Human Rights Act 1998 '[t]he approach of the ... common law to freedom of expression ... was hesitant and negative'.[46] While the courts often asserted that the common law and the Convention protected the same values,[47] this did not prevent the European Court of Human Rights finding violations of Article 10 ECHR.[48] Certainly freedom of expression did not receive unrestricted protection in English law, there were a number of pieces of legislation that substantially limited the extent to which individuals could express offensive or harmful speech, including the Public Order Act 1986, Race Relations Act 1976 and the law against blasphemy. Thus freedom of expression has never had the status in English law that the First Amendment has in US law: under the common law freedom of expression was often used as a defence or to qualify other rights; while freedom of expression under Article 10 ECHR is expressly framed as a qualified right which means that it has to be balanced against other competing rights and interests. In other words the right to freedom of expression is a right which must be balanced against privacy rather than a fixed measure to which the right to privacy must be fitted.

Disclosures of private information are litigated in England under the law of misuse of private information and it involves a mixture of private law and human rights. The courts have to apply and balance both freedom of expression and privacy. Both are regarded as fundamental rights, and neither right automatically trumps the other. The impact of these developments is such that if *Kaye* came before the courts now, they would be able to issue an injunction to prevent the publication.

The law of misuse of private information evolved out of breach of confidence. Traditionally there were three limbs to the law of breach of confidence as set out in *Coco* v. *AN Clark*

> The information itself ... must 'have the necessary quality of confidence about it' ...
>
> [It] must have been imparted in circumstances importing an obligation of confidence ...

45 Eric Barendt, *Freedom of Speech* (Oxford: Oxford University Press, 2005) 39.

46 *R (Laporte)* v. *chief Constable of Gloucestershire* [2006] UKHL 55, [34].

47 *Attorney General* v. *Guardian Newspapers (No. 2)* [1990] 1 AC 109, 283, *Derbyshire County Council* v. *Times Newspapers* [1993] AC 534, 551; *Rantzen* v. *Mirror Group Newspapers* [1994] QB 670, 691; and *R (Wagstaff)* v. *Secretary of State for Health* [2001] 1 WLR 292, 316–17.

48 *Sunday Times* v. *United Kingdom* (1979) 2 EHRR 245; *Observer and Guardian* v. *United Kingdom* (1991) 14 EHRR 153.

> [T]here must be an un-authorised use of the information to the detriment of the party communicating it.[49]

It was the second limb that was seen as a restriction upon the extent to which breach of confidence could be used in media privacy cases. Historically the second limb required a pre-existing relationship, for example, employer and employee or husband and wife, although even prior to the enactment of the Human Rights Act 1998 the courts were developing a more flexible approach to breach of confidence.[50] The second requirement had been developed to accommodate the imposition of confidentiality as a matter of conscience induced by the circumstances of receiving information. Nevertheless it was also the case that the courts did not systematically apply breach of confidence to personal privacy cases until after the enactment of the HRA 1998.[51]

The leading case post-HRA is the House of Lords decision in *Campbell* v. *MGN* where the Lords took the opportunity to develop the common law to provide a means of protecting individuals against the disclosure of personal information.[52] *Campbell* concerned the *Daily Mirror's* publication of the details of supermodel Naomi Campbell's drug treatment at Narcotics Anonymous. While it was conceded that the newspaper could legitimately reveal the fact that Ms Campbell was a drug addict (she had previously declared that unlike other supermodels she did not take drugs) and that she was receiving treatment, the House of Lords by a majority of 3:2 found the newspaper liable for publishing a photograph of supermodel Naomi Campbell outside a Narcotics Anonymous meeting and details of her treatment.[53] Ms Campbell was awarded £3,500 damages. The House of Lords took the opportunity to affirm that the law had developed a separate cause of action known as misuse of private information which had 'firmly shaken off' the need for a confidential relationship. It was clear following that decision that celebrities are entitled to some privacy even if the story will sell papers. But how do the courts reconcile the claimant's right to privacy with the defendant's right to freedom of expression?

### 9.3.2 *Method for balancing the right to privacy and freedom of expression*

There are two stages to the courts' analysis. First, the court considers whether the claimant had a reasonable expectation of privacy. Unlike the law of breach of confidence, the courts look at whether the information

[49] *Coco* v. *AN Clark* [1969] RPC 41, 47. [50] Phillipson and Fenwick, above n 43.
[51] *Ibid.* [52] *Campbell* [2004] UKHL 22. [53] *Ibid.*

was private rather than whether there should be an obligation of confidentiality. The reasonable expectation of privacy test can be answered in one of two ways, either the information itself is obviously private, or in the circumstances the individual had a reasonable expectation of privacy.[54] Examples of types of information that have been regarded as private include details of medical conditions and treatment and details of one's sex life. The bar for the reasonable expectation of privacy test is set lower in English law than the test for the disclosure of private facts tort in the United States, which requires that the disclosure be 'highly offensive to a reasonable person'.[55] In *Campbell* the House of Lords expressly rejected a requirement that the disclosure of personal information be 'highly offensive'.[56] Thus the scope of the English tort is significantly broader.

If the answer to the reasonable expectation of privacy test is positive, then the court must balance the Article 8 right to privacy[57] against the Article 10 right to freedom of expression.[58] In striking the balance, the courts are guided by the principles laid out in European case law. Under the European Convention on Human Rights, freedom of expression and privacy are granted equal status. In 1998 the Council of Europe, responding to the death of Princess Diana in a paparazzi chase in Paris, issued a Resolution asserting the relationship between the two Convention rights.

[54] For discussion see Kirsty Hughes, 'A Behavioural Understanding of Privacy and its Implications for Privacy Law' (2012) 75 *Modern Law Review* 806; and the chapter by Eric Barendt in this book.

[55] American Law Institute, Restatement (Second) of Torts (1977) §652D.

[56] *Campbell* [2004] UKHL 22.

[57] Convention for the Protection of Human Rights and Fundamental Freedoms, 4 November 1950, 213 UNTS 221, in force 3 September 1953, Art. 8 ('ECHR'): Right to respect for private and family life

1. Everyone has the right to respect for his private and family life, his home and his correspondence.
2. There shall be no interference by a public authority with the exercise of this right except such as is in accordance with the law and is necessary in a democratic society in the interests of national security, public safety or the economic wellbeing of the country, for the prevention of disorder or crime, for the protection of health or morals, or for the protection of the rights and freedoms of others.

[58] ECHR Art. 10, Freedom of expression

1. Everyone has the right to freedom of expression. This right shall include freedom to hold opinions and to receive and impart information and ideas without interference by public authority and regardless of frontiers. This Article shall not prevent States from requiring the licensing of broadcasting, television or cinema enterprises.
2. The exercise of these freedoms, since it carries with it duties and responsibilities, may be subject to such formalities, conditions, restrictions or penalties as are prescribed by law and are necessary in a democratic society, in the interests of national security, territorial integrity or public safety, for the prevention of disorder or crime, for the protection of health or morals, for the protection of the reputation or rights of others, for preventing the disclosure of information received in confidence, or for maintaining the authority and impartiality of the judiciary.

> It is often in the name of a one-sided interpretation of the right to freedom of expression, which is guaranteed in Article 10 of the European Convention on Human Rights, that the media invade people's privacy, claiming that their readers are entitled to know everything about public figures.
>
> Certain facts relating to the private lives of public figures, particularly politicians, may indeed be of interest to citizens, and it may therefore be legitimate for readers, who are also voters, to be informed of those facts.
>
> It is therefore necessary to find a way of balancing the exercise of two fundamental rights, both of which are guaranteed in the European Convention on Human Rights: the right to respect for one's private life and the right to freedom of expression.
>
> The Assembly reaffirms the importance of every person's right to privacy, and of the right to freedom of expression, as fundamental to a democratic society. These rights are neither absolute nor in any hierarchical order, since they are of equal value.[59]

The European Court of Human Rights has applied the Resolution in subsequent cases and the court has developed a set of criteria for balancing the Convention rights. These criteria were established in a series of cases relating to the publication of details of the private lives of celebrities beginning with the first *Von Hannover* v. *Germany* decision.[60] In *Von Hannover (No. 1)*, the court concluded that Germany had failed to protect Princess Caroline of Monaco's privacy by allowing magazines to publish photographs of the Princess engaging in everyday activities in public places. The court asserted that 'the decisive factor in balancing the protection of private life against freedom of expression should lie in the contribution that the published photos and articles make to a debate of general interest' as the photographs in question did not contribute to a debate of general interest, the publications violated the right to privacy. The decision of the Strasbourg court was controversial, in part because it was felt by some that the European court should have given a wider margin of appreciation to the reasoning of the German courts that had sought to strike a balance between the two rights.[61] The European Court of Human Rights revisited its approach in the later *Von Hannover* v. *Germany (No. 2)* proceedings and *Axel Springer* v. *Germany* in which the court identified a number of factors that the courts should take into consideration in determining where the balance should be struck between the two Convention rights.[62] Those

[59] *Right to Privacy*, Council of Europe Parliamentary Assembly, Res 1165, 24th sitting (26 June 1998) http://assembly.coe.int/main.asp?Link=/documents/adoptedtext/ta98/eres1165.htm.

[60] (2005) 40 EHRR 1.

[61] Rainer Grote, 'The ECHRs rulings in *Von Hannover* v. *Germany (No.2)* and *Axel Springer AG* v. *Germany*: Rebalancing Freedom of the Press with the Respect for Privacy' (2012) 55 *German Yearbook of International Law* 639.

[62] *Von Hannover* v. *Germany (No.2)* (2012) 55 EHRR 15; *Axel Springer* v. *Germany* (2012) 55 EHRR 6.

criteria are: (a) whether the information or photographs contribute to a debate of general interest; (b) how well known is the person concerned and what is the subject of the report; (c) prior conduct of the person concerned; (d) content, form and consequences of the publication; (e) and circumstances in which the photographs were taken. The first three of those factors can all be used to curtail the right to privacy of those who are in the public eye. When considering an interference with the right to freedom of expression under Article 10 ECHR, the court will also consider (a) the method by which the information was obtained and its veracity and (b) the severity of the sanction imposed.[63]

Applying the Strasbourg jurisprudence, the domestic courts have frequently recognised since the HRA 1998 that people's sex lives are essentially their own business.[64] Provided the participants are consenting adults, there is no question of exploiting the young or vulnerable,[65] and the situation does not give rise to favouritism or advancement through corruption,[66] there is no legitimate public interest in the disclosure of the existence of a sexual relationship, less still salacious details or intimate photographs. In many cases the defendant newspaper has offered no public interest argument at all and has not even attempted to justify the publication.[67] However, the courts have sometimes allowed one party to a sexual relationship who wishes to sell the story of the relationship to the press, to do so, provided the identity of the claimant is protected. Thus the courts directly determine the very issue that American courts are reluctant to engage with, namely the importance of speech.[68]

[63] *Ibid.*

[64] See, in this regard, Tugendhat J's decision in *TSE* v. *News Group Newspapers* [2011] EWHC 1308, [24]: 'For decades, both the English courts and the European Court of Human Rights have recognised a reasonable expectation of privacy in relation to sexual relationships, with sexual conduct being regarded as 'an essentially private manifestation of the human personality' (*Dudgeon* v. *United Kingdom* (1981) 4 EHRR 149, [52] and [60]). It is sometimes forgotten that, ten years before the HRA, the court in *Stephens* v. *Avery* [1988] Ch 449 afforded protection to information concerning an adulterous lesbian relationship. Sir Nicolas Browne-Wilkinson said: 'To most people the details of their sexual lives are high on their list of those matters which they regard as confidential'.

[65] *Mosley* v. *News Group Newspapers* [2008] EMLR 20, [100].

[66] *Campbell* v. *MGN* [2004] 2 AC 457, 475, where Lord Hoffmann gave the example of a sexual relationship between a politician and someone she has appointed to public office.

[67] For further discussion of this issue see 'Kirsty Hughes and Lord Grabiner QC – Written Evidence on privacy and Injunctions' in Joint Select Committee on Privacy and Injunctions, 'Privacy and Injunctions: Oral and Written Evidence (UK Parliament, November 2011) 37.

[68] The jurisprudence of the European Court of Human Rights has long determined that there is a hierarchy of expression with political expression at the apex, followed by artistic expression, which is afforded lesser protection, and commercial speech which is regarded as the lowest form of expression.

### 9.3.3 *Remedies*

Perhaps the biggest difference between American and English law is the approach to remedies. English law is more open to prior restraint, whereas American law has long been opposed to such measures. Remedies are controversial because the choice of remedy itself has implications for the protection of privacy and free speech. An injunction as a form of prior restraint precludes disclosure and therefore acts as complete fetter on free speech, whereas damages may not necessarily act as a complete fetter on free speech. The defendant is allowed to disclose the information, but needs to pay. Clearly, the greater the level of damages the more likely that the prospect of damages will have a chilling effect on free speech. Thus those that favour free speech generally oppose injunctions and also caution against large awards of damages. Conversely, from a privacy perspective damages are an inadequate remedy. Once the information is disclosed, the harm is done. Unlike defamation, an award of damages cannot restore reputation as the information is true. Thus from the perspective of the claimant – an injunction is the preferable remedy as it prevents the information from being disclosed in the first place.

In English law both damages and injunctions are available. In order to obtain an interim injunction the claimant must not only establish that his or her right to privacy is engaged, but also that the requirement set out in section 12(3) of the HRA is satisfied. Section 12(3) HRA provides that 'no such relief is to be granted so as to restrain publication before trial unless the court is satisfied that the applicant is likely to establish that publication should not be allowed'. In *Cream Holdings* v. *Banerjee* the House of Lords determined that: likely means 'more likely than not' in this context.[69] The court will also consider whether damages would be an adequate remedy, and where the balance of convenience lies between Article 8 and Article 10 ECHR. Thus it is not the case that claimants can advance spurious claims to block the publication of any news story. Two sub-categories of injunctions have been the subject of controversy and confusion and they have been misunderstood in both the United Kingdom and the United States in part due to some dubious press coverage. They are super-injunctions and anonymity orders. A super-injunction can properly be defined as follows:

> An interim injunction which restrains a person from: (i) publishing information which concerns the applicant and is said to be confidential or private; and, (ii) publicising or informing others of the existence of the order and the proceedings (the 'super' element of the order).[70]

[69] [2005] 1 AC 253, [22]–[23].

[70] *Report of the Committee of Super-Injunctions: Super-Injunctions, Anonymised Injunctions and Open Justice*, (Master of the Rolls, May 2011) paragraph 2.14 ('*Report of the CMS*').

An anonymised injunction is:

> An interim injunction which restrains a person from publishing information which concerns the applicant and is said to be confidential or private where the names of either or both of the parties to the proceedings are not stated.[71]

As both are forms of interim injunction, they must satisfy the criteria for an interim injunction set out above. Thus, as a matter of law, it is not the case that super-injunctions and anonymised injunctions are automatically, or indeed readily, granted. In 2011 super-injunctions were headline news and there was a press myth that the courts were readily giving out 'super-injunctions' to celebrities. But, while there was a rise in the number of cases in which interim injunctive relief was sought, and the courts granted injunctions, these generally took the form of anonymity orders or injunctions prohibiting the publication of specific details. They were not, as the *Report of the CMS* confirmed, super-injunctions.[72] Further, following clarification of the court's approach to granting super-injunctions in *Donald* v. *Ntuli*,[73] the circumstances in which that type of injunction can properly be made for anything other than a short period of time are extremely limited. Since 2011 the Ministry of Justice has published statistics on privacy injunctions; in January–June 2014 there were no privacy injunction proceedings.[74]

The reality is that in many cases in which a privacy injunction is sought, the defendant advanced no public interest argument. This does not, however, relieve the court of its obligation to consider the matter: section 12(4) of the HRA requires the court to have regard to whether publication is in the public interest, regardless of whether it is raised by the defendant or not. Nevertheless, this practice has been starkly highlighted by the *Guardian's* analysis of applications for privacy injunctions, which has revealed that, between 2007 and 2011, a public interest argument was advanced in only seven cases; 21 out of the 38 cases identified in the *Guardian*'s survey did not involve a public interest argument at all; and in the remaining cases, it is not clear whether a public interest argument was

[71] *Ibid.*, paragraph 2.14.

[72] *Ibid.*, page iv. The report dispelled the myth that the courts were issuing significant numbers of super-injunctions. It confirmed that only two known super-injunctions have been issued by the courts since the case of *Terry* v. *Persons Unknown* [2010] EMLR 16. One of those injunctions was set aside on appeal (*Donald* v. *Ntuli* [2011] 1 WLR 294), and the other was granted for a period of 7 days for anti-tipping-off reasons (*DFT* v. *TFD* [2010] EWHC 2335).

[73] [2011] 1 WLR 294.

[74] Ministry of Justice, 'Statistics on privacy injunctions: January to June 2014' (25 September 2014) www.gov.uk/government/uploads/system/uploads/attachment_data/file/358274/privacy-injunctions-statistics-january-june-2014.pdf.

put forward.[75] It is rare for a defendant to advance a public interest argument, and even rarer for a defendant to support such an argument with credible evidence.

## 9.4 Comparing the cases

There are thus real and meaningful differences between how the English misuse of private information tort and the American disclosure of private facts interact with constitutional protections for free expression. England balances two equally weighty constitutional rights, whereas under the American tort notions of privacy are curtailed by the dominance of the First Amendment. These differences are best illustrated by a series of comparative examples, (i) disclosures of information relating to government officials; (ii) disclosures of information relating to celebrities; (iii) disclosures of information relating to private individuals; and (iv) the dissemination or publication of photographs or video footage. Analysis across these core areas highlights a number of important differences, but also some points of similarity.

### *9.4.1 Government officials and heads of states*

Under American free speech law, it should be unsurprising that privacy and defamation cases involving government officials receive the greatest scrutiny under the First Amendment. Questions relating to the fitness of women and men for public office are at the core of the concept of a *matter of public concern*. *Sullivan*, of course, held that the greatest level of First Amendment protection was warranted when tort law was being used to deter discussion about the behaviour of public officials, and thus acting as a private law substitute for the old crime of seditious libel.[76] This idea was at the heart of the Warren and Brandeis theory as well, under which the proposed tort would not reach matters of public interest, such as those relating to the fitness of a candidate for public office.[77]

Under American law, the mere involvement of a public official in the litigation can render an entire set of facts newsworthy and immune from tort liability resulting from press reports. For example, in *Bartnicki* v. *Vopper*, the Supreme Court protected the disclosure of an intercepted telephone conversation by the press because the press had not participated in the interception, and the recording related to a matter of public

[75] Available online at the *Guardian:* www.guardian.co.uk/law/datablog/2011/aug/05/super injunctions-gagging-orders-injunctions-list#data

[76] *Sullivan*, 376 US 254, 297 (1964). [77] Warren and Brandeis, above n 1, 214–16.

import, a public school teacher's strike.[78] More controversially, in the leading case of *Sipple* v. *Chronicle Publishing*, a state court ruled that the disclosure tort could not be used to bar the *San Francisco Chronicle* from reporting that the plaintiff, Oliver Sipple, was gay. Sipple had saved the life of President Ford by thwarting an attempted assassination, and the court held that Sipple could not recover from being outed in press reports because his sexual orientation was relevant to dispelling 'the false public opinion that gays were timid, weak, and unheroic figures and to raise the equally important political question whether the President of the United States entertained a discriminatory attitude or bias against ... homosexuals'.[79] Ford had not thanked Sipple publicly, and because there had been speculation that Ford might have done this out of homophobia, the court ruled that Sipple's outing was protected by the First Amendment. (It later turned out that Ford had thanked Sipple with 'heartfelt appreciation' in a personal letter signed 'Jerry Ford'.[80])

Yet to say that all matters involving public officials are insulated by the First Amendment under American law would be significantly overstating things. Even under American law, First Amendment protection has important limits. The disclosure by the press of even newsworthy private facts can be regulated, at least when there is something like a duty of confidentiality in the case. Thus, in *Cohen* v. *Cowles Media*, the Supreme Court upheld a judgement against a newspaper for breaking a promise to withhold a source's name from a story, even though the story involved a scandal about a candidate for government, and the source was connected to the candidate's campaign.[81] And in *Boehner* v. *McDermott*, the DC Circuit Court of Appeals held that a Member of Congress could be held liable for sharing an illegally recorded tape of other Members plotting because it violated an internal House ethics confidentiality rule, even though the disclosing Member had not participated in the illegal interception and the disclosure was highly newsworthy.[82]

The Strasbourg jurisprudence on the rights of government officials to privacy is also mixed. At first glance it appears that the position is relatively simple, namely that politicians are entitled to less privacy than other individuals. The court has repeatedly stated in both defamation and privacy cases that the limits of permissible criticism are wider as regards politicians than other individuals. The court recognises that the press plays an important role as 'public watchdog' and that press coverage of the activities of politicians is crucial to democracy. Yet, while politicians

[78] *Bartnicki* v. *Vopper*, 532 US 514 (2001).
[79] 201 Cal. Rptr. 665 (Cal. Ct. App. 1984).
[80] Dan Morain, 'Sorrow Trailed a Veteran Who Saved a President's Life and Then Was Cast in an Unwanted Spotlight', *LA Times* (13 February 1989) Part 5, 1.
[81] 501 US 663, 665 (1991). [82] 484 F.3d 573 (D.C. Cir. 2007).

are entitled to less privacy, they are entitled to some semblance of a private life. Indeed in *Axel Springer* the court noted that

> A fundamental distinction needs to be made between reporting facts capable of contributing to a debate in a democratic society, relating to politicians in the exercise of their official functions for example, and reporting details of the private life of an individual who does not exercise such functions. Whilst in the former case the press exercises its role of 'public watchdog' in a democracy by imparting information and ideas on matters of public interest, that role appears less important in the latter case. Similarly, although in certain special circumstances the public's right to be informed can even extend to aspects of the private life of public figures, particularly where politicians are concerned, this will not be the case – even where the persons concerned are quite well known to the public – where the published photos and accompanying commentaries relate exclusively to details of the person's private life and have the sole aim of satisfying the curiosity of a particular readership in that respect.[83]

The rationale for this is clear, but it is difficult to discern where those limits will be drawn in practice and how this compares to the level of privacy offered to other public figures. In *Editions Plons* v. *France* the European Court of Human Rights held that an injunction prohibiting the disclosure of the former French president's terminal illness while head of state violated Article 10 ECHR, although it should also be noted that the court found that a temporary injunction prohibiting the disclosure of the information shortly after his death was justified.[84] The principles were applied in *Ruusunen* v. *Finland.*[85] *Ruusunen* was the former girlfriend of the former prime minister of Finland. She published an autobiography which described a period of their life together including details of their sex life. Finnish law criminalises the dissemination through mass media (or otherwise by making available to many persons) of information, insinuation or images of the private life of another person conducive to causing that person suffering or contempt. Enforcing these provisions the public prosecution office brought criminal proceedings against the applicant and the publishing company for disclosing information about the private life of the prime minister. The appellate court convicted the applicant and sentenced her to a 300 euro fine, the court also ordered the forfeiture of the proceeds of the crime, 4,270 euros, to the state. The Supreme Court upheld the conviction but quashed the forfeiture order. The applicant complained to the European Court of Human Rights. The court found that there was no violation of Article 10 ECHR.[86]

[83] *Axel Springer* v. *Germany* (2012) 55 EHRR 6, [91] citing *Von Hannover* v. *Germany (No.2)* (2012) 55 EHRR 15.

[84] *Editions Plons* v. *France* (2006) 42 EHRR 36.

[85] *Ruusunen* v. *Finland* (App. No. 73579/10, 14 January 2014) ('*Ruusunen*'), available on HUDOC: http://hudoc.echr.coe.int/sites/eng/pages/search.aspx?i=001-139989.

[86] As noted above we find the use of criminal law to protect the private life of a politician particularly troubling. It may be counter- argued that the use of criminal law may provide

The court reiterated that 'the limits of permissible criticism are wider as regards a politician than as regards a private individual' because the former 'inevitably and knowingly lay themselves open to close scrutiny of their words and deeds by journalists and the public at large, and they must consequently display a greater degree of tolerance', in doing so the court seemed to elide politicians and other 'persons in the public eye' noting that similar considerations apply to both.[87] Yet, while emphasising that politicians and public figures must expect a greater degree of scrutiny, the court also asserted that '[i]n certain circumstances, even where a person is known to the general public, he or she may rely on a 'legitimate expectation' of protection of and respect for his or her private life'.[88] The court then went on to balance the two convention rights applying the principles that it had set out in *Von Hannover (No. 2)* and *Axel Springer.* In applying those criteria the court acknowledged that the former prime minister could be expected to tolerate a greater degree of public scrutiny. Yet the court refused to scrutinise the analysis of the domestic courts, instead the court concluded that as the domestic court had applied the *Von Hannover (No. 2)* principles the European court should afford a margin of appreciation to the state in striking the balance between the competing interests. This demonstrates why the court should be cautious about determining that a wide margin of appreciation should inevitably follow when the state authorities are striking a balance between competing rights. The court's mechanical analysis offers no sense of insight into the significance of the issues at stake. In particular the fact that these were not civil proceedings between the former prime minister and the applicant, but were criminal proceedings in which the state's criminal justice was mobilised against the applicant to protect the prime minister. The court depressingly trivialised this issue by regarding the fine as reasonable and emphasising the fact that there was no entry on the applicant's criminal record. Yet this approach does not appear to be in line with the court's own analysis in *Axel Springer* in which the court asserted that the severity of the sanction imposed was one of the criteria for determining whether an appropriate balance had been struck between the Convention rights. While the authors of this article may disagree as to the question of whether politicians can ever restrict the publication of details of their

a faster and cheaper remedy than civil law proceedings, however, even if this is the case (and we do not know that it necessarily is true) this does not justify the use of the state prosecution system to protect the private life of politicians against citizens. The use of criminal law strikes at the heart of free speech and the democratic rationale for freedom of speech.

[87] *Ruusunen* (App. No. 73579/10, 14 January 2014) n. 86, [41]. [88] *Ibid.*

private lives, we are both of the view that the criminal justice system is not an appropriate mechanism for protecting such interests.

In a subsequent case currently under appeal to the Grand Chamber, the court held that an award of damages following the revelation of a member of the aristocracy's secret son constituted a violation of Article 10 ECHR. In *Couderc and Hachette Filipacchi Associés* v. *France* a newspaper had published a story disclosing the fact that Prince Albert of Monaco had secretly fathered a son.[89] The French courts had awarded 50,000 Euros in damages for invasion of privacy and the publisher appealed to the European Court of Human Rights. The court emphasised that the Prince was entitled to have his private life protected but that this needed to be 'weighed against the interests of open discussion of political issues, since exceptions to freedom of expression must be interpreted narrowly'.[90] In this case some aspects of the article were part of a debate of general interest, but others were not. As a Head of State, the Prince was clearly a public figure and the story raised issues concerning his hereditary function as Head of State. As the domestic courts had failed to distinguish between information forming part of that general debate and other details, there had been a violation of Article 10 ECHR.

### *9.4.2 Celebrities*

What about celebrities, loosely defined as people in the public eye who do not perform official functions? Under American law, celebrities are treated as 'public figures', and the publication of information about them receives essentially the same protection as that relating to public officials. Shortly after *Sullivan*, the Supreme Court decided the case of *Curtis Publishing* v. *Butts*, which involved a defamation suit brought by a famous football coach against a national sports magazine.[91] The court held that the full protection of the *Sullivan* actual malice standard applied to public figures because 'many who do not hold public office at the moment are nevertheless intimately involved in the resolution of important public questions or, by reason of their fame, shape events in areas of concern to society at large'.[92] Moreover, celebrities could respond to false statements about them easily because, 'as a class, these "public figures" have as ready access as "public officials" to mass media of communication, both to influence policy and to counter criticism of their views and activities'.[93] The broad protection of speech about celebrities under defamation law has been extended to disclosure tort cases as well. As early as 1940, the

[89] (App. No. 40454/07, 12 June 2014) available on HUDOC: http://hudoc.echr.coe.int/sites/eng/pages/search.aspx?i=001-145084.
[90] *Ibid.* [91] 388 US 130 (1967). [92] *Ibid.*, 164. [93] *Ibid.*

Second Circuit held in the famous *Sidis* case that a 'Where Are They Now?' feature on a reclusive former child prodigy was not actionable under the disclosure tort. The court explained, in reasoning that reflects American law to this day, that '[r]egrettably or not, the misfortunes and frailties of neighbors and "public figures" are subjects of considerable interest and discussion to the rest of the population. And when such are the mores of the community, it would be unwise for a court to bar their expression in the newspapers, books, and magazines of the day'.[94]

The Strasbourg court has held that celebrities are entitled to less privacy than private individuals, but more privacy than those exercising official functions. However, as the same principles apply to both politicians and celebrities, it is difficult to determine the implications of these different categories. As discussed earlier, the court has held that even politicians are entitled to keep private those details of their lives that do not relate to their official role. Thus in practice it is not clear what the sphere of privacy afforded to celebrities amounts to, and how it relates to the level of protection offered to politicians and ordinary individuals. What is apparent from the case law is that Article 8 ECHR may protect both anodyne and salacious stories. *Von Hannover (No. 1)* exemplifies the anodyne end of the spectrum the court held in that case that photographs of Princess Caroline of Monaco carrying out ordinary activities such as shopping, dining in a restaurant and visiting a beach club were protected by Article 8 ECHR. At the salacious end of the spectrum the court acknowledged in *Mosley* v. *United Kingdom* that details of a sado-masochistic sex romp involving the president of the Fédération Internationale de l'Automobile were protected by Article 8 ECHR; commenting that the publication of these details constituted a 'flagrant and unjustified invasion into the applicant's private life'.[95] Yet the court has also asserted that the news worthy nature of the story and the prior conduct of the applicant may also alter the balance which is struck between the celebrity's privacy right and freedom of expression. Thus in *Von Hannover (No. 2)* the court held that the magazines were entitled to publish a set of photographs of the Princess on holiday when they were published in connection to a story concerning the illness of her father and who was looking after him while she was on holiday.[96] In *Axel Springer* the court held that the anonymous celebrity in

[94] *Sidis* v. *F-R Publishing*, 113 F.2d 806, 809 (2nd Cir. 1940). See generally, Samantha Barbas, 'The Sidis Case and the Origins of Modern Privacy Law' (2012) 36 *Columbia Journal of Law and the Arts* 21.

[95] Mosley lost the pre-notification argument but it was accepted in the proceedings that the publication itself violated Article 8 ECHR. The domestic courts had awarded £60,000 damages.

[96] *Von Hannover* v. *Germany (No.2)* (2012) 55 EHRR 15.

question had courted publicity and therefore his privacy should be curtailed.[97] These findings were in spite of the fact that the Regional Court had found that the personal disclosures were limited and did not amount to waiver of his privacy. Even more bizarre was the court's conclusion that there was a greater public interest in the story (the revelation of the arrest of a celebrity for possession of cocaine) because the celebrity in question played a detective in a police drama 'whose mission was law enforcement and crime prevention'.[98] If that analysis is followed to its logical conclusion, it would mean that actors who play criminals or drug addicts are entitled to greater privacy than those who portray police officers and priests.

The court also declined to protect the privacy of celebrities in *Lillo-Stenberg and Saether* v. *Norway*.[99] This case concerned the publication of photographs of the arrival and departure of a bride and groom (a famous Norwegian actress and musician) at a private wedding ceremony conducted outdoors on an islet. The photographs were published in a weekly magazine as part of a two page article. The couple were unsuccessful in the proceedings in the Norwegian courts and subsequently brought proceedings to the European Court of Human Rights. The court found no violation of Article 8 ECHR. There are two issues which stand out from the judgement. First, the court was very deferential to the decisions of the Norwegian courts.[100] Second, the court's analysis of what constitutes a debate of general interest requires closer examination. The court followed the reasoning of the Norwegian courts that a wedding has a public element, the court then added of its own initiative that 'the publication of an article about a wedding cannot itself relate exclusively to details of a person's private life and have the sole aim of satisfying public curiosity'[101] and that therefore 'there was an element of general interest in the article about the applicant's wedding'.[102] The court's analysis here seems utterly implausible; it is hard to discern how the publication of photographs of a wedding does anything other than satisfy public curiosity. The very point of the publication is to show what the wedding looked like; there was no suggestion that it formed part of any broader debate. Thus it seems doubtful that there was 'an element of general interest in the article'. The old adage 'what is interesting to the public is not necessarily in the public interest' is apt.

Examining across the cases, it is not possible to draw a general rule about the balance which is struck between privacy and freedom of

[97] *Axel Springer* v. *Germany* (2012) 55 EHRR 6. [98] *Ibid.*, [99].
[99] *Lillo-Stenberg and Saether* v. *Norway* (App. No. 13258/09, 16 January 2014) available on HUDOC: http://hudoc.echr.coe.int/sites/eng/pages/search.aspx?i=001-140015.
[100] *Ibid.*, [44]. [101] *Ibid.*, [37]. [102] *Ibid.*

expression when the court is faced with cases concerning celebrities. Each case will be context-specific and will depend upon the application of the full set of criteria developed by the court. There are cases concerning trivial details of the life of a celebrity that have been protected (*Von Hannover (No. 1)* and cases in which similar details have not been protected (*Von Hannover (No. 2)*)). Likewise there have been front-page news stories which were protected by Article 8 ECHR (*Mosley* v. *UK* and *MGN* v. *UK*) and other scandalous stories in which Article 10 ECHR has outweighed Article 8 ECHR (*Axel Springer* v. *Germany*). What is increasingly apparent is that the court will defer to the state provided the state has employed the framework of principles set out in *Von Hannover (No. 2)*.[103] This could lead to some very different results in each jurisdiction depending on how much weight the domestic courts decide to give to each criterion.

In England and Wales the courts have dealt with the issues raised by celebrities under a number of different guises: (i) in some cases the courts have held that where a celebrity is a role model he or she may legitimately be the subject of public interest where he or she fails to live up to that role model status;[104] (ii) the courts have held that a celebrity has waived any expectation of privacy by courting publicity, although note here that the courts have rejected the argument that entire zones of a celebrity's life will be fair game and has held instead that this must be a fact sensitive enquiry;[105] and (iii) where a celebrity has made some sort of false statement, or false projection of their image the press is entitled to rectify this on grounds of hypocrisy.[106]

### 9.4.3 *Private individuals*

While the First Amendment robustly protects publications about public officials and public figures, it sweeps with much less force when private figures are the subjects of speech. As in other areas of privacy law, Supreme Court defamation cases have marked out the basic contours of the law, and privacy law has followed suit. Thus, in *Dun & Bradstreet* v. *Greenmoss Builders*, a splintered court suggested very strongly that 'private speech', in this case the issuance of a credit report to a small number of subscribers, received substantially lesser First Amendment protection than speech on matters of public concern, and that tort law imposing liability for speech of this sort would be subject to much lower First

[103] See for example *Lillo-Stenberg and Saether* v. *Norway* (App. No. 13258/09, 16 January 2014), [44].
[104] *Ferdinand* v. *MGN* [2011] EWHC 2454 (QB) ('*Ferdinand*'); *Terry* v. *Persons Unknown* [2010] EMLR 16.
[105] *Rocknroll* v. *News Group Newspapers* [2013] EWHC 24 (Ch)
[106] *Ferdinand* [2011] EWHC 2454 (QB) and *Campbell* [2004] UKHL 22.

Amendment regulation.[107] Thus, in the case of *Lake* v. *Wal-Mart Stores*, the disclosure tort was found to apply when nude photographs of two young women were circulated in the community without their consent.[108] Nevertheless, such lower protection applied only when the speech at issue is not on a matter of public concern. If the speech or publication is a matter of interest to the community, then the full protection of the First Amendment applies.[109] Thus, in a line of cases striking down prohibitions on the publication of the names of rape victims, the Supreme Court has repeatedly noted the public interest in the operation of the courts, or the identities of the victims of high-profile crimes.[110]

It is clear from the European Court of Human Rights' analysis that the court intends to give greater protection to the private life of ordinary individuals. There are a few cases in which the court has been faced with such circumstances. Perhaps the most notable is the case of *Armonienė* v. *Lithuania* in which the court held that the publication of the HIV status of the applicant's husband violated Article 8 ECHR.[111] In fact in that case the domestic courts had already concluded that the disclosure violated Article 8 ECHR but the level of damages awarded by the domestic courts was so low that the Strasbourg court found that this did not protect the right and therefore the state had violated the Convention right by failing to provide an appropriate remedy. Moreover, in *KU* v. *Finland* the court held that Finland had failed to protect the Article 8 ECHR right of a twelve-year-old boy that had been the subject of an advertisement of a sexual nature on an internet dating site. The boy's father had sought to sue the anonymous poster of the advertisement but under Finnish law the operator of the internet server could not be compelled to disclose the identity of the poster. The European Court of Human Rights held that Finnish law failed to provide a framework for striking an appropriate balance between the competing rights and interests at stake.[112]

### 9.4.4 *Video footage and photographs*

If discussions of public officials' fitness for office is the most-protected type of expression under American law, the non-consensual publication

[107] 472 US 749, 758–9 (1985). The Supreme Court reaffirmed this principle in *Snyder*, 562 US __ (2011) (No. 09-751).

[108] 582 N.W. 2d 231 (Minn. 1998). [109] *Snyder*, 562 US __ (2011) (No. 09-751).

[110] *Florida Star* v. *BJF*, 491 US 524, 541 (1989); *Smith* v. *Daily Mail Publishing*, 443 US 97, 103–4 (1979); *Oklahoma Publishing* v. *Oklahoma County District Court*, 430 US 308, 311–12 (1977); *Cox Broadcasting* v. *Cohn*, 420 US 469, 494–5 (1975).

[111] *Armonienė* v. *Lithuania* (App. No. 36919, 25 November 2008) available on HUDOC: http://hudoc.echr.coe.int/sites/eng/pages/search.aspx?i=001-89823.

[112] (2009) 48 EHRR 52.

of sexual images and videos receives substantially less protection. American law on this point is underdeveloped and sometimes contradictory. For example, in the case of *Michaels* v. *Internet Entertainment Group*, a federal court enjoined the distribution of a sex tape involving celebrities Pamela Anderson and Bret Michaels, though an unpublished opinion of the court subsequently allowed the publication of a news report with brief excerpts of the sex tape.[113] Yet in the United States at present, the best understanding of the law is that the non-consensual disclosure of sex videos and images of even celebrities can be regulated consistent with the First Amendment.[114] There is even more of a rising consensus that for ordinary people, the distribution of non-consensual pornography is a serious social problem that does not raise serious First Amendment issues,[115] and states are starting to pass laws criminally punishing the distribution of such images.[116]

The Supreme Court has not ruled on this precise question, but it recently suggested that explicit sexual videos and images would not be matters of public concern. In *Snyder*, as noted previously, the court determined that the Westboro Baptist Church's funeral protest should be understood as involving a matter of public concern. The court found that under the circumstances of that case the dominant theme of the church's protest was that God hates America for its sexual permissiveness and was punishing it as a result. If the church were correct and God was in fact punishing the United States, this would undoubtedly be a matter of public concern. Yet in making this finding, the court once again noted that the balance between privacy and free speech must be a careful one, and that only speech on matters of public concern could trump the tort interests in protection from severe emotional distress. The court cited two examples of truly private speech – the economic speech in Dun & Bradstreet, and a sexually-explicit video by a government employee in *San Diego* v. *Roe*. As the *Snyder* court described the sex video case, 'in the context of a government employer regulating the speech of its employees, videos of an employee engaging in sexually explicit acts did not address a

113 See *Michaels* v. *Internet Entertainment Group*, 5 F.Supp.2d 823 (C.D. Cal.1998); *Michaels* v. *Internet Entertainment Group*, 1998 WL 882848, 10 (C.D.Cal. 1998).

114 Richards, *Intellectual Privacy*, above n 1, 52–4.

115 Neil M. Richards and Danielle Citron, 'Regulating Revenge Porn Isn't Censorship', Al-Jazeera America, (11 February 2015) http://alj.am/1Mb8pZo.

116 Danielle Keats Citron and Mary Anne Franks, 'Criminalizing Revenge Porn' (2014) 49 *Wake Forest Law Review* 345. See also Mary Anne Franks and Danielle Citron, 'It's simple: criminalize revenge porn, or let men punish women they don't like' the *Guardian* (18 April 2014) www.theguardian.com/commentisfree/2014/apr/17/revenge-porn-must-be-criminalized-laws.

public concern; the videos 'did nothing to inform the public about any aspect of the [employing agency's] functioning or operation"'.[117]

The origins of English breach of confidence can be traced back to the protection of Prince Albert and Queen Victoria's private etchings in *Prince Albert* v. *Strange*, so it should be no surprise that images have a particularly special role in the law of confidence.[118] Yet despite this long history it is also apparent that the level of protection offered to photographs and video footage has been shifting in English law under the influence of the Convention.

It has long been clear that very strong protection is afforded to footage or photographs of a sexual nature in English law, even if there is a public interest in the story in question. Thus even in *Theakston* v. *MGN* a case in which Ouseley J refused to recognise sexual relations between a man and a prostitute as confidential, the judge held that photographs were different as they 'can be particularly intrusive'.[119] He refused to allow the publication of a photograph inside the brothel and held that the only freedom of expression at stake was the newspapers which was 'outweighed by the peculiar degree of intrusion in to the integrity of the Claimant's personality which their publication would entail'.[120]

The strong level of protection afforded to sexual footage and images was considered in more detail in *Mosley* v. *News Group Newspapers*, a case concerning the dissemination of video footage and photographs of Formula 1 boss Max Mosley engaging in sado-masochistic orgies. The defendant argued that there was a public interest in the dissemination of the material as there was a Nazi theme to the orgies, this was particularly important as the claimant's father was involved with the Nazis and the claimant had publicly renounced Nazism. However, Eady J held that even if there had been a public interest in the story (in fact the Nazi element was not established by the defendant), this 'objective [could] be achieved effectively without displaying the edited footage of bottoms being spanked'.[121] In other words public interest in the substance of the story will not necessarily mean that the images themselves need to be revealed, a description may suffice. Yet it should be noted that ultimately Eady J refused to order an injunction prohibiting the further dissemination of the material on the basis that the material was already so widely accessible that an order to prohibit it would make very little practical difference.[122] He acknowledged that this is particularly problematic where the defendant has released the material and then seeks to take advantage of the fact

[117] *Snyder*, 562 US ___ (2011) (No. 09-751) 7, quoting *San Diego* v. *Roe*, 543 US 77, 84 (2004) (per curiam).
[118] (1849) 18 LJ Ch 120. [119] [2002] EMLR 22. [120] [2002] EMLR 22, [79].
[121] [2008] EWHC 687 (QB), [32]. [122] *Ibid.*, [33]–[37].

that it is available to defend an application for an injunction, but nevertheless he concluded that when the 'dam has effectively burst', an injunction would be a 'futile gesture'.[123] Thus English law provides strong protection for intimate footage and photographs provided that the images are not already in the public domain. Although, on this latter point, see *Contostavlos* v. *Mendahun*, a case in which there was no public interest argument for the dissemination of the sex tape. The background to that case was that the rogue ex-boyfriend of X Factor judge Tulisa Contostavlos had been selling a sex tape featuring himself and Tulisa. There was nothing more to the story than prurient interest. In that case Tugendhat J issued an injunction and because the footage was 'particularly personal and intrusive' he refused to include a public domain proviso, thus there could be no justification for the continuing disclosure of material that was already in the public domain.[124]

Thus under both traditional breach of confidence tort and the post-HRA 1998 misuse of private information tort sexual images receive a strong degree of protection. The level of protection afforded to photographs and video footage has been bolstered by the Convention. The European court has developed strong protection for the right to one's image which it has applied to a number of cases concerning photographs since the first *Von Hannover* decision.[125] The extensive protection offered to individuals captured in anodyne photographs (*Von Hannover*) means that it is beyond doubt that the court would protect the privacy of those featured in sex tapes. It is likely that this would be the case even if the individual in question was a politician given the strong protection afforded to descriptions of the Finnish prime minister's sex life in *Ruusunen.* Although it should be noted that the court's matrix of principles leaves open the possibility of concluding in exceptional circumstances that the disclosure of a sex tape is justified under Article 10 ECHR. For example, if a sex tape had emerged during the Bill Clinton and Monica Lewinsky allegations, it would be feasible for the court to find that such a disclosure was justifiable applying the principles set out in *Von Hannover (No. 2)* and *Axel Springer.*

Where the European court has pushed ahead has been in cases concerning the publication of relatively trivial photographs. Since *Von Hannover* it has been apparent that the court offers strong protection to the right to one's image. This went far beyond anything in English law, as Baroness Hale noted in *Campbell*:

[123] *Ibid.*, [36]. [124] [2012] EWHC 850.
[125] See Kirsty Hughes, 'Photographs in Public Places and Privacy' (2009) 2 *Journal of Media Law* 159.

Unlike France and Quebec, in this country we do not recognise a right to one's own image: cf *Aubry* v. *Editions Vice-Versa Inc* [1998] 1 SCR 591. We have not so far held that the mere fact of covert photography is sufficient to make the information contained in the photograph confidential. The activity photographed must be private. If this had been, and had been presented as, a picture of Naomi Campbell going about her business in a public street, there could have been no complaint. She makes a substantial part of her living out of being photographed looking stunning in designer clothing. Readers will obviously be interested to see how she looks if and when she pops out to the shops for a bottle of milk. There is nothing essentially private about that information nor can it be expected to damage her private life. It may not be a high order of freedom of speech but there is nothing to justify interfering with it.[126]

Yet in *Von Hannover* it was precisely those sorts of activities that were protected by the court. There have been two developing concerns here (i) protecting claimants from harassment by the paparazzi, implicit in *Von Hannover* and explicit in Council of Europe Resolution 1165 of 1998 and (ii) the broader protection of image rights. In a number of cases post-*Von Hannover* the court has expanded the level of protection offered to claimants captured in photographs that were taken without their consent.[127] The domestic courts have only very recently been required to set out their position on the issue.[128] In *Weller* v. *Associated Newspapers* it was held that the children of musician Paul Weller had a reasonable expectation of privacy when on a family day out in Los Angeles.[129] The court then applied the balancing factors set out in *Von Hannover (No. 2)* and held that the balance came down in favour of Article 8 ECHR, in particular because the photographs concerned children and they did not contribute to a debate of general interest. £10,000 in damages was awarded to the children. From a comparative perspective, the case is particularly interesting because the court held that the publication of the photographs in England was unlawful even though the taking of the photographs was lawful in Los Angeles.

## 9.5 Is it problematic to have different approaches?

Our analysis thus far has revealed real differences, but perhaps more subtle differences than may be commonly thought. Contrary to the assumption by both Americans and Europeans that the First Amendment eliminates liability in privacy tort cases, a closer reading

[126] [2004] UKHL 22, [154]. [127] See Hughes, above n 126.

[128] This issue was at the heart of *Murray* v. *Express Newspapers* [2008] EWCA Civ 446; [2008] EMLR 12, but that was only an application for summary judgement and was eventually settled without a definitive ruling by the court.

[129] [2014] EWHC 1163 (QB).

of the opinions and their rationales suggests that in practice things are a little more complicated. American courts undoubtedly take a strong position against torts imposing liability in privacy and other tort cases of emotional harm. But this position is far from absolute. Where the speech is particularly harmful, where the speech is not on a matter of public concern (even though this is a broad category), or where the theory of liability sounds not in tort but in contract or confidentiality, the protections of the First Amendment slacken and ordinary principles of tort law apply once more.

Conversely, English law, which is heavily governed by the European Convention on Human Rights, uses a balancing methodology which in practice affords strong protection to details of even famous people's sex lives, medical information, and photographs. A core part of the European and English courts' analysis is whether or not the story contributes to a debate of general interest, an analogous but by no means identical concept to the American idea of 'matters of public concern'. This is a double-edged sword as far as the protection of privacy is concerned. On the one hand, the fact that there is no harm requirement means that it is easier to protect privacy. But on the other hand, the fact that the test is so strongly grounded in the public interest in the story could give freedom of expression the upper hand depending on how public interest is interpreted. In many of the cases that have been brought before the English courts, the defendant has not in practice advanced a public interest defence. At Strasbourg what constitutes a public interest defence may be shifting in some of the European cases as the Strasbourg court is returning control over balancing the two rights to the member states provided that they use the Strasbourg methodology.

It is important to note then that 'public interest' means very different things in the United States and England. In the United States, 'public interest' or 'public concern' can mean little more than a factual enquiry in practice, which sometimes boils down to whether the public is interested in a story or piece of information. Riddled with epistemic doubt, American judges often defer to journalistic judgements on whether something will sell. By contrast, 'public interest' in England requires a more normative enquiry by the court. In Europe this is a complex matter with layers of deference between both the European Court of Human Rights and domestic courts (reflecting state sovereignty), and between the Strasbourg and domestic courts and journalists (reflecting the importance of press freedom and editorial latitude). In some cases the courts adopt a more nuanced approach and are willing to rule that additional details and images are unnecessary, in others the courts are more willing to afford editorial latitude to the press.[130] This depends on the nature of the story and the nature of the details included.

There is probably no real difference in outcome between English and American courts when it comes to politicians and stories directly relating to their public functions, although what is brought within the scope of public functions may vary. There are real differences when it comes to details of the sex lives of politicians as Europe gives far greater weight to privacy. There are also differences in approach when it comes to gossip about the sex lives of celebrities and photographs of celebrities engaged in everyday activities.

Despite the moral and cultural flavour of these differences, they arise from important features of the constitutional framework in which each system has evolved. While freedom of speech is protected under the Constitution in the United States, the two rights are placed on an equal footing by the European Convention on Human Rights. It is therefore unrealistic to argue that the US should adopt a more equally balanced approach or that the English courts should give dominant protection to free speech. Both are shackled by their constitutional frameworks, whether the primacy of the First Amendment or the status of privacy and freedom of expression speech in the European Convention on Human Rights. One solution to these differences is simply to accept that these are the product of different constitutional frameworks. In many cases disclosures in the United States may be of limited relevance to England and Europe more generally and vice versa. Provided that the population of each jurisdiction is content with the balance struck in their own system then perhaps we should simply accept that we each do things differently.

However, in a global media landscape we cannot be as insular as we may have been in the past. Disclosures are not limited to a single jurisdiction or continent, but take place on the global stage. After all, it was the *Guardian* (UK) that broke the Edward Snowden revelations, while American media covers many British musicians, actors and other celebrities. We thus need a system that can work better in that global context.

A handful of cases in Europe are already beginning to test these matters. The *Weller* case highlights how even photographs lawfully taken in the US may be prohibited from publication in the UK.[131] Given the extent to which parts of the UK media rely upon paparazzi photography from outside the UK, this decision could have significant repercussions. Moreover, in *OPO* v. *MLA* the Court of Appeal granted an injunction

[130] Compare, for example, *Von Hannover* v. *Germany (No.2)* (2012) 55 EHRR 15 and *Couderc and Hachette Filipacchi Associés* v. *France* (App. No. 40454/07, 12 June 2014).

[131] [2014] EWHC 1163 (QB).

based on the tort of intentional infliction of emotional harm to prohibit the publication of an autobiographical book in the UK, which could emotionally harm the author's son who resided outside the UK.[132] There was evidence that the book would not be prohibited in the country in which the child resided, but this did not preclude the injunction as the 'threat to cause harm emanated from this jurisdiction'.[133] The case has prompted concerns about possible forum shopping, and the case is being appealed to the Supreme Court. The problems posed by digital media are far greater. Some of these matters have been the subject of contentious legal proceedings in Europe. In *Delfi* v. *Estonia*, the European Court of Human Rights held that there was no violation of Article 10 ECHR when the Estonian courts required an internet news portal to adopt a system of prior monitoring of third party comments on news stories, this could include comments posted from outside Europe; a decision which was affirmed by the majority of the Grand Chamber.[134] Moreover, the European Court of Justice ruling in *Google Spain SL, Google* v. *Agencia Española de Protección de Datos (AEPD) and Mario Costeja González* requires Google to operate a system which allows individuals to request deindexing of stories from Google searches, this was despite the fact that the actual indexing occurred in the United States.[135] All of these cases highlight the complex global issues that arise from data sharing and the potential difficulties of operating different legal frameworks in different jurisdictions. The globalisation of the press brought on by modern digital technology means that interoperability between the constitutional regimes on either side of the Atlantic is essential. Interoperability of some sort is also inevitable, even if it is the product of a messy compromise rather than a formal reconciliation. The days of journalists and constitutional lawyers on each side of the Atlantic sniffing at each other's seemingly bizarre systems are drawing to a close. But if a reconciliation (or modus vivendi) is inevitable, its form is not, and we should ensure that whatever form reconciliation takes, it respects the important constitutional commitments of both systems to both freedom of expression and privacy. Although these commitments vary on opposite sides of the Atlantic, we hope to have shown not only that some agreement already exists, but also the places where there is conflict in the hope that future discussions will be more fruitful if they revolve around a clearer understanding of the points of disagreement. If any progress is to be made on these matters, then it is important to understand the different constitutional frameworks within which each is operating.

[132] [2014] EWCA Civ 1277. [133] *Ibid.*
[134] (2014) 58 EHRR 29; (2015) ECtHR 64659/09 (16 June 2015).
[135] Case C-131/12; see also the chapter by David Lindsay in this book.

# 10 The 'right to be forgotten' by search engines under data privacy law: a legal and policy analysis of the *Costeja* decision

*David Lindsay*

## 10.1 Introduction

In May 2014 the Court of Justice of the European Union (CJEU) delivered a landmark ruling in *Google Spain SL, Google Inc.* v. *Agencia Española de Protección de Datos (AEPD) and Mario Costeja González* ('*Costeja*').[1] The ruling has been widely interpreted as establishing a 'right to be forgotten' (RTBF) under the current European data privacy law, the 1995 Data Protection Directive (DPD);[2] although, as this chapter explains, the RTBF terminology is controversial.[3] The judgement has fuelled an already complex debate about whether, and if so how, an RTBF should be introduced as part of a fundamental review of European data privacy law.[4]

Since the ruling, controversy has grown as a result of the number of requests made to Google Inc. ('Google') for removal of material from

Developments relating to the CJEU ruling in *Costeja*, including responses to the ruling, have been complex and rapidly moving. Accordingly, this chapter is primarily focussed on an analysis of the ruling itself. To the extent possible, material in the chapter is accurate to November 2014.

[1] Case 131/12, *Google Spain SL* v. *Agencia Española de Protección de Datos (AEPD) and Mario Costeja González* [2014] CMLR 50 (ECJ (Grand Chamber)) ('*Costeja*, ECJ').

[2] Directive 95/46/EC of the European Parliament and of the Council of 24 October 1995 on the protection of individuals with regard to the processing of personal data and on the free movement of such data, OJ 1995No No. L281, p. 31 (the 'DPD'). See Julia Hörnle, 'Google's Algorithms, Search Results and Relevancy under Data Protection Law – Whose Data Quality?' (2014) 25 *Entertainment Law Journal* 209; Steven James, 'The Right to Privacy catches up with Search Engines: The Unforgettable Decision in *Google Spain* v. *AEPD*' (2014) 20 *Computer and Telecommunications Law Review* 130.

[3] House of Lords, European Union Committee, *EU Data Protection Law: A 'Right to Be Forgotten'?* (2014 HL Paper 40).

[4] See David Lindsay, 'The "Right to be Forgotten" in European Data Protection Law' in Normann Witzleb, David Lindsay, Moira Paterson and Sharon Rodrick (eds), *Emerging Challenges in Privacy Law: Comparative Perspectives* (Cambridge: Cambridge University Press, 2014) 290. In December 2015 an agreement was reached between the European Commission, the European Parliament and the Council of the EU on a new General Data Protection Regulation (GDPR), to become applicable in two years. The compromise text of the GDPR includes an express 'right to erasure': Art 17.

search returns. According to its online transparency report, by mid-November 2014, Google had received almost 170,000 requests for removal of links to almost 600,000 URLs,[5] with links being removed to just over 40 per cent of the URLs.[6] To assist it with this task, Google established an expert Advisory Council on the Right to be Forgotten which, in 2014, held hearings as part of a process to provide guidance on how to respond to the ruling, and which issued a report in early 2015.[7] Meanwhile, in November 2014, the Article 29 Working Party (the 'Art. 29 WP'), an advisory body consisting of representatives of EU national data privacy authorities, published guidelines on the implementation of the ruling for search engines receiving requests.[8] At the time of writing, it was clear that working through the full implications of the *Costeja* judgement would take some time.

This chapter analyses the legal and policy issues regarding the application of the DPD to search engine operators (SEOs)[9] that were before the CJEU in *Costeja*. First, the chapter addresses terminological issues relating to the phrase, the RTBF. Second, the chapter provides an overview of the operation of search engines. The chapter then introduces the *Costeja* dispute; and explains and analyses the three main legal issues before the CJEU. These issues are analysed predominantly by comparing the approach taken by the Advocate-General with that taken by the CJEU. Following this, the chapter identifies gaps and ambiguities in the ruling, which have created considerable practical difficulties of implementation.

[5] See 'Google Transparency Report: European privacy requests for search removals', Google, accessed 18 November 2014, www.google.com/transparencyreport/removals/europeprivacy/?hl=en.

[6] Paul Bernal, 'Do we remember the point of the "right to be forgotten"?', Inforrm's Blog, 18 November 2014, http://inforrm.wordpress.com/2014/11/18/do-we-remember-the-point-of-the-right-to-be-forgotten-paul-bernal/.

[7] Brendan Van Alsenoy and Jef Ausloos, 'Google's Advisory Council Hearings: Things to Remember and Things to Forget', London School of Economics and Political Science: Media Policy Project Blog, 7 November 2014 http://blogs.lse.ac.uk/mediapolicyproject/2014/11/07/googles-advisory-council-hearings-things-to-remember-and-things-to-forget/; The Advisory Council to Google on the Right to be Forgotten, February 2015, https://drive.google.com/a/google.com/file/d/0B1UgZshetMd4cEI3SjlvV0hNbDA/view?pref=2&pli=1.

[8] Article 29 Data Protection Working Party: *Guidelines on the Implementation of the Court of Justice of the European Union Judgement on "Google Spain and Inc.* v. *Agencia Española de Protección de Datos (AEPD) and Mario Costeja González" C131-12* (adopted on 26 November 2014) http://ec.europa.eu/justice/data-protection/article-29/documentation/opinion-recommendation/files/2014/wp225_en.pdf.

[9] The chapter uses the term search engine operator (SEO) to refer to entities responsible for search engines, although it is also common to refer to such entities as search engine providers.

## 10.2 What is a 'right to be forgotten'?

In previous work, I have argued that what is known as the RTBF should be carefully distinguished from both the 'right to oblivion', which is a right to be free from one's judicial or criminal past, and the 'right to erasure', which is a right, recognised by data privacy law, to delete or remove personal data.[10] By way of contrast, the RTBF should be confined to a right to have *online* personal data removed, or to have access to that data restricted, and incorporates rights to removal of data from search engines and from online digital archives. Applying this terminology, it is not inaccurate to say that, in the *Costeja* ruling, the CJEU recognised that a version of RTBF exists under current EU data privacy law. Nevertheless, as suggested by the Art. 29 WP guidelines, it is more precise to refer to the *Costeja* ruling as creating a right to request the de-listing of links in search returns to third-party web pages.[11]

Considerable terminological confusion has been created in this area by the combination of an overly literal understanding of the term 'RTBF' and an understandable desire to avoid giving users unrealistic expectations that they will be able to have their online personal data effectively purged. This misunderstanding and these concerns form the background to views, such as those of the UK House of Lords in its report on the *Costeja* ruling, where it stated:

> The expression 'right to be forgotten' is misleading. Information cannot be deliberately 'forgotten'. It cannot be 'consigned to oblivion' (the expression used by the Spanish court in its request for a preliminary ruling).[12]

It is undeniable that, once information has been made available on the Internet, it is difficult, and often impossible, for that information to be completely removed. To give the impression that to be 'forgotten' is equivalent to all records being sanitised would clearly be misleading. But to use this elementary insight to argue against what has popularly come to be known as the RTBF is to fundamentally misunderstand the nature of the problem sought to be addressed by such measures. The near-ubiquitous, pervasive access to online personal data is a new phenomenon, which poses significant risks to individual privacy and personal autonomy. Given the ease with which digital data can be copied and distributed, the most that can be done is to reduce the accessibility of the data. Potentially the most effective way of doing this is to inhibit access to personal data by means of search engines.

Although the *Costeja* ruling is an interpretation of the current EU data privacy law, which applies the existing right to erasure to SEOs, it remains

[10] Lindsay, above n 4.
[11] Article 29 Data Protection Working Party, *Guidelines*, above n 8, [6].
[12] House of Lords, European Union Committee, above n 3, 9.

a mistake to conflate the right to erasure with the RTBF. This is a mistake because the policy issues raised by ubiquitous online access to personal data differ fundamentally from the policy issues raised by the deletion of personal data in traditional data processing. As this chapter explains, the *Costeja* ruling has created significant practical problems as a result of applying a regulatory regime – traditional EU data privacy law – to a problem that it was never designed to address. Strictly speaking, the most accurate explanation of the *Costeja* ruling is to regard it as recognising that the right to erasure in the DPD extends to a right to request delinking in search returns, which is a form of the RTBF. Accordingly, while the RTBF is an imprecise and potentially misleading term, as there remains a need to conceptually distinguish the traditional right to erasure from the right to remove, or restrict access to, ubiquitous online personal data, this chapter will continue to apply the RTBF terminology.

## 10.3 How does the Google search engine work?

Search engines are the main tools for locating and accessing information on the World Wide Web; and Google operates the most popular, profitable and influential search engine. A basic overview of how Google's search engine works is necessary to understand the ruling in *Costeja.*

Google's search engine is a complex combination of software and hardware,[13] but can be understood as consisting of three main components: an automated program or 'spider', known as the 'Googlebot', which continuously crawls the Internet to locate and catalogue web pages; a search index, known as 'Google's Indexer'; and a query processor, that compares search queries with the index and returns web pages which, in accordance with Google's algorithm, are most relevant.[14] As part of this process, Google takes a snapshot of each page that the Googlebot examines and stores this in a cache. The cached version of a page is used to determine if it is a good match to the search query. Google's Indexer is a database that is arranged alphabetically by search term, with a list of documents in which the terms appear. The query processor consists of a number of elements, including the 'engine' which evaluates queries and matches them with results in accordance with Google's famous 'PageRank' algorithm. When a user performs a Google search, the Google web server sends the query to Google's index server, which matches the query to web pages and ranks the

[13] *Google Spain SL* v. *Agencia Española de Protección de Datos (AEPD) and Mario Costeja González*, Case C-131, Opinion of Advocate-General Jääskinen delivered on 25 June 2013 ('*Costeja*, A–G'), fn 9.

[14] This overview of Google's search engine is based on the GoogleGuide, www.googleguide.com/.

results, which are then returned to the user and formatted with ‘snippets’ of the web pages.

Website owners can prevent their sites being indexed by Google, or other search engines, by applying exclusion codes, such as the robots.txt file or Noindex/NoArchive tag. The robots.txt file is used by website owners to specify web pages that are not to be indexed by web crawlers, such as the Googlebot.[15] More specifically, the robots exclusion protocol incorporates a number of meta tags, including: the <noindex> tag, which instructs Google not to index a specific web page; the <nofollow> tag, which instructs Google not to follow the links on a specific web page; the <noarchive> tag, which instructs Google not to store a cached copy of a web page; and the <nosnippet> tag, which instructs Google not to show a snippet from the web page in search returns.[16] While exclusion codes indicate that a site should not be indexed, compliance with a code is purely a matter for the SEO.

## 10.4 Procedural history of the *Costeja* ruling

In 2011 a large number of complaints were made to the Spanish data protection authority, the Agencia Española de Protección de Datos (AEPD), seeking removal of content from the Web and from Google search returns. Many of the complaints concerned material published online in the Spanish Official Gazette or in online news archives, some of which had been published as a result of an official order from a public authority.

The diversity of the factual circumstances in the complaints illustrates the complexity of the policy issues raised by attempts to remove online material. In one case, two sisters objected to a photograph in an archive of a 1985 news story about the brother of the mayor of Barcelona, where they appeared in prison and obviously suffering drug withdrawals.[17] In another case, a plastic surgeon objected to search return results of an

[15] For a general explanation of the operation of the robots.txt file see Dan Crow, ‘Controlling how search engines access and index your web site’, Google Official Blog, 26 January 2007 http://googleblog.blogspot.com.au/2007/01/controlling-how-search-engines-access.html.

[16] Dan Crow, ‘The Robots Exclusion Protocol’, Google Official Blog, 22 February 2007 http://googleblog.blogspot.com.au/2007/02/robots-exclusion-protocol.html. For the original robot exclusion protocol standard see Martijn Koster, ‘A Standard for Robot Exclusion’ www.robotstxt.org/orig.html.

[17] Artemi Rallo Lombarte, ‘The Origins and Importance of the Right to Be Forgotten’ (Keynote address presented at ‘The “Right to be Forgotten” and Beyond: Data Protection and Freedom of Expression in the Age of Web 2.0’, Oxford Privacy Information Law and Society Conference University of Oxford, 12 June 2012) available via www.csls.ox.ac.uk/conferences/oxpilsconference2012.

archived story from the *El Pais* newspaper of a 1991 malpractice suit, which failed to mention his subsequent acquittal at trial.[18] Yet another case concerned search engine links to reports of a father who, in 1989, had been charged with suffocating his child, but who had successfully pleaded the defence of mental illness.[19]

The particular facts before the CJEU concerned a Spanish lawyer, Mario Costeja González (Costeja), who was identified in two announcements, made pursuant to an order by the Spanish Ministry of Labour and Social Affairs, which were published in a widely circulated Catalonian newspaper, *La Vanguardia*, in early 1998. The newspaper items concerned a compulsory real estate auction of property owned by Costeja that resulted from attachment proceedings, as part of Spanish bankruptcy law, arising from unpaid social security debts. The announcements were subsequently uploaded to an online archive maintained by the newspaper. Costeja claimed that, as the attachment proceedings had been resolved, the online items were no longer relevant and should be removed.

After the newspaper refused to remove the notices, Costeja lodged a request with the AEPD to have the archived notices removed both at source and from the Google search links. While the AEPD found that the notices on the newspaper site were lawful, it ordered Google to remove links to the notices from its search results. Google Spain and Google Inc. appealed to the Audiencia Nacional (the Spanish High Court) which, on 9 March 2012, referred a series of questions to the CJEU for a ruling on the application of the DPD to the Google search engine. In June 2013, Advocate-General Jääskinen issued an Opinion effectively finding that SEOs, such as Google, had no legal responsibility under the DPD for personal data appearing on websites that they process. Although it is usual for the CJEU to agree with the Opinion of an Advocate-General, in this case the court reached a different conclusion.

## 10.5 The issues before the CJEU

The reference to the CJEU raised difficult legal questions about the application of the DPD to SEOs. Fundamental problems with interpreting the DPD and applying it to SEOs were well known in the data privacy

[18] Ciaran Giles, 'Spain Launches First "Right to be Forgotten" Case Against Google', *The Huffington Post*, updated 21 June 2011 www.huffingtonpost.com/2011/04/21/right-to-be-forgotten-google-spain_n_851891.html; Kashmir Hill, 'Plastic Surgeon's Legal Quest to Facelift Google Search Results', *Forbes* (online), 3 July 2011 www.forbes.com/sites/kashmirhill/2011/03/07/plastic-surgeons-legal-quest-to-facelift-google-search-results/.

[19] Lombarte, above n 17.

community, with some of the most contentious issues being the subject of Opinions delivered by the Art. 29 WP.[20]

The main legal issues before the CJEU were:

- the territorial scope of the application of the DPD to search engine operators, especially where an operator is effectively headquartered outside the European Union (EU) but with European subsidiaries;
- the extent to which an SEO is an entity regulated by the DPD, specifically whether or not it is a 'data controller'; and
- the extent to which the substantive rules under the DPD relating to data processing require an SEO to remove links to the relevant material from search results.

The reference to the CJEU was an opportunity for clarifying contentious provisions of the DPD, with some of the complexity illustrated by the differences between the Opinion of the Advocate-General and the court's ruling. While the CJEU ruling clarifies some points, however, as explained in this chapter, significant ambiguities and gaps in the ruling have created challenges for its practical implementation.

## 10.6 Territorial scope of the DPD

The territorial scope of the DPD is determined by Article 4(1), which provides that EU Member States shall apply the national laws implementing the DPD to data processing where:

(a) the processing is carried out in the context of the activities of an establishment of the controller on the territory of the Member State;
(b) the controller is not established on the Member State's territory, but in a place where its national law applies by virtue of international public law;
(c) the controller is not established on Community territory and, for purposes of processing personal data makes use of equipment, automated or otherwise, situated on the territory of the said Member State, unless such equipment is used only for purposes of transit through the territory of the Community.

There are considerable difficulties in the characterisation and application of Article 4(1), with Bygrave referring to it as 'arguably the most

[20] See Article 29 Data Protection Working Party, *Opinion 1/2008 on data protection issues related to search engines* (adopted on 4 April 2008) http://ec.europa.eu/justice/policies/privacy/docs/wpdocs/2008/wp148_en.pdf; *Opinion 1/2010 on the concepts of "controller" and "processor"* (adopted on 16 February 2010) http://ec.europa.eu/justice/policies/privacy/docs/wpdocs/2010/wp169_en.pdf; *Opinion 8/2010 on applicable law* (adopted on 16 December 2010) http://ec.europa.eu/justice/policies/privacy/docs/wpdocs/2010/wp179_en.pdf.

controversial, misunderstood and mysterious of the Directive's provisions'.[21] Regarding characterisation, there is uncertainty about how far the Article is concerned purely with applicable law and the extent to which it is also relevant to jurisdiction.[22] Although applicable law and jurisdiction may coincide, this is not necessarily the case.

While a distinction between applicable law and jurisdiction is drawn by Article 28(6) of the DPD, which implies that national data privacy authorities have competence over data processing that occurs within their jurisdiction regardless of the applicable law,[23] this is relevant only where the applicable law is the data privacy law of an EU Member State.[24] In practice, it seems that applicable law and jurisdiction are conflated, so that the question of applicable law under Article 4(1) is the primary question in determining the territorial scope of the DPD, such that it may be regarded as 'the cornerstone of the data protection edifice erected by' the DPD.[25] This may be justified by the high level of protection accorded to the data privacy of EU citizens as a fundamental right under the European human rights framework.[26] There has, nevertheless, been considerable variation in the implementation of Article 4(1) in EU Member States.[27]

Article 4(1) sets out two distinct points of attachment for the application of the data privacy law of an EU Member State to data processing: that the processing is carried out 'in the context of' the activities of the establishment of a controller on the territory of the Member State; or, in the absence of an establishment, the controller makes use of equipment for data processing that is situated on the territory of the Member State.

The concept of an establishment is expanded upon by Recital (19) of the DPD, which provides that establishment 'implies the effective and

[21] Lee A Bygrave, *Data Privacy Law: An International Perspective* (Oxford: Oxford University Press, 2014) 199.

[22] Dan Jerker B Svantesson, *Extraterritoriality in Data Privacy Law* (Copenhagen: Ex Tuto Publishing, 2013) 96; Christopher Kuner, *Transborder Data Flows and Data Privacy Law* (Oxford: Oxford University Press, 2013) 176; Liane Colonna, 'Article 4 of the EU Data Protection Directive and the Irrelevance of the EU-US Safe Harbour Program?' (2014) 4 *International Data Privacy Law* 203.

[23] Article 29 Data Protection Working Party, *Opinion 8/2010*, above n 20, 10.

[24] Svantesson, above n 22, 96–7.

[25] Douwe Korff, *EC Study on Implementation of Data Protection Directive: Comparative Summary of National Laws* (Cambridge, 2002) (Study Contract ETD/2001/B5-3001/A/49) 43.

[26] Jon Bing, 'Data Protection, Jurisdiction and the Choice of Law' (1999) 6 *Privacy Law & Policy Reporter* 92.

[27] Kuner, above n 22, 117–18; Commission of the European Communities (2003), *First Report on the implementation of the Data Protection Directive (95/46/EC)*, COM (2003) 265 final, 15 May 2003 http://eur-lex.europa.eu/legal-content/EN/TXT/PDF/?uri=CELEX:52003DC0265&from=EN; Korff, above n 25.

real exercise of activity through stable arrangements' and 'the legal form of such an establishment, whether simply branch or a subsidiary with a legal personality, is not the determining factor'. The application of the concept of an establishment to trans-border internet-based data processing gives rise to obvious difficulties. These difficulties are exacerbated by the organisation of Google's search engine activities. Google Inc. is incorporated in Delaware but has subsidiaries, such as Google Spain, that are incorporated under national laws. While Google Inc. controls and coordinates the search engine activities, the exact physical location of search engine functions, including the location of its servers, is not made public. Google Inc.'s national subsidiaries are not responsible for the operation of the search engine, but are responsible for the promotion and sale of keyword advertising within the relevant jurisdiction.

Advocate-General Jääskinen pointed to the interpretative difficulties arising from the drafting of Article 4(1), as well as the problems in applying this to the Internet, to conclude that the wording is unhelpful in addressing Google's search engine activities.[28] In particular, the Advocate-General pointed out that, although Google could be said to have several establishments in the EU it was unclear where its data processing occurred and, accordingly, whether the processing occurred 'in the context' of the activities of Google's establishment as a data controller in a Member State. Taking into account the injunction in Recital (19) that the legal form of an establishment is not determinative, the Advocate-General considered that the issue should be approached primarily by reference to the business model of Google's search engine. As the business model is premised on the sale of keyword advertising, the Advocate-General concluded that a national subsidiary which is responsible for selling targeted advertising in a Member State, is an establishment 'in the context of' the controller on that territory. On this analysis, Google has multiple relevant establishments within the EU. In the alternative, the Advocate-General considered that if Article 4(1)(a) required the identification of a single controller, rather than multiple controllers, on the basis of its economic activities Google should be regarded as a single unit.[29]

In its ruling, the CJEU emphasised that the overarching objective of the DPD, as set out in Article 1(1) and confirmed by the Recitals, is to 'protect the fundamental rights and freedoms of natural persons, and in particular their right to privacy with respect to the processing of personal data'.[30] Moreover, further Recitals to the DPD make it clear that it is to be given a particularly broad territorial scope, so as to prevent the

[28] *Costeja*, A–G. [29] *Ibid.*, [66]. [30] *Costeja*, ECJ, [53].

circumvention of protections, especially by extraterritorial data processing.[31] The CJEU therefore held that where an establishment in a Member State is intended to promote and sell advertising by a search engine, the data processing undertaken by the search engine is carried out 'in the context of the activities' of an establishment in the Member State.[32]

In sum, the court determined that the advertising activities of Google, conducted via Google Spain, were 'inextricably linked' to its data processing activities, as keyword advertising is the means for ensuring that the Google search engine is profitable.[33] Consequently, Google Spain's business activities in Spain in relation to the promotion and sale of advertising space were held sufficient to found the application of the Spanish data privacy law, despite Google Inc. being responsible for any data processing by its search engine, and irrespective of the precise location of equipment or data processing.

Both the Advocate-General and the CJEU adopted expansive interpretations of the phrase 'in the context of' to found a broad, extraterritorial application of the concept of establishment. In adopting this interpretation, the CJEU emphasised the importance of protecting the privacy rights of EU citizens against extraterritorial processing. This broad interpretation has significant implications for trans-border internet communications, especially as it relieves data privacy authorities and courts of the need to determine the physical location of data processing, which may often be difficult. By basing a point of attachment on business activities within a territory that have any sort of relationship with data processing, however, the expansive interpretation of 'establishment' opens the door to the application of EU law to much online processing, as well as to multiple, potentially inconsistent, laws of EU Member States applying to the same data processing.

## 10.7 Is Google a data controller?

The DPD applies minimum principles to all stages of data processing, and generally does not distinguish between collection, storage, use or disclosure of personal data. In doing so, it applies the fundamental principle that processing of personal data is impermissible except in certain enumerated circumstances, such as where: the data subject has given unambiguous consent; processing is necessary for performance of a contract to which the data subject is a party; or processing is necessary for compliance with a legal obligation of the data controller. This approach is

[31] See especially the DPD, recitals (18), (19). [32] *Costeja*, ECJ, [55]. [33] *Ibid.*, [56].

reinforced by a broad notion of the processing of personal data which, in Article 2(b), is defined to mean 'any operation or set of operations which is performed upon personal data, whether or not by automatic means, such as collection, recording, organisation, dissemination or otherwise making available, alignment or combination, blocking, erasure or destruction'.

The principal obligations established under the DPD are imposed on 'controllers', commonly referred to as data controllers. For example, Article 6(2) provides that '[i]t shall be for the controller to ensure that paragraph 1 [of the Article] is complied with'. Article 6(1) sets out the main principles relating to data quality, including that personal data must be processed 'fairly and lawfully' and that personal data must be kept in an identifiable form for no longer than is necessary for the purposes of collection or processing.

Article 2(d) of the DPD defines a 'controller' to mean:

> the natural or legal person, public authority, agency or any other body which alone or jointly with others determines the purposes and means of the processing of personal data ...

Advocate-General Jääskinen found that the 'core issue' in applying the DPD to Google was whether or not an SEO is a 'controller'.[34] To begin with, the Advocate-General had no difficulty in determining that Google's activities – consisting of locating information published on the Web by third parties, automatically indexing it, storing it and making it available – amount to the processing of personal data under the Article 2(b) definition. The characterisation of Google as a data controller is, however, a more difficult issue.

In its 2008 Opinion on search engines, the Art. 29 WP had concluded that SEOs might be classified as controllers in relation to some functions but not others.[35] In particular, the WP concluded that an SEO should not be regarded as a controller in so far as it acts purely as an 'intermediary' for providing access to data.[36] Nevertheless, in so far as SEOs go beyond a purely intermediary role, such as by caching Web content, the WP concluded that they could be regarded as controllers.[37]

The Advocate-General commenced his analysis of the concept of 'controller' by acknowledging that either a literal or purposive application of the expansive definitions in the DPD would lead to the logical conclusion that an SEO, such as Google, must be a 'controller'.[38] As the Advocate-General explained, however, since the DPD was drafted before the

[34] *Costeja*, A–G, [76].
[35] Article 29 Data Protection Working Party, *Opinion 1/2008*, above n 20. [36] *Ibid.*, 14.
[37] *Ibid.*, 14–15. [38] *Costeja*, A–G, [77].

development of search engines, there are real difficulties in applying its provisions to SEOs. Referring to the WP Opinion, the Advocate-General doubted that a 'blind literal' construction should be applied, as this could lead to internet users who simply download files containing personal data being held to be controllers.[39] Further, referring to the WP Opinion, as well as the substantive provisions of the DPD, the Advocate-General read down the concept of 'controller' to mean the person who is *responsible* for data processing 'in the sense that the *controller* is aware of the existence of a certain defined category of information amounting to personal data and the controller processes this data with some intention which relates to their processing *as* personal data'.[40] From this, the Advocate-General drew a distinction between purely automated data processing and intentional data processing, concluding that, 'the data processing must appear to ... [the entity] ... as processing of personal data, that is 'information relating to an identified or identifiable natural person' in some semantically relevant way and not a mere computer code'.[41]

Applying this analysis, the Advocate-General referred to the distinction drawn in the WP Opinion between purely intermediary functions, in relation to which the provider is not a controller, and other functions, where the provider may be a controller. While generally consistent with the views of the WP on this point, the Advocate-General identified a broader legal principle, drawn in part from Recitals to the DPD, that 'automated, technical and passive relationships to electronically stored or transmitted content do not create control or liability over it'.[42]

Although the Advocate-General agreed with the WP in distinguishing functions which will not render an SEO a controller from functions which will, he differed in identifying the circumstances in which an SEO is a controller. First, in so far as a search engine operates as an information location tool, he found that an SEO is not a controller as it does not exercise any control over personal data on third-party websites, and cannot change that data.[43] Second, he concluded that in relation to the provision of a search engine index, an SEO that determines the way an index is structured is a controller, as it decides whether or not exclusion codes are complied with.[44] Third, in relation to material stored in cache memory, the Advocate-General concluded that an SEO has no control over the automated caching of content, except to the extent that it fails to comply with exclusion codes, such as the robots.txt file, or does not update a cached website in response to a request.[45] On the basis of this analysis, the Advocate-General effectively concluded that the only

[39] *Ibid.*, [81]. [40] *Ibid.*, [82]. [41] *Ibid.*, [83]. [42] *Ibid.*, [87]. [43] *Ibid.*, [84], [86].
[44] *Ibid.*, [91]. [45] *Ibid.*, [93].

circumstances in which the provider could be compelled under the DPD to remove material from its search engine would be if it failed to comply with exclusion codes, or refused a request from a website to update cached material. In general, therefore, the Advocate-General considered that Google could not be required to remove material from its search index as it has insufficient *intentional* control over this material.

The CJEU differed fundamentally from the Advocate-General in its analysis of the concept of a data controller, and in the application of the concept to SEOs. In doing so, the CJEU applied the express words of the definition of 'controller' in Article 2(d) and rejected the Advocate-General's attempt to confine the concept to the person *responsible* for the processing.[46] The differences on this issue reflect a fundamental disagreement in relation to the starting point of the legal analysis: whereas the Advocate-General was concerned with the difficulties of applying the broad concepts of data processing and controller to internet-based activities, the CJEU considered that the broad definitions of the DPD support the objective of providing a high level of protection of the privacy of data subjects.

This approach, however, does not mean that the CJEU ignored the extent to which the functions of SEOs differ from more traditional data controllers, or from website publishers. On the contrary, the court considered that distinctive features of search engines mean that they pose significant threats to the privacy of data subjects. First, the CJEU pointed out that search engines play a decisive role in making personal data accessible in response to searches conducted on the basis of a person's name, including where this data would otherwise be difficult or impossible to access.[47] Second, the court referred to the role of search engines in organising and aggregating internet information, which can result in users obtaining a 'structured overview' of information about an individual, including the possibility of creating detailed profiles.[48] Rather than applying a minimalist approach to the definition of a 'controller', as proposed by the Advocate-General, the CJEU concluded that the distinctive privacy-threatening functions of search engines mean that the person responsible for determining the purposes and means of data processing by search engines should be regarded as a controller.[49]

The CJEU therefore concluded that the central consideration in the Advocate-General's analysis – whether or not a search engine operator complies with exclusion codes – is irrelevant to determining whether a search engine operator is a data controller.[50] According to the court, the only possible relevance of exclusion codes is that a failure to use them may

[46] *Costeja*, ECJ, [33]. [47] *Ibid.*, [36]. [48] *Ibid.*, [37]. [49] *Ibid.*, [38]. [50] *Ibid.*, [39].

potentially render publishers of websites controllers in relation to data processing undertaken by search engines, on the basis that they may determine the means of processing jointly with a search engine operator.[51]

## 10.8 Does the DPD incorporate a right to be forgotten?

Once an SEO, such as Google, is found to be a data controller, questions arise about the scope of its obligations. Whether Google may be required to remove links to personal data on third-party websites, and if so the circumstances in which it must do so, raises the issue of whether the DPD incorporates an RTBF, in the sense that term is used in this chapter.

The DPD provides for the erasure of personal data in two main provisions. First, Article 12(b), which provides for access and correction rights, requires Member States to give data subjects the right to obtain:

> as appropriate the rectification, erasure or blocking of data the processing of which does not comply with the provisions of . . . [the DPD], in particular because of the incomplete or inaccurate nature of the data.

This provision is subject to two important qualifications: first, the right arises only where data processing is contrary to the DPD; and, second, it is possible to interpret the clause beginning with 'in particular' as limiting the right to circumstances where the data are incomplete or inaccurate. In relation to the first qualification, the DPD requires compliance with the data quality principles set out in Article 6 and the criteria for making data processing legitimate set out in Article 7.

The second provision, Article 14(a), requires Member States to confer on a data subject the right:

> [T]o object at any time on compelling legitimate grounds relating to his particular situation to the processing of data relating to him, save where otherwise provided by national legislation.

As with Article 12(b), this right is subject to limitations. Importantly, it is expressly confined to where processing is permitted as being necessary in the public interest under Article 7(e), or for the legitimate interests of the data controller or another person under Article 7(f).

Although it was strictly unnecessary for Advocate-General Jääskinen to consider whether the DPD incorporates an RTBF, he nevertheless addressed the question of whether the data subject's rights to

[51] *Ibid.*, [40].

rectification, erasure, blocking and objection could apply to prevent indexing of personal data appearing on third-party websites.

First, turning to Article 12(b), the Advocate-General expressly interpreted the phrase beginning 'in particular' as confining the erasure right to where the data concerned is incomplete or inaccurate. He therefore concluded that this could have no application to a search engine, as neither the search engine index nor the contents of a cache could be regarded as incomplete or inaccurate.[52]

Second, in relation to Article 14(a), the Advocate-General held that the subjective preference of the data subject is not, in itself, a 'compelling legitimate ground' for objection.[53] Rather, he pointed out that the relevant enquiry under Article 14(a) requires an objective balancing of the purpose of processing and the interests served by it, on the one hand, and the interests of the data subject, on the other. Although the Advocate-General acknowledged that, if an SEO were classified as a controller it would be subject to Article 14(a), he cautioned that this would involve the operator abandoning its intermediary role and assuming responsibility for content on a third-party website, which could result in censorship.[54]

Consistent with its approach to interpreting the definitions in the DPD, the CJEU interpreted the substantive provisions in the light of the high level of protection of privacy required by the objectives set out in Article 1 and the Recitals. Moreover, as the court observed, this high level of protection is reinforced by the extent to which the general principles of EU law include the rights set out in the Charter of Fundamental Rights which, in Article 8, expressly includes a right to protection of personal data.[55]

In relation to Article 12(b), contrary to the Advocate-General's approach, the CJEU considered that the reference to incomplete or inaccurate data is not exhaustive.[56] Consequently, the right of rectification or erasure can arise from non-compliance with any of the substantive provisions of the DPD, especially the obligations relating to data quality in Article 6(1) and the criteria for making data processing legitimate in Article 7.[57] Regarding the specific obligations set out in Article 6, the CJEU interpreted Article 12(b) as requiring the controller to take 'every reasonable step' to ensure that data that do not comply with the data

[52] *Costeja*, A–G, [104,], [105]. [53] *Ibid.*, [108]. [54] *Ibid.*, [109].

[55] *Costeja*, ECJ, [68],[69]. For the role of the Charter in protecting privacy and personal data in the EU see Udo Fink, 'Protection of Privacy in the EU, Individual Rights and Legal Instruments' in Normann Witzleb, David Lindsay, Moira Paterson and Sharon Rodrick (eds), *Emerging Challenges in Privacy Law: Comparative Perspectives* (Cambridge: Cambridge University Press, 2014), 75.

[56] *Ibid.*, [70]. [57] *Ibid.*, [71].

quality principles are erased or rectified.[58] Regarding the criteria for legitimating data processing, the court pointed out that data processing by an SEO may be permissible, pursuant to Article 7(f), where it is necessary for the legitimate interests of the controller (or third parties), except where such interests are overridden by the fundamental rights of the data subject. Thus, as the CJEU observed, applying the Article 12(b) right to search engines 'necessitates a balancing of the opposing rights and interests concerned, in the context of which account must be taken of the significance of the data subject's rights arising from Articles 7 and 8 of the Charter'.[59]

In relation to Article 14(a), the CJEU concluded that the assessment of 'compelling legitimate grounds' for objection requires a balancing exercise that 'enables account to be taken in a more specific manner of all the circumstances surrounding the data subject's particular situation'.[60] Consequently, under neither Article 12(b) nor Article 14(a) do data subjects have a right to the automatic removal of personal data from Google's search returns; in all cases the data subject's rights must be balanced against the rights and interests of the data controller and those of other internet users. In the first instance, the balancing exercise is to be undertaken by Google as the data controller. If, however, Google fails to remove material, the data subject may complain under national laws to the relevant data protection authority, such as the AEPD, which then becomes responsible for the requisite balancing exercise, or to the courts.

## 10.9 Balancing rights and interests

Given that any decision to remove material involves a complex balance of competing rights and interests, some of the most significant parts of the CJEU's ruling concern the guidance it provides on the nature of the balancing exercise. Whereas the Advocate-General essentially considered that the intermediary role performed by a search engine operator meant that it should not be regarded as responsible for almost all of its data processing, the CJEU emphasised the extent to which the functions of search engines may significantly affect the fundamental rights of data subjects, especially by providing access to a 'structured overview' of information about an individual.[61]

Taking into account the high level of privacy demanded by the DPD, and the potentially serious consequences of the increased accessibility to personal data afforded by search engines, the CJEU considered that personal data processing undertaken by search engines could not be

[58] *Ibid.*, [72]. [59] *Ibid.*, [74]. [60] *Ibid.*, [76]. [61] *Ibid.*, [80].

justified by 'merely the economic interest' of a search engine operator.[62] On the other hand, the court regarded the balance between the data subject's right to privacy and the rights and legitimate interests of internet users in accessing personal data as more complex. Even there, however, the CJEU considered that the data subject's rights would generally override the interests of users, unless there was a public interest in access to the personal data, which may depend upon 'the role played by the data subject in public life'.[63]

The approach taken by the CJEU to the balancing of rights required under the DPD in the context of search engines may be contrasted with the Advocate-General's approach. While agreeing that the DPD must be interpreted consistently with the EU Charter and the jurisprudence of the European Court of Human Rights (ECHR), there are fundamental differences in the interpretation of the relevant rights. In particular, the Advocate-General placed considerable emphasis on the Article 11 Charter right to freedom of expression which, in his view, is especially important in the context of the Internet. Thus, the Advocate-General stated that the Article 11 right:

> ... concerns both information on the source web pages and the information provided by internet search engines. As I have already mentioned, the internet has revolutionised access to and dissemination of all kinds of information and enabled new forms of communication and social interaction between individuals.[64]

The central issue raised by the material facts in *Costeja* is the extent to which access to accurate material that has been lawfully published on a third-party website can be impeded by the DPD. The ECHR expressly addressed the application of the right to freedom of expression to online archives in the context of defamation law in *Times Newspapers* v. *The United Kingdom (nos. 1 and 2)*.[65] In that case, the ECHR held that there was considerable public value in the maintenance of news archives, but that publishers had more stringent obligations to ensure the accuracy of historical publications than current news reports.[66] In *Costeja*, however, the Advocate-General considered that this did not extend to requiring publication of digital material with content differing from the original news content, as this would result in 'falsification of history'.[67] By analogy, the Advocate-General expressed the view that restricting access to search information would infringe the fundamental right of users to seek information about other people and, in effect, result in a falsification of

[62] *Ibid.*, [81]. [63] *Ibid.* [64] *Costeja*, A–G, [121].
[65] Applications 3002/03 and 23676/03, [2009] ECHR 451. [66] *Ibid.*, [45].
[67] *Costeja*, A–G, [129].

search returns.[68] In addition, the Advocate-General considered that imposing an obligation to remove material would infringe an SEO's freedom to conduct a business, which is guaranteed by Article 16 of the Charter.

The Advocate-General therefore effectively interpreted the Article 11 right to freedom of expression as encompassing rights of users to access accurate historical information, including personal data, via a search engine. In approaching the issue from the perspectives of users and web publishers, the Advocate-General assimilated access to content via search engines with the continued availability of that content from the original site. The CJEU, however, was concerned to distinguish the activities of SEOs from those of web publishers. In this respect, the court emphasised that a different balance of rights and interests should be applied to SEOs, on the one hand, and web publishers, on the other. For example, the CJEU pointed out that quite different considerations apply in determining whether data processing is justified by the legitimate interests of a controller, pursuant to Article 7(f), depending upon whether the controller is a web publisher or an SEO.[69]

Moreover, while the Advocate-General focussed on the extent to which the ease of locating information by search engines enhances freedom of expression, the CJEU focussed on the privacy-invasive consequences of ease of access to personal data. In this respect, in one of the most significant passages of the judgement, the court stated that:

> ... since the inclusion in the list of results, displayed following a search made on the basis of a person's name, of a web page and of information contained on it relating to that person makes access to that information appreciably easier for any internet user making a search in respect of the person ..., it is liable to constitute *a more significant interference* with the data subject's fundamental right to privacy than the publication on the web page.[70]

The conclusion that necessarily follows from the CJEU's analysis is that an SEO may be required to restrict access to material by removing links even where the balance of rights and interests weighs against the removal of material, such as a stale news story, from the source website.

## 10.10 When should links be removed?

In assessing the consequences of imposing an obligation to remove material on SEOs, the Advocate-General was especially concerned with the consequences of requiring private parties, namely SEOs, to properly

[68] *Ibid.*, [130]. [69] *Costeja*, ECJ, [86]. [70] *Ibid.*, [87] (emphasis added).

balance the complex constellation of rights and interests.[71] In particular, the Advocate-General was concerned that SEOs would be likely to respond to requests to remove material by automatically withdrawing links, which would effectively 'amount to the censuring of . . . published content by a private party'.[72]

The conclusion of the CJEU that the DPD effectively includes a right to have links removed from search engine returns raises questions concerning the circumstances in which this may be required. As explained earlier, the CJEU interpreted Article 12(b) as conferring a right to erasure in circumstances of non-compliance with Articles 6 and 7, and as not being confined to erasure of incomplete or inaccurate data. In relation to Article 6, it is clear that there may be non-compliance not merely where data is incomplete or inaccurate, but also where data is no longer relevant, or is inadequate, in relation to the purposes of collection or processing.[73] Accordingly, the CJEU considered that, even where personal data has been initially lawfully processed, it may, over time, become incompatible with Article 6 by becoming no longer necessary for the purposes of collection or processing. On this basis, the court concluded that, where a person requests the removal of material from a search engine and it is found that, following a search on the basis of that person's name, the results include links to third-party web pages that contain information that is inadequate, irrelevant or excessive to the purposes of the processing by the SEO, the links (and the information underpinning the links) in the list of results must be erased.[74]

While the right to erasure under Article 12(b) arises where there is non-compliance with Articles 6 and 7, the right to object under Article 14(a) is confined to non-compliance with the criteria in Article 7(e) and (f), which effectively requires an assessment of the legitimate interests of the data controller and third parties. In this respect, the CJEU pointed out that the data processing must be justified for the entire period it is carried out, meaning that it might be legitimately processed by a search engine at one time – such as when the information is still 'news' – but later cease to be justified.[75] As explained earlier, however, the CJEU expressed the strong view that, in the context of the Charter rights to privacy and data privacy, the rights of the data subject should generally override the economic interests of search engine operators and the interests of users in accessing information, unless there is a public interest in continuing access.

[71] *Costeja*, A–G, [133]. [72] *Ibid.*, [134]. [73] See, especially, the DPD, Article 6(1)(c).
[74] *Costeja*, ECJ, [94]. [75] *Ibid.*, [95].

## 10.11 Gaps in the ruling

Significant difficulties in interpreting and implementing the *Costeja* ruling have arisen from ambiguities and gaps in the judgement, especially in relation to the scope of the rights of data subjects. The AEPD initially required Google to withdraw personal data from its search index and render future access impossible.[76] The reference from the Audiencia Nacional to the CJEU, on the other hand, sought a ruling as to whether the DPD extended to enable a data subject to prevent indexing of personal data on the basis that it might be prejudicial or that he or she wished it to be 'consigned to oblivion'.[77] In determining the rights under Articles 12(b) and 14(a), however, the CJEU ruled that 'it should inter alia be examined whether the data subject has a right that the information in question relating to him personally should, at this point in time, *no longer be linked* to his name by a list of results displayed following a search made on the basis of his name, without it being necessary in order to find such a right that the inclusion of the information in question in that list causes prejudice to the data subject'.[78]

The disparity between the precise question before the CJEU, which refers to the prevention of indexing, and the ruling, which is confined to the removal of links in search returns, reflects difficulties in determining precisely what an SEO is required to do to comply with the DPD. As explained earlier, the CJEU considered data processing by SEOs to be especially privacy-invasive on the bases that search engines enable a structured overview of information relating to individuals and appreciably increase accessibility to personal data.[79] Given the emphasis on the consequences of accessibility, it is understandable that the ruling focusses on restricting access by means of removal of links in search returns rather than preventing the collection of personal data to include in the Google cache or the processing and structuring of data as part of the Google index. Accordingly, the ruling does not require Google to remove personal data from its cache or its search index – even though both caching and indexing, on the CJEU's analysis, clearly amount to data processing.[80]

This conclusion seems to be at odds with the CJEU's analysis of whether an SEO is a data controller, which includes the statement that:

> ... the *organisation* and *aggregation* of information published on the internet that are effected by search engines with the aim of facilitating their users' access to that information may ... result in them obtaining through the list of results a structured overview of the information relating to that individual ...[81]

[76] *Costeja*, A–G, [22]. [77] *Ibid.*, [23]. [78] *Costeja*, ECJ, [99] (emphasis added).
[79] *Ibid.*, [80], [87]. [80] See *ibid.*, [28], [41]. [81] *Ibid.*, [37] (emphasis added).

This would suggest that, at the least, data subjects should have a right to complain about the indexing of personal data, and not merely the inclusion of links to personal data in search returns. Although it is not explicit in the ruling, however, it may be that the inclusion of personal data in a search engine index can be regarded as adequate, relevant and not excessive in relation to the purposes of collection and processing by an SEO, whereas the return of structured links to users may be regarded as excessive. Moreover, according to the reasoning of the CJEU, the processing of accurate personal data may initially be justified as necessary for the purposes of collection or processing but, over time, the processing may become incompatible with the DPD as the data become inadequate, irrelevant or excessive.[82] While this clearly provides a basis for the distinction drawn by the ruling between the balance required to be struck in relation to the availability of personal data on a source website (such as an online news archive) and the different balance required in relation to accessibility to structured data via a search engine, it may also enable a distinction between initial processing by a search engine and ongoing accessibility. In addition, it seems clear that the CJEU's ruling represents a pragmatic assessment of the difficulties of removing data from a search index. Unfortunately, the failure of the court to expressly address these complexities created the potential for uncertainty in applying the ruling.

The focus of the CJEU's ruling on the implications of the ubiquitous accessibility to personal data enabled by search engines therefore masks an absence of precision in the identification of the relevant data processing. This is mirrored by imprecision in what the ruling requires of SEOs. While it is clear from the ruling that there is no need for a data subject to affirmatively establish that the inclusion of personal data in a search return causes prejudice, the approach taken by the CJEU to the balancing of rights and interests assumes that increased accessibility to structured personal data prejudices the data subject inasmuch as it breaches the rights to privacy and data privacy. Much of the debate since the ruling has rightly concentrated on the real difficulties facing SEOs in balancing the right to privacy of data subjects with competing rights and interests, especially the right to freedom of expression.[83] Nevertheless, the trans-border operations of general purpose search engines create just as many difficulties. Google initially interpreted the ruling as requiring it to respond to complaints by removing links from country-specific search domains that operate in the EU, such as

[82] *Ibid.*, [93].

[83] While the Art. 29 WP guidelines include a list of common criteria to be used in handling complaints, as no single criterion can be determinative, the guidelines do not appreciably simplify the task facing SEOs: see Article 29 Data Protection Working Party: *Guidelines*, above n 8, 12–20.

<google.es> or <google.co.uk>.[84] Thus, when Google assessed a complaint as being justified, it removed links in returns for searches based on the name of the data subject from all EU-based country-specific search engines. Nevertheless, links to the relevant URLs remained accessible from EU countries via name-based searches via the <google.com> search engine. Moreover, links remain accessible via searches on EU-based search engines that use criteria other than the data subject's name, such as searches based on distinguishing characteristics of the data subject.

Google's initial interpretation of the CJEU's ruling was contentious. As explained earlier, the CJEU found that EU data privacy law could apply to Google Inc. on the basis that the operation of Google's search engine is carried out 'in the context of' the advertising activities undertaken in an EU member state.[85] Moreover, the CJEU found that this was confirmed by the extent to which search returns are accompanied by the display of the relevant advertising.[86] Unfortunately, the sections of the ruling that address the question of establishment refer simply to the 'processing of personal data for the purposes of a search engine' and do not distinguish between access via country-specific search domains and access via <google.com>. In this respect, the ruling concludes that jurisdiction may be established 'when the operator of a search engine sets up in a Member State a branch or subsidiary which is intended to promote and sell advertising space offered by that engine and which orientates its activity towards the inhabitants of that Member State'.[87] As keyword advertising marketed by Google's Spanish subsidiary will customarily appear in returns from searches made via <google.es>, but not necessarily in returns from searches made from Spain via <google.com>, it is potentially arguable that the ruling requires only the removal of links from <google.es>. This interpretation, however, would not justify Google's policy of removing links from all EU-based search engines. Furthermore, given that keyword advertising via Google Adwords in returns from searches using <google.com> is personalised by geographical location, determined by an IP address, a distinction between links returned via <google.es> and links returned to users located in Spain via <google.com> is impossible to sustain, at least on the basis of the CJEU's reasoning; after all, Google Spain sells advertising in Spain for <google.com> as well as for <google.es>. Emphasising the extent to which the CJEU's ruling is based on conferring

[84] Danny Sullivan, 'How Google's New 'Right to be Forgotten' Form Works: An Explainer', Search Engine Land, 30 May 2014 http://searchengineland.com/google-right-to-be-forgotten-form-192837. In May 2015, the French data regulator, the CNIL, ordered Google to apply the RTBF under the DPD to google.com; and in September 2015 it rejected an appeal from Google. Non-compliance with the order, which continues to be opposed by Google, can result in fines.

[85] See *Costeja*, ECJ, [55]. [86] *Ibid.*, [57]. [87] *Ibid.*, [60].

a high level of protection to data subjects, and preventing circumvention of EU law, the Art. 29 WP guidelines conclude that to be effective, delisting must apply to all domains, including google.com.[88] But the problem arises because the CJEU's ruling failed to explore this issue in sufficient depth, simply referring to data processing by search engines in abstract and general terms. While Google's initial response was a pragmatic attempt to deal with the trans-border complexities that arise from applying the ruling to a global search engine, such as google.com, the Art. 29 guidelines recognise the ease with which the *Costeja* ruling could be circumvented by users simply switching from the default national search engine to google.com. Following the publication of the guidelines, it is clear that Google must have a consistent policy for dealing with delinking requests across all search domains. Nevertheless, given that Google's Adwords service incorporates the ability to exclude IP addresses,[89] it seems unusual that the Art. 29 WP failed to at least evaluate the advantages and disadvantages of geo-blocking as a potential mechanism for limiting territorial over-reach of EU law.

In relation to the continued availability of links to personal data via searches based on criteria other than the data subject's name, the CJEU's ruling simply concludes that the rights of a data subject are limited to rights over results displayed following a search made on the basis of a name, rather than searches based on other identifiable characteristics, without any attempt to justify this limitation. Especially given that the definition of personal data in the DPD is not confined to personal names, the only possible explanation of this limitation is the pragmatic consideration that to attempt to cast a wider net would be unworkable. Similarly, the Art. 29 WP guidelines merely restate that the ruling is confined to name-based queries,[90] without any legal or policy analysis of the reasons for confining the ruling. It would, nevertheless, have been helpful if the CJEU's ruling or the Art. 29 guidelines had offered some explanation for the limitation, both as a matter of data privacy law and policy.

## 10.12 Conclusion

The CJEU ruling in *Costeja* has created considerable controversy, not least as it is one of the rare occasions where the Grand Chamber differed

[88] Article 29 Data Protection Working Party: *Guidelines*, above n 8, [20]. The majority of the Advisory Council to Google on the RTBF, however, supported confining the ruling to nationally directed versions of Google's search engine (with member Sabine Leutheusser-Schnarrenberger dissenting on this point).

[89] Google, 'Exclude IP addresses' https://support.google.com/adwords/answer/2456098?hl=en.

[90] Article 29 Data Protection Working Party: *Guidelines*, above n 8, [4].

fundamentally from the Advocate-General. The differences in approach between the CJEU and the Advocate-General arise from ambiguities in the drafting of key definitions and provisions of the DPD, and from difficulties in applying the DPD to search engines. Nevertheless, they are also based on fundamental differences in the assessment of the extent to which SEOs should adapt their operations to comply with the fundamental rights to privacy and data privacy. The Advocate-General considered that the automated operation of a search engine, and the great societal benefits provided by search engines in facilitating access to information mean that, in general, an SEO such as Google should not be subject to the DPD. In this, the Advocate-General was concerned that requiring SEOs to abandon a neutral intermediary role in relation to access to content might amount to censorship. The CJEU, on the other hand, emphasised the privacy threat posed by search engines – in the form of enhanced access to structured personal data – which, on the basis of the high level of privacy protection required by the DPD, justifies imposing restrictions on the accessibility of personal data via search engines. In this, the CJEU carefully distinguished the balancing exercise that applies to search engines from the balance that applies to source websites, to essentially conclude that privacy could be protected by restricting access, but not removing material from source. Given the ambiguous drafting of the DPD, and the importance of interpreting the provisions of the DPD in the light of European human rights law, the CJEU's ruling is, purely as a matter of European law, preferable to the Advocate-General's approach. Nevertheless, significant difficulties have arisen both in interpreting and in implementing the *Costeja* ruling.

At the time of writing this chapter, much attention has focussed on the practical challenges confronting Google and other SEOs (and potentially other intermediaries) in undertaking the balancing exercise required by the ruling on a case-by-case basis. As the balance between the right to privacy and competing rights and interests is often inherently complex, and context-dependent, this is clearly a difficult undertaking. It is, however, a necessary consequence of imposing a rights-based framework, which gives due recognition to the right to privacy, on general purpose search engines. A greater concern is whether this task should be left predominantly in the hands of private sector entities, such as Google, albeit with some supervision by data protection authorities and, ultimately, the courts. In this respect, it is obvious that the DPD, which was clearly not drafted to apply to search engines, in itself provides inadequate legal safeguards and guidance to SEOs.

As this chapter has explained, quite apart from the complexities and uncertainties associated with the application of the European human rights framework to SEOs, considerable difficulties have arisen from ambiguities and gaps in the CJEU's ruling. For example, there is no clear explanation of why the CJEU concluded that the DPD was confined to requiring Google to remove links from returns from searches conducted on the basis of a data subject's name, and did not extend to requiring actions in relation to other data processing conducted by Google, including the creation of the Google search index. Moreover, the ruling itself fails to expressly address the issue of whether it applies only to territorially-based search engines, such as <google.es>, or extends to require removal of links returned from <google.com>, an issue that has since created controversy. Reading between the lines, it would seem that, to a significant extent, the CJEU was concerned to balance a principled application of European human rights law to SEOs, on the one hand, against the considerable practical difficulties of regulating general purpose search engines, on the other. Nevertheless, as these practical issues must be addressed by both SEOs and EU data protection authorities in operationalising the ruling, it would have been preferable for the CJEU to have been more precise and explicit in explaining its reasoning, as well as in setting out the legal conclusions reached. Ultimately, the difficult practical and policy issues must be addressed as part of the interpretation of the new 'right to erasure' in the new EU data privacy law (the GDPR). Meanwhile, the experience gained in the process of implementing the CJEU's ruling in *Costeja* can contribute to our understanding of how far practical steps can be taken to protect privacy in an age of ubiquitous and instantaneous access to data via search engines, not only in Europe but elsewhere.

# 11 Privacy for the weak, transparency for the powerful*

*Melissa de Zwart*

In January 2011, while Julian Assange was fighting extradition from the UK to face sexual assault charges in Sweden, he entered into an agreement with UK-based publishers Canongate to produce a memoir, to be ghostwritten by Scottish author Andrew O'Hagan. The resulting book was published later that year as *Julian Assange: The Unauthorised Autobiography*, without the blessing of either Assange or the ghostwriter.[1] In 2014, O'Hagan published an extended account of his dealings with Assange during the ghostwriting process.[2] Each of these accounts refers to Assange's desire to publish a 'manifesto, a book that will reflect this great big generational shift'.[3] Of course, rather than being such a manifesto, O'Hagan's ghostwritten work was preoccupied with the childhood of Assange and influences that had shaped him, including his early exploits as a hacker, the foundation of WikiLeaks and details of his interactions in Sweden with the women who were to become his accusers. This self-proclaimed 'intimate account' of Assange's personal life, and

* Julian Assange with Jacob Applebaum, Andy Müller-Maguhn and Jérémie Zimmermann, *Cypherpunks: Freedom and the Future of the Internet* (New York: OR Books, 2012), 141.

1 Julian Assange, *Julian Assange: The Unauthorised Autobiography* (Melbourne: Text Publishing, 2011). The book contains 'A Note from the Publisher' which explains the decision to publish the book despite the fact that Assange had sought to cancel the contract with the publisher: 'Whether you read this book as a ghosted memoir or as a "literary interpretation of a conversation" (which is how Assange himself describes it), it may be the most insightful and intimate account of him that we will ever have'. For Assange's account see 'Julian Assange: Statement on the Unauthorised, Secret Publishing of the Julian Assange "autobiography" by Canongate', Julian Assange, 'Press Statement on the Unauthorised "Autobiography"' (22 September 2011, updated 27 September 2011), https://wikileaks.org/Julian-Assange-Statement-on-the.html.

2 Andrew O'Hagan, 'Ghosting', *London Review of Books* (6 March 2014) www.lrb.co.uk/v36/n05/andrew-ohagan/ghosting.

3 Ibid. See also 'A Note from the Publisher', in Assange, *Unauthorised Autobiography*, above n 1. O'Hagan cites from Assange's statement to the Associated Press (above n 1) regarding the book, noting that Assange signed the contract to produce the book 'part memoir, part manifesto – in order to fund legal defences and to contribute towards WikiLeaks' operating costs'.

the ensuing public spat between Assange, the publishers and the mainstream media regarding publication of the book, was reflective of the dysfunctional and hostile relationship that already existed between Assange and the mainstream media.[4] The breakdown of the publishing partnerships between WikiLeaks and major UK- and US-based news organisations is documented elsewhere, as are the statements by and on behalf of some of those organisations who attempted to distance themselves from the whistle-blowing platform.[5] However, it appears important at a time when we are evaluating the threats to privacy that result from major public–private partnerships, as well as government mass surveillance programs, that we remain undistracted by questions of personality and focus on the bigger picture of the new internet-enabled surveillance society, and what role, if any, concepts of privacy continue to have in that society.

In 2012, Assange, together with Jacob Appelbaum, Andy Müller-Maguhn and Jérémie Zimmermann, produced another book, this one prefaced with the words, 'This book is not a manifesto. There is not time for that. This book is a warning'.[6] In that book Assange asserts that the Internet 'has been transformed into the most dangerous facilitator of totalitarianism we have ever seen'.[7] Assange (and his collaborators) argue that the Internet is being transformed from a liberating and empowering platform for the free exchange of ideas to a massive, global network for surveillance.[8] Responding to suggestions that it had become impossible for governments to keep any secrets in the era of online whistle-blowing platforms such as WikiLeaks, Assange described WikiLeaks as but a 'shadow of a shadow' in the face of the enormous volume of user data being collected daily by governments and platform providers such as Google, Facebook and Apple.[9] Therefore, any belief that the existence of an online whistle-blowing platform sufficiently redressed the imbalance of power was misguided.

The publication of these books in 2011–2012 was followed by several others in 2013, in addition to a major Hollywood movie (*The Fifth Estate*) based on the book by former WikiLeaks staffer Daniel Domscheit-Berg

[4] See, e.g., Henry Porter, 'Julian Assange: The Unauthorised Autobiography – review', *The Guardian* (2 October 2011) www.theguardian.com/media/2011/oct/02/julian-assange-unauthorised-autobiography-review; Guy Rundle, 'Assange bio: not a manuscript anyone would intend to publish', *Crikey.com* (23 September 2011) www.crikey.com.au/2011/09/23/rundle-on-the-assange-bio-not-a-manuscript-that-anyone-would-intend-to-publish/ (including an account of an attempt by UK TV media to manufacture some public outrage regarding publication of the book).

[5] Melissa de Zwart, 'Whistleblowers and the Media: Friends or 'Frenemies'?'(2013) 38 *Alternative Law Journal* 250.

[6] Assange et al, *Cypherpunks*, above *, 1. [7] Ibid. [8] Ibid., 6. [9] Ibid., 145.

and a feature-length documentary (*We Steal Secrets*) which focussed on the upbringing and motivation of former US Army Private First Class Chelsea (formerly Bradley) Manning, sentenced in April 2013 to thirty-five years in prison for her role in leaking over 700,000 government files to WikiLeaks (notably the Afghan war logs, the Iraq war logs, the US Embassy cables and the footage of the US Apache helicopter gunning down a group of civilians, produced by WikiLeaks as the video 'Collateral Murder').[10] Much of this material focussed on the personality of Assange, or on the morals of whistle-blowing, rather than on the broader questions of analysing the claims and information that were being disclosed. However, Assange's largely ignored warnings regarding widespread use of the Internet for surveillance and data collection purposes have now been proven well founded.

In June 2013, former National Security Agency contractor Edward Snowden revealed the existence of vast programs being conducted by the US government to monitor and collect user data from US and foreign citizens.[11] Subsequent revelations by Snowden implicated not only other national governments in data collection and sharing, notably the Five Eyes alliance including Australia, Canada, New Zealand, UK and US, but also the major US internet companies in facilitating access to user data. WikiLeaks' own data releases paled beside the scale of the Snowden revelations regarding the metadata capture occurring globally, such as the PRISM and s215 programs in the US. These disclosures are discussed later.

Snowden is currently exiled in Russia, where he was granted temporary asylum in June 2013, after leaving Hong Kong which he chose to use as his base for providing the leaked material to the media.[12] Snowden managed his media disclosures very differently from WikiLeaks.

[10] Daniel Domscheit-Berg, *Inside WikiLeaks: My Time with Julian Assange at the World's Most Dangerous Website* (Melbourne: Scribe Publications, 2011); David Leigh and Luke Harding, *WikiLeaks: Inside Julian Assange's War on Secrecy* (London: Guardian Books, 2011); Charlie Beckett with James Ball, *WikiLeaks: News in the Networked Era* (Cambridge: Polity Press, 2012); Andrew Fowler, *The Most Dangerous Man in the World: The Inside Story on Julian Assange and WikiLeaks* (Melbourne: Melbourne University Press, 2012). The documentary was *We Steal Secrets: the Story of Wikileaks* (Directed by Alex Gibney, Jigsaw Productions, 2013) and the feature film (based on the Domscheit-Berg book) was *The Fifth Estate* (Directed by Bill Condon, Touchstone Pictures, 2013).

[11] Glenn Greenwald, 'NSA collecting phone records of millions of Verizon customers daily', *The Guardian* (online), (6 June 2013) www.theguardian.com/world/2013/jun/06/nsa-phone-records-verizon-court-order.

[12] Snowden's temporary asylum was extended in August 2013 for a further three years: Alec Luhn and Mark Tran, 'Edward Snowden given permission to stay in Russia for three more years', *The Guardian* (online) (7 August 2014) www.theguardian.com/world/2014/aug/07/edward-snowden-permission-stay-in-russia-three-years.

Viewing himself very much as source, a whistle-blower, rather than a media outlet, he carefully orchestrated the disclosure of his leaks to journalist Glenn Greenwald and documentary maker Laura Poitras.[13] Part of this strategy was to ensure that the focus was on the content of the disclosures rather than the personality and motivations of the leaker.[14] Nevertheless, there has been significant interest in and speculation regarding Snowden's personal life. In addition, Snowden was concerned to ensure that his actions were all in the open in the sense that there could be no suggestions that he was being motivated by money or acting as an agent for a foreign power. Nevertheless, Snowden has been charged with theft and two counts under the Espionage Act 1917 (US), namely 'unauthorized communication of national defense information' and 'willful communication of classified communications intelligence information to an unauthorized person'.

This chapter is concerned with the notion of privacy in a post-Snowden Internet, when, as Assange has observed, the ubiquitous services on the Internet upon which we all rely have themselves become a surveillance device. In particular it is interested in analysing the context within which the revelations regarding mass surveillance have occurred and the perceived hostility between the role of whistle-blowers and new media platforms in disclosing such surveillance and their media partners in reporting it. It attempts to address the frequently asked question about whether those who reveal state secrets should themselves be entitled to retain secrets of their own. In other words, it asks whether whistle-blowers should be regarded as retaining any rights to their own privacy in the light of their apparent lack of respect for the secrets of others. It concludes that it should be recognised that the message of Snowden and WikiLeaks is consistent with the conclusion that personal privacy is paramount. It will attempt to address issues of the rights of privacy of the individual in the global surveillance environment and the complexities of applying old concepts to new scenarios. Viewed in the context that privacy is a vital aspect of democratic participation, personal privacy should be respected and protected against indiscriminate (warrantless) government and corporate surveillance.

[13] For a detailed insight into Snowden's actions and motivations, see Glenn Greenwald, *No Place to Hide: Edward Snowden, the NSA and the Surveillance State* (London: Penguin Books, 2014); James Bamford, 'Edward Snowden: The Untold Story' *Wired*, Issue 22.09 September 2014, 78; and the documentary *Citizenfour* (Directed by Laura Poitras, Praxis Films, 2014).

[14] Alan Rusbridger and Ewan MacAskill, 'Edward Snowden interview – the edited transcript', *The Guardian* (online) (19 July 2014) www.theguardian.com/world/2014/jul/18/-sp-edward-snowden-nsa-whistleblower-interview-transcript.

## 11.1 Surveillance and mass data capture

As noted earlier, in the 2012 'not-manifesto' *Cypherpunks*, Assange had conjured up the spectre of the mass collection of data from ordinary citizens on a daily basis. In his interviews with O'Hagan in 2011, Assange had described the role of expert hackers in this new environment in detecting and fighting 'the cancer of modern power' which was invisible and unknown to the average member of society.[15]

It is likely that most people would have viewed these as the thoughts of an avid conspiracy theorist, but several public interest groups were already engaged in a legal battle with the US government to reveal what communications data was being monitored. A group of lawyers, NGOs, human rights, labour, and media organisations headed up by Amnesty International had brought an action in 2012 against James Clapper, the US Director of National Intelligence, seeking a declaration that §1881a of the Foreign Intelligence Surveillance Act (FISA) was unconstitutional, and a permanent injunction against §1881a-authorised surveillance.[16] In that matter, heard before the US Supreme Court, the respondents claimed that their work required them to engage in sensitive and sometimes privileged communications via telephone and email with their clients, colleagues, sources and other relevant parties who may be located outside of the US.[17] They claimed that some of the people with whom they exchanged information were likely to be targets of surveillance under §1881a, including those people 'the Government "believes or believed to be associated with terrorist organizations", "people located in geographic areas that are a special focus" of the Government's counterterrorism or diplomatic efforts, and activists who oppose governments that are supported by the United States Government'.[18] The threat of surveillance, they asserted, compromised their ability to communicate freely and effectively with their clients and other important sources, chilled their ability to communicate and required them to implement additional measures to protect the confidentiality of their communications, including incurring the expense and inconvenience of travelling overseas to meet their clients and sources face to face. The case revolved around the question of standing, whether the respondents could establish injury in fact based on their claim that there was a strong likelihood that their communications would be acquired under §1881a in the future thus causing them

[15] O'Hagan, 'Ghosting', above n 2.

[16] Foreign Intelligence Surveillance Act of 1978, 50 USC § 702 (1978); §1881a was added by the Foreign Intelligence Surveillance Act Amendments Act of 2008, 154 USC (2008).

[17] *Clapper* v. *Amnesty International USA* 568 US _, 7 (2013), Docket No. 11-1025 ('*Clapper*').

[18] Ibid.

injury, or alternatively that they were sustaining injury as a consequence of the fact that the risk of §1881a-authorised surveillance was requiring them to take 'costly and burdensome measures to protect the confidentiality of their international communications'.[19]

§1881a authorises the US Attorney-General and the Director of National Intelligence to acquire foreign intelligence information by jointly authorising the surveillance of individuals who are not 'United States persons' and are reasonably believed to be located outside of the United States.[20] Normally, the approval of the Foreign Intelligence Surveillance Court (FISC) is also required and, as the Supreme Court observed, is subject to 'statutory conditions, judicial authorization, congressional supervision, and compliance with the Fourth Amendment'.[21]

In February 2013, the US Supreme Court handed down its decision that the respondents lacked the requisite standing on the basis that they had no actual knowledge of the government's targeting practices under §1881a.[22] The Supreme Court held that claims of fears of widespread surveillance, such as those of the communications journalist Christopher Hedges, who stated, 'I have no choice but to assume that any of my international communications may be subject to government surveillance, and I have to make decisions ... in light of that assumption', were merely speculative.[23] Further, the respondents could not establish that the interception may be authorised under some other provision of FISA, nor could they demonstrate that even if the government sought to invoke surveillance of communications with their foreign contacts that the FISC would authorise such surveillance, that the communications could actually be acquired nor that their own communications would be caught up in such surveillance.[24] Any costs incurred by the respondents in attempting to avoid surveillance were based on their own 'fears of hypothetical future harm that is not certainly impending'.[25]

Breyer J filed a dissenting opinion, which concluded that, based on the nature of the communications engaged in by the respondents, the past conduct of the government and the capacity to undertake the surveillance, there 'is a high probability that the Government will intercept at least some electronic communication to which at least some of the plaintiffs are parties'.[26] It was therefore wrong to characterise the harm

[19] Ibid., 2.
[20] Foreign Intelligence Surveillance Act of 1978, 50 USC § 1801(i) (1978) states that 'United States person' includes US citizens, aliens admitted for permanent residence and certain associations and corporations.
[21] *Clapper*, 5.
[22] *Clapper*. The respondents argued that § 1881 violated the Fourth and First Amendments, Article III of the Constitution and the separation of powers principles.
[23] *Clapper*, 12. [24] Ibid., 14–15. [25] Ibid., 17. [26] Ibid., 10 (Breyer J dissenting).

threatened to the respondents as 'speculative' and at least some of the respondents were entitled to standing.[27]

Of course, just how 'speculative' these claims were was revealed with dramatic consequences only a few months later when the government was forced by Snowden's revelations to confirm the existence of major warrantless telephone and internet surveillance programs. It then had to consider how it could combat the massive anger of its own and foreign citizens and the consequent collateral damage it had inflicted on its own tech industry. What had been merely speculative in February 2013 was confirmed as widespread practice in June.[28]

In June 2013, former NSA contractor Edward Snowden revealed to journalists Glenn Greenwald, Laura Poitras and Ewen MacAskill that the US government, through its various agencies, was engaging in massive-scale collection of data from both its own and foreign citizens. This data collection was occurring in the context of two separate but similar programs: the first, known as 's 215', facilitated the collection of telephony metadata, capturing caller ID, numbers dialled, place of call, duration and other information, but not including the content of the call. One of Snowden's first leaks revealed that Verizon, a major US telecommunications provider, was compelled by order of the FISC to produce to the NSA daily records of all telephony metadata for communication between the US and abroad and wholly within the US, including local telephone calls.[29] In response to these disclosures the US government confirmed that such a program did in fact exist, pursuant to which 'the FBI obtains orders from the FISC pursuant to the USA Patriot Act[30] directing certain telecommunications service providers to produce to the NSA on a daily basis electronic copies of "call detail records"'.[31] The second of

[27] Ibid.

[28] It may be noted that when James Clapper was asked if the NSA collected any kind of data on millions of Americans at a US Senate Select Committee on Intelligence hearing on 12 March 2013, he responded: 'Not willingly. There are cases where they could, inadvertently, perhaps, collect, but not willingly'. There have been calls for Clapper to be charged with perjury with respect to this statement.

[29] Greenwald, 'NSA Collecting Phone Records of Millions of Verizon Customers Daily', above n 11.

[30] Uniting and Strengthening America By Providing Appropriate Tools Required To Intercept and Obstruct Terrorism Act ('USA Patriot Act') of 2001, 18 USC § 215 (2001).

[31] See *Klayman* v. *Obama* 957 F.Supp.2d 1 (DCC, 2013) slip op 7. This details the various public statements made by the Office of the Director of National Intelligence following Snowden's disclosures, see Office of the Director of National Intelligence, 'DNI Statement on Recent Unauthorized Disclosure of Classified Information' (Press Release, 6 June 2013) www.dni.gov/index.php/newsroom/press-releases/191-press-releases-2013/868-dni-statement-on-recent-unauthorized-disclosures-of-classified-information.

Snowden's leaks detailed the collection by the US government of user data directly from the servers of nine major US technology companies including Facebook, Microsoft, Skype, Google and Apple, as part of a program known as 'PRISM'.[32] The companies issued denials regarding their involvement in the mass collection of data, but they could not deny that they had been compelled to provide records to the US government.[33] They had not however been allowed to reveal their involvement in the program due to the fact they were prevented by court order. This complicity of the major tech companies with covert surveillance of global internet users threatened the very substance of the Internet, undermining the characterisation of the Internet as the engine of free speech, transforming it rather into 'a means of widespread surveillance'.[34] This revelation of the clear involvement of US technology companies in the collection of user data, chat, photographs, video and connection logs was perhaps the most damaging of all to US global interests.[35] Again the US government confirmed the existence of such a program, but claimed that it was targeted only at non-US citizens, and was authorised under the FISA.[36]

The fact that US technology companies had been the instrument of widespread user surveillance had also generated massive user backlash and a commercial headache for these companies who depend heavily upon user trust.[37] However, in addition to the section 215 and PRISM revelations, further disclosures had continued to flow from Snowden. Not only was the US now implicated in spying on governments of hostile nations, but had been caught tapping the phone of German Chancellor Angela Merkel.[38]

[32] Glenn Greenwald and Ewen MacAskill, 'NSA Prism Program Taps In To User Data of Apple, Google and Others', *The Guardian* (online) (8 June 2013) www.theguardian.com/world/2013/jun/06/us-tech-giants-nsa-data; Barton Gellman and Laura Poitras, 'U.S., British intelligence mining data from nine U.S. Internet companies in broad secret program' *The Washington Post* (online) (7 June 2013) www.washingtonpost.com/investigations/us-intelligence-mining-data-from-nine-us-internet-companies-in-broad-secret-program/2013/06/06/3a0c0da8-cebf-11e2-8845-d970ccb04497_story.html.

[33] Greenwald, above n 13, 108–18.

[34] Steven Levy, 'How the NSA Almost Killed the Internet', *Wired.com* (7 January 2014) www.wired.com/threatlevel/2014/01/how-the-us-almost-killed-the-internet/all.

[35] Snowden's leaked documents included a Power Point presentation prepared for the NSA which identified the key tech companies by name and logo, including details of their participation in the PRISM program collection of user data, see Levy, 'How the NSA Almost Killed the Internet', above n 34.

[36] Foreign Intelligence Surveillance Act of 1978, 50 USC § 702 (1978); Dan Roberts, Spencer Ackerman and Tania Branigan, 'Clapper Admits Secret NSA Surveillance Program to Access User Data', *The Guardian* (online) (8 June 2013) www.theguardian.com/world/2013/jun/07/clapper-secret-nsa-surveillance-prism.

[37] Levy, above n 34.

[38] Ian Traynor, 'Angela Merkel: NSA Spying On Allies Is Not On', *The Guardian* (online) (25 October 2013) www.theguardian.com/world/2013/oct/24/angela-merkel-nsa-spying-allies-not-on.

Further, several governments allied with the US, including the UK and Australia, had been implicated in mass surveillance practices, including spying on one another's citizens.[39] The Obama regime had to go into damage control.

## 11.2 US government responses

The surveillance practices of the US government were reviewed in the *Report and Recommendations of The President's Review Group on Intelligence and Communications Technologies: Liberty and Security in a Changing World*, commissioned by President Obama in August 2013 and released in December 2013. That Report flagged a number of key principles which should underpin intelligence collection in the future. In particular, the Report flagged the dualistic nature of the concept of 'security', encompassing both the traditional individual rights of US citizens under the Fourth Amendment to be 'secure in their persons, houses, papers, and effects, against unreasonable searches and seizures' and the concept of national security with the consequent need for information in the post-911 world to defend the US against its enemies.[40] The determination of the appropriate extent of surveillance could not however be determined by a simple balancing exercise of these two forms of security.

The Report made forty-six recommendations, beginning from the principle that for national and global safety purposes the US would need to continue to collect signals intelligence. It did recommend the end of bulk storage of telephone data under s215 and President Obama announced in January 2014 that this program would be terminated.[41] Telecommunications providers would themselves be required to hold the data for a prescribed period of time, which could then be accessed only by order of the FISC. Note, however, that this refers to telecommunications providers rather than internet service providers who will still be engaged in the bulk collection of data.

[39] Bernard Keane, 'Spy versus Spy, Gatekeeper versus Gatekeeper', *Crikey.com* (22 November 2013) www.crikey.com.au/2013/11/22/spy-versus-spy-gatekeeper-versus-gatekeeper/.

[40] Richard A Clarke, Michael J Morell, Geoffrey R Stone, Cass R Sunstein and Peter Swire, *Liberty and Security in a Changing World: Report and Recommendations of The President's Review Group on Intelligence and Communications Technologies* (Washington, DC: Office of the Director of National Intelligence, 2013), 14 www.whitehouse.gov/sites/default/files/docs/2013-12-12_rg_final_report.pdf.

[41] The White House, Office of the Press Secretary, 'Presidential Policy Directive/ PPD-28: Signals Intelligence Activities' (17 January 2014); 'Obama's Speech on NSA Phone Surveillance', *The New York Times* (online) (17 January 2014) www.nytimes.com/2014/01/18/us/politics/obamas-speech-on-nsa-phone-surveillance.html.

Amendments to the USA Patriot Act were passed by the House of Representatives in May 2014.[42] Those amendments implemented a range of responses to the Snowden revelations, in particular, the end of collection of bulk telephone metadata, but the reforms have been criticised for not going far enough in responding to US-based concerns regarding mass data collection. In June 2014 the House of Representatives voted to remove the power from the NSA to search 'warrantlessly through its troves of ostensibly foreign communications content for Americans' data, the so-called "back-door search" provision'.[43] In a joint statement by the chief sponsors of that Bill, the USA Freedom Act, Jim Sensenbrenner (Republican), Zoe Lofgren (Democrat) and Thomas Massie (Republican), observed that: 'There's no question Americans have become increasingly alarmed with the breadth of unwarranted government surveillance programs used to store and search their private data ... By adopting this amendment, Congress can take a sure step toward shutting the back door on mass surveillance'.[44] The passage of this Bill was not without controversy, with original sponsors of the Bill, including Lofgren, having withdrawn support from the watered-down version of the Bill, and then rejoining in bipartisan support of the Bill following further amendments. However, the Bill was stalled before the Senate for several weeks and the future of the s215 program remained uncertain, as without legislative amendment, the program was due to expire in June 2015.[45] In the face of this uncertainty, the NSA shut down the bulk collection of phone records on 31 May 2015. The USA Freedom Act was finally passed on 2 June 2015, resulting in a temporary 're-animation' of the s215 program while the collection of telephone metadata is transitioned to the phone companies.[46]

[42] Dan Roberts, 'NSA surveillance reform bill passes House by 303 votes to 121', *The Guardian* (online) (23 May 2014) www.theguardian.com/world/2014/may/22/nsa-reform-bill-usa-freedom-act-passes-house.

[43] Spencer Ackerman, 'House of Representatives moves to ban NSA's "backdoor search" provision', *The Guardian* (online) (21 June 2014) www.theguardian.com/world/2014/jun/20/house-bans-nsa-backdoor-search-surveillance.

[44] Zoe Lofgren, 'House to debate amendment to curb government access to private data' (Press Release, 19 June 2014) http://lofgren.house.gov/news/documentsingle.aspx?DocumentID=385102.

[45] Spencer Ackerman, 'Failure to pass US surveillance reform bill could still curtail NSA powers', *The Guardian* (online) (4 October 2014) www.theguardian.com/world/2014/oct/03/usa-freedom-act-house-surveillance-powers.

[46] Sabrina Siddiqui, 'Congress passes surveillance reform in vindication for Snowden', *The Guardian* (online) (3 June 2015) www.theguardian.com/us-news/2015/jun/02/congress-surveillance-reform-edward-snowden. In addition, the US Court of Appeals for the Second Circuit had held that the collection of telephone metadata was not authorised by s 215, *American Civil Liberties Union* v. *Clapper* 785 F. 3d 787 (2015). However, given the impending expiration of the program it had declined to grant an injunction to halt its operation.

Therefore, although Snowden's revelations may be seen to have caused significant concern to the public, government and business, US law-makers have been slow to respond with real change.

## 11.3 Fourth amendment protection: electronic searches and seizures

Both the section 215 and PRISM programs were designed around the fact that different legal frameworks apply in the US with respect to surveillance of 'foreign' and 'domestic' persons.[47] Any surveillance of a US person must comply with Constitutional and legal requirements, notably obtaining a warrant. However, legal restrictions upon surveillance without a warrant do not apply to non-US persons located outside of the US. Thus two very different surveillance frameworks exist in theory, but with global networks of communication and the centrality of the US to the global internet and communication industries, these boundaries appear to have become very blurred. As noted earlier, it appears that following the revelations of the surveillance programs, US citizens were appalled that their Constitutional rights under the Fourth Amendment appeared to have been violated.[48] Responses to these concerns have however become mired in political compromise and coloured by debates regarding national security, radicalisation and renewed threats of home-grown terrorism.[49]

The Fourth Amendment of the US Constitution provides as follows: 'The right of the people to be secure in their persons, houses, papers, and effects, against unreasonable searches and seizures, shall not be violated, and no warrants shall issue, but upon probable cause, supported by oath or affirmation, and particularly describing the place to be searched, and the persons or things to be seized'. Fourth Amendment interests are clearly implicated both through the targeted collection of data from non-US persons, through the likely and possible collection of communications data from the US citizens involved in expanding networks of

[47] USA Patriot Act, 18 USC § 215 (2001).

[48] Andrea Peterson, 'A year after Snowden revelations, government surveillance reform still a work in progress', *Washington Post* (online) (5 June 2014) www.washingtonpost.com/blogs/the-switch/wp/2014/06/05/a-year-after-snowden-revelations-government-surveillance-reform-still-a-work-in-progress/.

[49] Robert Wright, 'ISIS and the Forgotten, Deadly Threat of Homegrown Terrorism', *The Atlantic* (online) (19 September 2014) www.theatlantic.com/politics/archive/2014/09/will-obamas-isis-strategy-actually-worsen-the-terror-threat/380465/; Jerry Markon, 'Amid threats abroad, Homeland Security chief keeps eye on homegrown terrorism', *Washington Post* (online) (1 October 1014) www.washingtonpost.com/blogs/federal-eye/wp/2014/10/01/amid-threats-abroad-homeland-security-chief-keeps-eye-on-homegrown-terrorism/.

connections, and the accidental collection of data directly from US persons caught up in a data sweep.[50] Further, the indiscriminate collection of communications metadata reveals some very accurate and detailed information regarding those targets whose metadata is collected without their knowledge or consent.[51]

Existing Fourth Amendment law provides that information shared voluntarily with third parties may be collected on the basis that individuals have 'no reasonable expectation of privacy' in this information.[52] The continuing validity and scope of application of this line of authority in the digital era was raised but not resolved in *United States* v. *Jones*, which concerned the Constitutionality of the surveillance of an individual suspected of drug trafficking, by attaching a GPS to his car.[53] The court concluded (by majority) that the installation of the GPS was a 'search' within the meaning of the Fourth Amendment, but declined to further consider the argument that such surveillance was legitimate based on the argument than an individual's movements along public roads are voluntarily disclosed to third parties in accordance with *Miller* and *Smith*.[54]

[50] The § 215 telephone metadata program authorised a maximum of three 'hops' from a 'seed' telephone number: When a 'seed' or identified target telephone number is queried the NSA received a list of every telephone number that called or was called by that seed number in the past five years (the 'first hop'), the 'second hop' involved every number called or called by each of those numbers obtained in the first hop, and the third hop was to every number called or called by those second hop numbers, which could expand the list of numbers queried by the NSA to approximately 1,000,000: Clarke et al, above n 40, 102–3.

[51] Edward W Felten, 'Declaration of Professor Edward W Felten', Submission in *American Civil Liberties Union* v. *Office of the Director of National Intelligence*, 13-cv-03994 (WHP), 26 August 2013, 20–1 [61] (citations omitted):

> 'Researchers have discovered that individuals have unique calling patterns, regardless of which telephone they are using, they have figured out how to predict the kind of device that is making the calls (a telephone or a fax machine), developed algorithms capable of predicting whether the phone line is used by a business or for personal use, identified callers by social group (workers, commuters, and students) based on their calling patterns, and even estimated the personality traits of individual subscribers'.

[52] *Miller* v. *United States*, 425 US 435 (1976) (bank records) and *Smith* v. *Maryland*, 442 US 735 (1979) (telephone records).

[53] *United States* v. *Jones*, 132 S.Ct. 945 (2012). For an extended analysis of how the Internet challenges Fourth Amendment law, see Orin Kerr, 'The Fourth Amendment and the Global Internet' (2015) 67 *Stanford Law Review* 285.

[54] For example, Sotomayor J observed: 'it may be necessary to reconsider the premise that an individual has no reasonable expectation of privacy in information voluntarily disclosed to third parties ... This approach is ill-suited to the digital age, in which people reveal a great deal of information about themselves to third parties in the course of carrying out mundane tasks ... I would not assume that all information voluntarily disclosed to [others] for a limited purposes is, for that reason alone, disentitled to Fourth Amendment protection'. *United States* v. *Jones* 132 S.Ct. 945, 957 (2012). See Clarke et al, above n 40, 84–5.

Thus until *Miller* and *Smith* are reviewed by the Supreme Court, they remain good law, and create a low-threshold test regarding privacy of individual information. Essentially people must reveal personal information to banks, phone companies, health providers and so on in order to participate in modern society, so the question of whether the person has voluntarily consented to the disclosure of such information is moot. Further, there is a real concern that people are becoming increasingly aware of the fact that their personal information is being monitored, collated and used and therefore may be prevented from fully participating in society as a consequence, contrary to the purposes of the Fourth and First Amendments.[55]

## 11.4 Australian responses

The Australian government is now implementing a mandatory data retention regime which requires phone companies and ISPs to retain metadata for two years.[56] This is in the context of ongoing reviews of intelligence security, including the Parliamentary Joint Committee on Intelligence and Security *Report of the Inquiry into Potential Reforms of Australia's National Security Legislation*[57] and the review by the Senate Select Committee on Legal and Constitutional Affairs on a Comprehensive revision of the Telecommunications (Interception and Access) Act 1979.[58]

The Telecommunications (Interception and Access) Amendment (Data Retention) Act 2015 requires telecommunications providers to retain customer data for law enforcement and national security purposes for a period of two years (subject to some exemptions). Some specific details regarding the precise types of data to be retained remain to be prescribed by regulations; however, in general terms the Act requires the

[55] Clarke et al, above n 40, 110–11, citing National Research Council of the National Academy of Science, *Protecting Individual Privacy in the Struggle Against Terrorists: A Framework for Program Assessment* (Washington, DC: National Academic Press, 2008) 203.

[56] Josh Taylor, 'Data Retention is "the way western nations are going": Brandis', *ZDnet.com* (16 July 2014) www.zdnet.com/article/data-retention-is-the-way-western-nations-are-going-brandis/.

[57] Parliamentary Joint Committee on Intelligence and Security, House of Representatives, *Report of the Inquiry into Potential Reforms of Australia's National Security Legislation* (2013) www.aph.gov.au/parliamentary_business/committees/house_of_representatives_committees?url=pjcis/nsl2012/report.htm.

[58] Senate Legal and Constitutional Affairs Committee, *Comprehensive revision of the Telecommunications (Interception and Access) Act 1979 Interim Report*, (2014) www.aph.gov.au/Parliamentary_Business/Committees/Senate/Legal_and_Constitutional_Affairs/Comprehensive_revision_of_TIA_Act/Interim_Report.

retention of 'telecommunications data' but excluding content, internet browsing history, email titles, social media posts and URLs. Content of communications remains accessible only upon the terms of a warrant and other limited circumstances such as a life-threatening emergency. Mandatory retention of such data is justified on the basis that 'Telecommunications data is central to virtually every counter-terrorism, organized crime, counter-espionage and cyber-security investigation, as well as almost every serious criminal investigation, such as murder, rape and kidnapping'.[59]

The proposed mandatory retention regime attracted significant controversy, raising concerns ranging from the cost of storing this data, which will inevitably be passed on to consumers, to its potential use to identify illegal downloaders of copyright material.[60] The government has attempted to dampen such concerns with statements that there is 'no relationship' between copyright piracy and data retention.[61] Notably the Act also reduces the number of agencies who currently have access to customer data, by including a new definition of 'enforcement agency' and 'criminal law-enforcement agency' (Schedule 2). Previously approximately eighty Commonwealth and State agencies had access to such data under the Telecommunications (Interception and Access) Act and were required to report on access to customer data without a warrant (excluding the Australian Security Intelligence Organisation which is not required to make such a report).[62] The powers of the Commonwealth Ombudsman are also being extended to provide oversight of the compliance with the access to stored communications by agencies other than ASIO (Schedule 3).

In addition, legislation was enacted in October 2014 expanding ASIO's powers to access computers and computer networks and increasing the maximum jail sentence from two to ten years for intelligence officers who leak information to third parties, including journalists and other members

59 Explanatory Memorandum, Telecommunications (Interception and Access) Amendment (Data Retention) Bill 2014, 5.

60 Ben Grubb, 'Metadata and data retention changes explained', *Sydney Morning Herald* (online) (31 October 2014) www.smh.com.au/digital-life/consumer-security/metadata-and-data-retention-changes-explained-20141031-11euov.html.

61 Geordie Guy, 'Brandis's desperate and confused metadata laws are far from sold', *The Guardian* (online) (30 October 2014) www.theguardian.com/commentisfree/2014/oct/30/brandiss-desperate-and-confused-metadata-laws-are-far-from-sold.

62 In 2012–2013 approximately eighty enforcement agencies made over 300,000 requests for access, Commonwealth Attorney-General's Department, *Telecommunications (Interception and Access) Act 1979: Annual Report 2012–13* (Commonwealth of Australia, 2013), 47 www.ag.gov.au/NationalSecurity/TelecommunicationsSurveillance/Documents/TSLB-GAPSTIAActAnnualReport2012-13.pdf.

of the public.[63] Those reforms are clearly targeted at whistle-blowers such as Snowden. The Second Reading speech notes the 'risk presented by so-called "trusted insiders"' as a security threat.[64] The Bill creates new offences relating to unauthorised dealings with intelligence records, including copying, transcription, removal and retention. Such dealings with intelligence material have never been criminalised previously and will of course have significant impact on journalists who are provided with such material by whistle-blowing sources.[65] In addition, the Act introduced a new section 35P into the Australian Security Intelligence Organisation Act 1979 (Cth) providing that a person commits an offence, punishable by five years' imprisonment, if they disclose information relating to a 'special intelligence operation'.[66] These reforms reflect a

[63] National Security Legislation Amendment Act 2014 (Cth). See further, Senator George Brandis' Second Reading Speech for the National Security Legislation Amendment Bill 2014 (Cth): Commonwealth, *Parliamentary Debates*, Senate, 16 July 2014, 5157 (George Brandis); David Wroe and James Massola, 'Spies, internet firms in firing line of national security reforms', *Sydney Morning Herald* (online) (16 July 2014) www.smh.com.au/federal-politics/political-news/spies-internet-firms-in-firing-line-of-national-security-reforms-20140715-3bzfd.html.

[64] Second Reading Speech, National Security Legislation Amendment Bill 2014, above, 63.

[65] Ben Grubb, 'Edward Snowden's lawyer blasts Australian law that would jail journalists reporting on spy leaks' *Sydney Morning Herald* (online) (30 July 2014) www.smh.com.au/digital-life/consumer-security/edward-snowdens-lawyer-blasts-australian-law-that-would-jail-journalists-reporting-on-spy-leaks-20140730-zyn95.html; Gay Alcorn, 'Lachlan Murdoch attacks special laws to jail journalists for up to 10 years', *The Guardian* (online) (23 October 2014) www.theguardian.com/media/2014/oct/23/lachlan-murdoch-attacks-special-laws-to-jail-journalists-for-up-to-10-years.

[66] Section 35P provides:

(1) A person commits an offence if:
  (a) the person discloses information; and
  (b) the information relates to a special intelligence operation.

Penalty: Imprisonment for 5 years.

Note: Recklessness is the fault element for the circumstance described in paragraph (1)(b) – see section 5.6 of the Criminal Code.

(2) A person commits an offence if:
  (a) the person discloses information; and
  (b) the information relates to a special intelligence operation; and
  (c) either:
    (i) the person intends to endanger the health or safety of any person or prejudice the effective conduct of a special intelligence operation; or
    (ii) the disclosure of the information will endanger the health or safety of any person or prejudice the effective conduct of a special intelligence operation.

Penalty: Imprisonment for 10 years.

Note: Recklessness is the fault element for the circumstance described in paragraph (2)(b) – see section 5.6 of the Criminal Code.

Section 4 of the Act provides that 'special intelligence operation' is an operation:

(a) in relation to which a special intelligence operation authority has been granted; and

concerning definitional creep, imposing harsh obligations on the journalist who is neither an insider nor a source. This approach is reflective of a general trend of blurring the role of the reporter and the source in the online context, attempting to remove journalistic privileges regarding protection of sources by implying collusion between whistle-blowers and those journalists who choose to report their stories.[67] The Commonwealth Attorney-General attempted to allay concerns regarding prosecution of journalists for reporting on intelligence operations by issuing a directive to the Commonwealth Director of Public Prosecutions, instructing the DPP to obtain consent of the Attorney-General to any proposed prosecution of a journalist under these provisions.[68] However, the criminalisation of the reporting of these operations reflects the frustration that governments experienced worldwide in the face of the Manning and Snowden disclosures and places reporters such as Greenwald, and media platforms such as WikiLeaks in a very precarious situation.

## 11.5 Privacy and the whistle-blower

Until recently, the average internet user has had very little knowledge of the extent of information collected regarding their communications on a daily basis. Even the term 'metadata' has caused significant confusion among the public and lawmakers.[69] However, a full and open consideration of the complexities and consequences of surveillance, openness, public accountability and the role of privacy in the online environment has been muddied and distorted by muckraking and vilification of those who have sought to draw attention to these issues: as noted earlier, Assange is routinely the subject of articles which explore his personal life, habits and background, seemingly fascinated with matters of personal hygiene, eating habits and other aspects of his lifestyle. Manning has

(b) that is carried out for a purpose relevant to the performance of one or more special intelligence functions; and
(c) that may involve an ASIO employee or an ASIO affiliate in special intelligence conduct.

[67] de Zwart, 'Whistleblowers and the Media', above n 5; Henry A Giroux 'Totalitarian Paranoia in the Post-Orwellian Surveillance State' (2014) 29 *Cultural Studies* 108, 120–1.

[68] Lenore Taylor, 'George Brandis: attorney general must approve prosecution of journalists under security laws', *The Guardian* (online) (30 October 2014) www.theguardian.com/australia-news/2014/oct/30/george-brandis-attorney-general-approve-prosecution-journalists-security-laws.

[69] Sara Dingle, 'Meta-mess as George Brandis struggles with web terminology', *AM*, (7 August 2014), www.abc.net.au/news/2014-08-07/meta-mess-as-george-brandis-struggles-with-web/5654280.

more recently been pitied for her treatment and portrayed in certain quarters as the pawn in Assange's personal war on the US.[70] Snowden, with his emphasis on conducting his disclosures completely in the public eye appears to have fared slightly better, but it should be noted that both Snowden and Assange are subject to criminal warrants in the US and both live in exile. All three have been the subject of calls for their execution or assassination.[71] Most recently, Glenn Greenwald's partner was detained for nine hours at Heathrow Airport under Schedule 7 of the Terrorism Act 2000 in the UK on his way home to Rio de Janeiro, after visiting Laura Poitras in Berlin, and had electronics equipment including his mobile phone, laptop, camera, memory sticks, DVDs and games consoles confiscated.[72] The detention was the subject of a challenge but was declared legal by the UK High Court.[73] In July 2013 in one of the most bizarre and dramatic acts involved in the Snowden releases senior employees of *The Guardian* used angle grinders and other equipment to destroy the hard drives of computers which had been used to store the Snowden files, watched over by officers from GCHQ. Of course this was a symbolic act as the files were stored on servers belonging to *The Guardian* offshore.[74]

These actions suggest that capacity for individuals to effect acts of whistle-blowing will become much more difficult as they become the subject of increased penalties, and dealt with under anti-terrorism laws. Certainly the fates of Manning and Snowden would act as a significant deterrent to anyone contemplating such action. Yet the importance of

[70] This is certainly the suggestion of both the documentary *We Steal Secrets* (2013), above n 10; see also Robert Manne, 'We Steal Secrets: Alex Gibney, Wikileaks & Julian Assange', *The Monthly*, July 2013, www.themonthly.com.au/issue/2013/july/1372600800/robert-manne/we-steal-secrets-alex-gibney-wikileaks-julian-assange; and Daniel Domscheit-Berg, above n 10.

[71] Haroon Siddique and Matthew Weaver, 'US embassy cables culprit should be executed, says Mike Huckabee', *The Guardian* (online) (1 December 2010) www.theguardian.com/world/2010/dec/01/us-embassy-cables-executed-mike-huckabee; Erik Kirschbaum, 'Edward Snowden: There Are "Significant Threats" To My Life', *Huffington Post* (26 January 2014) www.huffingtonpost.com/2014/01/26/edward-snowden-threats_n_4670786.html.

[72] 'Glenn Greenwald's partner detained at Heathrow airport for nine hours', *The Guardian* (online) (19 August 2013) www.theguardian.com/world/2013/aug/18/glenn-greenwald-guardian-partner-detained-heathrow.

[73] *Miranda* v. *Secretary of State for the Home Department* [2014] EWHC 255. This decision is currently the subject of an appeal.

[74] Julian Borger, 'NSA files: why the Guardian in London destroyed hard drives of leaked files', *The Guardian* (online) (21 August 2013) www.theguardian.com/world/2013/aug/20/nsa-snowden-files-drives-destroyed-london; Luke Harding, 'Footage released of Guardian editors destroying Snowden hard drives', *The Guardian* (online) (31 January 2014) www.theguardian.com/uk-news/2014/jan/31/footage-released-guardian-editors-snowden-hard-drives-gchq.

whistle-blowing remains a key element of democratic society.[75] The risk in imposing serious criminal penalties and even going so far as to label whistle-blowers as terrorists and traitors worthy of the death penalty will act as an incentive to self-censor and to remain silent, even in the face of great wrong.[76] As Snowden observed regarding his own decision to disclose the NSA surveillance practices:

> The reality of working in [the] intelligence community is you see things that are deeply troubling all the time. I raised concerns about these programs regularly and widely, [to] more than 10 discreet colleagues that I have worked with – and that's both laterally and vertically in my work. I went to [them] and I showed [them] these programmes and said: 'What do you think about this? Is this unusual? How can we be doing this? Isn't this unconstitutional? Isn't this a violation of rights?' and 'Why are we intercepting more American communications than we're intercepting Russian communications?'
>
> The people that are staffing these intelligence agencies are ordinary people, like you and me. They're not moustache-twirling villains that are going, 'ah ha ha that's great', they're going: 'You're right. That crosses a line but you really shouldn't say something about that because it's going to end your career'.
>
> We all have mortgages. We all have families. And when you're working for a national security system that has these official secrets acts, that means even if you go to a chosen representative of Congress, a representative chosen by a reporter as opposed to a representative chosen by the intelligence community responsible for the wrongdoing to begin with, you can be prosecuted for it. And even if you're not prosecuted for it, you can lose your job over it.[77]

## 11.6 Is privacy dead?

Assange has now been the subject of a major feature film, a made-for-television movie, and a significant documentary, as well as countless magazine, blog, television and news items. Many of these have focussed on Assange the individual rather than Assange the editor-in-chief of WikiLeaks, and have therefore attracted the ire of Assange and his supporters, an issue which itself becomes a news item, as is the story behind the ghostwriter published by O'Hagan. In particular Assange's desire for personal privacy has been critiqued as inconsistent with his stance on accountability and transparency.

[75] 'In the modern age of institutions, whistleblowing is now established as one of the most important processes – if not the single most important process – by which governments and corporations are kept accountable to the societies they are meant to serve and service'. David Lewis, AJ Brown and Richard Moberly, 'Whistleblowing, its Importance and the State of the Research' in AJ Brown, David Lewis, Richard Moberly and Wim Vandekerckhove (eds), *International Handbook on Whistleblowing Research* (Cheltenham, UK: Edward Elgar, 2014), 33.

[76] Giroux, above n 67. [77] Rusbridger and MacAskill, above n 14.

Throughout his account of working with Assange on the ill-fated autobiography, O'Hagan refers to his belief that Assange did not want to do the book because he did not want to confront or reveal his own personal life story. O'Hagan observes:

> The man who put himself in charge of disclosing the world's secrets simply couldn't bear his own. The story of his life mortified him and sent him scurrying for excuses. He didn't want to do the book. He hadn't from the beginning.[78]

This observation begs the question as to whether there can be any such thing as personal privacy in the online environment, particularly for an advocate of radical transparency? What rights (if any) does the transparency advocate have to preserve his or her own secrecy? Many of the technology companies have famously said that in the age of the Internet, there is no privacy so get over it.[79] Platforms such as Facebook actively require and elicit disclosure of personal information in order to function. Consent operates in a new mode in the online context of social networking: if you want to be part of the platform you need to agree to 'share' your information.[80] The PRISM program discussed earlier is premised largely on the fact that millions of people are willing and required to share their personal information with the platform providers, granting the US government an open invitation to gather such voluntarily disclosed details.

Can it be said that Assange's own publication of secret documents voids any rights he has to personal privacy? Is there inconsistency in his approach to privacy for the individual and transparency for the powerful? Assange's attitudes towards personal privacy appear to be determined by his belief that true privacy is almost impossible to attain in the current legal and technological climate. Hence his 'call to cryptographic arms' in *Cypherpunks*: to resist the interception, monitoring and storage of 'the collective private intellectual output of humanity' through the use of encryption.[81] Further, responses to his own call for privacy are coloured

[78] O'Hagan, 'Ghosting', above n 2.

[79] Scott McNealy, former head of Sun Microsystems, said in 1999: 'You have zero privacy anyway... Get over it', Stephen Manes, 'Private Lives? Not Ours' (2000) 18(6) *PC World* 312; Eric Schmidt, CEO of Google, said in 2009: 'If you have something that you don't want anyone to know, maybe you shouldn't be doing it in the first place', Ryan Tate, 'Google CEO: Secrets Are for Filthy People' (12 April 2009) http://gawker.com/5419271/google-ceo-secrets-are-for-filthy-people.

[80] Of course the effectiveness of the concept of consent in this context is highly contested, the requirement of data disclosure for use of many online services renders the concept of consent meaningless; Daniel J Solove, 'Introduction: Privacy, Self-Management and the Consent Dilemma' (2013) 26 *Harvard Law Review* 1880, 1888–90.

[81] Assange et al, *Cypherpunks*, above *, 4.

by the fallout between Assange and his mainstream media partners over publication of unredacted documents by WikiLeaks in 2011.[82]

O'Hagan also acknowledges the fine line between fact and fiction inherent in the Assange story, a preoccupation of his own: 'However it came, and however I unearthed it or inflected it, the Assange story would be consistent with my instinct to walk the unstable border between fiction and non-fiction, to see how porous the parameters between invention and personality are'.[83] At one point in time Assange said to O'Hagan: 'People think you're helping me write my book ... but actually I'm helping you write your novel'.[84] O'Hagan justifies this approach by claiming that there is something inherently 'ghostwritten' in the nature of the Internet itself, the exemplar being the countless contributions that comprise Wikipedia, and the fact that hackers like Assange are 'interested in masks within masks'.[85] Thus matters of identity are marked as fluid, shifting and responsive to particular circumstances. Of course, this is relevant in many internet-related contexts as people use the online environment to explore and act out various aspects of their personality in chat rooms, dating sites, fan forums and even on Facebook. It seems especially relevant in the case of Assange who had to adopt different personas in order to maintain the appearance that WikiLeaks was anything more than a single person organisation. Again, O'Hagan notes that Assange seems most comfortable and at home as the hacker but was also forced to adopt the role of journalist, editor and spokesman. This lack of certainty and fluidity is regarded as evidence of dishonesty and lack of transparency and hence reason to disregard Assange's views on personal privacy. However, this is conflating and oversimplifying concepts of individual versus institutional privacy.

Rather than inconsistent, the clear message of Snowden and Assange is that privacy of the individual is paramount. It is an essential element of self-expression and fulfilment and invasions of individual privacy are harmful. Constant surveillance can operate as an impediment to self-expression and personal development and ultimately deter democratic

[82] Fowler, *The Most Dangerous Man*, above n 10, 201–10.

[83] O'Hagan, 'Ghosting', above n 2.

[84] It may be worth noting here Robert Manne's observation in his 2011 piece on Assange that: 'Journalists as senior as David Leigh of the *Guardian* or John F Burns of the *New York Times* in general accept on trust many of Assange's stories about himself. They do not understand that their subject is a fabulist. By contrast, when Daniel Domscheit-Berg, Assange's lieutenant at WikiLeaks between late 2007 and September 2010, heard that Assange was writing an autobiography he tells us in *Inside WikiLeaks* that his "first thought" was that it should be placed "in the fiction section"'. Robert Manne, 'The Cypherpunk Revolutionary', *The Monthly*, Issue 65 March 2011, 16, 17.

[85] O'Hagan, 'Ghosting', above n 2.

participation in society. Conversely, governments and institutions should be transparent and accountable to their members and citizens.[86]

## 11.7 Conclusion

As Manne explains:

> At the core of the cypherpunk philosophy was the belief that the great question of politics in the age of the internet was whether the state would strangle individual freedom and privacy through its capacity for electronic surveillance or whether autonomous individuals would eventually undermine and even destroy the state through their deployment of electronic weapons newly at hand.[87]

Does this suggest a need to remodel concepts of privacy for the surveillance society, indicating that privacy, rather than being a default status to which we are entitled with respect to all communications at home, between friends, colleagues and classmates, internet searches and transactions, must be a deliberate choice that is made by the user: to ensure privacy through the use of encryption?

In the current surveillance society it appears that any belief in the traditional sense of privacy in individual communications and transactions is misplaced. The threat of surveillance operates as a significant chill upon a citizen's exercise of civil engagement and freedom.[88] Further, as consumers of digital platforms, we are complicit in our own open disclosure and commodification of our personal information. The Fourth Amendment in the US has proven incapable of redressing these problems in the digital environment. In Australia the risks are even stronger as there is no such constitutional protection against search and surveillance.

Snowden recently urged all professionals to encrypt all of their communications in order to ensure that they can satisfy professional obligations of confidentiality.[89] Encryption, the hacker's tool, may need to become the new standard, replacing common law or statutory concepts of privacy which have proven too vague and too unenforceable to protect individual interests. As Assange urged in *Cypherpunks*, the balance between individuals and large public and private institutions may be

[86] Manne notes that Snowden was motivated to make his disclosures by two interrelated causes: first: opposition to mass surveillance, and second, integrity of the Internet as a place for freedom, exploration and self-actualisation. Robert Manne, 'The Snowden Files', *The Monthly*, Issue 104 September 2014, 38.

[87] Manne, 'The Cypherpunk Revolutionary', above n 84, 21.

[88] Neil M Richards, 'The Dangers of Surveillance' (2013) 126 *Harvard Law Review* 1934.

[89] Alan Rusbridger and Ewen MacAskill, 'Edward Snowden urges professionals to encrypt client communications', *The Guardian* (online) (18 July 2014) www.theguardian.com/world/2014/jul/17/edward-snowden-professionals-encrypt-client-communications-nsa-spy.

redressed through the recognition of individual privacy and institutional transparency, but this will need to be enacted through technological tools. The call for individual privacy should not be seen as hypocrisy on the part of one who has revealed the secrets of institutions, but rather should be characterised as consistent with the role of a whistle-blower in redressing the power imbalance between the weak and the powerful.[90]

[90] Luke Heemsbergen, 'Whistleblowing and Digital Technologies: An Interview with Suelette Dreyfus' (2013) 5 *Platform: Journal of Media and Communication* 67, 69.

# 12 The trouble with dignity

*Amy Gajda*

In Spring 2014, a court in France ordered *Closer* magazine, already infamous for publishing photographs of a topless Kate Middleton, to pay actress Julie Gayet the equivalent of $US20,000 in damages. Gayet, it seems, had been in a romantic relationship with François Hollande, the president of France, and *Closer* had revealed the affair in a news story and photo spread. The photos, all said to have been taken outside Gayet's apartment, included those of the actress arriving in the evening and leaving the next morning, along with a purposefully helmeted man said to be Hollande.[1]

The photos were apparently not staged and the affair was seemingly factual, so Gayet had sued not for defamation but for invasion of privacy. The story had, in her lawyer's description, turned her life upside down – and the court was convinced that that was enough for a plaintiff's verdict and ordered the damages award. It therefore punished *Closer* for revealing accurately that the president of France and a famous actress were seeing each other.

The original story of the affair made headlines in the United States as well. It is apparently of some interest among Americans that an elected official they know and an actress they don't were dating in secret, especially when earlier stories had revealed that Hollande's girlfriend of nine years, a woman considered to be the First Lady of France, had been hospitalised for what was later said to have been treatment related to her shock at the news of the affair.[2] Both types of news articles, especially as regarding public figures, appear routinely in the United States.

I am a law professor but I spent more than a decade working as a journalist, mainly for television and radio stations across the United States. My journalism work has also been published by *The New York Times* and other major publications. Thanks to Laura Fink, Mia Lindell, and Mitchell Tedesco for research assistance.

1 Reuters, 'Actress Julie Gayet gets $20,000 judgement against tabloid linking her to President Francois Hollande', *New York Daily News* (27 March 2014) www.nydailynews.com/news/world/french-actress-julie-gayet-wins-lawsuit-tabloid-affair-president-francois-hollande-article-1.1736750.

2 Peter Mikelbank, 'French President Francois Hollande and Valérie Trierweiler Split after Alleged Affair', *People* (25 January 2014) www.people.com/people/article/0,20779935,00.html.

But the story of the results of Gayet's lawsuit also made headlines for a decidedly different reason: the lawsuit's outcome was extraordinary for US audiences. If a court in the United States had ruled in favour of a public figure plaintiff in such a case, after all, it would not only be surprising, it would be considered by many to be unconstitutional.

This chapter explores the extraordinarily broad rights that news organisations have to publish information about public officials, public figures, and others in the United States. It examines the law that has for many years encouraged such expansive coverage, including the highly influential Restatement of Torts provisions concerning privacy. It also explores journalism ethics standards that, in turn, have kept some inflammatory information out of print despite such press-accommodating law. It suggests, however, that some newer media organisations, believing themselves protected by the First Amendment but unwilling to follow traditional ethics provisions, have the potential to change the course of First Amendment protections. It ends with the argument that the law must change in the United States to be more respectful of privacy, but must avoid a single-minded focus on human dignity that would unconstitutionally impact press freedoms.

One thing is certain: Today, if the president of the United States were having an affair with a Hollywood actress and the president's long-term girlfriend had been hospitalised for treatment related to the affair, the story would not only make the cover of gossip magazines, it would be the lead story in every major US newspaper and would be contained within breaking news emails sent to readers across the nation. CNN would almost certainly focus on the story above all else for several days if not weeks. Call it puritanism or nosiness driven by a culture of celebrity or concern stemming from worries about political integrity, but most Americans would both want to know and would absolutely consider it their business. As the law currently stands in the United States, it is, in fact, the public's business.

## 12.1 The president and (no) privacy

In William Prosser's famously influential 1960 law review article *Privacy*, he wrote this regarding news coverage about the president of the United States:

> Perhaps there is very little in the way of information about the President of the United States, or any candidate for that high office, that is not a matter of legitimate public concern.[3]

[3] William L Prosser, 'Privacy' (1960) 48 *California Law Review* 383, 417.

Such sweeping language, suggesting that nearly everything about the president of the United States is newsworthy, is not all that far from what Samuel Warren and Louis Brandeis had written in the similarly groundbreaking law review article 'The Right to Privacy'[4] some seventy years before. Even though the two authors in 1890 famously and decidedly favoured privacy over complete freedom of the press, they wrote broadly that '[t]he right to privacy does not prohibit any publication of matter which is of public or general interest'.[5] In doing so, they made a distinction between people who live their lives in private and those who achieved some sort of fame or infamy through politics, Hollywood films, or some other spotlight. The former deserved to be let alone. The latter had 'renounced the right to live their lives screened from public observation' and included public officials who, Warren and Brandeis wrote, could indeed be 'the subject of legitimate interest to their fellow citizens'.[6] Any notion of the 'private life' of such public people, they suggested, must necessarily be defined in 'its most limited sense'.[7]

The privacy principle in the United States, then, no matter its cultural basis, is that once someone runs for public office, that person's life becomes much more open to intrusion, investigation, and the publication of the fruits of such enquiry. It has been that way since at least 1890, at the arguable birth of privacy law in the US. And even though, remarkably, Warren and Brandeis had been influenced at least in part by hounding press coverage of President Grover Cleveland and his considerably younger bride who was once his 'charge', they recognised that when something is of public interest, including information regarding those in the public eye, it should not be repressed.

In 1977, William Prosser, the scholar who had written earlier that everything that the president of the United States did was newsworthy, had a second strong hand in influencing the way courts in the United States define privacy and what would be considered appropriately published information regarding those in the public eye and otherwise. He was the lead author of the privacy sections contained within the highly influential Second Restatement of Torts and his definition for legally appropriate news in 1977 was nearly as broad as his notions of appropriate presidential news coverage in 1960.[8] The Restatement privacy sections – still in effect[9] – suggest, for example, that '[t]here may be some intimate details of [an actress's] life, such as sexual relations,

[4] (1890) 4 *Harvard Law Review* 193. [5] Ibid., 214. [6] Ibid., 215.

[7] Ibid., 216 and its n 1.

[8] American Law Institute, *Restatement (Second) of Torts* (1977) § 652(D).

[9] The Restatement sections on privacy were being reviewed by the American Law Institute in recent years for possible changes.

which even the actress is entitled to keep to herself', but that language is tempered with this: 'the home life and daily habits of a motion picture actress may be of legitimate and reasonable interest to the public that sees her on screen'.[10]

Given that, it should be of little surprise that appropriately newsworthy information in the Restatement includes 'matters of genuine, even if more or less deplorable, popular appeal' and stops only at news springing from morbid and sensational prying done for its own sake.[11] Such a balance gave press the leeway to cover events that included:

> homicide and other crimes, arrests, police raids, suicides, marriages and divorces, accidents, fires, catastrophes of nature, a death from the use of narcotics, a rare disease, the birth of a child to a twelve-year-old girl, the reappearance of one supposed to have been murdered years ago, a report to the police concerning the escape of a wild animal and many other similar matters.[12]

Moreover, appropriate news as defined within the Restatement is not limited to so-called 'hard news', but includes information that is published 'for purposes of education, amusement or enlightenment, when the public may reasonably be expected to have a legitimate interest in what is published'.[13]

In the United States, then, even a college-aged intern who becomes involved with a public official could well suddenly find herself the subject of legitimate news interest, as Monica Lewinsky learned after her relationship with President Bill Clinton became known. '[P]ublishers' in the United States, the Restatement had explained many years before, 'are permitted to satisfy the curiosity of the public as to its heroes, leaders, villains and victims, and those who are closely associated with them'.[14]

The Supreme Court – a court that had significantly supported the press through its 1964 decision in *New York Times* v. *Sullivan*[15] when it protected the publishers of even untruthful reputation-harming information – continued what appeared to be a march towards a broad interpretation of the First Amendment press clause in dicta and otherwise. '[W]here a newspaper publishes truthful information which it has lawfully obtained', the court wrote in *Florida Star* v. *BJF*,[16] a 1989 case brought by a rape victim who had sued a newspaper that had identified her by name, 'punishment may lawfully be imposed, if at all, only when narrowly tailored to a state interest of the highest order'.[17] Protection of rape victims, such as the plaintiff in *Florida Star*, the court decided, failed to

[10] American Law Institute, *Restatement (Second) of Torts* (1977) § 652(D) cmt h.
[11] Ibid., cmt g. [12] Ibid. [13] Ibid., cmt j. [14] Ibid., cmt f. [15] 376 US 254 (1964).
[16] 491 US 524 (1989). [17] Ibid., 541.

reach the level of 'a state interest of the highest order' when balanced against the freedom of the press to decide what was appropriate news.

In doing so, the court paralleled the ideas in *Sullivan*. There, the court had written that there was a 'profound national commitment to the principle that debate on public issues should be uninhibited, robust, and wide-open' and would necessarily include the press's 'vehement, caustic, and sometimes unpleasantly sharp attacks on government and public officials'.[18] The First Amendment, the Justices wrote, required 'breathing space' to survive,[19] and worried that a decision against publishers could well lead to a 'pall of fear and timidity' and 'an atmosphere in which the First Amendment freedoms cannot survive'.[20] Courts, they explained, must protect even inaccurate reporting to help support the journalistic work that is central to democracy.

In the same year as *Sullivan*, the Justices wrote that journalists required protection especially in cases involving public officials. There is a 'paramount public interest in a free flow of information to the people concerning public officials, their servants', the Justices explained, '[and] [t]o this end, anything which might touch on an official's fitness for office [is] relevant' to public discourse, including 'dishonesty, malfeasance, or improper motivation, even though these characteristics may also affect the official's private character'.[21]

Just a few years later, in *Time* v. *Hill*,[22] the court reiterated the connection between a free press and publishers' freedoms, writing that '[a] broadly defined freedom of the press assur[ed] the maintenance of our political system and an open society' and that journalists should not be saddled with verifying all information in stories lest it 'create a grave risk of serious impairment of the indispensable service of a free press in a free society'.[23]

So strong was the protection of the press in the United States, the Restatement authors suggested, that it was possible that any distinction made by courts between legitimate and illegitimate news would be unconstitutional. In fact, in their eyes, press interests could well be absolute: '[I]t has not been established with certainty', the Restatement reads, 'that liability of this nature [that would uphold privacy interests over news decisions made by news media] is consistent with the free-speech and free-press concerns of the First Amendment to the Constitution, as applied to state law through the Fourteenth Amendment'.[24]

[18] 376 US 254, 271 (1964). [19] Ibid., 272. [20] Ibid., 278.
[21] *Garrison* v. *Louisiana*, 379 US 64, 77 (1964). [22] 385 US 374 (1967).
[23] Ibid., 389.
[24] American Law Institute, *Restatement (Second) of Torts* (1977) § 652(D), Special Note on Relation of § 652D to the First Amendment of the Constitution.

That legal framework – that a free press in the United States could well trump privacy interests in every single case – can be seen in holdings like that in *Sipple* v. *Chronicle Publishing*, a case in which a brave bystander saved President Ford from an assassination attempt and then was outed as being gay by a gossip columnist.[25] Family members who did not know were said to have rejected him because of his homosexuality and he sued the newspaper on invasion-of-privacy grounds. But a California appeals court held that it was decidedly newsworthy that a gay man had saved the president. There, because there was substantial legitimate public interest both in the event and the hero at its heart, 'a much greater intrusion into [the hero's] private life [would] be sanctioned', the court wrote in 1984, even if the man were an involuntary public figure, one thrust onto the public stage through his own act of courage.[26] More broadly and notably, the court worried about a 'chilling effect' that could well cripple media in its reporting should it find in favour of such plaintiffs on privacy grounds.

While that decision may be shocking to some, especially those who live in more privacy-protective countries, those concerned about media excesses in the United States should take some comfort in knowing that mainstream media publishers in the US generally have strong ethics codes that restrict some push-the-envelope coverage like that in *Sipple*. It is relevant, for example, that Sipple's homosexuality was first revealed by a gossip columnist.

To put it simply, ethics is an important and at times overriding concern in mainstream newsrooms in the United States. Most mainstream journalists in the US subscribe both to a personal and a professional code of ethics. The former, an internal ethics sense, leads mainstream reporters to discard certain information that would surely invade the privacy of someone who deserves protection. This might include, for example, a journalist who videotapes a witness to a crime or someone in mourning but then refuses to include such video in a story, knowing that such a revelation could prove emotionally or physically harmful. The latter, a professional code to which a journalist adheres, could well be the Society of Professional Journalists Code of Ethics. That code, the one with the greatest reach in the US, advises journalists to hold back on certain news that would invade privacy. As one example, journalists are advised to 'Minimize Harm' in language that very clearly supports privacy over what might be considered sensational coverage:

> Ethical journalists treat sources, subjects and colleagues as human beings deserving of respect.

[25] *Sipple* v. *Chronicle Publishing*, 154 Cal. App. 3d 1043 (Cal. Ct. App. 1984).
[26] Ibid., 1049.

Journalists should:

— Balance the public's need for information against potential harm or discomfort. Pursuit of the news is not a license for arrogance or undue intrusiveness.

— Show compassion for those who may be affected adversely by news coverage. Use heightened sensitivity when dealing with juveniles, victims of sex crimes, and sources or subjects who are inexperienced or unable to give consent. . . .

— Recognize that legal access to information differs from an ethical justification to publish or broadcast.

— Realize that private people have a greater right to control information about themselves than do public figures and others who seek power, influence or attention. Weigh the consequences of publishing or broadcasting personal information.

— Avoid pandering to lurid curiosity, even if others do.

— Balance a suspect's right to a fair trial with the public's right to know. Consider the implications of identifying criminal suspects before they face legal charges.

— Consider the long-term implications of the extended reach and permanence of publication . . . .[27]

Because of ethics and other concerns, mainstream journalists, for example, have suggested that they knew about Idaho Senator Larry Craig's alleged sexual encounters with men in public bathrooms – some had called it an open secret in Idaho – but did not initially report the story even though it had been noted by others on the Internet.[28] The journalists were necessarily careful for defamation-based reasons, of course, but also because they recognised the harm that would necessarily befall Craig, his wife, and his family once the information was reported in an official sense. In fact, many mainstream reporters today suggest that they will only reveal information regarding a public official's sex life if his or her behaviour is in some way hypocritical: when he or she votes against gay rights, for example, but is involved in a homosexual relationship.[29]

[27] Society of Professional Journalists Code of Ethics, available at www.spj.org/ethicscode.asp (last visited 21 November 2015). The SPJ Code of Ethics was amended slightly in 2014; an earlier code provision had more explicitly suggested that '[o]nly an overriding public need [could] justify intrusion into anyone's privacy.'

[28] The *Idaho Statesman* investigated internet claims for nearly half a year before publishing a story. See Dan Popkey, 'Men's room arrest reopens questions about Sen. Larry Craig', *Idaho Statesman* (28 August 2007) www.idahostatesman.com/2007/08/28/143801/mens-room-arrest-reopens-questions.html.

[29] Kelly McBride, 'Thresholds of Coverage: When to Say He's Gay', poynter.org www.poynter.org/news/mediawire/84245/thresholds-of-coverage-when-to-say-hes-gay/.

There are other examples of mainstream media's withholding of information that others would likely consider important, including information media knew about but decided not to publish because of national security concerns. CNN once reported, for example, that it 'ha[d] agreed to a request from an Obama administration official not to publish or broadcast additional details [regarding the closing of embassies after an intercepted terrorist message] because of the sensitivity of the information'.[30] Each time, journalists suppressed information for ethics reasons even though that information, if truthful, would be publishable in a legal sense.

Despite the public's perception, then, of eager journalists in the United States jumping at the chance to cover any salacious story about a public official or otherwise, those who work for mainstream media recognise that they and their colleagues know a lot of salacious, sensational secrets that they decide not to cover, halted in many cases by an ethics sense alone.

Because of those journalistic traditions, courts in the United States generally came to trust journalists – and, under those circumstances, the expansively protective language in *Sullivan, Florida Star*, and others is understandable. If judges respectfully gave journalists the breathing space that journalists argued was necessary to do good work, journalists would in turn be respectful of the privacy rights of individuals and would only rarely (and the journalists would argue, necessarily) go too far. It was, then, journalism's professionalism that helped protect it in the United States. And that protection was good while it lasted.

## 12.2 Pushing the envelope

It was, perhaps in hindsight, a predictable predicament. In the wake of journalistic efforts in the United States that had heroically uncovered president Richard Nixon's sins in the Watergate scandal and that had boldly portrayed the Vietnam War in all its tragedy, courts in the United States trusted journalists to do the right thing. Most judges, even at the highest levels, embraced an expansive definition for news in the name of democracy; such a broad definition limited personal privacy and allowed media to delve into the embarrassing histories and current-day lives of public officials, voluntary and involuntary public figures, and others who found themselves the subject of news. In giving journalists that freedom, judges thought of journalism as a noble profession deserving of

[30] Barbara Starr, Chris Lawrence and Tom Cohen, 'Intercepted al Qaeda message led to shuttering embassies, consulates', CNN.com (5 August 2013) http://edition.cnn.com/2013/08/04/politics/us-embassies-close/.

protection. Ethics codes, though suggestive rather than mandatory, effectively forced journalists to police themselves even when the law suggested otherwise.

There has been an important shift, however. The alarming growth of push-the-envelope programming on the Internet and elsewhere over the past decade marks an important change in journalism in its broadest sense. Helped along not only by expansive First Amendment protection but also by statutes like Section 230 of the Communications Decency Act that protect websites from liability for defamatory or privacy-invading information posted by others, some media organisations have started to test the limits of protection.

A fine example of a push-the-envelope publisher is Gawker, a website with a motto that suggests that its gossip today will become tomorrow's news. Gawker is the perfect case study because it decided to publish what a mainstream newspaper website never would: explicit excerpts of a sex tape featuring professional wrestler Hulk Hogan apparently surreptitiously recorded in Hogan's sex partner's bedroom. Hogan is fully nude – his penis is shown – and clearly engaging in sexual activity with a woman who is also fully nude. Gawker has described the tape as featuring only approximately thirty seconds of explicit sex. If that sounds like a short amount of time, a check of a clock's second hand will offer a different perspective.

Not surprisingly, Hulk Hogan sued Gawker for, among other things, invasion of privacy. It was, after all, a fairly clear violation. Recall that the Restatement suggests that even celebrities can keep their sex lives private and this, after all, was not just a story about an affair: it was a graphic depiction of a sexual act on video that had been recorded surreptitiously and publically posted against its subject's wishes. It was, it might be argued, precisely the sort of morbid and sensational prying for its own sake that even the permissive Restatement condemned.

Gawker's response was to wrap itself in the First Amendment and its promises of press protection. '[T]he Constitution does unambiguously accord us the right to publish true things about public figures' a Gawker writer wrote with regard to the tape, '[a]nd [a state trial judge's] order requiring us to take down not only a very brief, highly edited video excerpt from a thirty-minute Hulk Hogan [f—] session but also a lengthy written account from someone who had watched the entirety of that [f—] session, is risible and contemptuous of centuries of First Amendment jurisprudence'.[31]

[31] John Cook, 'A Judge Told Us to Take Down Our Hulk Hogan Sex Tape Post. We Won't', Gawker.com (25 April 2013) http://gawker.com/a-judge-told-us-to-take-down-our-hulk-hogan-sex-tape-po-481328088. Gawker used the profanity.

What is perhaps even more remarkable than that First Amendment-absolutist argument is that two courts, at least so far, have completely embraced it and sided with Gawker. Gawker initially convinced a federal trial court in Florida that Gawker's decision to post the videotape was in line with First Amendment protections. That court wrote that it hesitated to second-guess what Gawker editors had decided was newsworthy. Such a decision was, instead, 'appropriately left to [Gawker's own] editorial discretion'.[32]

After the case shifted to the Florida state court system, a court there also sided with Gawker.[33] The 'arguably inappropriate and otherwise sexually explicit content'[34] could well be of legitimate public interest and was necessarily left to Gawker's 'editorial discretion', the court wrote, because it addressed 'matters of public concern'.[35] Hulk Hogan himself, the court explained, had put his sex life at issue when he wrote about an affair in his autobiography. (Of important note, however, the passages to which the court refers in its opinion are decidedly innocuous and suggest only that he regretted his dalliance.) In finding that Gawker was protected from Hulk Hogan's request for a preliminary injunction that would have mandated the tape's removal from the website, both courts had necessarily decided that Hulk Hogan was likely to lose any underlying privacy lawsuit against Gawker. In short, the sex tape was newsworthy because Gawker said it was.

As I have previously suggested,[36] it is as if emboldened media organisations in the United States like Gawker believe that they are within their own protective First Amendment bubble. There, they believe that they can make whatever news decisions they would like without limit. Indeed, other push-the-envelope publishers have gone at least as far as Gawker in its interpretation of the press clause. Nik Richie, the brainchild behind a website known as The Dirty that is at times quite dirty, has said that he believes that 'you can say whatever you want on the internet'.[37]

Compare the surprising initial outcome in the Hulk Hogan case and that strident language from Nik Richie with the decision of the French court that found in favour of the actress pictured outside her apartment building, fully clothed, and fully visible to anyone else walking by. Why should a fully clothed woman photographed outside be successfully cloaked with privacy rights while a man engaging in explicit sexual activity

[32] *Bollea* v. *Gawker Media*, 40 Media L. Rep. 2601 (M.D. Fla. 2012).

[33] *Gawker Media* v. *Bollea*, 129 So. 3d 1196 (Fla. App. 2 Dist. 2014). [34] Ibid., 1210.

[35] Ibid., 1202.

[36] Amy Gajda, *The First Amendment Bubble: How Privacy and Paparazzi Threaten a Free Press* (Cambridge, MA: Harvard University Press, 2015).

[37] *Jones* v. *Dirty World Entertainment Recordings*, 840 F. Supp. 2d 1008 (E.D. Ky. 2012).

videotaped surreptitiously inside a house shouldn't be? Surely, as some courts in the United States have started to decide, the First Amendment cannot be so absolute. Surely, privacy springing from human dignity considerations should trump publication rights in certain cases even in the United States.

## 12.3 Mosley and more

In other parts of the world, dignity is an important part of privacy law[38] and there are examples beyond France and the Julie Gayet case outcome. As James Whitman explained in his Yale Law Review article 'The Two Western Cultures of Privacy: Dignity Versus Liberty', '[t]he right of free expression that protects the press is always balanced in continental Europe against an individual right to "dignity," "honour," or "personality"'.[39] And there, as seen in the Gayet case, much more often than in the United States, privacy wins out over press freedoms.

In Europe, the European Convention on Human Rights supports plaintiffs' privacy-related claims. The language in Article 8 is highly protective of privacy: 'Everyone', the ECHR suggests, 'has the right to respect for his private and family life, his home and his correspondence'. In the United Kingdom as well, the Human Rights Act of 1998 gives force to the same rights and helps give plaintiffs there the ability to bring privacy-related causes of action. There is an expression-based counter-balance, however, given equal weight with privacy: language in Article 10 of the ECHR contemplates 'the right to freedom of expression', including the right to 'impart information' without government interference. Those duelling rights, both given the same level of importance, however, lack the overarching constitutional strength – at least in its traditional sense – of First Amendment-based freedom of the press.

The power of this differing treatment of privacy is clear. Consider the case of Max Mosley, famous for leading Formula One racing and later for images featuring sadomasochistic dealings with prostitutes that were published in the British newspaper *News of the World* and otherwise. The images of the encounter, recorded surreptitiously by one of the prostitutes, had been described by *News of the World* as stemming from Nazi-related role play, which the British court found false, and therefore found no public interest in the images. In hearing Mosley's claims against the now-defunct newspaper, the court wrote more generally that public

[38] See, e.g., James Q Whitman, 'The Two Western Cultures of Privacy: Dignity Versus Liberty' (2004) 113 *Yale Law Journal* 1151.
[39] Ibid., 1197.

figures like Mosley were 'entitled to a private personal life [and that] [t]he notion of privacy covers not only sexual activities but personal relationships more generally'.[40] Compare that strong protection for public figures' personal privacy with the very weak privacy rights afforded Hulk Hogan in the United States.

Thereafter, in Mosley's effort to halt publication of the embarrassing but apparently accurate photographs more generally, he sued Google on privacy-related grounds in a French court, asking that links to the images of his encounter with prostitutes be removed from the internet search engine completely. Despite Google's strong protestations based in part upon freedom of expression, the French court sided with Mosley and ordered that the links to the nine images be removed.[41] Some of the images are still available in the United States through a Google search.

This is where considerations of American journalism's ethics provisions become important. The most intimate of the images seem to have been published not by websites operated by mainstream newspapers in the United States but by non-journalistic websites and other publishers, some based outside of the US, that would not necessarily have the same incentives to abide by the strong ethics provisions suggested by the SPJ Code of Ethics and otherwise.[42]

The Mosley example, then, seems to show the ethics-based tempering of the press in the United States as opposed to more expansively sensational news decisions made by news publications and otherwise in other parts of the world. The photographs of Max Mosley that apparently appeared in *News of the World* would likely never have been published by more mainstream ethics-abiding newspapers in the US such as the *Washington Post* or the *New York Times*. Even though US law may well have allowed the publication of such images of a public figure, as shown most strikingly in the Hulk Hogan case so far, mainstream newspapers seemed to have shunned the most explicit of the images, if not all of them.

It is of at least of some relevance that journalism in the United States has had ethics provisions in place in a formal sense since at least the 1920s. While it is true that the BBC has had editorial guidelines in place for years[43] and that these provisions have helped to guide other

[40] *Mosley* v. *News Group Newspapers* [2008] EWHC 1777, [101] (QB).

[41] Alexandria Sage, 'Google Ordered to Remove Max Mosley Sex Party Images', Reuters (6 November 2013) www.reuters.com/article/2013/11/06/france-google-idUSL5N0IR3SL20131106.

[42] A June 2014 search indicated that one or more of the images was available, for example, on a website calling itself sextape.com. The US-based website Huffington Post also published one of the images, though it obscured what appeared to be Mosley's buttocks.

[43] The current BBC Editorial Guidelines are available at www.bbc.co.uk/editorialguidelines/guidelines/ (last visited 11 June 2014).

journalists as well, an overarching journalism ethics code in the United Kingdom meant to reach all journalists, the Editors' Code of Practice, is said to have first been enacted in the 1990s, some seventy years after the US code. The UK ethics code protects privacy through language that suggests that '[e]veryone is entitled to respect for his or her private and family life, home, health and correspondence, including digital communications',[44] but, given the publication of the Mosley images, given the phone hacking scandal in the UK in which some journalists were alleged to have hacked into public figures' voicemail messages, and given other examples of tabloid culture there, it does not seem to have the same reach or the same level of acceptance as does the Society of Professional Journalists Code of Ethics in the United States.

Consider again the publication of Hulk Hogan's sex tape by the push-the-envelope website Gawker in the United States, however. The similarity between the editorial decision to publish the tape and the publication of the Max Mosley images signals a shift away from traditional ethics at least by nonmainstream media websites like Gawker. Such a publication, in addition to the courts' initial acceptance of such an editorial decision, shows not only the extreme protection of First Amendment press freedoms in the United States, but it also suggests that a shift in the law that has for decades blindly accepted journalistic decisions may well be suddenly necessary despite the far reach of the SPJ ethics code.

It is likely not coincidental that Nick Denton – Gawker's founder, virtual editor-in-chief, and a man who has suggested that his website purposefully shuns mainstream journalism's ethics provisions[45] – was born and grew to adulthood in England where, as the *New Yorker* magazine put it in a biography of Denton, 'the Fleet Street tabloid culture is cutthroat'.[46]

## 12.4 The trouble with dignity

Even though dignity considerations are not a part of tort privacy law by name in the United States, there are some cases in which courts explicitly find that human dignity is at the heart of privacy-based claims. In many of those cases, the ones seeking privacy win.

[44] The Editors' Code of Practice is available at www.pcc.org.uk/cop/practice.html (last visited 11 June 2014).

[45] Jeff Bercovici, 'A Candid Conversation with Gawker's Nick Denton', *Playboy* (March 2014) http://playboysfw.kinja.com/the-playboy-interview-a-candid-conversation-with-gawke-1527302145.

[46] Ben McGrath, 'Search and Destroy: Nick Denton's Blog Empire', *New Yorker* (18 October 2010) www.newyorker.com/magazine/2010/10/18/search-and-destroy-2.

In 1956, for example, a Michigan court wrote in a privacy-related case that '[w]hat [the court was] looking at, in essence, [was] simply a matter of human dignity, the right to live our own lives without the meddlesome interference of others, the simple right to be let alone'.[47] A federal court some years later decided that a man who had been surreptitiously recorded by media in his home practicing silly homeopathic remedies had a valid privacy claim. 'A different rule', the court wrote, 'could have a most pernicious effect upon the dignity of man'.[48] And when the wife of assassinated US president John F. Kennedy asked for an injunction against a highly aggressive paparazzo, the court found that the paparazzo could be forced to stay a certain distance away: 'Privacy essential to individual dignity and personal liberty underlies the fundamental rights guaranteed in the Bill of Rights', the court wrote.[49]

In *Shulman* v. *Group W Productions*,[50] the 1998 case that some believe marked the start of a bolder turn in the US courts against media, the court also looked to the dignity of the individual. It held that media could be liable for videotaping an unaware and profoundly injured accident victim at the scene of the accident and, later, in a rescue helicopter. 'It is in the intrusion cases that invasion of privacy is most clearly seen as an affront to individual dignity', the court wrote.[51]

More recently, a 2014 New York-based federal trial court refused media's request for the names of the victims of an infamous securities fraud scam and did so based in large part on dignity considerations.[52] Jordan Ross Belfort, the so-called 'Wolf of Wall Street', had been the one behind the scam and his dealings had led to headlines, a best-selling book, and a Hollywood movie. In other words, public interest in the information was high. The court, however, balanced the victims' dignity and privacy interests against strong public interest in the underlying information – and the personal dignity and privacy interests won out, even over strong First Amendment-based arguments from media. As regarding dignity, 'there is embarrassment', the court wrote, 'at being identified as a victim of a boiler-room scam'.[53] In each of those cases, the plaintiffs won despite the protective power of the First Amendment. In each, human dignity by name seemingly trumped, at least in part, the ideal of a truly free press and access to truthful information.

[47] *Hawley* v. *Professional Credit Bureau*, 76 N.W.2d 835, 843 (Mich. 1956).
[48] *Dietemann* v. *Time*, 449 F.2d 245, 249 (9th Cir. 1971).
[49] *Galella* v. *Onassis*, 487 F.2d 986, 995 (2d Cir. 1973).
[50] 955 P.2d 469, 489 (Cal. 1998).
[51] Ibid., citing Edward J Bloustein, 'Privacy as an Aspect of Human Dignity: An Answer to Dean Prosser' (1964) 39 *NYU Law Review* 962, 973–4.
[52] *United States* v. *Belfort*, 2014 WL 2612508 (E.D.N.Y. 2014).
[53] Ibid.

It is, therefore, perhaps intentional that the generally pro-media Restatement does not use the word 'dignity' in its definition for the privacy torts or within its lengthy discussion of appropriate privacy standards. It is also perhaps intentional that the Society of Professional Journalists Code of Ethics fails to include dignity by name as well. When the focus is on human dignity, it seems, at least some courts side with the plaintiff, thereby making First Amendment press rights secondary.

The trouble with dignity, then, is that a focus that is exclusively there can be decidedly dangerous for journalism. And yet some courts appear to be moving in that direction even when dignity is not considered by name. Take, for example, the decision of a federal trial court in *Conradt* v. *NBC Universal.*[54] In that opinion, one that never uses the word dignity but includes its ideals throughout, the court found that a television program that helped expose child sex predators could be liable for the intentional infliction of emotional distress of one of those would-be predators. William Conradt, a prosecutor who himself had handled child sex crimes, had committed suicide as police entered his home to arrest him for graphic sexual discussions with a boy he apparently thought to be 13. Even though there was no evidence that Conradt had known that NBC was outside his home videotaping his arrest, the court found that NBC could still be liable for Conradt's death. This is remarkable because, by tradition in the United States, arrests are newsworthy and such coverage occurs daily. In addition, this was would-be coverage of the arrest of a public official, coverage that long-standing law suggests is even more appropriate and necessarily of public interest.

The basis on which the court found potential liability was even more remarkable. NBC's journalists, the court reasoned, had failed to adhere to the Society of Professional Journalists' Code of Ethics, including three provisions of particular note:

- Recognise that gathering and reporting information may cause harm or discomfort
- Show good taste. Avoid pandering to lurid curiosity
- Recognise that private people have a greater right to control information about themselves than do public officials and others who seek power, influence or attention. Only an overriding public need can justify intrusion into anyone's privacy.

The *Conradt* case, therefore, embraces human dignity to the exclusion of free press concerns just as blindly as the Gawker courts had embraced the press clause to the exclusion of human dignity. After all, journalists

[54] 536 F. Supp. 2d 380 (S.D.N.Y. 2008).

fully understand that even the most innocuous of stories can cause 'discomfort', they understand that one person's 'lurid curiosity' is another's important news, and they understand that to publish only stories that the public needs to know could well mean the cessation of crime, celebrity, and other innocuous public interest-type news stories.

For journalism, then, the *Conradt* outcome is especially worrisome: The court found a valid intentional infliction of emotional distress claim because, in part, reporters were on the scene to cover the arrest of a public official who had the public's trust to prosecute the same sort of crime he himself was accused of committing. That the court would suggest (1) that the prosecutor's discomfort regarding the revelation of such information was relevant to an intentional infliction of emotional distress claim; (2) that a lack of a highly subjective 'good taste' could also be the basis for that claim; (3) that the court's or a jury's subjective sense of 'lurid curiosity' could well be a journalist-defendant's downfall; (4) that a public prosecutor who had previously been elected and had also previously run for judge might well be considered a private person worthy of protection; and that (5) that 'public need' and not 'public interest' was the appropriate standard for journalism clearly shows that some judges have set out to incorporate the ideals of human dignity without using the precise word.

But the *Conradt* decision is perhaps most jarring because it suggests that the arrest of a public official on child sex solicitation charges was not something that the public should know. While the Gawker decisions at the federal and state levels, then, give media too much leeway, *Conradt* goes too far in its condemnation of media and media practices.

How might courts in the United States do a better job of balancing the important interest in a free press – a freedom that has come to be synonymous with democracy in the United States and one that has led to important investigative journalism that has, among other credits, exposed government corruption at the highest level – with important interests in personal privacy and the right to be let alone? The answer could well be found in a word like dignity.

The trouble is that a focus on dignity exclusively could well lead to a stifling of press freedoms and an end to the necessary breathing space that is crucial to media in the United States. Note that the US Supreme Court could well and understandably have focussed on human dignity in a case like *Florida Star*. If it had, it would likely have decided the case differently and in favour of the rape victim who had been named against her will by the newspaper. Instead, the Justices suggested that there was a chance that it would be unconstitutional to *ever* limit the press, language it later pulled back on, but language that nonetheless shows how powerful freedom of the press is in the United States when it stands against privacy. To focus on dignity to the exclusion of free press concerns, therefore, would seemingly be unconstitutional in the United States.

But consider the power and the value of such a word. If Gawker had been tasked with considerations of human dignity, it quite possibly would not have published Hulk Hogan's sex tape. If the Gawker courts had been tasked with considerations of human dignity as well, they likely would not have been so fast to suggest that Gawker had the right to publish whatever it wished and that Hulk Hogan had no apparent privacy claims. If there were ever a case for considerations of human dignity, it would seem to be this one: one in which a human being is videotaped in what has traditionally been the most intimate of acts, an act in which privacy considerations are so strong that a celebrity's sexual relations are distinctly off limits even for the generally press-permissive Restatement authors.

While dignity is troublesome as a single consideration, it has significant value, however, when used in conjunction with the ideals of a free press. Given that, I have previously argued for the use of language such as this in determining newsworthiness in the United States:

> Because the Supreme Court has warned courts to be 'chary of deciding what is and what is not news',[55] the publication of any truthful information is presumptively newsworthy and of public interest and, therefore, is protected from tort-based and related claims. This presumption of newsworthiness may be overcome only in truly exceptional cases, when the degradation of human dignity caused by the disclosure clearly outweighs the public's interest in the disclosure.[56]

Under such language, dignity concerns would not be all-encompassing and would clearly not be of the type that led to successful claims in Europe for the publication of images of everyday (albeit newsworthy) life taken outside, such as those in the case brought by Julie Gayet in France. Instead, a successful dignity-based privacy claim would spring from the publication of information that is not merely embarrassing to some, but deeply shocking to most. This is a test in line with what one federal appeals court found to be the appropriate balance between privacy and press concerns.[57] As I have previously suggested, this dignity-relevant shocking information could well include aspects of private life generally kept private by tradition in the United States, including depictions of sex, nudity, deeply private or deeply embarrassing medical conditions, private expressions of grief, and other similar parts of life generally not exposed to others.

Such language and this more restrictive way of looking at human dignity is meant to protect NBC and other news media for covering the

[55] *Harper & Row, Publishers* v. *Nation Enterprises*, 471 US 539 (U.S.N.Y. 1985).
[56] Gajda, above n 19. [57] *Haynes* v. *Alfred A Knopf*, 8 F.3d 1222 (7th Cir. 1993).

arrest of a suspected child sex predator, especially one who is a public official as in the *Conradt* case, but is also meant to protect individuals like Hulk Hogan, who find the most intimate details of their personal lives published for world consumption against their wishes. It allows human dignity to trump privacy concerns, but only in cases that are truly exceptional. And it would also protect media in the United States that had the temerity to report on an affair between the president of a country and an actress.

## 12.5 Conclusion

It is certain that even under current law in the United States, French actress Julie Gayet would not have won her lawsuit against *Closer* magazine. Gayet is a public figure involved with the president of a country, a public official. In the United States, the law permits deeper enquiry into both such individuals and their romantic relationships. Photographs of the two of them, together or apart, have news value, both journalistically and in a legal sense.

What is not as clear is whether it will always be this way. Even though there is a rich jurisprudential history and tradition respecting press rights in the United States seen at its most striking in cases like the one decided in favour of Gawker and against Hulk Hogan, decisions like the one in *Conradt* show that some recent courts feel quite free to condemn media despite the protections of the First Amendment.

Considerations of human dignity could well be the perfect counterbalance to what is, in some minds, the all-encompassing power of the press in the US. Most fundamentally, if Gawker and its lawyers had had to consider human dignity because they knew that judges would do so, they might well have decided not to publish any part of Hogan's surreptitiously recorded sex tape. The simple suggestion that such a tape existed, with a quick, non-invasion description, is perfectly sufficient journalistically. Even a still image from the tape with strategically placed black boxes would be acceptable and would provide coverage of a story admittedly of some public interest.

Dignity, however, cannot be the sole consideration lest journalists in the United States lose their power to cover the issues that are important to many, including politicians' misdeeds, arrests of the famous and not-so-famous, and even the incongruous or simply interesting behaviour of Hollywood celebrities. Some may find such information unimportant, but, as the United States Supreme Court has described, appropriate news in a legal sense is broad, some of it is sensationalistic, and it is not limited to information of importance alone.

The balance suggested here, including a presumption of newsworthiness, is an attempt to protect both press and privacy, to protect both those journalists who would cover the arrest of a public official on sex solicitation charges, and those individuals, even celebrities, who find themselves exposed when they are at their most vulnerable.

# 13 The uncertain landscape of Article 8 of the ECHR: the protection of reputation as a fundamental human right?

*Tanya Aplin and Jason Bosland*

## 13.1 Introduction

The right to respect for private and family life under Article 8 of the European Convention on Human Rights (ECHR) is based on Article 12 of the Universal Declaration of Human Rights.[1] However, unlike Article 12 – and similar provisions in other human rights instruments[2] – Article 8 of the ECHR does not include express reference to the protection of 'reputation'. Instead, reputation only receives express mention in the ECHR in Article 10 as an *exception* to the right to freedom of expression. While the *travaux preparatoires* to the ECHR indicate that reputation was deliberately omitted from Article 8, no explanation is given for this decision.[3] Traditionally, the approach of the European Court of Human Rights (referred to hereafter as 'the Court' or 'Strasbourg') was to follow

The authors wish to thank the Faculty of Law of the University of New South Wales for hosting them as visiting scholars during the writing of this chapter. The authors also wish thank Andrew Kenyon, Janice Luck, Megan Richardson and David Rolph for helpful comments on an earlier draft.

[1] See Council of Europe, European Commission of Human Rights, 'Preparatory Work on Article 8 of the European Convention on Human Rights' (Information Document prepared by Secretariat of the Commission DH (56) 12, 9 August 1956) 2, available at www.echr.coe.int/LibraryDocs/Travaux/ECHRTravaux-ART8-DH%2856%2912-EN1674980.pdf.

[2] The International Covenant on Civil and Political Rights, New York, 19 December 1966, entered into force 23 March 1976, 999 UNTS 171, Art. 17 ('ICCPR').

[3] See the Report presented by PH Teitgen (Doc A 290), in the name of the Committee on Legal and Administrative Questions of the Consultative Assembly of the Council of Europe on 5 September 1949, [6]–[8], reported in Council of Europe, *Collected Edition of the Travaux préparatoires of the European Convention on Human Rights* (The Hague: Martinus Nijhoff, 1975), vol I, 192 et seq. See also 'Report to the Committee of Ministers submitted by the Committee of Experts instructed to draw up a draft convention of collective guarantee of human rights and fundamental freedoms' (Doc. CM/WP 1 (50) 15; 16 March 1950) reported in Council of Europe, *ibid.*, vol IV, 18 et seq. See also J Velu, 'The European Convention on Human Rights and the Right to Respect for Private Life, the Home and Communications' in Arthur Henry Robertson (ed), *Privacy and Human Rights: Reports and Communications Presented at the Third International Colloquy about the*

the plain text of the ECHR: freedom of expression was seen as the interest of paramount importance and any restriction on that right for the protection of reputation was treated as a narrowly construed exception.[4] There was no question, in other words, of 'balancing' two competing rights of equal importance.

In a development attacked by some commentators as contrary to the intention of the drafters,[5] this approach was dramatically altered in 2004 when Strasbourg recognised for the first time that reputation was protected as part of the right to 'respect for private life' under Article 8.[6] As a consequence, reputation and freedom of expression started to be treated as *equally competing* interests, with a 'fair balance' having to be struck between the two.[7] More recently, however, Strasbourg has partially retreated from this approach by finding that harm to reputation will not *always* engage Article 8. Thus, in cases where Article 8 is *not* found to be engaged, the protection of reputation will revert to being treated as a mere exception to the more fundamental right to freedom of expression. This further shift in approach is the result of a series of related doctrinal refinements that have been made by Strasbourg since 2009 regarding the relationship between reputation and Article 8. Importantly, Strasbourg has held that reputation and private life are conceptually distinct interests: it is the external evaluation of a person which makes up their reputation and, therefore, reputation per se is not related to private life.[8] In a further development, the Court has also held that harm to reputation must attain a certain threshold of seriousness before Article 8 comes into play.[9]

In this chapter, we critique Strasbourg's approach. In order to understand the connection between the concept of reputation and one's private life, we begin in Part II by exploring the theoretical literature on justifications for protecting reputation (as traditionally protected under defamation law). We show that the two most convincing justifications – the dignity and sociality rationales – are squarely based on concerns for aspects of private life and therefore provide a basis, at least at a theoretical

*European Convention on Human Rights* (Manchester: Manchester University Press, 1973) 12, 14–18.

[4] See, e.g., *Lingens* v. *Austria* (1986) 8 EHRR 407.

[5] See, e.g., Geoffrey Robertson and Andrew Nicol, *Media Law*, 5th edn (London: Penguin Books, 2007), xxiii.

[6] *Radio France* v. *France* (2005) 40 EHRR 29, [31]; see, also, the cases discussed at nn 55–71 and accompanying text.

[7] See, e.g., *Chauvy* v. *France* (2005) 41 EHRR 29, [70]; *Pfeifer* v. *Austria* (2009) 48 EHRR 8, [38].

[8] *Karakó* v. *Hungary* (2011) 52 EHRR 36, [23].

[9] *A* v. *Norway* (28070/06, 9 April 2009), [64]; *Karakó* v. *Hungary* (2011) 52 EHRR 36, [23]; *Axel Springer AG* v. *Germany* (2012) 55 EHRR 6, [83].

level, for connecting the protection of reputation with the right to private life in Article 8. We proceed in Part III to set out what we see as four chronological phases in the development of Strasbourg's Article 8 jurisprudence regarding the protection of reputation. While evidence of both the dignity and sociality rationales described in Part II can be discerned in the Court's reasoning, we argue that there has been neither adequate nor consistent guidance, doctrinally or theoretically, on *when or why* harm to reputation will engage Article 8[10] or how it is to be established.[11] Given this jurisprudential uncertainty, in Part IV we make an important contribution to the existing literature by putting forward what we think is the most doctrinally appropriate and theoretically sound approach to the protection of reputation under the right to private life in Article 8. In short, we argue that reputation *does not form part of* private life but that harm to reputation might *cause* harm to private life. Furthermore, we argue that incorporating the dignity and sociality rationales directly into the threshold seriousness test can provide a mechanism by which to assess on an objective basis whether any given publication harmful to reputation is sufficient to bring Article 8 into play.

## 13.2 Theoretical justifications for the protection of reputation

The protection of reputation is at the heart of defamation law.[12] But what is reputation and why do we seek to protect it? Almost three decades ago Robert Post aptly observed that there was 'relatively little discussion of the nature and importance of . . . protecting reputation'.[13] Despite Post's influential theoretical account of reputation and the subsequent efforts of scholars,[14] it is fair to say that reputation remains to this day

[10] For similar criticisms, see Alastair Mullis and Andrew Scott, 'The Swing of the Pendulum: Reputation, Expression and the Re-Centring of English Libel Law' (2012) 63 *Northern Ireland Legal Quarterly* 27, 28; Jan Oster, *Media Freedom as a Fundamental Right* (Cambridge: Cambridge University Press, 2015) 147–52.

[11] Alastair Mullis and Richard Parkes (eds), *Gatley on Libel and Slander*, 12th edn (London: Sweet & Maxwell, 2013), 16 [1.14]; Brid Jordan, 'Reputation and Article 8: *Karakó* v. *Hungary*' (2010) 21 *Entertainment Law Review* 109, 110–11.

[12] Van Vechten Veeder, 'The History and Theory of the Law of Defamation' (1903) 3 *Columbia Law Review* 546; Eric Barendt, 'What is the Point of Libel Law?' (1999) 52(1) *Current Legal Problems* 110, 112, 117; Eric Descheemaeker, '"Veritas non est defamatio"? Truth as a Defence in the Law of Defamation' (2011) 31 *Legal Studies* 1, 16–17; Eric Descheemaeker, 'Defamation Outside Reputation: Proposals for the Reform of English law' (2010) 18 *Tort Law Review* 133.

[13] Robert C Post, 'The Social Foundations of Defamation Law: Reputation and the Constitution' (1986) 74 *California Law Review* 691, 692.

[14] See, David Howarth, 'Libel: Its Purpose and Reform' (2011) 74 *Modern Law Review* 845; Laura A Heymann, 'The Law of Reputation and the Interest of the Audience' (2011) 52

under-theorised, particularly when compared with the vast scholarship on privacy.[15] From the limited literature that exists on reputation, we can, however, point to some agreement regarding the concept of reputation and the types of justifications that may support its protection.

Conceptually, there is broad consensus that reputation is something that is distinct from 'character'. Character 'refers to the actual attributes or personality of a person'[16] whereas reputation concerns the estimation by which the community holds a person.[17] As to *why* reputation should receive protection, four main justifications have emerged. Three of these – the property, honour and dignity justifications – stem from Post's influential article published in 1986[18] and have formed the starting point for much of the scholarship that has followed, while the sociality justification is a recent contribution to the theoretical literature by David Howarth.[19] The property and honour justifications are not considered any further in this chapter. They have only limited support[20] and do little to shed light on the relationship between reputation and private life. Justifications based on dignity and sociality, on the other hand, are more persuasive and – relevant to the present discussion – fundamentally grounded in notions of private life, which we see as broadly encompassing non-public aspects of the self.

### *13.2.1 Dignity justification*

The most enduring justification for protecting reputation is the concern for human dignity. Of the traditional justifications, it is the only one that

*Boston College Law Review* 1341; David Rolph, *Reputation, Celebrity and Defamation Law* (Aldershot: Ashgate, 2008); Lawrence McNamara, *Reputation and Defamation* (Oxford: Oxford University Press, 2007).

15 For a survey of this theoretical literature, see Nicole Moreham, 'Privacy Rights' in Mark Warby, Nicole Moreham and Iain Christie (eds), *Tugendhat and Christie: The Law of Privacy and the Media*, 2nd edn (Oxford: Oxford University Press, 2011), ch 2.

16 Barendt, above n 12, 115.

17 Ibid.; Eric Descheemaeker, 'Protecting Defamation: Reputation and Negligence' (2009) 29 *Oxford Journal of Legal Studies* 603, 609; Veeder, above n 12; McNamara, above n 14, 31, 229. See, e.g., *Plato Films* v. *Speidel* [1961] AC 1090, 1138. Cf Rolph, above n 14, 4–5 (who argues that it is 'important not to overstate the distinction between reputation and character so as to posit a false dichotomy between the two'); Robert N Bellah, 'The Meaning of Reputation in American Society' (1986) 74 *California Law Review* 743, 750 (who claims that '[i]n defending our reputation we are defending ourselves against defamation of our character').

18 Post, above n 13. 19 Howarth, above n 14.

20 See, e.g., McNamara, above n 14, 31; Bellah, above n 17, 17. The property conception of reputation is said to be inconsistent with various important defamation doctrines – in particular, the requirement that meaning be defamatory before it is actionable and the presumption of damages: see Post, above n 13, 697. The honour justification, on the other hand, is seen as outdated (see, Howarth, above n 14, 852).

offers a convincing account of the relationship between reputation and private life. As Post observes, there is strong rhetorical power in linking reputation with dignity, but the challenge is explaining how dignity, which is inherently private, can be affected by reputation, which is considered 'social and public'.[21] The answer to bridging this gulf, according to Post, is finding an 'implicit theory of the relationship between the private and public aspects of the self'.[22] Here Post utilises sociological accounts of how personality or identity is influenced or constructed by social perspectives and interactions.[23] He argues that 'our own sense of self-worth. . .. is perpetually dependent upon the ceremonial observance by those around us of rules of deference and demeanour', by which he means rules governing social conduct.[24] Defamation law, as the primary means by which the law protects reputation, is thus a mechanism for policing these rules and, in turn, protecting the individual's interest in dignity[25] and enforcing society's interest in maintaining its rules of social conduct.[26]

Various critiques of the dignity justification have been put forward by commentators. Alastair Mullis and Andrew Scott, for example, convincingly argue that human dignity 'does not amount to a specific justification' and 'is at once everything and nothing'.[27] In making this argument, they rely upon scholarship that sees dignity, particularly in a human rights context, as a complex, uncertain and malleable concept.[28] Thus, for Mullis and Scott, dignity only operates as an effective justification if it is used in conjunction with 'the more empirical concept of psychological integrity',[29] by which is meant 'self-esteem'. In particular, they adopt the

[21] Post, above n 13, 708. [22] Ibid.

[23] Ibid., citing George H Mead, *Mind, Self and Society from the Standpoint of a Social Behaviorist* (Chicago: University of Chicago Press, 1934); Erving Goffman, *Interaction Ritual: Essays on Face-to-Face Behavior* (Garden City, NY: Anchor Books, 1967); Charles H Cooley, *The Two Major Works of Charles H. Cooley: Social Organisation, Human Nature and the Social Order* (Glencoe: Free Press, 1956).

[24] Post, above n 13, 710.

[25] Dignity is defined as 'the respect (and self-respect) that arises from full membership in society': ibid., 711.

[26] Ibid. [27] Mullis and Scott, above n 10, 38.

[28] See, e.g., Christopher McCrudden, 'Human Dignity and Judicial Interpretation of Human Rights' (2008) 19 *European Journal of International Law* 655; David Feldman, 'Human Dignity as a Legal Value: Part 1' [1999] *Public Law* 68; David Feldman, 'Human Dignity as a Legal Value: Part 2' [2000] *Public Law* 61. But note, however, that in the context of 'group defamation', i.e., hate speech, Jeremy Waldron has posited a notion of dignity as a person's basic social standing and 'the basis of their recognition as social equals, and of their status as bearers of human rights and constitutional entitlements': See Jeremy Waldron, 'Dignity and Defamation: The Visibility of Hate' (2009) 123 *Harvard Law Review* 1596, 1610.

[29] Mullis and Scott, above n 10, 39.

'looking-glass self' theory[30] to argue that 'it is primarily the perceived level of esteem that we think others hold for us that affects our judgements of self-worth'.[31] As such, defamatory statements have the capacity to impact upon our self-esteem. Eric Barendt shares this view of dignity[32] and other commentators also support a dignity rationale.[33]

Howarth, on the other hand, challenges the 'looking-glass self' theory on two grounds.[34] First, he queries whether external evaluation really affects how individuals see themselves. Adult conceptions of the self, according to Howarth, are 'especially resistant to change as a consequence of evaluations by others', particularly where such evaluations are made by those who are 'not trusted' or who are outside a person's immediate group of family and friends.[35] Second, he argues that the theory relies upon a 'normatively loaded notion of self-esteem'.[36] For Howarth, 'it is far from clear that self-esteem should count as an unalloyed good and that loss of it should always count as harm'.[37] In making these critiques, Howarth notes the debates in the psychological literature about the value of pursuing self-esteem and concludes that 'it seems unwise to ground the law of defamation on such contested terrain'.[38]

While Howarth is right to query whether the 'looking-glass self' theory 'might not be true in any straightforward way',[39] we think that a wholesale dismissal of the dignity justification would seem entirely to discount the possibility that our internal evaluations can be influenced by the external evaluations of others.[40] Given the existing support for this theory, this is not a concession that can be made without particularly robust evidence. Further, while there is disagreement in the psychological literature about the individual importance and social utility of pursuing self-esteem,[41] this

[30] This terminology comes from Charles Horton Cooley, *Human Nature and the Social Order* (New York: Charles Scribner's Sons, 1922) ch V, 184.

[31] Alastair Mullis and Andrew Scott, 'Reframing Libel: Taking (All) Rights Seriously and Where it Leads' (2012) 63 *Northern Ireland Legal Quarterly* 3, 8. See also Mullis and Scott, above n 10, 41.

[32] Barendt, above n 12, 116.

[33] Rolph, above n 14; Heymann, above n 14, 1368–9, 1372–3; McNamara, above n 14, 57. See also Dean Spielmann and Leto Cariolou, 'The Right to Protection of Reputation Under the European Convention on Human Rights' in Dean Spielmann, M Tsirli and P Voyatzis (eds), *The European Convention on Human Rights, A Living Instrument: Essays in Honour of Christos L Rozakis* (Brussels: Bruylant, 2011) 571, 572–3.

[34] Howarth, above n 14, 854. [35] Ibid. [36] Ibid., 855. [37] Ibid. [38] Ibid.

[39] Ibid., 854.

[40] Nicholas Emler, 'A Social Psychology of Reputation' (1990) 1 *European Review of Social Psychology* 171, 181, who argues that a sense of self is not entirely subjective and that reputations are socially constructed, 'created collectively through processes of social communication'.

[41] Some argue that the importance of self-esteem is not whether it is high or low, but in how we strive for it and that our pursuit of self-esteem can have costs to learning, relatedness, autonomy, self-regulation and, over time, health: see, e.g., Jennifer Crocker and

does not mean that harm to self-esteem should be entirely dismissed. It cannot be assumed that there is no value at all in self-esteem or, if there is value, that the negative consequences of pursuing self-esteem – and protecting it through the law of defamation – will necessarily outweigh its benefits.[42] Therefore, despite Howarth's concerns, we believe there remains a solid basis for a dignity justification grounded in the 'looking-glass self' theory.

### *13.2.2 Sociality justification*

Howarth has recently argued for the protection of reputation on the alternative basis that there are fundamental interests in human sociality – that is, in our ability to form and maintain social relationships, whether they are 'strong ties' (such as intimate relationships) or 'weak ties' (such as those with acquaintances and business contacts).[43] As Howarth explains:

> Interference with a person's ability to associate with other people, which is the most obvious effect of damaging a person's reputation, not only brings indirect disadvantages in terms of lost opportunities to gain access to resources, it also causes direct damage in terms of a sustained reduction in well-being.[44]

Loss of reputation can therefore cause 'the pain of the threat of social isolation and rejection' and if isolation and rejection materialises this can cause harm to, among other things, our psychological and physical health.[45] The protection against such harm, according to Howarth, is both of private and public concern:

> The individual pain caused by a threat to sociality might be a private matter, but the functioning of human groups and networks is important to the welfare of all their members, not just to those threatened with exclusion.[46]

Katherine M Knight, 'Contingencies of Self-Worth' (2005) 14 *Current Directions in Psychological Science* 200; Jennifer Crocker and Lora E Park, 'The Costly Pursuit of Self-Esteem' (2004) 130 *Psychological Bulletin* 392; Joachim I Krueger, Kathleen D Vohs and Roy F Baymeister, 'Is the Allure of Self-Esteem a Mirage After All?' (2008) 63 *American Psychologist* 64.

42 See commentators who argue there is value to self-esteem: Mark R Leary, Ellen S Tambor, Sonja K Terdal and Deborah L Downs, 'Self-esteem as an Inter-personal Monitor: The Sociometer Hypothesis' (1995) 68 *Journal of Personality and Social Psychology* 518; Lisa Zadro, Kipling D Williams and Rick Richardson, 'How Low Can You Go? Ostracism by a Computer is Sufficient to Lower Self-reported Levels of Belonging, Control, Self-esteem, and Meaningful Existence' (2004) 40 *Journal of Experimental Social Psychology* 560; William B Swann Jr, Christine Chang-Schneider and Katie Larsen McClarty, 'Yes, Cavalier Attitudes Can Have Pernicious Consequences' (2008) 63(1) *American Psychologist* 65, 66.

43 Howarth, above n 14, 856. 44 Ibid., 849. 45 Ibid., 850. 46 Ibid., 859.

However, by Howarth's own admission, what remains unclear is whether impact to one's private life can be said to arise only where there is harm to strong ties (family, local community, etc.) or whether it extends to harm to weaker ties (acquaintances, professional and business relationships, etc.). For Howarth, it remains to be resolved exactly where the line should be drawn.[47] Despite this uncertainty, it is our view that the sociality theory nevertheless provides a persuasive justification for the protection of reputation, at least as it relates to strong social ties.

Although not directly responding to Howarth's theory, Mullis and Scott have rejected the proposition that reputational harm should fall within Article 8 because of the impact 'on the capacity of an individual to engage in relationships with other members of the community'.[48] Their primary objection to adopting this justification appears to be doctrinal, namely, that it is not supported by Strasbourg jurisprudence.[49] We address this objection in Part IV.[50] However, Mullis and Scott also object on conceptual grounds. They argue that if impact on personal relationships justifies the inclusion of reputation within Article 8, this might necessitate taking into account the responses of family, friends or associates to libellous imputations. It would, they argue, be a leap for private life – at least as understood under Article 8 – 'to encompass decisions made and actions taken by other people' and, as such, it 'is conceptually more sound' to limit protection to psychological impact under the looking-glass self theory.[51] While this objection raises a legitimate concern about how to evidence harm to the ability to form and maintain social relationships, it does not address the possibility that broken social bonds can affect the private life of the individual concerned – that is, the pain of threatened exclusion along with the clear consequences on private life in the event of actual exclusion. Mullis and Scott also suggest that if it arises such impact will usually coincide with an individual perceiving this shift, such that his or her psychological integrity is affected.[52] Thus, a sociality justification does not add much to a dignity justification. This criticism, however, does not appreciate a crucial difference between the two justifications: the dignity rationale focusses on the impact on self-esteem whereas the sociality rationale is concerned with the physical and psychological impact of forced isolation following a break or damage to social ties. While both constitute harm to private life and, indeed, may coincide in many instances, we nevertheless see them as separate and distinct.

[47] Ibid.

[48] Mullis and Scott, above n 10, 41, discussing Lord Rodger's comments in *Guardian News and Media Ltd* [2010] UKSC 1, [42].

[49] Ibid., 42.

[50] See, n 129 and accompanying text.

[51] Mullis and Scott, above n 10, 43.

[52] Ibid.

Our discussion of the rationales for protecting reputation shows that, despite some legitimate criticisms being raised, the dignity and sociality theories both provide persuasive justifications for the protection of reputation. This is true not only in terms of their normative appeal but also in their ability to connect harm to reputation with impact on private life. As we see in the following section, both of these rationales are also reflected, albeit inconsistently and superficially, at various points in the Strasbourg jurisprudence.

## 13.3 Strasbourg jurisprudence

There are four key chronological phases in the Strasbourg case law on the protection of reputation under Article 8. They are: the shift from Article 10(2) to reputation as a protected interest under Article 8; the introduction of the 'seriousness threshold' and the conceptual distinction between reputation and private life; the Grand Chamber's ruling in *Axel Springer* v. *Germany*;[53] and the post-*Springer* decisions.

### *13.3.1 From Article 10(2) to the protection reputation under Article 8*

The recognition of reputation as protected under Article 8 rather than as a mere exception to freedom of expression in Article 10(2) first occurred in the context of cases brought for violation of Article 10.[54] In 2004, in the case of *Radio France* v. *France*,[55] the Court observed in passing that: 'the right to reputation does indeed figure among the rights safeguarded by Article 8 of the Convention, as an element of the right to respect for private life'.[56] This was subsequently confirmed in *Chauvy* v. *France*,[57] where, in dismissing a complaint of violation of Article 10, the Court stated that it had to verify whether a 'fair balance' had been struck between the right to freedom of expression in Article 10 and the right to protection of reputation, said to be protected as 'part of' the right to private life in Article 8.[58] The Grand Chamber in *Cumpana* v.

[53] (2012) 55 EHRR 6.

[54] Note the European Commission on Human Rights was also initially reluctant to recognise reputation as falling within Article 8 (see *X* v. *Germany* (European Commission of Human Rights, Application No 2413/65, 16 December 1966); however, in *A* v. *Sweden* (11366/85) (1987) 9 EHRR CD551), a complaint about failed defamation proceedings, the Commission considered that 'honour' fell within Article 8 but held that there had not been a failure to strike a balance between the applicant's Article 8 rights and the Article 10 right to freedom of expression. Furthermore, in *Tee* v. *United Kingdom* (26663/95) (1996) 21 EHRR CD108, [2] the Commission observed that 'an interference with the professional reputation of an individual may, in certain circumstances, fall to be examined under Article 8'.

[55] (2005) 40 EHRR 29. [56] Ibid., [31]. [57] (2005) 41 EHRR 29. [58] Ibid., [70].

*Romania*[59] subsequently followed the balancing approach adopted in *Chauvy*,[60] observing that 'the protection of the reputation ... [is] an aspect of private life ... protected by Article 8 of the Convention'.[61]

Notably, despite introducing such a major shift, these cases contained no explanation as to why reputation should be seen as suddenly falling within the scope of Article 8. Judge Loucaides provided the earliest hint as to the possible justifications in a concurring opinion in a subsequent Article 10 case, *Lindon* v. *France*,[62] where it was recognised that protecting reputation under Article 8 was about protecting the dignity of individuals:

> [T]he case-law on the subject of freedom of speech has on occasion shown excessive sensitivity and granted over-protection in respect of interference with freedom of expression, as compared with interference with the right to reputation. Freedom of speech has been upheld as a value of primary importance which in many cases *could deprive deserving plaintiffs of an appropriate remedy for the protection of their dignity*. This approach cannot be in line with the correct interpretation of the Convention. The right to reputation should always have been considered safeguarded by Article 8 of the Convention, as *part and parcel* of the right to respect for one's private life.[63]

In addition to protecting human dignity, Judge Loucaides suggested that the protection of reputation also enhances the quality of speech, encourages participation in public life and promotes the publication of more accurate information.[64]

These Article 10 cases were soon followed by a series of cases brought under Article 8 where complaints were made about failed domestic defamation proceedings. In these cases, the Court confirmed that the right to reputation fell within the scope of private life.[65] In *Pfeifer* v. *Austria*,[66] the first case to uphold a violation of Article 8 on the basis of reputation, the Court was also willing to provide greater insight, albeit perfunctory, as to the justifications for the development. The applicant, Pfeifer, who was an editor of a magazine for Vienna's Jewish community, had published a commentary about an article written by a professor

[59] (2005) 41 EHRR 14.

[60] Followed in *Abeberry* v. *France* (Admissibility Decision) (Application No 58729/00, 21 September 2004); *Leempoel* v. *Belgium* (Application No 64772/01, 9 November 2006); *Petrina* v. *Romania* (Application No 78060/01, 14 October 2008).

[61] (2005) 41 EHRR 14, [91]. [62] (2008) 46 EHRR 35.

[63] Ibid., 40 (emphasis added). [64] Ibid., 42.

[65] *Gunnarsson* v. *Iceland* (Admissibility Decision) (Application No 4591/04, 20 October 2005) (recognised that 'reputation and honour ... are interests that may be taken into account' under Article 8). Clearer acknowledgements occurred in *White* v. *Sweden* (2008) 46 EHRR 3, [26]; *Pfeifer* v. *Austria* (2009) 48 EHRR 8, [33]–[35].

[66] (2009) 48 EHRR 8.

claiming it had neo-Nazi overtones. The professor, after failing in defamation proceedings and being charged with a criminal offence, later committed suicide. A right-wing magazine article was subsequently published in which it called the applicant a member of a hunting society that had hounded the professor to his death. The applicant's defamation proceedings in the domestic courts ultimately failed and the applicant subsequently took the case to Strasbourg arguing that his Article 8 rights had been violated. In upholding the application, the Court stated:

> ...the Court reiterates that *'private life' extends to aspects relating to personal identity...and furthermore includes a person's physical and psychological integrity; the guarantee afforded by art 8 of the Convention is primarily intended to ensure the development, without outside interference, of the personality of each individual in his relations with other human beings*. There is therefore a zone of interaction of a person with others, even in a public context, which may fall within the scope of 'private life' ...
>
> ...It has already been accepted in the Convention organs' case law that a person's right to protection of his or her reputation is encompassed by art 8 as being part of the right to respect for private life... The *Court considers that a person's reputation, even if that person is criticized in the context of a public debate, forms part of his or her personal identity and psychological integrity and therefore also falls within the scope of his or her 'private life'*.[67]

There is no express reference in this passage to dignity as in Judge Loucaides' concurring opinion in *Lindon*. Nevertheless, it is implicit in the statements that Article 8 includes a person's identity and psychological integrity that the Court's approach is based on a concern for human dignity.[68] It is possible, however, to also interpret *Pfeifer* as supporting the sociality thesis. As argued by Howarth, this is reflected in the Court's statement that Article 8 is 'primarily intended to ensure the development... of the personality of each individual *in his relations with other human beings*'.[69]

While the early cases of *Lindon* and *Pfeifer* can be seen as linking the protection of reputation to private life by relying upon both dignity and, to a lesser extent, sociality-style rationales, it is fair to say that the theoretical underpinnings for doing so were not interrogated in any depth. In relation to the dignity justification in particular, apart from broad references to 'personal identity' and 'psychological integrity' and the like, there is no explanation as to how a person's reputation and their dignity interests might be related.[70] This is perhaps not surprising given that the Court

[67] Ibid., [33], [35] (emphasis added). While Judge Loucaides dissented, he agreed that Article 8 includes the protection of reputation: ibid., [O-I11].
[68] Howarth, above n 14, 858.
[69] *Pfeifer* v. *Austria* (2009) 48 EHRR 8, [33] (emphasis added).
[70] Mullis and Scott, above n 10, 40, make a similar criticism of *Pfeifer*.

appeared to treat reputation as *directly* and *automatically* protected under Article 8 as part of private life and, as such, did not require that a precise link between reputation and private life be identified on the facts. Even so, this aspect of the Court's reasoning has remained opaque despite developments in more recent cases where, contrary to the approach just discussed, the Court has introduced a 'seriousness threshold' test in order to assess, on a case-by-case basis, whether reputational harm has sufficient impact on private life so as to engage Article 8.

### *13.3.2 The introduction of the 'seriousness' threshold and the conceptual distinction between reputation and private life*

The seriousness threshold first emerged in *A* v. *Norway*.[71] The applicant alleged that a failed defamation suit (prompted by the publication of newspaper articles suggesting that he was a suspect in a murder investigation and identifying his residence) constituted a failure to protect his right to reputation under Article 8. The Court followed *Pfeifer* in finding that a person's reputation forms *part of* his personal identity and psychological integrity and thus directly falls within the scope of his 'private life'.[72] However, while supporting the 'direct' protection of reputation under Article 8, the Court resiled from the *Pfeifer* approach of treating such protection as 'automatic' by adding an unexpected and unexplained qualification:

> In order for Article 8 to come into play, the attack on personal honour and reputation must attain a certain level of gravity and in a manner causing prejudice to personal enjoyment of the right to respect for private life . . . [73]

Although the article had not identified the applicant by name, the details supplied in the publication made it possible for persons who knew the applicant to identify him as the murder suspect. The applicant was subsequently persecuted by journalists and as a result suffered various adverse consequences, including being unable to continue in his employment, having to leave his home and being 'driven into social exclusion'.[74] Consequently, the Court found that the publication was harmful to the applicant's 'moral and psychological integrity and to his private life' and therefore that Article 8 was engaged.[75] The Court further held that a fair balance between the applicant's right to private life and the

[71] (Application No 28070/06, 9 April 2009). [72] Ibid., [64].

[73] Ibid. The threshold test in *A* v. *Norway* has been followed in: *Roberts* v. *United Kingdom* (2011) 53 EHRR SE23, [40]; *Pauliukienė* v. *Lithuania* (Application No 18310/06, 5 November 2013); *Popovski* v. *Former Yugoslav Republic of Macedonia* (Application No 12316/07, 31 October 2013), [88].

[74] Ibid., [73]. [75] Ibid.

newspapers' right to freedom of expression had not been struck by the domestic courts and upheld the complaint.[76]

Shortly after *A* v. *Norway*, in the important case of *Karakó* v. *Hungary*,[77] Strasbourg appeared to backtrack even further by deciding, contrary to the *Pfeifer* and *A* v. *Norway* line of reasoning, that reputation does not receive *direct* protection under Article 8.[78] The applicant in *Karakó*, a politician, had been standing for re-election when a flyer was distributed stating that he regularly voted against the interests of the district. A criminal complaint for libel was terminated by the Public Prosecutor's Office and the applicant's subsequent private prosecution was also dismissed by the Nyiregyahza District Court. The applicant argued that the authorities failed to protect his right to private life in not pursuing criminal libel proceedings.

The Court's majority decision began by recognising a distinction between personal integrity and reputation:

> For the court, *personal integrity rights falling within the ambit of art 8 are unrelated to the external evaluation of the individual, whereas in matters of reputation, that evaluation is decisive*: one may lose the esteem of society – perhaps rightly so – but not one's integrity, which remains inalienable.[79]

Notably, this statement accords with common understandings in defamation law and scholarship, discussed earlier, of reputation as the evaluation of a person by others.[80] The Court went on to state that 'reputation has traditionally been protected by the law of defamation as a matter related primarily to financial interests or social status'.[81] While such interests, of course, would ordinarily fall within the concept of reputation under Article 10(2), the Court clearly saw them as beyond the protection afforded to private life under Article 8.

Despite rejecting the proposition that reputation finds direct protection in and of itself under Article 8, the Court proceeded to explain that harm to reputation could nevertheless invoke the protection of Article 8 when there is impact on personal integrity:

> In the Court's case law, reputation has only been deemed to be an independent right sporadically and mostly when the *factual allegations were of such a seriously offensive nature that their publication had an inevitable direct effect on the applicant's private life*.[82]

[76] Ibid., [74]. [77] (2011) 52 EHRR 36.
[78] Cf Spielmann and Cariolou, above n 33, 582–8 who do not see a difference in approach between *Karakó* and *A* v. *Norway*.
[79] Ibid., [23] (emphasis added). [80] See above nn 16–17 and accompanying text.
[81] *Karakó* v. *Hungary* (2011) 52 EHRR 36, [22]. [82] Ibid., [23] (emphasis added).

It is important to note that this test significantly differs from the seriousness threshold test as expressed in *A* v. *Norway*. We deal with the various differences, and their potential consequences, in Part IV. On the facts, Article 8 was not engaged because the applicant had failed to demonstrate that the publication in question 'constituted such a serious interference with his private life as to undermine his personal integrity'.[83]

Given the Court's unequivocal statements in earlier cases that reputation falls within the protection of Article 8,[84] it seems disingenuous for the Court in *Karakó* to describe its jurisprudence as 'sporadic'. *Karakó*, nevertheless, makes a definite break from earlier case law by expressly drawing a firm conceptual distinction between reputation and the concept of private life in Article 8. But, what is unclear is the precise link between reputation and private life that must be established under the *Karakó* approach in order to invoke the protection of Article 8. The Court talks in broad terms of undermining 'personal integrity', which would appear to raise a dignity rationale. However, apart from requiring that the allegations reach a certain level of seriousness, the Court does not elaborate on how such allegations might impact on personal integrity in order to bring Article 8 into play. Furthermore, unlike in *Pfeifer*, the sociality rationale is absent from the Court's reasoning as a possible basis for establishing impact on private life.[85]

### 13.3.3 *The Grand Chamber in* Springer

Given the clear tensions between *Karakó* and the earlier *Pfeifer* line of cases, there was an opportunity for the Grand Chamber in *Axel Springer AG* v. *Germany*[86] to clarify its jurisprudence. Unfortunately, this did not occur. The applicant in this case was the publisher of a daily German newspaper, the *Bild*. It published two articles about X, a well-known television actor, famous for playing the part of a police superintendent

[83] Ibid.

[84] Note the partly concurring opinion of Judge Jociene who, while finding no violation of Article 8, disagreed that protection of reputation should not be included under Article 8. The judge noted that the jurisprudence had in fact been clearly developed on this point.

[85] Note, however, that Howarth argues that *Karakó* is not inconsistent with his sociality theory: Howarth, above n 14, 858–9. He argues that 'integrity' as it appears in *Karakó* is not limited to 'pure individuality' due to the reference to family life in Article 8. Presumably, Howarth means that integrity extends to protecting relations between family members (i.e., strong ties). Note also that in *Guardian News and Media* (2010) 2 AC 697, 717–8 Lord Roger's interpretation of *Karakó* is that Article 8 was engaged on the basis that the impact of the publication would have affected his relationships with members of his community (i.e., sociality reasoning). We agree with Mullis and Scott, above n 10, 42, that this is a misreading of *Karakó* and that Strasbourg did not find that Article 8 was engaged.

[86] (2012) 55 EHRR 6.

in a television series, which described how X had been arrested at Oktoberfest with a small amount of cocaine and subsequently convicted. Photographs accompanied the articles. The German courts had prohibited any further publication of the articles on the basis that they amounted to a serious interference with X's personality right and that this prevailed over the public's interest in being informed. The applicant company complained that this was a violation of Article 10.

Following *Pfeifer*, the Court reiterated that 'the right of protection of reputation is a right which is protected by Article 8 of the Convention as *part of* the right to respect for private life'.[87] Notably, no mention was made of the conceptual distinction that had been drawn earlier in *Karakó* between reputation and private life. However, while the Court reaffirmed that the right to reputation receives direct protection under Article 8, it also followed the *A* v. *Norway* approach of requiring that a threshold test be met before Article 8 is engaged. Thus, the Court held that:

> an attack on a person's reputation must attain a *certain level of seriousness* and in a manner causing prejudice to personal enjoyment of the right to respect for private life.[88]

In justifying the protection of reputation under Article 8, the Court made reference to the right to private life as encompassing 'physical and psychological integrity'.[89] It appears therefore that dignity interests were seen to be at stake. However, like the previous decisions of the Court, it was not specified how such interests specifically relate to reputation. Furthermore, as in *Karakó*, there was no reference to the sociality theory as a possible basis. No further guidance on the relationship between reputation and private life can be gleaned from the Court's decision. Indeed, while accepting that Article 8 and Article 10 were both engaged and therefore triggered a balancing exercise, the Court did not explain *how* on the facts the threshold test was met.[90] The test was simply stated but not applied.

A further difficulty with *Springer* is that the Court seemed to contradict itself in finding that Article 8 was engaged. This is because the Court expressly stated 'that Article 8 cannot be relied on in order to complain of a loss of reputation which is the foreseeable consequence of one's own actions such as, for example, the commission of a criminal offence'.[91] On the facts, the loss of reputation was a result of X's actual drug use and was presumably, therefore, a foreseeable consequence of his own actions. This is not to say that Article 8 could not have been engaged at all, it is

[87] Ibid., [83] (emphasis added). [88] Ibid. [89] Ibid. [90] Ibid., [83]–[84].

[91] Ibid., citing *Sidabras* v. *Lithuania* (Application Nos 55480/00 and 59330/00, 27 July 2004).

just that it would have been based on harm to 'private life' unrelated to reputation. This aspect of the case, however, was not explained.

### *13.3.4 Post-*Springer *cases*

Given the rather glib statements of principle in *Springer*, it is not surprising that the more recent jurisprudence of the Court has been inconsistent and has continued to show a lack of clarity. In terms of the conceptual relationship between reputation and private life, the Court has failed to provide any further guidance in the post-*Springer* cases on why reputation should receive protection under the right to private life in Article 8. The Court routinely cites *Pfeifer* without explanation. In only two cases – *Putistin* v. *Ukraine*[92] and *Someşan* v. *Romania*[93] – has the Court gone further and made specific reference to reputation as having a connection with personal identity and psychological integrity, albeit without explanation as to what the exact nature of that connection is. Furthermore, none of the cases since *Springer* has endorsed the Court's conceptual distinction in *Karakó* between reputation and private life.[94] Thus, in all of the cases it appears that reputation in and of itself is treated as an interest protected under Article 8.

But, despite accepting in the post-*Springer* cases that private life includes the right to reputation, the Court has nevertheless adopted varying approaches as to whether such protection is automatic or subject to the threshold test. In some cases brought under Article 8, the Court has remained faithful to *Springer* and *A* v. *Norway* in requiring that the threshold test be satisfied. Such cases include *Lavric* v. *Romania*,[95] *Pauliukienė* v. *Lithuania*,[96] and *Popovski* v. *Former Yugoslav Republic of Macedonia*.[97] In other more recent Article 8 cases, however, there appears to be a clear abandonment of the threshold test in favour of a return to the *Pfeifer* approach of providing direct and automatic protection to reputation. Such cases include *Someşan* v. *Romania*,[98] *Putistin* v. *Ukraine*,[99] and *Cârstea* v. *Romania*.[100] In these cases, the Court cites *Pfeifer* (and related earlier cases) but does not mention the threshold test nor does it appear to

[92] (Application No 16882/03, 21 November 2013), [32].
[93] (Application No 45543/04, 19 November 2013), [23], [29].
[94] The distinction is noted in *Putistin* v. *Ukraine* (Application No 16882/03, 21 November 2013), [32]–[33] but only as an afterthought and without analysis, endorsement or application.
[95] (Application No 22231/05, 14 January 2014).
[96] (Application No 18310/06, 5 November 2013), [44].
[97] (Application No 12316/07, 31 October 2013), [88].
[98] (Application No 45543/04, 19 November 2013).
[99] (Application No 16882/03, 21 November 2013).
[100] (Application No 20531/06, 28 October 2014).

apply the test to the facts.[101] Importantly, a return to *Pfeifer* is also reflected in the post-*Springer* Article 10 cases where complaints have been brought following successful defamation proceedings at the domestic level.[102] In these cases, the Court tends to cite *Springer* in relation to the balancing exercise that must be carried out where there are competing interests at play under Articles 8 and 10. However, in the majority of these cases the Court does not acknowledge the threshold test as a necessary precondition for invoking Article 8 and, even in the few instances where the threshold test *is* acknowledged,[103] the Court does not engage with whether it has been met. It seems that the Court simply assumes that Article 8 is engaged where harm to reputation is involved and no attempt is made to explain why.

## 13.4 Resolving the doctrinal and conceptual tensions: the proper approach to the protection of reputation under Article 8

It is apparent from our discussion of the developing case law in Part III that significant points of uncertainty arise from Strasbourg's approach to the protection of reputation under Article 8. In this section, we seek to resolve some of the tensions that pervade the jurisprudence. We do this by setting out what we think is the proper relationship, both doctrinally and theoretically, between reputation and the concept of private life in Article 8, and how the threshold test should operate in order to determine whether Article 8, in any given case, is engaged.

### *13.4.1 Relationship between reputation and Article 8*

There are three possible interpretations of the relationship between reputation and the right to private life under Article 8.

We begin with the approach reflected in the *Pfeifer* line of cases that harm to reputation per se is protected under Article 8 because reputation is considered to form an integral part of a person's private life. This view, as we have already explained, is contrary to the conceptual distinction

[101] Note, however, in *Someşan* v. *Romania* (Application No 45543/04, 19 November 2013) the court refers to seriousness considerations when balancing Articles 8 and 10: [29].

[102] *Hlynsdóttir* v. *Iceland* (Application No 43380/10, 10 July 2012), [58]; *Eidsdóttir* v. *Iceland* (Application No 46443/09, 10 July 2012), [64]; *Ziembiński* v. *Poland* (Application No 46712/06, 24 July 2012), [46]; *Jucha* v. *Poland* (Application No 19127/06, 23 October 2012), [37]; *Ungváry* v. *Hungary* (Application No 64520/10, 3 March 2014), [43]; *Erdoğan* v. *Turkey* (346/04 and 39779/04, 27 May 2014), [37].

[103] *Hlynsdóttir* v. *Iceland* (Application No 43380/10, 10 July 2012), [58]; *Eidsdóttir* v. *Iceland* (Application No 46443/09, 10 July 2012), [64].

drawn in *Karakó* between reputation as the external evaluation of a person and a person's interest in private life. Despite the fact that this distinction does not appear to have been followed by Strasbourg in any subsequent cases,[104] it is nevertheless undoubtedly correct. We therefore reject the *Pfeifer* approach on this basis. We also reject the approach in *Springer*. This is because, despite adopting a seriousness threshold test, the *Springer* line of cases continues to insist that reputation forms 'part of' the right to private life under Article 8 (albeit only when the seriousness test is met). This, in turn, highlights a significant contradiction in the reasoning in *Springer* (and *A* v. *Norway*): if reputation forms *part of* the right to private life, then the adoption of the seriousness test as a way of assessing the impact of harm to reputation on private life is nonsensical. This is because harm to reputation will inevitably constitute harm to private life. One possible way of reconciling this is to assume that reputation forms part of private life (a view which we reject), but will only receive the protection of Article 8 when the impact on private life reaches a certain degree of seriousness. The problem with this interpretation of the seriousness threshold, however, is that it involves the doctrinally unsound conflation of the question of the interference (i.e., whether the right is engaged) with the subsequent issue of the weight to be accorded to such interference (i.e., at the balancing stage).[105]

The second possible interpretation is that harm to reputation does not engage Article 8 unless the defamatory allegation also relates to an aspect of the person's private life. This would arise, for example, where the defamatory allegations are about the claimant's sex life or a medical condition (classic examples of private life).[106] This view may explain why the following cases engaged Article 8 – *Springer*[107] (cocaine conviction), *Küchl*[108] (homosexual activities of a priest) and *Someşan*[109] (extra-marital affair). These were all cases where one could point to private or sensitive information, the disclosure of which would harm one's integrity. This explanation, however, does not account for why Article 8 was engaged in cases such as *Lavric*[110] (professional corruption and

104 Note, it was referred to unenthusiastically in *Putistin* v. *Ukraine* (Application No 16882/03, 21 November 2013), [33].

105 Courts have disapproved of this conflation: e.g., see, *Campbell* v. *MGN* [2004] 2 AC 457, 466 (Lord Nicholls) and *Murray* v. *Express Newspapers* [2009] Ch 481, [26] and [39].

106 See also Normann Witzleb, 'Interim Injunctions for Invasions of Privacy: Challenging the Rule in *Bonnard* v. *Perryman*?' in Normann Witzleb, David Lindsay, Moira Paterson and Sharon Rodrick (eds), *Emerging Challenges in Privacy Law: Comparative Perspectives* (Cambridge: Cambridge University Press, 2014) 407, 429.

107 (2012) 55 EHRR 6.

108 *Küchl* v. *Austria* (Application No 51151/06, 4 December 2012).

109 (Application No 45543/04, 19 November 2013).

110 (Application No 22231/05, 14 January 2014).

misconduct), *Popovski*[111] (allegation of theft), *Mikolajová*[112] (assault on husband), *A* v. *Norway*[113] (alleged murder suspect), *Pfeifer*[114] (allegation the applicant's publication caused a person to suicide) or *Lindon*[115] (politician criticised in a novel). These cases involved the publication of allegations related to public matters, with Article 8 appearing to be engaged simply on the basis that they were defamatory (and where truth was not an available defence). A further conceptual difficulty with this interpretation, of course, is that the harm necessary to engage Article 8 is, in truth, clearly distinct from harm to reputation. That is, harm to reputation is not in and of itself sufficient to engage Article 8 but instead coincidentally sits *alongside* harm that does (i.e., private, albeit false, information). This, however, cannot be reconciled with Strasbourg's repeated focus on reputational harm as the basis for engaging Article 8.

The final interpretation of the relationship between reputation and the protection of private life in Article 8 is that damage to reputation can, on occasion, *cause* harm to private life.[116] There are two reasons why this 'causal' interpretation is the most doctrinally coherent and conceptually sound. First, and perhaps most fundamentally, it accords with the understanding adopted in *Karakó* of reputation as being conceptually distinct from private life. Thus, reputational harm will not *directly* engage Article 8, no matter how serious that harm might be; rather, any harm to reputation must result in further harm, in one way or another, to one's private life. Adopting this interpretation, of course, requires Strasbourg to refrain from incorrectly describing reputation as being 'part of' the right to private life. The continued use of such terminology is liable to confuse. Second, this interpretation also makes sense of the threshold test and avoids any potential tension with Strasbourg's broader interpretive methodology that we highlighted in objecting to the first interpretation. Thus, under the causal interpretation, the seriousness threshold is not being used to assess the weight of the harm but rather whether reputational harm in any given case has had, or is likely to have, the requisite impact on the person's private life such as to bring Article 8 into play. However, the acceptance of this 'causal' interpretation raises the further question of *when* reputational harm will be taken to have the requisite impact on private life. In answer to this, we support the application by Strasbourg of *both* the dignity (looking-glass self) and the sociality rationales for the protection of reputation, discussed in Part II, as dual convincing bases for establishing this necessary link.

111 (Application No 12316/07, 31 October 2013)
112 (Application No 4479/03, 18 January 2011).
113 (Application No 28070/06, 9 April 2009). 114 (2009) 48 EHRR 8.
115 (2008) 46 EHRR 35. 116 See Witzleb, above n 106, 429.

Importantly, the express adoption of such theories would bring much needed clarity to the extant case law. In terms of the dignity rationale, we have already seen that the Court has spoken of the impact of reputational harm on 'personal' and 'psychological integrity' but has failed to elucidate exactly how or why such an impact might arise. Rather than continuing to rely upon such broad and largely meaningless epithets, the Court should clarify the link between reputation and dignity interests by directly drawing upon, and making reference to, the looking-glass self theory in its analysis. It is important to note that the adoption of reasoning consistent with the looking-glass self theory to explain impact on private life is not unprecedented in Strasbourg's jurisprudence in other contexts. In *Aksu* v. *Turkey* the Grand Chamber acknowledged that negative racial stereotyping had the capacity to impact on a 'group's sense of identity and the feelings of self-worth and self-confidence of members of the group'.[117] The 'looking-glass self' theory has also been endorsed by Mullis and Scott as providing a suitable conceptual and doctrinal basis for establishing that reputational harm can impact on a person's Article 8 interests.[118] Howarth, on the other hand, has argued that the adoption of the theory cannot be reconciled with the distinction made in *Karakó* between reputation and private life. Thus, he argues that '[b]y drawing a distinction between external evaluation and inner integrity and denying any automatic connection between the two, *Karakó* is arguably rejecting the looking-glass theory itself'.[119] We, however, reject this criticism by suggesting an attenuated model of the 'looking-glass self' theory which does not assume that self-esteem is *automatically* affected by external evaluation but accepts that one's self-esteem *could* be harmed where particularly damaging allegations are published. This is an interpretation of the looking-glass self theory that we share with Mullis and Scott.[120]

As with the looking-glass self theory, the linking of reputational harm and private life based on the sociality theory also finds support in the broader Article 8 jurisprudence. Thus, in the 1976 case of *X* v. *Iceland*, the Commission held that the right to private life encompasses 'the right to establish and to develop relationships with other human beings...'[121] As the jurisprudence has developed, it has become clear that this right is broadly drawn to encompass any interference where a person's

[117] (Application Nos 4149/04 and 41029/04, 15 March 2012).
[118] Mullis and Scott, above n 10, 39–41. [119] Howarth, above n 14, 858.
[120] See also Mullis and Scott, above n 10, 40–1.
[121] *X* v. *Iceland* (Application No 6825/74, 18 May 1976). See also, eg, *Niemietz* v. *Germany* A/251–B (1992); 16 EHRR 97, [29]; *Von Hannover* v. *Germany* (2005) 40 EHRR 1, [50].

'interaction with others is affected'[122] and includes 'the totality of social ties' between a person and the 'community in which they are living'.[123] While Strasbourg has held that Article 8 will not protect relationships that are of 'such broad and indeterminate scope' that 'no conceivable direct link' to private life can be established,[124] it has certainly not confined the protection of Article 8 to intimate or personal relationships. Thus, on many occasions the right to private life has been held to include the protection of even professional and business relationships,[125] despite their 'strong public-context'.[126] It has been noted that 'this "social dimension" of Article 8 has not yet been fully worked out in the case law'[127] and it is 'not obvious' where the line should be drawn.[128] What *is* clear is that applying the sociality theory by reference to this body of jurisprudence would result in Article 8 being engaged where a broad range of relationships might be impacted by reputational harm and would potentially include relatively 'weak social ties' (to use Howarth's terminology). We raise no objection to the protection of weak social ties provided that a direct and genuine link between such ties and private life can be established. It is important to note, however, that the weight of the Article 8 interest where only 'weak' social ties are threatened is likely to be significantly less than would be the case where 'strong' social ties are threatened. This means that at the balancing stage, depending on the public interest nature of the publication, competing Article 10 interests in freedom of expression will often outweigh any Article 8 interests that might arise from compromised weak social ties.

Mullis and Scott argue that the sociality theory is not a suitable theory of harm for the Court to adopt because it cannot be reconciled with the Court's reasoning in *Karakó*. Mirroring Howarth's objection to the looking-glass self theory, they argue that the sociality theory is contrary to the finding that Article 8 does not protect the external evaluation of a

122 David J Harris, Michael O'Boyle, Edward P Bates, and Carla M Buckley, *Law of the European Convention on Human Rights*, 3rd edn (Oxford: Oxford University Press, 2014), 525.

123 See, e.g., *Üner* v. *Netherlands* (2007) 45 EHRR 14, [59] (Grand Chamber).

124 *Friend and Countryside Alliance* v. *UK* (Applications Nos 16072/06 and 27809/08). See, also, *Botta* v. *Italy* (1998) 26 EHRR 241; *Zehnalova and Zehnal* v. *Czech Republic* (Application No 38621/97).

125 *Niemietz* v. *Germany* (1992) 16 EHRR 97, [29]. See, also, *Taliadorou* v. *Cypress* (Application Nos 39627/05 and 39631/05, 16 October 2008) [53]; *Kyriakides* v. *Cypress* (Application No 39058/05, 16 October 2008); *Gillberg* v. *Sweden* (Application No 41723/06, 3 April 2012).

126 Spielmann and Cariolou, above n 33, 580.

127 Richard Clayton and Hugh Tomlinson, *Privacy and Freedom of Expression*, 2nd edn (Oxford: Oxford University Press, 2010) [12.299].

128 Harris, et al., above n 122, 525.

person.[129] We disagree with Mullis and Scott on this point. This is because we see their view as based on a mistaken conflation of two separate issues: harm to reputation (i.e., the external evaluation of a person which is not, at least according to *Karakó*, directly protected under Article 8) and the effect of that harm on a subject's relationships with others (i.e., broken social ties). In other words, contrary to Mullis and Scott's view, we see harm to reputation and consequential harm to a person's sociality as two related but nevertheless distinct matters.

### *13.4.2 Explaining the 'seriousness' threshold test*

If we are correct in our support of *Karakó* that reputation and private life are distinct concepts, and that the dignity and sociality theories both provide appropriate conceptual links between reputational harm and private life, we must also consider *how* it is that harm to private life is to be assessed on the facts of any given case. This requires a consideration of the various formulations of the seriousness threshold test that appear in *Springer* and *Karakó* and an examination of how these tests should operate in order to properly assess whether harm has been caused to private life when reputation is at stake.

The precise language of the seriousness threshold test has shown some variation. In *Springer*, the Court required that the attack on reputation 'attain a certain level of seriousness'[130] *and* that it be in 'a manner causing prejudice to personal enjoyment of the right to respect for private life'. *Karakó*, on the other hand, adopted what seems to be a significantly different formulation, requiring that the factual allegations be of such a 'seriously offensive nature that their publication had an inevitable direct effect on the applicant's private life'. These formulations differ in two important respects.[131] First, *Springer* focusses on the *attack on reputation* reaching a certain level of seriousness whereas *Karakó* focusses on the more limited question of the seriousness of the factual allegation itself. We prefer the *Springer* approach in this regard. This is because the impact of an allegation on a person's reputation – and, consequently, the possible impact on a person's private life – is determined not only by the inherent

[129] Ibid., 42.

[130] Note, in the *A* v. *Norway*, the Court uses the language of 'gravity' rather than 'seriousness'; we see this as inconsequential.

[131] Note, in *Mikolajová* v. *Slovakia* (Application No 4479/03, 18 January 2011), the Court appears to treat both formulations as having the same substantive effect by reciting the *Springer* formulation but citing *A* v. *Norway* and *Karakó* in support. Note, that a third formulation of the test was adopted in *Polanco* v. *Spain* (Application No 34147/06, 21 September 2010), citing *Karakó*: the tarnishment of reputation 'must be an infringement of his privacy so serious that his personal integrity is compromised' ([40]).

severity of the allegation itself (e.g., an allegation of terrorism or paedophilia) but also the broader circumstances of its publication. Such circumstances would include, for example, the scope and extent of the publication, the particular medium of publication, and whether an apology or correction has been issued.

Second, *Springer* appears to require *both* an attack on reputation that is sufficiently serious *and* prejudice to private life as a result. Under *Karakó*, on the other hand, seriousness does not seem to be a separate 'threshold' question; rather, it appears that seriousness is judged by reference to whether the allegation has had the required impact on private life. Given our view that the ultimate question is whether reputational harm has caused prejudice to private life, it would appear that the separate 'gatekeeper' question of seriousness in *Springer* is unnecessary. This aspect of the *Springer* formulation only makes sense if the seriousness of the attack on reputation is intended to act as a 'proxy' for judging whether there has been, or is likely to be, an impact on private life (as opposed to having to prove actual impact on private life). On whether this is the case, the *Springer* formulation (and its application on the facts) offers little guidance. *Karakó* is similarly unhelpful. There, the Court employs confusing and contradictory terminology, talking in terms of the allegations having to have an 'inevitable direct effect' on private life (suggesting an objective standard where harm to private life is presumed) and that they 'had' such an effect (in the past tense and presumably requiring subjective evidence of impact on private life).[132] It is unclear, therefore, *how* detriment to private life is to be shown. Is it enough for the applicant to demonstrate sufficient seriousness of the attack on reputation as a 'proxy' for judging harm to private life? Or, does the applicant have the burden of proving actual harm to private life?

Analysing the Strasbourg decisions where the seriousness threshold test has been applied, it appears that in most cases the Court employs a proxy approach in assessing impact on private life. For example, in *Lavric* v. *Romania*,[133] allegations of corruption, lack of professionalism and incompetence were made against a public prosecutor. Without considering any actual harm to the applicant's private life, the Court simply stated that the allegations 'were of a serious nature and were capable of affecting her in the performance of her duties and of damaging her reputation'.[134] Similarly, in *Roberts* v. *United Kingdom*, the Court considered that the defamatory allegations of dishonesty and threatening violence were 'serious' and, on this basis alone, was 'willing to accept' that their publication

[132] Spielmann and Cariolou, above n 33, 588.
[133] (Application No 22231/05, 14 January 2014). [134] Ibid., [41].

'had a direct effect on the applicants' private lives'.[135] Treating the seriousness of the allegations as a proxy for assessing harm to private life is also evident in the Court's reasoning in *Pauliukienė* v. *Lithuania* (allegations of repeatedly breaking the law)[136] and *Mikolajová* v. *Slovakia* (allegation that the applicant had committed a violent criminal offence).[137] On the other hand, in cases where there *is* evidence of actual harm, the Court's approach has shown significant variation. In *A* v. *Norway*, for example, there was evidence that an allegation published in a newspaper that the applicant had committed murder resulted in him being unable to continue in his employment, caused him to leave his home and forced him into social exclusion. On the basis of this evidence, the Court held that there was 'little doubt' that the publication was 'especially harmful' to his private life.[138] In other cases, however, evidence of actual impact on private life has not been expressly relied upon by the Court. Thus, in the cases where evidence of harm *is* available, the Court's assessment does not contain reference to such evidence and it is either simply stated[139] or it is assumed without discussion[140] that Article 8 is engaged. It is unclear in these cases, therefore, whether the Court has arrived at this conclusion on the basis of the seriousness of the allegations or on the basis of the evidence of actual impact on private life, or a combination of both.[141]

Our view is that, subject to the refinements discussed later, the Court's apparent preference for the proxy approach is justified. This is for two main reasons. The first is that in many instances it will be difficult to provide actual evidence that a particular defamatory allegation has had the requisite impact on private life. This is especially the case when it comes to applying the sociality theory of reputational harm. The Court has held that Article 8 is not just concerned with protecting *existing* 'relationships with other human brings' but also extends to a person's capacity to 'establish and develop' such relationships in the future.[142] The impact of a defamatory publication on the *future* development of a person's social ties, however, is not the subject of positive proof (at least not readily). Thus, an assessment of the severity of the attack on reputation is

[135] (2011) 53 EHRR SE23, [41]. [136] (Application No 18310/06, 5 November 2013).

[137] (Application No 4479/03, 18 January 2011). Arguably *Karakó* supports this approach because the allegations at issue (politician acting against the interests of his electorate) were fairly mild. This explains Howarth's view of *Karakó* (that the criticism was so mild that 'no one would believe that it amounted to a threat of ostracism or would result in a breach of even the weakest social tie'): Howarth, above n 14, 859.

[138] (Application No 28070/06, 9 April 2009), [67], [72]–[73].

[139] *Somesan* v. *Romania* (Application No 45543/04, 19 November 2013), [29].

[140] *Popovski* v. *Former Yugoslav Republic of Macedonia* (Application No 12316/07, 31 October 2013), [88]–[91].

[141] One exception to this is *Cardenas* v. *Norway* (Application No 12148/03, 4 January 2008).

[142] *X* v. *Iceland* (1976) 5 DR 86 [97]; *Niemietz* v. *Germany* (1992) 16 EHRR 97, [29].

the only practical way to assess the likelihood that the publication will have an impact on the ability for a person to forge social ties in the future. The second reason for preferring a proxy approach over an actual harm approach is that it allows for greater predictability for publishers, including the mass media. At the pre-publication stage, publishers need to be able to assess with a reasonable degree of certainty what legal constraints and consequences apply to a particular publication. The proxy approach allows for objective criteria to be utilised in judging the likely impact on private life, whereas the 'actual harm' approach depends on the subjective effect upon a particular claimant. Third parties and potential defendants, therefore, are better able to assess the scope of their obligations to protect reputation if they can point to an objective test based on the seriousness of the defamatory imputation and the circumstances of the publication.

While we support the proxy approach, we nevertheless recognise that the Court's current proxy methodology is problematic in two main respects. First, despite the test in *Springer* referring to the severity of the attack on *reputation*, the Court has a propensity to focus on the much narrower question of the severity of the *allegation*. As already explained, such an approach ignores the wider circumstances of the publication and should be rejected. Our second criticism of the current proxy approach is that we do not see it as going far enough in connecting harm to reputation *with* harm to private life. At present, the Court simply asks whether the harm to reputation has reached a level of seriousness such that private life would be impacted but no attempt appears to be made to assess this by reference to *how* reputational harm may impact on private life. Without inquiring as to this link the current test is largely meaningless and perhaps explains why the Court has found it to be satisfied, as far as we can see, in every case apart from *Karakó*. Thus, in light of our dual acceptance of the looking-glass self and the sociality theories as providing the sufficient theoretical and doctrinal foundations for connecting reputational harm with private life, we think that these theories should be the focus of, and therefore be directly incorporated into, the seriousness threshold test.

The precise approach to doing this should depend on which theory is being invoked as the basis of the complaint. If the looking-glass self theory is invoked by the applicant, the Court should ask whether, after taking into account all of the circumstances of the publication, there is a sufficiently serious attack on the applicant's reputation such that an ordinary person in the position of the applicant would likely suffer detriment to their own self-view? It is only then that reputational harm can be said to affect a person's psychological integrity. On the other hand, if it is the sociality theory being invoked, the enquiry should be whether, after taking into account all of the circumstance of the publication, there is a sufficiently serious attack on reputation such that ordinary recipients of that publication forming part of the applicant's group of existing or future social ties would be likely to shun or avoid the applicant? The types of recipients contemplated here would depend on the particular facts and might include groups of recipients who have either strong or weak ties to the applicant, or both. Applicants would also be at liberty to adopt either or both of the looking glass and the sociality approaches in their complaint. Unclear is the extent to which such a refocussing on the precise harms to private life in applying the threshold test would necessarily lead to different conclusions – although we assume that in many cases it would. The point is that such an approach provides a more nuanced, rational and, most importantly, focussed doctrinal framework for the Court to conduct its analysis in determining the central link between harm to reputation and impact on private life.

## 13.5 Conclusion

We have argued that Strasbourg's jurisprudence concerning when harm to reputation will engage the Article 8 right to private life has been inconsistent and confusing. The Court has veered between accepting reputation as directly and automatically protected by Article 8 to requiring that a 'seriousness' threshold be met before Article 8 is engaged. Despite the Grand Chamber's ruling in *Springer*, recent case law has continued to demonstrate this ambivalence. This is problematic, not least because it makes it difficult to predict when matters of reputation engage Article 8, such that a balancing methodology between competing rights is required. This chapter has sought to untangle the Strasbourg jurisprudence and articulate the proper relationship, both doctrinally and conceptually, between reputation and private life in Article 8. The preferable interpretation of the relationship between reputation and Article 8 is that reputation does *not* form part of private life but that harm to reputation *can* impact on private life in certain situations. Furthermore, we see the 'seriousness' threshold adopted in *Springer* and *Karakó* as establishing a proxy for assessing such impact. The current test, however, does not seek to identify or explain when or why harm to reputation results in harm to private life. Thus, we have argued that the dignity and sociality theories for the protection of reputation have a crucial role to play in the court's analysis and should be incorporated to form the central focus of the court's seriousness threshold test in determining whether Article 8 is engaged when a person has suffered harm to his reputation.

# 14 Vindicating reputation and privacy

*David Rolph*

## 14.1 Introduction

The recognition of a new legal right can have an impact on existing legal rights, particularly where the rights overlap or operate in similar spheres of activity. The movement towards the recognition of a direct, general, enforceable right to privacy in various ways in English, Australian and New Zealand law over the last fifteen years demonstrates this. The common law long adopted an anomalous and bifurcated treatment of personality interests. Reputation – principally the public self of the plaintiff[1] – was highly protected, while there was no direct protection of privacy.

The recent development of privacy protections aims to overcome this lacuna in the law. The potential consequences of recognising a right to privacy on existing defamation laws have not been systematically explored. Indeed, recent law reform processes about defamation and privacy in England, Australia and New Zealand still proceed to consider these areas largely in isolation, with some occasional reference to each other.[2] Cases in English and, to a lesser extent, New Zealand, courts have

The author wishes to thank Jackson Wherrett and Joanna Connolly for their excellent research assistance.

[1] *Plato Films Ltd* v. *Speidel* [1961] AC 1090, 1138 (Lord Denning); David Rolph, *Reputation, Celebrity and Defamation Law* (Aldershot: Ashgate, 2008), 6.

[2] As to privacy law reform largely without reference to defamation, see Australian Law Reform Commission, *For Your Information: Australian Privacy Law and Practice*, Report No 108 (2008); New South Wales Law Reform Commission, *Invasion of Privacy*, Report No 120 (2009); Victorian Law Reform Commission, *Surveillance in Public Places*, Final Report No 18 (2010); New Zealand Law Commission, *Invasion of Privacy: Penalties and Remedies – Review of the Law of Privacy, Stage 3*, Issues Paper No 14 (2009); Australian Law Reform Commission, *Serious Invasions of Privacy in the Digital Era*, Final Report No 123. As to defamation law reform largely without reference to privacy, see United Kingdom Parliament, *Bill Documents – Defamation Act 2013*, http://services.parliament.uk/bills/2012-13/defamation/documents.html. The last sustained analysis of defamation and privacy by a law reform body was the Australian Law Reform Commission's 1979 report, *Unfair Publication: Defamation and Privacy*, Report No 11.

explored some of the touching points between defamation and privacy.[3] Nevertheless, the distinction between defamation and privacy remains largely intact. A prominent way in which this distinction is maintained is the assertion that reputation can be vindicated by an award of damages, while privacy, once invaded, can never be restored. This view has been expressed by some judges, law reform bodies and academics. With respect, it is one which does not withstand close scrutiny for a range of reasons. The efficacy of defamation law to vindicate reputation and of an award of damages to achieve that end is questionable.

A major purpose of an award of damages for defamation is the vindication of the plaintiff's reputation. There is, however, disagreement as to what aspects of the defamation proceeding effect this vindication and, more fundamentally, whether a defamation trial is indeed efficacious in securing the vindication of a plaintiff's reputation. There is the related issue of the extent to which the vindicatory purpose can be satisfied where a defamation proceeding is not litigated to final judgement.

What is telling, though, about the emphasis on the difference between reputation and privacy is the apparent reason behind it. It is well established that defamation law takes a restrictive approach to the grant of injunctive relief, based significantly on the importance of freedom of speech and an aversion to prior restraint.[4] By insisting on the difference between defamation and privacy, defamation law's restrictive approach to injunctive relief can be maintained, while the readier grant of injunctive relief is permitted in the developing cause of action for invasion of privacy. However, it may be that, in order to ensure the coherent development of the law, the restrictive approach to injunctive relief in defamation claims will need to be revisited.

This chapter critically evaluates this putative difference between defamation and privacy for the purposes of remedies. In doing so, it examines in particular the concept of vindication, which is one of the main purposes of an award of damages for defamation, both in principle and in practice. It questions the efficacy of defamation law in vindicating reputations and queries whether reputations, like privacy, once damaged, can never be fully restored. It then considers what insights can be gleaned by

[3] See, e.g., *Hosking* v. *Runting* [2005] 1 NZLR 1; [2004] NZCA 34, [136]–[138] (Gault P and Blanchard J); *Terry* v. *Persons Unknown* [2010] EMLR 16, 420–5; [2010] EWHC 119 (QB), [74]–[96] (Tugendhat J).

[4] *Bonnard* v. *Perryman* [1891] 2 Ch 269, 284 (Lord Coleridge CJ); *Australian Broadcasting Corporation* v. *O'Neill* (2006) 227 CLR 57, 68, 72–3 (Gleeson CJ and Crennan J), 86–7 (Gummow and Hayne JJ); [2006] HCA 46. See also Benedict Bartl and Dianne Nicol, 'The Grant of Interlocutory Injunctions in Defamation Cases in Australia following the Decision in *Australian Broadcasting Corporation* v. *O'Neill*' (2006) 25 *University of Tasmania Law Review* 156, 175–8.

emphasising the similarities between defamation and privacy. After all, these causes of action aim to protect different aspects of the plaintiff's own persona. This chapter argues that awards of damages for invasion of privacy in English cases thus far have been relatively modest because the principal, if not the exclusive, head of damages is for mental distress. If a plaintiff's privacy has been invaded and an injunction has not been sought or granted, he or she should not only have an award of damages by way of consolation for the distress caused to him or her but should also have an award of substantial damages to mark the fact that the plaintiff's right to privacy has been unlawfully interfered with and to vindicate that right. This would mirror the purposes for an award of damages in defamation. Just as the right to reputation might need to be vindicated, so too might the right to privacy.

## 14.2 The distinction between defamation and privacy for the purposes of remedies

The view that defamation can be vindicated by an award of damages, whereas privacy, once invaded, can never be restored has only needed to develop after a direct, enforceable right to privacy started to be recognised. It was only then that the relationship between defamation and privacy and the proper remedy for each of these causes of action really needed to be considered. There have been a number of endorsements of this view. One of the earliest and most influential expositions is to be found in Eady J's judgement in *Mosley* v. *News Group Newspapers*. In considering the nature of compensatory damages in privacy claims, Eady J suggested that there was 'some scope for analogy' between defamation and privacy, given both of these causes of action were concerned with infringements of Article 8 of the *European Convention on Human Rights* ('ECHR'). Nevertheless, he stressed 'the distinctive functions of a defamation claim'.[5] Because of this, Eady J ultimately suggested that the analogy between defamation and privacy should not be overstated. He then observed:

> that libel damages can achieve one objective that is impossible in privacy cases. Whereas reputation can be vindicated by an award of damages, in the sense that the claimant can be restored to the esteem in which he was previously held, that is not possible where embarrassing personal information has been released for general publication. As the media are well aware, once privacy has been infringed,

[5] *Mosley* v. *News Group Newspapers* [2008] EMLR 20, 732; [2008] EWHC 1777 (QB), [214] ('*Mosley*').

the damage is done and the embarrassment is only augmented by pursuing a court action.[6]

This is not the only expression of this view. For example, in his final report, Leveson LJ also observed that:

In the case of defamation, that vindication is the public demonstration of success in the action, thereby neutralising the slander or libel. In the case of privacy, however, that which was private is no longer so and, irrespective of the condemnation that might flow from a judgement, what was placed in the public domain cannot be erased.[7]

There are many other statements to similar effect.[8] This view has been endorsed in the assessment of damages for libel and misuse of private information in a single claim.[9] It may be accepted that, once invaded, privacy can never be restored.[10] Having been made public, private information cannot be rendered private again. Thus, the disposition of courts to grant an injunction to restrain the public disclosure of private information is entirely understandable. What is open to question, however, is the extent to which defamation law in fact achieves one of its principal stated purposes, the vindication of a plaintiff's reputation, given that this is used to justify the differences between the treatment of reputation and privacy, and the extent to which the idea of vindication in defamation law is peculiar to that tort. If defamation is not effective in securing the vindication of a plaintiff's reputation, and the idea of vindication underpinning

[6] *Ibid.*, 736, [230].

[7] Right Honourable Lord Justice Brian Leveson, *An Inquiry into the Culture, Practices and Ethics of the Press*, HC 780 (2012), vol IV, [3.12].

[8] See, e.g., New South Wales Law Reform Commission, above n 2, [7.16]–[7.18]; Gavin Phillipson, 'Max Mosley Goes to Strasbourg: Article 8, Claimant Notification and Interim Injunctions' (2009) 1 *Journal of Media Law* 73, 74–5; House of Lords and House of Commons, Joint Committee on Privacy and Injunctions, *Privacy and Injunctions* (2012 HL 273 / HC 1443), [51]. See also Mark Warby, Nicole Moreham and Iain Christie (eds), *Tugendhat and Christie: The Law of Privacy and the Media*, 2nd edn (Oxford: Oxford University Press, 2011), [13.51].

[9] *Cooper* v. *Turrell* [2011] EWHC 3269 (QB), [102] (Tugendhat J): 'Damages for defamation are a remedy to vindicate a claimant's reputation from the damage done by the publication of false statements. Damages for misuse of private information are to compensate for the damage, and injury to feelings and distress, caused by the publication of information which may be either true or false'.

[10] *Mosley* [2008] EMLR 20, 736; [2008] EWHC 1777 (QB), [231] (Eady J). There is, of course, a live issue as to whether this approach to privacy treats the concept as secrecy or confidentiality, when other approaches are possible. For some discussion of the relationship between privacy, secrecy and confidentiality and the availability of other approaches, see Daniel J Solove, 'Conceptualizing Privacy' (2002) 90 *California Law Review* 1087, 1105–9. See also David Rolph, 'Irreconcilable Differences? Interlocutory Injunctions for Defamation and Privacy' (2012) 17 *Media & Arts Law Review* 170, 184–7.

the purposes is not particular to defamation, then the soundness of the distinction between defamation and privacy might need to be revisited.

## 14.3 The concept of vindication in defamation law

There are many statements of high authority, both judicial and extra-judicial, which assert or assume the effectiveness of a defamation verdict in vindicating a plaintiff's reputation.[11] In his *Commentaries on the Laws of England*, Sir William Blackstone described 'the chief excellence of the civil action for a libel' as being 'that it not only affords a reparation for the injury sustained, but it is a full vindication of the innocence of the person traduced'.[12] In *Dingle* v. *Associated Newspapers*, Lord Radcliffe opined that '[a] libel action is fundamentally an action to vindicate a man's reputation on some point as to which he has been falsely defamed, and the damages awarded have to be regarded as the demonstrative mark of that vindication'.[13]

The central role of vindication in an award of damages for defamation has been considered in a number of influential judgements in the High Court of Australia. In *Uren* v. *John Fairfax & Sons*, Windeyer J noted that a person's reputation is not a chattel so that damage to reputation cannot be measured – 'money and reputation are not commensurables'. He then explained the purpose of compensatory damages for non-economic loss in defamation thus:

> It seems to me that properly speaking, a man defamed does not get compensation for his damaged reputation. He gets damages because he was injured in his reputation, that is simply because he was publicly defamed. For this reason, compensation by damages operates in two ways – as a vindication of the plaintiff to the public and as consolation to him for a wrong done. Compensation is here a solatium rather than a monetary recompense for harm measurable in money.[14]

He characterised the assessment of compensatory damages for defamation as 'the product of a mixture of inextricable considerations'.[15]

In *Carson* v. *John Fairfax & Sons*, Mason CJ, Deane, Dawson and Gaudron JJ endorse this approach to assessment of damages for defamation, noting that the multiple purposes for which such damages are

[11] See, e.g., *Jameel* v. *Wall Street Journal Europe* [2007] 1 AC 359, 375 (Lord Bingham of Cornhill): 'The tort of defamation exists to afford redress for unjustified injury to reputation. By a successful action the injured reputation is vindicated. The ordinary means of vindication is by the verdict of a judge or jury and an award of damages' ('*Jameel*'). See also *Coyne* v. *Citizen Finance* (1991) 172 CLR 211, 240 (McHugh J); *John* v. *MGN* [1997] QB 586, 607.

[12] Sir William Blackstone, *Commentaries on the Laws of England*, Vol 3, Ch 8.

[13] [1964] AC 371, 396. [14] (1966) 117 CLR 118, 150. [15] *Ibid.*

awarded often 'overlap considerably'. Their Honours identified the purposes as:

> consolation for the personal distress and hurt caused to the appellant by the publication, reparation for the harm done to the appellant's personal and (if relevant) business reputation and vindication of the appellant's reputation. The first two purposes are frequently considered together and constitute consolation for the wrong done to the appellant. Vindication looks to the attitude of others to the appellant: the sum awarded must be at least the minimum necessary to signal to the public the vindication of the appellant's reputation.[16]

It is clear then that vindication is an important purpose of defamation. However, there is a lack of clarity or precision about what aspect of a defamation proceeding vindicates a plaintiff's reputation. It has been suggested that the trial itself, conducted in public, serves in part to vindicate the plaintiff's reputation.[17] As damages for defamation are now overwhelmingly assessed by judges,[18] the reasons for judgement provide another important means for vindicating a plaintiff's reputation and may serve as a basis for lessening the quantum of damages, in contrast to a jury's assessment of damages, which is unsupported by any reasons.[19] The publicity attracted by the reasons for judgement can also be another means of securing the vindication of the plaintiff's reputation. Given that the harm done to the plaintiff is damage to his or her perception in the eyes of others, publicising the reasons for judgement that clears the plaintiff's name can obviously have a vindicatory effect. It has been suggested that the fact of the judgement in favour of the plaintiff is important in securing the vindication of the plaintiff's reputation.[20] Beyond the fact of the judgement in favour of the plaintiff, the award of damages, particularly the size of the award, is commonly cited as the most important factor in

[16] (1993) 178 CLR 44, 60–1 ('*Carson*').

[17] *Ballina Shire Council* v. *Ringland* (1994) 33 NSWLR 680, 699 (Kirby P): 'Defamation trials can also, sometimes, provide a public means of vindicating the honour and reputation of the person defamed'. See also *Random House Australia* v. *Abbott* (1999) 94 FCR 296, 321 (Miles J); *Greene* v. *Associated Newspapers* [2005] QB 972, 994; [2004] EWCA Civ 1462.

[18] Juries are not available in defamation cases in South Australia, the Australian Capital Territory and the Northern Territory. See Juries Act 1927 (SA) s 5; Supreme Court Act 1933 (ACT) s 22; Juries Act 1962 (NT) s 6A. In all other Australian jurisdictions, juries are available but the role of assessing damages in defamation cases is allocated to judges. See Defamation Act 2005 (NSW) s 22(3); Defamation Act 2005 (Qld) s 22(3); Defamation Act 2005 (Tas) s 22(3); Defamation Act 2005 (Vic) s 22(3); Defamation Act 2005 (WA) s 22(3). In England and Wales, there is now a presumption against trial by jury in defamation cases. See Defamation Act 2013 (UK) s 11.

[19] *Applause Store Productions* v. *Raphael* [2008] EWHC 1781 (QB), [76] (Richard Parkes QC) ('*Applause Store*'). See also New South Wales Law Reform Commission, *Defamation*, Report No 75 (1995) [2.15].

[20] *Kiam* v. *MGN* [2003] QB 281, 303 (Sedley LJ).

securing the vindication of the plaintiff's reputation.[21] The quantum of damages needs to be 'sufficient to convince a bystander of the baselessness of the charge'.[22] As Mason CJ, Deane, Dawson and Gaudron JJ suggested in *Carson* v. *John Fairfax & Sons*, the size of the award of damages for defamation has to be sufficiently substantial to alter other people's perceptions of the plaintiff, which is to say, to vindicate the plaintiff's reputation.[23] However, given that awards of damages for defamation are now constrained by judge-made tariffs or statutory caps,[24] the vindicatory effect of awards of damages is surely diminished.

Although, in principle, vindication of a plaintiff's reputation is a significant, stated purpose, whether this occurs in practice is questionable. There is a well-developed and justifiable scepticism as to the efficacy of defamation law in vindicating a plaintiff's reputation. As Lord Nicholls of Birkenhead noted in his speech in *Reynolds* v. *Times Newspapers*, in the absence of effective vindication, 'a reputation can be damaged forever'.[25] The New South Wales Law Reform Commission also observed in its 1995 report on defamation that the vindication of a plaintiff's reputation currently relies upon an inference being drawn from the award of damages.[26] It does no more to secure the vindication of the plaintiff's reputation. It does not ensure that the inference is in fact drawn or that other available inferences are excluded. The NSWLRC suggests that it is undesirable for a tort to seek to secure its fundamental purpose in such an indirect way, The recognition that vindication of reputation is a dominant purpose of an award of damages for defamation is often accompanied or underscored by an acknowledgement that damages for defamation are an imperfect and ultimately pragmatic remedy for a range of reasons. In *Plato*

[21] See *John Fairfax & Sons* v. *Kelly* (1987) 8 NSWLR 131, 139 (Samuels JA); *Carson* (1993) 178 CLR 44, 66 (Mason CJ, Deane, Dawson and Gaudron JJ), 69–70 (Brennan J); *The Gleaner Co* v. *Abrahams* [2004] 1 AC 628, 647 (PC). See also *Jameel* [2007] 1 AC 359, 375 (Lord Bingham of Cornhill) (vindication of plaintiff's reputation through combination of verdict in plaintiff's favour as well as award of damages).

[22] *Broome* v. *Cassell* [1972] AC 1027, 1071 (Lord Hailsham of St Marylebone LC).

[23] (1993) 178 CLR 44, 61.

[24] As to tariffs on damages for defamation under English law, see *Cairns* v. *Modi* [2013] 1 WLR 1015, 1023 (*per curiam*); [2012] EWCA Civ 1382; *Flood* v. *Times Newspapers* [2013] EWHC 4075 (QB), [52] (Davies J) (current tariff £275,000). See also *Gur* v. *Avrupa Newspaper* [2008] EWCA Civ 594, [20] (Dyson LJ). As to statutory caps on damages for defamation under Australian law, see Civil Law (Wrongs) Act 2002 (ACT) s 139F; Defamation Act 2006 (NT) s 32; Defamation Act 2005 (NSW) s 35; Defamation Act 2005 (Qld) s 35; Defamation Act 2005 (SA) s 33; Defamation Act 2005 (Tas) s 35; Defamation Act 2005 (Vic) s 35; Defamation Act 2005 (WA) s 35 (current cap $355,500).

[25] [2001] 2 AC 127, 201. See also *ZAM* v. *CFW* [2013] EWHC 662 (QB), [61],[62] (Tugendhat J) (particularly noting the permanence of damage to reputation due to internet technologies). Thanks to Nicole Moreham for drawing this reference to my attention.

[26] New South Wales Law Reform Commission, *Defamation*, above n 19, [2.8].

*Films* v. *Speidel*, Viscount Simonds described a defamation trial as 'an imperfect instrument for doing justice in every case', pointing out that there are cases in which undeserving plaintiffs recover more damages for defamation than they deserve.[27] In *Broome* v. *Cassell*, Lord Hailsham of Marylebone LC observed that, from a pecuniary perspective, a plaintiff in a claim for defamation can be left in a better position by an award of damages, because, from a non-pecuniary perspective, such a plaintiff can never be adequately compensated.[28] The eminent torts scholar, John Fleming, criticised the award of damages for defamation as an inefficient means of vindicating a plaintiff's reputation but it was the remedy provided by defamation law in the absence of more efficacious remedies, such as retractions and rights of reply.[29] This criticism is echoed by a number of judges. For instance, Callinan J in *Australian Broadcasting Corporation* v. *Lenah Game Meats* observed that, in the absence of a right of reply, '[p]eople who are the subject of intrusive and offensive media attention have only one real, effective, and complete remedy, a vindicatory verdict (with or without an apology) in defamation proceedings'.[30]

To similar effect, Mahoney JA in *John Fairfax & Sons* v. *Carson* stated that:

> it is necessary to have in mind that the plaintiff has no other way of achieving vindication than by an award of damages. There is no power to force a defendant, by public advertisement or letter or otherwise, to provide a vindication of the plaintiff. In the case of defamation by a journalist or a newspaper, the common organs for vindication are within their control. Damages, and the size of the award, are the only means which ordinarily are available to attract the public or private attention involved in the vindication of the plaintiff's position.[31]

This criticism of general damages can be widened beyond defamation to other torts for which such damages are awarded. As Sedley LJ observed in *Kiam* v. *MGN*, '[t]he law governing general damages depends upon the fiction that suffering can be translated into money. Because it is a fiction, damages as a whole are arbitrary'.[32]

The complexity of defamation law, the prolixity of its pleadings and its propensity for interlocutory skirmishes as a consequence act as impediments to defamation law effectively vindicating reputations.[33] As Kirby J

[27] [1961] AC 1090, 1125. [28] [1972] AC 1027, 1071.

[29] John G Fleming, 'Retraction and Reply: Alternative Remedies for Defamation' (1978) 12 *University of British Columbia Law Review* 15, 15. See also *Ballina Shire Council* v. *Ringland* (1994) 33 NSWLR 680, 699 (Kirby P); *Cerutti* v. *Crestside* [2014] QCA 33, [35], [36] (Applegarth J).

[30] (2001) 208 CLR 199, 301–2; [2001] HCA 63, [260].

[31] (1991) 24 NSWLR 259, 300. [32] [2003] QB 281, 301.

[33] *Drummoyne Municipal Council* v. *Australian Broadcasting Corporation* (1990) 21 NSWLR 135, 149 (Kirby P).

observed in *Favell* v. *Queensland Newspapers*, the combination of these factors means that '[f]or ordinary Australians, suing a media defendant in defamation is a very risky way of vindicating wrong to one's good name. Usually, it is only for the foolhardy'.[34]

Finally, it should be noted that damages for defamation are often perceived as an imperfect remedy because, whatever the amount awarded and whatever publicity the judgement attracts, the words can never be unpublished so the damage to reputation is, in some sense, ineradicable. As Patrick George observes, 'the plaintiff will often feel that, regardless of the monetary compensation, the slur remains or the mud sticks, to be resurrected whenever the opportunity may arise. The defamation is remembered, not the outcome'.[35]

Given the dynamic nature of reputation as an interest, the defamation and the subsequent trial to vindicate the plaintiff's reputation can become part of the plaintiff's reputation. The plaintiff then can never really overcome the reputational harm that has been done to him or her.

An award of damages for defamation then is the principal remedy the law currently affords, not necessarily the optimal one. The extent to which reputations are actually vindicated by an award of damages for defamation should not then be overstated.

## 14.4 The concept of vindication in tort law

The central importance of vindication in defamation law as a stated purpose of its principal remedy, an award of damages, cannot be doubted. However, the idea of vindication is not infrequently perceived as being peculiar to defamation. In *Mosley* v. *News Group Newspapers*, Eady J accepted that, in an award of damages for privacy, there might need to be a component to vindicate the plaintiff's right to privacy, by marking the infringement of that right.[36] He emphasised that, in his view, vindication in that context was different from vindication of reputation as a purpose of the award of compensatory damages.[37] With respect, it is not self-evident why the concept of vindication should be understood and applied in these two different senses.

The attempt to treat vindication in defamation law as unique is part of a broader tendency to view defamation as a tort unlike any other.

[34] (2005) 221 ALR 186, 193; [2005] HCA 52, [22].

[35] Patrick George, *Defamation Law in Australia*, 2nd edn (Chatswood, NSW: LexisNexis, 2011), [37.1].

[36] *Mosley* [2008] EMLR 20, 732; [2008] EWHC 1777 (QB), [216]. See also *John Fairfax & Sons* v. *Kelly* (1987) 8 NSWLR 131, 139 (Samuels JA).

[37] *Mosley* [2008] EMLR 20, 732; [2008] EWHC 1777 (QB), [216].

Periodically, there are statements or assertions to the effect that basic principles of tort law, like causation and remoteness of damage, apply to defamation claims but the evidence for the systematic application of such principles is scant. More typical is the characterisation of defamation as a unique tort. The most evocative recent expression of this view was provided by Ipp JA, a judge of the New South Wales Court of Appeal, who described defamation as 'the Galapagos Islands Division of the law of torts'. Ipp JA went on: 'The tort of defamation has evolved all on its own and has created legal forms and practices unknown anywhere else. It has evolved its own dialect and adopted esoteric customs'.[38]

This is not an isolated observation or criticism.[39] Rather than emphasising the particularity of the tort of defamation, it might be useful to treat defamation like any other tort. For present purposes, an important consequence of doing this is to recognise that vindication in defamation law does not serve a distinctive purpose peculiar to this tort. The idea that a right is vindicated by an award of damages is a long-standing one in tort law.[40] One of the classic statements on this issue is provided by Holt CJ in *Ashby* v. *White*, wherein he stated: 'If the plaintiff had a right, he must of necessity have the means to vindicate and maintain it, and a remedy if he is injured in the exercise of the enjoyment of it'.[41]

Holt CJ then provides a number of illustrations of his general point:

> as in an action for slanderous words, though a man does not lose a penny by reason of the speaking of them, yet he shall have an action. So if man gives another a cuff on the ear, though it cost him nothing, no not so much as a little diachylon, yet he shall have his action, for it is a personal injury. So a man shall have an action against another for riding over his ground, though it did him no damage; for it is an invasion of his property and the other has no right to come there.[42]

It is clear that defamation is not the only tort in which an award of compensatory damages serves to vindicate the underlying right or interest protected by the tort. The interest protected by the tort of defamation is the plaintiff's reputation; an award of damages vindicates that interest. The interest protected by the tort of battery is the plaintiff's right to bodily integrity, to be free from physical injury or interference;[43] an award of damages vindicates that interest. The interest protected by the tort of trespass to land is the plaintiff's right to exclusive possession of his or her

[38] David Ipp, 'Themes in the Law of Torts' (2007) 81 *Australian Law Journal* 609, 615.
[39] See, e.g., *Crampton* v. *Nugawela* (1996) 41 NSWLR 176, 188 (Mahoney ACJ).
[40] *Ratcliffe* v. *Evans* [1892] 2 QB 524, 528 (Bowen LJ). See also *English and Scottish Co-operative Properties Mortgage and Investment Society* v. *Odhams Press* [1940] 1 KB 440, 455 (Slesser LJ).
[41] (1703) 2 Ld. Raym 938, 953; (1703) 92 ER 126, 136–7. [42] *Ibid.*
[43] *Collins* v. *Wilcock* [1984] 3 All ER 374, 378; [1984] 1 WLR 1172 (Robert Goff LJ);

land;[44] an award of damages vindicates that interest. This analysis is borne out by the legal principles applicable to other torts. For instance, the interest protected by the tort of false imprisonment is the plaintiff's liberty;[45] an award of damages vindicates that interest. Rather than being exceptional when it comes to the vindicatory purpose of an award of damages, defamation is similar to other torts. The vindication afforded by the award of damages for these torts is not ordinarily nominal. Not infrequently, substantial damages are awarded by way of vindication of the underlying interest for each of these torts.[46] It is important to note that the causes of action identified by Holt CJ in *Ashby* v. *White*, along with the tort of false imprisonment, share a number of common features. All of these torts are actionable per se. None requires a plaintiff to prove damage in order to establish liability. In addition, all of these torts protect interests which are fundamentally non-economic in nature. None of these interests is capable of 'pecuniary admeasurement'.[47] The award of damages always occurs after the infringement of the right has occurred and, although it is given by way of compensation, can never undo that infringement. The compensatory impulse of tort law, *restitutio in integrum*, operates in a particular way in relation to all of these torts, not just defamation. Vindication of reputation cannot restore a reputation to its previous position, wholly unaffected by the defamatory matter, any more than an award of substantial damages for trespass to land can restore exclusive possession, wholly unaffected by the defendant's intrusion; any more than an award of substantial damages for battery can undo the defendant's impermissible touching; any more than an award of substantial damages can restore the plaintiff's liberty after a plaintiff has already been deprived of it.

The concept of vindication has recently become a topic of considerable interest in tort law scholarship. The insights gleaned from this body of work might be usefully incorporated into reflections upon the remedies for defamation and privacy. For instance, in his book chapter, 'Private and Public: The Mixed Conception of Vindication in Torts and Private Law', Kit Barker argues that the concept of vindication in private law is 'mixed', in the sense that it is a purpose serving 'the plurality of public

[44] *Plenty* v. *Dillon* (1991) 171 CLR 635, 647 (Gaudron and McHugh JJ); *TCN Channel Nine* v. *Anning* (2002) 54 NSWLR 333, 339–40; [2002] NSWCA 82 (Spigelman CJ)

[45] *Bird* v. *Jones* (1845) 115 ER 668, 669; (1845) 7 QB 744 (Coleridge J); *Murray* v. *Ministry of Defence* [1988] 2 All ER 521, 529; [1988] 1 WLR 692.

[46] *Plenty* v. *Dillon* (1991) 171 CLR 635, 654–5 (Gaudron and McHugh JJ); *TCN Channel Nine* v. *Anning* (2002) 54 NSWLR 333, 365; [2002] NSWCA 82, [178] (Spigelman CJ).

[47] Robert C Post, 'The Social Foundations of Defamation Law: Reputation and the Constitution' (1986) 74 *California Law Review* 691, 694.

(social) and private (individualistic) aims'.[48] He suggests that there are four senses in which the vindication of rights can operate in private: by preventing infringement;[49] by declaring or marking the right;[50] by specifically enforcing the right;[51] and by reversing the effects of infringement.[52] In relation to torts actionable per se like defamation, vindication as a declaration or a marking of the right has the greatest application. As Barker points out, in private law, the declaration or the marking of right overwhelmingly occurs after the infringement of the right has occurred, thereby 'announcing the status of plaintiff and defendant as right-holder and wrongdoer *ex post facto* and thereby marking *both* the fact of the right *and* the fact of the wrong'.[53]

Barker acknowledges that all torts vindicate rights but singles out torts actionable per se as one serving a particular vindicatory function.[54] He treats awards of damages for non-economic harms, such as damage to reputation or interference with personal autonomy or dignity, as 'necessarily inexact' examples of vindicating the right at issue with a view to reverse the effects of its infringement.[55] Barker argues that vindication in defamation law operates not merely publicly to declare the right but also to reverse the effect of its infringement. He argues that:

> [s]ince reputational damage actually *consists in* a deleterious change in the *public perception* of a person, its remediation entails an equivalent change for the better in that perception and monetary sums are calculated symbolically with this objective in mind.[56]

Barker acknowledges that there is often a disparity between the vindicatory effect of defamation law in principle and in practice. He suggests that '[s]peedy, well-publicised judicial declarations of the slur's falsity' would probably be the most effective remedy for defamation, along with fully reasoned judgements, apologies, offers of amends and rights of reply.[57] Nevertheless, an award of damages is part of the process whereby the damage done to a plaintiff's reputation is sought to be reversed.[58]

Varuhas goes further than Barker in treating defamation like other torts and de-emphasising its particularity. In his article, 'The Concept of "Vindication" in the Law of Torts: Rights, Interests and Damages', Varuhas argues that vindication involves 'attesting to, affirming and

[48] Kit Barker, 'Private and Public: The Mixed Concept of Vindication in Torts and Private Law' in Stephen GA Pitel, Jason W Neyers and Erika Chamberlain (eds), *Tort Law: Challenging Orthodoxy* (Oxford: Hart Publishing, 2013) 59, 60.
[49] *Ibid.*, 69. [50] *Ibid.*, 69–73. [51] *Ibid.*, 73–4. [52] *Ibid.*, 74.
[53] *Ibid.*, 69 (original emphasis). [54] *Ibid.*, 66. [55] *Ibid.*, 75. [56] *Ibid.*, 76.
[57] *Ibid.*, 76–7. [58] *Ibid.*, 77.

reinforcing' the importance and value of the legal rights protected by tort law.[59] He acknowledges that, on one level, all torts are vindicatory in function.[60] However, he identifies torts that are actionable per se as having a primary vindicatory function. That is because the personal and proprietary interests protected by such torts are accorded such value that tort law protects them highly, against even slight interferences.[61] Defamation then is not a unique tort; it resembles other torts that are actionable per se. In relation to the award of damages, Varuhas argues that, for all torts actionable per se, the interference with the underlying interest is constructed as a form of damage, allowing the law to intervene to affirm the importance and value of the underlying interest.[62] According to Varuhas, the vindicatory function of torts actionable per se are 'engrained in their internal structures', allowing substantial damages to be awarded for an interference with the underlying interest in the absence of any actual loss.[63] In relation to defamation, Varuhas rejects the notion that there is any special or extra sense in which vindication operates. The interest protected by defamation is the plaintiff's reputation; the plaintiff's reputation is vindicated by an award of compensatory damages. This operates in a manner entirely consistent with the award of compensatory damages for other torts that are actionable per se.[64]

A significant impetus for both of these contributions was the heterodox suggestion in some of the judgements in the United Kingdom Supreme Court decision in *R (Lumba)* v. *Secretary of State for the Home Department* that there should be a discrete award of vindicatory damages.[65] One effect of this case was to refocus attention in tort law scholarship on what precisely was meant by the concept of vindication. As the authorities have long demonstrated and as Barker and Varuhas confirm, vindication has always been a central purpose of tort law, particularly for torts actionable per se. Vindication has not been historically, and should not be, treated as a separate head of damages. Rather, vindication is a central purpose of an award of ordinary compensatory damages for torts actionable per se, including defamation.

[59] Jason NE Varuhas, 'The Concept of "Vindication" in the Law of Torts: Rights, Interests and Damages' (2014) 34 *Oxford Journal of Legal Studies* 253, 254.

[60] *Ibid.*, 258. [61] *Ibid.*, 259. [62] *Ibid.*, 268. [63] *Ibid.*, 275.

[64] *Ibid.*, 276–7. Cf Normann Witzleb and Robyn Carroll, 'The Role of Vindication in Torts Damages' (2009) 17 *Tort Law Review* 16, 33–5.

[65] [2012] 1 AC 245; [2011] UKSC 12 ('*Lumba*'). For recent considerations of vindication in tort law predating *Lumba*, see Witzleb and Carroll, above n 64; Robyn Carroll and Normann Witzleb, '"It's Not Just About the Money" – Enhancing the Vindicatory Effect of Private Law Remedies' (2011) 37 *Monash University Law Review* 216.

## 14.5 A difficult issue of principle

It seems clear that a significant reason for emphasising the differences between defamation and privacy, for remedial purposes, is to avoid dealing with the issue of whether the restrictive approach to injunctive relief can be maintained in light of a fully developed right to privacy. This issue raises a range of conceptual and practical problems. The exploration and attempted resolution of this issue is beyond the scope of this chapter. However, it is sufficient to observe that it is well known that English, Australian and New Zealand law adopt a restrictive approach to injunctive relief, informed by a commitment to freedom of speech and an aversion to prior restraint.[66] This position was well established and consistently reinforced long before a direct, enforceable right to privacy began to be recognised. Yet English courts in particular have been willing to grant injunctions to restrain an apprehended disclosure of private information. In *Greene* v. *Associated Newspapers*,[67] the English Court of Appeal found that the rule in *Bonnard* v. *Perryman* was not inconsistent with the ECHR. This decision predated much of the recent consideration about the interaction of defamation and privacy in cases such as *Terry* v. *Persons Unknown*.[68] More significantly, it predated the acceptance of the view in English law that reputation is an aspect of the right to a private life under Article 8 of the ECHR[69] – a revolutionary change to the common law's traditional understanding of the relationship between defamation and privacy. It may be that *Greene* v. *Associated Newspapers* and the restrictive approach to injunctive relief in defamation more generally will need to be revisited.[70] In the interim, however, by emphasising the differences between defamation and privacy, it is possible to defer consideration of this complex issue. It cannot be deferred indefinitely. It may be accepted that defamation turns upon a dichotomy of truth or falsity and that privacy turns upon a dichotomy of whether the information is private or not.[71] These dichotomies, though, do not operate in parallel; they have necessary touching-points, overlaps and conflicts.

66 As to the position under English law, see *Bonnard* v. *Perryman* [1891] 2 Ch 269; *Greene* v. *Associated Newspapers* [2005] QB 972; [2004] EWCA Civ 1462. As to the position under Australian law, see *Australian Broadcasting Corporation* v. *O'Neill* (2006) 227 CLR 57; [2006] HCA 46. As to the position under New Zealand law, see *TV3 Network Services* v. *Fahey* [1999] 2 NZLR 129. See generally David Rolph, 'Showing Restraint: Interlocutory Injunctions in Defamation Cases' (2009) 14 *Media & Arts Law Review* 225.

67 [2005] QB 972; [2004] EWCA Civ 1462.

68 [2010] EWHC 119 (QB).

69 *In Re Guardian News and Media* [2010] 2 AC 697, 717–18; [2010] UKSC 1 (Lord Rodger of Earlsferry JSC). See also Rolph, above n 10, 196.

70 See, e.g., Richard Clayton and Hugh Tomlinson, *The Law of Human Rights*, 2nd edn (Oxford: Oxford University Press, 2009), [15.26]–[15.28].

71 *McKennitt* v. *Ash* [2008] QB 73, 102; [2006] EWCA Civ 1714 (Longmore LJ).

The principled negotiation of these touching-points, overlaps and conflicts will require careful consideration.

## 14.6 The vindication of privacy?

If, rather than treating defamation and privacy as different for remedial purposes, what might be gleaned from emphasising their similarities? If an injunction is not or cannot be granted to restrain an apprehended invasion of privacy and the plaintiff is compelled to rely on an award of damages, what considerations should be taken into account when assessing those damages?

A striking feature of the awards of damages in privacy claims is how modest they are. Naomi Campbell's award of £3,500 damages and the award of £3,750 damages each to Michael Douglas and Catherine Zeta-Jones are commonly cited high-profile examples of the relative parsimony of these judgements.[72] The award of £60,000 damages to Max Mosley is the largest ordered thus far by a court.[73] Most judgements, however, are much smaller than this.[74] Courts themselves have commented upon the modesty of awards in privacy cases.[75] As the jurisprudence develops, the level of damages will presumably rise. There has been a suggestion that substantial out-of-court settlements in privacy claims will cause the level of damages awarded by courts to rise,[76] although such settlements have no precedential value.[77] Importantly, the level of damages in privacy claims is modest when compared to defamation claims.[78]

[72] *Campbell* v. *MGN* [2004] 2 AC 457, 493 (Lord Hope), 502 (Baroness Hale), 505 (Lord Carswell); [2004] UKHL 22; *Douglas* v. *Hello! (No 3)* [2006] QB 125, 202 (*per curiam*); [2005] EWCA Civ 595.

[73] *Mosley* [2008] EMLR 20, 737; [2008] EWHC 1777 (QB).

[74] See, e.g., *Archer* v. *Williams* [2003] EMLR 38, 889; [2003] EWHC 1670 (QB) (Jackson J) (£2,500 damages); *Applause Store* [2008] EWHC 1781 (QB), [81] (Richard Parkes QC) (£2,000 damages); *Cooper* v. *Turrell* [2011] EWHC 3269 (QB), [107] (Tugendhat J) (£30,000 damages); *AAA* v. *Associated Newspapers* [2013] EMLR 2, 90; [2012] EWHC 2103 (QB) (£15,000 damages); *WXY* v. *Gewanter* [2013] EWHC 589 (QB), [59] (Tugendhat J) (£24,950 damages, including £5,000 aggravated damages); *Walsh* v. *Shanahan* [2013] EWCA Civ 411, [1], [55] (Rimer LJ) (£16,965); *Weller* v. *Associated Newspapers* [2014] EWHC 1163 (QB), [197], [200] (Dingemans J) (£10,000).

[75] See *Mosley* [2008] EMLR 20, 731–2; [2008] EWHC 1777 (QB), [212] (Eady J); *Applause Store* [2008] EWHC 1781 (QB), [81] (Richard Parkes QC). See also *Archer* v. *Williams* [2003] EMLR 38, 889; [2003] EWHC 1670 (QB) (Jackson J).

[76] *Spelman* v. *Express Newspapers* [2012] EWHC 355 (QB), [114] (Tugendhat J).

[77] *Mosley* [2008] EWHC 1777 (QB), [212] (Eady J).

[78] *Mosley* [2008] EWHC 1777 (QB), [212] (Eady J). It is worth noting that some legal systems which allow recovery for both defamation and privacy award damages and fines at a modest level. For example, as to the position under French law, see Alastair Mullis and Cameron Doley (eds), *Carter-Ruck on Libel and Privacy* (London: LexisNexis, 2010), [42.11]. Although the use of tariffs and statutory caps on damages for defamation are

There is no principled reason why this should be so. As recent tort law scholarship indicates, the importance and value of an interest is denoted by the level of damages awarded for a particular tort. Torts which are actionable per se are clear examples where substantial damages are awarded by way of vindication to reflect the importance and value underlying those causes of action. The Australian and particularly the English case law make it clear that the cause of action for privacy in both jurisdictions is, or should be, actionable per se.[79] Moreover, the Australian authorities imposing liability for invasion of privacy, such as they are, do so on the basis that the cause of action is tortious.[80] Although derived from the equitable cause of action for breach of confidence, the form of privacy protection that has developed under English law has been described as a 'tort of misuse of private information'.[81] In *Vidal-Hall* v. *Google*, Tugendhat J accepted that the 'tort of misuse of private information' was indeed a tort, notwithstanding its equitable origins, for the purpose of service of originating process outside the jurisdiction.[82] Treating invasion of privacy as a tort might have other consequences.

One of those consequences should be an acceptance that the award of damages for invasion of privacy should not be limited to an amount by way of solatium for the mental distress occasioned by the wrong. Like defamation, a significant component of the damages should be for the purpose of vindication, to demonstrate and affirm the importance and value of the right to privacy. There is no reason why these damages should be nominal. Like defamation, damages for invasion of privacy, in many cases, should be substantial, to reflect the significance attached to the right to privacy. The award of damages for invasion of privacy need not single out only mental distress for compensation but should be, as Windeyer J suggested in *Uren* v. *John Fairfax & Sons*, 'the product of a mixture of inextricable considerations'.

Taking into account the need to vindicate a plaintiff's right to privacy might require some careful consideration in certain circumstances. If a plaintiff has obtained an injunction to restrain further publication, that

used in English and Australian law respectively, they have not caused such a radical reduction in the level of damages awarded for defamation, not to a level comparable to those awarded under German or French law.

79 Australian Law Reform Commission, *Serious Invasions of Privacy in the Digital Era*, Discussion Paper No 80 (2014) [7.36]–[7.46], citing Mark Warby et al, *Tugendhat and Christie: The Law of Privacy and the Media*, 2nd edn (Oxford: Oxford University Press, 2011), [8.48].

80 *Grosse* v. *Purvis* (2003) Aust Torts Reports 81–706; [2003] QDC 151. See also *Doe* v. *Australian Broadcasting Corporation* [2007] VCC 281.

81 *Campbell* v. *MGN* [2004] 2 AC 457; [2004] UKHL 22, [14] (Lord Nicholls of Birkenhead).

82 [2014] EWHC 13 (QB).

will need to be taken into account when assessing damages in a privacy claim for such publication that has already occurred. In *WXY* v. *Gewanter*, Tugendhat J suggested that this was because the injunction is the most valuable form of vindication a plaintiff can receive.[83] Viewed another way, it could be argued that the grant of the injunction restrains the tortious conduct, thereby minimising the harm done and thus reducing the need for substantial damages. The exploration of these difficult issues in particular cases should not detract from the point that the vindication of the right to privacy should be reflected in an award of damages for invasion of privacy.

## 14.7 Conclusion

The notion that defamation law vindicates reputations, whereas privacy, once invaded, is irretrievably lost, does not withstand close scrutiny. This distinction has been used to justify continuing to award damages for defamation and injunctions rarely, while granting injunctions for apprehended disclosures of private information routinely and awarding only modest amounts of damages. It defers a fundamental reconsideration of the restrictive approach to injunctive relief in defamation, avoiding the issue of whether such an approach is sufficiently protective of privacy, which, in some cases, is inextricably linked with reputation. More fundamentally, it avoids engaging with the broader and complex issue of how the legal regulation of reputation and privacy – different aspects of a plaintiff's singular persona – should interact, in order to provide adequate protection of those rights, while ensuring that freedom of speech is not unduly curtailed. Defamation law has developed a finely calibrated, though not necessarily ideal, balance between the protection of reputation and freedom of speech. Considering the balance between the right to privacy and freedom of speech, without considering the right to reputation, carries with it the risk of unintentionally distorting or undermining existing defamation laws.[84]

Whatever the reason for advancing the putative distinction between defamation and privacy, the distinction rests on an overstatement of the vindicatory effect of an award of damages for defamation. There is understandably widespread scepticism about whether an award of damages for defamation can ensure the vindication of a plaintiff's reputation. An award of damages is not an ideal remedy for the harm done by the

[83] [2013] EWHC 589 (QB), [57], citing *Citation Plc* v. *Ellis Whitham* [2013] EWCA Civ 155.

[84] New South Wales Law Reform Commission, above n 19, [2.35].

publication of defamatory matter, if the only purpose is compensatory in the restorative sense. To a certain extent, then, the distinction also rests upon a misapprehension as to what constitutes vindication for the purposes of defamation law, and for tort law more generally. Defamation law has long recognised that compensatory damages for defamation are awarded by way of vindication because reputation, once damaged, can never be fully restored to its former state. The defamatory matter cannot be unpublished. Defamation is not a unique tort in this respect. A range of torts protect intangible interests and tort law expresses its concern for and affirms the importance and value of those interests by awarding substantial damages by way of vindication. There is no need to recognise a separate head of vindicatory damages. Vindication is already the purpose of an award of compensatory damages for torts actionable per se. By awarding compensatory damages, a court vindicates the right at issue. An award of compensatory damages for defamation vindicates a plaintiff's right to reputation. Similarly, a cause of action for invasion of privacy, particularly a 'tort' of misuse of private information, protects a right to privacy, and that right should be vindicated when damages are assessed. By stressing the similarities between defamation and privacy and by incorporating insights from tort law about the role of vindication, plaintiffs in privacy cases where they are having their damages assessed after the invasion has occurred should not be limited to awards of damages for mental distress by way of consolation.

# 15 Divining the dignity torts: a possible future for defamation and privacy

*Ursula Cheer*

## 15.1 Introduction

In a 2013 case, *Clague* v. *APN News and Media*, the New Zealand High Court declined an application for an interim injunction in a case involving anticipated publication of information about the plaintiff in mainstream media, even though it had considerable sympathy for the plaintiff's position.[1] The case involved an urgent application for interim relief to prevent the publication of a statement sent to media by the plaintiff's ex-wife which raised allegations he had assaulted her two years before that had been referred to police.

The plaintiff was the executive principal of a leading private school who advised the school board of the allegations and maintained that the incident was a minor domestic dispute involving a technical assault if any at all. The plaintiff now feared that he would be stood down if the matter got into the public domain and the reputation of the school would suffer. Among other submissions, he suggested the allegations were a private matter between himself and his ex-wife which would cause irreparable harm if published, especially if no criminal charges were laid. Justice Toogood found that the principal of a high-profile school could have no reasonable expectation of privacy in relation to an allegation that his past conduct was the subject of a police investigation. Further, although disclosure of that fact would be embarrassing and perhaps distressing to the plaintiff, it did not reach the threshold required in New Zealand of being publicity that is highly offensive or objectionable to a reasonable person of ordinary sensibilities.

The application was also based on a possible defamation claim. However, Justice Toogood concluded that there was no evidence that the newspaper involved intended to publish anything untrue about the

This chapter was written while the author was a Rutherford Visiting Scholar at Trinity College, Cambridge, 2014.

[1] *Clague* v. *APN News and Media* [2013] NZAR 99.

matter. In concluding, the Judge referred to the defendant as a responsible news media organisation which could reasonably be expected to give a balanced report on the matter. This meant the high threshold for injunctive relief based on anticipated publication had not been crossed.

*Clague* is a paradigm of what I shall call 'complex damaging speech' claims – cases where both reputational and privacy interests appear to have been breached and need to be untangled. It raised issues that are increasingly evident in UK cases as well. In these cases, the relevant information might or might not support a reasonable expectation of privacy. It might or might not be true. Was the plaintiff in *Clague* trying to protect his reputation or his privacy or both? The judge was forced to guess how the media might present the information. That affected how he saw the defamation claim. Publication was anticipated therefore injunction was the main remedy sought. Should the tests for granting an injunction be the same in defamation and privacy claims? How should a judge determine this?

In this chapter, I argue the intermingling of these torts is increasing, adding to the complexity of the law and damaging its coherence. In the first part of the chapter I attempt to analyse some of the similarities and differences in each tort to demonstrate that intermingling is real and substantial. In the second part, I make tentative suggestions for reform that might give more lucidity to this dynamic area of civil jurisprudence.[2]

## 15.2 Are defamation and privacy alike?

Western jurisdictions have had centuries to develop definitions of what makes a defamation claim. New Zealand definitions remain untouched by statute, and we rely solely on the cases.[3] It is agreed that the law of defamation protects the respect and esteem in which a person is held because that is the essence of reputation. We apply dated but still current English case law definitions such as: 'a statement that might tend to lower the plaintiff in the estimation of right-thinking members of society generally'[4]; and 'a false statement about a man to his discredit'.[5] These

[2] This chapter deals broadly with damage to reputation and invasion of privacy arising from publication or anticipated publication of information about a plaintiff. It does not focus on the tort of intrusion into seclusion recognised in the recent decision in *C* v. *Holland* [2012] 3 NZLR 672, although the options discussed in the second part of the chapter might embrace that tort also.

[3] See Ursula Cheer, *Burrows and Cheer Media Law in New Zealand*, 7th edn (Wellington: LexisNexis, 2015), 17.

[4] *Sim* v. *Stretch* [1936] 2 All ER 1237, 1240 (Lord Atkin).

[5] *Youssoupoff* v. *MGM Pictures* (1934) 50 TLR 581, 584 (Scrutton LJ).

speak strongly to loss of dignity and autonomy, with an emphasis on the falsity of the information.

Privacy on the other hand is newly minted compared to defamation, and notoriously difficult to define.[6] In New Zealand, we have settled on a formulation only a little more complex than the United Kingdom: a private statement is one about which the plaintiff has a reasonable expectation of privacy, and publication of it would be highly offensive to an objective, reasonable person.[7] Again, as in the UK, it was assumed at the birth of our tort that the relevant statements would be true, otherwise how could there be any reasonable expectation of privacy?

These definitions seem quite different. How, then, can there be overlap of these torts that have developed so separately in time? What is happening to our understanding of when freedom of expression might be limited by civil law? It has been suggested that privacy is an outgrowth of changes in the law of defamation.[8] It is conceivable that outgrowth has now taken hold, with defamation dying and privacy taking its place. Defamation claims both here and in the United Kingdom appear to be declining.[9] In New Zealand, there is also ample empirical and anecdotal evidence that defamation is becoming less of a concern to the media than the developing tort of privacy.[10] Furthermore, Palmer goes so far as to suggest that the tort of defamation might even fall into disuse in the next thirty years, as a relic of a previous media age.[11] While it is unclear whether this dramatic prediction will prove correct,[12] there are now ample examples of privacy's capacity to

[6] John Burrows, 'Invasion of Privacy' in Stephen Todd (ed), *The Law of Torts in New Zealand*, 6th edn (Wellington: Thomson Reuters 2013), 935. See also James Q Whitman, 'The Two Western Cultures of Privacy: Dignity Versus Liberty' (2004) 113 *Yale Law Journal* 1151, 1153.

[7] *Hosking* v. *Runting* [2005] 1 NZLR 1 (CA).

[8] David A Anderson, 'Defamation and Privacy: An American Perspective' in Simon Deakin, Angus Johnston, and Basil Markesinis, *Markesinis and Deakin's Tort Law*, 6th edn (Oxford: Clarendon Press, 2008) 865, 883.

[9] Hazel Genn, 'Civil Justice Reform and the Role of ADR' (Paper delivered as New Zealand Law Foundation Distinguished Visiting Fellow, Christchurch, 17 September 2009). Reform of procedural rules has led to a decline in civil claims generally. See also Human Rights Committee, *Consideration of Reports Submitted by States Parties Under Article 40 of the Covenant, Concluding observations of the Human Rights Committee*, 93rd session, UN Doc CCPR/C/GBR/CO/6 (30 July 2008).

[10] See Ursula Cheer, *Reality and Myth: The New Zealand Media and the Chilling Effect of Defamation Law* (PhD Thesis, University of Canterbury, Christchurch, New Zealand) http://hdl.handle.net/10092/3050.

[11] Geoffrey Palmer, 'The Law of Defamation in New Zealand – Its Recent Evolution and Problems', in John F Burrows, Jeremy Finn and Stephen Todd (eds), *Law, Liberty, Legislation: In Honour of John Burrows QC*, (Wellington: LexisNexis, 2008), 339, 357; GWR Palmer, *Reform: A Memoir* (Wellington: Victoria University Press, 2013), ch. 21.

[12] More recently, Inforrm has noted an apparent slight increase in the number of defamation claims for 2012: Judicial Statistics – defamation claims increased by 13 per cent http://inforrm.wordpress.com/2014/03/02/judicial-statistics-2012-defamation-claims-

'swallow up' significant parts of defamation. The evidence for increased entanglement of the two torts will now be considered.

### *15.2.1 Privacy has expanded to cover claims based on false facts*

Privacy claims no longer appear to be confined to true intimate statements, and can now be based on false facts as well. In *McKennitt* v. *Ash*,[13] Loreena McKennitt, a successful Canadian folk singer, complained of the publication of a book by Niema Ash, a former friend, that a substantial part of the book revealed personal and private details about her. Although she was a world-wide star, she very carefully guarded her personal privacy. The book contained details about Ms McKennitt's personal and sexual relationships, her personal feelings in relation to her deceased fiancé and the circumstances of his death, details of her health and diet and of her emotional vulnerability, and of a property dispute between Ms McKennitt and Ms Ash and another person.

The Judge at first instance found that most or all of the book's allegations about the property dispute were untrue and the defendant argued there could therefore be no claim in breach of confidence,[14] which usually protected true statements. However, the Court of Appeal held that the defendant cannot undermine a privacy claim simply by demonstrating that the matter is untrue. Buxton LJ rejected the suggestion that an allegation of falsity was inherent in the claim, saying: 'It would not reflect well on our law if that plea were to succeed. Ms McKennitt and her advisers cannot be criticised for choosing the wrong cause of action',[15] while Longmore LJ emphasised that '(t)he question in a case of misuse of private information is whether the information is private not whether it is true or false'.[16] In these circumstances, so long as a court considers the claim is not really a defamation claim in disguise, privacy will trump defamation and its absolute truth defence. This expansion of privacy is continuing with further privacy claims accepted by UK courts based not just on statements that turn out to be exaggerated, mistaken or partly true and partly false, but on complete fabrication.[17]

increased-by-13/ and the granting of no new privacy injunctions in the last six months of 2013: http://inforrm.wordpress.com/2014/03/19/news-privacy-no-new-injunctions-granted-in-last-6-months-of-2013/.

[13] *McKennitt* v. *Ash* [2008] QB 73 (CA).

[14] The English courts are now clearly recognising such claims as arising under a non-parasitic tort of privacy by misuse of personal information: *Vidal-Hall* v. *Google* [2014] EWHC 13 (QB); *Google* v. *Vidal-Hall* [2015] 3 WLR 409 (CA).

[15] *McKennitt* v. *Ash* [2008] QB 73 (CA) [79]. [16] *Ibid.*, [85].

[17] *Browne* v. *Associated Newspapers* [2007] EWHC 202 (QB); *P* v. *Quigley* [2008] EWHC 1051(QB). See John Hartshorne, 'An Appropriate Remedy for the Publication of False Private Information' (2012) 4 *Journal of Media Law* 93.

In *Clague*, the plaintiff pursued claims in both privacy and defamation. However, had the claim only been in privacy, and so long as the court found the true intention was to protect privacy and not reputation, it would not have mattered to the hearing of the claim if the allegations about spousal abuse were true or false. This appears to render the matter straightforward, and it is understandable why a court would want to ensure it is not the claimant's choice alone that determines the only cause of action, in order to avoid abuse of process.[18]

However, the question of the true motivation of the plaintiff is a difficult one which seems to require guesswork by the judges, especially where the claim is an interim one for an injunction to prevent publication. In *Terry* v. *Persons Unknown*,[19] the plaintiff's privacy claim failed because it was held to be likely that the nub of footballer John Terry's complaint about anticipated disclosure in a newspaper of the fact of his extra-marital affair was the protection of reputation and not private life. Tugendhat J reached this conclusion based on Terry's failure to put in evidence of any personal distress, his apparently very robust personality as a professional sportsman, and the assembling of the evidence by Terry's business partners, not his solicitors. The claim was seen as essentially a business matter from Terry's perspective, because of the way in which he delegated the preparation of the claim.[20] In these cases, the recognised principle that public figures have a lower expectation of privacy generally has produced cynicism about the motives behind privacy claims and this appears to make it very difficult for any professional person or true public figure to argue privacy where the relevant information is partly true and partly false or there is a general issue about truth or falsity. Indeed, there is the suspicion that such considerations influenced the determination in *Clague* that the plaintiff as the executive principal of a leading private school had no reasonable expectation of privacy in relation to the claim.

Although privacy has thus expanded to cover some of the ground sheltered by defamation, it has unfortunately done this in a way that further complicates the law and perhaps makes it difficult for particular classes of plaintiff to even establish the integrity of a privacy claim. Furthermore, the success of conjoined privacy and defamation claims is very much dependent on the pleadings, a characteristic for which defamation law is often and rightly criticised.

[18] The main concern in such cases is attempts to avoid the probably stricter requirements that apply to the granting of interim injunctions in defamation, as to which, see further later.

[19] [2010] EWHC 119 (QB); [2010] EMLR 16.

[20] [2010] EWHC 119 (QB); [2010] EMLR 16, [95].

### 15.2.2 *More complexity: defamation and privacy and the interim relief quandary*

Nowhere are tensions between the two torts in complex damaging speech cases more apparent than in relation to the granting of interim injunctions. The problem for UK law has been well stated by Parkes, as the question whether the same principles should govern the granting of interim injunctions in both defamation and privacy.[21] In English defamation law, prior restraint is not possible where a defendant indicates she or he will plead truth or another realistic defence at trial.[22] In privacy the test is different, because European law requires an intense focus on privacy and free speech rights in the context of the case with neither being given priority. Thus it appears to be easier to obtain interim injunctions in privacy, which may be a powerful incentive for plaintiffs to seek to frame reputational claims under the new tort, as found by the court in *Terry*. In this area, the overlap of the torts has produced remedial inconsistency and courts perhaps too sensitive to the possible undermining of existing principle.[23]

For defamation, New Zealand also adopted the restrictive rule laid down in *Bonnard* v. *Perryman*.[24] Additionally, since the passage of the New Zealand Bill of Rights Act 1990, the Court of Appeal has emphasised that it is not part of the function of the court to act as a censor, and that the jurisdiction to restrain is exceptional.[25] The leading case currently is *TV3 Network Services* v. *Fahey*,[26] where the Court of Appeal affirmed its view that an interim injunction will not be granted readily in a defamation case because of the need to preserve freedom of expression, therefore *clear and compelling* reasons are required before doing so.

21 Richard Parkes, 'Privacy, Defamation and False Facts' in Mark Warby, Nicole Moreham and Iain Christie (eds), *Tugendhat and Christie: The Law of Privacy and the Media*, 2nd ed (Oxford: Oxford University Press, 2011), [7.50]–[7.84].

22 Known as the rule in *Bonnard* v. *Perryman* [1891] 2 Ch. 269.

23 Parkes has suggested a modification of the rule in *Bonnard* v. *Perryman* in complex damaging speech claims, to that set out in s 12(3) of the Human Rights Act 1998, which would introduce a public interest factor into the equation: Parkes, above n 21, [7.83]. See also Godwin Busuttil and Patrick McCafferty, 'Interim Injunctions and the Overlap between Privacy and Libel' (2010) 2 *Journal of Media Law* 1, where the authors comment on *Terry* and suggest the rule in *Bonnard* v. *Perryman* requires amendment when applied to privacy, if claimants are to have meaningful effective rights under Art. 8 of the ECHR; and John Hartshorne, above n 17.

24 [1891] 2 Ch 269.

25 *Auckland Area Health Board* v. *Television New Zealand Ltd* [1992] 3 NZLR 406. See also *Australian Broadcasting Corporation* v. *O'Neill* [2006] HCA 46; 229 ALR 457.

26 *TV3 Network Services* v. *Fahey* [1999] 2 NZLR 129; *Hodgson* v. *Siemer* (Unreported, High Court of New Zealand, Ellen France J, 5 May 2005).

In privacy, the approach has been aligned with *Fahey*, but uncertainty remains. In the leading case, *Hosking* v. *Runting*,[27] the primary remedy for the newly recognised privacy tort was identified as damages, but injunctive relief was acknowledged as appropriate also.[28] Concerns about prior restraint were pressed very hard by the media in *Hosking*, and the court therefore discussed the stringent test requiring exceptional, clear and compelling reasons in New Zealand before injunctions are granted in defamation cases.[29] The judges noted that if the thresholds were to be different in privacy and defamation cases, plaintiffs could plead privacy in preference. The court recognised the need for consistency of approach and described a test for privacy cases which is probably the same: prior restraint is to be available where there is compelling evidence of most highly offensive intended publicising of private information and there is little legitimate public concern in the information.[30] However, privacy once gone is gone, and therefore restraint is arguably the most appropriate remedy in such cases.[31] At least one New Zealand Supreme court judge has argued that 'the analogy with interlocutory restraint in defamation proceedings is imperfect and needs to be treated with caution ... Whether freedom of information considerations should prevail depends on the circumstances of the particular case and all interests properly engaged'.[32] New Zealand judges may well address this issue again in a future case.

In *Clague*, the plaintiff was seeking an urgent interim injunction in relation to both his privacy and defamation claim. The privacy claim did not get past first base and so the question of the approach to injunction was not discussed. In relation to the defamation claim, the court noted the higher threshold requirement and concluded the plaintiff's case did not get beyond it. Yet if the privacy claim had been successful, Chief Justice Elias's reservations about applying the restrictive approach in defamation compellingly suggest a less restrictive approach may be justified in privacy, so long as freedom of expression is factored into the balance. More clarity within the remedial area of the law is desirable in New Zealand also.[33]

[27] *Hosking* v. *Runting* [2005] 1 NZLR 1 (CA). [28] *Ibid.*, [149]–[150].

[29] *Ibid.*, [151]–[155]; *TV3 Network* v. *Fahey* [1999] 2 NZLR 129 (CA).

[30] *Hosking* v. *Runting* [2005] 1 NZLR 1 (CA), [158].

[31] See *Greene* v. *Associated Newspapers* [2004] EWCA Civ 1462 (QB); [2005] EMLR 217; [2005] QB 972, and Hartshorne, above n 17, 103. Cf David Rolph in his chapter in this book 'Vindicating Reputation and Privacy', where he argues that invasion of privacy can in fact be vindicated by a significant award of damages.

[32] *Television New Zealand* v. *Rogers* [2008] 2 NZLR 277, [38] (Elias CJ).

[33] David Rolph has identified a similar potential tension in Australia, if a privacy tort develops there: David Rolph, 'Showing Restraint: Interlocutory Injunctions in Defamation Cases' (2009) 14 *Media & Arts Law Review* 255.

### *15.2.3 How defamation has always overlapped with privacy*

Thus far, this chapter has discussed how privacy has begun to encroach significantly into defamation law. This section will outline how defamation law has always contained elements that protect privacy to some degree, in ways that sit uncomfortably in defamation law.

Until quite recently, defamation defences in the United Kingdom and in New Zealand contained public interest requirements which meant aspects of privacy were protected in the tort. In the UK the fair comment defence could only apply if the publication was on a matter of public interest until as recently as the passing of the Defamation Act in 2013.[34] New Zealand had this requirement too, though abandoned it earlier with the passing of the Defamation Act 1992 when the defence was renamed honest opinion, as it has now been in the UK.[35]

Australia, until the passing of uniform defamation laws in 2005, was also notable because four states imposed public interest requirements for the truth defence in defamation. The requirement was accepted as protecting privacy to a limited degree in a country which has not yet recognised any form of tort, and thus its elimination in 2005 was seen by some as controversial and by others, as desirable for reasons of doctrinal purity.[36]

Additionally, the United Kingdom, New Zealand and Australia all now recognise varied forms of public interest defences in defamation.[37] These defences can apply where the truth defence fails or is impossible, with attendant conditions of responsibility. However, they do not allow the publication of private material.[38]

Finally, in defamation there are categories of speech recognised as potentially defamatory that arguably actually protect privacy. The first

[34] *Spiller* v. *Joseph* [2011] 1 AC 852. See now Defamation Act 2013 (UK) s 3.

[35] See Burrows and Cheer, above n 3, 188.

[36] David Rolph, 'Preparing for a Full-Scale Invasion? Truth, Privacy and Defamation' (2007) 25 *Communications Law Bulletin* 5. Should the jurisdiction, as seems inevitable, eventually recognise a claim protecting privacy, it is highly likely the tensions, overlaps and complexities between defamation and privacy identified above will arise.

[37] In the UK, a statutory defence under s 4 of the Defamation Act 2013, replacing the common law *Reynolds* defence; in New Zealand, a common law defence confirmed in *Lange* v. *Atkinson* [2000] 3 NZLR 385; in Australia in *Lange* v. *Australian Broadcasting Corporation*, the High Court of Australia extended the categories of qualified privilege to protect a communication made to the public on a government or political matter: (1997) 71 ALJR 818. See also Andrew T Kenyon, '*Lange* and *Reynolds* Qualified Privilege: Australian and English Defamation Law and Practice' (2004) 28 *Melbourne University Law Review* 406.

[38] In New Zealand, *Lange* allows discussion of the capacity of MPs to meet their public responsibilities, but this depends on 'a consideration of what is properly a matter of public concern rather than of private concern:' *Lange* v. *Atkinson* [2000] 3 NZLR 385, 390–1, 400 (CA).

is the 'shun and avoid' category. Tugendhat J treated the category in this light in *Terry*, saying:

> it is unlikely that it could be said that protection of reputation is the nub of the claim. These are cases where the information would in the past have been said to be defamatory even though it related to matters which were involuntary eg disease. There was always a difficulty in fitting such cases into defamation, but it was done because of the absence of any alternative cause of action.[39]

Similarly, it is arguable that some cases falling under the ridicule category are about privacy not reputation, in particular where a person is ridiculed for some personal and unfortunate trait, such as bad breath, or lack of personal hygiene, or poor sexual performance. Parkes suggests these categories are small and therefore do not undermine the coherence of defamation law in any significant way.[40] However, combined with the onslaughts of the developments in privacy law outlined earlier, these uneasy features of defamation law do appear more than insignificant.

### *15.2.4 Recognition in EU law*

Finally, and probably most significantly, European law now recognises privacy and defamation within the same Article of the European Convention on Human Rights. Article 8, which contains a right to respect for private life, has been expanded recently to protect the right to reputation.[41] In *Pfeifer* v. *Austria*,[42] the court held that 'a person's reputation, even if that person is criticised in the context of a public debate, forms part of his or her personal identity and psychological integrity'. In *Karakó*[43] it went so far as to suggest that some attacks on a person's reputation could be of such a seriously offensive nature as to have an inevitable direct effect on the victim's private life. This approach, though somewhat murky, reflects the potential for privacy to swallow up defamation, and has been applied by the UK Supreme Court.[44]

[39] *Terry* v. *Persons Unknown* [2010] EWHC 119 (QB); [2010] EMLR 16, [96].
[40] Parkes, above n 21, [7.28].
[41] *Petrina* v. *Romania* [2009] ECHR 2252; *Karakó* v. *Hungary* [2009] ECHR 712.
[42] (2007) 48 EHRR 175, 183 [35]. [43] *Karakó* v. *Hungary* [2009] ECHR 712.
[44] *Application by Guardian News & Media Ltd, HM Treasury* v. *Ahmed and ors* [2010] UKSC 1; [2010] 2 WLR 325. This merging is described by Rolph elsewhere in this book as a revolutionary change to the common law's traditional understanding of the relationship between defamation and privacy: David Rolph, 'Vindicating Reputation and Privacy', 340.

## 15.3 What are defamation and privacy claims about, really?

### *15.3.1 Shared roots – dignity and autonomy*

In addition to acknowledging increasing areas of overlap in defamation and privacy, it is possible to make convincing theoretical arguments that the torts share strong roots although they have developed centuries apart. As a very basic starting point, both are about protection from harms arising from published speech. Are those harms the same?

It is difficult to pin down what the protection of reputation is about although the tort of defamation is very old. The quaint old-fashioned language of the case law definitions commonly used in defamation claims referred to earlier do not in fact mention reputation at all and accordingly, Dent has described the concept of reputation as, in this sense, empty.[45]

However, Post has described three distinct concepts of reputation he detected in the common law of defamation, as property, honour and dignity.[46] The concept of property suggests reputation is the product of individual professional and personal exertion existing in a market where everyone is equal and reputation has protectable value. This notion sits well with current prevailing economic theory. Nevertheless, Post goes on to point out that important aspects of defamation law, such as the requirement for a defamatory meaning, and the presumption of harm, do not fit such a concept. Additionally, it does not sit well with aspects of injurious falsehood, which also protects similar loss.

Alternatively, the concept of honour is described by Post as based on an unequal, stratified society where individual honour is the personal reflection of the status that society gives to a person's social position. Honour is fixed and gives the value of a meaningful life. This concept is a public good, not a mere private possession, so maintaining honour maintains order in society. In contrast to reputation as property, damage to honour should be vindicated, not paid out in monetary terms. Post ultimately notes the demise of honour and the rise of egalitarianism in modern society, however. It is apparent the concept of honour may explain historical aspects of reputation, but it is a hopeless fit as a modern conception.

The final concept of dignity is described by Post as an authentic contemporary expression of understanding about defamation law. It suggests that a right to protect reputation is part of our essential dignity and worth

[45] Chris Dent, 'Compensation and/or correcting the record: A framework for the regulation of (defamatory) speech' (2011) 16 *Media & Arts Law Review* 123, 129 fn 25.

[46] Robert C Post, 'The Social Foundations of Defamation Law: Reputation and the Constitution' (1986) 74 *California Law Review* 691.

as human beings. Post sees the concept as thus uniting public and private parts of the self. Dignity is experienced as part of the self but is confirmed and made integral by the external respect shown by others. This dignity is the respect and self-respect that arises from full membership in society, based on rules of civility. Such a concept of reputation best explains the dual functions of defamation law in contemporary western society. Protecting reputation as dignity gives the individual social respect which is experienced both internally and externally, and maintains rules of social civility. The whole concept thus maintains social order. Dignity, then, is an excellent fit as a baseline concept for a modern theory of the interest protected by the tort of defamation.

In privacy, it has been recognised from the outset that the action is about protecting dignity and autonomy – in *Campbell* v. *MGN*[47] Lord Hope stated that the new form of privacy protection the House of Lords recognised in that case was about: 'the protection of human autonomy and dignity – the right to control the dissemination of information about one's private life and the right to the esteem and respect of other people'.[48] In *Hosking*, Tipping J in the majority said 'It is of the essence of the dignity and personal autonomy and wellbeing of all human beings that some aspects of their lives should be able to remain private if they so wish'.[49]

The proposition that both torts are about dignity has been well captured in the assertion by Parkes that 'If defamation is necessary to protect the reputation that a person has in the minds of *right*-thinking members of society generally, then privacy can be said to be necessary to protect the reputation a person has in the minds of *wrong*-thinking members of society'.[50] Rolph has expressed the view that defamation and privacy are separate, and defamation is uniquely concerned with the protection of the plaintiff's public face, (although in an essay in this book, he goes on to suggest both causes of action protect aspects of the plaintiff's own persona, and that there should be fewer remedial distinctions maintained).[51]

As the discussion of Post's work earlier demonstrates, the matter is complex. However, it is arguable that both torts look outwards at how others perceive us, which can impact on both public and personal

47 [2004] UKHL 22; [2004] 2 AC 457 (HL), [51].

48 As identified and endorsed by NA Moreham, 'Privacy in the Common Law: A Doctrinal and Theoretical Analysis' (2005) 121 *Law Quarterly Review* 628. See also the theorists noted by Moreham in her fn 34.

49 *Hosking* v. *Runting* [2005] 1 NZLR 1, [239] (CA). See also McGrath J in *Brooker* v. *Police* [2007] NZSC 30; [2007] NZLR 91, [225].

50 Parkes, above n 21, [7.15].

51 Rolph, 'Full-Scale Invasion', above n 36; David Rolph, 'Vindicating Reputation and Privacy', 305–7.

lives – in fact we can experience loss of public and personal dignity in both torts. Additionally, personal dignity can involve how we are perceived by an intimate group of others, but may embrace introspective dignity too, flowing from how we perceive ourselves. Loss of dignity, whatever form it may take, is reflected in damages for distress, hurt feelings and humiliation in both the defamation and privacy torts.

As to autonomy, Moreham has developed a concept of this within privacy law based on loss of choice.[52] Thus, even a captured image of individuals carrying on activities in a public place may breach a reasonable expectation of privacy because it makes the plaintiff more accessible than they actually were, and prevents them from adapting their behaviour to an unwanted wider audience – they have lost choice.[53] It is submitted that because claims in both defamation and privacy arise from forms of publication or anticipated publication by others, loss of autonomy is a strong feature of such claims. The injunction remedy available in both torts recognises this and attempts to restore autonomy over information by preventing, nullifying or bringing publication by the defendant to an end.

So if we look at *Clague*, it can be suggested both the plaintiff's claims expressed loss of dignity in his anticipated loss of status as a principal of a leading private school (quite apart from the possible loss of his job) and loss of the status of good husband. Both actions also expressed loss of autonomy over the information by claiming that the allegation made by the wife was exaggerated and private, and by objecting to the fact that the information had been sent to the media.

This survey of the similarities and overlaps between the defamation and privacy torts suggests that doctrinal purity of the two actions is under serious threat. The second part of this chapter advocates that the answer to these increasing difficulties is to look forward, not back.

## 15.4 Down the Yellow Brick Road to the Emerald City – merging defamation and privacy claims

### *15.4.1 Introduction*

Attempts to reconcile the similarities, encroachments and tensions within existing defamation and privacy tort law, or to minimise their effects, are essentially based on a desire for doctrinal purity. Rolph, for example, has argued that although both claims are founded on the personality of the

52 Moreham, above n 48.
53 NA Moreham, 'Privacy in Public Places' (2006) *Cambridge Law Journal* 606, 629–30.

plaintiff, they remain conceptually distinct legal interests. Properly understood, he suggests, it is not the function of defamation to protect privacy.[54] A similar view motivates other commentators, such as Parkes, to attempt to alleviate the identified tensions while preserving the separate torts.[55] Similarly, judges like Justice Tugendhat have attempted to downplay any loss of doctrinal coherence by suggesting that it is only in limited classes of cases that the law of privacy gives rise to an overlap with the law of defamation.[56]

The focus of this chapter, however, is on the possibility of uniting rather than dividing the torts, since they persist in jostling up against each other, and may do so increasingly in the future. This requires an analysis of shared characteristics at a more general level rather than a detailed focus on historical form and origin. The perspective, therefore, is not backward looking at what these claims have been, but forward-looking to what they might be. It is not, of course, being advanced that privacy has taken over all of defamation law nor that the two claims are completely alike. It seems doubtful defamation claims will disappear any time soon, and there will be claims based on false speech that have no private element at all, such as those which involve speech about companies, or individuals wrongly accused of terrible crimes such as murder and paedophilia whose lives have been destroyed.[57]

Nonetheless, although doctrinal clarity is a good idea in principle, adhering to it inflexibly ignores the reality that these two torts do appear to be drawing closer together as privacy develops and changes and as defamation ages, with a resulting loss of coherence in both. In that context, there appears to be some value in considering how privacy and defamation might be merged together in a form of civil action that seeks remedy for harms caused by published speech or seeks to prevent anticipated published speech. As suggested earlier, describing losses in terms of speech harms rather than attempting to force complex damaging speech claims into established defamation and privacy rubrics may be the key to developing an appropriate unitary claim. Potential actions might therefore, in varying degrees, take the emphasis off the nature of the words published and put it on remedying the harm. This part of the chapter traverses two possible forms such a unitary action might take. Examples from New Zealand law are used, however, the models have relevance to

[54] Rolph, 'Full-Scale Invasion', above n 36.

[55] See, e.g., Parkes, above n 21; and Hartshorne, above n 17, who suggests that claims for false privacy should be removed from the misuse of private information tort altogether.

[56] *Terry* v. *Persons Unknown* [2010] EWHC 119 (QB), [2010] EMLR 16, [96].

[57] See, e.g., *Lord McAlpine* v. *Bercow* [2013] EWHC 1342; *A-G* v. *MGN* [2011] EWHC 2074, [2012] EMLR 9, [3].

other jurisdictions, such as the United Kingdom and Australia. The discussion is, of necessity, somewhat exploratory and tentative.

### *15.4.2 A statutory model*

The defamation and privacy torts could of course simply be united in a statute. In *Hosking*, Gault P said: 'The law governing liability for causing harm to others necessarily must move to accommodate developments in technology and changes in attitudes, practices and values in society. These are drawn into the law in the main by legislation…'[58] Since NZ's parliament is sovereign in the Westminster style[59] and can pass any legislation it likes,[60] a statutory claim could take many forms, ranging from statements of very general propositions, to a very high level of detail. This chapter will not present an example of the latter, although it would be entirely possible for a good parliamentary counsel to draft a bill just clipping the current approach to the two torts together in some way. Such a statute could contain the common law definitions of the torts and preserve the separate defences for defamation and privacy depending on whether a statement was true or false. Similarly, different rules for prior restraint of true personal or untrue speech could be provided for if that was deemed desirable. However, this sort of provision would not represent a truly new unitary approach. Therefore, the two approaches that will now be discussed are presented as possible general reforming models, with the focus of discussion on the form rather than the exact content.

### *15.4.3 A harmful communications statute*

New Zealand is not afraid to pass detailed legislation dealing with speech harms. Parliament has recently passed a Harmful Digital Communications Act[61] which sets up a low-level civil regime dealing with such speech based on a set of communication principles that apply to digital (electronic) communication which, if seriously breached, can support complaints made to an appropriate agency. Proceedings in the District Court are

[58] *Hosking* v. *Runting* [2005] 1 NZLR 1, [3].

[59] International treaty obligations excepted.

[60] Subject to Bill of Rights consistency: see Claudia Geiringer, 'The Principle of Legality and the Bill of Rights Act: A Critical Examination of *R* v. *Hansen*' (2008) 6 *New Zealand Journal of Public and International Law* 59.

[61] Harmful Digital Communications Act 2015 http://www.legislation.govt.nz/act/public/2015/0063/latest/whole.html accessed 20 November 2015. The Act followed a report on Cyber-bullying prepared by the New Zealand Law Commission as part of a general review of regulation of the media: New Zealand Law Commission Ministerial Briefing Paper, *Harmful Digital Communications: The adequacy of the current sanctions and remedies*, August 2012, www.lawcom.govt.nz/sites/default/files/ministerial_briefing_-_harmful_digital_communications.pdf

then possible if the matter cannot be resolved by the agency, there has been a serious or repeated breach of a communication principle and the breach has caused or is likely to cause harm to a person. The Act also contains a criminal offence and provides for take-down orders, corrections, declarations and the like. Media are not exempt from the scheme.

This legislation covers some of the ground occupied by the defamation and privacy torts, relegating them to last resort status (if not there already). One possible form of statutory merging of defamation and privacy would be to expand this legislation to cover *all* harmful communications, not just digital. The Communication Principles in the Act which could have relevance to defamation and invasion of privacy are:

> *Principle 1* A digital communication should not disclose sensitive personal facts about an individual.
>
> *Principle 6* A digital communication should not make a false allegation.

However, as the full list makes clear,[62] breach of confidence, harassment, obscenity and offensive speech are also covered by the Principles. Indeed, they appear to cover most of the forms of harmful speech recognised in New Zealand law. There is in fact no good reason why the Act should not apply to all forms of communication rather than just digital. If this approach was taken, would the legislation cover the ground currently covered by defamation and privacy? While it is not possible to consider every detail of the Act, the major issues can be addressed here. It is

[62] The remaining principles are: Harmful Digital Communications Act 2015, s. 6:

> *Principle 2*: A digital communication should not be threatening, intimidating, or menacing.
>
> *Principle 3*: A digital communication should not be grossly offensive to a reasonable person in the position of the affected individual.
>
> *Principle 4*: A digital communication should not be indecent or obscene.
>
> *Principle 5*: A digital communication should not be used to harass an individual.
>
> Principle 7: A digital communication should not contain a matter that is published in breach of confidence.
>
> *Principle 8*: A digital communication should not incite or encourage anyone to send a message to an individual for the purpose of causing harm to the individual.
>
> *Principle 9*: A digital communication should not incite or encourage an individual to commit suicide.
>
> *Principle 10*: A digital communication should not denigrate an individual by reason of his or her colour, race, ethnic or national origins, religion, gender, sexual orientation, or disability.

(2) In performing functions or exercising powers under this Act, the Approved Agency and courts must—

(a) take account of the communication principles; and

(b) act consistently with the rights and freedoms contained in the New Zealand Bill of Rights Act 1990.

apparent there are some difficulties. However, none of these are unresolvable.

One problem is that Principle 6 refers simply to false allegations, which may not always be the same as defamatory allegations. For example, it is generally not defamatory to say of a living person that they have died, although it is a false statement. It is possible, then, that the principle would regulate more speech than the tort of defamation. However, the Act contains a number of safeguards against this. First, only an individual who has suffered harm can make a complaint. Harm is defined as serious emotional distress.[63] It is unlikely a person could show a false statement that he or she was dead has caused such harm. Thus the threshold is high, perhaps higher than the current threshold in the Defamation Act 2013 (UK). This would be a suitable threshold for privacy claims also. Second, a court can only consider a complaint if the agency has already attempted to deal with it, and then only if there has been a serious, repeated or threatened breach of one or more of the Principles, and this has caused or is likely to have caused harm.[64]

The next issue is whether there should be any fault element in such a regulatory regime. The Act addresses the issue of fault by requiring a court to consider a number of factors before making an order, including the purpose of the communicator, and in particular, whether the communication was intended to harm.[65] This does not mean lack of fault will result in no order being made. In some cases, even if there is no fault at all, it may still be a good idea to order removal of material from the Internet, or publication of a correction in a relevant form. However, the inclusion of this factor means that the issue of fault must be addressed and weighed in some way before any order is made.

Further, what might happen to defences that currently exist in defamation and privacy? The Act requires that the question whether the communication is in the public interest must also be addressed,[66] as well as the truth or falsity of the statement,[67] thus allowing for something akin to public interest and truth defences if relevant. A further requirement to consider the occasion, context and subject matter of the communication[68] would allow honest opinion to be treated leniently or excused, and for some communications to be treated as privileged. The requirement to act consistently with the rights and freedoms in the New Zealand Bill of Rights Act 1990 also reinforces the need to take account of defences that currently protect freedom of expression.[69]

[63] Harmful Digital Communications Act (2015), s. 4. [64] *Ibid.*, s. 12(1) and (2).
[65] *Ibid.*, s. 19(5)(b). [66] *Ibid.*, s. 19(5)(g). [67] *Ibid.*, s. 19(5)(f). [68] *Ibid.*, s. 19(5)(c).
[69] *Ibid.*, s. 6(2). Reference could be made to the ECHR in similar fashion if the Act was adopted in the UK.

What sort of remedies could be applied to deal with publication of defamatory or private information? The remedial powers in the Act are practical and extensive. The court may make interim orders pending determination of an application for a final order.[70] Both interim or final orders can take the following forms:

- an order to take down or disable material;
- an order that the defendant cease or refrain from the conduct concerned;
- an order that the defendant not encourage any other persons to engage in similar communications towards the affected individual;
- an order that a correction be published;
- an order that a right of reply be given to the affected individual;
- an order that an apology be published.[71]

The following orders can be made against content hosts:

- an order to take down or disable public access to material that has been posted or sent;
- an order that the identity of the author of an anonymous or pseudonymous communication be released to the court;
- an order that a correction be published in any manner that the court specifies in the order;
- an order that a right of reply be given to the affected individual in any manner that the court specifies in the order.[72]

There is also power to direct orders to apply to third parties, to order a declaration that a Principle has been breached, and to order suppression of names.[73]

The agency cannot make orders[74] and so the system makes no real provision for apprehended publication to be prevented by order because before a court can make an interim order, the agency must have tried to mediate or otherwise negotiate the complaint. If the agency cannot prevent publication through its processes, an order may come too late. This could be corrected by inclusion of a provision allowing applications for interim orders to prevent apprehended breach of the Principles to go direct to the court without the agency being involved at all. In any event, it is preferable for a court to deal with such applications, as the granting of these forms of interim orders requires consideration of sometimes complex legal issues, and involves the pre-censorship of speech.

Otherwise, the making of orders is fully nuanced. As well as the requirement to take account of any element of fault, public interest, truth and falsity, and context as outlined earlier, the court must consider the content of the communication and the level of harm caused, the

[70] *Ibid.*, s. 18. [71] *Ibid.*, s. 19(1). [72] *Ibid.*, s. 19(2) [73] *Ibid.*, s. 19(4).
[74] *Ibid.*, s. 8.

extent to which the communication has spread beyond the original parties, the age and vulnerability of the affected individual, the conduct of the defendant, including any attempt to minimise the harm, the conduct of the affected individual or complainant, the technical and operational practicalities and the costs of an order, and the appropriate individual or other person who should be subject to the order.[75] Thus, any differences arising from the nature of the information, depending on whether it is false or private, can be factored in, and an interim order may well be more justifiable where sensitive personal facts are involved than where false allegations have been made. Since all applications would be dealt with in this contextual manner, there would be little point in attempting to strategically argue complex speech claims as privacy claims when they are really intended to protect reputation. If a publication contained true sensitive material and false allegations as well, then complaint could be made under both Principles 1 and 6. All of the factors would then be applied in the full context of that unique claim.

The main advantages of this model would be increased coherence, accessibility and affordability of the law. It would truly deliver the low-level complaints process for harms arising from published speech that is frequently advocated by media and those who have been harmed by published speech. A weakness of this model would be that harm does not currently cover pecuniary loss, and complaints processes based on forms of mediation, and appeal-like resolution in a lower court, may not be appropriate in very serious cases where significant financial loss has occurred and there is very significant damage to dignity. Therefore, if a Harmful Communications Act was to oust the existing torts, it would need to be extended to cover pecuniary harms and provide additional remedial power to award damages, perhaps only where damage exceeds a minimum threshold level to keep the focus off damages and on the alternative non-pecuniary remedies. Alternatively, the torts could be preserved as a last resort for those cases, which is a less desirable solution as it would destroy the fully comprehensive nature of the statute.

If such legislation is intended to replace the torts (and other civil actions relevant to speech), then the media should not be exempt from it so long as freedom of expression is balanced when the Act is applied, as noted earlier. Media are exempt from the Privacy Act 1993 in New Zealand, which similarly relies on principles relevant to data collection. However, that exemption was made because it was recognised that the principles in the Privacy Act could impact on news gathering activities. Any negative impact on media under a Harmful Communications Act would simply

[75] *Ibid.*, s. 19(5).

replicate what already arises in relation to the existing torts. In fact, such an Act would provide more protection for media than current civil law, because it contains explicit direction that the Bill of Rights must be taken into account. At present, this is only done indirectly in New Zealand private law and somewhat inconsistently, depending on the inclination and experience of the particular judge involved.[76] Under a Harmful Communications Act, media would still be able to maintain their own varied regulatory complaints processes and complainants could choose to use those rather than the Act provisions.[77] This model would be workable, practical, coherent and genuinely reforming in New Zealand, the United Kingdom and Australia.

### 15.4.4 *Constitutional models*

The model considered earlier would create a new statutory claim, not a right. A more radical model would involve inserting an appropriate blended right into the New Zealand Bill of Rights Act 1990 (the Bill), based on the United Kingdom where a right blending reputation and privacy interests in Art. 8 of the ECHR is given indirect weak horizontal effect in domestic law.

The New Zealand Bill is not supreme law, and contains no judicial strike-down power, thus operating as an interpretative direction for the judiciary and other state servants.[78] The leading case *Hansen* v. *R*[79] mandates that the rights in the Bill are given effect through statutory construction. Thus, the question of whether limits to rights can be demonstrably

[76] Similarly, UK domestic law takes account of freedom of expression in Art. 10 of the European Convention of Human Rights by giving it weak indirect horizontal effect in private law. The New Zealand Bill of Rights Act is discussed further below.

[77] See Cheer, above n 3, 799.

[78] The key provisions are:

4. Other enactments not affected—

No court shall, in relation to any enactment (whether passed or made before or after the commencement of this Bill of Rights),—

(a) Hold any provision of the enactment to be impliedly repealed or revoked, or to be in any way invalid or ineffective; or

(b) Decline to apply any provision of the enactment – by reason only that the provision is inconsistent with any provision of this Bill of Rights.

5. Justified limitations—

Subject to section 4 of this Bill of Rights, the rights and freedoms contained in this Bill of Rights may be subject only to such reasonable limits prescribed by law as can be demonstrably justified in a free and democratic society.

6. Interpretation consistent with Bill of Rights to be preferred—

Wherever an enactment can be given a meaning that is consistent with the rights and freedoms contained in this Bill of Rights, that meaning shall be preferred to any other meaning.

[79] [2007] 3 NZLR 1 ('*Hansen*').

justified in a free and democratic society has been thrust to the centre of our Bill of Rights analysis.[80] It is answered by using the Canadian approach of asking whether the limiting measure serves a purpose sufficiently important to justify curtailing the right or freedom, and then querying whether it is rationally connected to its purpose, impairs the right no more than is reasonably necessary to achieve that purpose and is in due proportion to the importance of the objective.[81]

There is no statutory requirement in New Zealand to carry out a Bill of Rights analysis in relation to actions between private citizens. New Zealand's Bill was intended to have only vertical effects: it applies to the three branches of government and bodies exercising public functions,[82] and thus in general only protects private citizens from the state.[83] In spite of this, it is clear that, as in the United Kingdom in relation to ECHR convention rights, the New Zealand judiciary is giving the Bill horizontal effect when resolving disputes between private citizens and when developing the common law, including media law.[84] Because this process does not produce directly enforceable rights, the horizontal effect is usually regarded as weakly or strongly indirect.[85] It is given content in two ways, though sometimes in combination: the judges argue they are simply bound by the Bill as the judicial arm of the state, or that they are implicitly required to take account of the values expressed in the Bill.

What effect would inserting a new blended right covering both defamation and privacy into New Zealand's Bill have? Butler has recently made arguments for inserting a right of privacy into the Bill,[86] and has suggested that such inclusion would give symbolic recognition of the importance of privacy, increased legislative scrutiny of the impact of legislation on privacy interests and greater judicial certainty about the status of privacy

[80] See Geiringer, 'The principle of legality and the Bill of Rights Act: A critical examination of *R* v. *Hansen*', 59.

[81] *R* v. *Oakes* [1986] 1 SCR 103. See Tipping J in *Hansen*, [2007] 3 NZLR 1, [104] and Anderson J, [272].

[82] The New Zealand Bill of Rights Act 1990, s. 3.

[83] See Paul Rishworth, 'Human Rights' [2005] *New Zealand Law Review* 87.

[84] Philip A Joseph, *Constitutional and Administrative Law in New Zealand*, 3rd ed (Wellington: Thomson Brookers, 2007), 1176. See also *Simunovich Fisheries* v. *Television New Zealand* [2008] NZCA 350, [89]. Various approaches seem to have been accepted in the United Kingdom also – see, e.g., Jonathan Morgan, 'Privacy, Confidence and Horizontal Effect: "Hello" Trouble' (2003) 62 *Cambridge Law Journal* 444; Gavin Phillipson, 'Transforming Breach of Confidence? Towards a Common Law Right of Privacy under the Human Rights Act' (2003) 66 *Modern Law Review* 726; *McKennitt* v. *Ash* [2006] EMLR 10, [49].

[85] Jane Norton, '*Hosking* v. *Runting* and the Role of Freedom of Expression' (2004) 10 *Auckland University Law Review* 245, 249.

[86] Petra Butler, 'The Case for a Right of Privacy in the New Zealand Bill of Rights Act' (2013) 11 *New Zealand Journal of Public and International Law* 213.

interests. On the question of what form a right to privacy should have, she suggests a configuration based on Art. 8 of the Convention: 'Everyone has the right to respect for his private life, his home and his correspondence'.[87]

If the European approach to Art. 8 is applied to this wording in New Zealand, then Butler has in fact made arguments for a blended right to be inserted to the Bill, though she does not discuss this possibility, nor its implications. Alternatively, more explicit wording could be used, such as: 'Everyone has the right to respect for dignity and autonomy'.[88]

Whatever form is chosen, creating such a right could give symbolic recognition of the importance of dignity interests, increased legislative scrutiny of the impact of legislation on these and greater judicial certainty about the blended nature of defamation and privacy. But would it have the effect within private law of blending the two existing torts together? The answer is possibly, as should in fact be happening in the United Kingdom, because judges giving the Bill indirect horizontal effect should be prompted to move the torts together to reflect the constitutional right and would thus have more room to overcome the current difficulties and tensions outlined in the first part of this chapter. How long this might take is unknown, but development would likely be quicker than at present. Though more radical for New Zealand than the United Kingdom, which already has a blended right to apply indirectly in its domestic law, this model has the potential to make the law relating to the torts of defamation and privacy more coherent and consistent in the long term, and would put the focus on the interests protected as rights rather than mere claims. It would not have the immediate effect of a fused statutory claim, however.

## 15.5 Conclusion

This chapter has employed a comparative analysis to stimulate discussion of developments in the torts of privacy and defamation. It has suggested by traversing various examples that the torts are drawing closer together in a way that weakens them both because of increased tension and complexity. A forward-looking solution is proposed that abandons the search for doctrinal purity and focusses instead on seeking to merge the torts together. Two possible models for merging are suggested: a Harmful

[87] *Ibid.*, 254. Butler omits reference to family life because she considers this may go too wide and requires more in-depth consideration.

[88] Naturally this could impact on behaviour outside of use of information, and may therefore be too broad. However, the right would fall to be interpreted sensibly by the judges and, as pointed out by Butler, it would be constrained by being weighed against other rights under s. 5 of the Bill: *ibid.*, 254.

Communications Act, and the insertion of a blended right into a constitutional framework. Of these two, the first appears practical and workable. However, the second would go furthest, by creating a new right rather than simply a new form of claim. Both models require interpretation by a judiciary prepared to work outside existing forms with true visionary zeal.

# 16 Reverberations of *Sullivan*? Considering defamation and privacy law reform

*Andrew T. Kenyon and Megan Richardson*

In the pivotal decision in *New York Times* v. *Sullivan*,[1] the US Supreme Court embarked on a major rereading of the First Amendment and defamation law, responding to the political crisis of a country ravaged by resistance from southern states to desegregation policies being imposed from the north and the use of defamation law to quell public debate in northern news media. In the process, defamation law was reshaped to provide broad scope for public discussion of the conduct of public officials – an approach later extended to debate about public figures. Here, we consider reverberations of *Sullivan* in the US and some Commonwealth jurisdictions over the five subsequent decades. *Sullivan*'s influence led to a substantial reshaping of the law of defamation in the US and, to a lesser extent, it influenced the UK and Australian treatment of reputation and free speech. But also significant is the way that *Sullivan* exemplified a certain *style* of law reform. Subsequent defamation law reform has sometimes sought to emulate that style in treating reform as a response to a (perceived) public crisis with serious ramifications for free speech – a recent example being the UK reform process leading to the Defamation Act 2013.

In the contiguous field of privacy law, in contrast, reform during the same period has taken a different path. References to *Sullivan* have largely been eschewed outside the US where the Supreme Court, applying *Sullivan*, significantly limited privacy protection against public discussion of newsworthy material in cases including *Time* v. *Hill*.[2] This is not to say there have not been important legal changes related to privacy elsewhere in the common law world as well as various 'crises' which

This research has benefitted from Australian Research Council funding (Kenyon, DP0985337) and draws on a presentation by Kenyon at the International Communication Association 2014 conference in Seattle; thanks to Kyu Ho Youm for organising and chairing that 2014 conference panel which examined *Sullivan*'s international legacy. We are especially grateful to Jason Bosland for helpful discussions in the preparation and writing of this chapter.

[1] 376 US 254 (1964) ('*Sullivan*'). [2] 385 US 374 (1967) ('*Hill*').

efforts at law reform have sought to address. But outside the US privacy law has developed in quite another direction. This is seen, for example, with the development of a cause of action for misuse of private information by English courts premised on the right to private life in the European Convention on Human Rights (ECHR)[3] following the Human Rights Act 1998 (HRA). Courts in these jurisdictions have tended to avoid any *Sullivan*-style suggestion of effecting transformation to protect speech in response to crisis. Instead, as we have noted elsewhere,[4] the development of the English action for misuse of private information proceeded through case law in the direction of greater or enhanced privacy protection (with the process ongoing). Courts responded to the HRA and also drew on earlier developments in the law of confidence which predated the HRA and responded to earlier changes in technologies and media practices.

In these changes, the reverberations of *Sullivan* are complex. In the US, the Supreme Court commenced very substantial reforms to defamation law in *Sullivan* and, soon afterward, applied the principles to restrict markedly the possibility for privacy actions against media publications. The classic enunciation of First Amendment principles in *Sullivan* that led to these changes gradually came to haunt the law in at least some common law jurisdictions outside the US. For present purposes, two aspects of the reasoning in *Sullivan* are notable. First, Brennan J stated that the US has a 'profound national commitment' to the principle that debate on public issues should be 'uninhibited, robust and wide-open'.[5] Second, he emphasised that requiring a speaker to prove the truth of defamatory statements in court imposed too great a chill on speech.[6] In somewhat simplified terms, the second point about defamation law's chilling effect has been accepted in the UK and Australia. And similar patterns can be seen elsewhere, with Canada being a prime recent example.[7] But the first aspect of *Sullivan* about the value of robust public debate remains less recognised, at least in

[3] European Convention on Human Rights and Fundamental Freedoms, opened for signature 4 November 1950, 213 UNTS 222 (entered into force 3 September 1953).

[4] See Megan Richardson and Andrew T Kenyon, 'Fashioning Personality Rights in Australia' in Andrew T Kenyon, Ng-Loy Wee Loon and Megan Richardson (eds), *The Law of Reputation and Brands in the Asia Pacific* (Cambridge: Cambridge University Press, 2012) 86; and see generally Megan Richardson, Michael Bryan, Martin Vranken and Katy Barnett, *Breach of Confidence: Social Origins and Modern Developments* (Cheltenham: Edward Elgar, 2012) ch 7.

[5] *Sullivan*, 376 US 254, 270 (1964). [6] *Ibid.*, 277.

[7] See especially *Grant* v. *Torstar Corporation* [2009] 3 SCR 640, Hilary Young in this collection and eg Bob Tarantino, 'Chasing Reputation: The Argument for Differential Treatment of "Public Figures" in Canadian Defamation Law' (2010) 48 *Osgoode Hall Law Journal* 595.

relation to defamation law.[8] Thus defamation law in these non-US jurisdictions has been reformed, but in a manner that protects speech to a much lesser extent than the US law.

In the UK, a gradual recognition of the chilling effect of traditional defamation law, which was a central aspect of the *Sullivan* reasoning, led to modest judicial reform in *Reynolds*. But the ongoing contrast with the US position – exemplified by *Sullivan*'s apparently effective and clear model of protecting speech – meant pressure for more substantial defamation law reform remained. To a limited degree, that happened through subsequent cases that sought to emphasise the strength of protection that *Reynolds* privilege *should* offer. But beyond that, reform was made by the legislature that, on paper, makes some marked liberalisations (although future judgements will demonstrate the degree to which that intention has been achieved). Privacy law reform, however, took a different path. The ideas of constitutional rights, evident in *Sullivan*, arose more for privacy through the UK's HRA than through comparative case law. As a result, rights to private life and to freedom of expression were explicitly in play in the recent UK developments to privacy to a greater extent than could ever have been said before. That fact, coupled with the way in which English defamation law remained different from US law and far weaker in its protection of speech made it unsurprising that the US application of *Sullivan* principles to privacy had no real resonance across the Atlantic.

In Australia, the chilling effect of traditional defamation law was also recognised by the courts, around the same time as a relatively weak and narrow protection for speech was found to be implied in the Constitution. Recognising the chill, but less the value of robust public debate, meant the judicial reforms to defamation law were limited and even more modest in practice than *Reynolds* in the UK. The change was also followed by statutory reform, but in Australia, free speech arguments had less effect on the reforms and the process did not involve the sort of perceived crisis that existed before the UK's latest defamation legislation. In terms of privacy, it is unsurprising that *Sullivan's* legacy in US privacy law has not resonated in Australia. And, without the legislative human rights prompt that existed in the UK, Australian courts have made more incremental application of longstanding causes of action to offer some protection to privacy interests that, in principle, can apply against media publication.

[8] See, e.g., Andrew T Kenyon, 'What Conversation? Free Speech and Defamation Law' (2010) 73 *Modern Law Review* 697.

## 16.1 *Sullivan*'s transformations of US law

In the defamation case of *Sullivan*, the Supreme Court took the First Amendment as a reason to carve out significant protection for speech about public officials except in cases of 'actual malice', which requires the plaintiff to show the defendant's actual knowledge or reckless disregard of the publication's falsity with 'clear and convincing' evidence.[9] The decision in *Sullivan* was one of major significance, for the first time nationally and on the constitutional basis of the First Amendment giving wide latitude to discussions of public officials in the face of potential defamation claims. But equally significant is the way the case unfolded through the dramatic events of the early 1960s civil rights movement. A sense of crisis is suggested through the Supreme Court's reference to the defendants' advertisement in the *New York Times* seeking funds in support of Martin Luther King which led to the case, with its 'expression of grievance and protest on one of the major public issues of our time'. The publication (detailed in and appended to the judgement) consisted of a full-page advertisement in the *New York Times* titled 'Heed Their Rising Voices' which began by stating: 'As the whole world knows by now, thousands of Southern Negro students are engaged in widespread non-violent demonstrations in positive affirmation of the right to live in human dignity as guaranteed by the US Constitution and the Bill of Rights'. It continued: 'in their efforts to uphold these guarantees, they are being met by an unprecedented wave of terror by those who would deny and negate that document which the whole world looks upon as setting the pattern for modern freedom'; then gave a number of alleged examples; and concluded with an appeal for funds for support of the student movement, 'the struggle for the right-to-vote', and the legal defence of Martin Luther King against a perjury indictment then pending in Montgomery.[10]

The sense of crisis is also evident from the facts of the case, revealing southern state authorities resisting programs of racial integration from earlier Supreme Court decisions and attempting to censor northern media commentary about their actions against protesters. This attempted censorship included multiple libel suits brought against the *Times* resulting in very substantial verdicts rendered by local juries. As Black J records in his concurring opinion (joined by Douglas J), there was not only the Supreme Court proceedings involving a $500,000 verdict. A second $500,000 libel verdict against the *Times*, based on the same advertisement had already been awarded to another Commissioner, and further briefs

[9] *Sullivan*, 376 US 254, 280 (1964). [10] *Ibid.*, 256–7.

before the Supreme Court showed 'eleven libel suits by local and state officials against the *Times* seeking $5,600,000' were pending in Alabama, as well as 'five such suits against the Columbia Broadcasting System seeking $1,700,000'.[11] For the newspaper's lawyers, 'The stakes were enormous.'[12] Some suggested that 'Without a reversal of these verdicts there was a reasonable question of whether the *Times* . . . would survive.'[13] And it was doubtful whether broadcasters would have continued to 'do programs on the South',[14] further compromising the Supreme Court's views on change.[15] More generally, the decision was seen to open up possibilities for public debate on other contentious topics such as Watergate and Vietnam, where but for the Supreme Court's intervention those without authorised access to information would have little prospect of challenging official 'truths' and seeking change.[16]

Yet *Sullivan* did not merely create new law. It drew on older precedents – showing how even in such dramatic times processes that engage with longer debates may add a sense of legitimacy to case law reform. Thus, although *Sullivan*'s public official doctrine was new at the national level, the Supreme Court pointed to a range of precursors consistent with the change. There were references to earlier decisions that supported its approach, both to the First Amendment,[17] and to the wider protection of speech in defamation law,[18] as well as the more general statement that,

[11] *Ibid.*, 294–5.

[12] Nicholas F Burnett, '*New York Times* v. *Sullivan*' in Richard Parker (ed), *Free Speech on Trial: Communication Perspectives on Landmark Supreme Court Decisions* (Tuscaloosa: University of Alabama Press, 2003) 116, 118.

[13] See Anthony Lewis, *Make No Law: the Sullivan Case and the First Amendment* (New York: Random House, 1991) 35 (quoting James Goodale).

[14] *Ibid.*, 245 (quoting Eric Embry, with reference to CBS).

[15] Burnett, above n 12, 125. [16] Lewis, above n 13, 158.

[17] For instance, Brandeis J in *Whitney* v. *California*, 274 US 357, 375–6 (1927) ('public discussion is a political duty'); Black J in *Bridges* v. *California*, 314 US 252, 270 (1941) ('prized American privilege to speak one's mind'); Learned Hand J in *United States* v. *Associated Press*, 52 FSupp 362, 372 (1943); *Sullivan*, 376 US 254, 269–70 (1964).

[18] See *Sullivan*, 376 US 254, 280–1 (1964), noting that '[a]n oft-cited statement of a like rule . . . has been adopted by a number of state courts' (listing several of these and noting especially the Supreme Court of Kansas in *Coleman* v. *MacLennan*, 78 Kan 711, 724 (1908) as an exemplar). While some earlier cases used the term 'actual malice', it appears this was generally used as a synonym for express malice rather than in the sense used in the Supreme Court; see also David A Anderson, 'Weschler's Triumph' (2014) 66 *Alabama Law Review* 229, 241–2. The Supreme Court's citation to *Coleman* concerns the point in the judgement where an occasion of qualified privilege is found to exist, not the quality of malice that would make it unavailable. At other points in the judgement, e.g., 723, the *Coleman* court refers to 'actual malice' as part of the existing English law on qualified privilege. It also analyses and endorses US judgements which take a strong approach to protecting public speech, requiring plaintiffs to prove falsity and malice to defeat privilege.

we consider this case against the background of a profound national commitment to the principle that debate on public issues should be uninhibited, robust, and wide-open, and that it may well include vehement, caustic, and sometimes unpleasantly sharp attacks on government and public officials.[19]

In other words, the Supreme Court was suggesting that its ideas could be located in the history of the Bill of Rights, and especially the First Amendment, rather than simply being introduced in response to the social and political conditions of the 1960s. The impression of an ideal of deliberation and continuity is bolstered by references to such thinkers as John Milton and John Stuart Mill,[20] with some acknowledgment also of the influence of the contemporary scholar Alexander Meiklejohn, a recognised advocate of representative democracy in 1964.[21] Likewise, the open discussion of points of agreement and difference within the three judgements – Brennan J delivering the primary opinion and Black J and Goldberg J concurring – adds to the impression of judges participating in an almost Meiklejohnian-style debate (with negotiations proceeding through seven drafts[22]) with the final decision grounded in substantial albeit not complete consensus. The concurring judges, who argued against an actual malice restriction on the *Sullivan* doctrine, also looked to the First Amendment as authority. Black J noted 'the sturdy safeguard embodied in the First Amendment' and Goldberg J commented that '[w]e should be particularly careful . . . adequately to protect the liberties which are embodied in the First and Fourteenth Amendments'.[23] They would have provided even stronger protection against defamation suits.

If *Sullivan* exhibited relative consensus, it was a consensus which the Supreme Court was unable to emulate in some subsequent decisions extending the public official doctrine to public figures bringing defamation suits,[24] and more broadly any newsworthy discussion in suits for

[19] *Sullivan*, 376 US 254, 270 (1964).

[20] See *ibid.*, at footnote 19 where Brennan J quotes Mill's comment that 'even a false statement may be deemed to make a valuable contribution to public debate, since it brings about "the clearer perception and livelier impression of truth, produced by its collision with error"': *On Liberty* (Oxford: Blackwell, first published 1859, 1947 edn) 15; and further notes Milton's 'Areopagitica' (1644), in *Complete Prose Works of John Milton*, Vol II (New Haven: Yale University Press, 1959) 561.

[21] Only Black J cites Alexander Meiklejohn, *Free Speech and its relation to Self-Government* (New York: Harper, 1948) but Brennan J acknowledges the debt to Meiklejohn in William J 'The Supreme Court and the Meiklejohn Interpretation of the First Amendment' (1965) 79 *Harvard Law Review* 1, 14–19.

[22] See Kermit L Hall and Melvin I Urofsky, *New York Times* v. *Sullivan: Civil Rights, Libel Law, and the Free Press* (Lawrence: University Press of Kansas, 2011) 160–71.

[23] *Sullivan*, 376 US 254, 293, 300 (1964).

[24] The extension can be seen in *Curtis Publishing* v. *Butts*, 388 US 130 (1967); *Associated Press* v. *Walker*, 389 US 28 (1967); and *Rosenbloom* v. *Metromedia*, 403 US 29 (1971) in the latter case suggesting that even 'involuntary' public figures may be caught up in

invasion of privacy. A key case here is *Time* v. *Hill.*[25] The plaintiff, Hill, was neither a public official nor a public figure in a substantial sense. Rather he was a private individual who had been drawn into the public eye through his role as a hostage in a home invasion several years before the publication that gave rise to the case. Hill claimed that his privacy and that of his family had been breached by *Life* magazine's article about a Broadway play 'Desperate Hours' which falsely asserted that the play's 'tense' fictionalised account of a hostage situation reflected the actual experience of the family.[26] Thus the case centred on a false light invasion of privacy claim, not an especially easy platform on which to base an argument about violation of privacy as Dianne Zimmerman has noted, coming close to a claim of defamation in another guise.[27] Publication of private facts was not argued, and it was doubtful such a claim would have succeeded, given the terms of the New York Civil Rights Law's protection of privacy as narrowly construed by the New York courts.[28] The Supreme Court held that if the publication is judged to be in the public interest, meaning essentially that the information is newsworthy, a *Sullivan*-style doctrine applies[29] – and moreover did so in terms broad enough to suggest that the same should follow for other privacy torts as well where the First Amendment came into play.[30]

debates about matters of 'public or general interest' (Brennan J for the Supreme Court at 43–4). However, some limits were enunciated in the 'retreat' of *Gertz* v. *Robert Welch*, 418 US 323 (1974) so that private figures need not be subjected to the actual malice doctrine, although they could not have the benefit of traditional defamation law where publications involved matters of public interest. See, e.g., Rodney A Smolla, *The First Amendment: Freedom of Expression, Regulation of Mass Media, Freedom of Religion* (Durham: Carolina Academic Press, 1999) 474–8.

25 *Hill*, 385 US 374 (1967).

26 The *Life* article, included in the 'theatre' section and consisting of twelve lines of text followed by photographs, states: '[t]he play directed by Robert Montgomery and expertly acted is a heart-stopping account of how a family arose to heroism in a crisis. LIFE photographed the play during its Philadelphia tryout, transported some of the actors to the actual house where the actors were besieged': 'True Crime Inspires Tense Play', *Life*, February 28, 1955, 76.

27 Dianne Zimmerman, 'False Light Invasion of Privacy: The Light that Failed' (1989) 64 *New York University Law Review* 364.

28 See *Hill*, 385 US 374, 383–4 (1967), noting that in cases under the §§50–1 of the New York Civil Rights Law 1903 it is accepted that 'truth is a complete defense in actions . . . based upon reports of newsworthy people or events', citing *Spahn* v. *Julian Messner*, 18 NY 2d 324 (1966) ('*Spahn*').

29 *Hill*, 385 US 374, 383, 389 (1967). See also 379, 386 and n 8 for allusions to language of 'legitimate newsworthy information' and 'legitimate public interest' noting such language had been used in the Appellate Division in *Hill* and in *Spahn*. Of course in *Hill* there was also the actual malice test given this was a false light case: the case was remanded for further proceedings to determine the question of actual malice (but proceedings were not pursued).

30 *Hill*'s message that matters of 'public interest' or 'legitimate newsworthy information' were ones that the press may report on was picked up in later cases including *Cox*

On the surface the Supreme Court's majority judgement delivered by Brennan J might be read as a straightforward extension of *Sullivan* into privacy, and this could explain why the judgement is relatively short and contains little discussion of possible differences between defamation and privacy claims in free speech terms. Even so, there appear to be some challenges to the analogy – for instance, *Hill* was not so easily supported by ideas about representative democracy used in *Sullivan*, the Supreme Court in *Hill* displayed conflicts in their various judgements rather than any relative agreement (with strong dissents from Harlan J and Fortas J and a concurrence from Black J, joined by Douglas J, who reiterated their positions in *Sullivan* and emphasised that 'First Amendment freedoms can [not] be permanently diluted or abridged by this Court's action'),[31] and it was given before the scope of the public figure concept had been considered in later defamation cases and with less qualification than in those cases. Further, the decision probably had less support from earlier state authority than *Sullivan*. The principal earlier privacy cases that supported *Hill* were largely from New York, a state with major media interests and with a narrowly framed statutory protection of privacy which courts had also construed restrictively.[32] Even then, the New York courts had not gone as far as the Supreme Court in a newsworthiness doctrine, treating this as relevant only to newsworthy publications of facts by news media rather than fictionalised pseudo-biographical accounts of people and events.[33]

It may be that one reason why the First Amendment was allowed so easily to undermine privacy claims in cases such as *Hill*, was the perceived recent and tenuous character of these claims, emerging as they did in the first half of the twentieth century in response to Samuel Warren and Louis Brandeis' calls in their 1890 article 'The Right to Privacy'.[34] That

*Broadcasting Corp* v. *Cohn*, 420 US 469 (1975), a publication of private facts case, where the standard adopted was one of 'legitimate concern to the public'. The standard was applied there in the broadcaster's favour in broadcasting a rape victim's identity that had already been published on the court record (despite noting that in *Hill*, 385 US 374, 383, n 7 (1967) the question had been kept open whether truthful publication of very private matters unrelated to public affairs could be constitutionally proscribed). The American Law Institute's *Restatement (Second) of Torts* (1977) also includes a qualification for cases where the matter is 'of legitimate concern to the public'. Further, the *Restatement* clearly appreciates the very broad sweep of this standard, in a special note asking what remains of § 652D (publicity given to private life) after the Supreme Court's broad reading of the First Amendment in *Sullivan* and subsequent cases.

31 See *Hill*, 385 US 374, 398–9 (1967). 32 See above n 28.

33 For example, in *Spahn*, where it was said that *Sullivan*'s reasoning was inapplicable in a case involving neither a public official nor official conduct but concerning 'an individual's attempt to enjoin the publication of a fictitious biography': *Spahn*, 18 NY 2d 324, 329 (1966).

34 Samuel D Warren and Louis D Brandeis, 'The Right to Privacy' (1890) 4 *Harvard Law Review* 193. See also William L Prosser, 'Privacy' (1960) 48 *California Law Review* 383. The influence of these authors in identifying and shaping the privacy torts is extensively

Richard Nixon appeared for the plaintiff in front of his former 'enemies' on the Supreme Court, and that the claim was framed as one of false light publicity (when the apparent concern was having a family's ordeal raised again in the media), may not have assisted the plaintiff.[35] But another factor may have been the simple accident of timing, with the case coming so soon after *Sullivan* rather than raising any obvious free speech crisis of its own – concerning, as it did, an article about the human story behind a popular play.[36] Bernard Schwartz's *Unpublished Opinions of the Warren Court* reveals an intellectual disagreement in the Supreme Court following *Sullivan* between 'absolutists' and 'moderates', with the absolutists led by Black J ultimately influential in *Hill*.[37] This absolutism is also evident in the simple assertion in *Hill* that:

> The guarantees for speech and press are not the preserve of political expression or comment upon public affairs, essential as those are to healthy government. One need only pick up any newspaper or magazine to comprehend the vast range of published matter which exposes persons to public view, both private citizens and public officials. Exposure of the self to others in varying degrees is a concomitant of life in a civilized community. The risk of this exposure is an essential incident of life in a society which places a primary value on freedom of speech and of press.[38]

In the circumstances it may not be not surprising that, although the greater protection for criticism of public officials in *Sullivan* has been widely accepted and the extension to public figures has also been generally well received, the stringent approach adopted to privacy on newsworthy matters has raised some concern, even in the US. For instance, Anthony Lewis, a very strong supporter of *Sullivan*, expresses 'uneasiness' about the way the Supreme Court decided *Hill*.[39] And David Anderson has noted that US privacy law gives people 'no effective power to control use by the media of their very lives – the facts, incidents, ordeals, tragedies and emotions of their lives'.[40]

discussed in the US literature but see especially, for helpful historical perspective, Neil M Richards and Daniel J Solove, 'Prosser's Privacy Law: A Mixed Legacy' (2010) 98 *California Law Review* 1887.

[35] Nixon was reportedly concerned about taking on the case because 'some of his old ideological enemies now sat on the Court' and after losing the case reportedly said 'I always knew I wouldn't be permitted to win a big appeal against the press': see Leonard Garment, 'The Hill Case', *The New Yorker* (17 April 1989) 90, 104.

[36] Garment seems to think so, *ibid.*: 'Might the *Hill* decision have been affirmed if *Times*'s appeal to the Supreme Court had not followed so quickly on the heels of *Sullivan*?'

[37] Bernard Schwartz, *Unpublished Opinions of the Warren Court* (New York: Oxford University Press, 1985) ch 8.

[38] *Hill*, 385 US 374, 388 (1967).

[39] Lewis, above n 13, 189.

[40] David A Anderson, 'The Failure of American Privacy Law' in Basil S Markesinis (ed), *Protecting Privacy* (Oxford: Oxford University Press, 1999) ch 6, 146.

## 16.2 Reform elsewhere

A mixed pattern of reception can be seen in other common law jurisdictions, as issues of defamation and privacy law were addressed over later decades. In particular, courts and legislatures (as well as the weight of scholarship) largely accepted the basic idea in *Sullivan* that traditional defamation law imposed an unwarranted chilling effect on public speech, which underpinned reforms making more overt reference to constitutional and often human rights considerations. In addition, Australian and UK courts and legislatures reformed defamation largely through changing defences rather than the arguably far more significant challenges posed by remedies.[41] In that, they echo one central aspect of the approach in *Sullivan*. However, reforms did not give the same recognition to the significance of 'robust debate' in the US approach to defamation law. Thus the reforms went only some of the way towards *Sullivan*. *Sullivan*'s methodology – representing legal change as a transformation made in response to a crisis involving public debate – also has certain parallels elsewhere, even if the events were different in character, the solutions less dramatic, and their success more questionable in terms of reducing defamation law's 'chill'. While part of the reason for the differences may come down to the particular constitutional arrangements in jurisdictions such as the UK and Australia compared with the US, another part may lie in wider sociocultural differences and their influence within legal interpretation.[42] In the same jurisdictions, moreover, *Hill* and *Sullivan* have been treated as having little of value to say about the need for or shaping of privacy law reform.

In Australia, a sense of frustration emerged in some legal quarters in the early 1990s based on the failure to introduce a legislative Bill of Rights, as had occurred in Canada and New Zealand and as a Constitutional Commission had recommended in Australia.[43] As David Erdos points out, this did not translate into a broader public sense of 'perceived "crisis"

[41] See, e.g., John G Fleming, 'Retraction and Reply: Alternative Remedies for Defamation' (1978) 12 *University of British Columbia Law Review* 15; Andrew T Kenyon, 'Protecting Speech in Defamation Law: Beyond *Reynolds*-Style Defences' (2014) 6 *Journal of Media Law* 21; Alastair Mullis and Andrew Scott, 'Tilting at Windmills: The Defamation Act 2013' (2014) 77 *Modern Law Review* 87, 107–8.

[42] For instance, one of us has suggested that robust speech is more highly valued in the US, while more polite discourse is more highly valued in the UK: see Kenyon, above n 8; while the other has suggested that sociocultural and economic factors as well as journalistic practices leading to privacy law reform have been quite different, especially in the UK with repercussions with other jurisdictions such as Australia: see Richardson et al., *Breach of Confidence*, above n 4.

[43] See George Williams, *A Bill of Rights for Australia* (Sydney: UNSW Press, 2000) 12 and further ch 3.

within the constitutional order' prompting any public demand for legal change.[44] Indeed, as reportedly said by Sir Anthony Mason, 'I don't think there was strong support for a Bill of Rights until the 1980s and I'm not sure how strong the support for the Bill of Rights was even then.'[45] Nevertheless, the Mason High Court moved in the direction of a (rather limited) constitutional free speech standard, finding an implied freedom of political communication within the democratic principles of the Australian Constitution in cases from the early 1990s.[46]

The proposition that an implied freedom of political communication could now be read into the democratic principles of Australia's ninety-plus year old Constitution was controversial,[47] as was the High Court's treatment of the implied freedom in its 1994 *Theophanous* decision re-fashioning defamation law to include a new defence for political communication.[48] It may not have assisted the reception that the High Court seemed to go out of its way to emphasise the new defence, playing down the importance of the other step it took in *Theophanous* of expanding traditional qualified privilege to encompass cases involving public speech on political matters where the requirement of duty-interest for qualified privilege had previously been said not to apply. Now 'the public at large' was recognised as having a general interest in discussion of 'political matters'.[49] In fact, protecting political communication via 'traditional' qualified privilege in *Theophanous* appears to have been the more significant change for defamation law than the case's 'constitutional defence', although it did not endure in the *Lange* judgement, discussed below. Further, there was reference made in *Theophanous* to the US Supreme Court decision in *Sullivan* and to the House of Lords' support in *Derbyshire County Council* v. *Times Newspapers* for *Sullivan*'s reasoning about the chilling effect (discussed further below).[50] Mason CJ, Toohey and Gaudron JJ noted the way in which *Sullivan* spoke

[44] David Erdos, 'Elite Supply "Blockages" and the Failure of National Bill of Rights Initiatives in Australia: A Comparative Westminster Analysis' (2008) 46 *Commonwealth & Comparative Politics* 341.

[45] *Ibid.*, 353.

[46] Beginning with *Nationwide News* v. *Wills* (1992) 177 CLR 1 and *Australian Capital Television* v. *Commonwealth* (1992) 177 CLR 106 ('*ACTV*').

[47] For example, Williams questioned the legitimacy of the approach of interpreting a Constitution that 'was not drafted to include a Bill of Rights' in this way, and arguing that a legislative bill of rights was preferable: Williams, above n 43, 12.

[48] *Theophanous* v. *Herald & Weekly Times* (1994) 182 CLR 104, 137–8, 140 (Mason CJ, Toohey and Gaudron JJ) ('*Theophanous*'); cf *Stephens* v. *West Australian Newspapers* (1994) 182 CLR 211, 234.

[49] *Theophanous* (1994) 182 CLR 104.

[50] *Derbyshire County Council* v. *Times Newspapers* [1993] AC 534 ('*Derbyshire*'). See further below nn 66–67 and accompanying text.

'eloquently of the tendency of the law of defamation to inhibit the exercise of the freedom of communication – "the chilling effect"', and stated that existing defamation defences left the law 'significantly inhibiting free communication'.[51] All this reinforced the sense that *Sullivan*'s ideas had given rise to an Australian response. If so, it was something that certain judges found inappropriate. There were strong dissents in the early cases,[52] and continuing vocal critiques from some members of the High Court.[53]

In its 1997 decision in *Lange* v. *Australian Broadcasting Corporation*,[54] the High Court attempted to resolve its divisions through a compromise position on the basis and effects of the implied freedom. Judgements in *Theophanous* had differed as to whether the freedom acted only as a limitation on legislative power or might go further. Somewhat like the division in *Sullivan*, where Black J would have found an 'absolute' protection against defamation rather than the 'actual malice' standard adopted by the *Sullivan* majority, in *Theophanous* Deane J would have found a much stronger protection for political communication at least in relation to the official conduct and suitability for office of politicians and candidates. But as the High Court was otherwise evenly split, Deane J concurred with the result of the joint judgement which provided a constitutional defamation defence for political communication where publication was shown to be 'reasonable'. However, the later seven member unanimous judgement in *Lange*, noting that Deane J did not explain what would be required for reasonableness, held there was not an explicit majority in the *Theophanous* reasoning with regard to the implied freedom.[55] *Lange* thus re-examined all the issues.

As if to confer an aura of historical authority to the approach being adopted, the focus in *Lange* was on the constitutional 'text and structure' as founding an implied protection for political communication based on

[51] *Theophanous* (1994) 182 CLR 104, 131, 133.

[52] In particular, three of the seven judges of the High Court (Brennan, Dawson and McHugh JJ) dissented in *Theophanous* and *Stephens*.

[53] For instance, in *McGinty* v. *Western Australia* (1996) 186 CLR 140, 235–6, McHugh J described the reasoning in *ACTV* as 'fundamentally wrong and [an] alteration of the Constitution without the authority of the people under section 128 of the Constitution' and the then newest member of the High Court, Gummow J, also cautioned that '[t]o adopt as a norm of constitutional law the conclusion that a constitution embodies a principle or a doctrine of representative democracy or representative government (a more precise and accurate term) is to adopt a category of indeterminate reference': 269–70.

[54] *Lange* v. *Australian Broadcasting Corporation* (1997) 189 CLR 520 ('*Lange*').

[55] *Ibid.*, 554–6 (noting that '[a]lthough Deane J may have intended his concurrence with the answers in *Theophanous* to extend to the explanation of them in the joint judgement, the absence of an express agreement with the reasons in that judgement raises a question as to the extent to which he concurred with the terms of the answers').

the form representative and responsible government that had been selected in the Constitution at its adoption.[56] The decision set out a different form of common law qualified privilege, replacing the two defences from *Theophanous* – a constitutional defence which had required the defendant to show reasonableness of conduct and a duty-interest privilege which had not. The *Lange* form of qualified privilege required the defendant to show reasonableness, which was spelt out in quite stringent terms. Specified elements include that the defendant should generally have reasonable grounds for believing the imputation to be true, take proper steps to verify the information's accuracy, and seek and publish a response from the person defamed except where that 'was not practicable or it was unnecessary to give the plaintiff an opportunity to respond'.[57] At the same time the High Court omitted any explicit reference to *Sullivan* in terms of these reforms and the value in protecting public or political speech, let alone the role for robust public debate. In *Lange, Sullivan* is used to point to the different US constitutional arrangements and to emphasise the character of US common law as state-based rather than nationally uniform law, unlike in Australia.[58] The 'downplaying' of *Sullivan* may not be surprising when it is remembered that the High Court was *weakening* the protection to public debate that *Theophanous* appeared to have given, even if that protection was not so clearly established because it lacked the unanimous seven member judgement of *Lange*. For all the talk of adapting defamation law to 'the varied conditions' of modern social and political life,[59] the issue of broader reform of defamation law remained on the table.

The broader Australian reform instituted by the uniform Defamation Acts some eight years after *Lange* was nevertheless a fairly modest exercise.[60] The uniform laws brought about some specific changes including limiting the ability of many corporations to sue in defamation, removing a requirement of public benefit or public interest from the justification defence in the four jurisdictions where the requirement had existed, and extending nationwide a statutory 'reasonable publication' defence adapted from the former New South Wales Defamation Act 1974, which in *Lange* satisfied the minimum required by the Constitution's protection of political communication.[61] The reasonable publication defence, although not limited to the 'political communication' protected under *Lange*, has had little practical effect and offers a notable example of

[56] *Ibid.*, 560. [57] *Ibid.*, 574. [58] *Ibid.*, 563. [59] *Ibid.*, 571 and see especially 565–6.

[60] Defamation Act 2005 (NSW); Defamation Act 2005 (Qld); Defamation Act 2005 (SA); Defamation Act 2005 (Tas); Defamation Act 2005 (Vic); Defamation Act 2005 (WA); Defamation Act 2006 (NT); Civil Law (Wrongs) Act 2002 (ACT).

[61] *Ibid.*, 575. See, e.g., Defamation Act 2005 (NSW) s 30.

the uniform law reforms' limited ambition. One of us has argued elsewhere that the older Code defence of qualified protection, which applied in Queensland and some other Australian jurisdictions, was far stronger.[62] That Code defence was based on an understanding of nineteenth-century English common law that was similar to the understanding applied by US courts in cases such as *Coleman* v. *MacLennan*,[63] a notable precursor to *Sullivan*.

As a number of commentators have observed about the Australian statutory reforms, uniformity was probably their greatest achievement (and even then uniformity was not absolute).[64] Achieving uniformity may have been the main purpose of the States and Territories in agreeing to the new regime, especially when compared with the widely criticised federal bill that was being threatened by the then Attorney-General.[65] As such, it was probably a preferable solution to that threat. But there is little to suggest that more substantial reform is likely soon. The uniform defamation laws leave much of common law defamation in place and, given the existing statutory aim of promoting uniformity and the difficulty of reaching agreement across all jurisdictions for any future statutory reform, common law development through cases may be the most likely medium-term avenue for change in Australian defamation law.

It is worth contrasting here the steps taken in the UK to providing greater protection for speech within defamation law post-*Sullivan*. The transition was evident in 1993 with the House of Lords in *Derbyshire*.[66] At issue here was the question of whether the common law should extend its support for free speech to preclude a local authority (local council) from suing for defamation. The House of Lords held that it should. Lord Keith (with Lords Griffith, Goff, Browne-Wilkinson and Woolf concurring) stated:

> It is of the highest public importance that a democratically elected governmental body, or indeed any governmental body, should be open to uninhibited public criticism. The threat of a civil action for defamation must inevitably have an inhibiting effect on freedom of speech. ... [This idea was] endorsed by the Supreme Court of the United States in *New York Times Co* v. *Sullivan* ... While ... related most directly to the provisions of the American Constitution concerned with securing freedom of speech, the public interest considerations

[62] See Andrew T Kenyon and Sophie Walker, 'The Cost of Losing the Code: Historical Protection of Public Debate in Australian Defamation Law' (2014) 38 *Melbourne University Law Review* 554.

[63] 78 Kan 711 (1908) and see above n 18.

[64] See the discussion in Andrew T Kenyon. 'Six Years of Australian Uniform Defamation Law: Damages, Opinion and Defence Meanings' (2012) 35 *University of NSW Law Journal* 31, 31–2.

[65] *Ibid.*, 31. [66] *Derbyshire* [1993] AC 534.

which underlaid [the decision] are no less valid in this country. What has been described as 'the chilling effect' induced by the threat of civil actions for libel is very important.[67]

That explicit acceptance of *Sullivan*'s analysis of a chilling effect was a marked change from earlier judicial statements.[68] The robust reasoning in *Derbyshire* indeed suggested that free speech would gain greater protection in English defamation law – something that Lord Denning had argued was open in the early 1980s, when suggesting that qualified privilege should apply to mass media publications of public interest material based on responsible and reliable sources.[69] That sort of reform did not come until the end of the 1990s in *Reynolds* v. *Times Newspapers*.[70] Again reference was made to *Sullivan* although without suggesting it was a direct influence on the conclusions reached. Rather, the emphasis was on the imminent effect of the HRA making Article 10 of the ECHR a direct part of UK law,[71] as well as the existence of the chilling effect recognised in *Derbyshire*.[72] More generally there was reference to the need to give 'appropriate weight, in today's conditions, to the importance of freedom of expression by the media on all matters of public concern'.[73]

The approach in *Reynolds* to how free speech should affect defamation law was to acknowledge both the chilling effect recognised in *Derbyshire* and the constitutional change brought by the HRA but to present these as challenges that could be dealt with by a generous approach to existing defences.[74] As

[67] *Ibid.*, 547–8. [68] See e.g., *Blackshaw* v. *Lord* [1983] 2 All ER 311.

[69] Alfred Denning, *What Next in the Law?* (London: Butterworths, 1982) 192.

[70] *Reynolds* v. *Times Newspapers* [2001] 2 AC 127 ('*Reynolds*').

[71] In *Derbyshire* [1993] AC 534, 551 there was also reference made to Article 10 ECHR which although not yet implemented in the UK was a convention that the UK had 'adhered' to, but Lord Keith concluded:

> I have reached my conclusion upon the common law of England without finding any need to rely upon the European Convention. My noble and learned friend, Lord Goff of Chieveley, in *Attorney-General* v. *Guardian Newspapers Ltd (No 2)* [1990] 1 AC 109, at p 283–4, expressed the opinion that in the field of freedom of speech there was no difference in principle between English law on the subject and Article 10 of the Convention. I agree, and can only add that I find it satisfactory to be able to conclude that the common law of England is consistent with the obligations assumed by the Crown under the treaty in this particular field.

[72] See *Reynolds* [2001] 2 AC 127, 198 (Lord Nicholls). That *Sullivan* was only mentioned briefly suggests its details were not considered to be a suitable model for the UK; see also 208–9 (Lord Steyn) noting 'Counsel for the newspaper did not invite your Lordships to develop English law in line with the landmark case of *New York Times Co* v. *Sullivan*'.

[73] *Reynolds* [2001] 2 AC 127, 204 (Lord Nicholls).

[74] *Ibid.* As well, Lord Steyn noted a 'liberal' approach on the part of the European Court of Human Rights to questions such as the high value of 'speech about political matters' and 'the dynamics of the role of the press': *ibid.*, 215.

with the Australian High Court in *Lange*, change in England took the form of expanding qualified privilege. However, rather than limiting the defence to situations of political speech, it was extended to all matters of 'public concern'. This was seen to assist in complying with Article 10 and the judgements of the European Court of Human Rights. But it was also, Lord Nicholls suggested, the preferable way to frame the matter.[75] Concern to allow a broad scope for speech on matters of public interest may also be seen in Lord Nicholls' framing of the standard of 'responsible' publication with a range of enumerated factors wrapped up with a final statement that deference should be given to editorial judgement.[76] Further, by positing the reform as a response to changing social conditions,[77] but not entirely inconsistent with earlier authority,[78] Lord Nicholls sought to dissipate any suggestion that this was simply an exercise in forced 'Europeanisation' of English law as a result of the HRA. He framed the change instead as a moderate and deliberated exercise in law reform for the domestic environment.

The reasoning in *Reynolds* may help to explain the initial reaction. While many commentators hailed *Reynolds* privilege as a 'marked liberalisation' of defamation law,[79] some courts initially downplayed the doctrinal novelty of the responsible journalism defence put forward in *Reynolds*, leading to restrictive applications of the defence in judgements.[80] On the other hand, the effect of *Reynolds* on news production processes appears to have been greater (although not as great as *Sullivan*'s effect in the US).[81] In 2006, the House of Lords in *Jameel* v. *Wall Street Journal Europe* sought to clarify the scope of the defence by rejecting the restrictive approach of lower courts.[82] But it was not until the UK Supreme Court's decision in *Flood* v. *Times Newspapers*[83] that Lord Phillips confirmed (with other judges expressly or tacitly agreeing) the existence of a *Reynolds*

75 *Reynolds* [2001] 2 AC 127, 200–4. 76 *Ibid.*, 205.

77 *Ibid.*, 195 (noting '[t]he circumstances in which the public interest requires a communication to be protected in the absence of malice depend upon current social conditions. The requirements at the close of the twentieth century may not be the same as those of earlier centuries or earlier decades of this century').

78 *Ibid.* ('[t]hrough the cases [on qualified privilege] runs the strain that, when determining whether the public at large had a right to know the particular information, the court has regard to all the circumstances').

79 For instance, Kevin Williams, 'Defaming Politicians: The Not So Common Law' (2000) 63 *Modern Law Review* 748, 754.

80 Of the twenty '*Reynolds*' cases litigated prior to 2006, only three were successful: see Andrew Scott, 'The Same River Twice? *Jameel* v. *Wall Street Journal Europe*' (2007) 12 *Communications Law* 52.

81 See, e.g., Andrew T Kenyon, *Defamation: Comparative Law and Practice* (Abingdon: UCL Press, 2006) ch 7; Russell L Weaver, Andrew T Kenyon, David F Partlett and Clive P Walker, *The Right to Speak Ill: Defamation, Reputation and Free Speech* (Durham, NC: Carolina Academic Press, 2006) ch 8.

82 *Jameel* [2007] 1 AC 359. 83 *Flood* v. *Times Newspapers* [2012] 2 AC 273.

'public interest' defence now divorced from its doctrinal origins as a form of qualified privilege. Had it not been for other events that might have been the final contemporary step in fashioning a public interest defence in English defamation law – although reservations were still expressed about the final extent of the reforms, as well as their achievements to date in reducing the 'chilling effect' of defamation law.[84]

By this stage a number of controversies had emerged which had pushed into the public domain the question of English defamation law's ability to give adequate account of reputation and especially free speech. Concerns mounted towards something like a crisis. Perhaps most prominent was the fear widely ventilated in the media, parliamentary debates and other arenas about London becoming a destination for 'libel tourism'. This followed cases such as *Bin Mahouz* v. *Ehrenfeld*,[85] where a handful of UK publications online were deemed sufficient for proceedings to be launched by Saudi Arabian billionaire Bin Mahouz against American journalist Rachel Ehrenfeld whose book *Funding Evil* was the subject of his complaint. Through such cases, English law's perceived plaintiff-friendly character and generous geographical application resulted in a major political conflagration,[86] with legislative responses on both sides of the Atlantic.[87] And there were other popular causes, including the much-publicised dispute between the British Chiropractic Association and science writer Simon Singh.[88] That case, along with publicity around disputes over academic publication of scientific research, raised concerns about the law's potential for

[84] See, e.g., Eric Barendt, 'Reynolds Privilege and Reports of Police Investigations' (2012) 4 *Journal of Media Law* 1.

[85] *Bin Mahfouz* v. *Ehrenfeld* [2005] EWHC 1156.

[86] There is a large literature on libel tourism, including Richard Garnett and Megan Richardson, 'Libel Tourism or Just Redress: Reconciling the (English) Right to Reputation with the (American) Right to Free Speech in Cross-Border Libel Cases' (2009) 5 *Journal of Private International Law* 471; David Partlett and Barbara McDonald, 'International Publications and Protection of Reputation: A Margin of Appreciation but not Subservience' (2011) 62 *Alabama Law Review* 477; and Lili Levi, 'The Problem of Trans-National Libel' (2012) 60 *American Journal of Comparative Law* 507.

[87] On the US side results were prompt, with the federal legislative response taking the form of a 'Securing the Protection of our Enduring and Established Constitutional Heritage Act' 2010 (acronym the SPEECH Act). But this was a focussed exercise, passed to make clear that judgements given by English and other foreign courts in defamation cases would not be enforceable in the US unless US legal standards of liability would also have been met; query whether it was even necessary given the power already existed in US courts to deny enforcement on public policy grounds: see Garnett and Richardson, 'Libel Tourism or Just Redress', above n 86.

[88] See *British Chiropractic Association* v. *Singh* [2011] 1 WLR 133 and, e.g., the NGO Sense about Science's campaign 'Keep Libel Laws out of Science': www.senseaboutscience.org/pages/keep-libel-laws-out-of-science.html.

restricting critical commentary. Eventually these events were swept up in a thoroughgoing consultation about the need for defamation law reform,[89] with numerous experts along with interest groups and the media participating in the debate.[90]

Some of the new provisions in the Defamation Act 2013 were specific responses to particular raised concerns, including a form of single publication rule and restrictions on jurisdiction designed to limit the capacity for foreign libel disputes to use English courts.[91] However, other notable reforms were also made, such as replacing *Reynolds* with a statutory 'public interest' defence. It applies to publications on a matter of public interest where the defendant reasonably believed publication was in the public interest – although the degree to which that effects substantial change from *Reynolds* and the later cases is difficult to predict.[92] There is also a specific requirement for 'serious harm' as a threshold for what is 'defamatory', echoing requirements in some first instance judgements.[93] Further, a defence for defamatory statements in scientific and academic articles in peer reviewed journals may address some of the concerns about scientific debate.[94] It has been argued that more could have been done to support both free speech and reputation,[95] and in substantive terms the balance remains very different from in the US. Yet commentators have noted that it is remarkable that so much has been sought in one piece of legislation – with the new Act characterised as 'the most wide-ranging reforms that have ever been attempted to the law of defamation of England and Wales' and 'by any measure, a major achievement'.[96] In that sense at least, the reform package can be compared with the transformations of *Sullivan*.

On the other hand, we see little prospect of the US approach adopted to newsworthy publications in *Hill* gaining traction in the UK or other parts of the common law world when it comes to privacy law.[97] In Australia, for

[89] Including an 85-page report by a Libel Working Group convened by the Lord Chancellor and Ministry of Justice, which anticipated several of the Act's reforms: Report of the Libel Working Group, Ministry of Justice (March 2010). For an outline of the reform process, see James Price and Felicity McMahon (eds), *Blackstone's Guide to The Defamation Act 2013* (Oxford: Oxford University Press, 2013) 1–10.

[90] Popular public events, such as charity concerts in London's West End to raise funds and awareness of the calls for reform, could suggest the more inclusive public debate of analysts such as Dahlgren; see, e.g., Peter Dahlgren, *Media and Political Engagement: Citizens, Communication, and Democracy* (New York: Cambridge University Press, 2009).

[91] Defamation Act 2013 (UK) ss 8 and 9. [92] *Ibid.*, s 4.

[93] *Ibid.*, s 1. See, e.g., *Thornton* v. *Telegraph Media Group* [2011] 1 WLR 1985, [90],[91] (Tugendhat J).

[94] Defamation Act 2013 (UK) s 6. [95] For example, Mullis and Scott, above n 41.

[96] Matthew Collins, *Collins on Defamation* (Oxford: Oxford University Press, 2014) ix.

[97] A partial exception is New Zealand where the Court of Appeal fashioned a public disclosure of private facts tort in *Hosking* v. *Runting* [2005] 1 NZLR 1 with a defence for matters of 'legitimate public concern', referencing the Second Restatement private

example, courts by and large continue to rely on the traditional action for breach of confidence in the few cases before them, construed liberally to deal with modern situations of invasion of privacy,[98] and it is not entirely clear yet whether there will be a full 'public interest' defence (although some judges have hinted that there should be) in media cases.[99] In the UK, where a pressing consideration has been the effect of the HRA bringing into UK law the ECHR's Article 8 protection for private and family life along with Article 10 protection of freedom of expression, courts have pronounced a cause of action for misuse of private information drawing directly on the language of the Convention[100] as a next step beyond the development of breach of confidence during the lead-up to and immediately following the HRA's coming into force in 2000.[101] It is worth noting that some of these earlier developments occurred well before the HRA, and had to do with local socioeconomic conditions – including concerns about celebrity and tabloid journalism,[102] combined with some acknowledgment of the ECHR[103] – rather than any

facts tort (but even here it is clear that the Court of Appeal did not equate legitimate public concern simply with newsworthiness).

[98] See, e.g., the discussion of Gleeson CJ in *Australian Broadcasting Corporation* v. *Lenah Game Meats* (2001) 208 CLR 199 ('*Lenah*'), 224–5 and further *Giller* v. *Procopets* (2009) 24 VR 1 ('*Giller*'), 90 (Neave JA), and *Wilson* v. *Ferguson* [2015] WASC 15 (Mitchell J, following *Giller* in a sexting/revenge porn case); and see generally Megan Richardson and Michael Rivette, 'Australia' in NA Moreham and Mark Warby (eds), *Tugendhat and Christie: The Law of Privacy and the Media*, 3rd ed (Oxford: Oxford University Press, 2016).

[99] See especially *Lenah* (2001) 208 CLR 199, 224, where Gleeson CJ agreed with UK authorities on breach of confidence as subject to a public interest defence, although adding 'to adapt it to the Australian context, it is necessary to add a qualification concerning the constitutional freedom of political communication'.

[100] Notable authorities for the latter development include the Court of Appeal in *McKennitt* v. *Ash* [2008] QB 73 and *Murray* v. *Express Newspapers* [2009] Ch 481. See also Lord Nicholls in *Campbell* v. *MGN* [2004] 2 AC 457, 465: 'The continuing use of the phrase "duty of confidence" and the description of the information as "confidential" is not altogether comfortable ... The more natural description today is that such information is private. The essence of the tort is better encapsulated now as misuse of private information', and in *OBG* v. *Allan* [2008] 1 AC 1 at 72: '[a]s the law has developed breach of confidence, or misuse of confidential information, now covers two distinct causes of action, protecting two different interests: privacy, and secret ('confidential') information'. For overviews of the case developments, see the helpful discussion of Lord McFarlane MR and Sharp LJ in *Google* v. *Vidal-Hall* [2015] EWCA Civ 311 [17]–[51].

[101] For example, *Campbell* v. *MGN* [2004] 2 AC 457, 464–5 (Lord Nicholls); 472 (Lord Hoffmann); and 480 (Lord Hope) identifying Lord Goff in *Attorney-General* v. *Guardian Newspapers (No 2)* [1990] 1 AC 109 ('*Guardian Newspapers*') as setting the tone for modern breach of confidence as a doctrine that could be used to vindicate privacy as required under Article 8 of the European Convention.

[102] Richardson et al, *Breach of Confidence*, above n 4.

[103] See Lord Goff in *Guardian Newspapers* [1990] 1 AC 109, 283–4, and further discussion in *Derbyshire* [1993] AC 534 above nn 66–67 and accompanying text.

consideration of following the line laid down for privacy cases in *Hill* (or *Sullivan*, for that matter).

## 16.3 Conclusion: 'chilling effects' and 'robust' debate

*Sullivan* was a pivotal case in US law and one that clearly influenced law elsewhere. But that influence has only extended to part of *Sullivan*'s rationale. With respect to defamation, the changes have also followed some of the key arguments underpinning *Sullivan* but they have not engaged closely with the reasoning as a whole. In short, the chilling effect of traditional defamation law has been repeatedly recognised – examples are clear from England, Australia and elsewhere. But the value of public debate that is 'uninhibited, robust and wide-open' has received less recognition in defamation law outside the US.

As the US Supreme Court found in 1964, traditional defamation law is too restrictive of speech. In recent decades, Commonwealth courts agreed. The 'common convenience and welfare of society',[104] to use a rationale from traditional qualified privilege, now demands greater protection for speech. While one might note that doctrinal change came decades earlier in the US than elsewhere, it is also possible to see the recognition in nineteenth-century English cases.[105] The ideas from those cases were taken up in some US state decisions, such as *Coleman* v. *MacLennan*,[106] and were subsequently constitutionalised in the US through *Sullivan*. Thus, they 'returned' in a sense to Commonwealth law via *Sullivan*, but can also be seen to have 'domestic' origins.

Overall, however, the legacy of *Sullivan* for defamation law remains very different inside and outside the US. The *style* of the US law is different in at least two ways. First, *Sullivan* is not a defence but a set of rules imposing particular burdens on categories of plaintiff; the non-US developments are all privilege-like *defences*. This is an obvious element of the US doctrine, but probably worth emphasis. The US law classifies plaintiffs more than it provides particular defences for speech that is thought deserving of protection. Elsewhere, the defences focus on the types of speech, not the classification of plaintiffs. Second, the style of protection differs in the US because the law (overtly at least) takes a rule-based or categorical approach, whereas the Commonwealth approach is one of more overt balancing of particular factors within

[104] *Toogood* v. *Spyring* (1834) 1 Cr M & R 181, 193; 149 ER 1044, 1050 (Parke B).
[105] See, e.g., Ian Loveland, *Political Libels: A Comparative Study* (Oxford: Hart, 2000).
[106] 78 Kan 711 (1908).

each case in relation to the new defences at least. Of course, there remains great discretion in the US in applying apparently clear 'rules' – do particular actions by a publisher fall within or outside some doctrinal test? Does a particular action or omission suggest recklessness as to truth? Indeed, the range of factors that US courts have considered in actual malice cases bears quite some resemblance to the sort of enquiry made under tests like *Reynolds* about whether the publisher has met the standard of 'responsible journalism'. In the early 1990s research by Brian Murchison and colleagues investigated the journalistic behaviours at issue in more than 400 actual malice cases that had been decided up until 1990. The researchers concluded that US judges have created norms for journalism in relation to researching, writing and editing stories under the actual malice standard.[107] Thus one of the apparent key differences between the US and elsewhere – using rules in defamation doctrine or balancing factors in each given case – may contain an important similarity in terms of the examination of the actions of publishers.

While the style of protection differs, the greatest contrast between US defamation law and the other jurisdictions remains the *strength* of protection. That is the 'profound difference'.[108] Indeed, even lawyers who act for US defamation plaintiffs will tend to emphasise the First Amendment's vital importance.[109] That cultural attachment to a First Amendment understanding of free speech is, not surprisingly, stronger in the US than in England or Australia. As to the strength of protection, as well as doctrinal analysis and various interview-based research which supports the assessment that US protection is far stronger, it is worth noting that some analysis of media content also tends to support it. For example, one study conducted a decade ago compared US and Australian media newspaper content some years after the developments in *Theophanous* and *Lange* and many years after *Sullivan*.[110] It analysed more than 1,400 Australian and US newspaper articles and suggested that in the US, where many defamation plaintiffs face much heavier burdens, defamatory allegations against political and especially corporate actors were published more frequently – at nearly three times the

[107] See Brian C Murchison, John Soloski, Randall P Bezanson, Gilbert Cranberg and Roselle L Wissler, '*Sullivan*'s Paradox: The Emergence of Judicial Standards of Journalism' (1994) 73 *North Carolina Law Review* 7.

[108] See Kenyon, above n 81, 261 (quoting a US defamation lawyer).

[109] *Ibid.*, 254, 256.

[110] Chris Dent and Andrew T Kenyon, 'Defamation Law's Chilling Effect: A Comparative Content Analysis of Australian and US Newspapers' (2004) 9 *Media & Arts Law Review* 89, available via http://papers.ssrn.com/sol3/papers.cfm?abstract_id=586684.

rate – than in Australia.[111] While that is only one analysis of media content, there are no obvious reasons to suggest its sample is atypical, at least with regard to ordinary newspaper reporting and commentary in these countries at that time. The difference seen through content analysis is consistent with what could be expected from the differing laws.[112]

When it comes to privacy, in contrast, courts in these non-US jurisdictions have treated the law more through ongoing incremental development with occasional larger steps forward, increasing the protection for aspects of private life while, at least in the UK, seeking to take freedom of speech into account within that process of reform. With the HRA, rights to private life and to freedom of expression were both influential in the development of privacy protection under general law. While *Sullivan* has been influential in terms of traditional defamation law having an unwarranted chilling effect – and its call to protect robust public debate will continue as a standard by which Commonwealth defamation law can be judged – for privacy, the legacy of *Sullivan* appears to be almost entirely muted. In England, a different rights regime has taken precedence, and in Australia the lack of explicit constitutional rights means matters have been left to traditional legal actions. Despite all the debates about how the law could be improved with a statutory tort or cause of action,[113] without a more substantial sense of 'crisis' about the current shape of privacy law this may be

[111] The study used a purposive sample constructed to retrieve material likely to criticise political or corporate actors, and drew material from a similar number of mainstream newspapers in each country during periods that were not dominated by any particular scandal.

[112] The content analysis could be contrasted with Frederick Schauer's comment made at about the same time as that study: 'On the Relationship between Press Law and Press Content' in Timothy E Cook (ed), *Freeing the Presses: The First Amendment in Action* (Baton Rouge: Louisiana State University Press, 2005) 51, 54. Schauer suggested – based on his own observations from some time in Australia – that Australian media did not appear to be chilled in comparison with US media, despite Australian defamation law's much higher demands on publishers. Australian news was probably more direct, perhaps more abrasive, than in the US at that time, especially for 'quality' publications. However, systematically examining newspaper reports about political and business wrongdoing suggests greater difference. This is not to say that defamation law has overwhelming influence on media content; many wider factors are important, such as the role of civil society. This can be seen in, e.g., differences between news media content in Malaysia, Singapore and Australia, all of which have, on paper, similar defamation laws: Andrew T Kenyon, 'Investigating Chilling Effects: News Media and Public Speech in Malaysia, Singapore and Australia' (2010) 4 *International Journal of Communication* 440.

[113] See, e.g., the Australian Law Reform Commission, *Serious Invasions of Privacy in the Digital Era*, ALRC Report No 123 (2014); Paul Wragg, 'Enhancing Press Freedom through Greater Privacy Law: A UK Perspective on an Australian Privacy Tort' (2014) 36 *Sydney Law Review* 619.

unlikely to happen. If anything, the 'crises' that have occurred – for instance the UK's phone-hacking scandal, business and government surveillance practices – tend to point to the limits of privacy causes of action in dealing with many contemporary problems of 'privacy', prompting alternative legal responses. On the other hand, there has been little investigation of the 'chilling effect' of privacy laws for news reporting and perhaps the time has now come to conduct some.

# Bibliography


Aalberg, Toril and James Curran (eds), *How Media Inform Democracy: A Comparative Approach*, New York: Routledge, 2012

Ali, Zarqa S, 'Media Myths and Realities in Natural Disasters' (2013) 2 *European Journal of Business and Social Sciences* 125

Ammori, Marvin, 'The "New" New York Times: Free Speech Lawyering in the Age of Google and Twitter' (2014) 127 *Harvard Law Review* 2259

Anderson, David, 'Is Libel Law Worth Reforming' (1991) 140 *University of Pennsylvania Law Review* 487

'The Failure of American Privacy Law' in Basil S Markesinis (ed), *Protecting Privacy*, Oxford: Oxford University Press, 1999

'An American Perspective' in Simon Deakin, Angus Johnston and Basil Markesinis (eds), *Markesinis and Deakin's Tort Law*, 5th ed, Oxford: Clarendon Press, 2003

'Defamation and Privacy: An American Perspective' in Simon Deakin, Angus Johnston and Basil Markesinis, *Markesinis and Deakin's Tort Law*, 6th ed, Oxford: Clarendon Press, 2008

'Weschler's Triumph' (2014) 66 *Alabama Law Review* 229

Ardia, David S, 'Reputation in a Networked World: Revisiting the Social Foundations of Defamation Law' (2010) 45 *Harvard Civil Rights-Civil Liberties Law Review* 261

Assange, Julian, *Julian Assange: The Unauthorised Autobiography*, Melbourne: Text Publishing, 2011

Assange, Julian with Jacob Applebaum, Andy Müller-Maguhn and Jérémie Zimmermann, *Cypherpunks: Freedom and the Future of the Internet*, New York: OR Books, 2012

Baker, C Edwin, 'Scope of the First Amendment Freedom of Speech' (1978) 25 *UCLA Law Review* 964

Baker, Roy, 'Extending Common Law Qualified Privilege to the Media: A Comparison of the English and Australian Approaches' (2002) 7 *Media & Arts Law Review* 87

Balkin, Jack M, 'The Future of Free Expression in a Digital Age' (2009) 36 *Pepperdine Law Review* 427

Bambauer, Derek E, 'Shopping Badly: Cognitive Biases, Communications, and the Fallacy of the Marketplace of Ideas' (2006) 77 *University of Colorado Law Review* 649

Barbas, Samantha, 'The Death of the Public Disclosure Tort: A Historical Perspective' (2010) 22 *Yale Journal of Law and the Humanities* 171

'The Sidis Case and the Origins of Modern Privacy Law' (2012) 36 *Columbia Journal of Law and the Arts* 21

Barber, Nicholas W, 'A Right to Privacy' (2003) *Public Law* 602

Barendt, Eric, *Freedom of Speech*, Oxford: Clarendon Press 1996 and 2nd ed, Oxford: Oxford University Press, 2005

'What Is the Point of Libel Law?' (1999) 52 *Current Legal Problems* 110

'Reynolds Privilege and Reports of Police Investigations' (2012) 4 *Journal of Media Law* 1

'English Privacy Law in the Light of the Leveson Report' in Normann Witzleb, David Lindsay, Moira Paterson and Sharon Rodrick (eds), *Emerging Challenges in Privacy Law: Comparative Perspectives*, Cambridge: Cambridge University Press, 2014

Barker, Kit, 'Private and Public: The Mixed Concept of Vindication in Torts and Private Law' in Stephen GA Pitel, Jason W Neyers and Erika Chamberlain (eds), *Tort Law: Challenging Orthodoxy*, Oxford: Hart Publishing, 2013

Barrett, David A, 'Declaratory Judgments for Libel: A Better Alternative' (1986) 74 *California Law Review* 847

Bartl, Benedict and Dianne Nicol, 'The Grant of Interlocutory Injunctions in Defamation Cases in Australia following the Decision in *Australian Broadcasting Corporation* v. *O'Neill*' (2006) 25 *University of Tasmania Law Review* 156

Beckett, Charlie with James Ball, *WikiLeaks: News in the Networked Era*, Cambridge: Polity Press, 2012

Bellah, Robert N, 'The Meaning of Reputation in American Society' (1986) 74 *California Law Review* 743

Benn, Stanley I, 'Privacy, Freedom and Respect for Persons' in J Roland Pennock and John W Chapman (eds), *Privacy*, NOMOS vol XIII, New York: Atherton Press, 1971

Bernal, Paul, 'A Defence of Responsible Tweeting' (2014) 19 *Communications Law* 12

Bezanson, Randall P, 'Libel Law and the Realities of Litigation: Setting the Record Straight' (1985) 71 *Iowa Law Review* 215

'The Libel Suit in Retrospect: What Plaintiffs Want and What Plaintiffs Get' (1986) 74 *California Law Review*, 789

Bezanson, Randall P, Gilbert Cranberg and John Soloski, *Libel Law and the Press: Myth and Reality*, New York: Free Press, 1987

Bilboe, Wendy, 'The Thredbo Landslide: Was It Only Media Ethics That Came Tumbling Down?' (1998) 20 *Australian Journalism Review* 88

Bing, Jon, 'Data Protection, Jurisdiction and the Choice of Law' (1999) 6 *Privacy Law & Policy Reporter* 92

Blackstone, William, *Commentaries on the Laws of England* (1765–69), Chicago: University of Chicago Press, facsimile edition, 2002

Bloustein, Edward J, 'Privacy as an Aspect of Human Dignity: An Answer to Dean Prosser' (1964) 39 *NYU Law Review* 962

Boivin, Denis, 'Accommodating Freedom of Expression and Reputation in the Common Law of Defamation' (1997) 22 *Queen's Law Journal* 229

Bollinger, Lee C, *Uninhibited, Robust, and Wide-Open: A Free Press for a New Century*, New York: Oxford University Press, 2010

Bork, Robert H, 'Neutral Principles and Some First Amendment Problems' (1971) 47 *Indiana Law Journal* 1

Brennan, William J, 'The Supreme Court and the Meiklejohn Interpretation of the First Amendment' (1965) 79 *Harvard Law Review* 1

Brown, Jennifer E, 'News Photographs and the Pornography of Grief' (1987) 2 *Journal of Mass Media Ethics* 75

Brown, Sheila, 'What's the Problem, Girls? CCTV and the Gendering of Public Safety' in Clive Norris, Jade Moran and Gary Armstrong (eds), *Surveillance, Closed Circuit Television and Social Control*, Aldershot: Ashgate, 1998

Brüggemeier, Gert, Aurelia Ciacchi and Patrick O'Callaghan (eds), *Personality Rights in European Tort Law*, Cambridge: Cambridge University Press, 2010

Burnett, Nicholas F, '*New York Times* v. *Sullivan*' in Richard Parker (ed), *Free Speech on Trial: Communication Perspectives on Landmark Supreme Court Decisions*, Tuscaloosa: University of Alabama Press, 2003

Burrows, John F, 'Invasion of Privacy' in Stephen Todd (ed), *The Law of Torts in New Zealand*, 6th ed, Wellington: Thomson Reuters, 2013

*News Media Law in New Zealand*, Wellington: Sweet & Maxwell, 1974

*News Media Law in New Zealand*, 3rd ed, Auckland: Oxford University Press, 1990

Burrows, John and Ursula Cheer, *Media Law in New Zealand*, 4th ed, Auckland: Oxford University Press, 1999

*Media Law in New Zealand*, 5th ed, Auckland: Oxford University Press, 2005

*Media Law in New Zealand*, 6th ed, Wellington: LexisNexis, 2010

Busuttil, Godwin and Patrick McCafferty, 'Interim Injunctions and the Overlap between Privacy and Libel' (2010) 2 *Journal of Media Law* 1

Butler, Petra, 'The Case for a Right of Privacy in the New Zealand Bill of Rights Act' (2013) 11 *New Zealand Journal of Public and International Law* 213

Bygrave, Lee A, *Data Privacy Law: An International Perspective*, Oxford: Oxford University Press, 2014

Cane, Peter, *The Anatomy of Tort Law*, Oxford: Hart Publishing, 1997

Carroll, Robyn and Normann Witzleb, '"It's Not Just about the Money" – Enhancing the Vindicatory Effect of Private Law Remedies' (2011) 37 *Monash University Law Review* 216

Castle, Philip, 'Journalism and Trauma: Proposals for Change' (1999) 7 *Asia Pacific Media Educator* 143

Chadwick, Paul and Jennifer Mullaly, *Privacy and the Media*, Sydney: Communications Law Centre, 1997

Cheer, Ursula, *Reality and Myth: The New Zealand Media and the Chilling Effect of Defamation Law* (PhD Thesis, University of Canterbury, Christchurch, New Zealand) http://hdl.handle.net/10092/3050

Cheer, Ursula and Sarah Rosanowski, 'The Impact of Law on Media Reporting of Earthquakes in Christchurch 2010–2011' (2013) 18 *Media & Arts Law Review* 220

Cheung, Anne SY, 'Liability of Internet Host Providers in Defamation Actions: From Gatekeepers to Identifiers', University of Hong Kong Faculty of Law Research Paper No. 2014/013, 2014, http://ssrn.com/abstract=2428566

Citron, Danielle Keats and Mary Anne Franks, 'Criminalizing Revenge Porn' (2014) 49 *Wake Forest Law Review* 345

Clarke, Richard A, Michael J Morell, Geoffrey R Stone, Cass R Sunstein and Peter Swire, *Liberty and Security in a Changing World: Report and Recommendations of The President's Review Group on Intelligence and Communications Technologies* (Washington: Office of the Director of National Intelligence, 2013)

Clayton, Richard and Hugh Tomlinson, *Privacy and Freedom of Expression*, 2nd ed, Oxford: Oxford University Press, 2010

*The Law of Human Rights*, 2nd ed, Oxford: Oxford University Press, 2009

Collins, Matthew, *The Law of Defamation and the Internet*, Oxford: Oxford University Press, 2001; 2nd ed, 2005; 3rd ed, 2010

'Five Years On: A Report Card on Australia's National Scheme Defamation Laws' (2011) 16 *Media & Arts Law Review* 317

*Collins on Defamation*, Oxford: Oxford University Press, 2014

Colonna, Liane, 'Article 4 of the EU Data Protection Directive and the Irrelevance of the EU-US Safe Harbour Program?' (2014) 4 *International Data Privacy Law* 203

Cooley, Charles Horton, *Human Nature and the Social Order*, New York: Charles Scribner's Sons, 1922

*The Two Major Works of Charles H Cooley: Social Organisation, Human Nature and the Social Order*, Glencoe: Free Press, 1956

Council of Europe, *Collected Edition of the Travaux préparatoires of the European Convention on Human Rights*, The Hague: Martinus Nijhoff, 1975

Cowen, Zelman, *The Private Man: The Boyer Lectures 1969*, Sydney: Australian Broadcasting Commission, 1969

Cowling, M (ed), *Selected Writings of John Stuart Mill*, Cambridge: Cambridge University Press, 1968

Cram, Ian, 'Political Expression, Qualified Privilege and Investigative Journalism – An Analysis of Developments in English Defamation Law Post *Reynolds* v. *Times Newspapers*' (2005) 11 *Canterbury Law Review* 143

Crocker, Jennifer and Katherine M Knight, 'Contingencies of Self-Worth' (2005) 14 *Current Directions in Psychological Science* 200

Crocker, Jennifer and Lora E Park, 'The Costly Pursuit of Self-Esteem' (2004) 130 *Psychological Bulletin* 392

Dahlgren, Peter, *Media and Political Engagement: Citizens, Communication, and Democracy*, New York: Cambridge University Press, 2009

Danay, Robert, 'The Medium Is Not the Message: Reconciling Reputation and Free Expression in Cases of Internet Defamation' (2010) 56 *McGill Law Journal* 1

De Zwart, Melissa, 'Whistleblowers and the Media: Friends or "Frenemies"?' (2013) 38 *Alternative Law Journal* 250

Dearden, Richard and Wendy Wagner, 'Canadian Libel Law Enters the 21st Century: The Public Interest Responsible Communication Defence' (2009–2010) 41 *Ottawa Law Review* 351

DeCew, Judith Wagner, 'The Scope of Privacy in Law and Ethics' (1986) 5 *Law and Philosophy* 145

Denning, Alfred, *What Next in the Law?*, London: Butterworths, 1982

Dent, Chris, 'Compensation and/or Correcting the Record: A Framework for the Regulation of (Defamatory) Speech' (2011) 16 *Media & Arts Law Review* 123

Dent, Chris and Andrew T Kenyon, 'Defamation Law's Chilling Effect: A Comparative Content Analysis of Australian and US Newspapers' (2004) 9 *Media & Arts Law Review* 89

Deppa, Joan with Maria Russell, Dona Hayes and Elizabeth Lynne Flocke, *The Media and Disasters: Pan Am 103*, New York: New York University Press, 1994

Descheemaeker, Eric, 'Protecting Reputation: Defamation and Negligence' (2009) 29 *Oxford Journal of Legal Studies* 603

'Defamation Outside Reputation: Proposals for the Reform of English Law', (2010) 18 *Tort Law Review* 133

'"Veritas non est defamatio"? Truth as a Defence in the Law of Defamation', (2011) 31 *Legal Studies* 1

'"A Man Must Take Care not to Defame his Neighbour": The Origins and Significance of the *Reynolds* Defence', Research Paper No 2013/07, University of Edinburgh School of Law, February 13, 2013

Doley, Cameron and Alastair Mullis (eds), *Carter-Ruck on Libel and Privacy*, 6th ed, London: LexisNexis, 2010

Domscheit-Berg, Daniel, *Inside WikiLeaks: My Time with Julian Assange at the World's Most Dangerous Website*, Melbourne: Scribe Publications, 2011

Dudziak, Mary, '*Brown* as a Cold War Case' (2004) 91 *Journal of American History* 32

Duelfer, Charles, *Comprehensive Report of the Special Advisor to the DCI on Iraq's WMD*, Washington DC: Central Intelligence Agency, 2004

Durant, Alan, *Meaning in the Media: Discourse, Controversy and Debate*, Cambridge: Cambridge University Press, 2010

Dworkin, Ronald, *Taking Rights Seriously*, Cambridge, MA: Harvard University Press, 1978

Elliott, Deni, 'Family Ties: A Case Study of Coverage of Families and Friends during the Hijacking of TWA Flight 847' (1988) 5 *Political Communication and Persuasion* 67

Ellwood, John P, 'Outing, Privacy and the First Amendment' (1992) 102 *Yale Law Journal* 747

Emerson, Thomas I, 'Toward a General Theory of the First Amendment' (1963) 72 *Yale Law Journal* 877

Emler, Nicholas, 'A Social Psychology of Reputation' (1990) 1 *European Review of Social Psychology* 171

Englund, Liselotte, Rebecca Forsberg and Britt-Inger Saveman, 'Survivors' Experience of Media Coverage after Traumatic Injury Events' (2013) 22 *International Emergency Nursing* 25

Erdos, David, 'Elite Supply "Blockages" and the Failure of National Bill of Rights Initiatives in Australia: A Comparative Westminster Analysis' (2008) 46 *Commonwealth & Comparative Politics* 341

Farber, Daniel, 'Afterword: Property and Free Speech' (1999) 93 *Northwestern University Law Review* 1239

Fathaigh, Ronan Ó, 'The Recognition of a Right of Reply under the European Convention' (2012) 4 *Journal of Media Law* 322

Feldman, David, 'Secrecy, Dignity or Autonomy? Views of Privacy as a Civil Liberty' (1994) 47 *Current Legal Problems* 41

'Human Dignity as a Legal Value: Part 1' [1999] *Public Law* 68

'Human Dignity as a Legal Value: Part 2' [2000] *Public Law* 61

Fenwick, Helen and Gavin Phillipson, *Media Freedom under the Human Rights Act*, Oxford: Oxford University Press, 2006

Fink, Udo, 'Protection of Privacy in the EU, Individual Rights and Legal Instruments' in Normann Witzleb, David Lindsay, Moira Paterson and Sharon Rodrick (eds), *Emerging Challenges in Privacy Law: Comparative Perspectives*, Cambridge: Cambridge University Press, 2014

Fleming, John G, 'Retraction and Reply: Alternative Remedies for Defamation' (1978) 12 *University of British Columbia Law Review* 15

Fowler, Andrew, *The Most Dangerous Man in the World: The Inside Story on Julian Assange and WikiLeaks*, Melbourne: Melbourne University Press, 2012

Franklin, Marc A, 'A Declaratory Judgment Alternative to Current Libel Law' (1986) 74 *California Law Review* 809

Freund, Paul, 'Privacy: One Concept or Many?' in J Roland Pennock and John W Chapman (eds), *Privacy*, NOMOS vol XIII, New York: Atherton Press, 1971

Fried, Charles, 'Privacy' (1968) 77 *Yale Law Journal* 475

Gajda, Amy, *The First Amendment Bubble: How Privacy and Paparazzi Threaten a Free Press*, Cambridge, MA: Harvard University Press, 2015

Garnett, Richard and Megan Richardson, 'Libel Tourism or Just Redress: Reconciling the (English) Right to Reputation with the (American) Right to Free Speech in Cross-Border Libel Cases' (2009) 5 *Journal of Private International Law* 471

Gavison, Ruth E, 'Privacy and the Limits of the Law' (1980) 89 *Yale Law Journal* 421

'Too Early for a Requiem: Warren and Brandeis were Right on Privacy vs Free Speech' (1992) 43 *South Carolina Law Review* 437

Geiringer, Claudia, 'The Principle of Legality and the Bill of Rights Act: A Critical Examination of *R* v. *Hansen*' (2008) 6 *New Zealand Journal of Public and International Law* 59

Genn, Hazel, 'Civil Justice Reform and the Role of ADR' (Paper delivered as New Zealand Law Foundation Distinguished Visiting Fellow, Christchurch, 17 September 2009)

George, Patrick, *Defamation Law in Australia*, 2nd ed, Chatswood, NSW: LexisNexis, 2011

Gerety, Tom, 'Redefining Privacy' (1977) 12 *Harvard Civil Rights-Civil Liberties Law Review* 233

Gewirtz, Paul, 'Privacy and Speech' [2001] *Supreme Court Review* 139

Giroux, Henry A, 'Totalitarian Paranoia in the Post-Orwellian Surveillance State' (2015) 29 *Cultural Studies* 108

Glaeser, Edward and Cass R Sunstein, 'Does More Speech Correct Falsehoods?' (2014) 43 *Journal of Legal Studies* 65

Goffman, Erving, *Interaction Ritual: Essays on Face-to-Face Behavior*, Garden City, NY: Anchor Books, 1967

Goldman, Alvin I and James C Cox, 'Speech, Truth, and the Free Market for Ideas' (1996) 2 *Legal Theory* 1

Golvan, Colin and Michael McDonald, *Writers and the Law*, Sydney: Law Book Co, 1986

Gould, Douglas R, 'Is Editing What Judges Are For? Judicial Review of Journalists' Editorial Decisions in Defamation Cases in the United Kingdom and European Court of Human Rights' (2008) *46 Columbia Journal of Transnational Law* 732

Gould, Kim, 'Statutory Qualified Privilege Succeeds, but Too Early for the Media to Go "Dancing in the Streets"' (2011) 16 *Media & Arts Law Review* 241

Greenwald, Glenn, *No Place to Hide: Edward Snowden, the NSA and the Surveillance State*, London: Penguin Books, 2014

Greenwalt, Kent, 'Free Speech Justifications' (1989) 89 *Columbia Law Review* 119

Grote, Rainer, 'The ECHRs rulings in *Von Hannover* v. *Germany (No.2)* and *Axel Springer AG* v. *Germany*: Rebalancing Freedom of the Press with the Respect for Privacy' (2012) 55 *German Yearbook of International Law* 639

Gunther, Gerald, 'Learned Hand and the Origins of Modern First Amendment Doctrine: Some Fragments of History' (1975) 27 *Stanford Law Review* 719

Hall, Kermit L and Melvin I Urofsky, *New York Times* v. *Sullivan: Civil Rights, Libel Law, and the Free Press*, Lawrence: University Press of Kansas, 2011

Hallin, Daniel C and Paolo Mancini, *Comparing Media Systems: Three Models of Media and Politics*, Cambridge: Cambridge University Press, 2004

Handford, Peter, 'Intentional Negligence: A Contradiction in Terms?' (2010) 32 *Sydney Law Review* 29

Haravuori, Henna, Laura Suomalainen, Noora Berg, Olli Kiviruusu and Mauri Marttunen, 'Effects of Media Exposure on Adolescents Traumatized in a School Shooting' (2011) 24 *Journal of Traumatic Stress* 70

Harris, David J, Michael O'Boyle, Edward P Bates and Carla M Buckley, *Law of the European Convention on Human Rights*, 3rd ed, Oxford: Oxford University Press, 2014

Hartshorne, John, 'An Appropriate Remedy for the Publication of False Private Information' (2012) 4 *Journal of Media Law* 93

Hawkins, Nikki A, Daniel N McIntosh, Roxane Cohen Silver and Alison E Holman, 'Early Responses to School Violence: A Qualitative Analysis of Students' and Parents' Immediate Reactions to the Shootings at Columbine High School' (2007) 4 *Journal of Emotional Abuse* 197

Healy, Thomas, *The Great Dissent: How Oliver Wendell Holmes Changed His Mind – and Changed the History of Free Speech in America*, New York: Henry Holt and Company, 2013

Heemsbergen, Luke, 'Whistleblowing and Digital Technologies: An Interview with Suelette Dreyfus' (2013) 5 *Platform: Journal of Media and Communication* 67

Heymann, Laura A, 'The Law of Reputation and the Interest of the Audience' (2011) 52 *Boston College Law Review* 1341
Hörnle, Julia, 'Google's Algorithms, Search Results and Relevancy under Data Protection Law – Whose Data Quality?' (2014) 25 *Entertainment Law Journal* 209
Horwitz, Paul, 'Free Speech as Risk Analysis: Heuristics, Biases, and Institutions in the First Amendment' (2003) 76 *Temple Law Review* 1
'The First Amendment's Epistemological Problem' (2012) 87 *Washington Law Review* 445
Howarth, David, 'Libel: Its Purpose and Reform' (2011) 74 *Modern Law Review* 845
Hughes, Kirsty, 'Photographs in Public Places and Privacy' (2009) 2 *Journal of Media Law* 159
'No Reasonable Expectation of Anonymity?' (2010) 2 *Journal of Media Law* 169
'A Behavioural Understanding of Privacy and Its Implications for Privacy Law' (2012) 75 *Modern Law Review* 806
Hunt, Chris DL, 'Conceptualizing Privacy and Elucidating Its Importance: Foundational Considerations for the Development of Canada's Fledgling Privacy Tort' (2011) 37 *Queen's Law Journal* 167
International Commission of Jurists, 'The Legal Protection of Privacy: A Comparative Survey of Ten Countries' (1972) 24 *International Social Science Journal* 413
Ipp, David, 'Themes in the Law of Torts' (2007) 81 *Australian Law Journal* 609
Irving, Helen, 'The Over-Rated Mr Clark: Putting Andrew Inglis Clark's Contribution to the Constitution into Perspective' in *'The Truest Patriotism': Andrew Inglis Clark and the Building of an Australian Nation* (Papers on Parliament No. 61, May 2014)
James, Steven, 'The Right to Privacy Catches Up with Search Engines: The Unforgettable Decision in *Google Spain* v. *AEPD*' (2014) 20 *Computer and Telecommunications Law Review* 130
Jenkins, Roy, *Churchill*, London: Macmillan, 2001
Johnston, Angus, 'Putting the Cart before the Horse? Privacy and the Wainwrights' (2004) 63 *Cambridge Law Journal* 15
Joo, Thomas W, 'The Worst Test of Truth: The "Marketplace of Ideas" as a Faulty Metaphor' (2014) 89 *Tulane Law Review* 383
Jordan, Brid, 'Reputation and Article 8: *Karakó* v. *Hungary*' (2010) 21 *Entertainment Law Review* 109
Joseph, Philip A, *Constitutional and Administrative Law in New Zealand*, 3rd ed, Wellington: Thomson Brookers, 2007
Jourard, Sidney M, 'Some Psychological Aspects of Privacy' (1966) 31 *Law and Contemporary Problems* 307
Kahan, Dan M, Hank Jenkins-Smith and Donald Braman, 'Cultural Cognition of Scientific Consensus' (2011) 14 *Journal of Risk Research* 147
Kahneman, Daniel, *Thinking Fast and Slow*, New York: Farrar, Straus and Giroux, 2011
Kalven, Harry, Jr, 'The New York Times Case: A Note on "The Central Meaning of the First Amendment"' [1964] *Supreme Court Review* 191

'Privacy in Tort Law – Were Warren and Brandeis Wrong?'(1966) 31 *Law & Contemporary Problems* 326

Kant, Immanuel, *Grounding for the Metaphysics of Morals; with On a Supposed Right to Lie because of Philanthropic Concerns*, translated by J Ellington, 3rd ed, Indianapolis: Hackett Publishing, 1993

Katz, Ellen D, 'Hobby Lobby and the Pathology of Citizens United' (2014) 9 *Duke Journal of Constitutional Law and Public Policy* 23

Kenyon, Andrew T, '*Lange* and *Reynolds* Qualified Privilege: Australian and English Defamation Law and Practice' (2004) 28 *Melbourne University Law Review* 406

*Defamation: Comparative Law and Practice*, Abingdon: UCL Press, 2006

'What Conversation? Free Speech and Defamation Law' (2010) 73 *Modern Law Review* 697

'Investigating Chilling Effects: News Media and Public Speech in Malaysia, Singapore, and Australia' (2010) 4 *International Journal of Communication* 440

'Six Years of Australian Uniform Defamation Law: Damages, Opinion and Defence Meanings' (2012) 35 *University of NSW Law Review* 31

'Protecting Speech in Defamation Law: Beyond *Reynolds*-Style Defences' (2014) 6 *Journal of Media Law* 21

Kenyon, Andrew T and Sophie Walker, 'The Cost of Losing the Code: Historical Protection of Public Debate in Australian Defamation Law' (2014) 38 *Melbourne University Law Review* 554

Kerr, Orin, 'The Fourth Amendment and the Global Internet' (2015) 67 *Stanford Law Review* 285

Kinzie, David J, James Boehnlein, Crystal Riley and Lisa Sparr, 'A Cross-cultural Study of Reactivation of Posttraumatic Stress Disorder Symptoms: American and Cambodian Psychophysiological Response to Viewing Traumatic Video Scenes' (1998) 186 *Journal of Nervous and Mental Disease* 670

Koljonen, Kari, Pentti Raittila and Jari Väliverronen, 'Crisis Journalism at a Crossroads? Finnish Journalists' Reflections on Their Profession after Two School Shooting Cases' (2011) 5 *Journalism Practice* 719

Koltay, András, *Freedom of Speech: The Unreachable Mirage*, Budapest: CompLex, 2013

Korff, Douwe, *EC Study on Implementation of Data Protection Directive: Comparative Summary of National Laws* (Cambridge, 2002) (Study Contract ETD/2001/B5-3001/A/49)

Koziol, Helmut and Alexander Warzilek (eds), *The Protection of Personality Rights against Invasions by Mass Media*, New York: Springer Wein, 2005

Krauss, Stanton D, 'An Inquiry into the Right of Criminal Juries to Determine the Law in America' (1998) 89 *Journal of Criminal Law & Criminology* 111

Krotoszynski, Ronald J, Jr, 'Responding to a World without Privacy: On the Potential Merits of a Comparative Law Perspective' in Austin Sarat (ed), *A World without Privacy: What Law Can and Should Do?*, New York: Cambridge University Press, 2015

Krueger, Joachim I, Kathleen D Vohs and Roy F Baymeister, 'Is the Allure of Self-Esteem a Mirage After All?' (2008) 63 *American Psychologist* 64

Kuner, Christopher, *Transborder Data Flows and Data Privacy Law*, Oxford: Oxford University Press, 2013

Kwok, Kelvin Hiu Fai, 'Liability of Online Service Providers for Defamatory Content: The Case of Online Discussion Forums' (2014) 130 *Law Quarterly Review* 206

Laurie, Graeme, *Genetic Privacy: A Challenge to Medico-Legal Norms*, Cambridge: Cambridge University Press, 2002

Leary, Mark R, Ellen S Tambor, Sonja K Terdal and Deborah L Downs, 'Self-esteem as an Inter-personal Monitor: The Sociometer Hypothesis' (1995) 68 *Journal of Personality and Social Psychology* 518

Leigh, David and Luke Harding, *WikiLeaks: Inside Julian Assange's War on Secrecy*, London: Guardian Books, 2011

Leveson, Right Honourable Lord Justice Brian, *An Inquiry into the Culture, Practices and Ethics of the Press*, HC 780 (2012)

Levi, Lili, 'The Problem of Trans-National Libel' (2012) 60 *American Journal of Comparative Law* 507

Lewis, Anthony, '*New York Times* v. *Sullivan* Reconsidered: Time to Return to "The Central Meaning of the First Amendment"' (1983) 83 *Columbia Law Review* 603

*Make No Law: The Sullivan Case and the First Amendment*, New York: Random House, 1991

Lewis, David, AJ Brown and Richard Moberly, 'Whistleblowing, Its Importance and the State of the Research' in AJ Brown, David Lewis, Richard Moberly and Wim Vandekerckhove (eds), *International Handbook on Whistleblowing Research*, Cheltenham: Edward Elgar, 2014

Libow, Judith A, 'Traumatized Children and the News Media' (1992) 62 *American Journal of Orthopsychiatry* 379

Lidsky, Lyrissa Barnett, 'Nobody's Fool: The Rational Audience as First Amendment Ideal' [2010] *University of Illinois Law Review* 799

Lindsay, David, 'The "Right to Be Forgotten" in European Data Protection Law' in Normann Witzleb, David Lindsay, Moira Paterson and Sharon Rodrick (eds), *Emerging Challenges in Privacy Law: Comparative Perspectives*, Cambridge: Cambridge University Press, 2014

Lobb, Ano, Nancy Mock and Paul L Hutchinson, 'Traditional and Social Media Coverage and Charitable Giving following the 2010 Earthquake in Haiti' (2012) 27 *Prehospital and Disaster Medicine* 319

Lombarte, Artemi Rallo, 'The Origins and Importance of the Right to Be Forgotten' (Keynote address presented at 'The "Right to Be Forgotten" and Beyond: Data Protection and Freedom of Expression in the Age of Web 2.0', Oxford Privacy Information Law and Society Conference University of Oxford, 12 June 2012) available via http://www.csls.ox.ac.uk/conferences/oxpilsconference2012

Loveland, Ian, *Political Libels: A Comparative Study*, Oxford: Hart Publishing, 2000

McAlister, R and C Meehan, 'An Exploration of Media Reporting of Victims of Murder and Manslaughter in Northern Ireland', *Research Report for Support after Murder Manslaughter Northern Ireland*, University of Ulster, 2011

McCrudden, Christopher, 'Human Dignity and Judicial Interpretation of Human Rights'(2008) 19 *European Journal of International Law* 655

McDonald, Barbara, 'Tort's Role in Protecting Privacy: Current and Future Directions' in Simone Degeling, James Edelman and James Goudkamp (eds), *Torts in Commercial Law*, Pyrmont, NSW: Thomson Reuters, 2011

McFarlane, Alexander, 'Victims of Trauma and the News Media' (letter to editor) (1986) 145 *Medical Journal of Australia* 664

McGonagle, Marie, *A Textbook on Media Law*, 2nd ed, Dublin: Thomson Round Hall, 2003

McNamara, Lawrence, *Reputation and Defamation*, Oxford: Oxford University Press, 2007

Macfie, Rebecca, *Tragedy at the Pike River Mine: How and Why 29 Men Died*, Wellington: Awa Press, 2013

Matthiesson, Sophie and Eric Barendt, '*Carina Trimingham* v. *Associated Newspapers*: A Right to Ridicule?' (2012) 4 *Journal of Media Law* 309

Mayton, William T, 'Toward a Theory of First Amendment Process: Injunctions of Speech, Subsequent Punishment, and the Costs of the Prior Restraint Doctrine' (1982) 67 *Cornell Law Review* 245

Mead, George H, *Mind, Self and Society from the Standpoint of a Social Behaviorist*, Chicago: University of Chicago Press, 1934

Meiklejohn, Alexander, *Free Speech and Its Relation to Self-Government*, New York: Harper, 1948

*Political Freedom: The Constitutional Powers of the People*, New York: Oxford University Press, 1960

'The First Amendment is an Absolute' [1961] *Supreme Court Review* 245

Middlebrooks, Donald M, 'Reviving Thomas Jefferson's Jury: *Sparf and Hansen* v. *United States*, Reconsidered' (2004) 46 *American Journal of Legal History* 353

Milmo, Patrick and WVH Rogers, *Gatley on Libel and Slander*, 11th ed, London: Sweet & Maxwell, 2008

Mitchell, Paul, 'The Foundations of Australian Defamation Law' (2006) 28 *Sydney Law Review* 477

'The Nature of Responsible Journalism' (2011) 3 *Journal of Media Law* 19

Moreham, NA, 'Privacy in the Common Law: A Doctrinal and Theoretical Analysis' (2005) 121 *Law Quarterly Review* 628

'Privacy in Public Places' (2006) 65 *Cambridge Law Journal* 606

'Beyond Information: Physical Privacy in English Law' (2014) 73 *Cambridge Law Journal* 350

Moreham, NA and Mark Warby (eds), *Tugendhat and Christie: The Law of Privacy and the Media*, 3rd ed, Oxford: Oxford University Press, 2016

Moreham, Nicole, 'Privacy Rights' in Mark Warby, Nicole Moreham and Iain Christie (eds), *Tugendhat and Christie: The Law of Privacy and the Media*, 2nd ed, Oxford: Oxford University Press, 2010

Morgan, Jonathan, 'Privacy, Confidence and Horizontal Effect: "Hello" Trouble' (2003) 62 *Cambridge Law Journal* 444

Morison, WL, *Report on the Law of Privacy*, Sydney: Government Printer NSW, 1973

Mulheron, Rachel, 'A Potential Framework for Privacy? A Reply to *Hello!*' (2006) 69 *Modern Law Review* 679

Muller, Denis, 'Ethics and Trauma: Lessons from Media Coverage of Black Saturday' (2010) 18 *Australian Journal of Rural Health* 5

Muller, Denis, and Michael Gawenda, *Black Saturday: In the Media Spotlight*, Melbourne: Cussonia Press, 2011

Mullis, Alastair and Cameron Doley (eds), *Carter-Ruck on Libel and Privacy*, London: LexisNexis, 2010

Mullis, Alastair and Richard Parkes (eds), *Gatley on Libel and Slander*, 12th ed, London: Sweet & Maxwell, 2013

Mullis, Alastair and Andrew Scott, 'Reframing Libel: Taking (All) Rights Seriously and Where It Leads' (2012) 63 *Northern Ireland Legal Quarterly* 3

'The Swing of the Pendulum: Reputation, Expression and the Re-Centring of English Libel Law' (2012) 63 *Northern Ireland Legal Quarterly* 27

'Tilting at Windmills: The Defamation Act 2013' (2014) 77 *Modern Law Review* 87

Murchison, Brian C, John Soloski, Randall P Bezanson, Gilbert Cranberg and Roselle L Wissler, '*Sullivan*'s Paradox: The Emergence of Judicial Standards of Journalism' (1994) 73 *North Carolina Law Review* 7

Myrdal, Gunnar, *An American Dilemma: The Negro Problem and Modern Democracy*, New York: Harper & Row, 1962

Nagel, Thomas, 'Concealment and Exposure' (1998) 27 *Philosophy & Public Affairs* 3

National Research Council of the National Academy of Science, *Protecting Individual Privacy in the Struggle against Terrorists: A Framework for Program Assessment*, Washington: National Academic Press, 2008

Norton, Jane, '*Hosking* v. *Runting* and the Role of Freedom of Expression' (2004) 10 *Auckland University Law Review* 245

Nyhan, Brendan, Jason Reifler, Sean Richey and Gary L Freed, 'Effective Messages in Vaccine Promotion: A Randomized Trial' (2014) 133 *Pediatrics* e835 DOI:10.1542/peds2013–2365

O'Laughlin, Matt J, 'Exigent Circumstances: Circumscribing the Exclusionary Rule in Response to 9/11' (2002) 70 *UMKC Law Review* 707

Palacios, Agustín, José Cueli, José Camacho, Ramón Clériga, Pablo Cuevas, Jaime Ayala and Linda Cossoff, 'The Traumatic Effect of Mass Communication in the Mexico City Earthquake: Crisis Intervention and Preventive Measures' (1986) 13 *International Review of Psycho-Analysis* 279

Palmer, Geoffrey, 'The Law of Defamation in New Zealand – Its Recent Evolution and Problems', in JF Burrows, Jeremy Finn and Stephen Todd (eds), *Law, Liberty, Legislation: In Honour of John Burrows QC*, Wellington: LexisNexis, 2008

*Reform: A Memoir*, Wellington: Victoria University Press, 2013

Pantti, Mervi, Karin Wahl-Jorgensen and Simon Cottle, *Disasters and the Media*, New York: Peter Lang Publishing, 2012

Papandrea, Mary-Rose, 'Citizen Journalism and the Reporter's Privilege' (2007) 91 *Minnesota Law Review* 515

Parker, Richard B, 'A Definition of Privacy' (1974) 27 *Rutgers Law Review* 275

Parkes, Richard, 'Privacy, Defamation and False Facts', in Mark Warby, Nicole Moreham and Iain Christie (eds), *Tugendhat and Christie: The Law of Privacy and the Media*, 2nd ed, Oxford: Oxford University Press, 2011

Parkes, Richard and Alastair Mullis (eds), *Gatley on Libel and Slander*, 12th ed, London: Sweet & Maxwell, 2013

Partlett, David F, 'Tort Liability and the American Way: Reflections on Liability for Emotional Distress' (1997) 45 *American Journal of Comparative Law* 171

'The Libel Tourist and the Ugly American: Free Speech in an Era of Modern Global Communications' (2009) 47 *University of Louisville Law Review* 629

'Fifty Years Decline in Privacy: The Forgotten Right to be Forgotten and Forgiven', Uppsala University Sweden, September 2014

Partlett, David and Barbara McDonald, 'International Publications and Protection of Reputation: A Margin of Appreciation but Not Subservience' (2011) 62 *Alabama Law Review* 477

Payne, Christopher F, 'Handling the Press' (1994) 3 *Disaster Prevention and Management* 24

Pearson, Mark, *The Journalist's Guide to Media Law*, St Leonards: Allen & Unwin, 1997

Perez-Lugo, Marla, 'Media Uses in Disaster Situations: A New Focus on the Impact Phase' (2004) 74 *Sociological Inquiry* 210

Pfefferbaum, Betty, Robin H Gurwitch, Nicholas B McDonald, Michael J Leftwich, Guy M Sconzo, Anne K Messenbaugh and Rosemary A Schultz, 'Posttraumatic Stress among Young Children after the Death of a Friend or Acquaintance in a Terrorist Bombing' (2000) 51 *Psychiatric Services* 386

Phillipson, Gavin, 'Transforming Breach of Confidence? Towards a Common Law Right of Privacy under the Human Rights Act' (2003) 66 *Modern Law Review* 726

'Max Mosley Goes to Strasbourg: Article 8, Claimant Notification and Interim Injunctions' (2009) 1 *Journal of Media Law* 73

'The "Global Pariah", the Defamation Bill and the Human Rights Act' (2012) 63 *Northern Ireland Legal Quarterly* 149

'Leveson, The Public Interest and Press Freedom' (2013) 5 *Journal of Media Law* 220

Phillipson, Gavin and Helen Fenwick, 'Breach of Confidence as a Privacy Remedy in the Human Rights Act Era' (2000) 63 *Modern Law Review* 660

Pickard, Victor, *America's Battle for Media Democracy: The Triumph of Corporate Libertarianism and the Future of Media Reform*, New York: Cambridge University Press, 2015

Post, Robert C, 'The Social Foundations of Defamation Law: Reputation and the Constitution' (1986) 74 *California Law Review* 691

Powell, Di, 'Media Intrusion into Grief' (1990) 57 *Media Information Australia* 24

Price, James and Felicity McMahon (eds), *Blackstone's Guide to The Defamation Act 2013*, Oxford: Oxford University Press, 2013

Prosser, William L, 'Privacy' (1960) 48 *California Law Review* 383

Rabban, David M, *Free Speech in Its Forgotten Years, 1870–1920*, Cambridge: Cambridge University Press, 1997

Rachels, James, 'Why Privacy Is Important' (1975) 4 *Philosophy & Public Affairs* 323

Redish, Martin H, *Freedom of Expression: A Critical Analysis*, Charlottesville: Michie Co, 1984

Reiman, Jeffrey H, 'Privacy, Intimacy and Personhood' (1976) 6 *Philosophy & Public Affairs* 26

Richards, Neil M, 'The Puzzle of Brandeis, Privacy and Speech' (2010) 63 *Vanderbilt Law Review* 1295

'The Dangers of Surveillance' (2013) 126 *Harvard Law Review* 1934

*Intellectual Privacy: Rethinking Civil Liberties in the Digital Age*, Oxford: Oxford University Press, 2015

Richards, Neil M and Daniel J Solove, 'Privacy's Other Path: Recovering the Law of Confidentiality' (2006) 96 *Georgetown Law Journal* 123

'Prosser's Privacy Law: A Mixed Legacy' (2010) 98 *California Law Review* 1887

Richardson, Megan and Andrew T Kenyon, 'Fashioning Personality Rights in Australia' in Andrew T Kenyon, Ng-Loy Wee Loon and Megan Richardson (eds), *The Law of Reputation and Brands in the Asia Pacific*, Cambridge: Cambridge University Press, 2012

Richardson, Megan and Michael Rivette, 'Australia' in Moreham, NA and Mark Warby (eds), *Tugendhat and Christie: The Law of Privacy and the Media*, 3rd ed, Oxford: Oxford University Press, 2016

Richardson, Megan, Michael Bryan, Martin Vranken and Katy Barnett, *Breach of Confidence: Social Origins and Modern Developments*, Cheltenham: Edward Elgar, 2012

Rishworth, Paul, 'Human Rights' (2005) *New Zealand Law Review* 87

Roberts, Andrew J, 'A Republican Account of the Value of Privacy' (University of Melbourne, Melbourne Legal Studies Research Paper No. 673, 2013) http://ssrn.com/abstract=2369680

Robertson, Arthur Henry (ed), *Privacy and Human Rights: Reports and Communications Presented at the Third International Colloquy about the European Convention on Human Rights*, Manchester University Press: Manchester, 1973

Robertson, Geoffrey and Andrew Nicol, *Media Law*, 5th ed, Penguin Books: London, 2007

Rolph, David, 'Preparing for a Full-Scale Invasion? Truth, Privacy and Defamation' (2007) 25 *Communications Law Bulletin* 5

*Reputation, Celebrity and Defamation Law*, Aldershot: Ashgate, 2008

'A Critique of the National, Uniform Defamation Laws' (2008) 16 *Torts Law Journal* 207

'Showing Restraint: Interlocutory Injunctions in Defamation Cases' (2009) 14 *Media & Arts Law Review* 255

'Publication, Innocent Dissemination and the Internet after *Dow Jones & Co* v. *Gutnick*' (2010) 33 *University of NSW Law Journal* 562

'Irreconcilable Differences?' Interlocutory Injunctions for Defamation and Privacy' (2012) 17 *Media & Arts Law Review* 170

'Splendid Isolation? Australia as a Destination for Libel Tourism' (2012) 18 *Australian International Law Journal* 79

Rowbottom, Jacob, 'In the Shadow of the Big Media: Freedom of Expression, Participation and the Production of Knowledge Online' [2014] *Public Law* 491

Sawer, Geoffrey, *A Guide to Australian Law for Journalists, Authors, Printers and Publishers*, Melbourne: Melbourne University Press, 1949; 2nd ed, Melbourne: Melbourne University Press, 1968; 3rd ed, Melbourne: Melbourne University Press, 1984

Scanlon, Joseph T, Rudy Luukko and Gerald Morton, 'Media Coverage of Crises: Better than Reported, Worse than Necessary' (1978) 55 *Journalism Quarterly* 68

Scanlon, Joseph and Conrad McCullum, 'Media Coverage of Mass Death: Not Always Unwelcome' (1999) 14 *Australian Journal of Emergency Management* 55

Scanlon, Thomas, 'A Theory of Freedom of Expression' (1972) 1 *Philosophy & Public Affairs* 204

Schauer, Frederick, *Free Speech: A Philosophical Enquiry*, Cambridge: Cambridge University Press, 1982

'Reflections on the Value of Truth' (1991) 41 *Case Western Reserve Law Review* 699

'Uncoupling Free Speech' (1992) 92 *Columbia Law Review* 1321

'Can Public Figures Have Private Lives?' in Ellen Frankel Paul, Fred D Miller, Jr and Jeffrey Paul (eds), *The Right to Privacy*, Cambridge: Cambridge University Press, 2000

'On the Relationship between Press Law and Press Content' in Timothy E Cook (ed), *Freeing the Presses: The First Amendment in Action*, Baton Rouge: Louisiana State University Press, 2005

'Harm(s) and the First Amendment' [2011] *Supreme Court Review* 81

*'Free Speech on Tuesdays'* (University of Virginia, Public Law and Legal Theory Research Paper Series, Paper No. 2014-10) http://ssrn.com/abstract=2387009

Schils, Edward, 'Privacy: Its Constitution and Vicissitudes' (1966) 31 *Law and Contemporary Problems* 281

Schwartz, Bernard, *Unpublished Opinions of the Warren Court*, New York: Oxford University Press, 1985

Scordato, Marin, 'The International Legal Environment for Serious Political Reporting Has Fundamentally Changed: Understanding the Revolutionary New Era of English Defamation Law' (2007) 40 *Connecticut Law Review* 165

Scott, Andrew, 'The Same River Twice? *Jameel* v. *Wall Street Journal Europe*' (2007) 12 *Communications Law* 52

Seo, Mihye, Shaojing Sun, Andy J Merolla and Shuangyue Zhang, 'Willingness to Help Following the Sichuan Earthquake: Modelling the Effects of Media Involvement, Stress, Trust, and Relational Resources' (2012) 39 *Communication Research* 3

Shearer, Ann, *Survivors and the Media*, London: Broadcasting Standards Council, 1991

Shillito, Richard and Eric Barendt, 'Libel Law' (1999) 4 *Yearbook of Copyright and Media Law* 370

Simpson, Roger and William Coté, *Covering Violence: A Guide to Ethical Reporting about Victims and Trauma*, 2nd ed, New York: Columbia University Press, 2006

Smith, Anthony F, 'Actions for Breach of Confidence' in Carol Bartlett (ed), *Current Legal Developments: Media Law Seminars*, Clayton: Monash Law Press, 1985

Smolla, Rodney A, *The First Amendment: Freedom of Expression, Regulation of Mass Media, Freedom of Religion*, Durham, NC: Carolina Academic Press, 1999

Smolla, Rodney A and Michael J Gaertner, 'The Annenberg Libel Reform Proposal: The Case for Enactment' (1989) 31 *William & Mary Law Review* 25

Soloski, John and Randall P Bezanson (eds), *Reforming Libel Law*, New York: Guilford Press, 1992

Solove, Daniel J, 'Conceptualizing Privacy' (2002) 90 *California Law Review* 1087

'A Taxonomy of Privacy' (2006) 154 *University of Pennsylvania Law Review* 477

*The Future of Reputation: Gossip, Rumor, and Privacy on the Internet*, New Haven: Yale University Press, 2007

'Introduction: Privacy, Self-Management and the Consent Dilemma' (2013) 26 *Harvard Law Review* 1880

Spielmann, Dean and Leto Cariolou, 'The Right to Protection of Reputation under the European Convention on Human Rights' in Dean Spielmann, M Tsirli and P Voyatzis (eds), *The European Convention on Human Rights, A Living Instrument: Essays in Honour of Christos L Rozakis*, Brussels: Bruylant, 2011

Stapleton, Jane, 'In Restraint of Tort', in Peter Birks (ed), *The Frontiers of Liability*, vol 2, Oxford: Oxford University Press, 1994

'Duty of Care: Peripheral Parties and Alternative Opportunities for Deterrence' (1995) 111 *Law Quarterly Review* 301

'Duty of Care Factors: A Selection from the Judicial Menus', in Peter Cane and Jane Stapleton (eds), *The Law of Obligations: Essays in Honour of John Fleming*, Oxford: Clarendon Press, 1998

'Duty of Care and Economic Loss: A Wider Agenda' (1999) 107 *Law Quarterly Review* 249

'Comparative Economic Loss: Lessons from Case-Law Focused "Middle Theory"' (2002) 50 *UCLA Law Review* 531

'The Golden Thread at the Heart of Tort Law: Protection of the Vulnerable' (2003) 24 *Australian Bar Review* 135

Svantesson, Dan Jerker B, *Extraterritoriality in Data Privacy Law*, Copenhagen: Ex Tuto Publishing, 2013

Swann, William B, Jr, Christine Chang-Schneider and Katie Larsen McClarty, 'Yes, Cavalier Attitudes Can Have Pernicious Consequences' (2008) 63 *American Psychologist* 65

Tan, David, 'The Reynolds Privilege in a Neo-Confucianist Communitarian Democracy: Reinvigorating Freedom of Political Communication in Singapore' [2011] *Singapore Journal of Legal Studies* 456

Tarantino, Bob, 'Chasing Reputation: The Argument for Differential Treatment of "Public Figures" in Canadian Defamation Law' (2010) 48 *Osgoode Hall Law Journal* 595

Tsai, Robert L, *Eloquence and Reason: Creating a First Amendment Culture*, New Haven: Yale University Press, 2008

van den Haag, Ernest, 'On Privacy' in J Roland Pennock and John W Chapman (eds), *Privacy*, NOMOS vol XIII, New York: Atherton Press, 1971

Varuhas, Jason NE, 'The Concept of "Vindication" in the Law of Torts: Rights, Interests and Damages' (2014) 34 *Oxford Journal of Legal Studies* 253

Vasterman, Peter, C Joris Yzermans and Anja JE Dirkzwager, 'The Role of the Media and Media Hypes in the Aftermath of Disasters' (2005) 27 *Epidemiologic Reviews* 107

Veeder, Van Vechten, 'The History and Theory of the Law of Defamation' (1903) 3 *Columbia Law Review* 546

Velu, J, 'The European Convention on Human Rights and the Right to Respect for Private Life, the Home and Communications' in Arthur Henry Robertson (ed), *Privacy and Human Rights: Reports and Communications Presented at the Third International Colloquy about the European Convention on Human Rights*, Manchester University Press: Manchester, 1973

Volokh, Eugene, 'Freedom of Speech and Information Privacy: The Troubling Implications of a Right to Stop People from Speaking about You' (2000) 52 *Stanford Law Review* 1049

Wacks, Raymond, *The Protection of Privacy*, London: Sweet & Maxwell, 1980

*Privacy and Press Freedom*, London: Blackstone Press, 1995

*Privacy and Media Freedom*, Oxford: Oxford University Press, 2013

Waldron, Jeremy, 'Dignity and Defamation: The Visibility of Hate' (2009) 123 *Harvard Law Review* 1596

Walker, Clive and Russell L Weaver, 'Libelocracy' (2014) 41 *Journal of Malaysian and Comparative Law* 69

Walker, Sally, *The Law of Journalism in Australia*, Sydney: Law Book Co, 1989

Walsh-Childers, Kim, Norman Lewis and Jeff Neely, 'Twice Victimized: Lessons from the Media Mob at Virginia Tech', Research Paper, University of Florida, August 2008

'Listeners, Not Leeches: What Virginia Tech Survivors Needed from Journalists'(2011) 26 *Journal of Mass Media Ethics* 191

Warby, Mark, Nicole Moreham and Iain Christie (eds), *Tugendhat and Christie: The Law of Privacy and the Media*, 2nd ed, Oxford: Oxford University Press, 2011

Warren, Samuel D and Louis D Brandeis, 'The Right to Privacy' (1890) 4 *Harvard Law Review* 193

Waters, Richard D, 'Tracing the Impact of Media Relations and Television Coverage on US Charitable Relief Fundraising: An Application of Agenda-Setting Theory across Three Natural Disasters' (2013) 25 *Journal of Public Relations Research* 329

Weaver, Russell L, *Understanding the First Amendment*, 5th ed, New Providence, NJ: LexisNexis, 2014

Weaver, Russell L, Catherine Hancock, Donald E Lively, Steven I Friedland and Wendy B Scott, *Inside Constitutional Law: What Matters and Why*, Austin, TX: Wolters Kluwer Law & Business, 2009

Weaver, Russell L, Catherine Hancock, Donald E Lively, John C Knechtle, *The First Amendment: Cases, Problems and Materials*, 3rd ed, New Providence, NJ: LexisNexis, 2011

Weaver, Russell L, Andrew T Kenyon, David F Partlett and Clive P Walker, *The Right to Speak Ill: Defamation, Free Speech and Reputation*, Durham, NC: Carolina Academic Press, 2006

Westen, Drew, *The Political Brain: The Role of Emotion in Deciding the Fate of the Nation*, New York: Public Affairs, 2007

Westin, Alan F, *Privacy and Freedom*, New York: Atheneum, 1967

White, G Edward, 'Justice Holmes and the Modernization of Free Speech Jurisprudence: The Human Dimension' (1992) 80 *California Law Review* 391

'The First Amendment Comes of Age: The Emergence of Free Speech in Twentieth-Century America' (1996) 95 *Michigan Law Review* 299

Whitman, James Q, 'The Two Western Cultures of Privacy: Dignity versus Liberty' (2004) 113 *Yale Law Journal* 1151

Williams, George, *A Bill of Rights for Australia*, Sydney: UNSW Press, 2000

Williams, Kevin, 'Defaming Politicians: The Not So Common Law' (2000) 63 *Modern Law Review* 748

Witzleb, Normann, 'Interim Injunctions for Invasions of Privacy: Challenging the Rule in *Bonnard* v. *Perryman*?' in Normann Witzleb, David Lindsay, Moira Paterson and Sharon Rodrick (eds), *Emerging Challenges in Privacy Law: Comparative Perspectives*, Cambridge: Cambridge University Press, 2014

Witzleb, Normann and Robyn Carroll, 'The Role of Vindication in Torts Damages' (2009) 17 *Tort Law Review* 16

Wragg, Paul, 'A Freedom to Criticise? Evaluating the Public Interest in Celebrity Gossip after *Mosley* and *Terry*' (2010) 2 *Journal of Media Law* 295

'The Benefits of Privacy-Invading Expression' (2013) 64 *Northern Ireland Legal Quarterly* 187

'Enhancing Press Freedom through Greater Privacy Law: A UK Perspective on an Australian Privacy Tort' (2014) 36 *Sydney Law Review* 619

Youm, Kyu Ho, 'The Interaction between American and Foreign Libel Law: US Courts Refuse to Enforce English Libel Judgments' (2000) 49 *International and Comparative Law Quarterly* 131

Young, Hilary, 'But Names Won't *Necessarily* Hurt Me: Considering the Effect of Disparaging Statements on Reputation' (2011) 37 *Queen's Law Journal* 1

Zadro, Lisa, Kipling W Williams and Rick Richardson, 'How Low Can You Go? Ostracism by a Computer Is Sufficient to Lower Self-reported Levels of Belonging, Control, Self-esteem, and Meaningful Existence' (2004) 40 *Journal of Experimental Social Psychology* 560

Zimmerman, Dianne, 'Requiem for a Heavyweight: A Farewell to Warren and Brandeis's Privacy Tort' (1983) 68 *Cornell Law Review* 291

'False Light Invasion of Privacy: The Light That Failed' (1989) 64 *New York University Law Review* 364

Zines, Leslie, 'A Judicially Created Bill of Rights' (1994) 16 *Sydney Law Review* 166

*The High Court and the Constitution*, 5th ed, Annandale, NSW: Federation Press, 2008

Zipursky, Benjamin C, '*Snyder* v. *Phelps*, Outrageousness, and the Open Texture of Tort Law' (2011) 60 *DePaul Law Review* 473

# Index


*A* v. *B*, 142, 155
*A* v. *Norway*, 276–8, 288, 293
*AAA* v. *Associated Newspapers*, 107–8
*Abrams* v. *United States*, 58, 168–9
actual malice standard
  assessment of, 74
  in *New York Times* v. *Sullivan*, 86–7, 171, 335
Agencia Española de Protección de Datos (AEPD), 203–4
*Ajinomoto Sweeteners* v. *ASDA Stores*, 45–6
*Aksu* v. *Turkey*, 284
ALRC. *See* Australian Law Reform Commission
Ammori, Marvin, 63
Amnesty International, 228
Anderson, Pamela, 192
anonymity orders, in privacy law, 181–2
Aplin, Tanya, 14–15
Appelbaum, Jacob, 225
*Armoniene* v. *Lithuania*, 191
*Ashby* v. *White*, 300
Assange, Julian, 224–5, 241–4
  as fabulist, 243
  on Internet as facilitator of totalitarianism, 225, 228
  on mass data capture, 228–32, 239–40
*Attorney-General* v. *Guardian Newspapers Ltd (No 2)*, 345, 349
*Aubrey* v. *Editions Vice-Versa Inc*, 195
Australia
  damages awarded in, for privacy violations, 305–6
  data collection in, 236–9
    under Australian Security Intelligence Organisation Act 1979, 238–9
    under Telecommunications (Interception and Access) Amendment (Data Retention) Bill 2014, 236–7
  Defamation Act 1974 in, 37
  defamation cases involving media in, 24–5
  defamation in, public interest elements of, 316
  defamation law in, 1–2, 3–4, 82–4, 352
    reform of, 333, 340–4
  extension of qualified privilege in, 87–90
  free speech cases in, 64–5, 87–9
  implied rights in, 88
  journalism law in, 2–6
  *New York Times* v. *Sullivan* as legal influence in, 64–5
  privacy law in, 1–2, 80
  reasonable expectation of privacy in, 98–100
  reasonableness standard in, 37
*Australian Broadcasting Corporation* v. *Lenah Game Meats*, 98, 298, 349
*Australian Capital Television* v. *Commonwealth*, 87–9
Australian Law Reform Commission (ALRC), 1–2, 96–106
Australian Security Intelligence Organisation Act 1979, 238–9
*Author of a Blog* case, 112–13, 114
autonomy
  in commonwealth courts, 131–2
  defamation claims and, 318–20
  grief journalism as influence on, 131–5
  liberty and, 132
  through privacy, 131–5
  privacy claims and, 318–20
*Axel Springer* v. *Germany*, 146, 186–7
  privacy laws and, for celebrities, 188–90
  right of reputation in, 278–80, 286–90

*Ballina Shire Council* v. *Ringland*, 296
Barbas, Samantha, 169
Barendt, Eric, 3–4, 11–12, 270
Barker, Kit, 301–2
*Bartnicki* v. *Vopper*, 164–5, 183–4
Belfort, Jordan Ross, 259

Benn, Stanley, 126, 129
Bernal, Paul, 34
Bernstein, Carl, 73
Bill of Rights Act 1990 (New Zealand), 15
*Bin Mahouz* v. *Ehrenfeld*, 347–8
Blackstone, William, 295
blogs
  journalistic standards for, 30–1
  public interest communication defence by, 24–5
*Boehner* v. *McDermott*, 184
Bollinger, Lee, 171
*Bonnard* v. *Perryman*, 304, 314
*Bonnick* v. *Morris*, 43, 46
Bosland, Jason, 14–15
Brandeis, Louis, 166, 168–9, 248, 338–9
Brandis, George, 239
*Brooker* v. *Police*, 126–7
*Broome* v. *Cassell*, 297–8
Brown, Sheila, 130
Browne, John, 5
Burns, John F., 243
Burrows, John, 2–3

*Campbell* v. *MGN*, 96, 100, 131, 165, 177, 180, 195, 305, 319, 349
Canada. *See also Grant* v. *Torstar*
  defamation cases involving media in, 24–5
  defamation law in, 10, 82–4
  Supreme Court in, 18, 38–9
Canadian Association of Journalists, 31
*Cantwell* v. *Connecticut*, 85
*Carson* v. *John Fairfax & Sons*, 295–6, 297
*Cârstea* v. *Romania*, 280–1
Cash, William, 5
celebrities, privacy laws for, 187–90
*Chaplinsky* v. *New Hampshire*, 85
character, reputation compared with, 268
*Charleston* v. *News Group Newspapers*, 46
*Chase* v. *News Group Newspapers*, 44
*Chauvy* v. *France*, 273–4
Cheer, Ursula, 2–3, 15
children, reasonable expectation of privacy for, 108
civil rights
  implied rights, 88
  role of juries in protection of, 60
Civil Rights movement, 58–9
CJEU. *See* Court of Justice of the European Union
*Clague* v. *APN News and Media*, 309
claims, for defamation and privacy
  autonomy influenced by, 318–20
  complex damaging speech claims, 310
  constitutional models for, 327–9
  in EU, 317
  under Harmful Digital Communications Act, 15, 322–7
  merged of, 320–9
  under New Zealand Bill of Rights Act 1990, 327–9
  purpose of, 318–20
  statutory model of, 322
Clapper, James, 228–30
Clarke, Anthony, 101, 109
Clinton, Bill, 194
*Closer*, 246–7, 263
*Coco* v. *AN Clark*, 176–7
*Cohen* v. *California*, 79–80
*Cohen* v. *Cowles Media*, 184
*Coleman* v. *MacLennan*, 344, 350
*Commentaries on the Laws of England* (Blackstone), 295
common law systems
  constitutional court limits and, 79–80
  defamation law under, 9–11, 84–5
  dignity as value in, 80
  extension of qualified privilege in, 87–90
  First Amendment and, 75–8
  free speech in, 3–4, 74–5
  *New York Times* v. *Sullivan* and, 67–73
  privacy law in, 9–11, 84–5
  US law influenced by, 85–7
commonwealth courts, autonomy in, 131–2
Communications Decency Act, 63, 254
complex damaging speech claims, 310
conduct rule, 56
Conradt, William, 260
*Conradt* v. *NBC Universal*, 260–1
constitutionalism
  common law systems and, 79–80
  of defamation law, 9–11, 76–7
  human rights through, 61–2
  in UK, 197
  in US, 197
Contostavlos, Tulisa, 194
*Contostavlos* v. *Mendahun*, 194
Convention for the Protection of Human Rights and Fundamental Freedoms, 136
Costejo González, Mario, 204
*Costejo* ruling. *See Google Spain SL, Google Inc* v. *Agencia Española de Protección de Datos (AEPD) and Mario Costejo González*
*Couderc and Hachette Filipacchi Associés* v. *France*, 187

Court of Justice of the European Union (CJEU)
  DPD law and, 199, 204–17
    balance of rights and interests under, 214–16
    RTBF under, 212–14
    territorial scope of, 205–8
  Google and
    AEPD and, 203
    as data controller, 208–12
    RTBF requests for, 199–200
    SEOs and, 200, 202–3, 204–17
  *Google Spain SL, Google Inc* v. *Agencia Española de Protección de Datos (AEPD) and Mario Costejo González*, 198, 199–223
    DPD law and, 199, 204–17
    gaps in ruling, 218–21
    Google interpretation of, 220–1
    legal implications of, 221–3
    RTBF and, 199–202
  legals issues before, 204–17
    balance of rights and interests, 214–16
courts systems. *See also* Court of Justice of the European Union; European Court of Human Rights; US Supreme Court
  commonwealth, autonomy in, 131–2
Cowen, Zelman, 5
*Cox Broadcasting* v. *Cohn*, 164–5, 337–8
Craig, Larry, 252
*Cream Holdings* v. *Banjeree*, 181–2
criticism. *See* right to criticise
*CTB* v. *News Group Newspapers*, 165
*Cumpana* v. *Romania*, 273–4
*Curtis Publishing* v. *Butts*, 187
cypherpunk philosophy, 244
*Cypherpunks* (Assange), 225, 228

*Daboll* v. *DeMarco*, 26, 28
Dacre, Paul, 157, 161–2
damages. *See* vindication, through damages
data collection. *See also* Google
  Assange on, 228–32, 239–40
  in Australia, 236–9
    under Australian Security Intelligence Organisation Act 1979, 238–9
    under Telecommunications (Interception and Access) Amendment (Data Retention) Bill 2014, 236–7
  consent for, 242
  for defamation law, 6–8
  future of privacy rights with, 241–4
  Google as controller for, 208–12
  Manning on, 225–6, 239–40
  of metadata, 230, 235, 239
  under Patriot Act, 230
    amendments to, 233
  Snowden on, 226–7, 231, 239–40
  through surveillance, in US, 228–32
    under FISA, 228–30
    under Fourth Amendment, 234–6
    government responses to, 232–4
    under Patriot Act, 230, 233
    with PRISM program, 234–6
    search and seizures from, 234–6
    UK legal response to, 240
data privacy law, 6–8, 13–14. *See also* privacy law
  Google and
    AEPD and, 203
    as data controller, 208–12
    RTBF requests for, 199–200
    SEOs and, 200, 202–3, 204–17
  *Google Spain SL, Google Inc* v. *Agencia Española de Protección de Datos (AEPD) and Mario Costejo González* and, 198, 199–223
    CJEU and, 218–21
    DPD law and, 199, 204–17
    Google interpretation of, 220–1
    legal implications of, 221–3
    RTBF and, 199–202
Data Protection Act (DPA), 111
Data Protection Directive (DPD), 13–14, 199, 204–17
  balance of rights and interests under, 214–16
  RTBF under, 212–14
  territorial scope of, 205–8
data removal, from Google, 203
Davies, Nicola, 108
De Cew, Judith Wagner, 125
de Zwart, Melissa, 14
*Debs* v. *United States*, 60
declaration of falsity, 52
Defamation Act 1974 (Australia), 37
Defamation Act 1992 (New Zealand), 316
Defamation Act 2013 (UK), 10, 18, 40, 90
  declaration of falsity under, 52
  foundations of, 331
  free speech under, 66–7
  libel law reform under, 53
  new defamation provisions under, 348
  *Reynolds* v. *Times Newspapers* and, 90
  right to criticise under, 159
defamation claims. *See* claims, for defamation and privacy

defamation law, 83–4, 95. *See also* claims, for defamation and privacy; reputation, as right; single meaning rule
  actual malice and, assessment of, 74
  in Australia, 1–2, 3–4, 82–4, 352
    public interest elements of, 316
  autonomy influenced by, 318–20
  in Canada, 10, 17–39, 82–4 (*See also Grant* v. *Torstar*)
  in common law systems, 9–11, 84–5
  comparative analysis for, 8–9
  comparative reform of, 9–11
  constitutionalism and, 9–11, 76–7
  in courts, 2–6
  data collection for, 6–8
  in democracies, 83–4, 95
  dignity influenced by, 318–20
  discursive remedies in, 52–4
  disputes, without juries, 50
  in England and Wales, 2, 51, 82–4
  in EU, 317
  evolution of, 82–3
  free speech under, 3–4, 41
  group, 269
  as human rights issue, 5
  in journalism law, 2–6
  journalistic standards and, 53
  legislative reform proposals in, 2–6
  media reporting influenced by
    in Australia, 24–5, 94
    in Canada, 24–5
    in UK, 24–5, 91–2, 94–5
    in US, 24–5, 92–3
  negligence standards in, 33–4
  in New Zealand, 82–4, 309–30
    public interest elements of, 316–17
  privacy as distinct from, 292–3, 304–5, 310–12
    for purpose of legal remedies, 293–5
  privacy claims merged under, 320–9
  privacy law compared with, 14–16
  for public figures, 67–8, 83
  purpose of claims under, 318–20
  reasonable expectation of privacy and, 111–12
  reform of, 53
    in Australia, 333, 340–4
    after *New York Times* v. *Sullivan*, 331–50
    after *Reynolds* v. *Times Newspapers*, 345–50
    in UK, 333, 344–50
    in US, 334–9
  reporting technologies and, 6–8
  right to criticise under, 159
  severity of harm in, 34–5
  single meaning rule and, 51–7
  under Defamation Act 2013, 53
  under SPEECH Act, 347
  in UK, 310–12
    public interest elements of, 316–17
  in US, 2, 24–5, 33, 82–4, 85–7, 92–3
    reform movement for, 334–9
    Supreme Court cases, 79, 82, 85, 350
    under US Constitution, 85
  US states' determination of, 86–7
  vindication in, 295–9
    critique of, 298
*Delfi* v. *Estonia*, 198
democracy
  defamation law development under, 83–4, 95
  free speech and, 60–1
Denton, Nick, 258
*Derbyshire County Council* v. *Times Newspapers*, 341–2, 344–6
*Derry* v. *Peek*, 68
Descheemaeker, Eric, 19, 32
dignity
  defamation claims and, 318–20
  as justification for reputation as human right, 268–71
  looking-glass self theory and, 269–71, 272
  privacy claims and, 318–20
  privacy law and, 256–63
  self-esteem and, 269–71
  for Society of Professional Journalists Code of Ethics, 260
  as value, 80
*Dingle* v. *Associated Newspapers*, 295
The Dirty, 255–6
Domscheit-Berg, Daniel, 225–6, 243
*Donald* v. *Ntuli*, 182
*Douglas* v. *Hello*, 100, 305
DPA. *See* Data Protection Act
DPD. *See* Data Protection Directive
*Dun & Bradstreet* v. *Greenmoss Builders*, 67, 190–1

ECHR. *See* European Convention on Human Rights
*Editions Plons* v. *France*, 185
Ehrenfeld, Rachel, 347–8
England and Wales
  constitutional framework in, 197
  damages awarded in, for privacy violations, 305–6
  defamation law in, 2, 51, 82–4
  ECHR influence in, 196

European Charter on Human Rights in, 66
extension of qualified privilege in, 87–90
free speech in, 176
*de Libellis Famosis* in, 83
*New York Times* v. *Sullivan* as legal influence in, 66–7
privacy law in, 2, 4–5, 173–80
Public Order Act 1986 in, 176
Race Relations Act 1976 in, 176
reasonable expectation of privacy in, 100–3
right to criticise in, 157–61
Erdos, David, 340–1
European Convention on Human Rights (ECHR), 5–6, 66
Article 8
doctrinal and conceptual tensions for, 281–90
protected interests in, reputation as, 273–6
reputation as human right under, 265–7, 281–6
seriousness threshold in, 276–8, 286–90
Article 10(2), 273–6
English law influenced by, 196
free speech and, 178–9
privacy law and, 256
privacy rights under, 165, 178–9
for celebrities, 187–90
for private individuals, 190–1
reasonable expectation of privacy guidelines, 96, 103–4, 112
*Von Hannover* v. *Germany (no 2)*, public interest elements in, 151–4
European Court of Human Rights, 12–13
*Axel Springer* v. *Germany*, 146, 186–7
celebrity privacy and, 187–90
journalistic standards for, 37
jurisprudence of, 180
privacy rights and, 131–2, 136–7, 179–80
*Von Hannover* v. *Germany (no 1)*, 179–80, 188–90
*Von Hannover* v. *Germany (no 2)*, 137, 145–6, 179–80, 186–7
privacy rights in, 179–80

Falwell, Jerry, 77
*Favell* v. *Queensland Newspapers*, 298–9
*Ferdinand* v. *MGN*, 102, 109
First Amendment, US Constitution
in *Cantwell* v. *Connecticut*, 85
in *Chaplinsky* v. *New Hampshire*, 85
Civil Rights movement and, 58–9
common law rights and, 75–8
cultural power of, 165
free speech under, 3–4, 70, 86–7
freedom of press and, 140–1
Gawker's use of, 254–6
historical context for, 167–8
in *New York Times* v. *Sullivan*, 75–80, 86–7, 170, 171
*Patterson* v. *Colorado* and, 168
for private individuals, 190–1
*Smith* v. *People of the State of California* and, 85
FISA. *See* Foreign Intelligence Surveillance Act
Fleming, John, 298
*Flood* v. *Times Newspapers*, 90, 346–7
*Florida Star* v. *BJF*, 164–5, 249–50
Flynt, Larry, 77
Foreign Intelligence Surveillance Act (FISA)
data surveillance under, 228–32
US Supreme Court and, 229–30
*Foulidis* v. *Baker*, 26–7
Fourth Amendment, US Constitution, 234–6
France, privacy damages in, 305–6
free speech. *See also* First Amendment, US Constitution; freedom of press; *Grant* v. *Torstar*; *New York Times* v. *Sullivan*; public speech
in *Abrams* v. *United States*, 168–9
in Australia, 64–5, 87–9
Brandeis on, 166, 168–9
in common law systems, 3–4, 74–5
under Communications Decency Act, 63
under Defamation Act 2013, 66–7
under defamation law, 3–4, 41
democracy and, 60–1
in England and Wales, 176
European Convention on Human Rights and, 136, 178–9
European Court of Human Rights and, 179–80
under First Amendment, 3–4, 70, 86–7
Holmes on, 168
in *Jameel* v. *Wall Street Journal Europe*, 66
under *de Libellis Famosis*, 83
Mill on, 157
in *New York Times* v. *Sullivan*, 86, 167, 249
parody and, 77
privacy rights balanced with, 177–80
privacy-invading, benefits of, 141
rationale for, 138–42

free speech (cont.)
in *Reynolds* v. *Times Newspapers*, 66, 89–90
in UK, 13, 173–80
in US, 13, 166–73
methodology for, 172–3
in *Whitney* v. *California*, 168–9
freedom of press
economic survival argument for, 142–5
First Amendment arguments for, 140–1
in Germany, 145–50
under Human Rights Act 1998, 139
Impress Project and, 163
judicial approach to, 141–2
in *New York Times* v. *Sullivan*, 86, 167, 249
public figure doctrine and, 145–50
in *Axel Springer* v. *Germany*, 146
in *Von Hannover* v. *Germany (no 2)*, 137, 145–6
public interest arguments for, 137, 143
expansion of, 151–4
in *Von Hannover* v. *Germany (no 2)*, 151–4
rationale for, 138–42
right to criticise and
under Defamation Act 2013, 159
under defamation law, 159
in England and Wales, 157–61
on moral grounds, 161
role model argument for, 154–7
social value of, 139–40, 141
in UK, 142–5, 150–1
waiver argument for, 150–1
for Yellow Press, 164
*Fressoz and Roire* v. *France*, 104
*Funding Evil* (Ehrenfeld), 347–8

Gadja, Amy, 14
*Garrison* v. *Louisiana*, 86
Gavison, Ruth, 160
Gawker, 254–6, 258
Gayet, Julie, 246–7, 256, 262, 263
George, Patrick, 298–9
Gerety, Tom, 125
Germany. *See also Axel Springer* v. *Germany*; *Von Hannover* v. *Germany (no 1)*; *Von Hannover* v. *Germany (no 2)*
damages awarded in, for privacy violations, 305–6
freedom of press in, 145–50
privacy law in, for celebrities, 188–90
public figure doctrine in, 145–50
*Gertz* v. *Robert Welch*, 33, 336–7
Giggs, Ryan, 162, 165
Goodwin, Fred, 158
*Goodwin* v. *MGN*, 174
Google
as data controller, 208–12
data removal from, 203
interpretation of *Costejo* ruling, 220–1
RTBF requests for, 199–200
SEOs and, 200, 202–3
DPD application to, 204–17
link removal on, 216–17
*Google Spain SL, Google Inc* v. *Agencia Española de Protección de Datos (AEPD) and Mario Costejo González*
CJEU and, 198, 199–223
DPD law and, 199, 204–17
gaps in ruling, 218–21
Google interpretation of, 220–1
legal implications of, 221–3
RTBF and, 199–202
data privacy law in, 198, 199–223
procedural history of, 203–4
Googlebots, 202–3
Gould, R. Douglas, 36–7
*Grant* defence. *See* public interest communication defence
*Grant* v. *Torstar*, 10
elements of, 18–24
public interest communication defence in, 18–24
in applications besides journalism, 21–2
in applications besides publications to the world at large, 22–3
cost of risk avoidance analysis in, 35
journalistic standards references in, 30–2
jury questions in, 23–4
pleading of, 24–5
in practice, 24–9
public interest element in, 19
qualified privilege in, 22–3
reasonableness standard in, 32–8
responsible communication element in, 19–20
scope of, 20–3, 29–38
severity of harm aspect in, 34–5
social benefits of, 35
*Greene* v. *Associated Newspapers*, 304
Greenwald, Glenn, 139, 230, 239–40
grief journalism, 12
behavior of media in, 123, 125–31
breaches of privacy and, 124–5
components of, 119–20
interviewed participants in, 120, 121
justifications of, 120

pack phenomenon in, 122
physical presence of media and, 125–31
in Pike River disaster, 116–35
autonomy influenced by, 131–5
avoidance of media and, 132–3
behavior of media during, 123, 125–31
breaches of privacy and, 124–5
feelings of insecurity as result of, 128–31
feelings of safety as result of, 128–31
hiding of emotions as response to, 134–5
lack of empathy in, 127–8
personal dignity impacted by, 126–8
physical intrusiveness of media, 125–31
post-traumatic stress for interviewed persons, 121
psychological response to, 122
post-traumatic stress for interviewed persons, 121
psychological response to, 122
group defamation, 269

*Halford* v. *UK*, 103
*Hansen* v. *R*, 327–8
Harmful Digital Communications Act (New Zealand), 15, 322–7
Hogan, Hulk, 254–6, 258
Hollande, François, 246–7
Holmes, Oliver Wendell, 168
*Hosking* v. *Runting*, 97, 98–9, 131, 147, 315, 348–9
Howarth, David, 268, 270–3
Hughes, Kirsty, 13, 105, 110, 113, 136–7, 140–1
human rights. *See also* civil rights; privacy, as a right; reputation, as right
constitutional development of, 61–2
defamation law and, 5
implied rights, 88
privacy law and, 5, 173–80
Human Rights Act 1998 (UK), 139
privacy law under, development of, 175
privacy rights under, 165
*Hunter* v. *Chandler*, 28, 31
*Hustler Magazine* v. *Falwell*, 77
*Hutcheson* v. *News Group Newspapers*, 102

implied rights, 88
Impress Project, 163
Independent Press Standards Organisation (IPSO), 157
informational privacy, 124–5
injunctions, in privacy law, 181–2
International Covenant on Civil and Political Rights, 5
Internet
cypherpunk philosophy about, 244
as facilitator of totalitarianism, 225
IPSO. *See* Independent Press Standards Organisation

*Jameel* v. *Wall Street Journal Europe*, 7, 18, 66, 346–7
*John Fairfax & Sons* v. *Carson*, 298
Johnson, Boris, 143
journalism law, 2–6. *See also* grief journalism
public speech and, 7–8
journalistic standards. *See also* freedom of press
assessment of malice in, 74
for bloggers, 30–1
for Canadian Association of Journalists, 31
for courts compared with journalists, 36
defamation law and, 53
for European Court of Human Rights, 37
in *Grant* v. *Torstar*, 30–2
*New York Times* v. *Sullivan* and, historical context for, 73–4
pushing the envelope of, 253–6
Society of Professional Journalists Code of Ethics, 251–2
Twitter and, 30
journalists. *See also* freedom of press
standards for, 36
withholding of information by, 252–3
*Julian Assange: The Unauthorised Biography* (O'Hagan), 224–5
juries
civil rights and, 60
in *Grant* v. *Torstar*, 23–4
libel disputes without, 50

*K* v. *News Group Newspapers*, 137, 143
Kahan, Dan, 71
Kalven, Harry, 171
Kant, Immanuel, 126
*Karakó* v. *Hungary*, 277–8, 286–90
*Katz* v. *US*, 99
*Kaye* v. *Robertson*, 173–4
Kennedy, John F., 259
Kenyon, Andrew, 37, 50, 62
*Khashoggi* v. *IPC Magazines*, 43–4
*Kiam* v. *MGN*, 298
King, Martin Luther King, Jr., 170, 334. *See also New York Times* v. *Sullivan*
*KU* v. *Finland*, 191

*Lait* v. *Evening Standard*, 46, 48
*Lange* v. *Australian Broadcasting Corporation*, 94, 316, 342–4
*Lavric* v. *Romania*, 280–1
Leigh, David, 243
Lewinsky, Monica, 194
Lewis, Anthony, 339
libel law. *See* defamation law
*de Libellis Famosis*, 83
liberty, autonomy and, 132
Lidsky, Lyrissa, 72
*Lillo-Stenberg and Saether* v. *Norway*, 153, 189
*Lindon* v. *France*, 274
Lindsay, David, 13–14
Lofgren, Zoe, 233
looking-glass self theory, 269–71, 272, 284–5
*Lucas-Box* meaning, 44
*Lucas-Box* v. *News Group Newspapers*, 44
Lyon, Alexander, 5

MacAskill, Ewen, 230
male gaze, 130
*Mannai Investment* v. *Eagle Star Life*, 47–8
Manne, Robert, 243, 244
Manning, Chelsea, 225–6, 239–40
Mason, Anthony, 341
Massie, Thomas, 233
Maxwell, Robert, 92
*McCartan Turkington Breen* v. *Times Newspapers*, 139
McClaren, Steve, 149
McDonald, Barbara, 109
*McGinty* v. *Western Australia*, 342
*McKennit* v. *Ash*, 100–1, 113, 137, 312
*McLaren* v. *News Group Newspapers*, 102
media. *See also* journalistic standards; journalists; Pike River disaster
  in defamation cases
    in Canada, 24–5, 94
    in UK, 24–5, 91–2
    in US, 24–5, 92–3
  grief journalism and, 12
    autonomy influenced by, 131–5
    avoidance of media in response to, 132–3
    behavior of media, 123, 125–31
    breaches of privacy and, 124–5
    feelings of insecurity as result of, 128–31
    feelings of safety and, 128–31
    hiding of emotions as response to, 134–5
    lack of empathy in, 127–8
    personal dignity impacted by, 126–8
    physical intrusiveness of media, 125–31
    post-traumatic stress for interviewed persons, 121
    psychological response to, 122
  after *Lange* v. *Australian Broadcasting Corporation*, 94
  after *New York Times* v. *Sullivan*, 24–5, 92–3
  pack phenomenon in, 122
  during Pike River Disaster, 117, 135
  after *Reynolds* v. *Times Newspapers*, 24–5, 91–2, 94–5
Meiklejohn, Alexander, 336
*Merivale* v. *Carson*, 46
Merkel, Angela, 231
metadata, collection of, 230, 235, 239
*Michaels* v. *Internet Entertainment Group*, 192
*Mikolajová* v. *Slovakia*, 286, 288
Mill, John Stuart, 157, 175, 336
Milton, John, 74–5, 175, 336
morality, right to criticise and, 161
Moreham, Nicole, 12, 104–5, 106, 107, 109
*Mosley* v. *News Group Newspapers*, 102, 137, 157–61, 162, 165, 193–4, 256–8, 293–4, 299, 305
*Mosley* v. *United Kingdom*, 188
Müller-Maguhn, Andy, 225
Mullis, Alastair, 269–70, 272, 283–6
Murchison, Brian, 351
*Murray* v. *Express Newspapers*, 96–106, 195

Nagel, Thomas, 134–5
*Nationwide News* v. *Wills*, 87–9
negligence standards
  for defamation, 33–4
  in defamation law, 33–4
  in *Gertz* v. *Robert Welch*, 33
*New York Times* v. *Sullivan*, 2, 10–11, 15–16
  actual malice standard in, 86–7, 171, 335
  Australian law influenced by, 64–5
  civil rights context for, 58–9
  common law doctrine and, 67–73
  defamation law reform influenced by, 331–50
  elements of, 59, 170
  English law influenced by, 66–7
  epistemological issues in, 68–73
  First Amendment and, 75–80, 86–7, 170, 171
  free speech issues in, 86, 167, 249

freedom of press in, 86, 167, 249
historical context for journalism and, 73–4
isolation costs of, 67–8
legal impact of, 59–61, 62
media reporting after, 24–5, 92–3
privacy law reform influenced by, 331–50
privacy rights in, 167
qualified privilege defence in, 64–5
US Supreme Court and, 59–60, 86–7
New Zealand. *See also* Pike River disaster
Bill of Rights Act 1990 in, 15
Defamation Act 1992 in, 316
defamation in, 82–4
parameters of, 310–12, 314–15
public interest elements of, 316–17
Harmful Digital Communications Act in, 15, 322–7
privacy law in, 147
reasonable expectation of privacy in, 98–100
New Zealand Bill of Rights Act 1990, 327–9
Nixon, Richard, 253, 338–9
Nordic Conference on the Right to Privacy, 6
Northern Ireland, single meaning rule in, 57

*OBG* v. *Allan*, 349
O'Hagan, Andrew, 224–5, 241–4
*Oklahoma Publishing* v. *Oklahoma County District Court*, 164–5
*On Liberty* (Mill), 336. *See also* Mill, John Stuart
*OPO* v. *MLA*, 197–8
*Oriental Daily Publisher* v. *Ming Pao Holdings*, 46–7

parody, free speech and, 77
Partlett, David, 10–11
*Patterson* v. *Colorado*, 168
*Pauliukienė* v. *Lithuania*, 280–1, 288
*Pavesich* v. *New England Life Insurance*, 131–2
*Pfeifer* v. *Austria*, 274–5, 317
Phillipson, Gavin, 12–13, 114
photographs and video, under privacy laws, 191–5
Pike River disaster (New Zealand)
breaches of privacy during, 124–5
grief journalism in, 116–35
autonomy influenced by, 131–5
avoidance of media and, 132–3
breaches of privacy and, 124–5
feelings of insecurity as result of, 128–31
hiding of emotions as response to, 134–5
lack of empathy in, 127–8
personal dignity impacted by, 126–8
physical intrusiveness of media, 125–31
post-traumatic stress for interviewed persons, 121
psychological response to, 122
safety issues with, 128–31
media interest in, 117, 135
study of, 117–22
limitations of, 120–2
methodology for, 119
role of media presence in, 122–5
strengths of, 119–20
timeline of events, 116–17
*Plato Films* v. *Speidel*, 297–8
Poitras, Laura, 230, 239–40
*Polanco* v. *Spain*, 286
*Popovski* v. *Former Yugoslav Republic of Macedonia*, 280–1
presidents, US, privacy rights for, 247–53
*Prince Albert* v. *Strange*, 193
*Prince of Wales* v. *Associated Newspapers*, 107
*Privacy* (Prosser), 247
privacy, as a right. *See also* claims, for defamation and privacy; freedom of press; privacy law; reasonable expectation of privacy
autonomy and, 131–5
in *Campbell* v. *MGN*, 96, 100, 131
citizen's right to, 80
defamation as distinct from, 292–3, 304–5, 310–12
for purpose of legal remedies, 293–5
under DPA, 111
under ECHR, 136, 165, 178–9
European Court of Human Rights and, 131–2, 136–7, 179–80
expansion of, 312–13
free speech balanced with, 177–80
future of, 241–4
grief journalism and, 12, 124–5
in *Hosking* v. *Runting*, 97, 98–9, 131
under Human Rights Act 1998, 165
informational, 124–5
in journalism law, 2–6
male gaze and, 130
under *New York Times* v. *Sullivan*, 167
under public figure doctrine, 145–50
in UK, 177–80
remedies for, 181–3
in US, 166–73
for presidents, 247–53
remedies for, 181–3

privacy, as a right (cont.)
for whistleblowers, 227, 239–41
*Privacy and Media Freedom* (Wacks), 97
privacy claims. *See* claims, for defamation and privacy
privacy law. *See also* claims, for defamation and privacy; data privacy law; freedom of press; privacy, as a right; public figures, doctrine for; public interest arguments; reasonable expectation of privacy
anonymity orders in, 181–2
in Australia, 1–2, 80
in common law systems, 9–11, 84–5
comparative analysis for, 8–9
in courts, 2–6
defamation claims merged with, 320–9
defamation law compared with, 14–16
dignity as part of, 256–63
ECHR support of, 256
in England and Wales, 2, 4–5, 173–80
in EU, 317
expectations of, 11–13
in Germany, for celebrities, 188–90
under Human Rights Act 1998, 175
as human rights issue, 5, 173–80
journalistic practices under, 13–14
legal impact of, 11–13
legislative proposals in, 2–6
in New Zealand, 147
purpose of claims under, 318–20
rationale for, 11–13
reform of, *New York Times* v. *Sullivan* as influence on, 331–50
reporting technologies and, 6–8
Restatement of Torts provisions in, 247, 248–9
right to criticise under, 157–61
super-injunctions in, 181–2
in UK, 173–80
approach to remedies for, 181–3
for celebrities, 187–90
compared with US law, 183–95
for government officials, 183–7
for heads of state, 183–7
photographs and video in, 191–5
for private individuals, 190–1
in US, 2, 166–73
antecedents for, 166–7
approach to remedies for, 181–3
for celebrities, 187–90
compared with UK law, 183–95
for government officials, 183–7
for heads of state, 183–7, 247–53
photographs and video in, 191–5
for private individuals, 190–1
vindication of, through damages, 305–7
*Von Hannover* v. *Germany (no 2)* and, 179–80
for celebrities, 188–90
for photographs and video, 194–5
privacy-invading expression, 141
Prosser, William, 169–70, 247
public figures, doctrine for
in *Axel Springer* v. *Germany*, 146
for celebrities, 187–90
defamation law for, 67–8
*de Libellis Famosis* and, 83
expansion of concept, 148–9
freedom of press and, 145–50
for government officials, 183–7
for heads of state, 183–7, 247–53
in *Hosking* v. *Runting*, 97, 98–9, 131, 147
loss of privacy for, factors in, 150
reasonable expectation of privacy for, 145–50
role model argument, 154–7
in *Von Hannover* v. *Germany (no 2)*, 137, 145–6
public interest arguments
in defamation cases, 316–17
economic survival argument in, 142–5
for freedom of press, 137, 143
expansion of, 151–4
judicial support in, 144
right to criticise as, 157–61
role model argument, 154–7
in *Time* v. *Hill*, 337–8
in UK law, 196–7
in US law, 196–7
in *Von Hannover* v. *Germany (no 2)*, 151–4
public interest communication defence (Canada). *See also Grant* v. *Torstar*
application of, 25–9
by bloggers, 24–5
in *Daboll* v. *DeMarco*, 26, 28
in *Foulidis* v. *Baker*, 26–7
in *Grant* v. *Torstar*, 18–24
in applications besides journalism, 21–2
in applications besides publications to the world at large, 22–3
cost of risk avoidance analysis in, 35
journalistic standards references in, 30–2
jury questions in, 23–4
pleading of defence, 24–5
in practice, 24–9
public interest element in, 19

qualified privilege in, 22–3
reasonableness standard in, 32–8
responsible communication element in, 19–20
scope of defence, 20–3, 29–38
severity of harm aspect in, 34–5
social benefits of, 35
in *Hunter* v. *Chandler*, 28, 31
pleading of, 24–5
in *Roshard* v. *Saint Denis*, 27–8
in *Rubin* v. *Ross*, 27
in *Shavluk* v. *Green Party of Canada*, 29
success rate of, 25–6
by traditional journalists, 24
in *WIC Radio* v. *Simpson*, 18
Public Order Act 1986, 176
public speech, 7–8
publications to the world at large, 22–3
*Putistin* v. *Ukraine*, 280–1

qualified privilege, 22–3. *See also* Defamation Act 2013 (UK); *Grant* v. *Torstar*; *Lange* v. *Australian Broadcasting Corporation*; public interest communication defence (Canada); *Reynolds* v. *Times Newspapers*; *Theophanous* v. *Herald & Weekly Times*
in Australia, 87–90
in common law systems, 87–90
in England and Wales, 87–90
in *Lange* v. *Australian Broadcasting Corporation*, 87–9
in *New York Times* v. *Sullivan*, 64–5
in *Reynolds* v. *Times Newspapers*, 89–90, 346
*Quan* v. *Cusson*, 17

*R (Lumba)* v. *Secretary of State for the Home Department*, 303
*R* v. *Secretary of State for the Home Department ex parte Simms*, 175
Race Relations Act 1976, 176
Rachels, James, 124
*Radio France* v. *France*, 273
reasonable expectation of privacy, 96–8
abandonment of, 111–14
ALRC and, 96–106
in *Australian Broadcasting Corporation* v. *Lenah Game Meats*, 98
in Australian cases, 98–100
in *Author of a Blog* case, 112–13, 114
in *Axel Springer* v. *Germany*, 146
in *Campbell* v. *MGN*, 96, 100
for children, 108
defamation law and, 111–12
ECHR guidelines for, 96, 103–4, 112
in English cases, 100–3
in grief journalism, 124–5
in *Hosking* v. *Runting*, 97, 98–9
Hughes on, 105, 110, 113
in *Katz* v. *US*, 99
Moreham on, 104–5, 106, 107, 109
in *Murray* v. *Express Newspapers*, 96–106
in New Zealand cases, 98–100
origins of, 114
under public figure doctrine, 145–50
right of reputation and, 111–12
test of, in case law, 97, 98–103
arguments for, 104–7
incoherence of, 107–10
in *TSE* v. *News Group Newspapers*, 180
in *Von Hannover* v. *Germany (no 2)*, 137, 145–6, 179–80
reasonableness standard
in Australia, 37
in public interest communication defence, 32–8
remedies. *See* vindication, through damages
repetition rule, 56
reputation, as right
under Article 8, of ECHR, 265–7, 281–6
doctrinal and conceptual tensions for, 281–90
as protected interest, 273–6
seriousness threshold in, 276–8, 286–90
under Article 10(2), of ECHR, 273–6
in *Axel Springer* v. *Germany*, 278–80
character compared with, 268
looking-glass self theory and, 269–71, 272, 284–5
loss of, 271–2
reasonable expectation of privacy and, 111–12
self-esteem and, 269–71
theoretical justifications for, 267–73
for dignity, 268–71
property conception in, 268
sociality justification, 271–3
vindication of, through damages, 296
Restatement of Torts provisions, in privacy law, 247, 248–9
*Reynolds* v. *Times Newspapers*, 17, 18
Defamation Act 2013 and, 90
defamation law reform as result of, 345–50
expansion of qualified privilege in, 89–90
free speech in, 66, 89–90
media reporting after, 24–5, 91–2, 94–5

Reynolds v. Times Newspapers (cont.)
  public interest communication defence in, 32–3, 346
  qualified privilege in, 89–90, 346
  vindication in, 297
Richards, Neil, 13, 136–7, 140–1
Richardson, Megan, 15–16
Richie, Nik, 255–6
*Riegel* v. *Medtronic*, 79
right to be forgotten (RTBF)
  under DPD law, 212–14
  Google requests for, 199–200
  in *Google Spain SL, Google Inc* v. *Agencia Española de Protección de Datos (AEPD) and Mario Costejo González*, 199–202
right to criticise
  under Defamation Act 2013 (UK), 159
  under defamation law, 159
  in England and Wales, 157–61
  on moral grounds, 161
*The Right to Speak Ill* (Weaver et al.), 62
rights. *See* civil rights; human rights; privacy, as a right; reputation, as right; right to be forgotten; right to criticise
*Roberts* v. *United Kingdom*, 287–8
*Rocknroll* v. *News Group Newspapers*, 137
Rolph, David, 15, 319–21
*Rosenbloom* v. *Metromedia*, 336–7
*Roshard* v. *Saint Denis*, 27–8
Ross, Donald Q. C., 5
RTBF. *See* right to be forgotten
*Rubin* v. *Ross*, 27
*Ruusunen* v. *Finland*, 185–6

*San Diego* v. *Roe*, 192–3
Sawer, Geoffrey, 2
Schauer, Frederick, 68, 352
Schwartz, Bernard, 339
Scott, Andrew, 10, 269–70, 272, 281–6
search engine operators (SEOs), 200, 202–3
  DPD application to, 204–17
  link removal on, 216–17
Securing the Protection of our Enduring and Established Constitutional Heritage (SPEECH) Act, 347
self-esteem, 269–71
Sensenbrenner, Jim, 233
SEOs. *See* search engine operators
severity of harm, 34–5
*Shavluk* v. *Green Party of Canada*, 29
*Shulman* v. *Group W Productions*, 106, 259
single meaning rule
  in *Ajinomoto Sweeteners* v. *ASDA Stores*, 45–6
  in *Bonnick* v. *Morris*, 43, 46
  in *Charleston* v. *News Group Newspapers*, 46
  critique of, 42–6
  determination of meaning in, 51
  explanation of, 42–6
  extant rule and, 49–50
  function of, 40–1
  in *Lait* v. *Evening Standard*, 46, 48
  legal costs of, 49
  legal justifications for, 46–50
  libel law and, 51–7
  *Lucas-Box* meaning and, 44
  in *Mannai Investment* v. *Eagle Star Life*, 47–8
  in *Merivale* v. *Carson*, 46
  in Northern Ireland, 57
  in *Oriental Daily Publisher* v. *Ming Pao Holdings*, 46–7
  reform of, 55–7
  role of language in, 43
  in *Slim* v. *Daily Telegraph*, 42, 45–6, 48
  in UK law, 41
  in US law, 41
*Sipple* v. *Chronicle Publishing*, 183–4, 251
*Slim* v. *Daily Telegraph*, 42, 45–6, 48
*Smith* v. *Daily Mail Publishing*, 164–5
*Smith* v. *Maryland*, 235
*Smith* v. *People of the State of California*, 85
Snowden, Edward, 7, 14, 139, 197, 226–7, 239–40
  on US data collection, 230–2
*Snyder* v. *Phelps*, 63, 173
Society of Professional Journalists Code of Ethics, 251–2, 260
*Someşan* v. *Romania*, 280–1
SPEECH Act. *See* Securing the Protection of our Enduring and Established Constitutional Heritage Act
*Spelman* v. *Express Newspapers*, 102
*Stephens* v. *Western Australian Newspapers*, 88
Strasbourg court. *See* European Court of Human Rights
super-injunctions, in privacy law, 181–2
surveillance, mass data collection through, in US, 228–32
  under FISA, 228–32
  under Fourth Amendment, 234–6
  government response to, 232–4
  government responses to, 232–4
  under Patriot Act, 230, 233

with PRISM program, 234–6
search and seizures of, 234–6

*Tee* v. *United Kingdom*, 273
Telecommunications (Interception and Access) Amendment (Data Retention) Bill 2014, 236–7
*Terry* v. *Persons Unknown*, 304, 313
*Theakston* v. *MGN*, 193
*Theophanous* v. *Herald & Weekly Times*, 88, 341–2
*Time* v. *Hill*, 2, 171, 250, 337–9
*Times Newspapers* v. *United Kingdom (nos. 1 and 2)*, 215
Tinsley, Yvette, 12
tort law, vindication in, 299–303
*TSE* v. *News Group Newspapers*, 180
*TV3 Network Services* v. *Fahey*, 314
Twitter, tweeting and
journalistic standards for, 30
severity of harm and, 34

United Kingdom (UK). *See also* England and Wales; Northern Ireland; *Reynolds* v. *Times Newspapers*; single meaning rule
constitutional framework throughout, 197
Defamation Act 2013 in, 10, 18, 40, 90
declaration of falsity under, 52
foundations of, 331
free speech under, 66–7
libel law reform under, 53
*Reynolds* v. *Times Newspapers* and, 90
right to criticise under, 159
defamation cases involving media in, 24–5, 91–3, 94
defamation in, parameters of, 310–12
public interest elements of, 316–17
defamation law reform in, 333, 344–50
free speech in, 13, 173–80
remedies for, 181–3
freedom of press in, 142–5, 150–1
Human Rights Act 1998 in, 139, 165
privacy law in, 173–80
approach to remedies for, 181–3
for celebrities, 187–90
compared with US law, 183–98
for government officials, 183–7
for heads of state, 183–7
photographs and video in, 191–5
for private individuals, 190–1
privacy rights in, 177–80
public interest arguments in, 196–7
single meaning rule in, 41

United States (US). *See also* US Constitution
Civil Rights movement in, 58–9
common law as influence in, 85–7
Communications Decency Act in, 63
constitutional framework in, 197
data collection in, through surveillance, 228–32
under FISA, 228–30
under Fourth Amendment, 234–6
government responses to, 232–4
under Patriot Act, 230, 233
with PRISM program, 234–6
search and seizures from, 234–6
UK legal response to, 240
defamation cases involving media in, 24–5, 92–3
defamation law in, 2, 24–5, 33, 82–4, 85–7, 92–3
reform movement for, 334–9
under US Constitution, 85
US Supreme Court and, 79, 82, 85
free speech in, 13, 166–73
methodology for, 172–3
remedies for, 181–3
Freedom Act in, 233
Patriot Act in, 230, 233
privacy law in, 2, 166–73
antecedents for, 166–7
approach to remedies for, 181–3
for celebrities, 187–90
compared with UK law, 183–98
for government officials, 183–7
for heads of state, 183–7, 247–53
photographs and video in, 191–5
for private individuals, 190–1
public interest arguments in, 196–7
single meaning rule in, 41
states rights in, for defamation law, 85
*United States* v. *Jones*, 235
Universal Declaration of Human Rights, 5
*Unpublished Opinions of the Warren Court* (Schwartz), 339
US Constitution
defamation law under, 85
First Amendment
in *Cantwell* v. *Connecticut*, 85
in *Chaplinsky* v. *New Hampshire*, 85
Civil Rights movement and, 58–9
common law rights and, 75–8
cultural power of, 165
free speech under, 3–4, 70, 86–7
freedom of press and, 140–1
Gawker's use of, 254–6

US Constitution (cont.)
historical context for, 167–8
in *New York Times* v. *Sullivan*, 75–80, 86–7, 170, 171
*Patterson* v. *Colorado* and, 168
for private individuals, 190–1
*Smith* v. *People of the State of California* and, 85
Fourth Amendment, data collection under, 234–6
US Freedom Act, 233
US Patriot Act, 230, 233
US Supreme Court. *See also* specific cases
defamation law and, 79, 82, 85, 350
FISA and, 229–30
*New York Times* v. *Sullivan* and, 59–60, 86–7

Varuhas, Jason, 302–3
*Vidal-Hall* v. *Google*, 306
*Vigna* v. *Levant*, 30–1
vindication, through damages
under Australian law, 305–6
in defamation law, 295–9
critique of, 298
discursive, in libel law, 52–4
under English law, 305–6
under French law, 305–6
under German law, 305–6
in privacy law, 305–7
for privacy rights, 181–3
for public reputation, 296
in *Reynolds* v. *Times Newspapers*, 297
in tort law, 299–303
Volokh, Eugene, 140–1
*Von Hannover* v. *Germany (no 1)*, 179–80, 188–90, 194–5
*Von Hannover* v. *Germany (no 2)*, 137, 145–6, 179–80, 186–7
privacy law and, 179–80
for celebrities, 188–90
for photographs and video, 194–5
public interest elements in, 151–4

Wacks, Raymond, 5–6, 97
*Wainwright* v. *Home Office*, 174
Walden, Brian, 5
Waldron, Jeremy, 269
Wales. *See* England and Wales
Warren, Samuel, 166, 248, 338–9
Weaver, Russell, 11, 67
*Weller* v. *Associated Newspapers*, 137, 143, 195
Westin, Alan, 7
whistleblowers. *See also* Assange, Julian; Snowden, Edward; Wikileaks
corporate accountability through, 241
privacy rights for, 227, 239–41
Whitman, James, 256
*Whitney* v. *California*, 168–9
Whittall, Peter, 117
*WIC Radio* v. *Simpson*, 18
Wikileaks, 14, 225, 226–7, 243. *See also* Assange, Julian
*Wilkinson* v. *Downton*, 77
*Williams* v. *Reason*, 43
*Wood* v. *Commissioner of Police of the Metropolis*, 102–3
Woodward, Bob, 73
Wragg, Paul, 140–1, 153, 156–7
*WXY* v. *Gewanter*, 307
*Wyeth* v. *Levine*, 79

*X* v. *Iceland*, 284–5

Yellow Press, 164
Young, Hilary, 10

Zimmerman, Dianne, 140–1, 337
Zimmermann, Jérémie, 225

*Cambridge Intellectual Property and Information Law*

**Titles in the series (formerly known as *Cambridge Studies in Intellectual Property Rights*)**

Brad Sherman and Lionel Bently *The Making of Modern Intellectual Property Law*
Irini A. Stamatoudi *Copyright and Multimedia Products: A Comparative Analysis*
Pascal Kamina *Film Copyright in the European Union*
Huw Beverly-Smith *The Commercial Appropriation of Personality*
Mark J. Davison *The Legal Protection of Databases*
Robert Burrell and Allison Coleman *Copyright Exceptions: The Digital Impact*
Huw Beverly-Smith, Ansgar Ohly and Agnès Lucas-Schloetter *Privacy, Property and Personality: Civil Law Perspectives on Commercial Appropriation*
Catherine Seville *The Internationalisation of Copyright Law: Books, Buccaneers and the Black Flag in the Nineteenth Century*
Philip Leith *Software and Patents in Europe*
Geertrui Van Overwalle *Gene Patents and Clearing Models*
Lionel Bently, Jennifer Davis and Jane C. Ginsburg *Trade Marks and Brands: An Interdisciplinary Critique*
Jonathan Curci *The Protection of Biodiversity and Traditional Knowledge in International Law of Intellectual Property*
Lionel Bently, Jennifer Davis and Jane C. Ginsburg *Copyright and Piracy: An Interdisciplinary Critique*
Megan Richardson and Julian Thomas *Framing Intellectual Property: Legal Constructions of Creativity and Appropriation 1840–1940*
Dev Gangjee *Relocating the Law of Geographical Indications*
Andrew T. Kenyon, Megan Richardson and Ng-Loy Wee-Loon *The Law of Reputation and Brands in the Asia Pacific Region*
Annabelle Lever *New Frontiers in the Philosophy of Intellectual Property*
Sigrid Sterckx and Julian Cockbain *Exclusions from Patentability: How the European Patent Office is Eroding Boundaries*
Sebastian Haunss *Conflicts in the Knowledge Society: The Contentious Politics of Intellectual Property*
Helena R. Howe and Jonathan Griffiths *Concepts of Property in Intellectual Property Law*
Rochelle Cooper Dreyfuss and Jane C. Ginsburg *Intellectual Property at the Edge: The Contested Contours of IP*
Normann Witzleb, David Lindsay, Moira Paterson and Sharon Rodrick *Emerging Challenges in Privacy Law: Comparative Perspectives*
Paul Bernal *Internet Privacy Rights: Rights to Protect Autonomy*
Peter Drahos *Intellectual Property, Indigenous People and their Knowledge*
Susy Frankel and Daniel Gervais *The Evolution and Equilibrium of Copyright in the Digital Age*
Kathy Bowrey and Michael Handler *Law and Creativity in the Age of the Entertainment Franchise*

Sean Bottomley *The British Patent System and the Industrial Revolution 1700–1852: From Privileges to Property*
Susy Frankel *Test Tubes for Global Intellectual Property Issues: Small Market Economies*
Jan Oster *Media Freedom as a Fundamental Right*
Sara Bannerman *International Copyright and Access to Knowledge*
Andrew T. Kenyon *Comparative Defamation and Privacy Law*
Pascal Kamina *Film Copyright in the European Union, Second Edition*

For EU product safety concerns, contact us at Calle de José Abascal, 56–1°,
28003 Madrid, Spain or eugpsr@cambridge.org.

www.ingramcontent.com/pod-product-compliance
Lightning Source LLC
LaVergne TN
LVHW011530200926
848484LV00001B/212

* 9 7 8 1 1 0 7 1 2 3 6 4 9 *